READING
POLITICAL ECONOMY
ECONOMICS AS A SOCIAL SCIENCE
Third edition

Edited by
GEORGE ARGYROUS
FRANK STILWELL

First published in 1996 by
Pluto Press Australia Limited
Second edition published in 2003 by
Pluto Press Australia Limited
Third edition published in 2011 by
Tilde University Press Limited
PO Box 72 Prahran VIC 3181 Australia
www.tup.net.au   TUP-PoliticalEconomy-1e2p

Cover design by Christopher Besley, Besley Design.

Index by Neale Towart

Australian Cataloguing-in-Publication Data
Readings in Political Economy : Economics as a Social Science.
Third edition.

Bibliography.
Includes index.
ISBN 978 0 7346 1143 7.

1. Economics – Sociological aspects. 2. Economics –
Australia – Sociological aspects. 3. Australia – Economic
Policy. 4. Australia – Social policy. I. Argyrous, George, 1963–
II. Stilwell, Frank J. B. 1944–

CONTENTS

INTRODUCTION

Whether we like it or not, economic issues are of great importance. As individuals we are all concerned with the material conditions of existence: securing an income, managing that income, balancing saving against consumption, and so on. At a more aggregated level, nations also face similar problems, although it is sometimes observed that, for affluent nations, the problem of ensuring that everyone's material wants are satisfied is unequal income distribution rather than inadequate productive capacity. Economics concerns itself with the study of how these issues of production, distribution, exchange and growth are confronted by individuals, by social groups and by different types of societies.

The current economic conditions make exposure to economic analysis imperative since many problems have intensified in recent years. The economies of individual nations have become increasingly integrated through trade in goods and services, movements in capital and labor, and the operation of financial institutions so that people now often speak of a single global economy. However, the global economy faces continuing difficulties that impact on individual countries. International debt and trade imbalances pose major problems. Financial markets face periodic crises. It is not ecologically sustainable to base the economy on resource extraction and current forms of energy use. The capacity of states to engineer economic solutions is under increasing strain. The answers to such problems offered in the past no longer seem appropriate.

Can economics as a subject provide solutions for these contemporary concerns? One might reasonably expect it to do so. However, the discipline is bedeviled by its own problems. A student coming to the subject for the first time cannot expect to find ready and simple answers that explain how the economic system functions. There is a range of conflicting explanations of the operation and the problems of modern economies. Moreover, these varied explanations are typically linked with particular political positions.

This essential diversity is sometimes obscured by the dominance of the subject by a particular school of thought. This orthodoxy, based on neoclassical economic theory, forms the core of most standard textbooks and media commentaries on contemporary economic issues. Its influence on public policy proposals has been particularly evident in the last three decades. However, both as economic theory and as a basis for economic policy, this orthodoxy is subjected to continual challenge. Its dominance has been at the expense of alternative frameworks for understanding how the capitalist system functions, each of which provides insights that cannot be seen from the orthodox perspective.

The challenge to reformulate economics to take account of these insights involves reformulating economics more explicitly as a social science. It requires integrating economic analysis more closely with cognate disciplines such as sociology, political science, history, human geography, and anthropology. Economics deals with *people*, how they are organized for the purposes of production, how income and wealth are distributed among them, and how they interact in the process of exchanging goods and services. Thus, the study of the economy is necessarily linked with the study of *society*. A modern economist needs to understand the relationship between the economic system and the structure of social classes; the significance of economic power and of changes in economic institutions, such as the growth of the international financial system and its tendency to periodic crises; the changing character of government intervention in capitalist economies; and the varying relations between nation states. These are key issues for economics as a social science.

Approaching the subject in this way involves the reformulation of economics as political economy. This does not necessarily mean a return to the concerns of classical political economists writing two centuries ago. The character of economic life has changed so much in the meanwhile. However, the breadth of concerns of classical political economy does stand in striking contrast to the more narrowly constructed concerns of neoclassical economic theory. The further development of a modern political economy involves embracing the big questions about production, distribution, growth, and crises that have all-too-often been neglected in the neoclassical economic orthodoxy. It involves recognition that state, class, gender, race and ideology are key elements in shaping the 'social order' of modern capitalism, as well as 'the market' which is the primary focus of orthodox economists. It involves trying to understand the contradictory elements in economic systems and the forces generating evolutionary change. The real world will not stand still while we study it.

Modern political economy therefore can sensibly draw on the major currents of thought which have challenged the conventional wisdom of the dominant neoclassical economics – Marxian, institutional, Keynesian and post-Keynesian. It can also draw on the insights provided by contemporary social movements emphasizing 'green' and feminist agendas and on other perspectives that emphasize the 'have-nots' who have been marginalized by contemporary economic processes. It can also take account of developments in behavioral economics that link economics closer with social psychology. Drawing from these heterodox political economic approaches, modern political economy can address contemporary concerns about managing national economies, guiding structural economic change, regulating markets in the interests of equity and stability, and coping with the economic consequences of technological change. These are grand challenges to which there are no simple solutions.

This book provides a basis for such explorations. It is a new edition of a book previously titled *Economics as a Social Science*. The new version, compiled with the research assistance of Tim Roxburgh, retains the classical contributions but updates many of the previously published articles and adds 27 new articles to replace others. There is a mixture of classical and contemporary contributions. Many of the articles are condensed versions of longer originals, abridged in order to bring out key issues. Extracts have also been selected with a view to making the issues accessible to non-specialists who might otherwise shy away from the study of technical economic issues.

Calling the subtitle of the book *Economics as a Social Science* draws attention to the social purpose of economic inquiry. This is the essence of political economy as an academic and practical endeavour – understanding the world so that we can change it for the better. Whether the label 'science' is appropriate remains a moot point, however. The claim to scientific status sits uncomfortably with the inherently political nature of economic inquiry. Political questions are those over which reasonable people can reasonably disagree. However, if we are to avoid a chaotic free-for-all we have to be as systematic as possible, carefully considering alternative explanations of economic phenomena and weighing the evidence and arguments, given the existing (inherently imperfect) state of knowledge.

Therein lies the intriguing possibility of turning the 'dismal science,' as economics has traditionally been known, into a 'science of liberation.' Once the constraints on efficiency, equity, and sustainability are better understood, we may escape the dismal condition in which economic concerns are so dominant. Seen in this light, political economy can claim to be an essential element in social progress.

I
ECONOMY AND SOCIETY

CONTEMPORARY CHALLENGES

We live in an era of dramatic political economic challenges. The last couple of decades have seen a re-configuration of the world economy. Some hitherto 'Third World' nations such as the People's Republic of China and India have become newly industrialized, while other areas, particularly in Africa but also in parts of China and India, remain desperately poor. The forces of 'globalization' recurrently threaten the capacity for traditional forms of national economic management. The global financial crisis (GFC), which struck in 2007-8 and developed into a prolonged recession in the USA and many other nations, has been a major wake-up call. The challenge of climate change looms large over all these concerns, presaging ecological catastrophe unless fundamental changes to the existing economic arrangements are implemented.

A body of analysis developed in earlier political economic conditions must necessarily be subject to re-evaluation in these circumstances. Is it reasonable to continue with a set of economic orthodoxies that assume that the economy is an equilibrating system in which resource allocation is shaped mainly by competitive market forces? Subsequent sections of the book consider this orthodox legacy along with some alternative approaches to political economic analysis.

The articles in this opening section focus on some of the most challenging contemporary features of the world economy. Waldon Bello sets the scene, looking at how the processes of corporate globalisation are generating contradictions and counter tendencies. It makes a controversial start to the book by challenging the dominant view of globalisation as a relentless, even unstoppable, political economic process. The other articles in this opening section look at contemporary challenges associated with economic crises, income inequality, consumerism and environmental stress. Martijn Konings writes about the GFC, widely regarded as the biggest shock to the capitalist economy since the Great Depression of the 1930s that was triggered by the financial crash of 1929. Frank Stilwell then looks at the trend towards increased economic inequality, indicating various reasons why it is occurring and why it needs to be reversed. Mark Diesendorf discusses the crisis of climate change that overshadows the whole political economic situation in the current century. Finally, Clive Hamilton provides a critical perspective on consumerism, as a deeply entrenched culture in modern society that creates a profoundly dissatisfying 'affluenza'.

All these articles introduce themes that need to be further explored. They set the scene for the more careful analytical explorations that follow in later sections of this book, where we look at the major schools of thought that have addressed such issues and the approaches they have taken in dealing with them.

Readers interested in further discussions of major contemporary issues will follow up on these introductory articles by looking at international journals and magazines such as *Capital and Class* <www.cseweb.org.uk>, *New Internationalist* <www.newint.org> and *Dollars and Sense* <www.dollarsandsense.org>. Reference can also be made to the *Journal of Australian Political Economy* <www.jape.org> which is published every six months, and magazines such as *Dissent* and *Arena Magazine*.

Globalization in Retreat?
Walden Bello

When it first became part of the English vocabulary in the early 1990s, globalization was supposed to be the wave of the future. Fifteen years ago, the writings of globalist thinkers such as Kenichi Ohmae and Robert Reich celebrated the advent of the emergence of the so-called borderless world. The process by which relatively autonomous national economies become functionally integrated into one global economy was touted as 'irreversible'. And the people who opposed globalization were disdainfully dismissed as modern day incarnations of the Luddites that destroyed machines during the Industrial Revolution.

Fifteen years later, despite runaway shops and outsourcing, what passes for an international economy remains a collection of national economies. These economies are interdependent no doubt, but domestic factors still largely determine their dynamics. Globalization has reached its high water mark and is receding.

Bright predictions, dismal outcomes

During globalization's heyday, we were told that state policies no longer mattered and that corporations would soon dwarf states. In fact, states still do matter. The European Union, the USA government, and the Chinese state are stronger economic actors today than they were a decade ago. In China, for instance, transnational corporations (TNCs) march to the tune of the state rather than the other way around.

Moreover, state policies that interfere with the market in order to build up industrial structures or protect employment still make a difference. Indeed, over the last ten years, interventionist government policies have spelled the difference between development and underdevelopment, prosperity and poverty. Malaysia's imposition of capital controls during the Asian financial crisis in 1997-98 prevented it from unraveling like Thailand or Indonesia. Strict capital controls also insulated China from the economic collapse engulfing its neighbors.

Fifteen years ago, we were told to expect the emergence of a transnational capitalist elite that would manage the world economy. Indeed, globalization became the 'grand strategy' of the Clinton administration, which envisioned the USA elite being the *primus inter pares* – first among equals – of a global coalition leading the way to the new, benign world order. Today, this project lies in shambles. During the reign of George W. Bush, the nationalist faction overwhelmed the transnational faction of the economic elite. These nationalism-inflected states are now competing sharply with one another, seeking to beggar one another's economies.

A decade ago, the World Trade Organization (WTO) was born, joining the World Bank and the International Monetary Fund (IMF) as the pillars of the system of international economic governance in the era of globalization. With a triumphalist air, officials of the three organizations meeting in Singapore during the first ministerial gathering of the WTO in December 1996 saw the remaining task of "global governance" as the achievement of "coherence," that is, the coordination of the neoliberal policies of the three institutions in order to ensure the smooth, technocratic integration of the global economy.

But now Sebastian Mallaby, the influential pro-globalization commentator of the Washington Post, complains that "trade liberalization has stalled, aid is less coherent than it should be, and the next financial conflagration will be managed by an injured fireman." In fact, the situation is worse than he describes. The IMF is practically defunct. Knowing how the Fund precipitated and worsened the Asian financial crisis, more and more of the advanced developing countries are refusing to borrow from it or are paying ahead of schedule, with some declaring their intention never to borrow again. These include Thailand, Indonesia, Brazil, and Argentina. Since the Fund's budget greatly depends on debt repayments from these big borrowers, this boycott is translating into what one expert describes as "a huge squeeze on the budget of the organization."

The World Bank may seem to be in better health than the Fund. But having been central to the debacle of structural adjustment policies that left most developing and transitional economies that implemented them in greater poverty, with greater inequality, and in a state of stagnation, the Bank is also suffering a crisis of legitimacy.

But the crisis of multilateralism is perhaps most acute at the WTO. The Doha Round of global negotiations for more trade liberalization unraveled abruptly when talks among the so-called Group of Six broke down in acrimony over the USA refusal to budge on its enormous subsidies for agriculture. The pro-free trade American economist Fred Bergsten once compared trade liberalization and the WTO to a bicycle: they collapse when they are not moving forward. The collapse of an organization that one of its director generals once described as the "jewel in the crown of multilateralism" may be nearer than it seems.

Why globalization stalled

Why did globalization run aground? First of all, the case for globalization was oversold. The bulk of the production and sales of most TNCs continues to take place within the country or region of origin. There are only a handful of truly global corporations whose production and sales are dispersed relatively equally across regions.

Second, rather than forge a common, cooperative response to the global crises of overproduction, stagnation, and environmental ruin, national capitalist elites have competed with each other to shift the burden of adjustment. The Bush administration, for instance, pushed a weak-dollar policy to promote USA economic recovery and growth at the expense of Europe and Japan. It also refused to sign the Kyoto Protocol in order to push Europe and Japan to absorb most of the costs of global environmental adjustment and thus make USA industry comparatively more competitive. While cooperation may be the rational strategic choice from the point of view of the global capitalist system, national capitalist interests are mainly concerned with not losing out to their rivals in the short term.

A third factor has been the corrosive effect of the double standards brazenly displayed by the hegemonic power, the United States. While the Clinton administration did try to move the United States toward free trade, the Bush administration hypocritically preached free trade while practicing protectionism. Indeed, the trade policy seems to be free trade for the rest of the world and protectionism for the United States.

Fourth, there has been too much dissonance between the promise of globalization and free trade and the actual results of neoliberal policies, which have been more poverty, inequality, and stagnation. One of the very few places where poverty diminished over the last 15 years is China. But interventionist state policies that managed market forces, not neoliberal prescriptions, were responsible for lifting 120 million Chinese out of poverty. Moreover, the advocates of eliminating capital controls have had to face the actual collapse of the economies that took this policy to heart. The globalization of finance proceeded much faster than the globalization of production. But it proved to be the cutting edge not of prosperity but of chaos. The Asian financial crisis and the collapse of the economy of Argentina, which had been among the most doctrinaire practitioners of capital account liberalization, were two decisive moments in reality's revolt against theory.

Another factor unraveling the globalist project is its obsession with economic growth. Indeed, unending growth is the centrepiece of globalization, the mainspring of its legitimacy. While a recent World Bank report continues to extol rapid growth as the key to expanding the global middle class, global warming, peak oil, and other environmental events are making it clear to people that the rates and patterns of growth that come with globalization are a sure-fire prescription for ecological Armageddon.

The final factor, not to be underestimated, has been popular resistance to globalization. The battles of Seattle in 1999, Prague in 2000, and Genoa in 2001; the massive global anti-war march on February 15, 2003, when the anti-globalization movement morphed into the global anti-war movement; the collapse of the WTO ministerial meeting in Cancun in 2003 and its near collapse in Hong Kong in 2005; the French and Dutch peoples' rejection of the neoliberal, pro-globalization European Constitution in 2005 – these were all critical junctures in a decade-long global struggle that has rolled back the neoliberal project. But these high-profile events were merely the tip of the iceberg, the summation of thousands of anti-neoliberal, anti-globalization struggles in thousands of communities throughout the world involving millions of peasants, workers, students, indigenous people, and many sectors of the middle class.

Down but not out

While corporate-driven globalization may be down, it is not out. Though discredited, many pro-globalization neoliberal policies remain in place in many economies, for lack of credible alternative policies in the eyes of technocrats. With talks dead-ended at the WTO, the big trading powers are emphasizing free trade agreements (FTAs) and economic partnership agreements (EPAs) with developing countries. These agreements are in many ways more dangerous than the multilateral negotiations at the WTO since they often require greater concessions in terms of market access and tighter enforcement of intellectual property rights.

However, things are no longer that easy for the corporations and trading powers. Doctrinaire neoliberals are being eased out of key positions, giving way to pragmatic technocrats who often subvert neoliberal policies in practice owing to popular pressure. When it comes to FTAs, the global south is becoming aware of the dangers and is beginning to resist. Key South American governments under pressure from their citizenries derailed the Free Trade of the Americas (FTAA) – the grand plan of George W. Bush for the Western hemisphere – during the Mar del Plata conference in November 2005.

Also, one of the reasons many people resisted Prime Minister Thaksin Shinawatra in the months before the 2006 coup in Thailand was his rush to conclude a free trade agreement with the United States. In January of that year, some 10,000 protesters tried to storm the building in Chiang Mai, Thailand, where USA and Thai officials were negotiating. The government that succeeded Thaksin's has put the USA-Thai FTA on hold, and movements seeking to stop FTAs elsewhere have been inspired by the success of the Thai efforts.

The retreat from neoliberal globalization is most marked in Latin America. Long exploited by foreign energy giants, Bolivia under President Evo Morales has nationalized its energy resources. Nestor Kirchner of Argentina gave an example of how developing country governments can face down finance capital when he forced northern bondholders to accept only 25 cents of every dollar Argentina owed them. Venzuelan leader Hugo Chavez has launched an ambitious plan for regional integration, the Bolivarian Alternative for the Americas (ALBA), based on genuine economic cooperation instead of free trade, with little or no participation by northern TNCs, and driven by what Chavez himself describes as a "logic beyond capitalism."

Globalization in perspective

From today's vantage point, globalization appears to have been not a new, higher phase in the development of capitalism but a response to the underlying structural crisis of this system of production. Fifteen years since it was trumpeted as the wave of the future, globalization seems to have been less a "brave new phase" of the capitalist adventure than a desperate effort by global capital to escape the stagnation and disequilibria overtaking the global economy in the 1970s and

1980s. The collapse of the centralized socialist regimes in Central and Eastern Europe deflected people's attention from this reality in the early 1990s.

Many in progressive circles still think that the task at hand is to "humanize" globalization. Globalization, however, is a spent force. Today's multiplying economic and political conflicts resemble, if anything, the period following the end of what historians refer to as the first era of globalization, which extended from 1815 to the eruption of World War I in 1914. The urgent task is not to steer corporate-driven globalization in a "social democratic" direction but to manage its retreat so that it does not bring about the same chaos and runaway conflicts that marked its demise in that earlier era.

Walden Bello is Professor of Sociology and Public Administration, University of the Philippines Diliman, as well as Executive Director of Focus on the Global South. This chapter is adapted from Globalization in Retreat? *CounterPunch*, 6-7 January 2007. © 2007 Walden Bello. Reprinted with permission of the author.

The Global Financial Crisis
Martijn Konings

The Global Financial Crisis (GFC) will go into history as the most serious crisis since the Crash of 1929 and the Great Depression of the 1930s. It has fundamentally changed the contours of American and global capitalism, and it will continue to wreak havoc on the lives of people across the globe long after the pundits declare the world economy to have emerged from its protracted slump. They have lost houses, jobs and pension savings; they have seen their opportunities for advancement decimated and their children's life chances reduced to levels unknown since the Great Depression.

In the Summer of 2007, newspapers reported that a significant proportion of loans in the 'subprime' sector of the American mortgage market turned out to be 'bad debt'. The problem was magnified by the fact that this debt had been generated through a procedure known as 'securitization': the original debts had been sliced up, combined in complex ways with other kinds of debt and then sold on, so that they were now hidden in much larger pools of debt. During the first six months, while there was widespread agreement that a particularly profitable phase of financial growth had come to an end, most comparisons were with the stock market crash of 1987 and the dot-com meltdown at the turn of the century – events whose effects, while dramatic, did not reverberate so far as to cause a wholesale freezing of the financial system. Metaphors used to portray the situation were mostly pitched at the psychological level, emphasizing the lack of confidence and collective anxiety that had gripped markets as the major obstacles to recovery.

During the first half of 2008, the crisis began to take on entirely new dimensions. It gradually appeared that, rather than merely having to weather a period of slowdown, some of the world's most venerable financial institutions were heading for full-blown insolvency. The atmosphere of fundamental uncertainty had a disastrous effect on financial actors' willingness to take risk, and liquidity now froze up completely. As credit contracted and asset prices around the world began to drop, the effects quickly made themselves felt throughout the economic system at large. Economic growth came to a halt, the value of retirement savings plummeted, companies started to lay off workers, and even those homeowners who, with some forbearance, might have been able to maintain payments on their mortgages, were foreclosed upon. Governments (above all the American state) stepped in with unprecedented rescue packages to bail out the financial institutions that were 'too big to fail'.

Many commentators now began to consider the possibility that what we were witnessing was not a relatively localized financial meltdown, but rather the onset of a protracted economic depression that could well end up threatening the very foundations of capitalist order. Financial journalists increasingly resorted to natural metaphors (with 'perfect storm', 'tsunami' and 'hurricane' featuring prominently), as if to suggest that the forces of disintegration had begun to overpower society's mechanisms for exercising control over economic life.

The Global Financial Crisis was now born and the search for answers and solutions began. Comparisons with the Great Depression of the 1930s became commonplace. Indeed, the experience of early twentieth century capitalism has emerged as a key point of reference in public debate, serving not only as a source of causal analogies but equally as a mirror in which to examine and diagnose the moral and social warts of our age. But if public debate was now forced to go beyond the technicalities of financial markets to encompass the social, political and moral aspects of what had gone wrong, the dominant assessments of our subprime predicament have remained rather superficial.

At the heart of these discourses is the notion that an era of political irresponsibility has come to an end: the crisis is widely viewed as representing the breakdown of an economic model characterized by the abdication of public control over financial life, i.e. the regulatory indifference that allowed brokers to foist expensive mortgages on underprivileged Americans and investment managers to recklessly pour massive amounts of 'other people's money' into markets for lemons. We are all Keynesians again, aware of the need for government to regulate the unruly dynamics of free markets – so is the message. After three decades in which the mantra of 'less state, more market' reigned supreme, advocating for the proper regulation of economic activities has become respectable again.

The shallowness of this new Keynesian discourse should have been apparent from the very ease with which an ideological climate shaped so profoundly by decades of neoliberal hegemony gave way to a new common sense concerning the benefits of prudent regulation. Almost overnight, economists like Joseph Stiglitz and Paul Krugman, who for years had been portrayed as brilliant theoreticians that should be kept out of the real-world business of policymaking, sounded quite mainstream in their concerns about deregulation and their calls for re-regulation.

In the US, the change in political climate was already well underway during the last days of the Bush administration and subsequently consolidated to give rise to high hopes for a 'new New Deal'. While announcing his administration's proposal for the reform of the American financial system, President Obama put the need for a rebalancing of government and market front and centre: "It is an indisputable fact that one of the most significant contributors to our economic downturn was an unraveling of major financial institutions and the lack of adequate regulatory structures to prevent abuse and excess" (Obama 2009). This diagnosis of America's economic malaise corresponded to the remedies proposed by his administration in the Treasury's report on 'Financial Regulatory Reform', which outlined several ways to enhance the ability of regulators to supervise the financial services industry. While Obama was at pains to stress that his mission was "not to stifle the market, but to strengthen its ability to unleash … creativity and innovation", he also pointed out that the consequences of a failure to ensure transparency, fairness and prudence had been nothing short of catastrophic (Obama 2009). If the market cannot be expected to work its magic while being stifled by regulation, the Global Financial Crisis had made abundantly clear that government needs to define and police the rules of the game in order to ensure that market participants direct their efforts to the creation of wealth rather than the construction of complex speculative schemes.

Such themes and interpretations have by no means remained confined to the event-driven spheres of journalism and policymaking but have penetrated deeply into realms of public debate that should offer more opportunity for analysis and contemplation. There has been a veritable torrent of publications dealing with the causes, consequences and significance of the credit crunch. For all their differences, these contributions have converged around a common theme: the lack of regulation and the resulting acceleration of irresponsible speculation. Scholarly books tend to argue that lax and misguided policies allowed financial innovation to proceed unchecked, while the more anecdotal literature details the ways in which the unscrupulous lenders and traders that were thus given free rein exploited this lack of regulatory oversight.

Such events and personalities are no doubt important, but only as part of a much broader story of socio-economic change. The crisis and its aftermath need to be seen not just as a result of misguided policies but more fundamentally as a product of the social dynamics and economic institutions constructed over the course of many decades and consolidated during the neoliberal era. These include the dramatic rise in levels of inequality and the increasingly intense financial constraints on working people; the ways in which financial elites imposed a regime of austerity and discipline on corporations and their employees, as well as the rich world of opportunities that such growing indebtedness provided them with; and the ways in which such practices and power inequalities were consistently promoted and facilitated by political decisions to enlarge the room within which elite actors could maneuver while using public funds to socialize the risks they took in doing so.

The Keynesian understanding of the crisis suggests a communal interest in re-regulation that is hardly reflective of existing levels of inequality. Owing to the ease with which it can be invoked in calls to refrain from pointing fingers (at least once the bad apples have been dealt with), this apparently progressive discourse has been complicit in the legitimation of the most inegalitarian uses to which state power has ever been put. Public rescue efforts have overwhelmingly benefited those who already did very well for themselves during the preceding years of frantic financial growth, while the process whereby those benefits are supposed to trickle down to the rest of society remains fraught with uncertainty. The future of our financial order does not just involve a debate over better policies guided by a common interest but rather a confrontation of political projects and forces.

As Naomi Klein has reminded us, the effects of a crisis are often quite paradoxical and by no means necessarily progressive (Klein 2007). The impact of shock and trauma tends to be highly uneven, often further debilitating the political capacities of already marginalized actors while opening up new opportunities for elites. It is especially important to remember this when analyzing the particular brand of socio-economic life that has been constructed in the US over the course of the twentieth century and has gone global over the past decades. Its highly financialized nature means that participation in relations of credit and debt has come to be seen as the royal road to personal autonomy, and this in turn means that the maintenance or restoration of these relations has come to appear as an indisputable necessity.

This logic was evident in the aftermath of the dot-com crash at the start of the twentfirst century. When companies like Enron and WorldCom were revealed to have engaged in elaborate fraud schemes, the public outcry in the US was enormous. Yet the resulting legislation (the Sarbanes-Oxley Act) did little more than provide the American public with a minimal degree of protection from the most flagrant abuses of corporate privilege, while reinvigorating the ability of financial elites to tap into new sources of profit and accumulation. What connected in much more visceral ways with the anger of the American people was the public beheading of several 'bad apples'. While none of this did much to help those people who had seen their pensions evaporate, it was highly effective in dissipating the flurry of popular anger, thereby opening the door to a new episode of frantic financial expansion. Indeed, while the gap between rich and poor had been widening for decades, the astronomic fees that financiers were able to reap from private equity funds and securitization (which came on top of steadily growing basic compensation packages, the sum of which was taxed at lower rates than before) meant that inequality accelerated.

The vilification of financiers since the onset of the crisis has been swift and merciless, at times reminiscent of the days when ordinary people mistrusted banks and credit. Such sentiments were greatly intensified by the use of massive public funds for bailing out the very financial institutions whose irresponsible behavior had produced the crisis in the first place. But for all the widespread popular resentment these bailouts provoked, they have throughout been able to count on an appearance of dire necessity: the fortunes of ordinary Americans, so intricately bound up with a functioning financial infrastructure, were effectively held hostage by the bankers. In the absence of meaningful choice when it came to the political course of action, intense feelings of hostility have found their way into a highly moralistic discourse in which bloated bankers, once again wearing monocles and tophats, feature as villains. For all their unpleasantness, the prospect of redemption is central to such morality plays: their message is invariably that Wall Street can expect to be bailed out if it promises to change its errant ways and to ensure that henceforth financial intermediation will once again operate in the service of the public interest at large.

It is here – the belief in the possibility of using existing structures of political authority and regulation to effect reforms that will make the financial system more responsive to the public interest – that such populist narratives intersect with the Keynesian interpretation of the crisis that has been so widely espoused by scholars and commentators. The notion that once upon a time finance operated in the public interest has in the past often been a useful myth, allowing critics of capitalism to argue from a position that enjoys some degree of socially recognized validity. But at a time when our daily lives and personal ambitions have become so profoundly dependent on credit relations and their management by financial elites, it has become harder than ever for such ideologies of progressive reform to exact significant material concessions. Under such circumstances, to insist on the advent of a new era of Keynesian intervention and regulatory prudence means to allow intellectual capital to become instrumental in channelling popular anger into the highly manageable format of morality plays and the empty threats they pose.

Martijn Konings is Lecturer in Political Economy, School of Social and Political Sciences, University of Sydney. This chapter is adapted from the introduction to his edited book, *The Great Credit Crash*, Verso, London/New York, 2010. © 2010 Martijn Konings.

Economic Inequality
Frank Stilwell

Economic inequalities exist at different scales – global, national and local. The living conditions of people in different countries, regions and localities vary dramatically. At the global scale, measures of inequality are quite mind-boggling. For example it has been estimated that the richest 2 percent of adults owns more than half of global household wealth; and that the three richest people in the world have more wealth than the poorest 48 nations combined (World Institute of Development Economics Research 2006). North America (USA and Canada), with 5 percent of the world's population, has 24 percent of the world Gross Domestic Product. Africa, with over 10 percent of the population, has only a little more than 2 percent of total GDP. Some of the hitherto poorer nations, like the People's Republic of China and India, have markedly increased their overall economic wealth in the last couple of decades, but their internal economic inequalities – including regional inequalities – have grown concurrently.

Within the more affluent nations, major economic inequalities persist. Take the Australian case, for example. In the aggregate, it is a rich country but the increased wealth of Australians in recent years has been spread very unevenly. Contrary to the common perception of Australia as a classless, egalitarian society, its actual distribution of income and wealth is internationally mid-range, comparable to the UK and substantially more unequal than Japan and European nations like Sweden, Norway and Denmark. Some Australians have huge incomes, most notably the corporate executives whose prodigious remuneration packages, commonly exceeding $5 million and sometimes over $30 million annually, are often in the news. Meanwhile, poverty and entrenched disadvantage persist, despite the greater affluence of society as a whole. If the poverty line is set at half the median income for different types of Australian households, about 11 percent of households fall below it (Stilwell and Jordan 2007: 79) Particular groups, defined according to ethnicity, gender, location and socioeconomic status, are disproportionately represented among the poor; and they face persistent problems of economic marginality and social exclusion.

According to the report of the review of Australian taxation conducted by the head of the federal government Treasury in 2009, the top ten percent of Australian wealth holders receive 53 percent of all income from the ownership of capital, such as shares and real estate. This compares with the top ten percent of wage earners who receive 28 percent of all labour income. This is a pertinent reminder that inequality in the distribution of wage incomes is much less than inequality of capital incomes, confirming the class dimension of the overall inequalities.

Who cares?

Should the gulf between rich and poor – and the relative income shares of capital and labour – be a matter of public concern? Some say not. Complacent people accept whatever *is* as natural, even if it is a source of regret. Committed neoliberals have a more assertive ideological stance, asserting that a steep gradient between low and high incomes provides incentive for the efforts that create a thriving economy. The ungainly term 'incentivation' is sometimes used in this context. Although there is little systematic evidence that economic inequality produces high national productivity, proponents of this theory seek to give otherwise unacceptable inequalities a veneer of legitimacy.

Many other people have serious qualms about the current economic inequalities. Indeed, public opinion surveys recurrently reveal that most people think that the gulf between rich and poor is too wide: this is revealed for example, in the results of the official survey of Australian Social Attitudes (Wilson *et al.* 2005). Even relatively wealthy people often favour some degree of redistribution (Stilwell and Jordan 2007: Appendix A). So it is pertinent to ask on what basis such judgements can be made and what policies could be enacted. The challenge for proponents of a more egalitarian society is to establish the principles and policies that would reverse the general trend to inequality in the distribution of income and wealth.

Broadly speaking, there are three bases on which redistributive principles and policies can be established. One is the belief in egalitarianism as a general principle. Second is the expectation that people would be generally happier in a more equal society. Third are the benefits of greater equality for the economy, environment, political processes, social cohesion and public health.

Recognising the inherent equality of all humankind is a good starting point. Article 1 of the United Nations Declaration of Human Rights establishes this fundamental egalitarian principle in terms of innate and universal human rights. A local, folksy Australian variant is the popular belief in a 'fair go' for all. In practice, of course, people are not 'born equal': rather, they are born into situations where their life chances, even their chances of physically surviving infancy, are systematically unequal. So a good society is one that constantly seeks to 'level the playing field'.

Note, however, that this human rights principle stresses the desirability of equality of opportunity, rather than equality of outcome. From this perspective, what matters is not the gulf between high and low incomes, but whether everyone has an equal opportunity to attain the high incomes. So, notwithstanding the inherent appeal of the notion of equality of opportunity, it is not a principle that fundamentally challenges inequalities in the distribution of income and wealth. To take that further step requires more a direct consideration of the practical consequences of having major economic inequalities.

Fundamentally, we have to ask whether major economic inequalities impede the development of a contented society. Much evidence shows that they do. Wealthy people usually enjoy being wealthy, while people in poverty commonly experience personal distress. Most people try to make the best of whatever situation they face, but major divergences in economic circumstances accentuate the difficulties. Indeed, to the extent that people's perception of their happiness depends on what they have relative to others, then economic inequality is a reasonably reliable recipe for significant social discontent.

Evidence from the emerging social science of 'happiness research' confirms this broad generalization. Summarising this evidence, Wilkinson and Pickett (2009) show that more affluence has not, in general, been making societies happier. Over recent decades, there has not been any significant rise in people's average reported assessment of their own well-being, despite enormous increases in average incomes and Gross Domestic Product. The persistence of, and sometimes increase in, economic inequalities can help to explain why. Economic inequalities drive the process of 'conspicuous consumption', 'social emulation' and consumerism. For many people 'affluenza' has become a pervasive sickness, as Clive Hamilton points out in the following chapter in this book (see also Hamilton 2003 and Hamilton and Dennis 2005). Greater equality would not reliably resolve these problems, but could reduce their intensity. In other words, the recognition that people's well-being depends on their *relative* position in society, as well as their absolute living standards, requires continuous societal attention to distributional outcomes.

Unequal societies also tend to be unhealthier. Cross-country comparisons show that greater income inequality is associated with lower life expectancies and higher mortality rates. Another important study by Wilkinson (2005) suggests that this is because the psycho-social impacts of inequality, including "social stress, poor social networks, low self-esteem, high rates of depression, anxiety, insecurity [and] the loss of a sense of control", lead to higher rates of stress-related diseases, homicides and alcohol abuse. We have long known that poverty is strongly correlated with ill-health – because both physical and mental health problems arise when people have inadequate food, clothing and housing. However, we now know that inequality – the size of the gap between rich and poor – is also strongly correlated with ill-health. So just reducing poverty does not deal adequately with the problems of ill-health unless it is part of a broader process of creating a more even distribution of income and wealth.

Economic concerns

Greater equality can also have significant economic benefits. Neoliberal proponents of 'incentivation' may assert that productive effort is encouraged by inequalities, but neoclassical economic theory actually provides no general support for this view. High pay rates may indeed attract some people to work harder or longer, but they also may cause other people to take more leisure because they can generate the income they need by working fewer hours. In practice, inequality tends to impact adversely on cooperation in the workplace and thereby undermines labour productivity. People are more inclined to work cooperatively if they expect to get equitable shares in the fruits of those efforts.

Greater equality may also benefit economic growth more directly because of its effect on consumer spending. Rich people tend to save more than the poor. Boosting the disposable incomes of poor people therefore tends, other things being equal, to have positive macroeconomic effects. The Australian government recognised this when designing the economic stimulus package that it introduced to soften the local impact of the global financial crisis in 2008-9, making relatively poorer people fully entitled to the payments that the government made to households while wealthy people were not similarly eligible. The economic stimulus policy had beneficial macroeconomic outcomes for Australia, helping it to avoid the severe recession that many other countries experienced.

Greater economic equality may also help to reduce imbalances arising from international trade. Of course, both rich and poor people consume imported goods. However, if the proportion of consumer spending going on imported goods is greater for people in upper income groups than for people in lower income groups, economic inequality tends to increase the likelihood of there being a national current account deficit. Redistribution of income from rich to poor would be a very indirect way of dealing with trade problems, just as it is an indirect way of coping with economic crises, but there are some interesting interconnections there. Mainstream economists sometimes talk of a 'trade-off between efficiency and equity', but there are evidently policies that can have beneficial effects for *both* efficiency and equity.

The social, political and environmental costs of inequality

Another reason for being concerned with economic equality is its connection with social cohesion. Economic inequality can undermine the conditions for social stability. In the extreme case, the juxtaposition of a marginalized underclass and an affluent elite is conducive to the periodic breakdown of social order, as the experience of many other countries has shown. Differences in income inequality across countries are also closely associated with differences in rates of crime and violence. Economic inequalities require an ever greater share of society's economic resources to be used for maintaining security and stability.

Expenditures on transfer payments are also a fiscal burden for government in unequal societies. These costs of welfare provision have fuelled the attack on so-called 'welfare dependency', increasing public suspicion of those on welfare and increasing their sense of exclusion. Part of the appeal of greater equality is the prospect of resolving these problems 'at source' rather than putting more and more band-aids on the symptoms.

Turning next to the political arena, we can also see that economic inequalities can have other quite perverse impacts. Our political institutions are based on the fundamentally egalitarian principle of 'one person, one vote'. They work best when this political principle is aligned with economic conditions, such as reasonable equity in living standards, thereby giving a material basis for effective political participation and some degree of shared political economic interests. The fundamental *economic* principle of capitalism, on the other hand, is 'one dollar one vote', which sits awkwardly alongside the egalitarian character of the democratic political principle. So democracy and capitalism are uncomfortable partners, particularly when the capitalist economy produces a markedly uneven distribution of incomes, wealth and economic opportunities.

These tensions and contradictions arising from major economic inequalities pervade modern societies. The political institutions claim to provide universal rights and proclaim the equality of all citizens, while their economic institutions generate big disparities between those citizens in terms of their standards of living. Moreover, it is because economic inequality concentrates resources and power that the wealthy can 'capture' political institutions at the expense of broader national interests. In the extreme, the political process may be corrupted by economic inequality.

There is also an important environmental rationale for redressing existing economic inequalities. This is because some degree of equality is evidently a prerequisite for agreement to deal with environmental problems. Within individual nations, environmental consciousness is enhanced by the sense of shared and collective interests that is more likely to exist where there are no deep economic divisions. A similar tendency exists on an international scale. Many environmental problems are global, so their resolution requires agreement between poor and rich nations. As the 2009 Copenhagen climate change conference illustrated, it is difficult to get effective international agreements when people in the poorer countries see themselves being required to 'tighten their belts' to deal with problems generated disproportionately by people in the richer countries. More balanced economic outcomes are necessary for creating a common commitment to achieving ecologically sustainable development.

Policy responses

The existing patterns of economic inequality reflect the distribution of 'market' incomes and the influence of government policies that seek to redistribute those incomes. How much redistribution is appropriate? The troubling economic, social, political and environmental consequences of economic inequality noted in this chapter provide a case for making greater equality a guiding principle for public policy.

There is a wide array of public policy instruments that may be used for that purpose if there is the political will to act. Incomes policies can address distributional inequities at source. Upper limits could be put on excessive incomes, for example, such as the remuneration of corporate chief executive officers whose incomes have risen so disproportionately in recent years. Governments could also make tax policies more progressive so that they draw a larger share of revenue from rich people. Estate tax and land tax, for example, could be used to target accumulated wealth. Introducing an estate tax would be a means of taxing some of the wealth that is passed on through inheritance: many countries have inheritance taxation, but Australia is currently unusual in this respect. Taxing the unearned income that comes from inherited wealth would be a potent means of reducing economic inequalities and enhancing social mobility. Similarly, land tax, applied to all privately owned landed property, would be an effective means for capturing unearned increments of value for collective social purposes. The revenue thereby generated could fund a major increase in the stock of social housing, which would have the effects of directly helping low-income people and indirectly making housing generally more affordable. That would alleviate one of the main causes of poverty and social stress. Concurrently, other government expenditures could be more directly targeted at the provision of good quality and universally available public services, such as health, education and transport, that should not depend on individuals' ability to pay directly for what is essential to a good life and a healthy society.

On an international scale, the challenges are yet larger, of course. 'Closing the gap' between rich and poor countries is a worthy goal, but there are not currently the institutional arrangements for achieving it. Existing international institutions like the World Trade Organisation, World Bank and International Monetary Fund are demonstrably inadequate for the task of promoting more balanced global economic development. Direct aid by wealthy countries to poorer ones is typically miniscule, seldom more than one percent of GDP, and is often 'tied' to projects that mainly benefit companies in the richer nations. Some countries have forged ahead in economic growth regardless, while others – particularly in sub-Saharan Africa – have slipped backwards in the last three decades. Some radical rethinking of these global economic challenges is imperative.

The study of political economy necessarily raises these issues of intra-national and international equity, alongside concerns about efficiency and sustainability. Of course, there are legitimate differences of opinion about how much inequality is tolerable, even desirable, and how vigorously policies for 'closing the gap' should be pursued. Moreover, even mildly egalitarian policies face many obstacles: the power and economic resources of societal winners are seldom directed at resolving the difficulties of the losers. Many people continue to believe that more economic growth will solve all the problems without the need for redistribution. Generating more egalitarian outcomes requires a social and political movement with vision and commitment. As always, producing change requires political economic analysis, vision and action.

Frank Stilwell is Professor of Political Economy, School of Social and Political Sciences, University of Sydney. Economic Inequality © 2011 Frank Stilwell.

Climate Change and the Economy
Mark Diesendorf

Global warming is one of the greatest threats to civilisation that humans have ever known. But this should not be a cause for paralysis or panic. The threat has solutions, most of which are available now. Under the influence of powerful vested interests that are opposing change, most governments and businesses are not implementing these solutions beyond a token level. For those of us who are concerned, there is a way forward. It involves growing and empowering the community-based climate action movement until no government or business can resist it.

Global climate change, caused primarily by the emission of greenhouse gases from human activities, is accelerating. Temperature increases, averaged over 10-year periods, accelerated through the late twentieth century. Ten of the 12 years 1997-2008 inclusive have been the warmest recorded by instruments (Hansen *et al.* 2009). Melting of the Arctic ice cap and the vast majority of this planet's glaciers and snowfields is also accelerating. In 2006 climate scientists generally believed that the Arctic ice cap might have totally melted by the Summer of 2100 – but now several leading climate scientists believe that this could happen even before 2020 (Stroeve *et al.* 2007).

The acceleration of carbon dioxide (CO_2) emissions and its impact on sea-level can be seen by comparing data from the last 40 years or so with the past decade. According to measurements reviewed by the Intergovernmental Panel on Climate Change, the average rate of CO_2 emission into the atmosphere has increased from 1.4 parts per million (ppm) per year averaged over the period 1960-2005 to 1.9 ppm per year averaged over the period 1995-2005. Particularly worrying is the observation that the rate of sea-level rise has increased from 1.8 millimetres (mm) per year averaged over the period 1963-2003 to 3.1 mm per year over the 11-year period 1993-2003. (IPCC 2007a).

Global warming is triggering several processes that are feeding back to amplify the original warming. Unless the nations of this planet set and act on rigorous greenhouse targets, we are all facing potentially the worst environmental crisis of the twenty-first century (Hansen *et al.* 2008) and an economic crisis on the scale of the Great Depression of the 1930s and the world wars of the twentieth century. Only a nuclear war could compete in terms of the scale of potential devastation (Toon *et al.* 2007).

If we are to be successful in cutting greenhouse gas emissions and stabilising our planet's climate, we must diagnose correctly the source of Earth's fever. The vast majority of climate scientists recognise that most of the global warming that has occurred since the Industrial Revolution is the result of human activities that cause the emission of greenhouse gases.

Like the glass in a greenhouse, these invisible gases allow the life-giving rays of sunlight to pass unimpeded through the atmosphere. This warms the Earth and powers the process of photosynthesis, producing carbohydrates as stored solar energy. The warm Earth emits heat radiation that tries to escape the planetary bounds, but this infrared radiation is impeded on its way out by the greenhouse gases. A balance exists between energy flowing into the Earth from the Sun, mostly as visible sunlight, and the energy flowing outwards from the Earth, mostly as invisible infrared radiation. As concentrations of greenhouse gases in the atmosphere increase, this balance is maintained, but something has to give: the Earth's temperature rises.

Before we humans interfered with the climate, natural concentrations of greenhouse gases in the atmosphere kept Earth's average temperature at about 14 degrees Celsius. The principal natural greenhouse effect comes from water vapour, to which is added carbon dioxide (CO_2) and traces of methane and nitrous oxide. These greenhouse gases make possible the great abundance of life on Earth. However, human activities, especially those carried out since the Industrial Revolution, have increased the concentrations of greenhouse gases in the atmosphere. The principal activities of concern are the combustion of fossil fuels – coal, oil and gas – to generate electricity and heat and to provide the motive power for transportation, while emitting CO_2 as a byproduct. Other important greenhouse gas-emitting activities are forest clearing, which results in the emission of CO_2 and methane, and agriculture, which emits lots of methane together with nitrous oxide and some CO_2. There are also industrial emissions, in addition to those involving energy, comprising CO_2 and some rare but potent greenhouse gases such as HCFCs and PFC. Fugitive emissions, which are leaks of methane and other greenhouse gases from fossil fuel production and transportation, must also be taken into account (IPCC 2007a).

The basic physics, that increasing greenhouse gas concentrations cause global warming, has been well established since the late 1950s and is not scientifically controversial. Only the quantitative details, such as how much warming will result from a doubling of greenhouse gas concentrations, and the magnitude of the contribution of human activities, are subject to ranges of uncertainty and debate. The overwhelming evidence indicates that we humans are responsible for the major proportion of the industrial age global warming.

The impacts of global climate change are already with us. They include sea-level rise, droughts, heatwaves, bushfires, floods, loss of biodiversity and possibly an increase in the prevalence of intense cyclones/hurricanes (Pittock 2009). 'Sea-level rise' means "the initiation of ice-sheet disintegration and sea-level rise, out of humanity's control, eventually eliminating coastal cities and historical sites, creating havoc, hundreds of millions of refugees, and impoverishing nations" (Hansen 2008). 'Loss of biodiversity' means the extermination of a large fraction of the species on the planet. Climate change presages catastrophic consequences. Although it is scientifically difficult to attribute a single weather event to human-induced global warming – just as it is difficult to attribute a single case of cancer to smoking – the statistical evidence is strong and growing. Even in a few individual events, such as the 35,000 premature deaths from the European heatwave of 2003, a scientific case has been made that global warming greatly increased the severity and impact of a 'normal' heatwave (IPCC 2007b: 397). Similarly, global warming probably increased the severity of the bushfires that devastated Victoria (Australia) in February 2009 (Karoly 2009) and is increasing the likelihood of similar events around the world.

Solutions do exist, but we have to be discerning in our choices. Some currently proposed panaceas are deeply problematic. Coal power with CO_2 capture and sequestration (CCS), sometimes misleadingly marketed as 'clean coal', is an unproven technological system that is unlikely to be commercially available before the 2020s. CCS merits development, but not at the expense of cleaner and safer technologies that are ready now. Nuclear power, based on existing 'burner' reactor technology, would become a significant greenhouse gas emitter within several decades, when low-grade uranium ore has to be mined and milled using fossil fuels. Although alternative reactor designs (such as the fast breeder and the integral fast reactor) could, in theory, overcome this problem, they too cannot be commercially available before the 2020s, possibly even 2030. Since nuclear power is a very slow technology to be deployed, it is not a short-term part of the solution and it may not even prove to be a long-term contributor.

The more practical solutions are:

- efficient energy use;
- renewable sources of energy such as solar and wind power;
- natural gas, the least polluting fossil fuel, playing a transitional role while it lasts;
- improvements in urban public transport and better facilities for walking and cycling;
- an end to logging native forests;

- modifications to our lifestyles, including diet;
- modifications to agriculture to reduce methane emission from cattle and sheep and nitrous oxide emissions from soil, and to increase carbon sequestration in vegetation and soils.

These technologies and measures are ecologically sustainable and most of them are available now, although they may take some time to implement on a sufficiently large scale (Diesendorf 2007). They are not the complete solution, but together they can achieve such dramatic reductions in greenhouse gas emissions before 2020 that they can buy us time to address the more difficult challenges – changing our economic system to a steady-state and stabilising the population. In the longer term, by 2050, Australia could achieve zero net greenhouse gas emissions. If this could be achieved by Australia, the biggest per capita greenhouse gas emitter in the industrialised world, then most other countries can also achieve it.

New and improved technologies and practices are not implemented automatically, especially when they involve major changes to essential systems, such as energy demand and supply. To assist the transition, we need appropriate policies from government. Prior to 2009, the ecologically sustainable solutions were not favoured by the power-holders in the USA, the UK or Australia. Indeed, the governments of these countries have long-standing policies that favour fossil fuels and the nuclear industry. To implement the solutions to the anthropogenic climate crisis, we need new government policies to build markets for energy efficiency and renewable energy, foster research and development, and encourage and assist households, workers, business and industry to make the necessary changes. In the longer term, the barriers to ecologically sustainable solutions are not primarily technological or economic. Instead, they are political, institutional and cultural.

Although public concern has been growing rapidly around the world, the majority of governments continue to be dominated by vested interests, including the industries that are the biggest greenhouse gas polluters: coal, oil, aluminium, steel, cement, motor vehicles, forestry and agriculture. These vested interests lobby governments for policies to benefit themselves (Beder 2000). For example:

- the petroleum and motor vehicle industries lobby for tax deductions for petroleum exploration and for the use of company cars;
- the wealthy coal industry lobbies for approval of new coal-mines and new coal-fired power stations, for huge government grants and for taxpayer-funded infrastructure, such as ports, roads and railways for transporting coal;
- the aluminium industry lobbies for subsidised prices for its huge electricity purchases;
- the forestry industry lobbies for approval to log new areas of native forest;
- the livestock industry lobbies the government to market the country's beef and lamb overseas.

The dominant economic system fosters endless growth in consumption; waste of energy, materials and land; and technologies that appear to be cheap but impose huge indirect costs on society and the planet. The economic system creates institutions and cultures that reinforce itself: employment that depends on unsustainable economic growth; governments that subsidise the richest and most powerful industries and use taxpayers' money to bail them out when their speculations are unsuccessful; and a pervasive culture of consumerism.

Yet there is still hope. The economic power-holders and their representatives in government are a tiny minority of the population. The rapidly growing social movement for climate action is making itself felt in Europe, North America, Australia and elsewhere, recognising that the climate crisis and its response strategies are a universal problem, involving environmental protection, social justice, economic impacts, governance and ethics. It needs resources, strategies and tactics to expand the knowledge of its members and to increase its influence on government and industry. It also needs analysis from political economists concerned with these profound environmental challenges.

Mark Diesendorf is Associate Professor, University of New South Wales, and Deputy Director of the Institute for Environmental Studies. This chapter is based partly on his book *Climate Action: A Campaign Manual for Greenhouse Solutions*, UNSW Press, Sydney, 2009. © 2009 Mark Diesendorf. Reproduced with permission of the author.

Consumer Capitalism
Clive Hamilton

The 'economic problem' of reducing material deprivation that preoccupied classical economists has been solved. In Australia, for example, after the last six decades of economic growth the dominant characteristic is not deprivation but abundance. By any standard, it is an enormously wealthy country. Average real incomes are three times higher than they were in 1950 and the great bulk of Australians are prosperous beyond the dreams of their parents and grandparents. While pockets of poverty still exist, and are even less morally tolerable, similar features are evident in many other modern affluent societies.

The forces driving society have shifted from the sphere of production to the sphere of consumption – from workers to consumers, from want to excess, from class politics to identity politics. While the production sphere is associated with increased material output and conflict between suppliers of labour and owners of capital, the shift to the consumption sphere forces us to ask new questions about politics and social change.

Instead of asking how best to increase the rate of economic growth, the social objective under consumer capitalism must focus on the things that improve well-being in a post-scarcity society. But this is not a simple matter (Frey and Stutzer 2002; Myers and Diener 1996). At one level, the answer to the question is simple: The distance between what people have and what they want determines how contented they are. But this raises some awkward questions. How are people's wants determined? Is there a difference between what people say they want, and what they really want? Is what people want independent of what people have? Or does more 'having' drive up the level of wanting, so that the two can never meet and consumption is doomed to be a labour of Sisyphus?

While conventional economic thought regards consumption of goods as a straightforward process of satisfying human wants or desires, in fact the relationship of people to their possessions is full of psychological complexity. It is almost impossible today to buy any item that its producer has not attempted to invest with symbolic meaning (Csikszentmihalyi and Rochberg-Halton 1981; Schor 1998). Clothing, for example, is designed to send signals. Even underwear that may be seen by no-one is bought and sold because it makes the wearer feel a certain way about themselves – a pair of underpants can be sexy, sensible, muscular, vibrant, suave or whimsical. It can communicate a variety of sexual connotations – demure but willing, titillating, brazen, romantic or naughty – and the particular signals they are designed to send are the subject of meticulous commercial calculation.

That is the hallmark of consumer capitalism. For those without wealth in pre-industrial society, personal identity was derived from their daily activities, from their occupations. In today's consumer society people attempt to create an identity not from what they produce but from what they consume. In the words of the CEO of one of the world's largest producers of consumer products: "the brand defines the consumer. We are what we wear, what we eat, what we drive."

Market ideology asserts that free choice allows consumers to express their 'individuality'. But the individuality of modern urban life is pseudo-individuality, an elaborate pose that people adopt to cover up the fact that they have been buried in the homogenising forces of global consumer culture. The consumer self is garishly differentiated on the outside, but this differentiation only serves to conceal the dull conformity of the inner self.

In fact, to discover true individuality it is necessary to stage a psychological withdrawal from the market economy, since the latter is a place where one can buy only manufactured identities, masks purchased to provide the appearance of difference. The pseudo-individuality of modern consumer culture is profoundly isolating. The more isolated we are, the more we are preoccupied with what other people think of us, and the more inclined we are to manufacture an identity to project onto the world. The dramatic increase in the incidence of depression over the last few decades can be interpreted as a normal reaction to the conflict between the compulsive need to project an acceptable manufactured self onto the world, and the deep human need to live out who we are.

Consumer capitalism will flourish as long as what people desire consistently outpaces what people have. It is therefore vital to the reproduction of the system that people are constantly made to feel dissatisfied. The irony of this should not be missed: while economic growth is said to be the process by which people's wants are satisfied, in reality economic growth can be sustained only as long as people remain discontented. Economic growth does not create happiness; unhappiness sustains economic growth. Discontent must be fomented unrelentingly if modern capitalism is to survive, and this explains the indispensable role of the advertising industry.

The greatest danger to consumer capitalism is the possibility that people in wealthy countries will decide that they have more or less everything that money can buy. For each individual this is a small realisation, but one with momentous social implications. For an increasingly jaded population, deceived for decades into believing that the way to a contented life is material acquisition, the task of the advertising industry becomes ever more challenging. Consequently, a large portion of the creative genius of wealthy nations is channeled into the marketing machine (leaving us to speculate on the truly enriching cultural outpouring that would be possible if this genius were devoted to more productive ends).

Advertising long ago discarded the practice of selling a product on the merits of its useful features. The advertisers know that when consumers are at the point of making a purchase they are subconsciously asking themselves two questions: Who am I, and whom do I want to be? These questions of meaning and identity are the most profound questions humans are capable of posing, yet today they are manifested through the lines of a car and the shape of a softdrink bottle.

To protect itself the advertising industry hides behind an elaborate façade. The official story is that advertising helps discerning consumers make informed choices about how best to spend their money. The fiction is maintained in advertising codes of practice that verge on the risible. The British Code of Advertising Standards and Practice declares that "no advertisement may contain any descriptions, claims or illustrations which expressly or by implication mislead". In particular, "no advertisement may misleadingly claim or imply that the product advertised, or an ingredient, has some special property or quality that is incapable of being established".

If governments were serious about this criterion of ethical behaviour then the advertising industry would effectively be abolished. For is not the very purpose of advertising to give people the impression that the product has some special property or quality that is in fact entirely unrelated to the product itself? Do not advertisers attempt to persuade us that cars can give us sexual potency or express our level of achievement, that a certain tub of margarine can create happy and loving families, and that a certain brand of beer confers hard-working manhood? These claims are all manifestly and demonstrably misleading. Indeed, an advertising agency that failed to mislead potential consumers into believing that they could derive enhanced personal qualities from the product would not be in business for long.

Modern capitalism, then, differs in essence from capitalism as it emerged in Europe two to three hundred years ago. For the great majority of people in rich countries the human condition is no longer dominated by the ever-present need to provide for survival and accumulate assets to guard against lean times. The defining struggle today is no longer between proletarians and capitalists over how to divide the surplus of the production process; the defining struggle is how to live an authentic life in a social structure that manufactures 'individuality' and celebrates superficiality.

For the most part, capitalism itself has answered the demands that inspired nineteenth-century socialism – the demands for the end to exploitation at work, for an end to widespread poverty, for social justice and for representative democracy. But the attainment of these has only uncovered deeper sources of social unease – manipulation by marketers, environmental degradation, endemic alienation and mental illness.

In contrast to the historical trend – in which economic considerations have invaded and come to dominate more and more aspects of life and social organisation – a post-growth society would see the displacement of economic rationality by other forms of rationality so that economics would be confined to a smaller and smaller domain, indeed, to the domain where it properly belongs. It would see the flourishing of the rationality of community over that of self-interest and the spread of the ecological rationality of intrinsic value in place of the instrumental exploitation of the natural world. True sustainability would become possible in a society that had gone beyond economic growth and ever-increasing consumption.

Clive Hamilton is Professor of Public Ethics at the Centre for Applied Philosophy and Public Ethics, a joint centre of the Australian National University, Charles Sturt University and the University of Melbourne. This chapter is abridged from Economics in the Age of Consumer Capitalism, *Journal of Australian Political Economy*, no. 50, 2002, pp. 130-36. © 2002 Clive Hamilton. Reprinted with permission of the author.

ECONOMIC AND SOCIAL ORDER

Every society must have an economic foundation capable of generating the material preconditions of life. Moreover, it must be regarded as legitimate in the eyes of the majority of people, if not all people. If such conditions are not met, the divisions and problems that beset the economic system might tear society apart. So, political economists need to carefully study how the structure and functioning of the economy relates to the needs of society.

What are the elements that generally establish economic and social order? It is useful to identify seven: market, state, class, gender, ethnicity, social capital and ideology. *Markets* permit mutually advantageous exchanges that impose discipline on buyers and sellers in the use of economic resources. The *state* may simultaneously provide cohesion through regulation, redistribution, direct provision (e.g. of economic and social infrastructure) and, in the extreme, through repression. Relationships based on *class*, *gender*, and *ethnicity* structure the division of labor and shape the forms of competition and cooperation. *Social capital* may provide greater social cohesion in addition to being a source of increased material wealth. And *ideology* – particularly beliefs about the socio-economic system – shapes individual and collective behavior. How we act depends on what we believe, and therein lies the importance of economic thought as an aspect of capitalist ideology.

The operation of each of these seven elements, and their interaction, varies from society to society. Indeed, it is this variation that largely distinguishes different socio-economic systems. Understanding these elements is a key objective of political economy because it brings out the relationships between economy, society and polity – the connections between material conditions, social values and political activity.

The following articles illustrate these connections between economy, society and polity. Karl Polanyi's classic contribution shows that the development of the market economy, in historical context, was underpinned by distinctive social values and institutions. It is not a 'natural order.' In a similar vein, Evan Jones notes the folly of regarding the state as external to the economic system, as the terminology of 'government intervention' implies, since the state has been an integral part of capitalist development. The subsequent articles on class, gender, and ethnic divisions remind us that we are not all affected the same way by the functioning of the economic system. Rick Kuhn's article makes a strong case for class-based analysis and shows how we can view important aspects of modern Australian capitalism from this perspective. Gabrielle Meagher's article notes the importance and persistence of gender inequalities in economic life, while Phil Griffiths looks at the biases associated with racialization in modern society. Next, Ben Spies-Butcher emphasizes the importance of social capital as a glue holding everything together, and the difficulties associated with the systematic application of that contestable concept. Finally, Robert Heilbroner's piece turns our attention to the role of ideology. As Heilbroner shows, distinctive beliefs about private property and profits are needed to provide legitimacy for capitalism, not least of which is the need for the members of the capitalist class itself to have a set of economic and social theories justifying their own behavior.

For further reading on understanding economy and society, see Julie A. Nelson, 2006, *Economics For Humans*, University of Chicago Press, Chicago; Rick Kuhn (ed), 2005, *Class and Struggle in Australia*, Pearson, Australia; and Jim Stanford, 2008, *Economics for Everyone: A Short Guide to the Economics of Capitalism*, Pluto Press, London.

The Self-Regulating Market
Karl Polanyi

Never before our own time were markets more than accessories of economic life. As a rule, the economic system was absorbed in the social system, and whatever principle of behavior predominated in the economy, the presence of the market pattern was found to be compatible with it. The principle of barter or exchange, which underlies this pattern, revealed no tendency to expand at the expense of the rest. Where markets were most highly developed, as under the mercantile system, they throve under the control of a centralized administration that fostered autarchy both in the households of the peasantry and in respect to national life. Regulation and markets, in effect, grew up together. The self-regulating market was unknown; indeed the emergence of the idea of self-regulation was a complete reversal of the trend of development. It is in the light of these facts that the extraordinary assumptions underlying a market economy can alone be fully comprehended.

A market economy is an economic system controlled, regulated, and directed by markets alone; order in the production and distribution of goods is entrusted to this self-regulating mechanism. An economy of this kind derives from the expectation that human beings behave in such a way as to achieve maximum money gains. It assumes markets in which the supply of goods (including services) available at a definite price will equal the demand at that price. It assumes the presence of money, which functions as purchasing power in the hands of its owners. Production will then be controlled by prices, for the profits of those who direct production will depend upon them; the distribution of the goods also will depend upon prices, for prices form incomes, and it is with the help of these incomes that the goods produced are distributed amongst the members of society. Under these assumptions order in the production and distribution of goods is ensured by prices alone.

Self-regulation implies that all production is for sale on the market – and that all incomes derive from such sales. Accordingly, there are markets for all elements of industry, not only for goods (always including services) but also for labor, land, and money, their prices being called respectively commodity prices, wages, rent, and interest. The very terms indicate that prices form incomes: interest is the price for the use of money and forms the income of those who are in the position to provide it; rent is the price for the use of land and forms the income of those who supply it; wages are the price for the use of labor power, and form the income of those who sell it; commodity prices, finally, contribute to the incomes of those who sell their entrepreneurial services, the income called profit being actually the difference between two sets of prices, the price of the goods produced and their costs, i.e. the price of the goods necessary to produce them. If these conditions are fulfilled, all incomes will derive from sales on the market, and incomes will be just sufficient to buy all the goods produced.

A further group of assumptions follows in respect to the state and its policy. Nothing must be allowed to inhibit the formation of markets, nor must incomes be permitted to be formed otherwise than through sales. Neither must there be any interference with the adjustment of prices to changed market conditions – whether the prices are those of goods, labor, land, or money. Hence there must not only be markets for all elements of industry, but no measure or policy must be countenanced that would influence the action of these markets. Neither price, nor supply, nor demand must be fixed or regulated; only such policies and measures are in order which help to ensure the self-regulation of the market by creating conditions which make the market the only organizing power in the economic sphere.

To realize fully what this means, let us return for a moment to the mercantile system and the national markets that it did so much to develop. Under feudalism and the guild system land and labor formed part of the social organization itself (money had yet hardly developed into a major element of industry). Land, the pivotal element in the feudal order, was the basis of the military, judicial, administrative, and political system; its status and function were determined by legal and customary rules. Whether its possession was transferable or not, and if so, to whom and under what restrictions; what the rights of property entailed; to what uses some types of land might be put – all these questions were removed from the organization of buying and selling, and subjected to an entirely different set of institutional regulations.

The same was true of the organization of labor. Under the guild system, as under every other economic system in previous history, the motives and circumstances of productive activities were embedded in the general organization of society. The relations of master, journeyman, and apprentice; the terms of the craft; the number of apprentices; the wages of the workers were all regulated by the custom and rule of the guild and the town. What the mercantile system did was merely to unify these conditions. Mercantilism, with all its tendency towards commercialization, never attacked the safeguards which protected these two basic elements of production – labor and land – from becoming the objects of commerce.

Not before the last decade of the eighteenth century was the establishment of a free labor market even discussed; and the idea of the self-regulation of economic life was utterly beyond the horizon of the age. The mercantilist was concerned with the development of the resources of the country, including full employment, through trade and commerce; the traditional organization of land and labor he took for granted. He was in this respect as far removed from modern concepts as he was in the realm of politics, where his belief in the absolute powers of an enlightened despot was tempered by no intimations of democracy. And just as the transition to a democratic system and representative politics involved a complete reversal of the trend of the age, the change from regulated to self-regulating markets at the end of the eighteenth century represented a complete transformation in the structure of society.

A self-regulating market demands nothing less than the institutional separation of society into an economic and political sphere. Such a dichotomy is, in effect, merely the restatement, from the point of view of society as a whole, of the existence of a self-regulating market. It might be argued that the separateness of the two spheres obtains in every type of society at all times. Such an inference, however, would be based on a fallacy. True, no society can exist without a system of some kind that ensures order in the production and distribution of goods. But that does not imply the existence of separate economic institutions; normally, the economic order is merely a function of the social, in which it is contained. Neither under tribal, nor feudal, nor mercantile conditions was there, as we have shown, a separate economic system in society. Nineteenth century society, in which economic activity was isolated and imputed to a distinctive economic motive, was, indeed, a singular departure.

Such an institutional pattern could not function unless society was somehow subordinated to its requirements. A market economy can exist only in a market society. A market economy must comprise all elements of industry, including labor, land, and money. (In a market economy the last also is an essential element of industrial life and its inclusion in the market mechanism has, as we will see, far-reaching institutional consequences.) But labor and land are no other than the human beings themselves of which every society consists and the natural surroundings in which it exists. To include them in the market mechanism means to subordinate the substance of society itself to the laws of the market.

We are now in the position to develop in a more concrete form the institutional nature of a market economy, and the perils to society which it involves. We will, first, describe the methods by which the market mechanism is enabled to control and direct the actual elements of 'industrial life; second, we will try to gauge the nature of the effects of such a mechanism on the society which is subjected to its action.

It is with the help of the commodity concept that the mechanism of the market is geared to the various elements of industrial life. Commodities are here empirically defined as objects produced for sale on the market; markets, again, are empirically defined as actual contacts between buyers and sellers. Accordingly, every element of industry is regarded as having been produced for sale, as then and then only will it be subject to the supply-and-demand mechanism interacting with price. In practice this means that there must be markets for every element of industry; that in these markets each of these elements is organized into a supply and a demand group; and that each element has a price that interacts with demand and supply. These markets – and they are numberless – are interconnected and form One Big Market.

The crucial point is this: labor, land, and money are essential elements of industry; they also must be organized in markets; in fact, these markets form an absolutely vital part of the economic system. But labor, land, and money are obviously not commodities; the postulate that anything that is bought and sold must have been produced for sale is emphatically untrue in regard to them. In other words, according to the empirical definition of a commodity they are not commodities. Labor is only another name for a human activity which goes with life itself, which in its turn is not produced for sale but for entirely different reasons, nor can that activity be detached from the rest of life, be stored or mobilized; land is only another name for nature, which is not produced by man; actual money, finally, is merely a token of purchasing power which, as a rule, is not produced at all, but comes into being through the mechanism of banking or state finance. None of them is produced for sale. The commodity description of labor, land, and money is entirely fictitious.

Nevertheless, it is with the help of this fiction that the actual markets or labor, land, and money are organized; they are being actually bought and sold on the market; their demand and supply are real magnitudes; and any measures or policies that would inhibit the formation of such markets would *ipso facto* endanger the self regulation of the system. The commodity fiction, therefore, supplies a vital organizing principle in regard to the whole of society affecting almost all its institutions in the most varied way, namely, the principle according to which no arrangement or behavior should be allowed to exist that might prevent the actual functioning of the market mechanism on the lines of the commodity fiction.

Now, in regard to labor, land, and money such a postulate cannot be upheld. To allow the market mechanism to be sole director of the fate of human beings and their natural environment, indeed, even of the amount and use of purchasing power, would result in the demolition of society. For the alleged commodity 'labor power' cannot be shoved about, used indiscriminately, or even left unused, without affecting also the human individual who happens to be the bearer of this peculiar commodity. In disposing of a man's labor power the system would, incidentally, dispose of the physical, psychological, and moral entity 'man' attached to that tag. Robbed of the protective covering of cultural institutions, human beings would perish from the effects of social exposure; they would die as the victims of acute social dislocation through vice, perversion, crime, and starvation. Nature would be reduced to its elements, neighborhoods and landscapes defiled, rivers polluted, military safety jeopardized, the power to produce food and raw materials destroyed.

Finally, the market administration of purchasing power would periodically liquidate business enterprise, for shortages and surfeits of money would prove as disastrous to business as floods and droughts in primitive society. Undoubtedly, labor, land, and money markets *are* essential to a market economy. But no society could stand the effects of such a system of crude fictions even for the shortest stretch of time unless its human and natural substance as well as its business organization was protected against the ravages of this satanic mill.

The extreme artificiality of market economy is rooted in the fact that the process of production itself is here organized in the form of buying and selling. No other way of organizing production for the market is possible in a commercial society. During the late Middle Ages industrial production for export was organized by wealthy burgesses, and carried on under their direct supervision in the home town. Later, in the mercantile society, production was organized by merchants and was not restricted any more to the towns; this was the age of 'putting out' when domestic industry was provided with raw materials by the merchant capitalist, who controlled the process of production as a purely commercial enterprise. It was then that industrial production was definitely and on a large scale put under the organizing leadership of the merchant. He knew the market, the volume as well as the quality of the demand; and he could vouch also for the supplies which, incidentally, consisted merely of wool, wood, and, sometimes, the looms or the knitting frames used by the cottage industry. If supplies failed it was the cottager who was worst hit, for his employment was gone for the time; but no expensive plant was involved and the merchant incurred no serious risk in shouldering the responsibility for production. For centuries this system grew in power and scope until in a country like England the wool industry, the national staple, covered large sectors of the country where production was organized by the clothier. He who bought and sold, incidentally, provided for production – no separate motive was required. The creation of goods involved neither the reciprocating attitudes of mutual aid; nor the concern of the householder for those whose needs are left to his care; nor the craftsman's pride in the exercise of his trade; nor the satisfaction of public praise-nothing but the plain motive of gain so familiar to the man whose profession is buying and selling. Up to the end of the eighteenth century, industrial production in Western Europe was a mere accessory to commerce.

As long as the machine was an inexpensive and unspecific tool there was no change in this position. The mere fact that the cottager could produce larger amounts than before within the same time might induce him to use machines to increase earnings, but this fact, in itself, did not necessarily affect the organization of production. Whether the cheap machinery was owned by the worker or by the merchant made some difference in the social position of the parties and almost certainly made a difference in the earnings of the worker, who was better off as long as he owned his tools; but it did not force the merchant to become an industrial capitalist, or to restrict himself to lending his money to such persons as were. The vent of goods rarely gave out; the greater difficulty continued to be on the side of supply of raw materials, which was sometimes unavoidably interrupted. But, even in such cases, the loss to the merchant who owned the machines was not substantial. It was not the coming of the machine as such but the invention of elaborate and therefore specific machinery and plant which completely changed the relationship of the merchant to production. Although the new productive organization was introduced by the merchants – a fact which determined the whole course of the transformation – the use of elaborate machinery and plant involved the development of the factory system and therewith a decisive shift in the relative importance of commerce and industry in favor of the latter. Industrial production ceased to be an accessory of commerce organized by the merchant as a buying and selling proposition; it now involved long-term investment with corresponding risks. Unless the continuance of production was reasonably assured, such a risk was not bearable.

But the more complicated industrial production became, the more numerous were the elements of industry the supply of which had to be safeguarded. Three of these, of course, were of outstanding importance: labor, land, and money. In a commercial society their supply could be organized in one way only: by being made available for purchase. Hence, they would have to be organized for sale on the market – in other words, as commodities. The extension of the market mechanism to the elements of industry – labor, land, and money was the inevitable consequence of the introduction of the factory system in a commercial society. The elements of industry had to be on sale. This was synonymous with the demand for a market system. We know that profits are ensured under such a system only if self-regulation is safeguarded through interdependent competitive markets. As the development of the factory system had been organized as part of a process of buying and selling, therefore labor, land, and money had to be transformed into commodities in order to keep production going. They could, of course, not be really transformed into commodities, as actually they were not produced for sale on the market. But the fiction of their being so produced became the organizing principle of society. Of the three, one stands out: labor is the technical term used for human beings, in so far as they are not employers but employed; it follows that henceforth the organization of labor would change concurrently with the organization of the market system. But as the organization of labor is only another word for the forms of life of the common people, this means that the development of the market system would be accompanied by a change in the organization of society itself. All along the line, human society had become an accessory of the economic system.

We recall our parallel between the ravages of the enclosures in English history and the social catastrophe which followed the Industrial Revolution. Improvements, we said, are, as a rule, bought at the price of social dislocation. If the rate of dislocation is too great, the community must succumb in the process. The Tudors and early Stuarts saved England from the fate of Spain by regulating the course of change so that it became bearable and its effects could be canalized into less destructive avenues. But nothing saved the common people of England from the impact of the Industrial Revolution. A blind faith in spontaneous progress had taken hold of people's minds, and with the fanaticism of sectarians the most enlightened pressed forward for boundless and unregulated change in society. The effects on the lives of the people were awful beyond description. Indeed, human society would have been annihilated but for protective countermoves which blunted the action of this self-destructive mechanism.

Social history in the nineteenth century was thus the result of a double movement: the extension of the market organization in respect to genuine commodities was accompanied by its restriction in respect to fictitious ones. While on the one hand markets spread all over the face of the globe and the amount of goods involved grew to unbelievable proportions, on the other hand a network of measures and policies was integrated into powerful institutions designed to check the action of the market relative to labor, land, and money. While the organization of world commodity markets, world capital markets, and world currency markets under the aegis of the gold standard gave an unparalleled momentum to the mechanism of markets, a deep-seated movement sprang into being to resist the pernicious effects of a market-controlled economy. Society protected itself against the perils inherent in a self-regulating market system – this was the one comprehensive feature in the history of the age.

Karl Polanyi was Professor at Oxford University and the University of London. This chapter is abridged from The Self-Regulating Market. *The Great Transformation*, Beacon Press, New York, 1944, ch. 6, pp. 68-76. © 1944 Karl Polanyi.

Government Intervention
Evan Jones

'Government intervention' is orthodox economic language for the presence of the state in the capitalist economy. The label has powerful connotations: there is the tacit presumption that the state is 'outside' the economic sphere; that the state's role in the economic sphere is 'unnatural'; and that the workings of the economic sphere have been 'distorted' by the state's role.

Loaded language here substitutes for argument. The most significant tacit implication of the label's usage is that the natural structure of the economic sphere is a system of 'free market forces'. An even more deeply embedded presumption is that a system of free market forces works towards the public interest. The connection is now treated in an elusive manner in respectable orthodox economic theory, professional economists having backed off from the certainties of the turn of the last century, when they still talked with some assurance of people's happiness and the means to its achievement through the competitive market mechanism. The qualifications are absent in popular and political discourse – an explicit connection between unhampered market forces and the public interest has been the hallmark of 'neoliberal' ideology since the end of the long post-war boom in the mid-1970s. Thus, the clamor for 'deregulation' and privatisation becomes a natural policy response to the ideological implications of 'intervention' – the role of the state as unnatural and distorting.

This vision of the role of the state is, of course, both inaccurate and unworkable. There is no such thing as a pure economic system of free market forces, there never has been in the past and there could not be in the future.

The state has been integral in the *creation* of capitalism. The heyday of British capitalism, the long boom from the late 1840s to the mid-1870s, was the presumed pinnacle of *laissez faire*. Yet it was premised domestically on the long-term transformation of the British state to serve 'bourgeois' interests, and internationally on the colonizing activities and naval power of the British state. There has been a close historical association between the proponents and beneficiaries of free trade and the possession of economic might. In nineteenth-century Germany and Japan, the development of the capitalist mode of production was not merely dependent on the state; rather, capitalism was a *vehicle* for the stability of the state and the integrity of the nation – a newly created nation in Germany's case. American capitalism was vitally dependent upon a series of state-secured wars in the creation of nationhood, and upon economic support from governments at both the federal and State levels, most clearly represented in the ascendancy of the Republican Party after the Civil War. Again, the state's role was vital in the development of capitalism in Australia, for example, in the control of the location and character of settlement and in the provision of infrastructure.

The state has also been integral in providing the conditions for the *continuing success* of capitalism. Capitalist competition (so-called 'market forces') has required perennial state assistance – in the form of subsidies or rationalization measures, especially in times of crisis. It is in the mediation of international relations that the state's integral role has been most visible – managing tariffs, export subsidies, cartelization support, not to mention gunboat diplomacy (brilliantly manifest in the nineteenth-century partitions of China and Africa).

Finally, the state has been integral in the absorption and processing of claims from the victims of capitalist competition against its adverse effects. State-directed social security measures, factory legislation, public amenities, etc. form part of the so-called *legitimation* of the organization of society along capitalist lines.

Thus the state has been integral in the creation of capitalism, in providing for its continuity by supporting profit generation, and in providing the conditions for the system's legitimacy. Capitalism without the nation state (especially that of the superpowers) would be like a body without its skeleton. The so-called market mechanism does not have a backbone of its own – it is a social construct rooted in regulatory structures. Capitalist competition was preceded by 'bureaucratisation' and it, in turn, produces bureaucratisation.

Although the state's integral role has been pointed out many times, this does not appear to have made a significant impact on the still dominant economic vision of a purist version of the 'market mechanism'. Thus late nineteenth-century Australia has been labeled as 'colonial socialism' because this dominant vision cannot be reconciled with detailed inquiry into Australian economic history (Butlin, Barnard and Pincus 1982). According to this view, which treats capitalism as synonymous with market forces, the evidence on the major role of the state must indicate some form of socialism.

Given this distorted image, how is it possible for the calls for 'deregulation' to be taken seriously? Governments which are formally committed to reducing 'intervention' across the board are engaged, in practice, in a *restructuring of the state's* role. Regulations are removed selectively, welfare measures are reduced (e.g. public housing, government schooling, women's refuges, etc.), but industry assistance and 'law and order' expenditure is enhanced. In this context, a persistence with the concept of 'intervention' involves a calculated act of public deception. Behind the language, peak business organizations and Right-of-centre parties share with Marxist intellectuals a recognition of the structural impossibility of taking the government 'out' of private enterprise.

Paradoxically, however, there is a sense in which the term 'intervention' is meaningful. This is in reference to acts that are conscious, strategic and designed to effect a *transformation* of the existing polity. A different perspective is available from this interpretation. Firstly, much of the state's role, indeed the bulk, cannot be automatically so classified as 'intervention' – it is an integral part of the existing politico-economic structure. Elements of this role may be the result of decisive interventions in the past, but but these have become institutionalized. Such, for example, has been the existence of the Reserve Bank in Australia, as an institutionalized instrument of monetary policy. The state-owned railways in Australia provide a similar example.

Secondly, institutions other than the state engage in acts of strategic intervention – in particular, business corporations. Corporate groupings have engaged in systematic activities of strategy coordination, lobbying and propaganda, as a means of altering their public image, their benefits from the state, and their balance of power with labor. As indicated above, the very language that structures our thinking is an object of such interventions.

Moreover, labor has engaged in strategic intervention, fundamentally as a means of offsetting what it perceives as its structured subordination in capitalist society. Historically, the two most significant forms of intervention have been the formation of collective organizations in the workplace (trade unions) and the creation of working-class based political parties. In addition, loose groupings have waxed and waned, providing coalitions for social intervention, especially in periods of perceived crisis. Scores of welfare organizations or other self-help organizations have arisen in times of genuine destitution of working-class communities.

In the present context, it is worthwhile elaborating on the character of a genuine intervention by the state. To repeat, we are concerned with *strategic* acts by which the state attempts to transform, sometimes dramatically, the inherited politico-economic structure. Of course, 'the state' comprises a number of distinct instrumentalities – government, parliament, the public sector bureaucracies, the judiciary, etc. Each of these institutions may be variously the instigator and subject of strategic intervention, though popular wisdom vests in parliament the greatest legitimacy for the instigation of change.

In Australia, the Curtin-Chifley years in the middle of last century stand out as a good example of parliamentary intervention in a progressive direction; so also do certain elements of the Whitlam government program in the 1970s, such as the sheer breadth of the welfare measures enacted and the attempted creation of the Petroleum and Minerals Authority. Interventions, however, may also be of a reactionary character. The systematic attacks on labor by Labor-Nationalist governments under Billy Hughes after 1915 and the anti-union legislation and dramatic cuts in the social wage by the Fraser Coalition government later in the 1970s provide examples. So too do more recent government industrial relations policies that focus on individual labor contracts, culminating in the WorkChoices legislation of the Howard Coalition Government in 2006.

There is an important lesson here. Governments that are characterized ideologically as opposed to 'intervention' are aggressively interventionist. For example, deregulation of financial institutions, as undertaken by the Labor government in the 1980s, was an aggressive act of intervention. From this perspective, the Thatcher government in the UK must be seen as one of the most interventionist governments in postwar history. In quantitative terms, the Reagan Administration's commitment to US military build-up provided an excellent example of strategic intervention, as does the more recent bipartisan invasion and occupation of Afghanistan and Iraq since 2001.

By viewing the label 'intervention' in this different light we are exposed to a substantial transformation in the way in which we interpret capitalist development and the state. The concept of a self-contained free market mechanism with links to an external detached state is an unreal idealistic construction. The capitalist state develops symbiotically with the development of capitalism. If any metaphor is apt, the state's involvement is one of chemical fusion rather than one of mechanical linkages.

At least three implications follow from this conception. First, one must attempt to comprehend government behavior not in terms of the operation of some detached 'collective will' that might be rational or irrational depending on one's own ideological position, but in terms of the end product of centuries of political struggle directed by the ebb and flow of the balance of forces. Second, one can more readily appreciate the differences in government behavior across capitalist countries as reflecting the specific balance of forces behind each country's development. Finally, the calls and actions towards so-called 'small government' and 'deregulation' are not moves against a generalized government presence; they are rather class-interested interventions in their own right, and demand to be met both by critical counter-propaganda and counter-interventions of a progressive nature. The issue is not one of market economy versus government intervention, but one of reactionary intervention versus progressive intervention in which various instrumentalities of the state constitute an important arena of conflict and struggle.

Evan Jones is Research Associate in Political Economy, University of Sydney. This chapter is an updated extract adapted from Government Intervention. *Journal of Australian Political Economy*, no. 17, November 1984, pp. 53-60. © 1984 Evan Jones. Reprinted with permission of the author.

Why Class Matters
Rick Kuhn

How we get an income has a profound influence on our lives. The few who manage large numbers of people or own valuable assets have very different experiences from the rest of us. These economic inequalities have a class dimension.

An important indicator of inequality is differences in ownership of assets, such as cash, shares or houses. In 2006 the richest ten percent of households in Australia owned 44 percent of the total wealth (Commonwealth of Australia 2010a: 140). The richest 20 percent owned 61 percent of the wealth, so each of those households had wealth, on average, 63 times that owned by a houehold in the poorest fifth. That top group of households owned 86 percent of shares, held 78 percent of cash deposits, 81 percent of investment real estate, and 97 percent of households' own incorporated businesses. The bottom group owned less than a half of one percent of these kinds of assets (ABS 2007b).

Incomes are more evenly spread than the distribution of wealth: the richest 20 percent gained 41 percent of all income in 2008 (ABS 2009). Yet there are massive incentives to legally minimise your taxable income, if you can afford accountants, solicitors and barristers. The trend has been for income inequality to increase since the mid 1990s.

Our incomes and wealth profoundly shape our lives – what we eat and wear, the kinds of homes we inhabit, our access to education and information, whether or not we spend time in gaol and the range of personal choices available to us.

Where we are in the society's hierarchy to a large extent reflects our parents' positions. There is some social mobility between generations, but the existence of profound inequality remains an important aspect of Australian society whether or not there is social mobility between generations. Our individual capacities and talents, whose development is also influenced by family background, and chance can also play a role in determining how much control we have over our lives.

Taken separately, social patterns of wealth and income distribution, education, health and housing, *describe* important aspects of our world. Such inequalities don't *explain* much: they are symptoms. People at the top and many lower down believe that inequality just reflects the fact that some people are harder working or more clever than others. But this common sense explanation makes huge assumptions. First, leaving aside morality tales about poor but bright or dedicated kids making good, there is no solid evidence that the rich really do work harder and have greater intellectual capacities than the rest of us. This explanation takes as given, secondly, that it is natural for differences in intelligence or single-mindedness to result in profound social inequality.

It is not possible to account for patterns of inequality simply in terms of individual characteristics and behaviour. That leaves out relationships amongst people and therefore ignores the effects of social power. To explain how and why these patterns occur, their connections and their influence on politics, it is essential to go beyond surface appearances, beyond 'common sense' to examine social structures. This is what class analysis can do. By identifying class, grounded in social relationships of production, as the basis of power in our society, a Marxist approach to class, such as that outlined below. That approach also provides a framework for understanding the treatment of oppressed groups and social conflict as symptoms of a class divided society.

Class, power and production

Class today arises from the ownership and control that a tiny minority of employers, senior private and public sector managers and politicians exercises over productive resources like factories, offices, machinery and land or, in more abstract form, money that can purchase these things. Employers need the labour of other people to bring such resources into motion. With a part of their capital, bosses buy the right to direct workers' activities, that is to make use of employees' ability to work (labour power) over a specific time. The new value created by labour power is the basis of employers' profits.

The capitalist class (bourgeoisie) is made up of those who own or control productive resources and compete with each other to make profits. People whose only means of making a living is to sell their ability to work to an employer are members of the working class (proletariat). This includes spouses and children dependent on a wage. Most unemployed people, who cannot get a job or are unable to labour and therefore have to try to survive on meagre social security payments, are also part of the working class.

In Australia, the capitalist class is a tiny minority while a very large majority of people are working class. Understood as employees whose main tasks are not supervisory, the working class includes most teachers, nurses and clerical workers, alongside technicians and trades people, miners, transport, construction and production line workers. Together they comprised about 70 percent of the workforce in 2008 (calculated from ABS 2010).

Not everyone in the Australian workforce is either a boss or a worker. There are middle layers that share some characteristics with capitalists and others with the majority of wage earners. People in the traditional middle class (petty bourgeoisie) own small amounts of productive resources. Their ownership of a truck, a shop, computers or other kinds of equipment is often only possible because of heavy indebtedness. Unlike capitalists, members of the petty bourgeoisie are primarily dependent on their own labour, perhaps aided by family or a small number of employees. Some professionals, such as independent solicitors, accountants and doctors, operate in a similar way. A 'new middle class' also exists, made up of diverse groups of employees of large organisations in a hierarchy of senior supervisors, professionals and middle managers (Callinicos and Harman 1987; Carchedi 1975). Specialised professionals, engineers, lawyers or accountants in such bureaucracies may have considerable autonomy in their work. Supervisors have power over subordinates and limited authority to decide how productive resources are used. But they don't participate in major decisions about levels of employment or the kind of business done by their organisation. The number of people in the middle classes is much smaller than the number of workers, but they far outnumber the members of the capitalist class.

All the employees of a large business or government department – cleaners, technicians, managers and even the chief executive officer – may get their income in the form of a wage or salary. But this is less important in shaping their lives and, usually, in determining the level of their income than their role in production: whether they do what they are told at one extreme or make the key decisions and give the most important orders at the other.

Class relations are not just about economics. Human beings are fundamentally creative: they shape the non-human material world and their relationships with each other. Capitalist relations of production radically limit our scope to realise our creative capacities by depriving us of control over the means of production, the products of our labour, our relations with other people at work and our biological selves (in the form of our physical activity). This alienation influences many other aspects of human existence, including our relations with others outside work, how we think and how we feel. It does so for two reasons. First, work is essential for survival and takes up such a large proportion of our waking lives. Secondly, conflicts between bosses and workers and competition amongst capitalists are built into capitalist relations of production so that no one is in overall control of social processes (Ollman 1976).

Bosses have more control over circumstances and events than workers, but their creative capacities are also limited by capitalism. Members of the capitalist class are forced, through competition between businesses and states, to try to improve their profitability at the expense of workers and their competitors. Their personal relations, like ours, are affected by the fact that the capitalist mode of production encourages all of us to treat everything and everyone like a commodity. The priority of profit making over the maintenance of diverse and sustainable ecologies affects their health and pleasure too, although members of the capitalist class are in better position to escape the effects of pollution and the destruction of the natural environment.

Our positions in the relations of production may be a life and death matter, quite apart from the kind of medical care we can afford. The more control people exercise over their jobs, the less stress they suffer and the healthier they are. Even allowing for the effects of heredity, education and differences in lifestyle, people on lower incomes are more likely to suffer from stress-related diseases (Wilkinson and Marmot 1998; Wilkinson and Pickett 2009).

Appearance and reality

Capitalism is the first class system in history that pretends not to be one. It has a self-camouflage mechanism, which Karl Marx (1976: 163-77) labelled the fetishism of commodities. The defining social relationship of capitalism, that between bosses and workers, appears to be one between equals. Normally, in the wage contract, they really do exchange equivalents: a portion of the employers' capital (in the form of wages) against labour power of the same value. Exploitation takes place because employers own the products that result from the application of labour power.

Capitalists get to own the new value produced by workers without the kind of direct coercion that accompanied the extraction of surplus from peasants or slaves under previous modes of production. There is, however, indirect coercion and a radical imbalance between the power of individual employees and employers. Behind the apparent equal relationships between individuals lie class relations (Lukács 1971). If workers are not to suffer from very low living standards and, in some capitalist societies, even to starve, they have to sell their labour power to those who have the money to employ them. Once employed, the threat of dismissal for not following orders is generally a serious one.

Apparent equality in the production process extends to the formal equality of workers and bosses as citizens, in relation to the state. Yet, despite the appearance of impartiality, states are vital guarantors of capitalist class interests.

Class analysis will always be controversial. The people who control the most powerful mechanisms for generating and shaping ideas – media barons, government ministers, vice chancellors – are amongst the main beneficiaries of capitalism. They naturally oppose theories that highlight the inherent inequalities, injustices, and tendencies towards crisis in our society. Capitalists and their spokespeople are not shy about identifying their own interests with those of the entire society. They invent and promote ideas that dispute or ignore the significance of class and hinder the constitution of the working class as an effective and conscious actor capable of achieving social change.

Oppression and ideologies can only be understood in the context of class. This is true of the oppression of women, the repression of sexuality (especially when it is not expressed in monogamous and heterosexual relationships), racism and nationalism (Kuhn 2005).

The family plays a crucial role in reproducing labour power. Unpaid domestic labour makes the preparation of family members for work the next day and the creation of new generations of workers cheap. Think how much higher wages would have to be if all the cooking, cleaning and childcare services that take place at home had to be bought on the market. Women disproportionately do this unpaid labour. Sexism treats this as natural and justifies paying women in the workforce less than men.

The oppression of gays and lesbians is the flip side of politicians', churches' and the mass media's insistence that 'real' families consist of mum dad and the kids. If we don't match this image – and don't reproduce labour power in the accepted way – we aren't 'normal', don't deserve the same rights as other people, especially not the right to marry our partners. The repression of sexuality in general, from a young age, means that we get used to subordinating our desires to the expectations of others, an important characteristic of obedient workers.

Divisions between men and women, gays and straights, also make it more difficult for workers to unite against the capitalist class. So do racism and nationalism They create imagined communities and illusory social contradictions that are real in the sense that they have practical effects but are also fabrications whose appearance and continued existence is explicable in terms of ruling class interests. Racism and nationalism encourage us to identify other races and nations as threats and our bosses and rulers as allies. When politicians aim to win votes from racists, by attacking refugees, Muslims or Aborigines, their actions reinforce racism and serve capitalist class interests by dividing the working class, even as they deny that a capitalist class, as a ruling group, exists.

Racism distracts attention from the real causes of problems like unemployment, job insecurity, poor hospital and public transport services, longer work hours, low wages, expensive housing or environmental degradation, by blaming them on scapegoats. The racist treatment of Indigenous Australians has also justified the theft of Aboriginal land.

Nationalism is one of the most pervasive and least questioned of class ideologies and underpins mainstream political debate in Australia. The idea of the national interest assumes, first, that Australians are fundamentally different from people of other nationalities. Most nations make claims about their own special or unique unity of purpose. The assertion of Australian specialness has often been reinforced by explicit or implicit appeals to racism. A second assumption is that the national community is more important than the internal differences or divisions and, by implication, that cleavages between nations are fundamental (Howard 2001; Rudd 2007). But just how much do women gutting chickens on a Steggles production line share with the overwhelmingly male directors and top managers of the company they work for? Within and across national boundaries, nationalism operates in a similar way to racism as an antidote to workers' solidarity.

When the veil of national consciousness is removed, national interests are revealed as the naked self-interests of the dominant class. National prosperity depends on the profitability of capital invested in Australia. National security is the ability of those who own and control capital to see off threats to their rights, whether from opponents at home or overseas. National interests are ideological, conditional on national consciousness. In contrast, class interests derive directly from the objective existence of classes, whether they are consciously perceived or not (Davidson 2002: 13).

Class struggle

The everyday experience of doing what you're told at school, university and work, the fetishism of commodities and ideologies promoted by the capitalist class foster conservative attitudes. Together, they generally encourage us to accept that the existing order is natural and inevitable, that workers are incapable of bringing about change and that class differences are unimportant. One aspect of capitalism, however, tends to promote working class consciousness. Struggle between the capitalist and working classes is a necessary consequence of capitalist relations of production. For both sides it is a matter of survival. Competition amongst bosses over profits, markets and investments forces them to try to limit and, where possible, reduce their employees' wages, while increasing hours and the pace of work. The living standards of workers, on the other hand, depend on success in defending, if not improving, their pay and conditions. Bosses and workers therefore have contradictory interests, arising directly from the relations of production that give rise to *class struggles*.

At times such struggles are out in the open. Lockouts, reorganising work, reducing pay and conditions, attacking employees' ability or rights to organise, raising working hours, and cutting labour forces are all measures bosses use to secure their profits. Workers may pursue their interests by striking, banning certain kinds of work, occupying their workplaces or engaging in political protests. But class struggle is often less obvious and dramatic. Supervisors may tighten up existing rules or work practices concerning the length of a lunch break or the pace of work. Individual workers may slack off, take sickies, add a few minutes to breaks, or try to undermine the authority of supervisors.

Because individual workers lack power compared to individual bosses, to be effective their struggle usually has to be collective. If one employee dawdles, stops working or protests, she or he can easily be replaced or ignored. Groups of workers that strike, demonstrate, go slow or occupy their workplaces exert far more pressure on their bosses. This collective action can give rise to ongoing working class organisations and class consciousness.

The trade unions and the Labor Party (ALP) reflect the way large numbers of workers have a partial awareness of the implications of class. They appeal to workers by challenging some of the *consequences* of capitalism even though they accept the existence of capitalism as a system. While the unions and ALP are expressions of class consciousness, they can also act as brakes on its further development. Full-time officials are essential for effective union organisation but they are not workers employed by capitalists. They are intermediaries between capital and labour, negotiating a deal for their members within the framework of capitalism. They generally enjoy pay and conditions superior to those of the bulk of their members. This gives them a direct interest in maintaining the existing capitalist order.

Labor politicians are even more distant from the working class. The ALP has drawn its core support from the working class and, compared with the Liberal-National Coalition and even the Greens, a significantly higher proportion of its vote comes from workers. Workers' basic self-defence organisations, trade unions are integrated into the ALP through affiliation and the prominent role of union officials within it. On the other hand, Labor's goal is to achieve government and manage Australian capitalism. The ALP is therefore a capitalist workers' party and has never been a socialist workers' party (Bramble and Kuhn 2010: 6-24).

In open class conflicts, the politically creative and organisational capacities of ordinary people become apparent, as workers take on responsibilities and do things – from addressing meetings, writing leaflets and making banners, to coordinating picket lines, collecting funds and arranging large events – that lie outside their normal range of activities.

The greater the scale of class struggles, the more they can undermine conservative ideas amongst workers. In the course of class conflicts, the importance of overcoming divisions in the working class, by challenging racism, sexism and homophobia can become clearer. During intense struggles, the counterposed interests of the capitalist and working classes can seem obvious to large numbers of people. They can recognise that capitalism is an exploitative system and that working class interests lie not only in winning short term improvements in living standards, by reducing the level of exploitation, but ultimately in overthrowing capitalism.

Rising consciousness of class interests, and developing actions that advance or damage them, are subjective processes that are individual but also shared with other members of a class. The outcomes of particular struggles and debates within and between classes may advance or set back class consciousness, cohesion and organisation. Along with relations of production, they influence the outlooks and actions of individuals and therefore the behaviour of the classes to which they belong. Through class struggle, the working class can become a self-aware collective actor, an historical subject. The proletariat, an objective consequence of the relations of production, can become, in Marx's terms a "class for itself" (Marx 1975: 159-60).

Rick Kuhn is a Reader in Politics in the School of Politics and International Relations, Research School of Social Sciences, College of Arts and Social Sciences, Australian National University. Why Class Matters © 2011 Rick Kuhn.

The Political Economy of Gender
Gabrielle Meagher

Theories of economic division in society typically look at the unequal distribution of power and resources through the prism of class. Class is important, but only part of the story. There exists another social cleavage of comparable significance. Measures of the distribution of economic, social and political power in rich and poor countries alike continue to show that women are disadvantaged relative to men (World Economic Forum 2009). Thus, feminists have argued, social theory that ignores structures of gender power fails to grasp a crucial determinant of economic and social organization.

In advanced capitalist societies, payment for work supports a majority of households, determining to a large extent their standard of living. In addition to providing income, participation in paid work is an important expression of social citizenship. Yet paid work and its rewards are not evenly distributed among the adult population. Why do women, on average, work fewer hours and earn less than men in the labor market? Why is it that women and men do different jobs? Why do women continue to be responsible for the bulk of non-market work, in particular, domestic labor and child rearing? These questions focus our attention squarely on the political economy of gender relations.

Economists and other social theorists have tried to explain differences in how men and women participate in economic activity in diverse and often conflicting ways. Some start with perceived inherent differences between men and women, and so see the sexual division of labor as the natural order of things. On this view, women's responsibility for housework and child rearing derives from their biological role in human reproduction. Charged with the care of small children, many women find continuous full-time paid work impracticable. Discontinuous work participation undermines the value of investments in education. Women would be silly to spend time and money gaining skills they will not use and so are likely to be less skilled and therefore less productive than men. They work less, produce less – and so are paid less. Quite as it should be.

Or is it? Cross cultural evidence about the sexual division of labor shows that few, if any, tasks are the exclusive preserve of either men or women in all societies. This has led many social theorists to reject claims that any particular sexual division of labor is 'natural'. Instead, they argue, the sexual division of labor is a social construct, evolving through history and shaped by the social practices producing power structures within institutions. If women are disadvantaged in relation to men, then that disadvantage is the product of these institutions and social practices. Of course, given current technology, only women gestate, give birth to, and breastfeed babies. But there is no necessary link between these biological processes and the gender hierarchy built upon them. Instead, this hierarchy must be explained by reference to social processes – discrimination, exclusion, coercion, prevailing ideas about sex-roles, and so on. Explanations in terms of choice or nature ignore the dimension of power.

The sexual division of labor

When explanation starts with power we can begin to see how systematic material and ideological processes divide society along gendered lines. From ancient times, in different ways, social relations and institutions have been organised in part around a division between the public realm of citizenship and the private or domestic domain of life. Like so many distinctions organizing our thoughts and our world, the division between the public and the private contains an hierarchical opposition which values the masculine over the feminine. In classical Greece women and slaves remained in the private sphere, the realm of necessity, the 'economy'. Men alone were citizens of the *polis*, occupants of the realm of freedom and political action, power, and status.

Today the division between the public and the private is not so stark as in ancient times. The necessities of daily life are produced both inside and outside the domestic sphere. With capitalist industrialization, the 'economy' has become all those businesses, whether small or large, government or privately owned, that produce goods and services for the market. In liberal democratic societies, men and women of all races and classes now share the same formal rights as citizens before the law, and discrimination on the basis of sex or race is often legally prohibited. Yet in spite of these fundamental changes in social organization, women remain responsible for the work of daily life in the domestic domain and their opportunities in the world of work continue to be limited. In deep and often subtle ways masculine power is still supported and reproduced in both public and private spheres.

Historians disagree about how the current division between public and private spheres came to take the form it does. Honeyman and Goodman (1991) argue that the contemporary sexual division of labor in western societies is partly the result of two intense periods of gender conflict in the workplace, one lasting from the late fifteenth to the end of the sixteenth century, and the other from the early nineteenth century. During these periods of profound economic change, male artisans and other skilled craftsmen feared that their social and economic power was threatened. They acted to restrict the employment of women, to more clearly designate certain jobs as male or female, to reduce the value placed on women's work, and to emphasize women's domestic role.

During the late middle ages in Europe, production for the market was increasing and women's participation in market production endangered existing structures of male dominance. Honeyman and Goodman identify two processes at work in this period. First, the family production units in which household members produced goods and services for the market, rather than selling their labor directly, began to give way to small commodity and capitalist production. As a consequence, women lost the opportunities for high status work and considerable control over access to raw materials and distribution that family production offered. At the same time, men in urban craft guilds acted to exclude women from a wide variety of artisanal trades in which they had previously worked. The range of occupations available to women was thereby expressly restricted. Those remaining available became defined as 'women's work', and were no longer attractive to men.

Guildsmen also sought to redefine the relationship between the market and the household, by excluding goods produced in households from the market, and so pushing women out of productive work. In rural areas, beyond the control of guilds, women's work was critical to the expansion of industrial production, particularly in textile manufacture. However, by the late seventeenth century, women's work in urban Europe was confined primarily to textile manufacture and the clothing trades, retailing, and domestic service. The privileges and trappings of artisanal work had become the exclusive preserve of skilled males.

In the second period of profound economic transformation in the nineteenth century, Honeyman and Goodman argue that changes in production methods again threatened to disrupt the established gender order. In the early stages of industrialization in Europe, women and children crowded into factories. The sexual division of labor reinforced in the preceding centuries now operated for the benefit of capitalists. The low cost of female and child labor deriving from their subordination to men made them attractive employees indeed. This wholesale re-entry of women into productive employment in urban labor markets precipitated fears that men would lose their primary place in the world of work, and that social breakdown would ensue. Over the second part of the nineteenth century, women and children were removed from much productive activity in the public sphere as protective legislation, the family wage, and the ideology of domesticity worked together with the restrictive practices of skilled male workers to establish the hierarchical structure of employment still evident now. As a consequence, the viability of working class domestic life and so the successful reproduction of the working class itself were assured, with women providing their labor free to their husbands, and their husbands' employers.

Historians Edna Ryan and Anne Conlon (1989) tell a similar story about gender relations in Australian industrial history. In Australia, male workers were particularly successful in getting their work recognized as skilled. Organised into craft-based unions on the British model, their assertive use of the industrial arbitration system from the late nineteenth century ensured the establishment of a complex system of awards that enshrined hierarchies of skill and largely excluded women. Another turning point was the Harvester judgment of the Australian Industrial Court in 1907, which set down the family wage principle for the determination of the basic wage for men. In concert with a pro-natalist population policy, the family wage reinforced women's domestic roles, and kept women's pay down.

As a consequence, the Australian labor market remains strongly segregated by sex. Equal pay has been a goal of women industrial activists since World War 2, but sex segregation in the labor market has prevented many women's occupations achieving wage rates comparable to those in men's occupations. Inequalities remain in spite of the official demise of the family wage principle with arbitration decisions and legislation in support of the principle of equal pay in various jurisdictions since the late 1960s. That women are much more likely to be employed part-time and are less likely to achieve managerial positions only exacerbates differences in male and female average incomes.

Men have actively gained economic power at women's expense by claiming men's work as skilled work, by gaining control over crucial technological innovations, and by defining the appropriate relation between men and women as between breadwinner and dependent. Even though such strategies are increasingly difficult to pursue, their historical legacy remains, embodied in a working day too long to be compatible with community and family life, in gendered organizational and occupational cultures, and in existing rates of pay in sex segregated occupations.

Other historians have criticized arguments like these, which pose an alliance of capitalist and working class men against women. Writers like Jane Humphries (1979) and Wally Seccombe (1986) argue that the exclusion of women and children from the industrial workforce during the nineteenth century was as much the result of working class resistance to the encroachment of industrialization as of the assertion of male power. Women's jobs were not well paid, and family life itself was threatened by mass proletarianization. Both men and women of the working class gained from the 'breadwinner-dependents' wage model, in the context of the apparently unstoppable juggernaut of capitalist development.

Conclusion

Economic analysis is properly aimed at understanding the social relationships in which life is produced and reproduced in human societies. Critical examination of how work and skill are defined, distributed, and rewarded are crucial elements of such an analysis. By looking through the prism of gender, we can see much that is otherwise obscured. Feminist reconstructions of economics are now well underway. The process of redressing the invisibility of women and femininity in economic analysis is continuing, and new ways of thinking about economic processes are emerging. These innovations, along with the recognition that racial and ethnic hierarchies have existed in labor markets across the entire span of capitalist development, will improve the capacity of economists to understand our world and act intelligently in it.

Gabrielle Meagher is Professor of Social Policy, Faculty of Education and Social Work, University of Sydney. The Political Economy of Gender © 2011 Gabrielle Meagher.

The Political Economy of Racism
Phil Griffiths

The last thirty years have seen a dramatic revival of organised racism in the world's rich countries. Neo-Nazi and far right, anti-immigrant political parties have become a major force in countries across Europe, and some are now partners in government. In the United States, young African Americans are lucky to avoid starting adult life without a term in prison. In Australia, billions of dollars have been spent on locking up refugees and intervening in Northern Territory Aboriginal communities in an exercise which has criminalised Indigenous men, made thousands unemployed, imposed draconian restrictions on welfare, while failing to make any significant improvement to the problems faced by communities.

The main targets of racism across much of the west are immigrants, refugees, Muslims and people from Middle-eastern backgrounds.

Racism is one of the great barbarisms of modern society. For the people affected, it can mean discrimination, verbal abuse, humiliation, random acts of violence or targeted harassment by police and state officials, and murder. The human cost can be only dimly seen in the shorter life expectancy of Indigenous Australians, the mass deprivation in South Africa's 'townships', the poverty of African Americans, or the mental breakdowns suffered by asylum seekers locked up in detention centres in Australia, Europe and North America.

Many critics have focused on revealing and deconstructing the discourses of racism. The contribution of political economy is to focus on material interests and social structure. So we ask: Who benefits? Whose interests does this particular form of human oppression serve? A problem as widespread as racism is not an accident. How, we ask, is racism structured by society? What is its relationship to the fundamental features of modern capitalism, such as class and the market economy?

Racism was first used in modern society to justify the enslavement of millions of African people on the plantations of the West Indies and the United States. When slavery was challenged by liberals, who argued for a system of freedom, individual rights and wage labour, the slave-owners replied that black people were sub-human and 'savages'. They developed and promoted racism to protect the system of exploitation that had made them rich. These ideas did not disappear with slavery. After the American civil war, the new rulers of the South (and the North) continued to use anti-black racism to divide the working class and poor farmers.

When the great European powers grabbed their colonial empires, they promoted the most horrendous racism to justify the brutality they used. The mass starvation of Irish and Indian peoples, the genocide of Indigenous people in Australia and North America, the slaughter of Africans and the radical disruption of so many pre-existing economies and societies were all justified as necessary to bring the gifts of civilisation to 'the lower races'. Colonialism enriched European bankers, manufacturers, traders and governments. It can be no surprise, therefore, that the great conservative parties of Europe embraced racial superiority as a core part of their beliefs from the late nineteenth century onwards. Today, alongside the tabloid media, they continue to promote vicious and contemptuous stereotypes of the formerly colonised peoples who have migrated there.

In Australia, it was the great pastoralists who benefited from driving Aboriginal people from their lands, and bringing in sheep and cattle. Australia's anti-Aboriginal racism has its origins in the need to justify and extend this dispossession.

The nineteenth century saw the start of those great waves of migration that have come to characterise capitalism. The Irish famine and the grinding poverty of much of rural Europe drove millions to seek new lives in the United States of America, Australia, and South America. Millions too moved from China and India. The new class of industrial capitalists saw migrants as potentially cheaper labour, and encouraged as much division within the working class as possible. Racism was a potent tool for them. Karl Marx brilliantly summed up the dynamic of anti-immigrant racism in Britain in 1870:

> Every industrial and commercial centre in England now possesses a working class divided into two *hostile* camps, English proletarians and Irish proletarians. The ordinary English worker hates the Irish

worker as a competitor who lowers his standard of life. In relation to the Irish worker he regards himself as a member of the *ruling* nation and consequently he becomes a tool of the English aristocrats and capitalists … The Irishman … sees in the English worker both the accomplice and the stupid tool of the *English rulers in Ireland*. This antagonism is artificially kept alive and intensified by the press, the pulpit, the comic papers, in short, by all the means at the disposal of the ruling classes. *This antagonism is the secret of the impotence of the English working class*, despite its organisation. It is the secret by which the capitalist class maintains its power.

This dynamic has been reproduced in every great capitalist nation. In nineteenth century Australia, anti-immigrant attitudes focused on Chinese people and Irish Catholics. Opinion polls in the post-war decades consistently showed a majority wanted an end to immigration by Greeks and Italians. In the 1980s Asian immigrants were targeted, and today it is Muslims and refugees.

Opposition to immigrants is often focused on the fear that it will cost locally-born workers jobs. If that were true, unemployment in Australia should be astronomical. Around a quarter of Australia's population is foreign born. What happened to all the people whose jobs these immigrants supposedly 'took'? Why aren't they unemployed? The answer in part is that immigrants have also created millions of jobs, not least in providing for their needs – in housing construction, education, health, building our cities, retail, food processing, transport and hospitality. Employment and unemployment are shaped by the decisions of government and calculations of profit and loss, not by immigrants.

Racism against immigrants has been of enormous benefit to business. The great post-war immigration began as a raging economic boom took hold. Severe labour shortages appeared and by 1948, workers had used their bargaining power to drive up wages and win the 40-hour week. Protecting employers from working class militancy became the priority for government, and immigration was partly designed to deliver cheap labour to big capital. After 1951, the conservative government of Robert Menzies turned towards encouraging migrants from southern Europe: Italians, Greeks, Maltese, Yugoslavs and Spaniards. They were pushed into the dirtiest and most dangerous work, and forced to accept wages well below the level demanded by the Australian-born. Migrants from Britain and Northern Europe were able to gain work in skilled trades, business and the professions. The result was a workforce deliberately, if partially, divided on ethnic lines. From the 1950s to 1981 in Melbourne, some 50 percent of southern European men were employed in just 15 percent of jobs, mostly production and labouring, and mostly low paid. For over 20 years, BHP used newly arrived southern European migrants to work in its Port Kembla (NSW) steel mill to avoid paying market-rate wages, and the federal government gave the company priority in supplying new labour.

These economic and managerial gains for employers would not have been possible without promoting racism, to divide Australian-born and immigrant workers. Through the 1950s and 1960s, conservative governments demanded that migrants 'assimilate' into Australian society, and leave their previous customs, languages and cultures behind. It was very difficult to assimilate into a suspicious and hostile society, and the demand for assimilation sent a message that migrants were not really 'Australian', adding to the sense of isolation they felt. Assimilation told the Australian-born (as it does again today) that the poverty and isolation of immigrants was their own fault, a product of their refusal to assimilate and not a problem caused by racism or government policy.

But no group of people likes to be oppressed, and racist segmentation of the workforce created profound bitterness amongst immigrants. From the 1960s onwards, migrant workers started and led some of the most militant strikes against ruthless employers: at General Motors in Melbourne in 1964 and Ford in 1973. Vietnamese workers played a major role in a long strike at the Toyota-ANI factory in Melbourne, in 1980, and were the most active picketers during the 1985 strike at the Redfern Mail Exchange in Sydney.

Migrant militancy had the effect of building links with both Anglo-Australians and amongst national groups. The industrial power of the NSW Builders Labourers Federation in the late 1960s and early 1970s was built on migrant anger at their treatment, and through a conscious union policy of involving all national and language groups in the life and decision-making of the union, for instance, by pioneering the use of translators at union meetings. From the late 1960s, many unions decided to explicitly fight racism, because they came to see the strength it gave to employers, and the way it undermined the collective strength of their membership.

It was the migrant, union and left wing resistance to racism in the 1960s and 1970s that led many western governments to scrap their policy of assimilation and introduce multiculturalism; the idea that modern societies were composed of people from many different language, religious and national backgrounds, and that this cultural diversity should be accepted and celebrated. Multiculturalism had many limits, including the attempt to get people to identify by national origin, rather than their class position. However, when the progressive movement faltered, and pro-business activists looked for opportunities to attack unions, they also came out attacking multiculturalism for supposedly 'dividing' the nation.

Most writers on racism within the working class see it as driven by workers from the dominant national grouping attempting to preserve their wages, conditions and privileges from lower-cost competitors. In this view, the "white" working class is naturally, spontaneously racist. However this has been challenged by research done in the United States in the 1970s and 1980s. This focused on the racial division between black and white, and showed that where the gap between black and white wages was greatest, the wages of average white workers were lower than in areas where the racial gap was narrower. In other words, racism tended to reduce the wages of white workers as well as black, and to increase the incomes of the richest white people. This is because racism undermines class solidarity and weakens the bargaining position of all workers.

Both racism and class solidarity reflect the contradictory experience of workers within capitalism. On the one hand, we are all atomised and forced to compete – for jobs, places at university and decent services for our communities. This works to divide us, and provides the deep foundation for racism to work. On the other hand, capitalism takes billions of atomised workers and brings us together in large workplaces, to work alongside strangers to produce goods and services for our wages. The experience of collective work provides the basis for collective organisation and struggle against our employers. Trade unionism, class solidarity and mass anti-racism have their ultimate foundations in this very different material reality. The fundamental aim of our employers and governments is to keep us working together harmoniously, while limiting our ability to struggle together. British activist, Sivanandan, once argued that British colonialism in Sri Lanka, "divided in order to rule what it integrated in order to exploit". This sums up the role of racism for capitalism more generally.

Racism as a key element of ideology

The argument so far has focused on racism as functional for capitalists and government. In other words, there is a clear and direct benefit to slaveowners, colonialists and business people from promoting racism to justify brutal exploitation, or to divide the working class.

But racism also works to shape the overall world-view of people. It forms a significant part of the ideology – the web of ideas – that maintains support for, or at least tolerance of, the capitalist system by the working class and poor. A strong and durable ideology is one of the reasons that capitalism has been so durable, despite the horrors it has inflicted on so many.

While we are told that our political system treats everyone equally, the reality is one of vast inequalities. Racism represents a world-view in which inequality is natural, a product of the different levels of "civilisation" of the world's people, or differences in culture. Racist ideas suggest that the world's people are divided between those fit to run modern, powerful societies, and those whose "race" or culture are so backward that they need to be kept in line so that they don't disrupt everyone else. It insists that a dominant population deserves the right to control and benefit from a national economy, and to exclude others, or dictate the terms on which they participate.

The great achievement of the labour movement and the left in the 1960s and 1970s was to create a global movement for equality, for independence from imperialism, for decent welfare for the poor, for an end to sexism, and for social solidarity between people from different backgrounds.

When the first great post-war economic crisis hit the world in the early-mid 1970s, ruling classes set out to wind back wages and welfare and this required weakening trade unions. This was the agenda of the Fraser government in Australia (1975-83), but Fraser's victories were too modest for many business leaders. They wanted a more thoroughgoing attack on union militancy and welfare, so that profits could be raised, and taxes cut for businesses and the rich. They wanted us to be thoroughly disciplined by the laws of the market. Around the world, this neoliberal revolution eventually created widespread disgust as public services were privatised, government spending was slashed, and unions hammered. Few people wanted society changed in this way. To make it happen with the minimum political resistance, the ideas of equality and caring for others had to be undermined. In part this was done through economic arguments about the need for competitiveness. But racism was also important.

The changes imposed included a wave of casualisation, new rules to make it easier and cheaper to sack workers, a restructuring of jobs so that we all worked harder. While wages rose a little in most western countries (but not the US), large numbers of workers were pushed onto individual contractors, or even forced to become "independent" sub-contractors. Whole areas of manufacturing were sent offshore and workers left to a lifetime of unemployment. Millions felt far less secure, and far less confident about taking industrial action to defend their collective interests. Amongst poor people, there was deprivation.

There were two responses to this disruption; social solidarity and racist division, represented in Australia by Pauline Hanson and her movement in the late 1990s. Hanson, originally a Liberal candidate for the federal election of 1996, and then elected as an independent, railed against deregulation and privatisation, and linked these to Asian immigration, refugees and government funding for Aboriginal people.

John Howard disagreed with Hanson's economics, but sympathised with her racism. The leading conservative journalist, Paul Kelly (1994), summed up his strategy:

> The issue can be stated simply – free markets have the potential to destroy the social status quo. They can uproot communities, transfer capital and labour from one location to another and demolish long-established social ties and employment habits. Many consequences flow from this reality – that the more people grasp the meaning of free market economics, the more apprehensive they will become ...

> Howard relied upon two central ideas. He sought to project the security and reliability of the traditional family as a source of deliverance from social turmoil, and to advance a chauvinistic nationalism which emphasised the responsibility upon minority groups and new arrivals to subscribe to the Australian way and to ensure that cultural diversity did not diminish Australian values, institutions and customs.

In other words, racism would be used to give people comfort and a sense of identification even as Howard's economic policy destroyed their real security. For Howard, it wasn't the responsibility of government to help the losers; life is a matter of individual responsibility. For him, this individualism was one of the core strengths of the English tradition. To the extent that people signed up to Howard's racism, they were implicitly signing up to the very ideology that created so many stresses in their lives.

Around the world, neoliberalism went hand in hand with a new campaign to entrench racism. In the United States, police racially profiled African Americans, and the number in jail went up by six times in 20 years. In Europe, conservative and labourist governments both attacked immigrants.

The attack on refugees in Australia can serve as an example. Every single argument raised against people arriving by boats was also an argument for working class and poor people to accept the ruling class attack on their rights.

Refugees, we were told, were jumping the queue. This came when millions of people were angry over hospital queues and queues for public housing were decades long. The sub-text of the criticism of refugees was that queues were unavoidable, and that we should just accept them. Accepting the brutal treatment of refugees made it harder to fight the new deprivation that government cuts were imposing on ordinary Australians.

Australia, we were told, is the most generous country in the world towards refugees. It was a lie, of course, but when people swallowed it, they also weakened their ability to attack the ungenerous cuts imposed by Howard on health, welfare and education. One of these deprived poor people of free dental care, a measure that has led to an explosion in the most horrific dental diseases.

The Howard government set up a division between "good" refugees, and "bad", "deserving" and "undeserving". The "deserving" refugee waited patiently in a squalid refugee camp, hungry, cold and desperate, while Western countries thought about whom they might help. The 'deserving' refugee didn't care that there were another 22 million like them, and was not phased by the prospect that it could be a thousand years before they got an offer of resettlement. And whatever else they did, the "deserving" refugee never protested against their treatment in a detention centre; never tried to escape, never tried to harm themselves.

The 'deserving' refugee bore all the hallmarks of an earlier product of cruel ruling class mythology; the 'deserving' poor. These were people who accepted their station in life, meekly queued for a miserable amount of charity, and lived dark, moral abstemious lives and never disturbed the tranquillity of the ruling class. They were poor people who never wasted their money on alcohol or cigarettes; who accepted whatever dreadful, low paid job they were offered and did it cheerfully; who sent their children spick and span to work and sacrificed for their education. The 'deserving' poor were those super-humans who were oblivious of all the pain and humiliation that poverty involved. This view of refugees reinforced the idea that Australia's poor might also be divided between the 'deserving' and 'undeserving'. Around the world, the attack on refugees helped smooth the way for a relentless attack on welfare, and the rights of people on welfare.

In Australia, the Tampa crisis and the Children Overboard scandal of 2001, and the Labor Party's support for an attack on refugee rights, played a major role in helping Howard to a massive election. The terrorist attacks of 9/11 sealed the deal, because the refugees being attacked by the Coalition were mostly Afghan and Iraqi. Now they could be painted as possible terrorists as well. The racism of 2001 worked to divert widespread anger over the introduction of the GST in 2000, and to legitimise support for the US 'war on terror'. Legitimising war, and diverting anger are two more of the functional roles played by racism.

Hope for the future

Australia has a long history of racism. But it also has a long history of solidarity, between Australian-born and immigrants; between Indigenous and non-Indigenous. That solidarity has sometimes been built on the pragmatic need for unity in struggle, sometimes on an awareness that 'divided we fall'. If we desperately need a new struggle against racism, we also need a new struggle for our rights at work, and against all attempts to subordinate our lives to the needs of capital. The argument of this chapter is that these two struggles are one, and should be understood as such.

Phil Griffiths is Lecturer in Political Economy, University of Southern Queensland. The Political Economy of Racism © 2011 Phil Griffiths.

Social Capital
Ben Spies-Butcher

Social capital broadly refers to the range of social resources that enable people to cooperate and societies to function more effectively. While definitions vary, key elements include social norms and networks, obligations and trust, voluntary associations and the broader notion of the 'social fabric'. Proponents argue that social capital is what enables 'neighborhood watch' schemes to operate and what prevents a society becoming even more litigious. It facilitates cooperative action, providing the trust necessary for most exchange and employment relations.

Some have viewed an apparent decline in social capital in many developed nations as a source of acute concern. On the other hand, the possibility that social capital could enable development in the Third World has made it a source of hope to many, including the World Bank. Accompanying the rising debate around social capital has been increasing interest in the role of the community and civil society in both engaging with and moderating the influences of the market and the state. Some view social capital as the basis for a 'third way', an alternative to reliance on the market or the state as the vehicles for social and economic progress.

So it is important to have a clear analysis of social capital if we are to understand how the economy and society interlink and the options for different paths of economic and social development. Unfortunately, that is where the problems start. Without a clear definition the notion of social capital has become an increasingly unwieldy theoretical device. Although it has brought attention to the importance of social relations for economic outcomes, it is debatable that it has yet offered any real insights into social or economic processes.

Competing conceptions of social capital

The concept of social capital has only become a popular one in economics or the social sciences since the 1990s, although use of the term has been traced back as far as the early 1900s. The term's obvious linguistic appeal, bringing together the key themes of sociology on the one hand and economics on the other, has proved popular. However, there remains no clear single definition of social capital.

Lack of conceptual consistency can be perhaps explained by reference to the concept's origins. Emerging out of the interaction of economics and sociology, social capital was developed by a number of theorists in different ways simultaneously, with different theorists apparently unaware of each others' work.

Among those credited with developing the concept are sociologists Pierre Bourdieu (1986) and James Coleman (1988). Initially many saw commonalities in the two men's work, however, more recently there has been a growing acceptance of important differences. Whereas Bourdieu viewed social capital as a resource which helps maintain and reproduce class relations of differential power, Coleman's notion is situated within a 'rational choice' framework and denotes a relatively neutral resource for action. For Bourdieu social capital included an individual's networks to the rich and powerful, highlighting how these networks helped to maintain and reproduce inequality.

Coleman's understanding of social capital has been the more influential, partly as a result of his work being taken up by Robert Putnam whose 1993 book, *Making Democracy Work*, popularized the concept, although more recently some sociologists have returned to Bourdieu. Putnam drew on Coleman's analysis to argue that different levels of institutional performance and economic development between the North and South of Italy were due to different levels of social capital. The better developed social capital of the North was held to account for its superior economic living standards. Putnam's analysis of social capital, both in Italy and in other countries, has focused on the role of voluntary associations, linking increased participation in these associations with better economic and democratic outcomes.

This analysis has, however, been subject to a number of criticisms. It is unclear how social capital is differentiated from its effects. Is social capital added to by increased voter turnouts at elections, or increased newspaper readership, or are these effects of existing accumulations of social capital? It is also easy to point to instances where social ties and norms can have negative effects for society as a whole, such as when social norms enforce racist or sexist practices or when social ties allow criminal gangs to form. If social capital is to be regarded as a positive resource then these forms of antisocial relations need to be distinguished from forms that may have socially beneficial consequences.

One response to these concerns has been to differentiate between 'bonding' and 'bridging' social capital. The former is taken to refer to social ties between members of the same social group, be it within an ethnic, occupational, geographic or other form of community. These 'bonding' connections can be useful because they allow people to develop forms of collective insurance, such as by enforcing norms that ensure people look after the sick. But they can also be divisive at a macro level if different communities do not have some connection to each other, such as the situation between black and white America or between rival Hutu and Tutsi communities in Rwanda. Bonding within communities and conflict between them can be two sides of the same coin.

In contrast, 'bridging' social capital refers to ties that cross these cultural or socio-economic boundaries. This form of social capital has been viewed as particularly important for encouraging economic prosperity and democratic political institutions.

The insights being offered here are not necessarily new. The theory of 'bonding' versus 'bridging' social capital mirrors almost exactly the distinction made in the 1970s by sociologist Mark Granovetter (1973) between 'strong' and 'weak' social ties. Even the link between participation in voluntary associations and economic and political progress has its origins in the civic republican tradition (of which Putnam is part) emanating from the work of Alexander de Toqueville. This connection is also a contentious one, with some evidence suggesting that involvement in many voluntary organizations does little to engage people in democracy, and can even be an escape from larger macro social and political issues (Eliasoph 1998).

Putnam's and Coleman's work has since been taken up in a number of contexts, including consideration of how social capital relates to economic development, the future of the welfare state and more theoretical debates within neoclassical economic growth theory. Social capital has also been taken up in a number of non-economic contexts. This sheer diversity of application is the focus of much of the criticism of social capital, which critics see it as more of a buzz word than a serious conceptual tool. If we are to understand the implications for how social capital is to be addressed by economics as a social science, it is useful to examine a few of the applications to which the concept of social capital has been put.

Economic development

Interest in social capital as a solution to the problem of the under development of poorer nations has been championed in large part by the World Bank, which has developed a social capital library and commissioned a range of research projects on the subject. Following on from Putnam's account of Italian society, the World Bank has tended to emphasize the decentralist nature of social capital. In this view social capital is built in civil society, not by the state, and indeed the causation often runs the other way, with low social capital contributing to poor institutional performance by the state.

From this perspective, the answer to development therefore lies in mobilizing communities and encouraging people to participate in associations and other forms of civic engagement. While offering useful insights into the important role of micro community relations for development outcomes, highlighting the importance of taking seriously the needs and wishes of those people who live in poor communities, this analysis has been criticized in two ways. First, it often equates very different social resources. Social capital has been used to include social networks, participation in voluntary associations and trust between individuals or groups. But it is not clear how these different social phenomena are linked. For example, how is trust within the family similar to trust in government? And can the trust developed at a regular bowling league be used for another purpose, and if so under what conditions? If different social resources have different properties, then generalizing between them may be counter-productive. Second, social capital often focuses on micro issues of participation and trust to the exclusion to macro issues such as inequality and power.

More recently, the World Bank has been less focused on social capital. Critics like Ben Fine (2010) argue that social capital was used within the Bank as a way of regaining legitimacy in the wake of growing resistance to the Bank's neoliberal policies. There is some evidence that non-economists within the Bank were also using the concept to engage their economic colleagues in a broader conversation about the social determinants of development. Certainly, the use of social capital coincided with a shift in approach at the Bank, although the problems of creating a consistent definition now appear more widely accepted and its use has declined.

The welfare state

What strikes a casual observer is the sheer variety of positions apparently supported by social capital theory. Proponents of the concept of social capital use it variously to justify increased government intervention, different forms of government intervention and a withdrawal of government intervention.

The first position has been associated with a traditional social-democratic understanding of the state as expressing the collective interests of its citizens. Social capital here is defined in analogous terms to social trust or the social fabric. The state helps ensure trust by promoting universalism through health and unemployment insurance, by promoting tolerance of difference to ensure social harmony, and even by promoting voluntary civic engagement (for example, Cox 1995). Some empirical research suggests that people are more likely to trust strangers in social democratic nations, like Sweden, then in the more classically liberal countries of the English speaking world (Rothstein 2001), although this connection remains contentious. More recent research has shown that high levels of inequality worsen many social outcomes (see Wilkinson and Pickett 2009), like crime and poor health, and so equality itself might help development. In general, the claim is that social capital and an extensive role for government are harmonious, indeed mutually supportive.

Taking a politically opposite view, other proponents of the concept of social capital have used it to support neoliberal policy prescriptions. Here social capital is associated with voluntary associations that allow people to look after each other. As the state takes on more welfare functions it displaces voluntary organizations, such as mutuals, cooperatives and charities, that once performed this work, leading to a sort of 'crowding out' thesis of social capital. Not only does the state perform these tasks less efficiently, it also demoralizes people, by encouraging them to rely on the state rather than their own resourcefulness, thus promoting a culture of laziness and poverty. The solution is to wind back the welfare state and let families and communities fill the void.

Both these approaches appear to have done little more than superimpose the language of social capital onto existing political positions about the appropriate role for the state. Social capital theory thereby serves more as a linguistic device to advance different policy positions, rather than a means of shedding light on policy problems. The one possible exception to this has been the role of social capital in the development of Third Way politics. The connection between social capital and the Third Way is highlighted by some within the British Labour Party who have hailed social capital as a scientific justification of 'Third Way' politics (Szreter 1999). Here social capital is closely related to the concept of community as the third force between the market and the state. The welfare state is criticized as atomizing people by failing to recognize individual differences. The state is seen to lack the flexibility necessary to respond to individual needs. Because it provides standardized payments (like unemployment benefits) to all, it does not develop a human relationship with those it serves.

Rather than getting rid of the state, advocates of the Third Way argue for a different type of welfare state, one that works with communities and non-government organizations to provide a more individualized service and to help communities 'help themselves'. Advocates of the Third Way, often quite explicitly, accept the free trade, deregulation agenda of neoliberalism, but attempt to deal with the undesirable social implications of economic globalization through encouraging community participation.

The last twenty years has seen growing attention on the spatial distribution of inequality, with evidence that social and economic disadvantage cluster in particular locations. Social capital has been seen as a possible solution to this, because it is a collective resource that might be mobilized by disadvantaged communities. However, this analysis is subject to much the same critique as the World Bank arguments about the role of social capital in economic development. Macro processes that have caused the spatial and generational concentration of disadvantage, such as economic restructuring, tax cuts for high-income earners and the casualisation of the workforce, are largely ignored. Instead, social capital acts like 'self help' for communities, rather than individuals, placing the onus on the disadvantaged.

Engaging the voluntary sector also raises a number of other issues currently being realized in Australia. Recent welfare reforms have seen many non-government organizations (NGOs) take on roles traditionally performed by the state, such as employment services, in return for state funds. NGOs are thought to have better links to the community and provide a more human, individualized service. However, many NGOs are now worried that their dependence on government funding has reduced their capacity to advocate against government policies. Competitive tendering for funds has also meant contracts go to the largest providers, potentially undermining the advantages of involving non-government agencies.

Social capital and economic theory

At first sight social capital seems to be outside the concerns of conventional economic theory. The neoclassical analysis that has dominated economic theory views the economy as comprising atomistic utility maximizing individuals. A concept like social capital seems to imply a more collective dimension of social behavior than this theory can normally accommodate.

Some interesting attempts have been made to apply the idea of social capital within the neoclassical project. The most prominent example is probably that of Gary Becker, the winner of the Nobel Prize for Economic Science, also credited with developing human capital theory. Becker's work is notorious for its extension of neoclassical economic theory into the study of social behavior. Becker's model (1996) incorporates social capital as a variable in an individual's utility function, along with personal capital, goods purchased and goods produced within the household. Thus an individual acts to maximize overall utility from the combination of all these factors. The result is that social capital, like most variables in neoclassical economics, is reduced to something measured by a single index – 'utility'. The qualitative distinctions between different forms of social relations, to the extent that they cannot be captured in a single measure, are lost.

Similar approaches have attempted to integrate social capital into game theory, defining social capital as a resource that helps individuals overcome collective action problems like the 'free rider' problem. Again, social capital is understood as a resource that is developed through the rational decisions of individuals as 'utility maximizers'. However, this approach has partly inspired work within new institutional economics that has highlighted the importance of social norms in managing collective resources – like waterways and fish stocks. Social capital has been part of a broader shift within the economics community to acknowledge that history, social relations and institutions are important factors in determining economic outcomes.

Conclusion

The popularity of social capital indicates a growing recognition of the importance of social relations in shaping how, and how well, economies work in a 'socially embedded' context. Our economic actions, individually and collectively, are shaped in practice by broader social structures, norms and conventions.

The problem for economics as a social science is how to systematically analyze the influence of the social on the economic. Perhaps the root difficulty stems from treating social relations and resources as a single entity called social capital. The obvious danger is that such a concept will act to conceal important theoretical distinctions between different social resources and structures and, if thought of as a collective resource, between different sections of communities. It may also reinforce an understanding of the economic being separate from the social. Marxists, for example, would argue that all capital is social in the sense that objects only become capital as a result of capitalist property relations, so to call some capital social hides the fact that even 'economic' capital is really a product of social relations.

There are attempts that confront these dangers and use the concept of social capital to draw attention to the importance of social resources in a broader sense, disaggregating and distinguishing resources and bearers along the way. This is currently the most promising research work in the social capital field. Yet, other than being a useful heuristic, social capital on this view has little definitive content beyond what is already captured in existing notions such as 'social fabric' or 'community solidarity'.

If research on the nature and influence of social capital is able to bring issues of social cohesion to the fore of academic and policy debates then the use of social capital as a concept may have a positive impact. But using new language for old ideas is a dangerous game. It can obscure our understanding as well as aiding it. Political economy and sociology have a much richer language for describing the complex nature of social relations than social capital can provide. While bringing the social back into economics is an important project, and social capital is clearly potentially useful as a broad term to capture the importance of social resources, it is important it does not substitute for a genuine social science.

Ben Spies-Butcher is Lecturer, Department of Sociology, Faculty of Arts, Macquarie University. Social Capital © 2011 Ben Spies-Butcher.

The Ideology of Capital
Robert Heilbroner

Ideology is the deeply and unselfconsciously held views of the dominant class in any social order. Here it is important to begin by distinguishing these beliefs from views held in a more pietistic or even cynical fashion, to manipulate or form the opinions of those who are not members of the ruling class. Unlike such propaganda, ideologies are systems of thought and belief by which dominant classes explain to *themselves* how their social system operates and what principles it exemplifies. Ideological systems therefore exist not as fictions but as 'truths' – and not only evidential truths but moral truths.

Capitalist ideology has exactly the same explanatory function as does that of feudal or tributary systems of belief. But as with other aspects of capitalism, it differs in decisive ways from earlier belief systems. Samir Amin (1980: 52) has pointed out that the ideologies of earlier social formations were typical 'world' religions – Hinduism, Confucianism, Islam, the divine rulerships of early Mesoamerican and Near Eastern kingdoms, Christianity. As such, these ideologies further expressed the essential unity of tributary societies. The full authority of a priesthood sanctioned the exercise of worldly rule, including its use for the collection of the surplus; and this surplus was used, in turn, to support religious institutions. A single legitimating view, sacred in origin, thereby fortified the existing regime.

The ideological aspect of capitalism differs fundamentally from this imperial form. It is not sacred but secular, not monolithic but many-faceted. Its emplacement therefore requires more than a palace coup in which one absolute belief displaces another. The installation of the ideology of capitalism rather resembles a popular revolution, not only calling on new forms of social explanation but seeking a new source – in actuality, new sources – of legitimacy powerful enough to challenge the authority of a universal church.

Historically, the development of bourgeois self-clarification proceeded along several fronts. One of these was the forging of a new attitude towards the central activity of the capitalist socio-economic system – the search for profit. In every pre-capitalist society we find acquisitive activity disliked or despised – in part as a projection of aristocratic attitudes (true aristocrats do not 'need' money); in part as an expression of popular revulsion against money lenders and exploitative local traders; in part perhaps as a deep-rooted protest against the de-personalization of monetary dealings. Nowhere was this distaste more pronounced than within Christianity, where the taking of ordinary interest was declared to be an excommunicable offence as late as the Council of Vienne in 1311, and where three centuries later a disapproving view of wealth-seeking continued to inform Protestant as well as Catholic religious sentiments, even after both churches had made their formal truce with profits and interest.

This low estimation of acquisitiveness does not disappear with the rise in the power and influence of the bourgeois class. "In the numerous treatises on the passions that appeared in the seventeenth century", writes Albert Hirschman in *The Passions and the Interests* (1997: 4), "no change whatever can be found in the assessment of avarice as 'the foulest of them all' or in its position as the deadliest Deadly Sin that it had come to occupy toward the end of the Middle Ages." Even in the worldly eighteenth century, it is very much in the spirit of the age that Adam Smith regards acquisitiveness, in both the *Theory of Moral Sentiments* and *The Wealth of Nations*, as a useful but never admirable characteristic, leading to the pursuit of things that, viewed with philosophic detachment, appear "contemptible and trifling", or simply "vulgar".

That which did change, making it possible by the seventeenth or eighteenth century to create an acceptable belief system around activities that only a few centuries earlier would have been regarded as anathema and that continued to be denigrated, was the appraisal of the consequences of acquisitive behavior. Here we see two separate movements. One of them involved the reinterpretation of avarice or love of lucre, not as a disruptive 'passion' but as a steadying 'interest'. As such the drive for wealth was perceived as a calming influence compared with the unruly disposition over which no similar rational, calculating attribute exerted its restraints. In the guise of commerce, acquisitiveness is thus seen to exert a civilizing effect – *le doux commerce* – a point we find expressed again in Adam Smith, who writes that "probity and punctuality" are virtues that invariably accompany the introduction of commercial relations into society.

The second movement towards the rationalization of acquisitive behavior lies in the development of a 'science' of acquisition. This is, of course, the discipline of political economy, later economics, that emerges in the seventeenth, and achieves its full-fledged expression in the eighteenth century. The very possibility of such a science itself implies that acquisitive behavior has lost its connection with the unruly passions and has come to be regarded as a steady principle of human 'motion', capable of measurement and restraint. The ideological aspect of the new science emerges, however, when we inquire into the purpose of political economy or economics. It is an explanation of how the commercial or nascent industrial system works, *from the point of view of the ruling class*. This does not imply a willful distortion of the collective effects of the process, while excluding others.

One crucial aspect of this ideological view of the economic process is the fetishism of commodities – the extraordinary spell cast by the commodity form of labor (and its precondition, capital). It is this fetishism that still causes economists to perceive the process of production as carried on by M. le Capital and Mme La Terre (in Marx's words), as well as by the 'factor of production' called labor. It is largely as a consequence of this unconscious attitude that modern-day economics has no concept of any 'surplus' that is systematically transferred into the hands of a dominant class. Economics explains the flows of interest and dividends and rent, of trading gains, industrial profits, or technological advantage as the 'earnings' of capital. It thereby confuses the incomes that accrue to the owners of capital *because they have agreed not to withhold their property from use* with the actual physical contribution these resources create when placed in use. It follows that economics has no explanation for the origin of profits other than the 'imperfections' (such as monopoly or transient technological rents) that separate the real world from the state of general static equilibrium that is presumed to represent the logic of the system. Thus the very category of economic life that more than any other distinguishes the regime of capital from all others disappears from sight.

Rather than belabor this aspect of economics as ideology, I wish to call attention to a less commonly remarked aspect of the 'science', exemplified in Locke. Locke sets out to demonstrate that *unlimited* private acquisition, for centuries the target of the most scathing religious and philosophic criticism, was in fact compatible with both the dictates of Scripture and the promptings of right reason.

The objections to unlimited acquisition, Locke points out, are two: that acquisitiveness may impoverish others, and that it may waste goods that could be used by others. Thus the injunctions imposed on acquisition by Scripture and reason are that 'enough and as good' must be left behind for all, and that 'Nothing was made by God for man to spoil or destroy'. These injunctions would seem to constrain private accumulation to that of petty proprietorships. But Locke shows that no such inhibitions need in fact obtain. For an accumulator who encloses and cultivates land *increases its yield*, so that the act of acquiring land creates more wealth, which is presumably available to others.

Thus Locke disposes of a question that had almost monopolized the attention of social critics of the past, namely the moral significance of acquisition. By dwelling on the capacity of acquisitiveness to increase the amount of wealth, Locke changes the generation of a surplus from a zero sum game, where every gain is someone's loss, into a positive sum process in which every person's enrichment is at least potentially the occasion for the enrichment of all. The ideological – as contrasted with analytic – contribution of this argument does not lie in the empirical validity of Locke's claim which passes too easily over the question of how widely the gains from accumulation will be shared. The ideological breakthrough concerns a reinterpretation of an aspect of the acquisitive process that had formerly exerted a steady negative influence, often ignored in fact but never forgotten in principle. This was the morally destructive impact of the accumulation of wealth *on the gatherer himself.* The legend of Midas speaks volumes here, for Midas's curse had nothing to do with any impoverishment that his passion for gold would impose on others. It was to this ancient threat of self-destruction that Locke applies the remedy of an assurance that the accumulation of wealth violated neither the canons of right reason nor the Scriptures, so that the question of moral unease could in good conscience be set to one side.

Adam Smith's position on this issue is interesting because Smith was by no means oblivious to the moral costs of acquisitiveness. In his Glasgow lectures, delivered more than ten years before the publication of *The Wealth of Nations*, he balanced his praise of commerce for bringing probity and punctuality by pointing out that it also "sinks the courage of mankind, and tends to extinguish martial spirit ... By having their minds constantly employed on the arts of luxury (the people) grow effeminate and dastardly". Later, in the *Wealth*, Smith often lashes out at the motives of merchants and deplores the ignorance and apathy into which the working classes fall as a direct consequence of their exposure to that accumulation process, with its use of the mechanical division of labor. Yet despite these strictures, as outspoken as any that Marx was to offer, Smith's estimation of the positive effects of accumulation clearly outweighs his assessment of their costs. For all its balance, the *Wealth* is a book dedicated to the legitimation of an acquisitive, capital-amassing society, and that final balance could not be struck if the moral costs of such a society were not, in Smith's mind, overbalanced by its material benefits.

In Smith's hands the interplay of material progress and moral decline takes the form of a subtle dialectic that invests his work with its remarkable depths. In the hands of his successors the dialectic disappears, and the evaluation of economic growth emphasizes its material aspects without any concern as to untoward moral consequences, in terms of either motives or social outcomes. This de-emphasis of the moral aspect of economic life takes a final and decisive turn in the early nineteenth century with the advent of Bentham's utilitarian philosophy. Now any last lingering doubts about greed and rapacity, as well as exploitation and luxury, are removed by the demonstration that the happiness of all can be achieved by the self-regarding pursuit of the happiness of each. If the accumulation of wealth yields happiness for the individual, it follows that it will provide it for the society.

This is not the place to analyze the premises of utilitarianism, except to mention that it achieved its brilliant analytic results by ruling out of bounds the very question to be answered: namely, whether ancient canons of 'virtue' and 'justice' – canons that were always founded on a scrutiny of motives and an 'external' assessment of social results – could be replaced by a system that declared these canons to be arbitrary, and therefore null and void. What is significant for our purposes is that the utilitarian framework provided the final resolution of the moral dilemmas of the economic process by its assertion that whatever served the individual served society. By logical analogy, whatever created a profit (and thereby served the individual capitalist) also served society, so that a blanket moral exemption was, so to speak, extended over the entire range of activity that passed the profit-and-loss test of the marketplace.

The consequences of this ideological clarification were, and continue to be, far greater than is commonly understood. The demoralization of economic activity not only removed any need to justify the logic of capitalism, provided that it did not directly violate the law or outrage the deepest moral standards of society, but it made meaningless such questions as: Which of two equally profitable undertakings is the better? Can one call wasteful any undertaking that returns a satisfactory profit? Is it possible to condemn on moral grounds legal and profitable actions, such as the decision to relocate a plant at the cost of community disruption? Thus a kind of moral pardon is applied to all licit activities of the capital-accumulating sector, although in the so called public sector, where the absorption of losses rather than the accumulation of capital takes place, no such justification is available, so that moral obloquy and standards are constantly brought to bear.

As a result there is a further widening of the schism of realms: one 'private', profitable, and above intrinsic reproach; the other public, unprofitable, and without the presumptive innocence of the private sector. The ideology of economics plays an indispensable part in holding apart activities that, from our perspective, can be seen to intermingle, and in determining what criteria are regarded as appropriate for the assessment of each.

Here I must add once again that the purpose of an ideology is not to mystify but to clarify; not to mislead the lower classes but to enlighten all classes, in particular the ruling classes. Economics does not 'legitimate' activities that the ruling class knows in its heart of hearts to be wrong. It succeeds, rather, in offering definitions of right and wrong that exonerate the activities and results of market activity. This is accomplished in part because the motives of acquisitiveness are reclassified as interests and not passions; in part because the benefits of material gain are judged to outweigh any deterioration in the moral quality of society; and last and most important because the term 'goodness' is equated with *private* happiness, absolving all licit activity from any need to justify itself on others grounds. These powerful prescriptions, ground into the lenses through which the ruling class observes its own actions, provide the moral self-assurance without which it could not carry on its historic mission with such dedicated conviction.

A second, equally fraught consequence of the ideology of economics concerns the widely recognized phenomenon of the 'commercialization' of life. From one capitalist nation to the next, the thresholds and boundaries over which economic activity is allowed to step may vary, but looking backward for a generation or two, it is clear that in all capitalist nations more and more of 'private', that is, self-determined, life becomes public life, insofar as it is determined by the regime of capital. Thus to take two familiar instances, athletic prowess, one of the oldest and proudest activities of private individuals, has everywhere become a matter of commercial 'sport', and the self-determination of life patterns, the most private of all activities, is everywhere deliberately subjected to the influence of 'advertising', the purpose of which is to induce individuals, without knowing anything of them, to change their mode of living. These instances of a relentless commercialization, perhaps the single most self-destructive process of modern capitalist civilization, could be multiplied manifold.

What is needed is to understand the process as part of the nature of the system. Commercialization is a consequence of commodification – the continuous search of business for areas of social activity that can be subsumed within the capital-generating circuit. The expansion of capital is aided and abetted by the declaration that moral and aesthetic criteria – the only dikes that might hold back the floodtide of capital's expansion – are *without relevance* within the realm of economic activity.

Robert Heilbroner was Norman Thomas Professor of Economics, New School for Social Research. This chapter is abridged from The Ideology of Capital. *The Nature and Logic of Capital*, Norton, New York, 1985, ch. 5, pp. 107-18. © 1985 Robert L. Heilbroner. Reproduced with permission of the author.

WHAT MATTERS TO ECONOMISTS?

We need political economic analysis to understand the current challenges and the relationships between economy and society discussed in the previous chapters of this book. More than two hundred years of development in economic analysis has left an impressive legacy that can be drawn on for this purpose. It is not unified, however. Rather, it comprises competing 'schools of thought'. Each school of thought has certain analytical characteristics, strengths and weaknesses, and is associated with particular social values and policy prescriptions. In other words, each school of thought embodies a distinct 'world-view' as to how the economic universe is constituted.

Thomas Kuhn (1970) argued that the competition between competing schools of thought in the physical sciences leads a scientific community to choose one school to be the 'paradigm' over the others. A paradigm is a model which suggests certain questions as being worthy of scientific analysis (and others unworthy), and which offers the framework and tools by which these questions can be addressed. Having settled on a particular paradigm, and the world-view which underpins it, a scientific community proceeds to employ that paradigm in conducting the day-to-day puzzle-solving activity Kuhn called 'normal science'. For a period a dominant paradigm receives the unquestioning support of scientists as they explore and extend its field of application. However, the paradigm eventually exhausts its usefulness, or else encounters a puzzle to which it should offer a means of solution but cannot. As this puzzle draws more attention and yet remains difficult to solve, it becomes an anomaly that suggests that the paradigm itself is somehow deficient. At this point, the allegiance to the paradigm wanes, and more and more scientists look to alternative schools for a new paradigm. Such a period of scientific revolution eventually leads to the emergence of a new paradigm that provides the basis for a new period of normal science. Thus the Ptolemaic view of the universe which positioned the Earth in the centre, with the other planets and stars revolving around it, gave way to the Copernican Revolution, which placed the sun at the centre of the solar system. Other examples abound where few would dispute the progressive character of such revolutions in intellectual activity.

While Kuhn's model of scientific evolution was developed to explain the history of the natural sciences, it has had profound consequences for the interpretation of the social sciences as well. The extent to which it can be directly applied without modification to a field such as economics is open for debate. To any observer of the history of economic thought, it is clear that since the 1870s (at least in the English speaking world) economics has been dominated by the neoclassical paradigm. One can see this paradigm 'in action' in any orthodox textbook, or in the journals to which most economists subscribe. And lurking behind the simple textbook supply and demand explanation of market equilibrium lies a distinct view of the world that is loaded with social and political values. That dominant paradigm is influential in the formulation of economic policy, e.g. in the free market agenda popularly associated with the politics of neoliberalism.

However, economics has not totally conformed to the Kuhnian model. Despite the overwhelming dominance of the neoclassical approach within the economics profession, alternative schools of thought have not been driven out of existence. Indeed, the history of economic thought has been a long contest of competing frameworks for understanding the capitalist economy. Some schools of thought have remained important dissenting traditions throughout the period of neoclassical dominance. These heterodoxies have provided key elements in the development of contemporary political economy.

We may speculate, before turning to an exposition of these various schools of thought, as to why economics has not completely conformed to the Kuhnian model of scientific progress. One important reason concerns the role of *ideology*. All schools of thought in all sciences are intrinsically ideological in the sense that they offer a particular and partial view of the world. The problem in economics is that these ideologies are most directly connected to the vested interests and political practices that are in continuous contestation. Thus, it is not so much that economics is intrinsically ideological (which science isn't?), but that it is peculiarly placed in relation to the political struggles that feature in social life. While all major scientific revolutions alter in some way the established relationships of power and social order (as happened when the Copernican Revolution altered people's perceptions of the world by removing the Earth from the centre of the universe), the repercussions are rarely as direct and overt as when a choice between competing economic frameworks is to be made.

Another factor that differentiates economics as a social science from the physical sciences is that the subject matter is constantly changing. Certainly, the universe is changing, but there is also a sense in which the universe that Ptolemy wrote about in constructing his theory of astronomy was essentially the same as the universe about which Copernicus theorized. However, the social universe that Adam Smith wrote about in the *Wealth of Nations* is not the same as that which Karl Marx explored in *Capital*, nor which Keynes discussed in his *General Theory*. Theories that may have been adequate in explaining the economic conditions at one point of time may become outdated and irrelevant for a later period, so that episodes of normal science are relatively short.

Lastly (and possibly the most important reason for modifying the Kuhnian analysis in economics), the theories developed to explain the social world become elements of that world themselves, and the means of changing it. No matter which theory we choose for studying the movement of planets, the theory will not affect the way the planets behave: only our perception will have changed. Knowing how the planets and stars move does not allow us to then reposition the Earth into the centre of the universe. However, theories of how the economy functions allow us to alter its operation: to recreate the world (at least to some extent) in the image of the theory.

The conclusion that follows from these considerations is that a pluralist approach to the study of political economy is desirable. It is not possible to construct a single theory that will be satisfactory in all times and in all places. John King begins this section of the book by putting the case for a pluralist approach that explicitly acknowledges the diversity of methods we may use in studying 'the economy'. The articles that follow then argue as to why history, theory and policy matter. Paul David's article takes the history of the typewriter as an example, showing that the adherence to the QWERTY keyboard is explicable only in a historical and political economic context. Paul Krugman's following article argues the case for model-building in economic analysis based on theoretical abstractions. Geoff Dow then shows that policy issues have been a central concern to diverse currents in the development of political economic thought. All approaches to political economy have, to various degrees, been concerned with a method of enquiry that has these three aspects – history, theory and policy – but the emphasis differs markedly, as we will see.

For a more detailed account of the concerns of the major schools of political economy, see Frank Stilwell, 2006, *Political Economy: The Contest of Economic Ideas*, Oxford University Press, South Melbourne. For discussion of heterodox alternatives to economic orthodoxy, see also the *Real World Economics Review* <www.paecon.net/PAEReview/>.

Arguments for Pluralism in Economics
J.E. King

My friend Kurt Rothschild once told me how, a few years ago, he had googled 'heterodox' and 'economics', and got 50,000 hits. Then he googled 'heterodox' and 'sociology', and got six hits. He may have exaggerated the numbers a little, but the point he wanted to make is very clear. The opposite of 'heterodox' is 'orthodox' or 'mainstream'. In economics there is a very well-defined orthodoxy, and those outside it define themselves as heterodox. In sociology there is no single, monolithic mainstream, and so there is no need for anyone to take on the label 'heterodox'.

And it is not just sociology. A recent collective volume on the history of the social sciences since 1945 has separate chapters on psychology, political science, sociology, social anthropology and human geography, in addition to economics (Backhouse and Fontaine 2010). In each of the chapters on the other six social sciences, pluralism is shown to be the norm. In some cases – sociology and human geography, for example – there was once a single, powerful orthodoxy, but this has now fragmented and seems unlikely ever to be put together again. In others – psychology and social anthropology, at least – there has never been a mainstream like the one in economics.

Why, then, is economics so different? Why do mainstream economists believe that there is only one correct way to do economics? Why are they wrong? Is there any prospect that a single correct alternative to orthodox economics will come to replace it, any time soon? Is pluralism unavoidable, and indeed desirable?

To do mainstream economics properly you must construct a model, collect relevant data and then test it. The model itself must be consistent with the fundamental principle of methodological individualism: that is to say, it must be based on the assumption of optimising behaviour by rational agents. The tests must employ the most advanced econometric techniques rather than – or at least in addition to – descriptive statistics. For the defenders of mainstream economics these simple rules are what make it a science, which is envied and increasingly imitated by the practitioners of less favoured disciplines in the areas of management and social studies: 'economics imperialism', as it is sometimes described (Lazear 2000).

This is a seductive story, and it is widely believed, inside and outside economics (Fine and Milonakis 2009). When applied to the more disreputable branches of business 'thought' there is probably something to be said for it. If, however, it is taken as mandating the liquidation of sociology, political theory, social psychology and social anthropology as autonomous bodies of scholarly knowledge it is obvious nonsense. As a methodological prescription for economics it is, quite simply, wrong. But this does not mean that there is a single alternative to today's mainstream out there, created by heterodox economists, just waiting for the opportunity to become the orthodoxy of tomorrow.

In a brief paper on 'the limits of economics', the philosopher Daniel Hausman touches on these questions. He discusses the frequent failure of mainstream economists to apply the scientific method to their subject, and the disappointing results that are often obtained when they do. Orthodox economists make totally unrealistic assumptions; they hedge their bets with unfalsifiable *ceteris paribus* clauses; they rarely test their basic theories, and ignore evidence that casts doubt upon them; and they waste their time developing useless, abstract mathematical models. To a very considerable extent, Hausman argues, these failings are due to the peculiar nature of the economist's subject matter. He identifies "three such difficulties: (i) economists are generally unable to perform controlled experiments; (ii) the subject matter of economics is 'complex' – a large number of different *kinds* of causal factors influence economic phenomena;

and (iii) the subject matter of economics is changing – the relative importance of different kinds of causal factors differs at different times" (Hausman 1992: 103, original stress).

The first problem that Hausman refers to is perhaps less serious than he imagines. In some areas of microeconomics experiments are possible, and they form an important part of the rapidly growing sub-discipline of behavioural economics. (Of course, controlled experiments will never be feasible – or ethically acceptable – in macroeconomics). The second and third difficulties are more significant, but precisely what they entail for the practice of economics is contentious. Hausman is sympathetic to the mainstream, and orthodox economists often use similar reasoning as a defence against heterodox criticism. Heterodox economists themselves might draw a very different conclusion: the complexity and fluidity of economic phenomena provide two weighty arguments for pluralism.

First, economic reality certainly is very complicated. The questions that economists ask are therefore inherently difficult, and it is unlikely that they have simple answers. Since no theory can consider all relevant factors in any particular economic context, there is a strong *prima facie* case for theoretical pluralism. Different theories will often be complementary rather than alternative, so that "to seek dominance for one theory over all the others with the possible result that all the rival theories are extinguished amounts to advocating scientific regress. To paraphrase Voltaire: in a subject as difficult as economics a state of doubt may not be very comfortable, but a state of certainty would be ridiculous" (Kurz and Salvadori 2000: 237). As Geoff Hodgson, another well-known heterodox economist, puts it, "there are several problems with general theorizing in the social sciences. One is of analytical and computational intractability. Facing such computational limits, general theorists typically simplify their models, thus abandoning the generality of the theory. Another related problem with a general theory is that we are confined to broad principles governing all possible structures within the domain of analysis. In practice, a manageable theory has to confine itself to a relatively tiny subset of all possible structures. Furthermore, the cost of excessive generality is to miss out on key features common to a subset of phenomena" (Hodgson 2001:16).

Second, there is the inescapable fluidity of the subject matter itself. This means that the quest for a single, 'general' theory applicable to human behaviour in all societies, at all points in time, is a dangerous delusion that has led astray not only mainstream economists but also some heterodox theorists. Hodgson claims that failure to appreciate the need for historical specificity in economic theorising has not only blighted the work of several generations of general equilibrium theorists, but also reduced the analytical achievements of some of their strongest opponents, including John Maynard Keynes. Hodgson's own proposal for the reconstruction of economic theory, putting the history back, is innately and profoundly pluralistic (2001: chs 18-23).

This has important implications for the use of mathematical modeling in economics, as Victoria Chick and Sheila Dow (2001) explain. Formalising an argument is not, they suggest, an unambiguous improvement, as orthodox economists believe. On the contrary, it is a matter of costs and benefits. Formalism entails a particular view of the world. It must display event regularities strong enough for it to approximate to a closed system. Moreover, the meaning of economic terms must be fixed rather than context-specific, and they must be separable rather than internally related. If these assumptions are rejected, classical or formal logic is inapplicable and what Keynes described as 'ordinary logic' may be needed in its place. Ordinary, common-sense or human logic "generates knowledge which is imperfect, partial or vague", and provides "reasoned grounds for belief which are nevertheless not conclusively demonstrable" (Chick and Dow 2001: 711, 714). Economic statements may therefore be true in some historical and institutional circumstances, but false in others.

Here Chick and Dow share common ground with Hodgson, since their argument casts doubt on "the possibility of finding immutable laws applicable to, say, feudalism and capitalism alike, or even to capitalism in various stages of its development. From this perspective, a theory can be 'right' at one time and become 'wrong' (more accurately, outdated) at another. The notion of imbuing a closed theoretical system with meaning is thus not an objective procedure; it requires the exercise of judgement" (Chick and Dow 2001: 709). In this way their critique of formalism leads them to pluralism, not just in substantive theory but also in method, since Keynes's ordinary logic "supports a methodology which encompasses a range of methods in order to build up knowledge" (2001: 719; see also Dow 1997).

Note that Chick and Dow do not completely deny the legitimacy of formalism in economics, in all circumstances, for all purposes. On the contrary: some problems lend themselves to closed-system thinking and cry out for precise, formal solutions. They argue only that it is a serious mistake to suppose that all economic problems are of this type. If pluralism does not rule out formalism, but merely puts it in its place, what does it exclude? Unqualified relativism, for one thing; logical incoherence, for another. Hodgson is the most outspoken in denying that 'anything goes', and the most sternly critical of postmodernist claims in this regard. "An acceptable policy of pluralism", he suggests, "concerns the policy of institutions towards the funding and nurturing of science. Such a policy involves 'pluralism in the academy'. But it would not extend to the individual practices of science itself. This confusion, between encouraging contradictory ideas in the academy and encouraging them in our own heads, is widespread in post-modernism ... There is much to be said for tolerance of many and even antagonistic scientific research programmes within an academic discipline or university. But we should not tolerate the existence of inconsistent ideas within our own heads. The policy towards science must be pluralistic and tolerant, but science itself must be intolerant of what it regards as falsehood ... Any failure of social science to erect an adequate and coherent general theory is not rectified by applauding incoherence" (Hodgson 2001: 35). Horses for courses, as Geoff Harcourt has always put it (see Comim 1999), but they must each have four legs and a jockey and proceed anti-clockwise around the course.

Sheila Dow has also defended the principle of consistency against its postmodernist and constructivist opponents. Thus she proposes that a clear distinction be drawn between 'pure' and 'modified' pluralism. To be a pure pluralist entails "a refusal to appraise methodologies and thus also [a refusal] to advocate one method rather than a plurality". This, she maintains, offers "no scope for scientific (or indeed any) discourse". According to modified pluralism, however, 'no one system of knowledge can claim to have captured reality; each is partial, reflecting one vision of reality. Each school can support its approach to knowledge with reason while recognizing the legitimacy of alternative approaches ... World-view and theory of knowledge cannot be eradicated; yet recognition of differences at this level allows for more reasoned debate over appraisal criteria and analysis of different methodologies" (Dow 1996: 45-6; see also Dow 1997).

Personally, I think it is possible to be a unitarist in principle and a (modified) pluralist in practice. I would very much like to believe that, one day, a single unifying heterodox economic theory will be agreed on, a theory that will provide a framework for the explanation of all economic phenomena and for the evaluation of all manner of economic policies. Maybe it will, but almost certainly not in my lifetime – or, probably, in yours. In practice, the complexity and fluidity of the economist's subject matter that Hausman idenitifies as the main cause of discipline's failures are also the main reasons why we need to encourage pluralism in economics.

No single case for pluralism in economics emerges from this brief discussion, and indeed it would be a cause for concern if one had; Garnett, Olsen and Starr (2010) provide no less than 20 different arguments for pluralism. Similarly, there is no single version of 'unscientific' heterodox economics to stand in opposition to mainstream economic 'science'. Sraffians, institutionalists and post-Keynesians do quite different things, often in radically different ways – as do Marxists, social economists, feminists, greenies and other schools of heterodox political economy. The e-journal *Real World Economics Review* (formerly entitled, for good historical reasons, *Post-Autistic Economics Review*) will give you the flavour of the resulting debates <www.pae.econ.org>. Kurt Rothschild, with whom I began, has had at least one foot in several of these camps over a 70-year heterodox career.

As the radical anti-war campaigner Abbie Hoffman is supposed to have said, in the course of the 1968 Chicago conspiracy trial: 'Conspire? We couldn't agree on lunch'. But they did agree to keep on talking, which in the last resort is what pluralism is all about.

John King is Professor in the School of Economics and Finance, La Trobe University. This chapter is adapted from Three Arguments for Pluralism in Economics, *Journal of Australian Political Economy*, no. 50, 2002. © 2011 John E. King.

History Matters: Clio and the Economics of QWERTY
Paul A. David

Cicero demands of historians, first, that we tell true stories. I intend fully to perform my duty on this occasion, by giving you a homely piece of narrative economic history in which 'one damn thing follows another.' The main point of the story will become plain enough: it is sometimes not possible to uncover the logic (or illogic) of the world around us except by understanding how it got that way. A *path-dependent* sequence of economic changes is one of which important influences upon the eventual outcome can be exerted by temporally remote events, including happenings dominated by chance elements rather than systematic forces. Stochastic processes like that do not converge automatically to a fixed-point distribution of outcomes, and are called *non-ergodic*. In such circumstances 'historical accidents' can neither be ignored, nor neatly quarantined for the purpose of economic analysis; the dynamic process itself takes on an *essentially historical* character. Standing alone, my story will be simply illustrative and does not establish how much of the world works this way. That is an open empirical issue and I would be presumptuous to claim to have settled it, or to instruct you in what to do about it. Let us just hope the tale proves mildly diverting for those waiting to be told if and why the study of economic history is a necessity in the making of economists.

The story of QWERTY
Why does the topmost row of letters on your personal computer keyboard spell out QWERTYUIOP, rather than something else? We know that nothing in the engineering of computer terminals requires the awkward keyboard layout known today as 'QWERTY,' and we all are old enough to remember that QWERTY somehow has been handed down to us from the Age of Typewriters. Clearly nobody has been persuaded by the exhortations to discard QWERTY, which apostles of DSK (the Dvorak Simplified Keyboard) were issuing in trade publications such as *Computers and Automation* during the early 1970s. Why not? Devotees of the keyboard arrangement patented in 1932 by August Dvorak and W. L. Dealey have long held most of the world's records for speed typing. Moreover, during the 1940s US Navy experiments had shown that the increased efficiency obtained with DSK would amortize the cost of retraining a group of typists within the first ten days of their subsequent full-time employment. Dvorak's death in 1975 released him from forty years of frustration with the world's stubborn rejection of

his contribution; it came too soon for him to be solaced by the Apple IIC computer's built-in switch, which instantly convert[ed] its keyboard from QWERTY to virtual DSK, or to be further aggravated by doubts that the switch [was] not often flicked.

If, as Apple advertising copy [once said], DSK "lets you type 20 to 40% faster," why did this superior design meet essentially the same rejection as the previous seven improvements on the QWERTY typewriter keyboard that were patented in the United States and Britain during the years 1909-24? Was it the result of customary, nonrational behavior by countless individuals socialized to carry on an antiquated technological tradition? Or, as Dvorak himself once suggested, had there been a conspiracy among the members of the typewriter oligopoly to suppress an invention which they feared would so increase typewriter efficiency as ultimately to curtail the demand for their products? Or perhaps we should turn instead to the other popular 'Devil Theory,' and ask if political regulation and interference with the workings of a 'free market' has been the cause of inefficient keyboard regimentation? Maybe it's all to be blamed on the public school system, like everything else that's awry?

You can already sense that these will not be the most promising lines along which to search for an economic understanding of QWERTY's present dominance. The agents engaged in production and purchase decisions in today's keyboard market are not the prisoners of custom, conspiracy, or state control. But while they are, as we now say, perfectly 'free to choose,' their behavior, nevertheless, is held fast in the grip of events long forgotten and shaped by circumstances in which neither they nor their interests figured. Like the great men of whom Tolstoy wrote in *War and Peace*, "(e)very action of theirs, that seems to them an act of their own free will, is in an historical sense not free at all, but in bondage to the whole course of previous history..." (Bk IX, ch. 1).

This is a short story, however. So it begins only little more than a century ago, with the fifty-second man to invent the typewriter. Christopher Latham Sholes was a Milwaukee, Wisconsin printer by trade, and a mechanical tinkerer by inclination. Helped by his friends, Carlos Glidden and Samuel W. Soule, he had built a primitive writing machine for which a patent application was filed in October 1867. Many defects in the working of Sholes' "Type Writer" stood in the way of its immediate commercial introduction. Because the printing point was located underneath the paper carriage, it was quite invisible to the operator. 'Non-visibility' remained an unfortunate feature of this and other up-stroke machines long after the flat paper carriage of the original design had been supplanted by arrangements closely resembling the modern continuous roller-platen. Consequently, the tendency of the typebars to clash and jam if struck in rapid succession was a particularly serious defect. When a typebar stuck at or near the printing point, every succeeding stroke merely hammered the same impression onto the paper, resulting in a string of repeated letters that would be discovered only when the typist bothered to raise the carriage to inspect what had been printed.

Urged onward by the bullying optimism of James Densmore, the promoter-venture capitalist whom he had taken into the partnership in 1867, Sholes struggled for the next six years to perfect "the machine." From the inventor's trial-and-error rearrangements of the original model's alphabetical key ordering, in an effort to reduce the frequency of typebar clashes, there emerged a four-row, upper case keyboard approaching the modern QWERTY standard. In March 1873, Densmore succeeded in placing the manufacturing rights for the substantially transformed Sholes-Glidden "Type Writer" with E. Remington and Sons, the famous arms makers. Within the next few months QWERTY's evolution was virtually completed by Remington's mechanics. Their many modifications included some finetuning of the keyboard design in the course of which the 'R' wound up in the place previously allotted to the period mark '.' Thus were assembled into one row all the letters which a salesman would need to impress customers, by rapidly pecking out the brand name: TYPE WRITER

Despite this sales gimmick, the early commercial fortunes of the machine, with which chance had linked QWERTY's destiny remained terrifyingly precarious. The economic downturn of the 1870s was not the best of times in which to launch a novel piece of office equipment costing $125, and by 1878, when Remington brought out its Improved Model Two (equipped with carriage shift key), the whole enterprise was teetering on the edge of bankruptcy. Consequently, even though sales began to pick up pace with the lifting of the depression and annual typewriter production climbed to 1200 units in 1881, the market position which QWERTY had acquired during the course of its early career was far from deeply entrenched; the entire stock of QWERTY embodying machines in the United States could not have much exceeded 5000 when the decade of the 1880s opened.

Nor was its future much protected by any compelling technological necessities. For, there were ways to make a typewriter without the up-stroke typebar mechanism that had called forth the QWERTY adaptation, and rival designs were appearing on the American scene. Not only were there typebar machines with 'down-stroke' and 'frontstroke' actions that afforded a visible printing point; the problem of typebar clashes could be circumvented by dispensing with typebars entirely, as young Thomas Edison had done in his 1872 patent for an electric print-wheel device which later became the basis for teletype machines. Lucien Stephen Crandall, the inventor of the second typewriter to reach the American market (in 1879) arranged the type on a cylindrical sleeve: the sleeve was made to revolve to the required letter and come down onto the printing-point, locking in place for correct alignment. (So much for the 'revolutionary' character of the IBM 72/82's 'golf ball' design.) Freed from the legacy of typebars, commercially successful typewriters such as the Hammond and the Blickensderfer first sported a keyboard arrangement which was more sensible than QWERTY. The so-called "Ideal" keyboard placed the sequence DHIATENSOR in the home row, these being ten letters with which one may compose over 70 percent of the words in the English language.

The typewriter boom beginning in the 1880s thus witnessed a rapid proliferation of competitive designs, manufacturing companies, and keyboard arrangements rivalling the Sholes-Remington QWERTY. Yet, by the middle of the next decade, just when it had become evident that any micro-technological rationale for QWERTY's dominance was being removed by the progress of typewriter engineering, the US industry was rapidly moving towards the standard of an upright front-stroke machine with a four-row QWERTY keyboard that was referred to as "the Universal." During the period 1895-1905, the main producers of non-typebar machines fell into line by offering 'the Universal' as an option in place of the Ideal keyboard.

Basic QWERTY-nomics

To understand what had happened in the fateful interval of the 1890s, the economists must attend to the fact that typewriters were beginning to take their place as an element of a larger, rather complex system of production that was technically interrelated. In addition to the manufacturers and buyers of typewriting machines, this system involved typewriter operators and the variety of organizations (both private and public) undertook to train people in such skills. Still more critical to the outcome was the fact, that in contrast to the hardware subsystems of which QWERTY or other keyboards were a part, the larger system of production was nobody's design. Rather like the proverbial Topsy, and much else in the history of economies besides, it "jes' growed."

The advent of 'touch' typing, a distinct advance over the four-finger hunt-and-peck method, came late in the 1880s and was critical, because this innovation was from its inception adapted to the Remington's QWERTY keyboard. Touch typing gave rise to three features of the evolving production system which were crucially important in causing QWERTY to become 'locked in' as the dominant keyboard arrangement. These features were *technical interrelatedness, economies of scale*, and *quasi-irreversibility* of investment. They constitute the basic ingredients of what might be called QWERTY-nomics.

Technical interrelatedness, or the need for system compatibility between keyboard 'hardware' and the 'software' represented by the touch typist's memory of a particular arrangement of the keys, meant that the expected present value of a typewriter as an instrument of production was dependent upon the availability of compatible software created by typists' decisions as to the kind of keyboard they should learn. Prior to the growth of the personal market for typewriters, the purchasers of the hardware typically were business firms and therefore distinct from the owners of typing skills. Few incentives existed at the time, or later, for any one business to invest in providing its employees with a form of general human capital which so readily could he taken elsewhere. (Notice that it was the wartime. Navy, not your typical employer, that undertook the experiment of retraining typists the Dvorak keyboard.) Nevertheless purchase by a potential employer of a QWERTY keyboard conveyed a positive pecuniary externality to compatibly trained touch typists. To the degree to which this increased the likelihood that subsequent typists would choose to learn QWERTY, in preference to another method for which the stock of compatible hardware would not be so large, the overall user costs of a typewriter system based upon QWERTY (or any specific keyboard) would tend to *decrease* as it gained in acceptance relative to other systems. Essentially symmetrical conditions obtained in the market for instruction in touch typing.

These decreasing cost conditions – or *system scale economies* – had a number of consequences, among which undoubtedly the most important was the tendency for the process of intersystem competition to lead towards de facto standardization through the predominance of a single keyboard design. For analytical purposes, the matter can be simplified in the following way: suppose that buyers of typewriters uniformly were without inherent preferences concerning keyboards, and cared only about how the stock of touch typists was distributed among alternative specific keyboard styles. Suppose typists, on the other hand, were heterogeneous in their preferences for learning QWERTY-based 'touch,' as opposed to other methods, but attentive also to the way the stock of machines was distributed according to keyboard styles. Then imagine the members of this heterogeneous population deciding in random order what kind of typing training to acquire. It may be seen that, with unbounded decreasing costs of selection, each stochastic decision in favor of QWERTY would raise the probability (but not guarantee) that the next selector would favor QWERTY. From the viewpoint of the formal theory of stochastic processes, what we are looking at now is equivalent to a generalized 'Polya urn scheme.' In a simple scheme of that kind, an urn containing balls of various colors is sampled with replacement, and every drawing of a ball of a specified color results in a second ball of the same color being returned to the urn; the probabilities that balls of specified colors will be added are therefore increasing (linear) functions of the proportions in which the respective colors are represented within the urn. A recent theorem due to Arthur *et al.* (1983; 1985) allows us to say that when a generalized form of such a process (characterized by unbounded increasing returns) is extended indefinitely, the proportional share of one of the colors will, with probability one, converge to unity.

There may be many eligible candidates for supremacy, and from an *ex ante* vantage point we cannot say with corresponding certainty which among the contending colors – or rival keyboard arrangements – will be the one to gain eventual dominance. That part of the story is likely to be governed by 'historical accidents,' which is to say, by the particular sequencing of choices made close to the beginning of the process. It is there that essentially random, transient factors are most likely to exert great leverage, as has been shown neatly by Arthur's (1983) model of the dynamics of technological competition under increasing returns. Intuition suggests that if choices were made in a forward-looking way, rather than myopically on the basis of comparisons among the currently prevailing costs of different systems, the final outcome could be influenced strongly by expectations. A particular system could triumph over rivals merely because the purchasers of the software (and/or the hardware) expected that it would do so. This intuition seems to be supported by recent formal analyses by Michael Katz and Carl Shapiro (1983), and Ward Hanson (1984), of markets where purchasers of rival products benefit from externalities conditional upon the size of the compatible system or 'network' with which they thereby become joined. Although the initial lead acquired by QWERTY through its association with the Remington was quantitatively very slender, when magnified by expectations it may well have been quite sufficient to guarantee that the industry eventually would lock in to a de facto QWERTY standard.

The occurrence of this 'lock in' as early as the mid-1890s does appear to have owed something also to the high costs of software 'conversion' and the resulting *quasi-irreversibility of investments* in specific touch-typing skills. Thus, as far as keyboard conversion costs were concerned, an important asymmetry had appeared between the software and the hardware components of the evolving system: the costs of typewriter software conversion were going up, whereas the costs of typewriter hardware conversion were coming down. While the novel, non typebar technologies developed during the 1880s were freeing the keyboard from technical bondage to QWERTY, typewriter makers were by the same token freed from fixed-cost bondage to any particular keyboard arrangement. Non-QWERTY typewriter manufacturers seeking to expand market share could cheaply switch to achieve compatibility with the already existing stock of QWERTY-programmed typists, who could not. This, then, was a situation in which the precise details of timing in the developmental sequence had made it privately profitable in the short run to adapt machines to the habits of men (or to women, as was increasingly the case) rather than the other way around. And things have been that way ever since.

Message

In place of a moral, I want to leave you with a message of faith and qualified hope. The story of QWERTY is a rather intriguing one for economists. Despite the presence of the sort of externalities that standard static analysis tells us would interfere with the achievement of the socially optimal degree of system compatibility, competition in the absence of perfect futures markets drove the industry prematurely into standardization *on the wrong system* – where decentralized decision-making subsequently has sufficed to hold it. Outcomes of this kind are not so exotic. For such things to happen seems only too possible in the presence of strong technical interrelatedness, scale economies, and irreversibilities due to learning and habituation. They come as no surprise to readers prepared by Thorstein Veblen's classic passages in *Germany and the Industrial Revolution* (1915), on the problem of Britain's undersized railway wagons and "the penalties of taking the lead" (see pp. 126-27); they may be painfully familiar to students who have been obliged to assimilate the details of deservedly less-renowned scribblings (see my 1971, 1975 studies) about the obstacles which ridge-and-furrow placed in the path of British farm mechanization, and the influence of remote events in nineteenth-century US factor price history upon the subsequently emerging bias towards Hicks' labor-saving improvements in the production technology of certain branches of manufacturing.

I believe there are many more QWERTY worlds lying out there in the past, on the very edges of the modern economic analyst's tidy universe; worlds we do not yet fully perceive or understand, but whose influence, like that of dark stars, extends nonetheless to shape the visible orbits of our contemporary economic affairs. Most of the time I feel sure that the absorbing delights and quiet terrors of exploring QWERTY worlds will suffice to draw adventurous economists into the systematic study of essentially historical dynamic processes, and so will seduce them into the ways of economic history, and a better grasp of their subject.

Paul A. David is Professor of Economics, Stanford University. This chapter was first published as Clio and the Economics of QWERTY, *American Economic Review Papers and Proceedings*, May 1985, pp. 332-7. © 1985 American Economic Association. Reprinted with permission of the author and the AEA.

Modelling Matters: Two Cheers For Formalism

Paul Krugman

Attacks on the excessive formalism of economics – on its reliance on abstract models, on its use of too much mathematics – have been a constant for the past 150 years. [Yet] formalism is crucial to progress in economic thought – even when it turns out that the ideas initially developed with the help of formal analysis can in the end, with some work, be expressed in plain English.

McCloskey (1997) has recently made an eloquent appeal for a return to a 'Marshallian' style of economic discourse: a style based on verbal, intuitive exposition rather than formal modelling. Marshall (quoted in Sills and Merton 1991: 151) himself famously described his method:

> (1) Use mathematics as a shorthand language, rather than as an engine of inquiry. (2) Keep to them till you have done. (3) Translate into English. (4) Then illustrate by examples that are important in real life. (5) Burn the mathematics. (6) If you can't succeed in 4, burn 3.

Was he right? Marshall's dictum can usefully be divided into two parts: how one should arrive at an economic idea, and how one should communicate it.

Should one use mathematics as an 'engine of inquiry'? This is actually an ambiguous phrase. It might mean getting one's ideas entirely from mathematical logic; if so, that is a practice very few economists engage in. What is true, however, is that many economists use mathematics not merely as a way to check the internal consistency of their ideas, but as an 'intuition pump'; they start with a vaguely formulated idea, try to build a model that conveys that idea, and allow the developing model in turn to alter their intuitions. One way to interpret what Marshall was saying, then, is that one should avoid this process – one should use mathematics only to check intuitions, never to help develop them.

What was Marshall thinking of when he said this (if that was what he meant to say)? Probably he had in mind his own youthful explorations of general-equilibrium trade theory, and in particular his development of the 'offer-curve' technique for analyzing the determination of the terms of trade. Offer-curve analysis, it turned out, forces one to a conclusion that the modeller might not have expected or wanted: a large country, with the ability to affect world prices, can always raise its real income by imposing a small tariff. Marshall's sense was that this conclusion, however much it might be a necessary consequence of the mathematical logic, was wrong or at least unimportant as a practical matter, and presumably this experience was what led him to conclude that one should only use math to check conclusions, not to arrive at them.

And yet general-equilibrium trade analysis is one of those areas in which models are a crucial aid to intuition. Consider the questions posed by the rise of newly industrializing economies. The common perception of most people who think about the issue at all is that the emergence of new competitors must surely reduce real incomes in the established economies – indeed, that this has already happened. On the other hand, some business enthusiasts are quite sure that the expansion of world markets will bring vast prosperity to everyone. Thanks to the models of Hicks (1953) and especially Johnson (1955) well-trained economists eventually learn why both intuitions are deeply wrong. Growth in other countries can either help or hurt us: it depends on the effect on our terms of trade, an effect that in turn depends on the bias of that growth. This position can eventually be made to seem intuitive, but it would have been very hard to arrive at without the aid of models – in particular, without the aid of Marshall's offer-curve construction.

This is not an isolated example. It is crucially important in itself, and it is also representative. Most of the topics on which economists hold views that are both different from 'common sense' and unambiguously closer to the truth than popular beliefs involve some form of adding-up constraint, indirect chain of causation, feedback effect, etc. Why can economists keep such things straight when even highly intelligent non-economists cannot? Because they have used mathematical models to help focus and form their intuition.

Of course, this gain in intuition sometimes comes at a cost: the modeller can become a prisoner of the assumptions embodied in his model. One often hears accusations, in particular, that model-based economics inevitably biases the field toward standard economic assumptions like constant returns, perfect competition, and perfect information. Yet this need not be true. In fact, economists like myself who have worked at length on imperfect markets have found modelling an essential discipline in the process of exploring new territory. Trade theory is again a case in point. By the late 1970s there had been decades of discontent with conventional trade theory – discontent often manifested by complaints that conventional theory neglected increasing returns and imperfect competition. Many manifestos denouncing the conventional views had been published. Yet in all that literature of discontent it is hard to find any clear, let alone, useful ideas. Only when the 'new trade theory' began to emerge, driven by mathematical models that both embodied and shaped intuition, did compelling new ways of looking at international trade actually take shape.

Still, while it may be a good idea to use mathematical models to help develop one's ideas, shouldn't one then follow Marshall's precepts in communicating those ideas?

The answer, surely, is that it depends on the audience. Marshall's advice is exactly appropriate when an economist is writing for an intelligent, literate audience of non-economists. To reach such an audience, to help them get a grasp of some important economic point, it is essential to find a way to express the crucial ideas without the formal apparatus. Nor is this a demeaning exercise: on the contrary, finding a way to convey good economic reasoning without the usual equations and jargon can be both a valuable discipline and an exhilarating experience. And even professional economists, especially those who specialize in different areas, can find non-technical expositions of economic concepts very useful.

But professional economists also have another task: to communicate with each other, and in so doing to help economics as a discipline progress. In this task it is important for your colleagues (and students) to understand how you arrived at your conclusions, partly so that they can look for weak points, partly so that they may find other uses for the technical tricks you used to think an issue through. I like to think that I can manage to explain international economic concepts pretty convincingly to a broader public without ever drawing an offer curve; I can give a pretty good account of the 'home market effect' on trade patterns without ever mentioning Dixit-Stiglitz monopolistic competition and iceberg transport costs. However, I would be doing my graduate students a grave disservice if I never taught them offer curves and Dixit-Stiglitz-iceberg trade models: the point of their education is to learn methods, not answers. And publication in professional journals is or at least should be a form of education: it is how economists teach each other about their work. Tjalling Koopmans (1957) once complained about Marshall's "diplomatic style" – his emphasis on persuasion, his mingling of theory and evidence, his willingness to sweep awkward points under the rug. I am a great admirer of Marshall, yet Koopmans had a point. Marshall's style – the style some insider critics think we need to recapture – was entirely appropriate for a general audience, even a highly educated and intellectual one. But Marshall adopted the same style when writing for economists and their students. To do so is in effect to turn professional economics into the repetition of received truths rather than a continual process of exploration. Indeed, one can do no better on this than to quote Marshall again:

Economic doctrine ... is not a body of concrete truth, but an engine for the discovery of concrete truth (quoted in Sills and Merton 1991: 150).

How are students and colleagues supposed to learn how to use this engine if you burn the evidence of the engine at work?

What, then, is left of the accusation of excessive formalism in economics? Perhaps the moral should be that there are not enough economists doing what Marshall did: writing economics in a way that makes it accessible and persuasive to a broader, though hardly mass, audience. How many good economists actually do write carefully constructed, well-targeted articles, based on serious economic analysis, for a wider audience? I believe that the number in the United States can be counted on the fingers of one hand. This is absurdly low given both the size of the profession and the stakes involved: such articles, together with non-technical books aimed at a broader audience, can sometimes exert a startling influence on public discussion and even on policy. Yet for the most part good economists have simply abandoned this kind of writing, leaving the field wide open for the sort of person who hates economists because they insist that his arguments add up.

Here, then, is a revised version of Marshall's rules:

1. Figure out what you think about an issue, working back and forth among verbal intuition, evidence, and as much math as you need.
2. Stay with it till you are done.
3. Publish the intuition, the math, and the evidence – all three – in an economics journal.
4. But also try to find a way of expressing the idea without the formal apparatus.
5. If you can, publish that where it can do the world some good.

In short, two cheers for formalism – but reserve the third for sophisticated informality.

Paul Krugman is Professor of Economics and International Affairs at the Woodrow Wilson School of Public and International Affairs at Princeton University, and recipient of the Nobel Prize in Economic Science. This chapter is abridged from Two Cheers for Formalism, *The Economic Journal*, vol. 108, November 1998, pp. 1829-36. © 1998 Royal Economic Society. Reprinted with permission of the author.

Policy Matters in Political Economy
Geoff Dow

The purpose of policy is to achieve outcomes that would not have been likely without it. The pervasive concern with economic policy in practice fundamentally changes the type of economic analysis we need. Much of orthodox economics focuses on the 'logic of the market'. However, if policy interventions prevent the market from exerting its determinate influence, or modify its influence, on the economy, orthodox presumptions about maximizing behavior, individual calculation and optimizing tendencies lose their validity. Indeed, the usefulness of abstract conceptions of the economy evaporates. Thus the imposition of political conditions onto economic activity alters the very nature of 'an economy' and how we think about it.

The 'embeddedness' of the economy in social and political arrangements means that the economy is not identifiable separately from its society or its political process. In practice how the economy works depends on which political principles and institutions prevail. Political disputes recur as modern societies alternate between the endorsement of liberal principles (which try to replicate in reality the ideal textbook market economy) and attempts to construct alternatives to market modes of interaction or to protect people from their deleterious effects. The tensions between public and private auspices, between politics and markets as competing mandates for economic behavior, and between the state and the economy, as the locus of legitimate decision-making have always shaped understandings in political economy.

The classical traditions in political economy recognized the impurity of markets and, consequently, have contributed more to our understanding of contemporary human dilemmas than is usually thought. Even the towering figure of Adam Smith, only selectively appropriated by his proselytizers, was acutely aware of the negative effects of the capitalist division of labor and of the need for policy processes to do something about it. In the *Wealth of Nations* (1776, Book 5: 366-7), he wrote:

> The man whose whole life is spent in performing a few simple operations, of which the effects too are, perhaps, always the same or very nearly the same, has no occasion to exert his understanding, or to exercise his invention in finding out expedients for removing difficulties which never occur. He naturally loses, therefore, the habit of such exertion, and generally becomes as stupid and ignorant as it is possible for a human creature to become. The torpor of his mind renders him, not only incapable of relishing or bearing a part in any rational conversation, but of conceiving any generous, noble, or tender sentiment, and consequently of forming any just judgment concerning many even of the ordinary duties of private life … But in every improved and civilized society this is the state into which the laboring poor, that is, the great body of the people, must necessarily fall, unless government takes some pains to prevent it.

Here Smith is conceding the possibility of an anti-rationalist political economy. He is postulating that the logic of purely economic development as embodied in the division of labor (and specialization and economies of scale and the extension of markets) will be disrupted, and ought to be, by political constraints upon that logic. Earlier, in *The Theory of Moral Sentiments*, written before his encounters with the Physiocrats that persuaded him of the virtues of *laissez faire*, he had admired the "great systems of government" and "institutions which tend to promote the public welfare" (1759: 352). Economic conditions are not determined by economic parameters alone.

However, political activity is more contingent and open-ended than economic activity (and thereby less susceptible to formal or predictive analysis); it is driven as much by anti-rationalist impulses, those which depend on varying ideational, learned and cultural motivations, as by those which provide economics and political economy alike with their claims to methodological uniqueness. If government is to intervene, on the grounds Smith suggests are warranted, or on any other grounds, then the processes of wealth creation and capital accumulation and their concomitants (class conflict, crisis, evolution of the mode of production) will not adhere to any formal logic.

In fact, most traditions of heterodox political economy have endorsed one or more forms of social or political intervention into market economies; and it is these 'distortions' that render analyses and prescriptions based on the integrity and rationality of market processes methodologically inapplicable. Before Marx, but after Smith, Friedrich List in Germany had advocated 'infant industry' protection for nations wanting to catch up with more productive or more powerful ones. *The National System of Political Economy* (1841) was a tirade against English liberalism and the doctrines of free trade that List considered to be for export (from England). The British navy, rather than the doctrine of free trade, had actually been responsible for English economic development. Nations following the *laissez faire* doctrine were destined to lose their creative manufacturing capacities. Protection was therefore justified in all the countries pursuing 'late industrialization', particularly when increasing returns to scale could be observed.

The peculiarities of national development needed to be prioritized, not cosmopolitanism (Levi-Faur 1997).

Following List, the German Historical School (coalescing around Gustav Schmoller's *Verein für Sozialpolitik* from the 1870s) attempted to develop an empirical tradition in economic analysis, retaining an organic, society-centred conception of economic activity and human motivation while policy would limit competition, defend national peculiarities and redress the influence of mis-informed liberal ideas. Eventually, this school, like its English counterpart, lost the intellectual battle to the formalistic strictures that became economic orthodoxy, largely because its methodological disposition was more sociological, less abstract, with fewer claims to universal validity, than the emerging 'science of allocation' could accommodate (Jones 1999; Rueschemeyer and van Rossen 1996; Toynbee 1884).

Nonetheless, the distrust of rationalist method survived in the related discipline of economic sociology. Émile Durkheim, in the 1890s, initiated a critique of liberal economics based on an assertion that the understanding of market processes would lead to misunderstanding of economic processes. In other words, there could never be an autonomous economy (nor a methodologically constricted discipline to analyze it) because economies are inevitably 'embedded' in social conditions. Economies need social supports, some of which constitute constraints on individual and entrepreneurial freedoms; it is unreasonable for policy to try to remove many of the inflexibilities and rigidities that characterize actual economies, because the non-economic foundations may be important. External moral constraints on economic activity, perhaps monitored by such intermediary associations as guilds, trade unions and producer collectives, may be functionally necessary (Streeck 1997; Wilensky 2002).

Max Weber's critique of market rationality went further. Though celebrating the distinctive rationality of the capitalist epoch, he nonetheless argued, in *Economy and Society* (1922), that formally rational modes of calculation could occasionally lead to substantively irrational and unwanted outcomes. Therefore, each modern polity could be expected to retain the capacity to override decisions dictated by 'bottom line' evaluations if deliberative processes were likely to produce more desirable outcomes, and if the costs could reasonably be borne. Weber's plea for public adjudicative competences, able to influence economic outcomes in accordance with a political rather than market logic, has been re-awakened in industry policy debates in recent decades and also in the recent resurgent interest in conceptions of 'state capacity'.

At the same time as economic sociology was claiming that apparently unimportant facets, such as the general spiritual and cultural well-being of the populace, might be important, an approach to economic analysis now labelled the 'social economy' tradition was consolidating. Originally known as catholic social thought, this anti-enlightenment strand of political economy contended that economies do not, and should not, operate in the ways presumed by orthodox approaches. Social conditions precede individuals; people are often cooperative; their engagement in economic activity is often motivated by duty or justice or tradition or emulation; organizations are developed to bias production towards certain pursuits, and against others, for political or cultural reasons; long-lived institutions such as unions are devised precisely to politicize the deployment and remuneration of labor; welfare measures exist to provide unearned income and other forms of protection or compensation for those disadvantaged by the market; the rich are sometimes persuaded to take responsibility for the poor; the costs of instability can be socialized; and public policy can impose anti-liberal criteria onto private individuals and firms. A key documentary example is Pope Leo XIII's encyclical *Rerum Novarum* (Pecci 1891) that is more Marxist than Marx in its denunciation of 'labor markets' and in its enthusiasm for experiments in industrial democracy. Social rather than economic imperatives are seen as rightly determinant. The social economy tradition, despite these views, has defended the principle of private property and the right of inheritance, as well as being generally disrespectful of socialism and a strong state, preferring intermediate-level organizational controls (referred to as 'subsidiarity') (McHugh 1993).

The institutionalist tradition also de-emphasizes the autonomy of individual economic agents, focussing instead on the interaction between them and their environment. Thorstein Veblen's essays from the late 1890s argued that economics needed to be an evolutionary science because the economy's constituent institutions change (mature and stagnate) over time and, therefore, the methods available to people to engage in purposive action are subject to improvement or depreciation (as discussed by Geoff Hodgson later in this book). Institutional evolution is not necessarily developmental nor the amplification of 'worthy ends'; 'imbecile institutions' can persist and undermine human achievement. Nonetheless, humans are naturally curious and inventive, this proclivity being the catalyst for novelty, for change, for disruption to the 'relatively invariant' aspects of organization. In fact, productivism or 'workmanship' or purposefulness or substantive competency may require changes to patterns of behavior and appropriate institutional design. New productive (and other creative) possibilities constantly emerge from past institutional accomplishments, these 'emergent possibilities' being scarcely predictable from their elements (Hodgson 2000, 2001, 2004). Humanity is committed not just to income but to 'work', which therefore can never be regarded as an unambiguous disutility.

Joseph Schumpeter, from the 1910s to the 1940s, extended the understanding of innovation, especially in its entrepreneurial form, into a theory of capitalism's 'creative destruction', a conception which opened up the never-settled question of societal responsibility for the destructive aspects of dynamic progress (uncoordinated structural change). His views differed from those of Smith and the classicals insofar as he never imagined tendencies towards harmony or equilibrium, but rather the competitive system's rough efficacy, its capacity to motivate and to get things done. He consequently anticipated that success would lead to bigness, to the 'trustification' of large productive organizations and, eventually, to the 'social form of the society of the future' (1918: 114). Restrictive practices and economies of scale were inevitable and not necessarily undesirable; there was even a suggestion that policy processes might be required to slow the rate of technological innovation if the costs to social order were too great.

At roughly the same time, John Maynard Keynes set out to show that a capitalist economy could be managed, its boom and slump cycle subjected to counter-cyclical policy interventions. The propensity to under-employment reflected a permanent weakness in a market-coordinated economy, with production being chronically lower than potential unless public processes were developed to iron out the fluctuations. The most important policy recommendation of *The General Theory of Employment, Interest and Money* was that a "somewhat comprehensive socialization of investment" (1936: 378) would be able to achieve full employment, that is, to ensure that economic outcomes were determined not by the logic of the market but by deliberative political processes. Without really discussing the policy and practical implications of his critique of orthodoxy (though the topic had been broached in many of his wireless broadcasts in the early 1930s), Keynes was suggesting the need for new political institutions to take on tasks of industrial change and macroeconomic management. Not unexpectedly, the extent to which his views were incorporated into official policy varied across nations in accordance with the extent to which the polity as a whole could incorporate anti-liberal developments.

In a prodigious overlap between his own ideas and those of the historicists, Keynes mounted a critique of Ricardo's approach (and a defence of Malthus's) which reverberates through political economy to this day: Economics would become a 'dangerous science' if it sought 'general principles' instead of highlighting the irregular and impermanent dimensions of economic advance (1933: 117). This implies an empirical-inductive, not abstract-deductive, methodology.

Karl Polanyi's *The Great Transformation: The Political and Economic Origins of Our Time* (1944, part of which is reproduced earlier in this book) also reflected dissatisfaction with the intellectual preferences of mainstream economics. In policy-making, he questioned both commodification and market modes of regulation. From an anthropological viewpoint, 'market society' could not be seen as natural, and policy conclusions centring on free trade or *laissez faire* would be misguided. People in fact were entitled to develop whatever protective arrangements they were prepared to pay for whenever risk or uncertainty or insecurity demanded. The cosmopolitan outlook that informed the classical English economists tended to undermine a nation's ability to develop productive capacities, and the commodification of labor, in particular, was seen as the most repugnant achievement of the liberal era.

Increasingly since 1945, the disjunction between a conventional body of theory urging disengagement of the state from processes of economic development in liberal polities and the emergence of a developmental state in other contexts, especially East Asia, has been difficult to ignore. Conservative academic commentary, rather than Marxism, has examined many of these statist experiments and provided its own critique of liberalism. The Asian 'late-industrializers', as well as the protection-led development of Germany and the USA in the nineteenth century, have provided neo-Weberian statism since the 1980s with empirical support for its argument that public policies and institutions can positively affect structural change. Much of this tradition of analysis highlights the effects of the 'infrastructural power' of the state, that is, the capacities that can be developed to mobilize private activity in publicly-sanctioned directions. Authority rather than market mechanisms, including policy bordering on authoritarian, has been able to sponsor domestic networks, manage the challenges of global pressures on domestic economies, and maintain politically-determined but ongoing capital accumulation (Mann 1993; Skocpol 1985; Weiss 1998, 2003). In the modern world these sentiments manifest as volatile distrust of elite-driven rationalist reforms, particularly in non-urban areas.

Post-Keynesian theory, insisting that the 'Keynesian revolution' was aborted by the refusal of most Anglo-Saxon governments to commit to permanent full employment (due to the political objections), began with Joan Robinson's and Michal Kalecki's critiques of orthodoxy in the 1950s. This tradition also criticized the deflationary bias of the monetarist experiments of the 1970s and 1980s, calling instead for incomes policies to control inflationary conflicts over income distribution. In more recent versions, post-Keynesianism has argued that, in the mature economies, growth 'transforms' the economic structure away from one which can be comprehended by market analogies, thus confirming the Malthusian and the economic sociologists' approach. A particular concern in the early twenty-first century is the realization that wealth-creation now routinely outpaces employment-creation; this means that policies to redress the perceived and recessive imbalance between consumption and investment need to be augmented by policies which favor 'unproductive' investment. New post-liberal institutions could then be mandated to reduce the independence of the finance sector and to re-integrate economic with social development (Robinson 1971a, 1971b; Kalecki 1943; Nell 1998; Harcourt 2006: 145-157).

In response to policy failures and societal disaffection since the 1980s, mercantilist approaches to understanding and to policy formation have re-emerged. The neo-mercantilists, revealing affinities with List's and Veblen's confrontations with orthodoxy and partly impressed by the successful industrial sponsorship and upgrading capacities deployed by late-comers to affluence, are now attempting to reinstate a production focus in political economy. The major claim is that different forms of economic activity have different macroeconomic effects; there is therefore a case for an activist-interventionist state to prioritize some, rather than other, industries. Whenever economic activity depends on knowledge-intensive 'capital', on 'human wit and will', rather than on simple resource inputs, there will be systemic effects from its deployment. Then there will be synergies and positive feedback or 'virtuous cycle effects' from production – so it will be desirable to share fixed costs and risks, to allow increasing returns and 'cumulative

The unknown rise — a sharp-fall.

causation' to generate higher living standards, through higher wages and incomes rather than through cost cutting and lower prices. Competitiveness is an inappropriate criterion for national policy if the abnormal incomes (rent) generated by successful enterprises, but unavailable to the rest of the world, can be 'captured' for the whole society and productive capacities further enhanced (Reinert 1995, 1999, 2007; Reinert and Reinert 2006).

Comparative political economy derived its major fillip from the post-1974 experience of unemployment and inflation throughout most of the OECD economies. It has made a major contribution to the critique of orthodox economic policy by highlighting the observation that all low unemployment countries in the decades from 1974 had unusual political institutions, such as corporatist arrangements which allowed trade unions and employers – the 'actors' which cause problems such as inflationary wage demands or under-investment respectively – into the policy process. Labor confederations and the political organizations of capital impose distinctive criteria onto decision-making, especially when decisions are subject to negotiation and bargaining. If cross-national differences between policies and institutions (implying 'varieties' of interaction between politics and markets) are the ultimate determinants of differences between the economic performances of nations during a period of significant, globally-induced economic restructuring, an important challenge to the integrity of the formalist approaches to economic analysis has been registered (Streeck and Yamamura 2001; Milonakis and Fine 2009). In addition, insofar as the balance of policy influence shifts away from market prerogatives, microeconomic concerns and short-term calculation, not only does unemployment tend to fall, but the balance of power shifts towards those who are normally disadvantaged. Comparative analysis has consequently confirmed many of the theoretical expectations of post-Keynesian political economy (Boreham, Dow and Leet 1999).

The 'regulation school', the 'social structures of accumulation' approach, and the 'social systems of production' or 'business systems' approaches comprise a series of unorthodox approaches to economic analysis, influenced by Marxism, that also have anti-rationalist implications (Boyer 1990; Dore 2000; Parker 2001; Jessop and Sum 2006). The regulation school derives its name from observations that different stages of capital accumulation require different forms or 'modes' of regulation. Similarly, different types or 'regimes' of accumulation develop idiosyncratic regulatory arrangements (the regulation referred to here is more a 'regularization' of the accumulation process than strict regulation, and the term does not refer to state regulation but to the processes by which normal activity is reproduced). The mode of regulation appropriate to a manufacturing-based economy, for example, will tend to downplay the autonomy of financial institutions and to include institutionalized relations between capital and labor (to minimize industrial disruption). Conversely, in a more 'post-industrial' setting, banks may assert more influence so that less emphasis is placed on the regular involvement of the organizations of labor in macro-management (decentralized arrangements and marginalization of trade unions may constitute the preferred 'mode of regulation'). Labor relations, finance-industry relations and the way the domestic industry is integrated with the rest of the world are the most obvious ways in which regimes become regularized, and they are regime-specific (they allow the accumulation process to cohere, at least for finite periods, such as through the long postwar boom).

Patterns of accumulation will normally be guaranteed by 'settlements', 'compromises' or 'accords' between class groupings. The postwar settlement was an implicit agreement which conceded welfare state security, industrial relations standing and a measure of shared participation in the fruits of the long boom to labor; business received a stable environment, some surety that its 'right to manage' would not be challenged, and the legitimation of state supports to education, training and subsidized research and development. Such *rapprochement* could not prevail indefinitely and was transformed during the course of restructuring or recession in the post-1974 period. The implied social institutions link the economy to its societal supports; they are said to comprise a 'social structure of accumulation' which stabilizes challenges to market relations of production that are always latent in capitalist economies. The regime of accumulation, or social structure of accumulation, it has been said is "external to the decisions of individual capitalists", but "internal to the macrodynamics of capitalist economies" (Gordon, Edwards and Reich 1982: 16; see also Kotz 2008; McDonough 2008).

All these non-orthodox traditions in political economy together demonstrate that the actual behavior of capitalist economies is in large measure not predictable from an understanding of pure capitalism. As economies do not necessarily conform with the logic of markets, their evolution is indeterminate, and 'market reforms' do not amount to improvements. This observation has methodological implications for Marxist analysis as well as for liberal approaches. Marx's political economy, from *The Communist Manifesto* to *Capital III*, refused to contemplate social or political interventions that would disrupt the determinate analysis he wished to develop; and this has imparted to Marxian political theory its distinctive pessimism concerning the possibilities of politics. Marx would probably have endorsed the progressive aspects of the developments in actual capitalism outlined above because his analysis obviously permits the conclusion that market mechanisms (conceived as the 'social relations of capitalist production') would increasingly 'fetter' ongoing economic development, apparently implying that 'labor's mission', labor's involvement in policy-making under its own auspices, would expand. But it is non-Marxist political economy that has done most to elaborate the 'embeddedness' of markets in 'non-economic' conditions.

For more two-and-a-half centuries political economy has had an object of analysis that differs from the subject matter of what now passes for economic orthodoxy. Actual economic development, in rich and poor countries alike, does not follow the script imagined in abstract economic enquiry. It is, instead, a function of policies and institutions, usually policies and institutions devised precisely to effect outcomes that depart from the 'logic' of accumulation. Humanity has recurrently claimed the right to control its destiny through institution-building and policy-formation which, in turn, enhance both opportunities and responsibilities.

The high levels of uncivilized private behavior and corporate licentiousness that today characterize the liberalized corporate world provide cogent evidence that 'sweet commerce' needs sedulous regulation. The unemployment and disruptive structural change that have typified the rich countries for most of the past four decades are evidence that all societies need permanent mechanisms to prevent market mechanisms from determining economic conditions. The political economy traditions outlined above show that previous generations of social science knew more than most economists are currently prepared to concede.

Geoff Dow is Reader in Political Economy and Political Science, School of Political Science and International Studies, University of Queensland. Policy Matters in Political Economy © 2011 Geoff Dow.

CLASSICAL POLITICAL ECONOMY

The era of classical political economy, epitomized by the works of Adam Smith and David Ricardo, laid the foundations for the analysis of a capitalist economy. In Britain in the eighteenth century, capitalism was still emerging from feudalism and was not established as the dominant economic system until the nineteenth century. Smith and Ricardo sought to understand the characteristics of the emerging economic order and to grapple with the questions of economic policy relevant to the era. Their analyses, and those of other classical political economists including the Reverend Thomas Malthus, Jean Baptiste Say and John Stuart Mill, were wide-ranging and were concerned with social and political as well as more narrowly economic questions. Ethical issues were also explicitly considered.

Analyses of value, distribution and growth were recurrent themes in classical political economy. They remain so today in modern political economy. So, looking back to the works of the classics is not purely of historical interest. The selections included here illustrate some of these themes. Smith's piece on the division of labour comes from the opening chapter of his famous book *An Inquiry into the Nature and Causes of the Wealth of Nations*. Ricardo's piece on rents, prices and profits is from an essay responding in part to arguments put by Reverend Malthus. Both have been heavily edited to make them readily accessible to the modern reader who may not be attuned to the style of language used two centuries ago. They are followed by a contribution from John Eatwell, a modern British economist who is a member of the House of Lords, reflecting on the socio-economic context in which these classical ideas were developed and their impact on how the market economy came to be understood. The section concludes with an article by James Clifton that argues that a classical notion of competition is crucial for understanding the dynamics of the modern capitalist economy shaped by large corporations.

Readers interested in the classical economists and their writings will find the History of Economic Thought Website <homepage.newschool.edu/het/> and *History of Economics Review* <hetsa.fec.anu.edu.au> useful sources.

The Division of Labour
Adam Smith

The greatest improvement in the productive powers of labour, and the greater part of the skill, dexterity, and judgment with which it is anywhere directed, or applied, seem to have been the effects of the division of labour.

The effects of the division of labour, in the general business of society, will be more easily understood by considering in what manner it operates in some particular manufactures. It is commonly supposed to be carried furthest in some very trifling ones; not perhaps that it really is carried further in them than in others of more importance: but in those trifling manufactures which are destined to supply the small wants of but a small number of people, the whole number of workmen must necessarily be small; and those employed in every different branch of the work can often be collected into the same workhouse, and placed at once under the view of the spectator. In those great manufactures, on the contrary, which are destined to supply the great wants of the great body of the people, every different branch of the work employs so great a number of workmen that it is impossible to collect them all into the same workhouse. We can seldom see more, at one time, than those employed in one single branch. Though in such manufactures, therefore, the work may really be divided into a much greater number of parts than in those of a more trifling nature, the division is not near so obvious, and has accordingly been much less observed.

To take an example, therefore, from a very trifling manufacture; but one in which the division of labour has been very often taken notice of, the trade of the pin-maker; a workman not educated to this business (which the division of labour has rendered a distinct trade), nor acquainted with the use of the machinery employed in it (to the invention of which the same division of labour has probably given occasion), could scarce, perhaps, with his utmost industry, make one pin in a day, and certainly could not make twenty. But in the way in which this business is now carried on, not only the whole work is a peculiar trade, but it is divided into a number of branches, of which the greater part are likewise peculiar trades. One man draws out the wire, another straights it, a third cuts it, a fourth points it, a fifth grinds it at the top for receiving, the head; to make the head requires two or three distinct operations; to put it on is a peculiar business, to whiten the pins is another; it is even a trade by itself to put them into the paper; and the important business of making a pin is, in this manner, divided into about eighteen distinct operations, which, in some manufactories, are all performed by distinct hands ... they could, when they exerted themselves, make ... among them upwards of forty-eight thousand pins in a day. Each person, therefore, making a tenth part of forty-eight thousand pins, might be considered as making four thousand eight hundred pins in a day. But if they had all wrought separately and independently, and without any of them having been educated to this peculiar business, they certainly could not each of them have made twenty, perhaps not one pin in a day...

The division of labour ... occasions, in every art, a proportionable increase of the productive powers of labour. The separation of different trades and employments from one another seems to have taken place in consequence of this advantage. This separation, too, is generally called furthest in those countries which enjoy the highest degree of industry and improvement; what is the work of one man in a rude state of society being generally that of several in an improved one. In every improved society, the farmer is generally nothing but a farmer; the manufacturer, nothing but a manufacturer. The labour, too, which is necessary to produce any one complete manufacture is almost always divided among a great number of hands ... The nature of agriculture, indeed, does not admit of so many subdivisions of labour, nor of so complete a separation of one business from another, as manufactures ... The most opulent nations, indeed, generally excel all their neighbours in agriculture as well as in manufactures; but they are commonly more distinguished by their superiority in the latter than in the former ...

This great increase of the quantity of work which, in consequence of the division of labour, the same number of people are capable of performing, is owing to three different circumstances; first, to the increase of dexterity in every particular workman; secondly, to the saving of the time which is commonly lost in passing from one species of work to another; and lastly, to the invention of a great number of machines which facilitate and abridge labour, and enable one man to do the work of many.

First, the improvement of the dexterity of the workman necessarily increases the quantity of the work he can perform; and the division of labour, by reducing every man's business to some one simple operation, and by making this operation the sole employment of his life, necessarily increased very much the dexterity of the workman ...

Secondly, the advantage which is gained by saving the time commonly lost in passing from one sort of work to another is much greater than we should at first view be apt to imagine it. It is impossible to pass very quickly from one kind of work to another that is carried on in a different place and with quite different tools ... A man commonly saunters a little in turning his hand from one sort of employment to another. When he first begins the new work he is seldom very keen and hearty; his mind, as they say, does not go to it, and for some time he rather trifles than applies to good purpose. The habit of sauntering and of indolent careless application, which is naturally, or rather necessarily acquired by every country workman who is obliged to change his work and his tools every half hour, and to apply his hand in twenty different ways almost every day of his life, renders him almost always slothful and lazy, and incapable of any vigorous application even on the most pressing occasions. Independent, therefore, of his deficiency in point of dexterity, this cause alone must always reduce considerably the quantity of work which he is capable of performing.

Thirdly, and lastly, everybody must be sensible how much labour is facilitated and abridged by the application of proper machinery. It is unnecessary to give any example. I shall only observe, therefore, that the invention of all those machines by which labour is so much facilitated and abridged seems to have been originally owing to the division of labour. Men are much more likely to discover easier and readier methods of attaining any object when the whole attention of their minds is directed towards that single object than when it is dissipated among a great variety of things. But in consequence of the division of labour, the whole of every man's attention comes naturally to be directed towards some one very simple object. It is naturally to be expected, therefore, that some one or other of those who are employed in each particular branch of labour should soon find out easier and readier methods of performing their own particular work, wherever the nature of it admits of such improvement. A great part of the machines made use of in those manufactures in which labour is most subdivided, were originally the inventions of common workmen, who, being each of them employed in some very simple operation, naturally turned their thoughts towards finding out easier and readier methods of performing it. Whoever has been much accustomed to visit such manufactures must frequently have been shown very pretty machines, which were the inventions of such workmen in order to facilitate and quicken their particular part of the work ...

All the improvements in machinery, however, have by no means been the inventions of those who had occasion to use the machines. Many improvements have been made by the ingenuity of the makers of the machines, when to make them became the business of a peculiar trade; and some by that of those who are called philosophers or men of speculation, whose trade it is not to do anything, but to observe everything; and who, upon that account, are often capable of combining together the powers of the most distant and dissimilar objects. In the progress of society, philosophy or speculation becomes, like every other employment, the principal or sole trade and occupation of a particular class of citizens. Like every other employment too, it is subdivided into a great number of different branches, each of which affords occupation to a peculiar tribe or class of philosophers; and this subdivision of employment in philosophy, as well as in every other business, improves dexterity, and saves time. Each individual becomes more expert in his own peculiar branch, more work is done upon the whole, and the quantity of science is considerably increased by it.

It is the great multiplication of the productions of all the different arts, in consequence of the division of labour, which occasions, in a well-governed society, that universal opulence which extends itself to the lowest ranks of the people. Every workman has a great quantity of his own work to dispose of beyond what he himself has occasion for; and every other workman being exactly in the same situation, he is enabled to exchange a great quantity of his own goods for a great quantity, or, what comes to the same thing, for the price of a great quantity of theirs. He supplies them abundantly with what they have occasion for, and they accommodate him as amply with what he has occasion for, and a general plenty diffuses itself through all the different ranks of the society.

Observe the accommodation of the most common artificer or day-labourer in a civilized and thriving country, and you will perceive that the number of people of whose industry a part, though but a small part, has been employed in procuring him this accommodation, exceeds all computation … if we examine, I say, all these things, and consider what a variety of labour is employed about each of them, we shall be sensible that, without the assistance and co-operation of many thousands, the very meanest person in a civilized country could not be provided, even according to what we very falsely imagine the easy and simple manner in which he is commonly accommodated …

Of the principle which gives occasion to the division of labour

This division of labour, from which so many advantages are derived, is not originally the effect of any human wisdom, which foresees and intends that general opulence to which it gives occasion. It is the necessary, though very slow and gradual consequence of a certain propensity in human nature which has in view no such extensive utility; the propensity to truck, barter, and exchange one thing for another …

In civilized society a man stands at all times in need of the cooperation and assistance of great multitudes, while his whole life is scarce sufficient to gain the friendship of a few persons … But man has almost constant occasion for the help of his brethren, and it is in vain for him to expect it from their benevolence only. He will be more likely to prevail if he can interest their self-love in his favour, and show them that it is for their own advantage to do for him what he requires of them. Whoever offers to another a bargain of any kind, proposes to do this. Give me that which I want, and you shall have this which you want, is the meaning of every such offer; and it is in this manner that we obtain from one another the far greater part of those good offices which we stand in need of. It is not from the benevolence of the butcher, the brewer, or the baker that we expect our dinner, but from their regard to their own interest. We address ourselves, not to their humanity but to their self-love, and never talk to them of our own necessities but of their advantages. Nobody but a beggar chooses to depend chiefly upon the benevolence of his fellow-citizens …

As it is by treaty, by barter, and by purchase that we obtain from one another the greater part of those mutual good offices which we stand in need of, so it is this same trucking disposition which originally gives occasion to the division of labour … And thus the certainty of being able to exchange all that surplus part of the produce of his own labour, which is over and above his own consumption, for such parts of the produce of other men's labour as he may have occasion for, encourages every man to apply himself to a particular occupation, and to cultivate and bring to perfection whatever talent or genius he may possess for that particular species of business.

The difference of natural talents in different men is, in reality, much less than we are aware of; and the very different genius which appears to distinguish men of different professions, when grown up to maturity, is not upon many occasions so much the cause as the effect of the division of labour. The difference between the most dissimilar characters, between a philosopher and a common street porter, for example, seems to arise not so much from nature as from habit, custom, and education … But without the disposition to truck, barter, and exchange, every man must have procured to himself every necessary and conveniency of life which he wanted. All must have had the same duties to perform, and the same work to do, and there could have been no such difference of employment as could alone give occasion to any great difference of talents.

As it is this disposition which forms that difference of talents, so remarkable among men of different professions, so it is this same disposition which renders that difference useful … Among men, on the contrary, the most dissimilar geniuses are of use to one another; the different produces of their respective talents, by the general disposition to truck, barter, and exchange, being brought, as it were, into a common stock, where every man may purchase whatever part of the produce of other men's talents he has occasion for.

That the division of labour is limited by the extent of the market

As it is the power of exchanging that gives occasion to the division of labour, so the extent of this division must always be limited by the extent of that power, or, in other words, by the extent of the market. When the market is very small, no person can have any encouragement to dedicate himself entirely to one employment, for want of the power to exchange all that surplus part of the produce of his own labour, which is over and above his own consumption, for such parts of the produce of other men's labour as he has occasion for.

There are some sorts of industry, even of the lowest kind, which can be carried on nowhere but in a great town … As by means of water-carriage a more extensive market is opened to every sort of industry than what land-carriage alone can afford it, so it is upon the sea-coast, and along the banks of navigable rivers, that industry of every kind naturally begins to subdivide and improve itself, and it is frequently not till a long time after that those improvements extend themselves to the inland parts of the country …

Since such, therefore, are the advantages of water-carriage, it is natural that the first improvements of art and industry should be made where this conveniency opens the whole world for a market to the produce of every sort of labour, and that they should always be much later in extending themselves into the inland parts of the country. The inland parts of the country can for a long time have no other market for the greater part of their goods, but the country which lies round about them, and separates them from the sea-coast, and the great navigable rivers. The extent of their market, therefore, must for a long time be in proportion to the riches and populousness of that country, and consequently their improvement must always be posterior to the improvement of that country.

Adam Smith was a prominent British political economist. This chapter is abridged from *An Inquiry into the Nature and Causes of the Wealth of Nations*, 1776.

An Essay on Profits
David Ricardo

In treating on the subject of the profits of capital, it is necessary to consider the principles which regulate the rise and fall of rent; as rent and profits, it will be seen, have a very intimate connection with each other … In the first settling of a country rich in fertile land, and which may be had by any one who chooses to take it, the whole produce, after deducting the outgoings belonging to cultivation, will be the profits of capital, and will belong to the owner of such capital, without any deduction whatever for rent.

Thus, if the capital employed by an individual on such land were of the value of two hundred quarters of wheat, [and] … the value of the remaining produce were one hundred quarters of wheat, or of equal value with one hundred quarters of wheat, the neat profit to the owner of capital would be fifty percent or one hundred profit on two hundred capital.

For a period of some duration, the profits of agricultural stock might continue at the same rate, because land equally fertile, and equally well situated, might be abundant, and therefore, might be cultivated on the same advantageous terms, in proportion as the capital of the first, and subsequent settlers augmented.

Profits might even increase, because the population increasing, at a more rapid rate than capital, wages might fall; and instead of the value of one hundred quarters of wheat being necessary for the circulating capital, ninety only might be required: in which case, the profits of stock would rise from fifty to fifty-seven percent. Profits might also incr ease, because improvements might take place in agriculture, or in the implements of husbandry, which would augment the produce with the same cost of production. If wages rose, or a worse system of agriculture were practised, profits would again fall.

These are circumstances which are more or less at all times in operation – they may retard or accelerate the natural effects of the progress of wealth, by rising or lowering profits – by increasing or diminishing the supply of food with the employment of the same capital on the land.

We will, however, suppose that no improvements take place in agriculture, and that capital and population advance in the proper proportion, so that the real wages of labour continue uniformly the same: – that we may know what peculiar effects are to be ascribed to the growth of capital, the increase of population, and the extension of cultivation to the more remote, and less fertile land ...

After all the fertile land in the immediate neighbourhood of the first settlers were cultivated, if capital and population increased, more food would be required, and it could only be procured from land not so advantageously situated ... The necessity of employing more labourers ... would make it necessary that more capital should be permanently employed to obtain the same produce. Suppose this addition to be of the value of ten quarters of wheat, the whole capital employed on the new land would be two hundred and ten, to obtain the same return as on the old; and, consequently the profits of stock would fall from fifty to forty-three percent or ninety on two hundred and ten.

On the land first cultivated, the return would be the same as before, namely, fifty percent or one hundred quarters of wheat; but, the general profits of stock being regulated by the profits made on the least profitable employment of capital on agriculture, a division of the one hundred quarters would take place, forty-three percent or eighty-six quarters would constitute the profit of stock, and seven percent or fourteen, quarters, would constitute rent. And that such a division must take place is evident, when we consider that the owner of the capital of the value of two hundred and ten quarters of wheat would obtain precisely the same profit, whether he cultivated the distant land, or paid the first settler fourteen quarters for rent. In this stage, the profits on all capital employed in trade would fall to forty-three percent.

If, in the further progress of population and wealth, the produce of more land were required to obtain the same return, it might be necessary to employ, either on account of distance, or the worse quality of land, the value of two hundred and twenty quarters of wheat, the profits of stock would then fall to thirty-six percent or eighty on two hundred and twenty, and the rent of the first land would rise to twenty-eight quarters of wheat, and on the second portion of land cultivated, rent would now commence, and would amount to fourteen quarters. The profits on all trading capital would also fall to thirty-six percent.

Thus by bringing successively land of a worse quality, or less favourably situated, into cultivation, rent would rise on the land previously cultivated, and precisely in the same degree would profits fall; and if the smallness of profits do not check accumulation, there are hardly any limits to the rise of rent, and the fall of profit ...

It will be seen that during the progress of a country the whole produce raised on its land will increase, and for a certain time that part of the produce which belongs to the profits of stock, as well as that part which belongs to rent will increase; but that at a later period, every accumulation of capital will be attended with an absolute, as well as a proportionate diminution of profits, – though rents will uniformly increase ...

This is a view of the effects of accumulation which is exceedingly curious, and has, I believe, never before been noticed ... In a progressive country, rent is not only absolutely increasing, but that it is also increasing in its ratio to the capital employed on the land ... The landlord not only obtains a greater produce, but a larger share.

Rent then is in all cases a portion of the profits previously obtained on the land. It is never a new creation of revenue, but always part of a revenue already created.

Profits of stock fall only because land equally well adapted to produce food cannot be procured; and the degree of the fall of profits, and the rise of rents, depends wholly on the increased expense of production. If, therefore, in the progress of countries in wealth and population, new portions of fertile land could be added to such countries, with every increase of capital, profits would never fall, nor rents rise.

If the money price of corn, and the wages of labour, did not vary in price in the least degree, during the progress of the country in wealth and population, still profits would fall and rents would rise; because more labourers would be employed on the more distant or less fertile land, in order to obtain the same supply of raw produce; and therefore the cost of production would have increased, whilst the value of the produce continued the same.

But the price of corn, and of all other raw produce, has been invariably observed to rise as a nation became wealthy, and was obliged to have recourse to poorer lands for the production of part of its food; and very little consideration will convince us, that such is the effect which would naturally be expected to take place under such circumstances.

The exchangeable value of all commodities rises as the difficulties of their production increase. If then new difficulties occur in the production of corn, from more labour being necessary, whilst no more labour is required to produce gold, silver, cloth, linen, &c. the exchangeable value of corn will necessarily rise, as compared with those things. On the contrary, facilities in the production of corn, or of any other commodity of whatever kind, which shall afford the same produce with less labour, will lower its exchangeable value. Thus we see that improvements in agriculture, or in the implements of husbandry, lower the exchangeable value of corn; improvements in the machinery connected with the manufacture of cotton lower the exchangeable value of cotton goods; and improvements in mining, or the discovery of new and more abundant mines of the precious metals, lower the value of gold and silver, or which is the same thing, raises the price of all other commodities. Wherever competition can have its full effect, and the production of the commodity be not limited by nature, as in the case with some wines, the difficulty or facility of their production will ultimately regulate their exchangeable value. The sole effect then of the process of wealth on prices, independently of all improvements, either in agriculture or manufactures, appears to be to raise the price of raw produce and of labour, leaving all other commodities at their original prices, and to lower general profits in consequence of the general rise of wages.

This fact is of more importance than at first sight appears, as it relates to the interest of the landlord, and the other parts of the community. Not only is the situation of the landlord improved, (by the increasing difficulty of procuring food, in consequence of accumulation) by obtaining an increased quantity of the produce of the land, but also by the increased exchangeable value of that quantity.

...

It follows then, that the interest of the landlord is always opposed to the interest of every other class in the community. His situation is never so prosperous, as when food is scarce and dear: whereas, all other persons are greatly benefited by procuring food cheap. High rent and low profits, for they invariably accompany each other, ought never to be the subject of complaint, if they are the effect of the natural course of things.

They are the most unequivocal proofs of wealth and prosperity, and of an abundant population, compared with the fertility of the soil. The general profits of stock depend wholly on the profits of the last portion of capital employed on the land; if, therefore, landlords were to relinquish the whole of their rents, they would neither raise the general profits of stock, nor lower the price of corn to the consumer. It would have no other effect, as Mr Malthus has observed, than to enable those farmers, whose lands now pay a rent, to live like gentlemen, and they would have to expend that portion of the general revenue, which now falls to the share of the landlord.

A nation is rich, not according to the abundance of its money, nor to the high money value at which its commodities circulate, but according to the abundance of its commodities, contributing to its comforts and enjoyments. Although this is a proposition, from which few would dissent, many look with the greatest alarm at the prospect of the diminution of their money revenue, though such reduced revenue should have so improved in exchangeable value, as to procure considerably more of all the necessaries and luxuries of life.

If then, the principles here stated as governing rent and profit be correct, general profits on capital, can only be raised by a fall in the exchangeable value of food, and which fall can only arise from three causes: first, the fall of the real wages of labour, which shall enable the farmer to bring a greater excess of produce to market; second, improvements in agriculture, or in the implements of husbandry, which shall also increase the excess of produce; and third, the discovery of new markets, from whence corn may be imported at a cheaper price than it can be grown for at home.

The first of these causes is more or less permanent, according as the price from which wages fall is more or less near that remuneration for labour, which is necessary to the actual subsistence of the labourer.

The rise or fall of wages is common to all states of society, whether it be the stationary, the advancing, or the retrograde state. In the stationary state, it is regulated wholly by the increase or falling off of the population. In the advancing state, it depends on whether the capital or the population advance, at the more rapid course. In the retrograde state, it depends on whether population or capital decrease with the greater rapidity.

As experience demonstrates that capital and population alternately take the lead, and wages in consequence are liberal or scanty, nothing can be positively laid down, respecting profits, as far as wages are concerned. But I think it may be most satisfactorily proved, that in every society advancing in wealth and population, independently of the effect produced by liberal or scanty wages, general profits must fall, unless there be improvements in agriculture, or corn can be imported at a cheaper price ...

Profits then depend on the price, or rather on the value of food. Every thing which gives facility to the production of food, however scarce, or however abundant commodities may become, will raise the rate of profits, whilst on the contrary, every thing which shall augment the cost of production without augmenting the quantity of food, will, under every circumstance, lower the general rate of profits. The facility of obtaining food is beneficial in two ways to the owners of capital, it at the same time raises profits and increases the amount of consumable commodities. The facility in obtaining all other things only increases the amount of commodities.

If, then, the power of purchasing cheap food be of such great importance, and if the importation of corn will tend to reduce its price, arguments almost unanswerable respecting the danger of dependence on foreign countries for a portion of our food, for in no other view will the question bear an argument, ought to be brought forward to induce us to restrict importation, and thereby forcibly to detain capital in an employment which it would otherwise leave for one much more advantageous.

If the legislature were at once to adopt a decisive policy with regard to the trade in corn – if it were to allow a permanently free trade, and did not with every variation of price alternately restrict and encourage importation, we should undoubtedly be a regularly importing country. We should be so in consequence of the superiority of our wealth and population, compared to the fertility of our soil over our neighbours. It is only when a country is comparatively wealthy, when all its fertile land is in a state of high cultivation, and that it is obliged to have recourse to its inferior lands to obtain the food necessary for its population; or when it is originally without the advantages of a fertile soil, that it can become profitable to import corn …

That great improvements have been made in agriculture, and that much capital has been expended on the land, it is not attempted to deny; but, with all those improvements, we have not overcome the natural impediments resulting from our increasing wealth and prosperity, which obliges us to cultivate at a disadvantage our poor lands, if the importation of corn is restricted or prohibited. If we were left to ourselves, unfettered by legislative enactments, we should gradually withdraw our capital from the cultivation of such lands, and import the produce which is at present raised upon them. The capital withdrawn would be employed in the manufacture of such commodities as would be exported in return for the corn. Such a distribution of part of the capital of the country would be more advantageous, or it would not be adopted.

David Ricardo was a prominent British political economist. This chapter is abridged from *An Essay on the Influence of a low Price of Corn on the Profits of Stock*, 1815.

Voices in the Air
John Eatwell

The market economy is a mysterious thing. It is *a* system in which, in principle, all economic life – all production, all distribution – is organised through buying and selling; in which flows of money determine the scale, location and content of economic life; in which vitally inter-related decisions are made by countless individuals and companies on the basis of price calculations alone, with little or no direct communication among themselves.

Now, in a local area, with a limited number of people involved, this might be a plausible picture. But from its very beginnings the market system has operated on a world scale. The industrial revolution was built on cotton, a raw material brought from the New World, processed in Britain and then sold all over the globe. At least as important, therefore, as the technological innovations of the eighteenth and nineteenth centuries we all learn about at school – the spinning jenny, Crompton's mule, Watt's steam engine and so on – were the changes in economic organisation that gathered pace in the eighteenth century and then swept aside the old system of economic organisation.

For example, the making of knives, forks and spoons had been controlled in Sheffield by the Cutlers' Company. The company was incorporated by Act of Parliament in 1624, so that regulations which had been built up over the preceding hundred years were given the force of law. Membership of the company required an apprenticeship of seven years under a Master and, as each Master was allowed only one apprentice at a time, the quantity – as well as the quality – of output was strictly controlled.

Moreover, Company regulations in 1662 prohibited members from buying the components for making knives from anyone who was not also a member of the Company. The Company even had its own police force, the Searchers, who by a statute of 1625 were authorized "from time to time to enter into any house or houses, shops, cellars or warehouses, of the said Company, to search for deceitful wares and for those who work, buy or sell contrary to the statute".

But by the end of the eighteenth century the power of the guilds and corporations was on the wane. By 1806 the effective power of the Cutlers' Company had gone, and with it the mechanism of controls on production and trade which characterised Tudor England. The system of controls had been complex, though it is easy to see how it worked. Now it was swept away and replaced by – nothing. Length of apprenticeship could no longer be used to limit production, and quality was no longer regulated by statute: instead, the final arbiter was to be the market.

What effect would this abdication to the market have? Anarchy and chaos, it might reasonably have been supposed. Yet this was not so. The market system may be successful or unsuccessful. It may unleash a boom of innovative activity, or it may perpetuate an enduring slump. But it isn't chaos. It *is* a system with its own internal laws of behavior – laws which regulate, coordinate, direct and discipline all participants in the market economy: that is, everyone. The laws are there, demanding to be revealed.

At least that is what all economists believe!

If the market system is guided by hidden laws, we ought to know what they are. Perhaps they can be manipulated to achieve desirable results: full employment, for example, or a respectable rate of growth. Some sort of analytical apparatus is required to dig beneath the surface complexities and reveal just what these laws are. Economics is supposed to provide this apparatus.

But economic ideas do not arise from simple intellectual curiosity. When vested interests in society clash, ideas are one of the weapons used in the struggle. A group putting forward a particular point of view will try to show not only that it has a uniquely correct understanding of how the system works, but also that, as a consequence, its policies conform to 'natural justice', or are in the 'national interest'. Economic analysis thus plays a vital role in political controversy. But it would be wrong to imagine that this role is pursued entirely cynically. Economists' ideas do not lead events, they follow them. Brilliant political fashions are often economically old-hat. Ideas are picked up, dropped, revived, given more attractive covering (mathematics being the fashionable top-dressing at the moment) and presented as penetrating and new. Nothing is quite so powerful as an idea whose time has come.

Therefore, once a particular interpretation has been invented of how the system works, it may be transformed and developed in a way which is totally independent of the conflict in which it originated. An idea which began merely as an argument 'in a particular cause' acquires a 'scientific aspect'. It appears to be independent of political controversy, and so becomes a yet more powerful propaganda weapon.

Although economists are often the intellectual hired guns of political interests, this does not mean that they don't sometimes identify some elements of the process by which the market mechanism actually works. But it does mean that we should always be aware of just where ideas come from. For even the most abstract bit of theorising is erected round the skeleton of its ideological origins.

Adam Smith and the birth of the market economy

The birth of the market economy was painful and slow. The infant was almost stifled at birth by the vested interests that were themselves threatened by the rise of the market – the remnants of feudal privilege, the guilds, the companies trading under Royal patent and the 'landed interest'. Adam Smith's *Wealth of Nations* provided the intellectual ammunition in the battle for market freedom. The Cutlers' Company was cited by Adam Smith as a typical example of the 'corporations' which regulated production and trade, restrained competition and were, all in all, 'a

conspiracy against the public'. He was particularly incensed by the apprenticeship regulations, based on the Elizabethan Statute of Apprenticeship, which enacted that no person "should for the future exercise any trade, craft, or mystery at that time exercised in England, unless he had previously served to it an apprenticeship of seven years at least". All monopolies, rights and privileges, including the rights of workers, were to be swept aside and every individual and company left to fend for itself in the market place. The new freedom would release a wave of innovative endeavor, raising the rate of growth. Roads and canals would be built, opening up new markets, raising demand for the products of the new factories, encouraging technical change through the division of labour, enhancing the wealth and power of the nation.

The market, moreover, would not be anarchic, but would provide a mechanism of co-ordination, directing individual self-interest toward social benefit through the driving force of competition. The struggle for more, enforced by competition, would ensure that resources flowed to areas in which they might most profitably be used, and that new techniques were adopted that cheapened production. Anyone who refused to take the plunge would be swept aside. Competition produced change, novelty, innovation and growth; competition produced wealth. Adam Smith's book was a manifesto for the new market system.

In the early years of the nineteenth century the conflict over the liberation of free market forces focused on one clear-cut issue: free trade – or, more precisely, free trade in corn. The campaign for the abolition of the Corn Laws was a political struggle between, on the one hand, agriculture, the landlords and the countryside – the past – and, on the other, industry, manufacturers and their workers, and the towns – the future. The agricultural interests campaigned for restrictions to be maintained on the importation of corn, so that the price of domestic grain would be kept high. The industrial interests wanted imports of cheap foreign grain, so that the pressure on wages would be reduced and the profits that would fund new investment, and hence future growth, raised. As in any major economic struggle, each side had economists arguing its case.

Ricardo and the manufacturing classes

The chief economist supporting the industrial classes was David Ricardo (1772-1823), a brilliant young stockbroker who, having made his fortune on the Exchange, bought several large country estates and in his early forties turned to politics (he became an M.P. in 1819) and to the study of economic theory. In 1815 he published a pamphlet entitled *An Essay on the Influence of a low Price of Corn on the Profits of Stock Shewing the Inexpediency of Restrictions for Importation* (an extract from which appears as the preceding chapter of this book). It proved to be a best-seller, a second printing being required only a few days after the first. This was not, as hindsight might suggest, because it was destined to become a classic in economic analysis, but rather because it was a fundamental attack on the Corn Laws and on the economic arguments of the landlords. "The interest of the landlord", Ricardo was to write later, "is always opposed to that of the consumer and the manufacturer".

Ricardo's argument was built on two basic propositions: first, that the wage of each worker was given at, or near, subsistence; secondly, that the surplus produced over and above the wage was divided between landlords and capitalists in the form of rents and profits according as land was scarce or plentiful.

The Corn Laws, by prohibiting the import of foreign grain, kept up the demand for expensive home-produced gain and so raised the rent that landlords could command for the use of their land. High rents bit into profits, cutting investment and growth. As the economy grew, the number of industrial workers would grow with it. Since the workers' subsistence was based on grain, the pressure on domestic agricultural resources would rise, forcing rents yet higher and cutting profits yet further. Ultimately, increasing rents would bring growth to a painful halt.

If the Corn Laws were abolished, on the other hand, the price of corn and the level of rents would both fall, and profits would rise. The growing industrial labour force could be fed from the wheatlands of the world, and there would be no limit on the growth of the economy. Everyone would benefit – even perhaps, in the end, the landlords – from the greater prosperity.

Implicit in Ricardo's case was the assumption that the social classes played different roles in the economy. The workers merely subsisted; the landlords squandered their share of the product in riotous living, indulgence in the delights of the countryside, and in wine, persons and song; the capitalists, the greater the level of investment, and hence the greater the rate of growth.

This characterization of the role of social classes was not peculiar to Ricardo, but was broadly accepted by all economists at the time, including those who attempted to defend the Corn Laws and the role of the landlords. The champion of the landlords' interest was T.R. Malthus (1766–1834), famous for his pessimistic *Essay on the Principle of Population*. Smith, Ricardo, Malthus and John Stuart Mill (1806–1873) were leading figures of what has come to be known as the English School of Classical Political Economy, one of the interesting characteristics of which is that none of these leading figures was English. Smith, Malthus and Mill were all Scots, and Ricardo was of Dutch-Portuguese ancestry, his father having emigrated from Amsterdam in about 1760.

Ricardo's argument was presented in a system of precise mathematical logic, in terms of what is now called a 'model'. Construction of a model involves abstracting from reality what are believed to be the most relevant factors that affect a particular situation, and working out their relationships and interactions within the analytical vacuum. The clarity of Ricardo's argument rested on key simplifying assumptions – that the wages of the workers, for example, might be regarded as consisting only of corn – without which the antagonism between rents and profits would have been difficult to reveal unambiguously. In economics there is always a temptation to choose assumptions that are convenient rather than realistic – a vice that afflicts all economists, though some more than others. But, as was shown after his time, Ricardo's results do not depend on his rather limiting assumptions. In particular, the idea for which he was to be most criticized – that profits are determined by the surplus of output over wages – has been triumphantly vindicated. Analytical model-building has been the method of economic theorizing ever since Ricardo wrote. Adam Smith had defined what economics was about. Ricardo showed how it was to be done.

The debate over the Corn Laws was not resolved for another thirty years, and remained a bitter, divisive element in British politics. But when abolition eventually came, it proved to be something of an anti-climax. Agriculture was not ruined. On the contrary, the growing urban economy ensured an expanding demand for home-produced agricultural goods for the next twenty years, until British arable farming was overwhelmed by competition from the prairies. Moreover, many of the landlords had themselves invested in mines, or canals, or manufacturing, and the lines of the old class conflict between Land and Capital became blurred.

Capital and labour

Ricardo's ideas expressed the economic philosophy of the manufacturing classes. But as the nineteenth century wore on and the conflict between Land and Capital faded into history, a new and more bitter conflict began to dominate social and political life, the conflict between Capital and Labour. This created a problem for the economists. For, despite his eminent respectability, Ricardo had, as an incidental part of his analysis, portrayed wages and profits, as well as profits and rents, as mutually antagonistic. From the point of view of those in authority the growth of the trade-union movement, and the emerging political demands of an increasingly self-confident working class gathering into socialist parties, did not sit well with an economics that suggested that the operations of the market economy should be seen in terms of class conflict. As early as

1831 economists could be found who were prepared to accuse Ricardo and his followers "not merely or errors, but of crimes", for:

> in their theory of rent, they have insisted that landlords can thrive only at the expense of the public at large, and especially of the capitalists: in their circumstances by depressing those of the labouring and numerous class: ... In one and all of their arguments they have studiously exhibited the interests of every class in society as necessarily at perpetual variance with every other class! (Scrope, *Quarterly Review*, November 1831)

It was Karl Marx who took up the theoretical tools forged by Ricardo in the interests of the capitalists and transformed them in such a way as to expose the true class conflict and repression on which the market system was based, charting that system's internal contradictions and revealing the substance of its ultimate self-created destruction. The bourgeois economics of Smith and Ricardo thereby culminated in a set of ideas that haunted the privileged and the powerful, ideas that inspired revolutionary movements committed to the *rejection* of the market system.

John Eatwell is Member of the British House of Lords and President of Queens' College, Cambridge. This chapter is abridged from *Whatever Happened to Britain?* Duckworth, London, 1982, pp. 31-38. © 1982 John Eatwell. Reprinted with permission of the author.

Competition and Capitalist Development
James A. Clifton

Capitalism is an epoch in history, a period distinguished by its own economic laws, of which competition is one. Since capitalism is a mode of production, itself subject to development, a critical issue must be resolved before a general theory of price based on a concept of competition can be conceived. Does a mode of production itself unfold over time, gradually developing its own tendencies and characteristics, or does it emerge from another epoch immediately in its purest, most highly developed form and become increasingly imperfect with its own development?

Classical economics was founded on a perception of competition derived from the analysis of a new economic order. Ricardo, for example, held the view that "the principle which apportions capital to each trade in the precise amount that is required, is more active than is generally supposed" (Ricardo 1951: 90). In Ricardo's theory, a portion of each firm's invested capital was floating capital, capital borrowed from a bank, the demand for which fluctuated depending upon demand in the industry in which the firm produced.

The primary purpose of classical political economy was to understand such basic economic laws in abstraction from the concrete environment of its own day; to formulate a theory of capitalism. The secondary purpose of classical political economy was to defend on the basis of the theory this highly *imperfect* new order. Capitalism, far from pervading and dominating the economic system as a whole in the era of the classical economists, was an infant in a very few spheres of production, struggling for its survival in an economy dominated by forms of economic organisation inherited from the feudal epoch. To portray this era as one in which the economy as a whole was ideally suited to the operation of the laws distinguishing capitalism is historically inaccurate. In defending the new order, the classical economists emphasised the need to break down the economic, social and political barriers that were severely hindering the operation of free competition. In short, the actual world in which very small firms were owned and operated by individual capitalists was hardly one best suited to the economic laws distinguishing capitalism.

The alternative view from that implicit in the evolution of neoclassical price theory is that capitalism has gradually unfolded over the past two hundred years. Were it not for the powerful sway that neoclassical theory holds over our interpretation of the world, this alternative would appear at once much more plausible in the light of the facts of history and of contemporary life. Over the past two hundred years, capitalist organisation has come to dominate economic life almost completely in the developed countries and to a smaller but ever increasing degree in much of the third world. Through organisation and ever improving means of communication and transportation, factor mobility is much more highly developed today than ever before in history.

The question for price theory then becomes: how does one characterise the adjustment mechanism, given the view that capitalism has gradually unfolded over time, revealing its economic laws in the day-to-day operation of the economy ever more fully as the system has developed?

It is not sufficiently recognised that Adam Smith's concept of competition was intended for a world of merchant capital rather than a world of industrial or fixed capital. In the former context the conditions of free capital mobility are established direcdy through exchange. Commodities whose rates of return are expected to be high are purchased by the merchant. Whether or not his expectations are later borne out at the time of the sale, his capital is restored to liquidity. Since no portion of his capital remains tied up in commodities, it is entirely free to pursue another purchase in whatever area the highest returns are expected. Through the influx and outflow of merchant capital to areas of higher returns from those of lower returns, there is established a tendency towards a uniform rate of profit.

The situation is quite different, however, in a world of industrial or fixed capital. Where finance is committed to production activity it is at once immobilised. Only that portion of fixed capital used up within the period of production becomes restored to liquidity through the sale of produced commodities. The small firm of two hundred years ago, producing a single product in a single industry, was far less free to employ that finance in any sphere, as the merchant could. On the contrary, in order to preserve its fixed investment, the firm was generally committed to expanding production in its own sphere by reducing costs of production through economies of scale.

Was there any tendency towards the establishment of competition for the economy as a whole in the early stages of industrial capitalism? Ricardo, who was certainly in a position to know, believed there was, as the earlier citation makes evident. In Ricardo's concept of the adjustment mechanism, however, banks played the leading role. Banks without question help perform the same role today and in all likelihood with far greater efficiency and accuracy. But there was in Ricardo's time little discretion for the firm itself to establish, directly through investment, economy-wide competition with other firms. Direct competition was limited to single markets taken in isolation, rather than being a general process.

With its own growth, however, the capitalist firm has been able to overcome the limits to free capital mobility inherent in the nature of fixed capital. The conditions of free capital mobility for units of fixed capital have not been established fundamentally in the exchange process, as they were for merchant capital, but gradually in the systematic organisation of production across many geographical areas and industries, and through a broader range of competitive strategies applied to the market more methodically and intensively. Diversification is the *structural* element in the emergence of free capital mobility for the firm. The range and intensity of competitive strategies is the *operational* element of free capital mobility.

The fixed capital of the firm has become increasingly mobile as the firm has grown, by industrial and geographical diversification, out of its original sphere of production. Such a firm may be called a 'unit of general production', because it organises production across a wider spectrum of the full range of production possibilities than the single product firm in one locale. An important effect of this structural condition is to allow the firm itself to achieve a more efficient allocation of its capital between several activities and regions, in accordance with changing market conditions. This process of capital mobility among sectors is accomplished as an internal flow of funds within the corporation and without the intervention of the capital market as in Ricardo's day.

Another result of this structural element of the adjustment process is evident from the work of Alfred D. Chandler, Jr. Chandler has traced this process through the changes in the organisational structure of the most advanced capitalist firms at various stages of capitalist development in the United States. His analysis of organisation charts reveals the emergence of the modern corporation first in the separation between staff and line functions, and then later in the development of the distinction between the general corporate office and the various operating divisions. While the latter manage production and earn profits in different spheres, the general corporate office manages the firm as a single financial entity. Since it is the reinvestment of earnings from each division into areas promising the highest overall rate of return for the corporation that constitutes the major activity of the general office, it follows that the corporate identity should be this pool of finance, rather than production activity itself. The corporate identity can only be what is common to the diverse production activities. Each is a centre of profit making.

The structural condition of free capital mobility renders competition among firms in the dominant corporate sector more abstract, since it is more general or economy wide in nature. The abstract character is evident in the fact that it is now direct competition among cohesive sums of self-expanding finance that dominates the economic process, rather than competition among producers of soap on the one hand and producers of books on the other. Because production for each firm is general, firms are directly competing with a much larger number of firms than those in any one of its operating divisions. Further, the tremendous number of commodities produced by each firm and the dominant strategy of growth through product innovation add enormous complexity and changeability to the competitive interrelationships among firms.

Capitalism is an inherently dynamic process. For the firm as a cohesive unit of fixed capital, the conditions of free capital mobility have also developed on an operational basis. At all stages of capitalist development the growth of the firm has been the requisite for survival among competing firms. What has changed with the adjustment process is not merely the structural conditions through which competition is carried on. The number of competitive strategies available to the firm from economies of large scale organisation and the intensity of the search for competitive advantages available from large budgets and staffs have also increased.

Competition was first exhibited as a cheapening of commodities as basic industrial processes were developed and improved. Although it has in general been superseded by other forms of competition, price competition is still one of the competitive strategies available to the firm. Many other strategies are in use as well, however. In Chandler's analysis of organisational evolution, two of the more important ones come into focus during two hundred years of American corporate development. The first is the gradual separation of the purchasing and sales division into separate divisions and the growth of the sales division from that point onward. The increasing intensity and scope of the sales division as a competitive strategy are especially evident in the growth of the advertising budget.

The second competitive strategy that has become part of the operational condition of free capital mobility for the firm is a direct result of the origin and tremendous growth of a permanent research and development staff within the corporate structure. The research and development staff has become an integral part of the firm's major competitive strategy of product innovation.

Indeed, as the adjustment process has unfolded over two centuries, product innovations have come to occupy a larger share of the research and development budget than cost-reducing process innovations, which were the basis of the dominant competitive strategy at an earlier stage of capitalist development.

The number of competitive strategies the firm may pursue in its own struggle for growth also includes legal maneuvering, such as takeovers and divestitures, as well as further diversification. The increased number of competitive strategies gives the firm added flexibility in responding to changes in market conditions and in initiating them. In short, it means that the large firm is far more competitive.

It is also, however, the intensity and scope with which these competitive strategies may be applied which increase the operational mobility of the large firm's capital in pursuit of its own self-expansion. Many more products are tested on the market than ever develop fully to a commercial stage. Large budgets permit market research by the sales staff, which facilitates an optimal positioning of new products in the market, given consumer tastes. Intensive sales campaigns can systematically alter consumer tastes even for well-established products, altering the market to include different income groups, ages or sexes.

The operational conditions of free capital mobility pursued by each firm within the corporate sector add a further dimension to the general or economy-wide nature of competition in the contemporary capitalist economy. Product innovations and advertising are intense competitive pressures applied to the market, which transform it from a set of isolated spheres with minimal contact into a fluid mass of purchasing power, by continuously breaking down consumer habits and established traditions. With the historical adjustment of the firm and the capitalist economy as a whole to competitive conditions, the market is becoming increasingly fluid in the yearly and even monthly conditions of contemporary life.

It is the range of competitive strategies available to the large firm and the intensity with which they may be applied to the market in the search for competitive advantage that makes the contemporary capitalist economy dominated by such firms far more competitive than ever before. This intensity of the search for competitive advantage under conditions which for each firm approximate free capital mobility does not express itself as a stronger tendency towards industrial or market equilibrium. Nor does it express itself as a smoothly operating economic process with a high degree of continuity and stability through time. Rather, it expresses itself as a continuous increase in the rate of economic change and pace of economic life, an increase in the *speed* with which the modern corporation can operate the adjustment process in its own search for competitive advantage. It is not merely a reduction in the time necessary for corporations to take advantage of given areas of higher returns. The omnipresent variations in returns are in large part also caused by the very dynamism inherent in the corporation's drive to improve its rate of return and enhance its rate of growth. The movement from 'areas' of lower returns to areas of higher returns, if it can any longer be meaningfully called such, consists as much of firms introducing new products onto the market and withdrawing old ones as it consists of moving among given markets and given commodities.

Under such highly developed competitive conditions, the competitive process of the individual firm is directed more at securing the most favourable terms of growth than the most favourable terms of trade *per se*, although the latter remain important, especially during periods of economic recession. It is only in this wider context of competition and growth that corporate planning takes on meaning. It is not so much the ability of the firm to maintain existing shares of given commodities in given industries that is central to its competitiveness *vis-à-vis* other firms that are highly developed. Rather, it is the ability to maintain its share of the value of the economic surplus and, consequently, its own rate of expansion *vis-à-vis* other firms that is the criterion of competitiveness.

Concluding observations

The conditions of free capital mobility that permit maximum flexibility and intensity for an independent unit of capital to directly search out the highest possible rate of return in the market are most closely approximated in the modern corporation. Therefore it is interaction among firms within the corporate sector, not the neoclassical world of 'small' firms, that best approximates the assumption of a uniform rate of profit in the general theory of price.

The development of competition in this sense is an integral part of the development of the capitalist mode of production. Capital is always searching out its highest reward at all stages of capitalist development. The fact that it is typically the modern corporation rather than the independent capitalist that pursues this search today does not at all imply a lessening of competition in the capitalist economy. Nor does the fact that the freedom of movement of such large units of capital severely restricts the operating space of small businesses imply a decline of competition historically. In contrast to the vision of neoclassical theory, free capital mobility is not synonymous with the ability of small firms to move freely throughout the economy; it is merely the freedom of capital, however organised, so to move. Whatever the isolated cases of monopoly that occur at all stages of capitalist development and among all size classes of firms, it seems clear that the large firms which dominate the economic process as a whole cannot in general be so characterised, for that process is a highly competitive one. The concept of corporate power derived from neoclassical price theory, based on barriers to free capital mobility, is fundamentally unsound.

This chapter is abridged from Competition and the Evolution of the Capitalist Mode of Production. *Cambridge Journal of Economics*, vol. 1, 1977, pp. 137-51. © 1977 Oxford University Press. Reprinted with permission of Oxford University Press.

MARXIST ECONOMICS

Marxist economics provides a basis for the analysis and critique of the capitalist economy. Its general advantages from a political economic perspective are obvious: Marxism is firmly grounded in the study of history; it emphasizes the interactions between economic and political and social variables; and it focuses on key questions about the production and distribution of income. The focus on capital and labor, not merely as inputs into making goods and services but also in terms of class relationships, provides a means of understanding the systemic character of distributional inequalities and conflict. Marxist analysis can also help to illuminate the forces generating periodic economic crises. Moreover, the class analysis and the explicit analysis of the role of the state provide interdisciplinary links with other aspects of social and political science. On these various grounds, Marxist economists have often claimed to have the key to understanding – and transcending – the capitalist economy.

Nevertheless, the status of Marxist economics remains highly contentious. There is a popular view that the collapse of the former USSR and the reorientation of China towards more capitalist economic development signalled the demise of Marxism as a political practice and guiding ideology in the late twentieth century. Certainly, there is a need for a fundamental re-thinking of the contemporary relevance of Marxism and of other socialist ideas, but Marxism as an analysis of capitalism is not a direct casualty of the difficulty of constructing a viable socialist alternative in practice. Indeed, the global financial crisis of 2008-9 launched a new wave of interest in Marxist analysis as a framework for understanding the contradictions that bedevil modern capitalism. It also raised interest in the possibilities for the different models of socialism appropriate for the twenty-first century.

The articles in this section introduce these controversial issues. The extract from Marx and Engels sets the historical context, illustrating the original concerns and distinctively polemical style of this political tract, which is very different from the more labored theoretical passages in Marx's major three-volume work, *Capital*. The following article by Bertell Ollman gives an overview of the Marxist approach to political economy, written in more modern language. Robert Heilbroner provides an exposition of the principal stages in the process of capital accumulation that is both Marxian in spirit and contemporary in application. He shows how problems at each stage of capital accumulation can precipitate crises: capitalist business managers would surely agree that these problems are indeed recurrent, although they would not typically see the problems as rooted in the nature of the capitalist system itself! Perry Anderson notes some limitations and unfinished business on the Marxist agenda. Finally, Ben Fine and Alfredo Saad-Filho provide a basis for considering the relevance of Marxism today, giving particular attention to class, the state, globalization and the environment. Two articles later in the book – by James O'Connor in the section on Green Economics, and by Paul Sweezy in the section on Development for Whom? – provide further illustrations of modern applications of the Marxian method of political economic analysis.

For further reading see the Marxists Internet Archive <www.marxists.org>. For a comprehensive account of the history of Marxist economics see M.C. Howard and J.E. King, 1992, *A History of Marxian Economics*, various volumes, Princeton University Press, Princeton; and for an overview of Marxist economics see Ben Fine and Alfredo Saad-Filho, *Marx's Capital*, fifth edition, Pluto Press, London, 2010.

The Communist Manifesto
Karl Marx and Friedrich Engels

… The history of all hitherto existing society is the history of class struggles. Freeman and slave, patrician and plebian, lord and serf, guild-master and journeyman, in a word, oppressor and oppressed, stood in constant opposition to one another, carried on an uninterrupted, now hidden, now open fight, a fight that each time ended, either in a revolutionary reconstitution of society at large, or in the common ruin of the contending classes.

In the earlier epochs of history, we find almost everywhere a complicated arrangement of society into various orders, a manifold gradation of social rank. In ancient Rome we have patricians, knights, plebeians, slaves; in the Middle Ages, feudal lords, vassals, guild-masters, journeymen, apprentices, serfs; in almost all of these classes, again, subordinate gradations.

The modern bourgeois society that has sprouted from the ruins of feudal society has not done away with class antagonisms. It has but established new classes, new conditions of oppression, new forms of struggle in place of the old ones.

Our epoch, the epoch of the bourgeoisie, possesses, however, this distinct feature: it has simplified class antagonisms. Society as a whole is more and more splitting up into two great hostile camps, into two great classes directly facing each other – bourgeoisie and proletariat …

The bourgeoisie

The bourgeoisie, historically, has played a most revolutionary part. The bourgeoisie, wherever it has got the upper hand, has put an end to all feudal, patriarchal, idyllic relations. It has pitilessly torn asunder the motley feudal ties that bound man to his 'natural superiors', and has left no other nexus between people than naked self-interest, than callous 'cash payment'. It has drowned out the most heavenly ecstacies of religious fervor, of chivalrous enthusiasm, of philistine sentimentalism, in the icy water of egotistical calculation. It has resolved personal worth into exchange value, and in place of the numberless indefeasible chartered freedoms, has set up that single, unconscionable freedom – Free Trade. In one word, for exploitation, veiled by religious and political illusions, it has substituted naked, shameless, direct, brutal exploitation …

The bourgeoisie, by the rapid improvement of all instruments of production, by the immensely facilitated means of communication, draws all, even the most barbarian, nations into civilization. The cheap prices of commodities are the heavy artillery with which it forces the barbarians' intensely obstinate hatred of foreigners to capitulate. It compels all nations, on pain of extinction, to adopt the bourgeois mode of production; it compels them to introduce what it calls civilization into their midst, i.e. to become bourgeois themselves … it creates a world after its own image.

The bourgeoisie has subjected the country to the rule of the towns. It has created enormous cities, has greatly increased the urban population as compared with the rural, and has thus rescued a considerable part of the population from the idiocy of rural life. Just as it has made the country dependent on the towns, so it has made barbarian and semi-barbarian countries dependent on the civilized ones, nations of peasants on nations of bourgeois, the East on the West.

The bourgeoisie keeps more and more doing away with the scattered state of the population, of the means of production, and of property. It has agglomerated population, centralized the means of production, and has concentrated property in a few hands. The necessary consequence of this was political centralization. Independent, or but loosely connected provinces, with separate interests, laws, governments, and systems of taxation, became lumped together into one nation, with one government, one code of laws, one national class interest, one frontier, and one customs tariff.

The bourgeoisie, during its rule of scarce one hundred years, has created more massive and more colossal productive forces than have all preceding generations together. Subjection of nature's forces to man, machinery, application of chemistry to industry and agriculture, steam navigation, railways, electric telegraphs, clearing of whole continents for cultivation, canalization or rivers, whole populations conjured out of the ground – what earlier century had even a presentiment that such productive forces slumbered in the lap of social labor?

We see then: the means of production and of exchange, on whose foundation the bourgeoisie built itself up, were generated in feudal society. At a certain stage in the development of these means of production and of exchange, the conditions under which feudal society produced and exchanged, the feudal organization of agriculture and manufacturing industry, in one word, the feudal relations of property became no longer compatible with the already developed productive forces; they became so many fetters. They had to be burst asunder; they were burst asunder.

Into their place stepped free competition, accompanied by a social and political constitution adapted in it, and the economic and political sway of the bourgeois class.

A similar movement is going on before our own eyes. Modern bourgeois society, with its relations of production, of exchange and of property, a society that has conjured up such gigantic means of production and of exchange, is like the sorcerer who is no longer able to control the powers of the nether world whom he has called up by his spells. For many a decade past, the history of industry and commerce is but the history of the revolt of modern productive forces against modern conditions of production, against the property relations that are the conditions for the existence of the bourgeois and of its rule. It is enough to mention the commercial crises that, by their periodical return, put the existence of the entire bourgeois society on its trial, each time more threateningly. In these crises, a great part not only of the existing products, but also of the previously created productive forces, are periodically destroyed.

In these crises, there breaks out an epidemic that, in all earlier epochs, would have seemed an absurdity – the epidemic of over-production. Society suddenly finds itself put back into a state of momentary barbarism; it appears as if a famine, a universal war of devastation, had cut off the supply of every means of subsistence; industry and commerce seem to be destroyed. And why? Because there is too much civilization, too much means of subsistence, too much industry, too much commerce. The productive forces at the disposal of society no longer tend to further the development of the conditions of bourgeois property; on the contrary, they have become too powerful for these conditions, by which they are fettered, and so soon as they overcome these fetters, they bring disorder into the whole of bourgeois society, endanger the existence of bourgeois property. The conditions of bourgeois society are too narrow to comprise the wealth created by them.

And how does the bourgeoisie get over these crises? One the one hand, by enforced destruction of a mass of productive forces; on the other, by the conquest of new markets, and by the more thorough exploitation of the old ones. That is to say, by paving the way for more extensive and more destructive crises, and by diminishing the means whereby crises are prevented.

The weapons with which the bourgeoisie felled feudalism to the ground are now turned against the bourgeoisie itself. But not only has the bourgeoisie forged the weapons that bring death to itself; it has also called into existence the men who are to wield those weapons – the modern working class – the proletarians.

The proletariat

In proportion as the bourgeoisie, i.e. capital, is developed, in the same proportion is the proletariat, the modern working class, developed – a class of laborers, who live only so long as they find work, and who find work only so long as their labor increases capital. These laborers, who must sell themselves piecemeal, are a commodity, like every other article of commerce, and are consequently exposed to all the vicissitudes of competition, to all the fluctuations of the market.

Owing to the extensive use of machinery, and to the division of labor, the work of the proletarians has lost all individual character, and, consequently, all charm for the workman. He becomes an appendage of the machine, and it is only the most simple, most monotonous, and most easily acquired knack, that is required of him. Hence, the cost of production of a workman is restricted, almost entirely, to the means of subsistence that he requires for maintenance, and for the propagation of his race. But the price of a commodity, and therefore also of labor, is equal to its cost of production. In proportion, therefore, as the repulsiveness of the work increases, the wage decreases. What is more, in proportion as the use of machinery and division of labor increases, in the same proportion the burden of toil also increases, whether by prolongation of the working hours, by the increase of the work exacted in a given time, or by increased speed of machinery, etc.

Modern Industry has converted the little workshop of the patriarchal master into the great factory of the industrial capitalist. Masses of laborers, crowded into the factory, are organized like soldiers. As privates of the industrial army, they are placed under the command of a perfect hierarchy of officers and sergeants. Not only are they slaves of the bourgeois class, and of the bourgeois state; they are daily and hourly enslaved by the machine, by the overlooker, and, above all, in the individual bourgeois manufacturer himself. The more openly this despotism proclaims gain to be its end and aim, the more petty, the more hateful and the more embittering it is.

The less the skill and exertion of strength implied in manual labor, in other words, the more modern industry becomes developed, the more is the labor of men superseded by that of women. Differences of age and sex have no longer any distinctive social validity for the working class. All are instruments of labor, more or less expensive to use, according to their age and sex.

No sooner is the exploitation of the laborer by the manufacturer, so far at an end, that he receives his wages in cash, than he is set upon by the other portion of the bourgeoisie, the landlord, the shopkeeper, the pawnbroker, etc.

The lower strata of the middle class – the small tradespeople, shopkeepers, and retired tradesmen generally, the handicraftsmen and peasants – all these sink gradually into the proletariat, partly because their diminutive capital does not suffice for the scale on which Modern Industry is carried on, and is swamped in the competition with the large capitalists, partly because their specialized skill is rendered worthless by new methods of production. Thus, the proletariat is recruited from all classes of the population ...

But with the development of industry, the proletariat not only increases in number; it becomes concentrated in greater masses, its strength grows, and it feels that strength more. The various interests and conditions of life within the ranks of the proletariat are more and more equalized, in proportion as machinery obliterates all distinctions of labor, and nearly everywhere reduces wages to the same low level. The growing competition among the bourgeois, and the resulting commercial crises, make the wages of the workers ever more fluctuating. The increasing improvement of machinery, ever more rapidly developing, makes their livelihood more and more precarious; the collisions between individual workmen and individual bourgeois take more and more the character of collisions between two classes. Thereupon, the workers begin to form combinations (trade unions) against the bourgeois; they club together in order to keep up the rate of wages; they found permanent associations in order to make provision beforehand for these occasional revolts. Here and there, the contest breaks out into riots.

Now and then the workers are victorious, but only for a time. The real fruit of their battles lie not in the immediate result, but in the ever expanding union of the workers. This union is helped on by the improved means of communication that are created by Modern Industry, and that place the workers of different localities in contact with one another. It was just this contact that was needed to centralize the numerous local struggles, all of the same character, into one national struggle between classes. But every class struggle is a political struggle. And that union, to attain which the burghers of the Middle Ages, with their miserable highways, required centuries, the modern proletarian, thanks to railways, achieve in a few years.

This organization of the proletarians into a class, and, consequently, into a political party, is continually being upset again by the competition between the workers themselves. But it ever rises up again, stronger, firmer, mightier. It compels legislative recognition of particular interests of the workers, by taking advantage of the divisions among the bourgeoisie itself. Thus, the Ten-Hours Bill in England was carried.

The future

Hitherto, every form of society has been based, as we have already seen, on the antagonism of oppressing and oppressed classes. But in order to oppress a class, certain conditions must be assured to it under which it can, at least, continue its slavish existence. The serf, in the period of serfdom, raised himself to membership in the commune, just as the petty bourgeois, under the yoke of the feudal absolutism, managed to develop into a bourgeois. The modern laborer, on the contrary, instead of rising with the process of industry, sinks deeper and deeper below the conditions of existence of his own class. He becomes a pauper, and pauperism develops more rapidly than population and wealth. And here it becomes evident that the bourgeoisie is unfit any longer to be the ruling class in society, and to impose its conditions of existence upon society as an overriding law. It is unfit to rule because it is incompetent to assure an existence to its slave within his slavery, because it cannot help letting him sink into such a state, that it has to feed him, instead of being fed by him. Society can no longer live under this bourgeoisie, in other words, its existence is no longer compatible with society.

The essential conditions for the existence and for the sway of the bourgeois class is the formation and augmentation of capital; the condition for capital is wage labor. Wage labor rests exclusively on competition between the laborers. The advance of industry, whose involuntary promoter is the bourgeoisie, replaces the isolation of the laborers, due to competition, by the revolutionary combination, due to association. The development of Modern Industry, therefore, cuts from under its feet the very foundation on which the bourgeoisie produces and appropriates products. What the bourgeoisie therefore produces, above all, are its own grave-diggers. Its fall and the victory of the proletariat are equally inevitable

…

We have seen above that the first step in the revolution by the working class is to raise the proletariat to the position of ruling class to win the battle of democracy.

The proletariat will use its political supremacy to wrest, by degree, all capital from the bourgeoisie, to centralize all instruments of production in the hands of the state, i.e. of the proletariat organized as the ruling class; and to increase the total productive forces as rapidly as possible.

Of course, in the beginning, this cannot be effected except by means of despotic inroads on the rights of property, and on the conditions of bourgeois production; by means of measures, therefore, which appear economically insufficient and untenable, but which, in the course of the movement, outstrip themselves, necessitate further inroads upon the old social order, and are unavoidable as a means of entirely revolutionizing the mode of production.

These measures will, of course, be different in different countries.

Nevertheless, in most advanced countries, the following will be pretty generally applicable.

1.   Abolition of property in land and application of all rents of land to public purposes.

2. A heavy progressive or graduated income tax.
3. Abolition of all rights of inheritance.
4. Confiscation of the property of all emigrants and rebels.
5. Centralization of credit in the banks of the state, by means of a national bank with state capital and an exclusive monopoly.
6. Centralization of the means of communication and transport in the hands of the state.
7. Extension of factories and instruments of production owned by the state; the bringing into cultivation of waste lands, and the improvement of the soil generally in accordance with a common plan.
8. Equal obligation of all to work. Establishment of industrial armies, especially for agriculture.
9. Combination of agriculture with manufacturing industries; gradual abolition of all the distinction between town and country by a more equable distribution of the populace over the country.
10. Free education for all children in public schools. Abolition of children's factory labor in its present form. Combination of education with industrial production, etc.

When, in the course of development, class distinctions have disappeared, and all production has been concentrated in the hands of a vast association of the whole nation, the public power will lose its political character. Political power, properly so called, is merely the organized power of one class for oppressing another. If the proletariat during its contest with the bourgeoisie is compelled, by the force of circumstances, to organize itself as a class; if, by means of a revolution, it makes itself the ruling class, and, as such, sweeps away by force the old conditions of production, then it will, along with these conditions, have swept away the conditions for the existence of class antagonisms and of classes generally, and will thereby have abolished its own supremacy as a class.

In place of the old bourgeois society, with its classes and class antagonisms, we shall have an association in which the free development of each is the condition for the free development of all [...]

The Communists disdain to conceal their views and aims. They openly declare that their ends can be attained only by the forcible overthrow of all existing social conditions. Let the ruling classes tremble at a communist revolution. The proletarians have nothing to lose but their chains. They have a world to win.

Proletarians of all countries, unite!

Karl Marx and Friedrich Engels were revolutionaries. This chapter is abridged from *Manifesto of the Communist Party*, 1848.

What is Marxism?
Bertell Ollman

Karl Marx sought to understand how our capitalist society works (for whom it works better, for whom worse), how it arose out of feudalism and where it is likely to lead. Concentrating on the social and economic relations in which people earn their livings, Marx saw behind capitalism's law and order appearance a struggle of two main classes: the capitalists, who own the productive resources, and the workers, or proletariat, who must work in order to survive. 'Marxism' is essentially Marx's analysis of the complex and developing relations between these two classes.

Origins

The main theories that make up this analysis – the theory of alienation, the labor theory of value, and the materialist conception of history – must all be understood with this focus in mind. Even Marx's vision of socialism emerges from his study of capitalism, for socialism is the unrealized potential inherent in capitalism itself (something our great material wealth and advanced forms of organization makes possible) for a more just and democratic society in which everyone can develop his/her distinctively human qualities.

Some socialist ideas can be traced as far back as the Bible, but Marxism has its main intellectual origins in German philosophy, English political economy, and French utopian socialism. It is from the German philosopher, Hegel, that Marx learned a way of thinking about the world, in all its fluid complexity, that is called 'dialectics.' The British political economists, Adam Smith and David Ricardo, provided Marx with a first approximation of his labor theory of value. From the French utopians, especially Charles Fourier and the Comte de Saint-Simon, Marx caught a glimpse of a happier future that lay beyond capitalism. Along with the paradox of an Industrial Revolution which produced as much poverty as it did wealth, these are the main ingredients that went into the formation of Marxism.

Marxist philosophy

Marx's study of capitalism was grounded in a philosophy that is both dialectical and materialist. With dialectics, changes and interaction are brought into focus and emphasized by being viewed as essential parts of whatever institutions and processes are undergoing change and interaction. In this way, the system of capitalism, the wider context, is never lost sight of when studying any event within it, an election or an economic crisis for example; nor are its real past and future possibilities, the historical context, ever neglected when dealing with how something appears in the present. Whatever Marx's subject of the moment, his dialectical approach to it ensures that his fuller subject is always capitalist society as it developed and is still developing. The actual changes that occur in history are seen here as the outcome of opposing tendencies, or 'contradictions', which evolve in the ordinary functioning of society.

Unlike Hegel's dialectic, which operates solely on ideas, Marx's dialectic is materialist. Marx was primarily concerned with capitalism as lived rather than as thought about, but people's lives also involve consciousness. Whereas Hegel examined ideas apart from the people who held them, Marx's materialism puts ideas back into the heads of living people and treats both as parts of a world that is forever being remade through human activities, particularly in production. In this interaction, social conditions and behavior are found to have a greater affect on the character and development of people's ideas than these ideas do on social conditions and behavior.

Alienation

Marx's specific theories are best understood as answers to his pointed questions about the nature and development of capitalism. How do the ways in which people earn their living affect their bodies, minds and daily lives? In the theory of alienation, Marx gives us his answer to this question. Workers in capitalist society do not own the means – machines, raw materials, factories – which they use in their work. These are owned by the capitalists to whom the workers must sell their 'labor power', or ability to do work, in return for a wage.

This system of labor displays four relations that lie at the core of Marx's theory of alienation: (1) The worker is alienated (or cut off) from his or her productive activity, playing no part in deciding what to do or how to do it. Someone else, the capitalist, also sets the conditions and speed of work and even decides if the worker is to be allowed to work or not, i.e. hires and fires him. (2) The worker is alienated from the product of that activity, having no control over what is made or what happens to it, often not even knowing what happens to it once it has left his hands.

(3) The worker is alienated from other human beings, with competition and mutual indifference replacing most forms of cooperation. This applies not only to relations with the capitalists, who use their control over the worker's activity and product to further their own profit maximizing interests, but also to relations between individuals inside each class as everyone tries to survive as best they can. (4) Finally, the worker is alienated from the distinctive potential for creativity and community we all share just because we are human beings. Through labor which alienates them from their activity, product and other people, workers gradually lose their ability to develop the finer qualities which belong to them as members of the human species.

The cutting of these relationships in half leaves on one side a seriously diminished individual physically weakened, mentally confused and mystified, isolated and virtually powerless. On the other side of this separation are the products and ties with other people, outside the control and lost to the understanding of the worker. Submitted to the mystification of the marketplace, the worker's products pass from one hand to another, changing form and names along the way – 'value', 'commodity', 'capital', 'interest', 'rent', 'wage' – depending chiefly on who has them and how they are used. Eventually, these same products – though no longer seen as such – re-enter the worker's daily life as the landlord's house, the grocer's food, the banker's loan, the boss's factory, and the various laws and customs that prescribe his or her relations with other people.

Unknowingly, the worker has constructed the necessary conditions for reproducing his own alienation. The world that the worker has made and lost in alienated labor reappears as someone else's private property which he only has access to by selling his labor power and engaging in more alienated labor. Though Marx's main examples of alienation are drawn from the life of workers, other classes are also alienated to the degree that they share or are directly effected by these relations, and that includes the capitalists.

Theory of value

What is the effect of the worker's alienated labor on its products, both on what they can do and what can be done with them? Smith and Ricardo used the labor theory of value to explain the cost of commodities. For them, the value of any commodity is the result of the amount of labor time that went into its production. Marx took this explanation more or less for granted. His labor theory of value, however, is primarily concerned with the more basic problem of why goods have prices of any kind. Only in capitalism does the distribution of what is produced take place through the medium of markets and prices. In slave society, the slave owner takes by force what his slaves produce, returning to them only what he wishes. While in feudalism, the lord claims as a feudal right some part of what is produced by his serfs, with the serfs consuming the rest of their output directly. In both societies, most of what is produced cannot be bought or sold, and therefore, does not have any price.

In accounting for the extraordinary fact that everything produced in capitalist society has a price, Marx emphasizes the separation of the worker from the means of production (whereas slaves and serfs are tied to their means of production) and the sale of his or her labor power that this separation makes necessary. To survive, the workers, who lack all means to produce, must sell their labor power. In selling their labor power, they give up all claims to the products of their labor. Hence, these products become available for exchange in the market, indeed are produced with this exchange in mind, while workers are able to consume only that portion of their products which they can buy back in the market with the wages they are paid for their labor power.

'Value', then, is the most general effect of the worker's alienated labor on all its products; exchange – which is embodied in the fact that they all have a price – is what these products do and what can be done with them. Rather than a particular price, value stands for the whole set of conditions which are necessary for a commodity to have any price at all. It is in this sense that

Marx calls value a product of capitalism. The ideal price ('exchange value') of a commodity and the ways in which it is meant to he used ('use value') likewise exhibit in their different ways the distinctive relationships Marx uncovered between workers and their activities, products and other people in capitalist society.

'Exchange value' reflects a situation where the distinct human quality and variety of work has ceased to count. Through alienation, the relations between workers has been reduced to the quantity of labor that goes into their respective products. Only then can these products exchange for each other at a ratio which reflects these quantities. It is this which explains Smith's and Ricardo's finding that the value of a commodity is equal to the amount of labor time which has gone into its production. While in use value, the physical characteristics of commodities – planned obsolescence, the attention given to style over durability, the manufacture of individual and family as opposed to larger group units, etc. – give unmistakable evidence of the isolating and degraded quality of human relations found throughout capitalist society.

Surplus value, the third aspect of value, is the difference between the amount of exchange and use value created by workers and the amount returned to them as wages. The capitalist buys the worker's labor power, as any other commodity, and puts it to work for eight or more hours a day. However, workers can make in, say, five hours products which are the equivalent of their wages. In the remaining three or more hours an amount of wealth is produced which remains in the hands of the capitalist. The capitalists' control over this surplus is the basis of their power over the workers and the rest of society. Marx's labor theory of value also provides a detailed account of the struggle between capitalists and workers over the size of the surplus value, with the capitalists trying to extend the length of the working day, speed up the pace of work, etc., while the workers organize to protect themselves. Because of the competition among capitalists, workers are constantly being replaced by machinery, enabling and requiring capitalists to extract ever greater amounts of surplus value from the workers who remain.

Paradoxically, the amount of surplus value is also the source of capitalism's greatest weakness. Because only part of their product is returned to them as wages, the workers cannot buy a large portion of the consumables that they produce. Under pressure from the constant growth of the total product, the capitalists periodically fail to find new markets to take up the slack. This leads to crises of 'overproduction', capitalism's classic contradiction, in which people are forced to live on too little because they produce too much.

Historical tendencies

How did capitalism originate, and where is it leading? Marx's materialist conception of history answers the first part of this question with an account of the transformation of feudalism into capitalism. He stresses the contradictions that arose through the growth of towns, population, technology and trade, which at a certain point burst asunder the feudal social and political forms in which production had been organized. Relations of lord to serf based on feudal rights and obligations had become a hindrance to the further development of these productive forces; over an extended period, and after a series of political battles, they were replaced by the contractual relation of capitalists to workers. With capitalists free to pursue profits wherever they might take them and workers equally 'free' to sell their labor power to the capitalists however they might use it, the productive potential inherent in the new forces of production, especially in technology and science, grew to unmeasured proportions.

However, if maximizing profits leads to rapid growth when rapid growth results in large profits, then growth is restricted as soon as it becomes unprofitable. The periodic crises which have plagued capitalism from about 1830 on are clear evidence of this. Since that time, the new forces of production that have come into being in capitalism, their growth and potential for producing wealth, have come increasingly into contradiction with the capitalist social relations in which production is organized. The capitalists put the factories, machines, raw materials, and labor power all of which they own into motion to produce goods only if they feel they can make a profit, no matter what the availability of these 'factors of production', and no matter what the need of consumers for their products. The cost to society in wealth that is never produced (and in wealth which is produced but in forms that are anti-social in their character) continues to grow and with it the need for another, more efficient, more humane way of organizing production.

Within this framework the actual course of history is determined by class struggle. According to Marx, each class is defined chiefly by its relation to the productive process and has objective interests rooted in that relation. The capitalists' interests lie in securing their power and expanding profits. Workers, on the other hand, have interests in higher wages, safe working conditions, shorter hours, job security, and – because it is required to realize other interests – a new distribution of power. The class struggle involves everything that these two major classes do to promote their incompatible interests at each other's expense. In this battle, which rages throughout society, the capitalists are aided by their wealth, their control of the state, and their domination over other institutions – schools, media, churches – that guide and distort people's thinking. On the workers' side are their sheer numbers, their experience of cooperation – however alienated – while at work, trade unions, working class political parties (where they exist), and the contradictions within capitalism that make present conditions increasingly irrational.

In capitalism, the state is an instrument in the hands of the capitalists that is used to repress dangerous dissent and to help expand surplus value. This is done mainly by passing and enforcing anti-working class laws and by providing the capitalists with various economic subsidies ('capitalist welfare'). Marx also views the state as a set of political structures interlocked with the economic structures of capitalism whose requirements – chiefly for accumulating capital (means of production used to produce value) – it must satisfy, if the whole system is not to go into a tailspin. And, finally, the state is an arena for class struggle where class and class factions contend for political advantage in an unfair fight that finds the capitalists holding all the most powerful weapons. An adequate understanding of the role of the capitalist state as a complex social relation requires that it be approached from each of these three angles: as an instrument of the capitalist class, as a structure of political offices and processes, and as an arena of class struggle.

In order to supplement the institutions of force, capitalism has given rise to an ideology, or way of thinking, which gets people to accept the *status quo* or, at least, confuses them as to the possibility of replacing it with something better. For the most part, the ideas and concepts which make up this ideology work by getting people to focus on the observable aspects of any event or institution, neglecting its history and potential for change as well as the broader context in which it resides. The result is a collection of partial, static, distorted, one-sided notions that reveal only what the capitalists would like everyone to think. For example, in capitalist ideology, consumers are considered sovereign, as if consumers actually determine what gets produced through the choices they make in the supermarket; and no effort is made to analyze how they develop their preferences (history) or who determines the range of available choices (larger system). Placing an event in its real historical and social context, which is to say studying it 'dialectically,' often leads (as in the case of 'consumer sovereignty') to conclusions that are the direct opposite of those based on the narrow observations favored by ideological thinking. As the attempted separation of what cannot be separated without distortion, capitalist ideology reflects in thought the fractured lives of alienated people, while at the same time making it increasingly difficult for them to grasp their alienation.

As the contradictions of capitalism become greater, more intense, and less amenable to disguise, neither the state nor ideology can restrain the mass of the workers, white and blue collar, from recognizing their interests (becoming 'class conscious') and acting upon them. The overthrow of capitalism, when it comes, Marx believed, would proceed as quickly and democratically as the nature of capitalist opposition allowed. Out of the revolution would emerge a socialist society that would fully utilize and develop much further the productive potential inherited from capitalism. Through democratic planning, production would now be directed to serving social needs instead of maximizing private profit. The final goal, toward which socialist society would constantly build, is the human one of abolishing alienation. Marx called the attainment of this goal 'communism'.

Marxism today

Capitalism has obviously changed a lot since Marx wrote. In the basic relations and structures which distinguish capitalism from feudalism and socialism, however, it has changed very little, and these are the main features of capitalism addressed in Marx's theories. Workers, for example, may earn more money now than they did in the last century, but so do the capitalists. Consequently, the wealth and income gaps between the two classes is as great or greater than ever. The workers' relations to their labor, products and capitalists (which are traced in the theory of alienation and the labor theory of value) are basically unchanged from Marx's day. Probably the greatest difference between our capitalism and Marx's has to do with the more direct involvement of the state in the capitalist economy (primarily to bolster flagging profits) and, as a consequence of this, the expanded role of ideology to disguise the increasingly obvious ties between the agencies of the state and the capitalist class.

From its beginnings, Marxism has been under attack from all sides, but the major criticisms have been directed against claims that Marx never made. For example, some have mistakenly viewed Marx's materialism as evidence that he ignored the role of ideas in history and in people's lives. Viewed as an 'economic determinism', Marxism has also been criticized for presenting politics, culture, religion, etc. as simple effects of a one-way economic cause. (This would be un-dialectical.) Viewed as a claim that labor is the only factor in determining prices (equated here with 'value'), the labor theory of value has been wrongly attacked for ignoring the effect of competition on prices. And viewing what are projections of capitalism's tendencies into the future as inviolable predictions, Marx has been accused of making false predictions.

Some, finally, point to the anti-democratic practices of many Communist countries [in the twentieth century] and claim that authoritarianism is inherent in Marxist doctrine. In fact, Marx's theories concentrate on advanced industrial capitalism with its imperfect but still functioning democratic institutions and he never thought that socialism could achieve its full promise in relatively poor, politically underdeveloped nations.

Marxism, as defined here, has had its main influence among workers and intellectuals in capitalist countries, especially in Europe, who have used it as a major tool in defining their problems and constructing political strategies. In the Western countries, even non-Marxist intellectuals, particularly sociologists and historians, have drawn considerable insights from Marx's writings. In the Third World, Marxism – considerably modified to deal with their special mixture of primitive and advanced capitalist conditions – has clarified the nature of the enemy for many liberation movements. In the Communist countries, selected doctrines of Marx have been frozen into abstract principles to serve as the official ideology of the regimes. The influence of these three varieties of Marxism is as different as their content.

Modern capitalism cannot erase poverty, provide full employment, guarantee decent housing or an adequate diet or good health care to its people. Meanwhile the rich get richer. Only Marxism, as an account of the rational unfolding of a basically irrational capitalist system, makes sense of the chaos. In class struggle it also points the way out. The rest is up to us.

Bertell Ollman is Professor, Department of Politics, New York University. This chapter is abridged from *What is Marxism? A Bird's-eye View*, 1982 © 1982 Bertell Ollman. Reprinted with permission of the author.

Beyond Boom and Crash
Robert Heilbroner

How does capitalism as a system generate economic growth in the first place? Here I find it useful to adopt a view of the economy first described by Marx. Marx depicts the process much as a businessman would – namely, as the complicated way in which money makes money and business capital expands.

Marx pictures this as a great accumulation 'circuit' that can be divided into three distinct phases or stages. In the first phase, businessmen hire labor and buy the raw or semi-finished goods needed to start up production. In other words, they turn their money capital into labor power and supplies of various kinds. Moreover, if their business is to grow, they must turn ever *more* money into labor power and materials. Generalized to include the entire system, this means that a growing economy requires the hiring of more and more labor, and the buying of larger and larger quantities of materials, not only to turn out more consumable goods, but also to build new plant and equipment, the process economists call investment.

This initial phase of Marx's 'circuit' of accumulation immediately identifies two potential sources of crisis. The first is the crucial role played by businessmen's expectations. If capitalists do not anticipate growth – if the state of business confidence is poor – they will not invest in additional plant and equipment, and may not even seek to convert all their existing cash into payrolls and supplies. Expectations obviously play a critical role in determining the pace of advance or in determining whether there will be *any* advance.

But a second obstacle, of no less importance, also resides in the first stage. Money will not even begin its tortuous journey through the system if a labor force cannot be hired, or if supplies of materials or plant and equipment are not available. When workers strike, capitalist growth comes to a total halt, at least insofar as that particular portion of the economy is concerned. For the system as a whole this stoppage may be trivial, as when a small local union goes on strike, but it can also bring to a halt a very large section of industry.

Of course, it is not only a strike that can paralyze the initial phase in which money seeks to 'become' labor power and materials. If workers are unwilling to work at the wages that employers want to pay, the circuit is interrupted as effectively as if there were a strike. Or if needed inputs are unavailable or too expensive, the circuit is cut just as effectively as by the high price of labor. The OPEC oil shock in the 1970s was precisely such an event – a blow to the first phase of the accumulation process sufficiently severe to bring about a marked reduction in the scale of activity in every industrial nation.

Let us suppose, however, that money-capital is successfully converted into payrolls and stocks of materials and equipment. This now brings us to the second phase of the production process as Marx describes it – a part of the circuit located entirely within the factory rather than in the marketplace. Here no money is directly involved. Rather, the money that has been turned into labor power, raw materials, and other necessities for production is now further turned into the finished products that will emerge from the factory gate. Labor energies, and the physical and chemical properties of the materials and equipment with which labor works, now make steel out of iron, gasoline out of petroleum, cloth out of yarn.

And here again a set of potential obstacles to the accumulation process must be surmounted. Labor must perform its tasks efficiently and in a disciplined fashion. The engineering processes must function smoothly. Raw materials must be of proper grade and kind. Obviously the difficulties encountered in this second phase of the circuit are of a different nature from those of the first. Interruptions to labor discipline, such as absenteeism, sabotage, 'work-to-rule' slowdowns, vandalism, or indifference will damage the process by which money, embodied in labor power and materials, becomes transformed into saleable outputs. So are disruptions to the flow of production when raw materials are below grade, or goods in process defective, or plant and machinery inadequate. To the extent that the ability of a company to sell its products is damaged by a reputation for poor workmanship, the ability of that company to recoup its money-capital is hurt as severely as if a strike had shut its plants. Generalized to a sufficient degree (as in the automobile industry, where poor engineering and sloppy work have forced the recall of millions of cars), the problems of the second phase of the circuit of accumulation can threaten the profitability of an entire industry.

Finally, there is the third phase, the one most familiar to businessmen and economists alike. This is the phase in which capital, now embodied in a finished good, must complete its metamorphosis back into money. The metamorphosis takes place by selling the good, an act that commands the principal attention of the business world, although we can now see that selling is only the last, and not necessarily the most critical, of the links in the chain.

The obstacles faced in this third stage are again of a different kind than those of the previous ones. Changes in buyers' wants or needs, whether the consequence of changes in fashion or technology, can reduce the value of output to a fraction of its expected worth. Events over which an individual business has no control – indeed, events over which the collective business world, or the nation-state itself, have no control can cause markets to disappear into thin air, or on occasion can create profitable sales opportunities out of equally thin air. Thus the process of completing the circle of capital accumulation by selling the output of business is always attended by anxiety and uncertainty. In one way or another it is essential that the last loop of the process be closed if business is to recoup its original money outlays, but closing that loop is often difficult and sometimes impossible. Thus three separate obstacle courses must be negotiated if capital, in the form of money, is to return to its original hands, ready for still another round of metamorphoses. In view of the complexity and the dangers of these successive stages, our first reaction is to wonder how the process can ever be completed at all. Rather than accounting for the recurrent fact of crises – that is, of breakdown somewhere in the system – the burden seems shifted: how, we ask, can such a labyrinthine journey hope to be safely undertaken, not once, but again and again, as part of the 'mechanism' of the system?

The answer lies in becoming aware that the mechanism is not some kind of tutelary deity that smiles over the capitalist process, but is lodged in the living, breathing – often very hard breathing – bodies of millions of persons whose full-time endeavor is to *make* the process work. For example, the initial process by which money is turned into labor power and materials is successfully concluded only because workers and their union leaders are as eager to come to terms with employers as employers are with them. The labor market in which hiring takes place is motivated by pressures of need as well as greed, of aspiration as well as defeat. Labor and capital come together as iron filings to the pole of a magnet, each 'particle' of labor drawn to an employer, and the 'pole' of capital drawn to the mass of workers. So too, similar efforts bring together the suppliers of raw materials and equipment with the firms who must spend money to procure them. Purchasing agents, brokers, executives of both buying and selling concerns, all spend their energies in finding supplies of materials of the right kind and price so that production may begin.

The same outpouring of energy seeks to assure the completion of the production stage, where labor and materials are joined to create goods for sale. This is the domain of the foreman, the efficiency expert, the personnel manager, and the production boss. Here is where PhDs trained in psychology seek to remove obstacles of behavior, while other PhDs, trained in engineering and business management, seek to remove those of space, time, and organization; where union shop stewards and local managers work to prevent grievances from exploding into disruptions to the work process, and safety engineers install precautionary devices to prevent accidents from slowing or stopping production lines; where statistical sampling procedures detect variations in the quality of output before it is too late, and computer printouts inform men in shirtsleeves whether the rivers of sub-assemblies are advancing in proper coordination. Thus, like the metamorphosis of money into labor power and goods, the interaction of labor power with goods takes place not by the workings of a mysterious 'mechanism', but because it is the object of the intense concern, attention, expertise, and will of millions of individuals.

The same is true again when we reach the final stage in which commodities turn back into money, like frogs into princes. This time, of course, the process takes place as the consequence of an army of persons concerned with selling – copywriters, television actors with stentorian voices, models with pretty faces, merchandisers with clever ideas, ordinary sales clerks behind counters. At the same time, this crucial final closure of the total circuit is also expedited by two other extremely important groups who anxiously superintend the process at a remove. One consists of the financial institutions – banks, finance companies, savings and loan associations – who help complete the closure (as they also help business initiate it in the first phase) by lending buyers money. Second is the government, watching anxiously over the confused process in which all three loops of the capital regeneration process are inextricably intertwined. Although the government intervenes at many points in all three stages, its main attention is fixed on the buying power of the households and businesses who must create princes by waving the magic wand of money. By its fiscal and monetary policies that is, by raising and lowering expenditures and taxes, or by adjusting the supply of money – the government tries mightily to assure that the wand is waved and the process brought to a successful termination, prior to its instant recommencement. Thus, at the apex of the economy, as at its base, the economy 'works' because an enormous fraction of the total life energies and intelligence of society is developed to making it work.

When we look at the process of capitalist growth in this fashion, the question changes once more: how can the process fail to work? When so much energy and intelligence, drive and adaptation go into the various sub-processes that constitute the whole, how can the accumulation process falter? One reason, of course, is that the actors who strive so earnestly can make mistakes. If they are small mistakes, they cancel out, one person's shortfall balanced by another's windfall. From time to time very large mistakes are made, and huge enterprises go under because they cannot begin production, or because they are unable to discipline the work process, or through a failure of marketing.

But even giant failures do not create more than temporary pauses in the ongoing accumulation process of the entire economy. A more likely candidate for the role of villain is mistaken or wrong-headed action taken by the government itself. A considerable part of the explanation for the poor performance of the American (and most European) economies after the 'oil shock' was the imposition of conscious monetary restraints by governments seeking to put a halt to inflation, even at the expense of recession, or indeed by the very means of an engineered recession. Capitalist economies have encountered regular crises long before governments were meddling in the economic process, and the collapses of giant firms, usually in finance, generally took placc as a consequence, rather than a direct cause, of recessions. Thus we shall have to search elsewhere for explanations of the recurrence of crisis. Indeed, we shall have to see if we cannot find causes for crisis that are the outgrowth of the very success of capitalist growth.

One such endemic 'counter-process' is relatively easy to locate. It is the inherent spoiling effect of a period of boom on the labor and materials markets of the first phase of the accumulation process. For the more successful is this first phase – the more steadily money becomes transformed into labor power and goods – the more do the prices of labor and materials tend to rise. As Adam Smith already saw, the accumulation of wealth bids up the price of labor, and as David Ricardo added, it also raises the price of any other commodities whose supply cannot be quickly increased, or whose supply can be increased only at higher cost.

Thus the successful completion of the first stage tends to tighten loose markets for labor, materials, space, money – because the growing demand for the factors of production tends to raise their prices. As every businessman knows, booms jack up costs. Rising costs in turn squeeze business income. As the pressure against profits mounts, the general enthusiasm of the early days of the boom gives way to a growing unease about labor's 'demands' and raw materials' prices.

As the squeeze intensifies, the willingness or the ability to go on producing declines. Businesses cancel plans for expansion as too expensive. They decide to hang onto their money rather than to risk it in the accumulation process. The process begins to falter. A recession is at hand. There is, I must emphasize, nothing mechanical or certain about this. A tight labor market may be relieved if cheap labor can be imported from abroad, or if automation can be quickly introduced. A rise in materials' prices may simply lead to the use of substitutes or the rapid exploitation of new sources of supply. Credit shortages can be eased by government policy. Or the business outlook may remain buoyant, despite a rise in costs, because businessmen are convinced that 'they' won't allow a recession to occur. In a word, expansion can continue in the face of rising costs, or rising costs may themselves set into motion corrective processes that temper the rise in wages and prices.

So there is nothing in the self-spoiling propensities of a successful boom that is certain to abort the overall circuit of capital accumulation. Rather, a potential for disruption lies in the tendency of a boom to raise prices and thereby to constrict profits. Whether such a potential constriction actually takes place hinges on innumerable circumstances and cannot be predicted. It is enough to recognize that it could.

A second source of disruption, likewise rooted in the success of the accumulation process, lies within the second phase, where labor power and materials are combined to create saleable commodities. Here the problem has nothing to do with money. It is to be found in the difficulty of maintaining a smooth flow of production during an extended period of prosperity. In turn, this difficulty rests on the nature of the labor process within industrial capitalism. Industrial labor requires an extraordinary amount of discipline. This is because labor under capitalism is systematically reduced to what Marx called 'detail labor' – the performance of operations that have no significance in themselves, but are important only as units of a larger whole. Industrial production requires the steady, coordinated, dependable performance of tasks each one of which has little or no meaning, aesthetic satisfaction, tradition, art, pleasure, or completion. Compared with the work of artisans, or even of peasant farmers, the work of men and women in factories and offices is fragmented, pointless, empty of intrinsic meaning, however much money it may earn for its protagonist. (This is probably what Marx meant when he said that the worker under capitalism became ever more 'impoverished', whether his wage was high or low.)

To perform this labor with the machine-like regularity on which the production process as a whole depends requires that men and women submit to a routine that few do not find irksome. In the main the great majority of working people do submit, partly from the need to earn a living, partly from the social pressure to conform, partly from the absence of any imaginable alternative. But the irksomeness of the work process, like a hair shirt, is never lost to consciousness. And when prosperity continues, and the bargaining position and economic security of working people improve, the necessary discipline becomes harder to obtain. Absenteeism increases. Unions demand and get more job perks. Wildcat strikes break out over trifles. The authority of foremen diminishes. The issue of 'work satisfaction' comes to the fore.

It is clear that a very large potential for the interruption of capitalist accumulation resides in the lurking indiscipline of the labor process. General strikes have on occasion paralyzed England, France, Italy, Austria, The Netherlands, Sweden, and other nations. Even in countries that lack a unified and militant labor force, the problem of indiscipline is an ever-present threat to the smooth regeneration of capital. Moreover, the threat of indiscipline worsens as the general prosperity of the workforce improves, and bright prospects for employment elsewhere encourage labor to express its dissatisfactions. Consequently, we find efforts to lessen the irksomeness of labor by breaking up the monotony of assembly lines, as in the famous Volvo team system first tried in Sweden and now being used in a number of firms elsewhere; or to instill a sense of self-respect through trim uniforms, piped-in music, 'personalized' cubicles, special training for foremen in the dynamics of group psychology, company sports, outings, and morale-building activities.

A third, separate source of potential difficulty, also generated by the boom itself, lies in the last of the three phases of the accumulation process, where commodities must be converted into money. Here the difficulty is simply stated. It is that production tends to glut markets. Goods come off assembly lines faster than consumers can absorb them. Inventories pile up. Eventually, production has to be cut back.

Every businessman knows that gluts can spoil individual markets. The great question – one that has been debated in economics for a century and a half – is whether there can be 'general gluts', gluts for everything. Most economists today say no, that total demand is for all intents and purposes limitless and insatiable, spreading out from necessities towards infinite luxuries.

The problem of the third phase, however, is not one of spoiling total demand. It is rather that an economy that has enjoyed a boom may find it very difficult to rearrange production to suit the changing patterns of demand as particular markets get filled up. Production processes that are city blocks long and months 'deep' are not easily switched off or turned around. Gluts for products such as automobiles or ships or planes or export crops lead to pockets of unused labor and equipment that cannot be rapidly redeployed to meet other possible demands. These pockets become centres of depression whose infectious power is very great.

In addition, there is the larger problem of matching demand against supply, not just in one market or another, but in terms of the total amount of purchasing power generated back in phase one and the total value of goods produced in phase two. Here the question is not one of glut, but one of a balance between buying power and *expected* revenues. Perhaps all the existing output can be sold, but if it must be unloaded at prices less favorable than were originally hoped for, the expectations that drive the accumulation process will receive a setback. It is also true that if goods are sold at prices greater than those originally hoped for, business will receive a very strong stimulus. Thus the matching of buying power, on the one hand, and expected revenues on the other, holds out the possibility of disappointments that can lead to reduced production, or of windfalls that can lead to increased prices. In the phrase of Sir Roy Harrod, capitalism walks a 'knife-edge' between recession on one side and inflation on the other.

Thus the third phase of the overall process of capitalist reproduction and growth is a centre of constant tragedy and near tragedy, as well as of triumph or lucking-out. Gluts, or mismatches between supply and demand, are the stuff of everyday market life, as the business pages of any newspaper will testify, and a vast amount of effort goes into seeking to avert or rescue such gluts through sales, write-downs, write-offs, promotions, and the like. On a larger scale, the mismatch of whole sectors of outputs, such as crops or raw materials or housing, may lead to government intervention to prevent disasters from spreading. And, not least, the fiscal and monetary authorities are constantly scanning the economic scene for indications of mismatches between the volume of production and the volume of money incomes. The difficulties of the third phase, like those of the first two, do not dictate an 'inevitable' breakdown. It would be better to say that gluts, either for particular sectors or on a larger scale, are the principal reason for short circuits in this last of the three distinguishable stages of accumulation. They result in what Marx called 'realization crises' – failures to 'realize' the capital tied up in commodities because they cannot be sold at profitable prices.

The above is not, of course, anything like a full description of the causes of economic crisis, much less a systematic tracing through the interconnections by which crises exert their effects.

But it must be clear that the susceptibility to crisis lies directly within the process of capitalist expansion itself. It is the success of the system – its solution to the problem of converting money into goods and labor, and then reconverting the resultant production into new money, that increases the tension of the accumulative process. The tension is eventually snapped by a change in expectations or behavior, or in physical or social realities, somewhere along the lengthy path of money-making. Crisis thus appears to be not so much an exceptional occurrence as an event whose appearance is expected, although one never quite knows where or when. The system is crisis-prone not because it cannot make its sub-circuits operate, but because the very act of successfully operating them creates tensions that make the economy vulnerable to breakdown.

Robert Heilbroner was Norman Thomas Professor of Economics, New School for Social Research. This chapter is abridged from *Beyond Boom and Crash*, Norton, New York, 1978, ch. 2, pp. 18-37. © 1978 Robert L. Heilbroner. Reprinted with permission of the author.

Considerations on Western Marxism
Perry Anderson

The greatness of Marx's overall achievement needs no reiteration here. Indeed it was the very range of his general vision of the future which in a certain sense induced the local illusions and myopias in his scanning of the present of his own time. Marx could not remain so politically and theoretically central to the later twentieth century, if he had not at times been out of synchrony with the later nineteenth century in which he lived. His mistakes and omissions may be said to have typically been the price of his foresights. It is the sum of scientific knowledge now available about the history of capitalism – so much greater than that at his disposal – which should permit historical materialism today to surpass them. It is in this respect that there are three areas where Marx's work appears centrally uncertain, from a contemporary perspective.

(i) The first of these is his treatment of the capitalist state. His early writings started to theorize, in effect, the structures of what was later to be bourgeois democracy, before it existed anywhere in Europe – but at a very abstract and philosophical level. Then in 1848-50 he wrote a concrete, historical study of the peculiar dictatorial state created by Napoleon III in France – his only such venture. Thereafter, he never directly analyzed the English parliamentary state under which he lived for the rest of his life. If anything, he tended to generalise 'Bonapartism' abusively as the typical form of the modern bourgeois state, because of his political memories of its counter-revolutionary role in 1848. He was consequently unable to analyze the Third Republic in France, when it emerged after the defeat of 1870. Finally, because of his preoccupation with 'militarist' Bonapartism, he seems by contrast to have tended to underestimate the repressive capacity of the 'pacifist' English, Dutch and American states, at times appearing to think that socialism could be achieved in these countries by peaceful and electoral means alone. The result was that Marx never produced any coherent or comparative account of the political structures of bourgeois class power at all. There is a notable disjuncture between his early politico-philosophical writings and his later economic writings.

(ii) Allied to this failure seems to have been an incomprehension of much of the nature of the later epoch through which he lived. Although Marx was alone in his lifetime in understanding the economic dynamism of the capitalist mode of production after 1850, which was to transform the world, he seems never to have registered the great shift in the international state system that accompanied it. The defeats of 1848 appear to have convinced Marx that bourgeois revolutions could no longer occur, because of the fear that capital now everywhere had of labor (hence the betrayals in France and Germany of that year). In fact, the rest of his life witnessed a succession of triumphant capitalist revolutions in Germany, Italy, the USA, Japan and elsewhere. These all occurred under the banner of nationalism, not of democracy. Marx assumed that capitalism would progressively mitigate and annul nationality in a new universalism. His inability to perceive this resulted in a series of grave political mistakes during the 1850s and 1860s, when the major dramas of European politics were all interconnected with nationalist struggles. Hence his hostility to the Risorgimento in Italy, his neglect of Bismarckism in Germany, his adulation of Lincoln in the USA, and his approval of Ottomanism in the Balkans (the latter determined by the other 'anachronistic' preoccupation of 1848, his fear of Russia). A central theoretical silence on the character of nations and nationalisms was left, with very damaging consequences, to later generations of socialists.

(iii) The economic architecture of *Capital* itself, Marx's greatest achievement, is not immune to a number of possible doubts. The most insistent of these concern the very theory of value advanced by Marx. Apart from the difficulties associated with his exclusion of scarcity as a determinant, there is the problem of the dating of the labor inputs themselves, and above all the troubling difficulty so far of converting the latter into prices as a quantifiable medium (in contradiction with the normal canons of scientificity, and the conventional comparisons of the discovery of surplus value with that of oxygen). Another uneasy aspect of the whole theory of value is the distinction between productive and unproductive labor itself that, although essential to it, has never yet been codified theoretically or established empirically by Marx or his successors.

The most hazardous conclusions that the system of *Capital* yielded were the general theorem of the falling rate of profit, and the tenet of an ever-increasing class polarisation between bourgeois and proletariat. Neither has yet been adequately substantiated. The first implied an economic breakdown of capitalism by its inner mechanisms; the second a social breakdown by way – if not of an immiseration of the proletariat – of an ultimate absolute preponderance of a vast industrial working class of productive laborers over a tiny bourgeoisie, with few or no intermediary groups. The very absence of any political theory in the late Marx may thus be logically related to a latent catastrophism in his economic theory, which rendered the development of the former redundant.

Perry Anderson is Professor of History and Sociology, University of California Los Angeles. This chapter is abridged from *Considerations on Western Marxism*, Verso, New York, 1979, pp. 113-16. © 1979 Perry Anderson. Reprinted with permission of the author.

Marxism and the Twenty-First Century
Ben Fine and Alfredo Saad-Filho

The popularity and prominence of Marxism rises and falls with intellectual fashions and with the rhythm of world events. These two influences are far from independent of one another and, further, what is understood to be the content and emphasis of Marxism is equally variable across time, place and context. It ranges from being a critique of capitalism, currently to the fore in the presumed era of globalisation, to providing alternatives to it, as with the (previously) socialist countries and the struggles to construct post-colonial alternatives to capitalism. Marxism has also been heavily embroiled in all the major academic debates across the social sciences, although, once again, the weight and content of its presence have been both diverse and uneven over time, topic and discipline.

Marx's political economy has continuing salience for the study of contemporary issues, including 'non-economic' issues. Two intimately connected issues in particular come to the fore – one concerns the nature of class and the other the nature of the (capitalist) state. Concerns with the environment and the aftermath of capitalism are also examined below.

Class

The major criticism made against Marxism with respect to class is its supposed inability to deal with the complexity and diversity of class relations within advanced capitalist society, variously dubbed as post-industrial, democratic, welfarist, and so on. The critique has two separate components, one concerning class *structure*, the other concerning the *implications* of that structure. In short, and partly because Marx allegedly predicted increasing polarisation in class structure (including, wrongly, the presumption that Marx supports the notion of the 'absolute' pauperisation of the workers), it is argued that the division between bourgeoisie and proletariat is too crude, and, not least because of Marx's revolutionary aspirations for the working class, class action and ideology have presumably failed to match his expectations and those corresponding to his posited class structure. For example, why do wage-workers vote for right-wing governments, and why do conservative governments introduce reforms that benefit working people? These questions are taken up below. At a methodological level, concerns are voiced over both the structure of Marx's theory and its causal content. For example, it is deemed to be too deterministic and reductionist – supposedly it implies that everything flows from the economic, with the economic itself identified primarily with production and class relations.

No doubt many Marxists have been guilty of these analytical sins of oversimplification and the omission of other factors, if in part in the attempt to expose the fallacies of 'freedom', 'efficiency' and 'equality' that are too readily paraded as virtues of capitalism. Hopefully, though, enough of Marx's political economy and method has already been presented to show that Marx himself could not reasonably be accused of these shortcomings. Indeed, Marx once declared himself as not a Marxist, in view of the way his method had been abused in his own lifetime!

More specifically, in the case of class, Marx's political economy reveals the crucial and core component of the class structure of capitalism – that capital and labour necessarily confront one another over the buying and selling of labour power. Further, Marx's political economy is concerned with the consequences of this class structure for accumulation, reproduction, uneven development, crises, and so on. Thus, far from reducing all other economic and social phenomena to such analysis, Marx's political economy does no more than to open the way for broader, systematic and more complex investigation of the structure, relations, processes and consequences of capitalism – although what it does do is a great deal and of crucial importance.

Thus, Marx's political economy does not reduce the class structure to that of capital and labour. On the contrary, other classes are located *in relation* to capital and labour, whether as an essential or contingent part of the capitalist mode of production. Within capitalism itself, for example, scope is created for the self-employed to emerge and for 'professionals' to prosper because, for different reasons, they are able to retain the full fruits of their labour despite being paid a wage or, more exactly, a salary – although this can take different forms, including fees, commissions, and so on. Formally, this can be represented by the idea that such strata receive the full reward for their living labour, rather than remuneration at the value of labour power. More important, though, is to explain why such strata, and their associated activities and conditions of work, are not appropriated by capital and driven down in skill and/or social status to that of wage labour.

[handwritten note at top: L Merton? university staff?]

A number of general arguments can be given, some structural and some contingent. Thus, for example, a precondition for advanced capitalism is the emergence of sophisticated credit and commercial systems in which handsome rewards accrue to those who actively mobilise and allocate funds and commodities on behalf of others. The same applies to the professions needed to oil or safeguard the circulation of capital in all its aspects, and its social reproduction more generally, although these activities vary in weight and significance across time and place and, where professional associations prove ineffective, are subject to proletarianisation. There are, after all, huge differences between the 'self-employed' casual building worker or contracted-out cleaner and the specialist doctor or management consultant.

Finally, and drawing upon the above, what is perceived to be the greatest challenge to the political economy of class is the rise of the middle class, itself a highly diverse stratum in terms of its composition and characteristics. Advanced capitalism has witnessed the decline of the industrial worker and the rise of services, significantly those employed by the state and, thereby, potentially removed from direct commercial motivation and calculation. In short, does the growing army of health, education and other workers employed by the state, quite apart from those in the private services sector, undermine analysis predicated upon a class structure composed of capital and labour?

Posing the problem in these terms points to the continuing relevance of economic class, with labour defined in terms of its dependence upon a wage. This is not to deny that the class of labour is heavily differentiated within itself, even in economic terms – by sector, skill (manual and mental), labour process; between industry and commerce; and between the public and the private sectors. Such differentiations do not invalidate the concept of class; but they highlight the fact that class interests and actions do not always, or even predominantly, exist as an immediate consequence of class structure. Rather, class interests are formed economically, politically and ideologically in ways that arise socially and historically out of the class relations from which they derive. *[handwritten: can we come from]*

Thus, it is not a matter of slotting one or other individual into this or that class on the basis of their *individual* characteristics – manual workers, trade unionists, members of workers' parties, for example – but of tracing out the relations by which the working class is reproduced concretely and represented in material and ideological relations. On this basis, there can be no presumption of a neat or fixed correspondence between economic and other social characteristics; but nor are these entirely independent of one another. That the working class (i.e. wage earners in general, rather than the much narrower subset of blue-collar industrial workers) depends upon wages for its reproduction conditions every aspect of contemporary social life, even where it appears to be otherwise, but it does not subject them to iron determination in incidence and content. ✓

[handwritten: mediation comes here / economic can ... ... culture]

The state and globalisation

These general observations on class have relevance for the theory of the capitalist state. Once again, Marxism has been subject to criticism in the form of parody, with its theory of the state perceived as reducing to the simple proposition that it serves the ruling class and, hence, capitalist interests. This is immediately open to the objection that the state often implements policies that benefit working people, especially through welfare reform. Marxism is then crudely portrayed as defending itself through understanding reform as a devious strategy on the part of the ruling class to pre-empt revolution – where it is not otherwise securing a working class better able to produce (and fight wars) on its behalf. *[handwritten: devious strategy has players not ... here.]*

As before, the historical record fails to bear out such simple motives for the timing and content of reform, and nor is it sufficient to explain provision of health, education and welfare as simply the means by which to enhance short- or long-term labour productivity. Another popular misrepresentation of Marxist theory is to view the ('relatively autonomous') state as essential in mediating between conflicting interests *within* the capitalist class, rather than between capital and labour. In this case, the main function of the state is to prevent capitalists from cheating one another, and the intensity of competition from being unduly dysfunctional. Like the theory of the state as the instrument of one class against another, this approach sheds only limited light on the complexity and diversity of the state's role and actions.

The problem in each of these cases is that the state is seen as an internally homogeneous institution, clearly separated from 'the market', and an instrument serving readily identifiable interests – of capital against labour, or for capital as a whole against the destructive inclinations of its individual elements, or even for 'the nation' against rival nations and capitals. But such interests do not and cannot always exist in such highly abstract and yet easily recognisable forms. Rather, classes and class interests are formed through economic, political and ideological actions, conditioned if not rigidly determined by the accumulation and restructuring of capital and the patterns of social reproduction upon which class formation depends to a greater or lesser extent and in diverse ways. (These patterns include employment structures, conditions of work, trade union and other forms of activity, and daily reproduction at home, in the workplace and elsewhere).

In each of these areas, the capitalist state occupies an increasingly central role. The circulation of capital carves out an economic sphere of activity that is structurally separate from the non-economic but, simultaneously, dependent upon and supporting it. Workers' compliant observance of property relations and the legitimation of economic and other inequalities need to be reproduced at least as much as immediate value relations. Thus, the structural necessity of the capitalist state is created largely by its non-economic role, in social as opposed to, but in conjunction with, economic reproduction. Even so, the state is always heavily and directly embroiled in the economic life of capitalism – appropriating and disbursing (surplus) value through taxation and expenditure, regulating accumulation, restructuring capital as it goes through its cyclical patterns, manipulating exchange rates through monetary and other macroeconomic policies, and influencing distributional relations through taxation, spending and incomes policy.

Unfortunately, these critically important insights of Marxism have often been overlooked, even when Marx has been commended for his foresight in anticipating globalisation or for recognising similar processes at an earlier historical stage. Certainly Marx does emphasise the international character of capitalism and its restless search for profits wherever they can be found. This forges affinities with those who understand globalisation in terms of the withering away of the nation state as it becomes more and more powerless against an increasingly internationally mobile capital that is perceived to roam as effortlessly as the transfer of finance through electronic trading (or of culture through the media).

However, whatever the level of internationalisation of capital in its three forms (of money, commodities and production), the non-economic reproduction of capitalism inevitably requires and even strengthens the role of the nation state, although pressure to conform to the one-dimensional imperatives of commerce does not lead to uniformity. In a sense, this has been recognised by those who constructively oppose 'globalisation', pointing to and posing alternatives to what are taken to be its deleterious manifestations. Such views remain limited, with capitalism being understood as merely globalisation – from which all its evil consequences can easily be read off and, in principle, corrected through the implementation of 'adequate' policies. However, globalisation, in whatever aspect and however understood, should be seen as the effect of capitalism's international reproduction and, consequently, as *the form taken by the laws of political economy in the current period.* In short, whatever meaning is to be attached to globalisation in its application across economic, political and ideological aspects, its fundamental attachment to the production and appropriation of surplus value needs to be sustained analytically.

Capital's environment

Consider now the problem of environmental degradation. Here Marxism has been accused of privileging the social at the expense of the natural, underestimating the potential for reform, and even of precluding consideration of the natural because of excessive preoccupation with the economic. Whilst Marx had much to say about what we would now term the 'environment', he only rarely addressed it directly. But his theories of commodity fetishism and of the labour process offer excellent insights into his simultaneous emphasis upon both social *and* material factors, as value is always use value production with a physical, and so environmental content. This offers an appropriate approach to the environment. It should be understood first and foremost in terms of environmental relations (and corresponding structures and conflicts) characteristic of *capitalism*. This contrasts with the idea of a trans-historical conflict between ecological and social systems, or between the environment and the economy. However, these environmental relations are driven by capitalist relations of production. Thus, as is readily recognised, the drive for profitability leads, through the rising organic composition of capital, to the working up of ever more raw materials into commodities and the corresponding extraction and use of energy and minerals, without immediate regard to their environmental impact.

Yet, capitalism is also capable, not least through the development of new materials and through state regulation, of tempering or even reversing, at least in part, such environmental degradation. In this respect, it is important to recognise the multidimensional nature of the environment and the diverse range of issues and outcomes involved, from pollution, through biotechnology, to drugs, vaccines and artificial body parts. Again, the lessons to be drawn from commodity fetishism are significant. Marx argues that commodity relations are social relations expressed as relations between things, appearing at a superficial level purely as monetary magnitudes, thereby concealing as much as is revealed. What is not apparent is the underlying class relations of exploitation, the dynamics to which they give rise, and the reasons for them. By the same token, how commodities have been created as use values, with their corresponding attachment to the environment, is no more revealed to us than the geographical origins of the commodity or its dependence (or not) on sweated or child labour, unless these be overtly deployed, legitimately or not, as a selling point.

Not surprisingly, these 'hidden' aspects of the commodity, and its systems of production, distribution and exchange, are inevitably brought to our attention, inducing reactions against them. Struggles against child labour, in order to reveal its incidence and to campaign against it from the point of production through to the point of sale, are after all directed at the *nature* of humanity and its reproduction in material and cultural respects. By the same token, the reproduction of environmental relations, optimistically dubbed 'sustainability', is inevitably a shifting confrontation with a range of aspects of capitalist commodity relations. As long as these relations persist, so will the system of production to which they are attached, with the corresponding tendencies to appropriate, transform and degrade the environment, however much this may be tempered by regulation, which tends to be obstructed or evaded by competitive pressures.

Socialism

What is socialism, and does it offer better prospects in social, environmental and other respects? Socialist experiments in the twentieth century closely associated themselves with Marx(ism), and have been seen as Marxist in popular understanding. However, long before the collapse of the Eastern European bloc, controversy had long raged among Marxists over the nature of the Soviet Union, with stances ranging from uncritical support to condemnation as (state) capitalism.

In the event, the Soviet Union, over what is in relative terms a brief historical period, went through a remarkable transformation, well captured in Marx's notion of primitive accumulation.

For what was primarily a semi-feudal society, with a large proportion of its workforce in agriculture, succeeded in creating at breakneck speed a wage-labour market and a relatively advanced and well-integrated industrial base. The period since the collapse of the USSR has witnessed the completion of this transition through the re-emergence of a class of capitalists and private ownership of most of the means of production. Some have argued that such an end result was inevitable, given the low initial productive base and the relentless international hostility faced by the Soviet Union throughout its history. Even so, the pace, direction and consequences of such a transition to capitalism are far from predetermined, as is evident from the (as yet) less cataclysmic, if equally dramatic, adoption of 'market forces' in China.

Thus, whilst Marx is well known for his criticisms of capitalism as an exploitative system, he is probably just as often thought of as having inspired failed twentieth-century attempts at constructing socialism. Even though there is little work by Marx dealing directly and exclusively with the economics of socialism, Marx does, contrary to much opinion, have a great deal to say on the topic, not least in the *Critique of the Gotha Programme*. Generally, he is less interested in designing utopian blueprints than drawing upon, and extrapolating from, developments within capitalism itself, proceeding in two separate but closely related ways.

First, he sees capitalism as increasingly socialising life – through the organisation of production, the economy more generally, and through state power – but in ways that are fundamentally constrained by the private nature of the market, private property and the imperative of profitability. Competition tends to socialise capitalist production through the increasingly intricate division of labour on the shop floor and in society as a whole. In addition to this, the increasing role of the state in welfare provision, redistribution and production itself, through planning or nationalised industries, for example, all anticipate some of the economic and social forms of a future socialism. The same applies to the formation of such things as worker co-operatives, with or without state support. Yet these embryonic forms are inevitably constrained in content, form and even survival by their confinement within capitalist society, the direct or indirect imperatives of profitability, and the economic and social system that imposes commercial imperatives. Some forms of socialisation – the planning of production within large-scale firms to the exclusion of the market, or the broader and deeper role of money through the financial system – have a very different affinity to socialism than have the provision of health, education and welfare through the state. In this respect, the popular slogan 'people before profit' expresses socialist values within an acceptance of capitalism, since profit is allowed as long as it is not privileged. Here there is a neat correspondence with Marx's critique of Proudhon's notion that 'property is theft', for Proudhon both condemns and accepts property (without which there cannot be theft).

Second, then, Marx's anticipation of socialism derives from the contradictions within capitalism, irrespective of whether these have evolved into embryonic socialist forms. Most notable is the revolutionary role to be played by the working class – with capitalism creating, expanding, strengthening and organising labour for the purposes of production, but necessarily exploiting the working majority and failing to meet its broader economic and social aspirations and potential. In the telling phrase of the *Communist Manifesto*, "what the bourgeoisie … produces, above all, is its own gravediggers. Its fall and the victory of the proletariat are equally inevitable."

Such is the means for socialist revolution. Motivation arises out of the various aspects of exploitation, alienation and human debasement characteristic of capitalism, and how they may be superseded. Under capitalism, the working class is deprived of control of the production process, of its results in products themselves, and of comprehensive knowledge of, and influence upon, the workings of society and its development. The workers are also subjected to severe limitations in their prospects and potential achievements, and continuous upheaval in their living conditions, whose fortunes shift with the ebb and flow of the profit imperative and the fortunes of the economy. This is highly wasteful both in economic and, more importantly, in human terms. This has led to workplace resistance and political confrontation and, historically, has provided a powerful stimulus for social reforms and anti-capitalist rebellion.

For Marx, the abolition of capitalism marks the end of the prehistory of human society. However, the transition to communism is neither inexorable nor unavoidable. The social relations at the core of capitalism will change only if overwhelming pressure is applied by the majority. Failing that, capitalism may persist indefinitely, in spite of its rising human and environmental costs. Nonetheless, the passage to socialism can only be achieved in stages, rather than being magically completed on demand, with its first phase being marked by the continuing influence of the heavy historical baggage of capitalism. Marx argues that, at a later stage, when the division of labour and the opposition between mental and manual labour have been overcome, and the development of the productive forces has reached a level that is sufficiently high to permit the all-round development of individuals, the advanced phase of socialism (communism) can be reached. As he put it in the *Critique of the Gotha Programme*, "from each according to his ability, to each according to his needs"!

Ben Fine is Professor of Economics and Alfredo Saad-Filho is Professor of Political Economy at the University of London's School of Oriental and African Studies. This chapter is abridged from Ben Fine and Alfredo Saad-Filho, *Marx's Capital*, fifth edition, Pluto Press, London, 2010, ch. 14. © 2010 Pluto Press. Reproduced with permission of the authors and Pluto Press.

NEOCLASSICAL ECONOMICS

Our consideration of neoclassical economics follows that of Marxist economics, but not because it is subordinate in status or lesser in influence. On the contrary, it has been the dominant paradigm for the last century. Chronologically though, neoclassical economics represents a break with the tradition of classical political economy, a tradition from which Marx drew many of his ideas. The dominance of neoclassical economics has resulted in a narrowing of the focus of economic inquiry from the evolution of economic society to exchange relationships. Neoclassical economics theorises about markets as mechanisms for reconciling the objectives of buyers and sellers, leading to the establishment of prices which act as signals for all economic agents and ensure a more-or-less efficient allocation of resources.

Embodied in neoclassical economic analysis are particular assumptions about 'economic man' (to use the conventional gender-biassed terminology) or *homo economicus*. Methodological individualism is pervasive. So too is liberal ideology. Although claims are made for a positive or value-free status, normative elements enter explicitly via prescriptions for ensuring allocative efficiency. The analysis focuses on a pure market economy. However, neoclassical economic reasoning can also be used to analyse the functioning of government, leading to the development of a distinctive set of theories of 'public choice', infused with similar values and assumptions as that in the theories of consumer and business behavior.

The following articles give an indication of the political economic character of neoclassical economics. An extract from Alfred Marshall's classic, *Principles of Economics*, comes first to illustrate the foundations laid for this tradition in the late nineteenth century. Some of Marshall's other writing had a more historical-institutional orientation, but this extract (quite heavily edited, like the earlier classic contributions by Smith and Ricardo) emphasizes equilibrium analysis. The points at which neoclassical theorizing departs from classical political economy and Marxism come out in the next reading by William Barber. This provides the historical context, describing the origin and salient characteristics of this school of thought. The next article by Milton and Rose Friedman illustrates the neoclassical economists' general view of the virtues of the price system, not only as a device for generating information, but as a structure of incentives and as a means of distributing income. Pursuing this theme, George Stigler, another influential Chicago economist, argues that government attempts to regulate business behavior do more harm than good. These two articles show how neoclassical economics operates as "the ideology of capitalism" (Fusfeld 2002). Jack Hirshleifer's article then considers the 'imperialist' process whereby neoclassical theory is extended to the study of social phenomena. Looking at diverse social issues from the perspective of neoclassical theory is a counter to allegations that the orthodoxy is too narrow. However, critics argue that the more widely neoclassical economics is applied, the more its constricted character is revealed. The final article in this section, by Steve Keen, shows some of the fundamental problems of this neoclassical approach to economic theory. Much modern political economy starts from this sort of critique, leading on to the study of the alternative frameworks of analysis considered in the rest of the book.

Readers interested in exploring neoclassical economics more fully should consult any standard microeconomics textbook. For a critical introduction see, Yanis Varoufakis, 1998, *Foundations of Economics: A Beginner's Companion*, Routledge, London. For a defence of orthodox economics see Diane Coyle, 2007, *The Soulful Science*, Princeton University Press, Princeton.

Demand, Supply and Equilibrium
Alfred Marshall

The ultimate regulator of all demand is … consumers' demand …

There is an endless variety of wants, but there is a limit to each separate want. This familiar and fundamental tendency of human nature may be stated in the law [of] … diminishing utility thus:- The total utility of a thing to anyone (that is, the total pleasure or other benefit it yields him) increases with every increase in his stock of it, but not as fast as his stock increases. If his stock of it increases at a uniform rate the benefit derived from it increases at a diminishing rate. In other words, the additional benefit which a person derives from a given increase of his stock of a thing, diminishes with every increase in the stock that he already has.

That part of the thing which he is only just induced to purchase may be called his marginal purchase, because he is on the margin of doubt whether it is worth his while to incur the outlay required to obtain it. And the utility of his marginal purchase may be called the marginal utility of the thing to him. Or, if instead of buying it, he makes the thing himself, then its marginal utility is the utility of that part which he thinks it only just worth his while to make. And thus the law just given may be worded:- The marginal utility of a thing to anyone diminishes with every increase in the amount of it he already has.

There is however an implicit condition in this law which should be made clear. It is that we do not suppose time to be allowed for any alteration in the character or tastes of the man himself. It is therefore no exception to the law that the more good music a man hears, the stronger is his taste for it likely to become; that avarice and ambition are often insatiable; or that the virtue of cleanliness and the vice of drunkenness alike grow on what they feed upon. For in such cases our observations range over some period of time; and the man is not the same at the beginning as at the end of it. If we take a man as he is, without allowing time for any change in his character, the marginal utility of a thing to him diminishes steadily with every increase in his supply of it …

The larger the amount of a thing that a person has the less … will be the price which he will pay for a little more of it: or in other words his marginal demand price for it diminishes. His demand becomes efficient, only when the price which he is willing to offer reaches that at which others are willing to sell.

… We cannot express a person's demand for a thing by the 'amount he is willing to buy,' or by the 'intensity of his eagerness to buy a certain amount,' without reference to the prices at which he would buy that amount and other amounts. We can represent it exactly only by lists of the prices at which he is willing to buy different amounts …

So far we have looked at the demand of a single individual. And in the particular case of such a thing as tea, the demand of a single person is fairly representative of the general demand of a whole market: for the demand for tea is a constant one; and, since it can be purchased in small quantities, every variation in its price is likely to affect the amount which he will buy. But even among those things which are in constant use, there are many for which the demand on the part of any single individual cannot vary continuously with every small change in price, but can move only by great leaps. For instance, a small fall in the price of hats or watches will not affect the action of every one; but it will induce a few persons, who were in doubt whether or not to get a new hat or a new watch, to decide in favor of doing so.

There are many classes of things the need for which on the part of any individual is inconstant, fitful, and irregular. There can be no list of individual demand prices for wedding-cakes, or the services of an expert surgeon. But the economist has little concern with particular incidents in the lives of individuals. He studies rather 'the course of action that may be expected under certain conditions from the members of an industrial group,' in so far as the motives of that action are measurable by a money price; and in these broad results the variety and the fickleness of individual action are merged in the comparatively regular aggregate of the action of many.

In large markets, then – where rich and poor, old and young, men and women, persons of all varieties of tastes, temperaments and occupations are mingled together – the peculiarities in the wants of individuals will compensate one another in a comparatively regular gradation of total demand. Every fall, however slight in the price of a commodity in general use, will, other things being equal, increase the total sales of it; just as an unhealthy autumn increases the mortality of a large town, though many persons are uninjured by it. And therefore if we had the requisite knowledge, we could make a list of prices at which each amount of it could find purchasers in a given place during, say, a year.

The total demand in the place for, say, tea, is the sum of the demands of all the individuals there … There is then one general law of demand:- The greater the amount to be sold, the smaller must be the price at which it is offered in order that it may find purchasers; or, in other words, the amount demanded increases with a fall in price, and diminishes with a rise in price. There will not be any uniform relation between the fall in price and the increase of demand. A fall of one-tenth in the price may increase the sales by a twentieth or by a quarter, or it may double them.

The price will measure the marginal utility of the commodity to each purchaser individually: we cannot speak of price as measuring marginal utility in general, because the wants and circumstances of different people are different.

The demand prices in our list are those at which various quantities of a thing can be sold in a market during a given time and under given conditions. If the conditions vary in any respect the prices will probably require to be changed; and this has constantly to be done when the desire for anything is materially altered by a variation of custom, or by a cheapening of the supply of a rival commodity, or by the invention of a new one …

Equilibrium of normal demand and supply

We have next to inquire what causes govern supply prices, that is prices which dealers are willing to accept for different amounts … We have to consider the volume of production adjusting itself to the conditions of the market, and the normal price being thus determined at the position of stable equilibrium of normal demand and normal supply.

In this discussion we shall have to make frequent use of the terms cost and expenses of production; and some provisional account of them must be given before proceeding further.

We may revert to the analogy between the supply price and the demand price of a commodity. Assuming for the moment that the efficiency of production depends solely upon the exertions of the workers, we saw that 'the price required to call forth the exertion necessary for producing any given amount of a commodity may be called the supply price for that amount, with reference of course to a given unit of time.' But now we have to take account of the fact that the production of a commodity generally requires many different kinds of labor and the use of capital in many forms. The exertions of all the different kinds of labor that are directly or indirectly involved in making it; together with the abstinences or rather the waitings required for saving the capital used in making it: all these efforts and sacrifices together will be called the real cost of production of the commodity. The sums of money that have to be paid for these efforts and sacrifices will be called either its money cost of production, or, for shortness, its expenses of production; they are the prices which have to be paid in order to call forth an adequate supply of the efforts and waitings that are required for making it; or, in other words, they are its supply price …

We may then arrange the things that are required for making a commodity into whatever groups are convenient, and call them its factors of production. Its expenses of production when any given amount of it is produced are thus the supply prices of the corresponding quantities of its factors of production. And the sum of these is the supply price of that amount of the commodity ...

As far as the knowledge and business enterprise of the producers reach, they in each case choose those factors of production which are best for their purpose; the sum of the supply prices of those factors which are used is, as a rule, less than the sum of the supply prices of any other set of factors which could be substituted for them; and whenever it appears to the producers that this is not the case, they will, as a rule, set to work to substitute the less expansive method. And further on we shall see how in a somewhat similar way society substitutes one undertaker for another who is less efficient in proportion to his charges. We may call this, for convenience of reference, *the principle of substitution*.

The applications of this principle extend over almost every field of economic inquiry.

The position then is this: we are investigating the equilibrium of normal demand and normal supply in their most general form; we are neglecting those features which are special to particular parts of economic science, and are confining our attention to those broad relations which are common to nearly the whole of it. Thus we assume that the forces of demand and supply have free play; that there is no close combination among dealers on either side, but each acts for himself, and there is much free competition; that is, buyers generally compete freely with buyers, and sellers compete freely with sellers. But though everyone acts for himself, his knowledge of what others are doing is supposed to be generally sufficient to prevent him from taking a lower or paying a higher price than others are doing. This is assumed provisionally to be true both of finished goods and of their factors of production, of the hire of labor and of the borrowing of capital. ... [W]e assume that there is only one price in the mark *et al.* one and the same time; it being understood that separate allowance is made, when necessary, for differences in the expense of delivering goods to dealers in different parts of the market; including allowance for the special expenses of retailing, if it is a retail market.

In such a market there is a demand price for each amount of the commodity, that is, a price at which each particular amount of the commodity can find purchasers in a day or week or year ... [B]ut in every case the more of a thing is offered for sale in a market the lower is the price at which it will find purchasers ...

The unit of time may be chosen according to the circumstances of each particular problem: it may be a day, a month, a year, or even a generation: but in every case it must be short relatively to the period of the market under discussion. It is to be assumed that the general circumstances of the market remain unchanged throughout this period; that there is, for instance, no change in fashion or taste, no new substitute which might affect the demand, no new invention to disturb the supply ...

[L]et us assume that the normal supply price of any amount of that commodity may be taken to be its normal expenses of production (including gross earnings of management) by that firm. That is, let us assume that this is the price the expectation of which will just suffice to maintain the existing aggregate amount of production; some firms meanwhile rising and increasing their output, and others falling and diminishing theirs; but the aggregate production remaining unchanged. A price higher than this would increase the growth of the rising firms, and slacken, though it might not arrest, the decay of the falling firms; with the net result of an increase in the aggregate production. On the other hand, a price lower than this would hasten the decay of the falling firms and slacken the growth of rising firms; and on the whole diminish production ...

When therefore the amount produced (in a unit of time) is such that the demand price is greater than the supply price, then sellers receive more than is sufficient to make it worth their while to bring goods to market to that amount; and there is at work an active force tending to increase the amount brought forward for sale. On the other hand, when the amount produced is such that the demand price is less than the supply price, sellers receive less than is sufficient to make it worth their while to bring goods to market on that scale; so that those who were just on the margin of doubt as to whether to go on producing are decided not to do so, and there is an active force at work tending to diminish the amount brought forward for sale. When the demand price is equal to the supply price, the amount produced has no tendency either to be increased or to be diminished; it is in equilibrium.

When demand and supply are in equilibrium, the amount of the commodity which is being produced in a unit of time may be called the equilibrium-amount, and the price at which it is being sold may be called the equilibrium-price.

Such an equilibrium is stable; that is, the price, if displaced a little from it, will tend to return, as a pendulum oscillates about its lowest point; and it will be found to be a characteristic of stable equilibria that in them the demand price is greater than the supply price for amounts just less than the equilibrium amount, and vice versa. For when the demand price is greater than the supply price, the amount produced tends to increase ...

When demand and supply are in stable equilibrium, if any accident should move the scale of production from its equilibrium position, there will be instantly brought into play forces tending to push it back to that position; just as, if a stone hanging by a string is displaced from its equilibrium position, the force of gravity will at once tend to bring it back to its equilibrium position. The movements of the scale of production about its position of equilibrium will be of a somewhat similar kind.

But in real life such oscillations are seldom as rhythmical as those of a stone hanging freely from a string ... For indeed the demand and supply schedules do not in practice remain unchanged for a long time together, but are constantly being changed; and every change in them alters the equilibrium amount and the equilibrium price, and thus gives new positions to the centres about which the amount and the price tend to oscillate.

These considerations point to the great importance of the element of time in relation to demand and supply, to the study of which we now proceed. We shall gradually discover a great many different limitations of the doctrine that the price at which a thing can be produced represents its real cost of production, that is, the efforts and sacrifices which have been directly and indirectly devoted to its production. For, in an age of rapid change such as this, the equilibrium of normal demand and supply does not thus correspond to any distinct relation of a certain aggregate of pleasures got from the consumption of the commodity and an aggregate of efforts and sacrifices involved in producing it: the correspondence would not be exact, even if normal earnings and interest were exact measures of the efforts and sacrifices for which they are the money payments. This is the real drift of that much quoted, and much-misunderstood doctrine of Adam Smith and other economists that the normal, or 'natural,' value of a commodity is that which economic forces tend to bring about in the long run. It is the average value which economic forces would bring about if the general conditions of life were stationary for a run of time long enough to enable them all to work out their full effect. But we cannot foresee the future perfectly. The unexpected may happen; and the existing tendencies may be modified before they have had time to accomplish what appears now to be their full and complete work. The fact that the general conditions of life are not stationary is the source of many of the difficulties that are met with in applying economic doctrines to practical problems ...

We might as reasonably dispute whether it is the upper or the under blade of a pair of scissors that cuts a piece of paper, as whether value is governed by utility or cost of production. It is true that when one blade is held still, and the cutting is effected by moving the other, we may say with careless brevity that the cutting is done by the second; but the statement is not strictly accurate, and is to be excused only so long as it claims to be merely a popular and not a strictly scientific account of what happens ...

[A]s a general rule, the shorter the period which we are considering, the greater must be the share of our attention which is given to the influence of demand on value; and the longer the period, the more important will be the influence of cost of production on value. For the influence of changes in cost of production takes as a rule a longer time to work itself out than does the influence of changes in demand. The actual value at any time, the market value as it is often called, is often more influenced by passing events and by causes whose action is fitful and short lived, than by those which work persistently. But in long periods these fitful and irregular causes in large measure efface one another's influence; so that in the long run persistent causes dominate value completely. Even the most persistent causes are however liable to change. For the whole structure of production is modified, and the relative costs of production of different things are permanently altered, from one generation to another.

Alfred Marshall held the first Chair in Economics at the University of Cambridge. This chapter is abridged from *Principles of Economics*, eighth edition, pp. 78-291.

Origins of Neoclassical Economics
William Barber

In the world of neoclassical economics [dawning in the 1870s] the focus of analytical attention was directed to the process through which a market system allocates an economy's resources. This theme, though not altogether absent from the classical and Marxian traditions, had been far overshadowed in these theoretical systems by the paramount concern with interrelationships between long-period dynamic change and the distribution of income among the various orders of society. The approach to economic analysis developed by neoclassical theorists reversed the earlier orderings of analytical priorities. In their type of theoretical structure, market behavior within carefully delimited spans of time supplied the organizing principle of thought. Meanwhile, the grand themes of long-period development faded far into the background.

The reorientation in economic thinking brought by neoclassicists was connected with changes in the economic environment of western societies. Men of the high Victorian age could, with considerable justification in events, hold that de-emphasis of the problems with which the classical tradition had been preoccupied was appropriate. Western economies had enjoyed prosperity in unprecedented measure and without the checks anticipated by the classical and Marxian traditions. Continued economic expansion, though not unimportant, appeared to be capable of taking care of itself. Moreover, in the face of observable improvements in real wages, the Cassandra calls of Marx and his classical forerunners about the likely consequences of growth for the condition of the working class appeared to be misplaced.

From the point of view of the neoclassical economists the problem deserving study was the functioning of the market system and its role as an allocator of resources. Clearly a rethinking of this issue was timely. In the years since the classicists had written about the economy's natural order the economic structure had altered significantly. Industrial concentrations had grown in size and in capacity to wield unchecked economic power. Trade unions, though still in their infancy, were beginning to claim a voice in wage setting. In the language of classical writers, it could no longer be taken for granted that the normal operation of the economy would tend to make 'natural' and 'market' prices converge.

Changes in the economic environment, however, could go only part way towards accounting for the reorientation in thought represented by neoclassical economics. Intellectual currents of the time also influenced the choice of theoretical issues and the manner in which they were treated. In the main, neoclassical writers absorbed the late nineteenth-century faith in progress and in the benevolence of its consequences. Their conclusions pointed to the existence of certain 'imperfections' in the economic system that called for policy remedies. Nevertheless, they restored a temper of optimism to economic discourse that – with only a few exceptions – had been suppressed since Malthus. Progress, they could hold, appeared to resolve social tensions rather than aggravate them.

These influences converged to direct the attention of economic theorists to an analysis of economic behavior focusing on its decision-making units – households, firms and industries – and on the ways in which choices made by their economic agents were converted into an orderly process. The answers supplied at least purported to demonstrate that the market system was essentially an instrument of integration through which the resources at the disposal of the economy could be allocated to the most socially beneficial uses. With this concentration on the behavior of small units of the system (as opposed to the dominant concern of earlier theoretical traditions with aggregate income and its share-out between profits, wages and rents), microeconomics – i.e. the study of economic behavior of households, firms and industries – was brought to the centre of the stage.

This adjustment of analytical priorities was to have sweeping implications for the organization of economic thought and for the selection of issues deemed worthy of attention, One of its immediate consequences was to elevate the status of the theory of market price. For the purposes of analyzing the behavior of the market system, an understanding of the factors shaping the prices of both outputs and inputs took on a paramount importance. No longer was the discussion of price subordinated to concerns about natural 'value' and its long-period determinants. It became instead the linchpin of the whole network of micro-economic relationships. The elaborate embellishments to the analysis of market price formation worked out by the neoclassical economists opened up analytical horizons undreamed of by the John Stuart Mill of 1848, who had declared the theory of value to be complete.

The primacy of price-theory, however, necessarily implied a downgrading of other themes – and particularly of the long-period growth and distribution concerns of the classical and Marxian traditions. Even so, most major neoclassical theorists felt obliged to offer a few comments in passing about the longer term prospects of the economy. This matter, however, was not close to their hearts and was, in the main, treated rather cursorily. From their standpoint the important issues were more immediate in time, One commentator has described this shift in emphasis as a displacement of the big classical questions of growth and distribution by such little ones as "why does an egg cost more than a cup of tea!" (Robinson 1953: 221).

It was not simply by chance that neoclassical modes of reasoning should have been so far removed from those adopted in earlier theoretical traditions. Indeed, some of the pioneer formulators of neoclassical theory consciously designed their categories of analysis as refutations to Marx. In their hands economics was effectively removed from historical time and detached from the 'laws' of history. The search for the laws of motion of society was largely abandoned to be replaced by the investigation of market processes and their allocative properties.

Human behavior (or at least a stylized interpretation of its economic mainsprings) became the point of departure. On this basis neoclassical writers addressed their attention to the decisions reached by producers and consumers in market situations and to the analysis of their consequences. Worlds separated this approach from Marx's conviction that human behavior was driven by impersonal forces beyond challenge or control. Within a neoclassical perspective the scope for conscious choice and policy initiative was enormously widened. Though many who worked within this theoretical framework opposed governmental intervention in economic life, they were still prepared to argue that policies of the state could alter the course of economic affairs.

While neoclassical analysts shunned the fatalistic overtones of earlier traditions (and of Marxism in particular) they continued to look to the natural scientists for inspiration. The images and vocabulary of the natural sciences emerged most clearly in the propensity of neoclassical economists to construct much of their argument around 'pure' cases. Economic investigation, they maintained, should proceed in a manner analogous to research in a scientific laboratory. Some allowance had to be made for the fact that economic events could not be studied under controlled experimental conditions. The ideal situation could be simulated, however, through the formulation of abstract models of the economy's behavior in which the frictions and untidiness of the world were neglected. Admittedly, such formal systems could claim to be no more than approximations. Nevertheless, they were defended on two principal grounds: first, they isolated for inspection the central nerves of the economic process; and secondly, they provided a benchmark against which the performance of the flesh-and-blood economy could be measured.

This *modus operandi* lent itself readily to the use of mathematics in economic analysis and particularly to the application of the differential calculus. Even so, the widespread adoption of mathematical notation in economic debate did not altogether satisfy Malthus's appeal in the early decades of the century for a standardized set of definitions in the discipline. Each theorist exercised his prerogative to define symbols in a manner of his own choosing. Nevertheless, findings that could be reported in mathematical notation did lend an aura of universality to the subject. Moreover, this manner of argument both elevated the rigor of economic discussion and placed a premium on logically tight and consistent argument – even if, at times, the price of consistency was detachment from close contact with real problems.

The era of neoclassical economics differed from that of its predecessors in yet another respect. For the first time, economic theorizing at a high level became a thoroughly international activity. By contrast with classicism – the overwhelming bulk of the contributors to which were British – insights of fundamental significance to the formal treatment of neoclassical problems were generated by nationals of many countries. While the fertility of the English tradition was undiminished, important schools of neoclassicism emerged in Vienna, Lausanne, Sweden, and in the United States. Each played its own variations on the common neoclassical theme: the analysis of the allocative properties of a market system.

In the world of neoclassicism, economics became more universal and more scientific in its claims – and less dismal in its conclusions.

William Barber is Andrews Professor of Economics Emeritus, Wesleyan University. This chapter is abridged from Origins of Neoclassical Economics, *A History of Economic Thought*, Penguin, Harmondsworth, 1967. © 1967 William Barber. Reprinted with permission of the author.

The Power of the Market
Milton and Rose Friedman

The key insight of Adam Smith's *The Wealth of Nations* is misleadingly simple: if an exchange between two parties is voluntary, it will not take place unless both believe they will benefit from it. Most economic fallacies derive from the neglect of this simple insight, from the tendency to assume that there is a fixed pie, that one party can gain only at the expense of another.

This key insight is obvious for a simple exchange between two individuals. It is far more difficult to understand how it can enable people living all over the world to cooperate to promote their separate interests.

The price system is the mechanism that performs this task without central direction, without requiring people to speak to one another or to like one another. When you buy your pencil or your daily bread, you don't know whether the pencil was made or the wheat was grown by a white man or a black man, by a Chinese or an Indian. As a result, the price system enables people to cooperate peacefully in one phase of their life while each one goes about his own business in respect of everything else.

Adam Smith's flash of genius was his recognition that the prices that emerged from voluntary transactions between buyers and sellers – for short, in a free market – could coordinate the activity of millions of people, each seeking his own interest, in such a way as to make everyone better off. It was a startling idea then, and it remains one today, that economic order can emerge as the unintended consequence of the actions of many people, each seeking his own interest.

Prices perform three functions in organizing economic activity: first, they transmit information; second, they provide an incentive to adopt those methods of production that are least costly and thereby use available resources for the most highly valued purposes; third, they determine who gets how much of the product – the distribution of income. These three functions are closely interrelated.

Transmission of information

Suppose that, for whatever reason, there is an increased demand for pencils – perhaps because a baby boom increases school enrolment. Retail stores will find that they are selling more pencils. They will order more pencils from their wholesalers. The wholesalers will order more pencils from the manufacturers. The manufacturers will order more wood, more brass, more graphite – all the varied products used to make a pencil. In order to induce their suppliers to produce more of these items, they will have to offer higher prices for them. The higher prices will induce the suppliers to increase their workforce to be able to meet the higher demand. To get more workers they will have to offer higher wages or better working conditions. In this way ripples spread out over ever widening circles, transmitting the information to people all over the world that there is a greater demand for pencils – or, to be more precise, for some product they are engaged in producing, for reasons they may not and need not know.

The price system transmits only the important information and only to the people who need to know. The producers of wood, for example, do not have to know whether the demand for pencils has gone up because of a baby boom or because 14,000 more government forms have to be filled out in pencil. They don't even have to know that someone is willing to pay more for wood and that the higher price is likely to last long enough to make it worthwhile to satisfy the demand. Both items of information are provided by market prices – the first by the current price, the second by the price offered for future delivery.

A major problem in transmitting information efficiently is to make sure that everyone who can use the information gets it without clogging the 'in' baskets of those who have no use for it. The price system automatically solves this problem. The people who transmit the information have an incentive to search out the people who can use it and they are in a position to do so. People who can use the information have an incentive to get it and they are in a position to do so. The pencil manufacturer is in touch with people selling the wood he uses. He is always trying to find additional suppliers who can offer him a better product or a lower price. Similarly, the producer of wood is in touch with his customers and is always trying to find new ones. On the other hand, people who are not currently engaged in these activities and are not considering them as future activities have no interest in the price of wood and will ignore it.

The transmission of information through prices is enormously facilitated these days by organized markets and by specialized communication facilities. It is a fascinating exercise to look through the price quotations published daily in, say, the *Wall Street Journal*, not to mention the numerous more specialized trade publications. These prices mirror almost instantly what is happening all over the world. There is a revolution in some remote country that is a major producer of copper, or there is a disruption of copper production for some other reason. The current price of copper will shoot up at once. To find out how long knowledgeable people expect the supplies of copper to be affected, you need merely examine the prices for future delivery on the same page.

Few readers even of the *Wall Street Journal* are interested in more than a few of the prices quoted. They can readily ignore the rest. The *Wall Street Journal* does not provide this information out of altruism or because it recognizes how important it is for the operation of the economy. Rather, it is led to provide this information by the very price system whose functioning it facilitates. It has found that it can achieve a larger or a more profitable circulation by publishing these prices – information transmitted to it by a different set of prices.

Prices not only transmit information from the ultimate buyers to retailers, wholesalers, manufacturers, and owners of resources; they also transmit information the other way. Suppose that a forest fire or strike reduces the availability of wood. The price of wood will go up. That will tell the manufacturer of pencils that it will pay him to use less wood, and it will not pay him to produce as many pencils as before unless he can sell them for a higher price. The smaller production of pencils will enable the retailer to charge a higher price, and the higher price will inform the final user that it will pay him to wear his pencil down to a shorter stub before he discards it, or shift to a mechanical pencil. Again, he doesn't need to know why the pencil has become more expensive, only that it has.

Anything that prevents prices from expressing freely the conditions of demand or supply interferes with the transmission of accurate information. Private monopoly – control over a particular commodity by one producer or a cartel of producers – is one example. That does not prevent the transmission of information through the price system, but it does distort the information transmitted.

Important as private distortions of the price system are, these days the government is the major source of interference with a free market system – through tariffs and other restraints on international trade, domestic action fixing or affecting individual prices, including wages, government regulation of specific industries, monetary and fiscal policies producing erratic inflation and numerous other channels.

One of the major adverse effects of erratic inflation is the introduction of static, as it were, into the transmission of information through prices. If the price of wood goes up, for example, producers of wood cannot know whether that is because inflation is raising all prices or because wood is now in greater demand or lower supply relative to other products than it was before the price hike. The information that is important for the organization of production is primarily about relative prices – the price of one item compared with the price of another. High inflation, and particularly highly variable inflation, drowns that information in meaningless static.   ✓

Incentives

The effective transmission of accurate information is wasted unless the relevant people have an incentive to act, and act correctly, on the basis of that information. It does no good for the producer of wood to be told that the demand for wood has gone up unless he has some incentive to react to the higher price of wood by producing more wood. One of the beauties of a free price system is that the prices that bring the information also provide both an incentive to react to the information and the means to do so.

This function of prices is intimately connected with the third function – determining the distribution of income – and cannot be explained without bringing that function into the account. The producer's income – what he gets for his activities – is determined by the difference between the amount he receives from the sale of his output and the amount he spends in order to produce it. He balances the one against the other and produces an output such that producing a little more would add as much to his costs as to his receipts. A higher price shifts this margin.

In general, the more he produces, the higher the cost of producing still more. He must resort to wood in less accessible or otherwise less favorable locations; he must hire less skilled workers or pay higher wages to attract skilled workers from other pursuits. But now the higher price enables him to bear these higher costs and so provides both the incentive to increase output and the means to do so.

Prices also provide an incentive to act on information not only about the demand for output but also about the most efficient way to produce a product. Suppose one kind of wood becomes scarcer and therefore more expensive than another. The pencil manufacturer gets that information through a rise in the price of the first kind of wood. Because his income, too, is determined by the difference between sales receipts and costs, he has an incentive to economise on that kind of wood. To take a different example, whether it is less costly for loggers to use a chain saw or handsaw depends on the price of the chain saw and the handsaw, the amount of labor required with each, and the wages of different kinds of labor. The enterprise doing the logging has an incentive to acquire the relevant technical knowledge and to combine it with the information transmitted by prices in order to minimize costs.

To go much further afield to more remote effects: insofar as the relative price of wood was raised by the higher cost of producing it or by the greater demand for wood as a substitute source of energy, the resulting higher price of pencils gave consumers an incentive to economise on pencils! And so on in infinite variety.

We have discussed the incentive effects so far in terms of producers and consumers. But it also operates with respect to workers and owners of other productive resources. A higher demand for wood will tend to produce a higher wage for loggers. This is a signal that labor of that type in greater demand than before. The higher wage gives workers an incentive to act on that information. Some workers who were indifferent about being loggers or doing something else may now choose to become loggers. More young people entering the labor market may become loggers. Here, too, interference by government, through minimum wages, for example, or by trade unions, through restricting entry, may distort the information transmitted or may prevent individuals from freely acting on that information.

Information about prices – whether it be wages in different activities, the rent of land, or the return to capital from different uses – is not the only information that is relevant in deciding how to use a particular resource. It may not even be the most important information, particularly about how to use one's own labor. That decision depends in addition on one's own interest and capacities – what the great economist Alfred Marshall called the whole of the advantages and disadvantages of an occupation, monetary or non-monetary. Satisfaction in a job may compensate for low wages. On the other hand, higher wages may compensate for a disagreeable job.

Distribution of income

The income each person gets through the market is determined, as we have seen, by the difference between his receipts from the sale of goods and services and the costs he incurs in producing those goods and services. The receipts consist predominantly of direct payments for the productive resources we own – payments for labor or the use of land or buildings or other capital. The case of the entrepreneur – like the manufacturer of pencils – is different in form but not in substance. His income, too, depends on how much of each productive resource he owns and on the price that the market sets on the services to those resources, though in his case the major productive resource he owns may be the capacity to organize an enterprise, coordinate the resources it uses, assume risks, and so on. He may also own some of the other productive resources used in the enterprise, in which case part of his income is derived from the market price for their services. Similarly, the existence of the modern corporation does not alter matters. We speak loosely of the 'corporation's income' or of 'business' having an income. That is figurative language. The corporation is an intermediary between its owners – the stockholders – and the resources other than the stockholders' capital, the services of which it purchases. Only people have incomes and they derive them through the market from the resources they own, whether these be in the form of corporate stock, or of bonds, or of land, or of their personal capacity.

The accumulation of physical capital – of factories, mines, office buildings, shopping centres; highways, railroads, airports, cars, trucks, planes, ships; dams, refineries, power plants; houses, refrigerators, washing machines, and so on and on in endless variety – has played an essential role in economic growth. Without that accumulations the kind of economic growth that we have enjoyed could never have occurred. Without the maintenance of inherited capital the gains made by one generation would be dissipated by the next.

But the accumulation of human capital – in the form of increased knowledge and skills and improved health and longevity – has also played an essential role. And the two have reinforced one another. The physical capital enabled people to be far more productive by providing them with the tools to work with. And the capacity of people to invent new forms of physical capital, to learn how to use and get the most out of physical capital, and to organize the use of both physical and human capital on a larger and a larger scale enabled the physical capital to be more productive. Both physical and human capital must be cared for and replaced. That is even more difficult and costly for human than for physical capital – a major reason why the return to human capital has risen so much more rapidly than the return to physical capital.

The amount of each kind of resource each of us owns is partly the result of chance, partly of choice by ourselves or others. Chance determines our genes and through them affects our physical and mental capacities. Chance determines the kind of family and cultural environment into which we are born and as a result our opportunities to develop our physical and mental capacity. Chance determines also resources we may inherit from our parents or other benefactors. Chance may destroy or enhance the resources we start with. But choice also pays an important role. Our decisions about how to use our resources, whether to work hard or take it easy, to enter one occupation or another, to engage in one venture or another, to save or spend – these may determine whether we dissipate our resources or improve and add to them. Similar decisions by our parents, by other benefactors, by millions of people who may have no direct connection with us will affect our inheritance.

The price that the market sets on the services of our resources is similarly affected by a bewildering mixture of chance and choice. Frank Sinatra's voice was highly valued in twentieth-century United States. Would it have been highly valued in twentieth-century India, if he had happened to be born and live there? Skill as a hunter and trapper had a high value in eighteenth- and nineteenth-century America, a much lower value in twentieth-century America. These are all matters involving chance and choice – in these examples, mostly choices made by consumers of services that determine the relative market prices of different items. But the price we receive for the services of our resources through the market also depends on our own choices – where we choose to settle, how we choose to use those resources, to whom we choose to sell our services, and so on.

In every society, however it is organized, there is always dissatisfaction with the distribution of income. All of us find it hard to understand why we should receive less than others who seem no more deserving – or why we should be receiving more than so many others whose needs seem as great and whose deserts seem no less. The farther fields always look greener – so we blame the existing system. In a command system envy and dissatisfaction are directed at the rulers. In a free market system they are directed at the market.

One result has been an attempt to separate this function of the price system – distributing income – from its other function – transmitting information and providing incentives. Much government activity during recent decades in the United States and other countries that rely predominantly on the market has been directed at altering the distribution of income generated by the market in order to produce a different and more equal distribution of income. There is a strong current of opinion pressing for still further steps in this direction.

However we might wish it otherwise, it simply is not possible to use prices to transmit information and provide an incentive to act on that information without using prices also to affect, even if not completely determine, the distribution of income. If what a person gets does not depend on the price he receives for the services of his resources, what incentive does he have to seek out information on prices or to act on the basis of that information? If your income will be the same whether you work hard or not, why should you work hard? Why should you make the effort to search out the buyer who values most highly what you have to sell if you will not get any benefit from doing so? If there is no reward for accumulating capital, why should anyone postpone to a later date what he could enjoy now? Why save? How would the existing physical capital ever have been built up by the voluntary restraint of individuals? If there is no reward for maintaining capital, why should people not dissipate any capital which they have either accumulated or inherited? If prices are prevented from affecting the distribution of income, they cannot be used for other purposes.

Milton Friedman was Paul Snowden Russell Distinguished Service Professor Emeritus of Economics at the University of Chicago, and recipient of the Nobel Prize in Economic Science. Rose Friedman was his wife and co-author of *Free to Choose*. This chapter is abridged from *Free to Choose*, Penguin, Harmondsworth, 1980, ch. 1, pp. 27-43. © 1980 Milton and Rose Friedman. Reprinted with permission of Milton Friedman.

Can Regulatory Agencies Protect the Consumer?
George Stigler

The consumer – and the investor and laborer – have always been subjected to vicissitudes arising out of chance, ignorance, neglect, and fraud. Some are largely avoidable, but sometimes at costs more onerous than the vicissitudes: consider how much would be required thoroughly to test ten competing brands of a product. That may very well be the reason there is no business which supplies leading brands of goods for experiment by the prospective buyer.

For long centuries during which the state concerned itself little with such problems, the consumer had two main resources in dealing with the possible vicissitudes of purchasing, lending, working, and living. The first resource was his own intelligence, enshrined in the doctrine of *caveat emptor* ('let the buyer beware'). That phrase poorly describes the situation, and for at least three reasons:

1. The consumer did not have to beware of everything: he could contract with the seller for express warranties with respect to the commodity, and these warranties were and are enforceable.

2. There were implied warranties that the goods were of merchantable quality: the seller was required to reveal defects which would not be discoverable with ordinary examination.
3. The seller then, as now, had a good deal to beware of too. Anyone who thinks that there are more careless, irresponsible, or dishonest sellers than buyers obviously has never been a seller.

There was a second resource of the consumer to deploy against the vicissitudes of inferior performance, and that was the great engine of competition. It is widely assumed that if company A produces shoddy goods, rival B must also lower the quality of its goods to compete in price. That is exactly the opposite of the typical sequence: it is usually profitable to compete by improving quality, reliability, and safety.

Of course, neither the diligence of ordinary mortals nor the competitive energies of an extraordinary economy will detect and prevent or correct all the mishaps and negligences and frauds of life. So it is natural to turn to that centre of authority, that depository of virtue and benevolence, that fountain of justice, the state, to provide further and fuller protection to the consumer.

The question is what the government can do to help the consumer.

The overwhelmingly popular level of discourse is deductive and hortatory. Appoint to a commission seven highly intelligent men who have unflagging zeal to serve the public interest, and only the public interest, equip them with the resources to find out what to do, and give them the legal power to do it. Then automobiles will be safe, stock exchanges will charge reasonable commissions, and mutual funds will not spend too much on selling costs. If on occasion the commissioner is less than superb, replace him; if on occasion the commission does something wrong, reprimand it; if the commission does too little, enlarge its powers and fatten its appropriations. With at most an occasional searching glance from the legislature, the agency will take care of monopolistic railroads, or profit-grubbing television, or deceptively quoted interest rates, or whatever. In this easy world we would need only fashion a new agency to solve this problem: one agency equals one problem solved.

If commissioners have often been lazy or timid, or deeply subservient to the industry they purport to regulate, it is inexcusably romantic to assume that all future appointments will be regulatory saints. If, whatever the quality of commissioners, quite often the law dictates inherently anti-consumer policies, what purpose is there in unctuously demanding better laws from better Congresses? Or perhaps we should have a commission to regulate Congress? The regulatory experience is now sufficiently varied and lengthy so that we can isolate the essential characteristics of the regulatory process, characteristics which determine what, in fact, the consumer may expect from regulation.

And now to the main thesis: public regulation weakens the defences the consumer has in the market and often imposes new burdens upon him, without conferring corresponding protections. The doctrine of *caveat emptor* has not lost its force: the only change is that now the consumer must beware of different threats, and threats which he is less well equipped to defend against.

Competition, like other therapeutic forms of hardship, is by wide and age-long consent, highly beneficial to society when imposed upon – other people. Every industry that can afford a spokesman has emphasized both its devotion to the general principle and the overriding need for reducing competition within its own markets because this is the one area in which competition works poorly. The doctors must protect their patients against (unlicensed) quacks, and the medical profession must be right because heaven has rewarded its benevolence with the highest earnings of any profession. Farmers must protect the consumer against famine, and this is best done by the subtle path of restrictions upon output and subsidies to producers.

Regulatory bodies are remarkably loyal in their acceptance of this two-edged philosophy – as indeed they should be, since they owe their existence to it. Regulation and competition are rhetorical friends and deadly enemies: over the doorway of every regulatory agency save two should be carved: 'Competition Not Admitted'. The [US] Federal Trade Commission's doorway should announce, 'Competition Admitted in Rear', and that of the Antitrust Division, 'Monopoly Only by Appointment'.

I have neither inclination nor evidence to deny the regulatory process occasional triumphs. The delay in introducing thalidomide [a pharmaceutical which, when used by pregnant women, led to child abnormalities] in the United States presumably was a splendid success, and should receive full credit. But we must base public policy not upon signal triumphs or scandalous failures but upon the regular, average performance of the policy. If the policies that delayed thalidomide would delay a new penicillin at least as long – as seems highly probable – we must reckon this in the costs of the program.

The ultimate, inescapable fact of life for the consumer is that he must beware – as much today as in the past. I began by saying that, under the earlier regime of *caveat emptor*, the consumer was protected basically by his own care and intelligence and by the most powerful of allies, competition. Public regulation weakens and sometimes destroys these defences against fraud and negligence, without replacing the protections they used to afford.

Consider a regulatory activity – perhaps the federal milk marketing boards which have so carefully cartelized the production and distribution of milk in the United States, to the substantial economic detriment of the consumer. If one milk company exploits or misleads its customers, each consumer has an incentive to seek out a more reliable or more efficient supplier. The larger the misdeeds of this company, and the larger the consumption of milk by the consumer, the greater his rewards if he can uncover a new source of supply. Profit-seeking outsiders will strive mightily to respond to this demand for lower but profitable prices. These incentives provide a strong sanction even on a monopolist. (There is a widespread view that a monopolist profits by lowering the quality of goods compared with what competition would provide, and this view is simply erroneous economic theory. There is an equally popular view – often held by the very same people! – that competition leads to continuous reductions of quality and it is equally erroneous.)

What is the consumer's recourse if he is being exploited by a federal marketing order which either neglects his interests or positively arms and protects a cartel in exploiting this consumer? His sole defence is to organize a political campaign to change or eliminate that marketing scheme. For the individual consumer this is a bleak prospect. The costs – in time, effort, and money – to change legislation are large; the reward to any one consumer from joining a consumer lobby is negligible. The milk marketing board in Chicago, according to a competent economist's analysis, raised the price of milk at least 2 cents per quart in the mid-1960s – or perhaps $10 to $20 per family per year. If a family were to devote a sum such as this to stirring up opposition to the marketing order, and even if the battle could be restricted to Chicago (the underlying legislation is federal), it would be a wretched option: the family would receive negligible benefits from its own activity.

The sheltered farmers, milk companies, and laborers in the industry have much larger stakes, and they can and do mount the legislative drives which create and dominate such legislation. The individual consumer has no real defence, given the nature of our political process, which allows compact groups with substantial *per capita* interests to win out over diffused masses of consumers, no one of whom can effectively combat special interest legislation.

Occasionally the consumer will be protected in the legislature by another industry which happens to share the consumer's goal but not his impotence. This fortuitous and uncommon circumstance aside, he is the victim without recourse of our political system which is inaccessible to groups that may be large but whose members as individuals have only small stakes in a controversy.

The superiority of the traditional defences of the individual – reliance upon his own efforts and the power of competition lie precisely in the characteristics which distinguish them from public regulation. Each of the traditional defences is available and working at all times – self-interest and competition are never passing fads. Each of the traditional defences is available to individuals and small groups – changes in policy and adaptation to new circumstances do not require changes in the ponderous, expensive, insensitive machinery of a great state. It is of regulation that the consumer must beware.

George Stigler was Charles R. Walgreen Distinguished Service Professor Emeritus, University of Chicago, and recipient of the Nobel Prize in Economic Science. This chapter is abridged from Can Regulatory Agencies Protect the Consumer? *The Citizen and the State*, Chicago University Press, Chicago, 1982, ch. 1, pp. 178-88. © 1982 Chicago University Press. Reprinted with permission of Chicago University Press.

The Expanding Domain of Economics
Jack Hirshleifer

In dealing with economics as an expansive imperialist discipline, a geopolitical metaphor may be illuminating. Our heartland is an intellectual territory carved off by two narrowing conceptions: (1) of man as a rational, self-interested decision-maker, and (2) of *social interaction* as typified by market exchange. However, the logic of ideas irresistibly draws economists beyond these core areas. Rational self-interested choice plays a role in many domains of life other than markets, for example, in politics, warfare, mate selection, engineering design, and statistical decisions. Conversely, even within the domain of market behavior, economists can hardly deny that what people want to buy and sell is influenced by cultural, ethical, and even 'irrational' forces more customarily studied by social psychologists and anthropologists. And how people go about their dealings in the market touches upon issues also involving law and sociology.

Responding to these intellectual attractions, the rhetoric of an economic imperialist like Gary Becker is notably more muscular:

> The combined assumptions of maximizing behavior, market equilibrium, and stable preferences, used relentlessly and unflinchingly, form the heart of the economic approach (1976: 4).

This approach has powered the imperialist expansion of economics into the traditional domains of sociology, political science, anthropology, law, and social biology – with more to come.

It is ultimately impossible to carve off a distinct territory for economics, bordering upon but separated from other social disciplines. Economics interpenetrates them all, and is reciprocally penetrated by them. *There is only one social science*. What gives economics its imperialist invasive power is that our analytical categories – scarcity, cost, preferences, opportunities, etc. – are truly universal in applicability. Even more important is our structured organization of these concepts into the distinct yet intertwined processes of optimization on the individual decision level and equilibrium on the social level of analysis. Thus economics really does constitute the universal grammar of social science. But there is a flip side to this. While scientific work in anthropology and sociology and political science and the like will become increasingly indistinguishable from economics, economists will reciprocally have to become aware of how constraining has been their tunnel vision about the nature of man and social interactions. Ultimately, good economics will also have to be good anthropology and sociology and political science and psychology.

The history of imperialist economics illustrates that the model of economic man has indeed been productive, but only up to a point. Each of our expansionist invasions has typically encountered an initial phase of easy successes, where postulating rational self-interested behavior in a new field of application has yielded sudden sharp results. In the field of politics it was like a breath of fresh air when Anthony Downs boldly proposed as 'axioms' that men seek office solely for income, prestige, and power and that every political agent acts rationally to achieve goals with minimal use of scarce resources (1957: 137). Or in the field of crime when Gary Becker (1968) and Isaac Ehrlich (1973) chose to set aside the possibly 'deviant' personalities of criminals and instead treat them as individuals rationally responding to opportunities in the form of punishment and reward. These, and similarly oriented explorations into domains of study such as law, marriage and the family, and war and conflict, have led to a rapid intellectual flowering of exciting results. But then comes a second phase, when doubts begin to emerge. In the partially conquered new territories some of the evidence persists in remaining intractable, difficult to square with the postulate of rational self-interested behavior. In politics these include the fact of voting, the willingness to provide public goods, the grip of ideology. As to crime, it remains true that faced with the same incentives some people commit offences while others respect the law. So more than a suspicion remains that, after all, criminals are to a degree 'deviant' personalities. In some of the fields of imperialist extension of economics we are still in the first phase, reaping easy results. But my emphasis will be upon the more interesting second stage, and what we can learn from the difficulties encountered. In what follows I will examine what our imperialist explorations have taught us about the two crucial aspects of economic man – *self-interest* and *rationality*.

Self-interest

Adam Smith, as usual, said it best: "We are not ready to suspect any person of being defective in selfishness" (1976 [1759]: 482). And of course there are is his famous lines:

> It is not from the benevolence of the butcher, the brewer, or the baker that we expect our dinner, but from their regard to their own interest (1937 [1776]: 14).

From the neoclassical era a characteristically strong statement comes from F. Y. Edgeworth (1881: 16), who stated that "the first principle of Economics is that every agent is actuated only by self-interest". And finally, a modern quotation from Richard Posner (1977: 3), the celebrated legal scholar who – like the convert more Catholic than the Pope – has become one of the most outstanding of our economic imperialists:

> Economics … explores and tests the implications of assuming that man is a rational maximiser of his ends in life, his satisfactions – what we shall call his 'self-interest'.

There is one problem here, which Posner promptly raises. Suppose a person's ends in life include the well-being of others. If so, do their interests become his 'self-interest'? Posner, like many others, answers in the affirmative – an evasion that robs the concept of self-interest of any distinguishable content. But it is not so easy to separate 'self-interested' satisfactions from the psychic sensations generated by the experiences of others.

A distinction proposed by Amartya Sen (1977: 327) illustrates the nature of the difficulty:

> And of course there are his famous lines: If the knowledge of torture of others makes you sick, it is a case of sympathy; if it does not make you feel personally worse off, but you think it is wrong ... it is a case of commitment ... [B]ehaviour based on sympathy is in an important sense egoistic, for one is

oneself pleased at others' pleasure and pained at others' pain, and the pursuit of one's own utility may thus be helped by sympathetic action. It is action based on commitment rather than sympathy which would be non-egoistic in this sense.

Thus Sen would count the emotion of sympathy as self-interested, leaving only an abstract intellectualized moralism as non-egotistic – which does not seem a very appealing categorization. For present purposes, the following commonsense interpretation will serve: someone is non-self-interested to the extent that he or she attaches utility to the impact of events upon the bodies or psyches of other parties. When my mother says, "Drink your milk", that is her benevolent concern for my bodily well-being. And if I drink it only to please her, that is my benevolent concern for her psychic comfort. (Ultimately, the difficulty can be resolved only in the light of bioeconomic considerations which allow us to separate the motivational from the functional aspects of self-interest.)

It is important to distinguish motivations, aspects of individuals' utility or preference functions, from actions. (Even entirely egoistic individuals, we economists know, may be led to engage in mutually helpful actions by an appropriate set of penalties and rewards.) Self-interested or egoistic motivations represent an intermediate point on a spectrum that has benevolence at one extreme and malevolence at the other.

Rationality

When it comes to rationality, economics as an imperialist discipline finds itself in an unwontedly defensive position. Damaging attacks upon rational man have come from the direction of psychology. But this is all to the good if, as I have maintained, economics must ultimately become coextensive with all of social science. Generalized economics will have to deal with man as he really is – self-interested or not, fully rational or not. Rationality is an instrumental concept. In the light of one's goals (preferences), if the means chosen (actions) are appropriate the individual is rational; if not, irrational. 'Appropriate' here refers to method rather than result. Rational behavior is action calculated on the basis of the rules of logic and other norms of validity. Owing to chance, good method may not always lead to good result.

Few real men and women behave rationally all the time, and many of us scarcely any of the time. How then can economics maintain the postulate of rationality? Several answers can be given, in parallel with the responses offered when the self-interest postulate was challenged: (1) We could redefine all choice as rational. ('If I chose to do X, I must have thought that X was best.') This gets us nowhere. (2) We could retreat to a fallback position, asserting that the rationality postulate yields useful predictions in the field where economists customarily apply it – to wit, in market decisions. Such modesty, as argued above, is an improper evasion of the scientific challenge. Ultimately we must be ready to abandon the rationality paradigm to the extent that it fails to fit the evidence about human behavior.

Rationality may fail in two quite distinct ways. First, individuals often commit errors in logical inference even when doing their best to reason logically. Second, what is quite a different matter, actions are often 'unthinking'; when governed by habit or passion, people do not even attempt rational self-control.

At least as important as failure to reason correctly is the fact that, in some contexts, people do not even attempt to think rationally at all (or do so only in a very limited way). Habit is surely a way of economizing on scarce reasoning ability. Indeed, in many contexts habit may be faster and more accurate than thinking no-one can play the piano or drive a car effectively without engaging in a host of complex unthinking actions. But I am not aware of any studies of the psycho-economics of habit.

Under the heading of 'bounded rationality', Herbert Simon (1955; 1959) has contended that a person faced with a complex mental task will not attempt to strictly optimize but will be content instead merely to 'satisfice'. That is, he aims to find not the best but a good solution – one which achieves a given proximate target or aspiration level. Simon (1959: 263) argues that:

> Models of satisficing behavior are richer than models of maximizing behavior, because they treat not only of equilibrium but of the method of reaching it as well ... (a) When performance falls short of the level of aspiration, search behavior ... is induced. (b) At the same time, the level of aspiration begins to adjust itself downward until goals reach levels that are practically attainable. (c) If the two mechanisms just listed operate too slowly to adapt aspiration to performance, emotional behavior – apathy or aggression, for example – will replace rational adaptive behavior.

Simon's steps (a) and (b), it might at least be argued, constitute a valid successive-approximation technique for optimisation that economizes on humans' limited information and reasoning ability. Only step (c), the emotional response to frustration, seems clearly dysfunctional in terms of rational adaptation. However, it can be shown, even 'irrational' emotions may serve a useful adaptive function.

I will conclude this discussion of the psychology of rationality on a properly aggressive imperialist note. Economists, for example Akerlof and Dickens (1982) and David Alhadeff (1982) to my mind have been over-respectful of what psychology is supposedly able to tell us. While rich in data, the theoretical level of psychology remains a confusing clamor of competing categories; there is no integrating theoretical structure. I will be so bold as to predict that such a structure, when achieved, will be fundamentally economic – or more specifically bioeconomic – in nature. That is, it will show how mental patterns have evolved as optimizing solutions subject to the constraints of scarcity and competition.

Jack Hirshleifer was Professor of Economics, University of California Los Angeles. This chapter is abridged from The Expanding Domain of Economics. *American Economic Review*, vol. 75, no. 6, 1985, pp. 53-68. © 1985 American Economics Association. Reprinted with permission of the author and the American Economics Association.

Madness in their Method
Steve Keen

Before economics can have any hope of being a science, it has to wean itself from the belief that it is futile to challenge the assumptions used to devise a theory, and instead that a theory can only be judged by the accuracy of its predictions. This belief is bad philosophy, leading to pseudo-scientific behavior rather than real science. Ironically, it is also the primary reason why neoclassical economists, in general, spectacularly failed this very test in their complete failure to predict the largest economic event of the last half century: the economic crisis that began in 2007.

Do assumptions matter?

Students of economics often complain that the theories they are required to study are unrealistic. The classic defence against this claim draws from the famous argument by the neoclassical economist, Milton Friedman. According to Friedman, a theory can properly be judged only by the consistency of its *predictions* with real world experiences, not by the extent to which its underlying *assumptions* conform to observable features of the real world. This is the basis for the claim that 'assumptions don't matter'. Friedman actually went further to suggest that unrealistic assumptions were in fact the hallmark of a good theory. In what Samuelson later dubbed 'the *F*-twist', Friedman (1953) argued that:

> Truly important and significant hypotheses will be found to have 'assumptions' that are wildly inaccurate descriptive representations of reality, and, in general, the more significant the theory, the more unrealistic the assumptions … the relevant question to ask about the 'assumptions' of a theory is … whether they are sufficiently good approximations for the purpose in hand. And this question can be answered only by seeing whether the theory … yields sufficiently accurate predictions.

This proposition appears scientific, in that most scientists would agree that their theories can never exactly describe reality. It also implies a healthy dose of theoretical agnosticism, in that the economist is allegedly really interested in 'the facts'. But despite its superficial appeal, this 'instrumentalist' view is fundamentally flawed. As Alan Musgrave pointed out, there are three classes of assumptions, and Friedman's dictum is only partially true in relation to the least important of them.

Negligibility assumptions state that some aspect of reality has little or no effect on the phenomenon under investigation. Much of Friedman's musings were reasonable in this domain, but even here it is possible to rephrase these 'unrealistic' statements as 'realistic' ones. As Musgrave (1981) put it, such assumptions:

> are not necessarily 'descriptively false', for they do not assert that present factors are absent but rather that they are 'irrelevant for the phenomena to be explained' … Galileo's assumption that air-resistance was negligible for the phenomena he investigated was a true statement about reality, and an important part of the explanation Galileo gave of those phenomena.

The second class of assumptions comprises *domain assumptions*. A domain assumption specifies the conditions under which a particular theory will apply. If they don't apply, then neither does the theory.

For example, economists often assume that risk can be used as a proxy for uncertainty. But risk applies to situations in which the regularity of past events is a reliable guide to future events, whereas uncertainty applies when past events cannot be extrapolated into the future. A somewhat intimate example might illustrate the fallacy of identifying uncertainty with risk. Imagine that you are very attracted to a particular person, and he/she has gone out with 20 percent of those who have asked him/her out in the past. Does this mean that you have a 20 percent chance of being lucky if you 'pop the question'? Of course not. Each instance of attraction is a unique event, and the past behavior of the object of your desires provides no guide as to how your advances will be received.

A similar observation can be made about each new business investment. The assumption that risk can be used as a proxy for uncertainty when evaluating investments is unrealistic, and a theory that makes such an assumption is quite clearly not better than an alternative one which does not – quite the opposite in fact. This assumption says that the domain of relevance of the theory is a world in which the future is simply subject to chance, and in such a world the possibility of extreme events – like, for example, the Dow Jones Industrial Index falling by 6 percent in one day – can be utterly ruled out since the odds of such a change happening are miniscule. In the Dow Jones case, such a huge movement would only happen once every 2500 years.

Since there is no such world, the domain of applicability of theories which make such an unrealistic assumption is 'nowhere'. Instead, in the real world in which we live, extreme events like those ruled out by the assumption that statistically predictable risk is a proxy for uncertainty occur all the time – the Dow Jones, for example had over 100 "once in two and a half millennia" events last century.

Such assumptions should be made only if they are *heuristic assumptions.* This is the third class of assumptions. A heuristic assumption is one which is known to be false, but which is made as a first step towards a more general theory. For instance, when developing the theory of relativity, Einstein assumed that the distance covered by a person walking from one side to the other of a moving train was equal to the sum of the distance covered by the train, and the width of the carriage. He continued that "We shall see later that this result … cannot be maintained; in other words, the law that we have just written down does not hold in reality. For the time being, however, we shall assume its correctness" (Einstein 1961). When this heuristic assumption was dropped, the theory of relativity was born. The greater realism at the heart of Einstein's theory transformed our understanding of reality, and dramatically expanded the physical and intellectual capabilities of our species. Yet if we accept Friedman's methodology, we would have to argue that Einstein's theory was poorer than Newton's because it was more realistic. In general then, and contrary to Friedman, abandoning a factually false heuristic assumption will normally lead to a better theory – not a worse one.

Theories can therefore be evaluated by their assumptions, if one has an intelligent taxonomy of assumptions. A theory may well draw power from 'unrealistic' assumptions if those assumptions assert, rightly, that some factors are unimportant in determining the phenomena under investigation. But it will be hobbled if those assumptions specify the domain of the theory, and real world phenomena are outside that domain. They may be justified if they are simply heuristic devices used to derive a more general theory – but only if that more general theory is in fact derived. Economists often imply that the unrealistic assumptions in introductory economics are dropped in more advanced theory. In fact, the assumptions used in advanced theory are often even more unrealistic than those presented in introductory economics.

Scientific realism versus instrumentalism

Most scientists reject an instrumental view of science in favor of 'scientific realism' – the belief that scientific theories should not merely predict reality but should, in some sense, represent it. Ironically, this is actually the belief that most economists have about economic theory. Though they profess that the assumptions don't matter, economists continue to use the same small class of assumptions over and over again: rational utility maximizing individuals, profit maximizing firms, and so on. These assumptions are used because economists believe they capture essential elements of reality, and regard any theory that does not use these building blocks as 'unrealistic'. This belief is most clearly seen in the manner in which the 'Bibles' of economics, its academic journals, filter out papers that do not make this core set of assumptions.

The proposition that assumptions don't matter implies that economists would be quite willing to accept a theory that assumed irrational behavior if the model generated results which accorded with observation. It also implies that the development of economic theory would be driven primarily by the desire to produce theories that provide a closer fit to observed data. Both these implications are strongly at variance with reality. It is almost impossible to have an article accepted into a neoclassical academic journal unless it has the full panoply of neoclassical assumptions including rationality (as neoclassical economics defines it!), equilibrium, risk as a proxy for uncertainty, etc. Contrary to Friedman's dictum, little else matters apart from preserving the set of assumptions that defines economic orthodoxy.

I had recent personal experience of this when I submitted papers (based on the argument I developed in *Debunking Economics*) showing that the theory of perfect competition was logically false. The basis of the fallacy, as I explained in the chapter called 'Size Does Matter', was that it was logically impossible to derive horizontal demand curves for individual firms from a downward-sloping demand curve for the entire market.

Much to my amazement, I found that this point had also been made by the arch-conservative neoclassical economics George Stigler in 1957. Stigler showed that the slope of the demand curve facing an individual competitive firm was exactly the same as the market demand curve, using one of the fundamental rules of mathematics, the 'Chain Rule'. ✓

The Chain Rule lets you break a single process – in this case, how the price that a competitive firm sells its output at changes as it changes its output – into two steps: how much market price changes as the market quantity changes, times how much the individual firm's change in output changes market output. Economic theory assumes that the overall process has a value of zero: that the price a single firm gets for its output is unaffected by the amount that firm produces (the so-called 'price-taker' assumption).

But neoclassical economics also assumes (1) that market price falls as the quantity supplied to the market rises, so that the first step in the chain is a non-zero, negative number ('the market demand curve slopes downwards', as textbooks put it), and (2) that competitive firms are "atomistic", that is, other firms in the industry either ignore or don't know what other firms are doing. This last assumption means that, if a single firm increases its output by (say) 100 units, then market output will also rise by 100 units. The second step in the chain is therefore equal to 1 – the change in market output divided by change in the output of a single firm equals 1.

A negative number – the slope of the market demand curve – times 1 is a negative number, not zero: yet that's what neoclassical textbooks say is the slope of the firm's demand curve.

My critique went much further than that (see Keen 2004; Keen and Standish 2006), but it was rejected by a referee for the *Journal of Economics Education* simply on the basis that the Chain Rule shouldn't be applied in economics!:

> Stigler's many attempts to save neoclassical theory have always caused more problems than they have solved. His version of the chain rule is contrary to the partial equilibrium method and thus is irrelevant.

This illustrates the lengths to which neoclassical economists are willing to go to defend their treasured assumptions from criticism, and I am sure other non-orthodox economists could add hundreds of similar examples.

Not only do neoclassical economists defend their assumptions even at the cost of contradicting mathematical logic, the manner in which they have developed their theory over time has been propelled by the desire to make it conform more closely to these preferred assumptions. Macroeconomics, when it first began, bore little resemblance to microeconomics, but today it is effectively a branch of microeconomics. A major factor behind this was the belief that, regardless of its predictive validity, macroeconomics was unsound *because its assumptions did not accord with those of microeconomics*. It was therefore extensively revised to make it more consistent with microeconomic assumptions. Assumptions drove the 'development' of macroeconomic theory.

Assumptions matter in a more profound sense because assumptions can be logically incoherent (Keen 2001: ch. 7). A theory that contains logically inconsistent assumptions will be a bad theory; and economics is replete with logical inconsistencies.

This is a science?

The behavior of economists hardly fits the stereotype of scientists as dispassionate seekers of truth. But their behavior does fit modern, sociological theories of how scientists behave. These theories argue that each 'science' is both a society and an intellectual discipline. Scholars share a perspective on what defines their discipline, and what constitutes scientific behavior. This shared mind set includes a 'hard core' of beliefs that cannot be challenged, a 'protective belt' of ancillary beliefs that are somewhat malleable and whose function is to protect the hard core from attack, a set of analytic techniques, and as yet unsolved problems to which these techniques should be applied.

The scholars expect that their techniques will be able to solve the outstanding problems, thus increasing the explanatory power of their science. If they fail, the first response is to adjust the protective belt. Only when the problem proves both intractable and crucial is there any possibility that core beliefs will be abandoned, leading to the formation of a new school of thought – or the ascendancy of an existing rival school. While a school of thought is expanding what it can explain then it is said to be a 'progressive' scientific research program that manifests a 'positive heuristic'. The opposite position is to be 'degenerative' with a 'negative heuristic'.

It is possible for more than one such collection of scholars to exist in a science at any one time, so that it makes sense to speak of schools of thought. Each will compete with the others, emphasizing their weaknesses and its own strengths.

Clearly this sociological description of a science fits the historical record of economics; but even at this level, economics can be distinguished from true sciences – since if economics were as fully a science as, for example, astronomy, eventually its litany of failures would lead to at least a general acknowledgement of crisis. ?

The incredible inertness of economics

What makes economics different from and inferior to other sciences is the irrational tenacity with which it holds to its core beliefs in the face of either contrary factual evidence, or theoretical critiques that establish fundamental inconsistencies in its intellectual apparatus. The discovery, for example, that firms believe they experience constant or falling marginal costs, and generally set prices by placing a mark-up on average cost, led not to the abandonment of the conventional economic theory of how markets set prices. It led instead to a welter of academic papers arguing that in a competitive market, the effect of mark-up pricing was the same as if firms did consciously equate marginal cost to marginal revenue. As a result, students in the twentyfirst century are receiving much the same instruction about how firms set prices as did their counterparts at the end of the nineteenth century.

Physical sciences hold onto their core beliefs with some tenacity, but nowhere near this much. As a result, revolutions in physical sciences – where one dominant paradigm is replaced by another – occur much more frequently than they do in economics. Often, these revolutions outpace the popular understanding of a science. Think of the many revolutions in our understanding of the physical world that occurred in the twentieth century. Any scientist from the nineteenth century would be bewildered by what is commonplace today.

Economics, in contrast, has had only one acknowledged revolutionary episode in the last century – the Keynesian revolution during the 1930s. Yet, at the start of the twentyfirst century, the dominant school of thought in economics retains almost nothing from that revolution, and in fact appears as a direct descendant of pre-Keynesian neoclassical economics.

Why is economics so resistant to change? Is it because everything economists believed at the end of the nineteenth century was correct? Hardly! Instead, to understand the incredible inertness of economics, we have to consider an essential difference between social sciences in general and the physical sciences, and consider the thorny topic of ideology.

In the nineteenth century, scientists and philosophers of science generally believed that what distinguished the social sciences from the physical sciences was that the latter could undertake experiments to test their theories, whereas the former could not. In the twentieth century, Popper instead argued that the distinction between a science (like physics) and a non-science (like astrology) was not that one could undertake experiments and the other could not, but that one made falsifiable statements, while the other did not. Popper's distinction between science and non-science wasn't completely relevant to the 'experiments versus no experiments' distinction, but it did tend to play down the importance of experimentation in deciding what was and what was not a science.

The history of economics implies that Popper's distinction does not give sufficient attention to whether or not a falsifiable statement can in fact be experimentally falsified. Unless it develops a means to undertake experiments to test rival theories, economics may be unable to break from the grip of ideology. *This misunderstand ideology*

Equilibrium and an invisible ideology

Economics as a discipline arose at a time when English society was in the final stages of removing the controls of the feudal system from its mercantile/capitalist economy. The feudal structure was nothing if not ordered, but this order imposed severe restrictions on the increasingly important classes of merchants and industrialists. Economic theory – then rightly called political economy – provided the merchants with a crucial ideological weapon, the argument that the equilibrium of the market would replace the enforced order of feudalism.

More importantly, whereas the feudal order endowed only the 'well-born' with welfare, the equilibrium of the market would guarantee the best possible welfare for all members of society. The level of individual welfare would reflect the individual's contribution to society: people would enjoy the lifestyle they deserved rather than the lifestyle into which they had been born. If, instead of equilibrium and meritocracy, economists had promised that capitalism would deliver chaos and inequality, then they could have hindered rather than helped the transition to capitalism (though they more likely would have been ignored).

By the middle of the nineteenth century, the transition to capitalism was complete but, rather than the promised equilibrium, nineteenth century capitalism was wracked by cycles and enormous disparities of wealth. A new political challenge arose: that of socialism. Once again, economics rose to the challenge, and once again equilibrium was a central tenet. This time the defence was mounted by what we today call neoclassical economics, since classical economics had been turned into a weapon against capitalism by the last great classical economist, Karl Marx. In contrast to the hand-waving of Adam Smith, the neoclassical economists of the late nineteenth century provided a substantive mathematical analysis of how equilibrium could be achieved by an idealized market economy, and how this equilibrium could be fair to all. The defensive imperative, and the role of equilibrium in that defence, cemented equilibrium's role as a core belief of economic theory.

Today, most economists imperiously dismiss the notion that ideology plays any part in their thinking. Yet ideology innately lurks within 'positive economics' in the form of the core belief in equilibrium. The defence of this core belief is what has made economics so resistant to change, since virtually every challenge to economic theory has called upon it to abandon the concept of equilibrium. It has refused to do so, and thus each challenge has been repulsed, ignored, or belittled.

This is why economists tend to be extreme conservatives on major policy debates, while simultaneously believing that they are non-ideological, and are in fact motivated by knowledge rather than bias.

If you believe that a free market system will naturally tend towards equilibrium – and also that equilibrium embodies the highest possible economic welfare for the highest number – then, *ipso facto*, any system other than a complete free market will produce disequilibrium and reduce economic welfare. You will therefore oppose minimum wage legislation and social security payments – because they will lead to disequilibrium in the labor market. You will oppose price controls – because they will cause disequilibrium in product markets. You will argue for private provision of services – such as education, health, welfare, perhaps even police – because governments, untrammeled by the discipline of supply and demand, will either under or oversupply the market (and charge too much or too little for the service). In fact, the only policies you will support are ones that makes the real world conform more closely to your economic model. Thus you may support anti-monopoly laws – because your theory tells you that monopolies are bad. You may support anti-union laws, because your theory asserts that collective bargaining will distort labor market outcomes. And you will do all this without being ideological!

Most economists genuinely believe that their policy positions are informed by scientific knowledge, rather than by personal bias or religious-style dogma. Economists are truly sincere in their belief that their policy recommendations will make the world a better place for everyone in it – so sincere, in fact, that they often act against their own self-interest. But being non-partisan in self-belief does not mean being non-partisan in reality. The slavish devotion by economists to the concept of equilibrium, which both encapsulates and obscures so many ideological issues, leads economists into politically reactionary and intellectually contradictory positions. Far from assumptions not mattering, they are the core of what is wrong with modern, neoclassical economics.

The 'Great Recession' as the ultimate economic experiment

I concluded *Debunking Economics* with the observation that economics was incapable of reforming itself, and that the only hope for reform lay, paradoxically, in a serious economic crisis that would be caused in large measure by neoclassical economics (Keen 2001: 312). That crisis came about in 2007, with the near collapse of the global financial system – a collapse that was only prevented by bailouts and fiscal stimuli that amounted to the largest government intervention in the economy in history. Economics has since been subject to criticism as never before – with once compliant economic journalists like Anatole Kaletsky (2009) now openly calling for a revolution in economics:

> Was Adam Smith an economist? Was Keynes, Ricardo or Schumpeter? By the standards of today's academic economists, the answer is no. Smith, Ricardo and Keynes produced no mathematical models. Their work lacked the 'analytical rigour' and precise deductive logic demanded by modern economics. And none of them ever produced an econometric forecast (although Keynes and Schumpeter were able mathematicians). If any of these giants of economics applied for a university job today, they would be rejected. As for their written work, it would not have a chance of acceptance in the *Economic Journal* or *American Economic Review*. The editors, if they felt charitable, might advise Smith and Keynes to try a journal of history or sociology.

There are some economists too who admit that maybe, just perhaps, economic theory itself deserved some blame for the financial crisis, and possibly some amendments to theory are in order. But neoclassical economists will not make the realisation that neoclassical economics is fundamentally flawed. Their methodology insulates them from the real world, even as the real world that their theories largely helped construct collapses. Regrettably, change in economics must come from outside the economics profession: new approaches to economics that are based on realism rather than fantasy are far more likely to develop in departments of sociology and history – and engineering and physics – than they are in economics.

This leads me to one more contradiction between what neoclassical economists preach and what they practice. They are the champions of the free market and of competition: everything, it seems, will work better if we just add some more competition. And yet economics departments have acted ruthlessly to preserve their monopoly over the topic of 'economics': opposing any other department that wishes to use the words 'economic' in any of its subject titles, and insisting that any service courses in economics insociology, for example, be taught by its academics.

Let's end this clearly uncompetitive monopoly and add competition to the development of economic ideas as well. Let any academic department, from sociology to physics, put on economics courses based on its own methodology, and not that of neoclassical economics itself. Then we might finally get a science of economics that is worthy of the name.

Steve Keen is Associate Professor of Economics and Finance, University of Western Sydney. This chapter is an updated version of material in *Debunking Economics*, Pluto Press, Sydney, 2001, ch. 7, pp. 148-64. © 2011 Steve Keen.

INSTITUTIONAL ECONOMICS

Institutional economics has immediate appeal to many political economists because it has characteristics opposite to those of neoclassical theory. It seems to offer an escape from the problems described in the last chapter. It does not seek to abstract from historical processes in seeking to construct a formal theory. Its methodology is more inductive, emphasizing the description of institutional detail and the processes of change rather than the specification of equilibrium conditions for idealized market structures. Institutionalist economics is interdisciplinary, not in the imperialist sense of applying an existing economic analysis to social and political phenomena, but in learning and borrowing from other disciplines in the pursuit of a more holistic social science.

This tradition of economic thought had its origins in a number of countries, but was largely based in the twentieth century in the United States. Some of the writings of prominent institutionalists, from Veblen to Galbraith, have been iconoclastic, full of jibes at the expense of their more orthodox colleagues in the profession. Some have involved the painstaking assembly of empirical information, while other institutional economists have pursued detailed studies of the policy process. Yet other contributions involve advocacy – particularly of economic reforms that could make the economy a more effective servant of social needs and aspirations. J.K. Galbraith's article later in this book is a clear example of this approach, based on a view of the state as necessary for steering the economy and redistributing the fruits of economic growth.

Institutional economics is a diverse tradition, not sharply differentiated from some aspects of economic history, economic sociology and industrial relations. This breadth makes for certain tensions in institutional economics. How to sift through the mass of institutional detail is a recurrent question. Institutionalism tends to involve 'plausible story telling.' The persistent need for plausibility is a useful antidote to neoclassical theory, but there is a difficulty in identifying the specific analytical guidelines. This may help to explain why some political economists argue for a blending of institutionalism with Marxist and/or post-Keynesian economics in a pursuit of a more structured analytical framework within which historical and institutional information can be generated.

The following articles show some of the main contours of the institutionalist tradition. The first extract comes from Thorstein Veblen, widely heralded as the founding father of institutional economics. His musings on 'pecuniary emulation' provide a significant forerunner to modern political economic concerns with consumerism. It also illustrates Veblen's sociological approach to economic issues. The next reading by Ha-Joon Chang makes a strong case for preferring an institutional economics approach to neoclassical theory of 'market failure'. Then comes a contribution by George Argyrous, who argues that the notion of cumulative causation provides a unifying theme in institutional economics, allowing economics to borrow, with important modifications, the metaphor of evolution from biology. The final article by the modern institutionalist Geoff Hodgson distinguishes between this 'old' and 'new' institutionalism, and argues that the former has been generally superior in recognizing how individual economic behavior is shaped by social institutions and norms. The importance of habit is given particular attention as a recurrent feature of individual behavior. Hodgson posits a positive future for institutional analysis at the core of modern political economy.

Readers interested in the institutional school should consult past issues of its key journals, the *Journal of Economic Issues*, and the *Journal of Institutional Economics*. These will give readers a sense of the major concerns and methodological approaches of institutionalists when addressing economics problems.

Pecuniary Emulation
Thorstein Veblen

The end of acquisition and accumulation is conventionally held to be the consumption of the goods accumulated – whether it is consumption directly by the owner of the goods or by the household attached to him and for this purpose identified with him in theory. This is at least felt to be the economically legitimate end of acquisition, which alone it is incumbent on the theory to take account of. Such consumption may of course be conceived to serve the consumer's physical wants – his physical comfort – or his so-called higher wants – spiritual, aesthetic, intellectual, or what not; the latter class of wants being served indirectly by an expenditure of goods, after the fashion familiar to all economic readers.

But it is only when taken in a sense far removed from its naive meaning that consumption of goods can be said to afford the incentive from which accumulation invariably proceeds. The motive that lies at the root of ownership is emulation; and the same motive of emulation continues active in the further development of the institution to which it has given rise and in the development of all those features of the social structure which this institution of ownership touches. The possession of wealth confers honor; it is an invidious distinction. Nothing equally cogent can be said for the consumption of goods, nor for any other conceivable incentive to acquisition, and especially not for any incentive to accumulation of wealth.

It is of course not to be overlooked that in a community where nearly all goods are private property the necessity of earning a livelihood is a powerful and ever present incentive for the poorer members of the community. The need of subsistence and of an increase of physical comfort may for a time be the dominant motive of acquisition for those classes who are habitually employed at manual labor, whose subsistence is on a precarious footing, who possess little and ordinarily accumulate little; but it will appear in the course of the discussion that even in the case of these impecunious classes the predominance of the motive of physical want is not so decided as has sometimes been assumed. On the other hand, so far as regards those members and classes of the community who are chiefly concerned in the accumulation of wealth, the incentive of subsistence or of physical comfort never plays a considerable part. Ownership began and grew into a human institution on grounds unrelated to the subsistence minimum. The dominant incentive was from the outset the invidious distinction attaching to wealth, and, save temporarily and by exception, no other motive has usurped the primacy at any later stage of the development.

Property set out with being booty held as trophies of the successful raid. So long as the group had departed and so long as it still stood in close contact with other hostile groups, the utility of things or persons owned lay chiefly in an invidious comparison between their possessor and the enemy from whom they were taken. The habit of distinguishing between the interests of the individual and those of the group to which he belongs is apparently a later growth. Invidious comparison between the possessor of the honorific booty and his less successful neighbors within the group was no doubt present early as an element of the utility of the things possessed, though this was not at the outset the chief element of their value. The man's prowess was still primarily the group's prowess, and the possessor of the booty felt himself to be primarily the keeper of the honor of his group. This appreciation of exploit from the communal point of view is met with also at later stages of social growth, especially as regards the laurels of war.

But as soon as the custom of individual ownership begins to gain consistency, the point of view taken in making the invidious comparison on which private property rests will begin to change. Indeed, the one change is but the reflex of the other. The initial phase of ownership, the phase of acquisition by naive seizure and conversion, begins to pass into the subsequent stage of an incipient organization of industry on the basis of private property (in slaves); the horde develops into a more or less self-sufficing industrial community; possessions then come to be valued not so much as evidence of successful foray, but rather as evidence of the prepotence of the possessor of these goods over other individuals within the community. The invidious comparison now becomes primarily a comparison of the owner with the other members of the group. Property is still of the nature of trophy, but, with the cultural advance, it becomes more and more a trophy of successes scored in the game of ownership carried on between the members of the group under the quasi-peaceable methods of nomadic life.

Gradually, as industrial activity further displaced predatory activity in the community's everyday life and in men's habits of thought, accumulated property more and more replaces trophies of predatory exploit as the conventional exponent of prepotence and success. With the growth of settled industry, therefore, the possession of wealth gains in relative importance and effectiveness as a customary basis of repute and esteem. Not that esteem ceases to be awarded on the basis of other, more direct evidence of prowess; not that successful predatory aggression or warlike exploit ceases to call out the approval and admiration of the crowd, or to stir the envy of the less successful competitors; but the opportunities for gaining distinction by means of this direct manifestation of superior force grow less available both in scope and frequency. At the same time opportunities for industrial aggression, and for the accumulation of property, increase in scope and availability. And it is even more to the point that property now becomes the most easily recognized evidence of a reputable degree of success as distinguished from heroic or signal achievement. It therefore becomes the conventional basis of esteem. Its possession in some amount becomes necessary in order to any reputable standing in the community. It becomes indispensable to accumulate, to acquire property, in order to retain one's good name. When accumulated goods have in this way once become the accepted badge of efficiency, the possession of wealth presently assumes the character of an independent and definitive basis of esteem. The possession of goods, whether acquired aggressively by one's own exertion or passively by transmission through inheritance from others, becomes a conventional basis of reputability. The possession of wealth, which was at the outset valued simply as an evidence of efficiency, becomes, in popular apprehension, itself a meritorious act. Wealth is now itself intrinsically honorable and confers honor on its possessor ...

In the nature of the case, the desire for wealth can scarcely be satiated in any individual instance, and evidently a satiation of the average or general desire for wealth is out of the question. However widely, or equally, or 'fairly', it may be distributed, no general increase of the community's wealth can make any approach to satiating this need, the ground of which is the desire of every one to excel every one else in the accumulation of goods. If, as is sometimes assumed, the incentive to accumulation were the want of subsistence or of physical comfort, then the aggregate economic wants of a community might conceivably be satisfied at some point in the advance of industrial efficiency; but since the struggle is substantially a race for reputability on the basis of an invidious comparison, no approach to a definitive attainment is possible.

What has just been said must not be taken to mean that there are no other incentives to acquisition and accumulation than this desire to excel in pecuniary standing and so gain the esteem and envy of one's fellow-men. The desire for added comfort and security from want is present as a motive at every stage of the process of accumulation in a modern industrial community; although the standard of sufficiency in these respects is in turn greatly affected by the habit of pecuniary emulation. To a great extent this emulation shapes the methods and selects the objects of expenditure for personal comfort and decent livelihood.

Thorstein Veblen was a US political economist and pioneer of the institutional tradition of political economy. This chapter is abridged from *The Theory of the Leisure Class*, Macmillan, New York, 1899, ch. 2.

From 'Market Failure' to Institutions
Ha-Joon Chang

The term, 'market failure', refers to a situation when the market does not work as is expected of the ideal market. But what is the ideal market supposed to do? In the neo-liberal framework, the ideal market is equated with the 'perfectly competitive market' of neoclassical economics. However, the neoclassical theory of the market is only one of many legitimate theories of market and not a particularly good one at that. There are, to borrow Hirschman's phrase, many 'rival views of market society' (Hirschman 1982). And therefore the same market could be seen as failing by some people while others regard it as normally functioning, depending on their respective theories of the market. Let us illustrate this point with some examples.

Many people think that one of the biggest 'failures' of the market is its tendency to generate an unacceptable level of income inequality (whatever the criteria for acceptability may be). However, in neoclassical economics, this is not considered a market failure, because the ideal neoclassical market is not supposed to generate equitable income distribution in the first place. This is not to deny that many well-intentioned neoclassical economists may dislike the income distribution prevailing in, say, Brazil, and may support some 'non-distortionary' lump-sum income transfers to reduce inequality. However, even these economists would argue that an equitable income distribution is not what we should expect from the ideal market and therefore that there is no market failure in Brazil in this sense.

To take another example, a non-competitive market is one of the most obvious examples of a failing market for neoclassical economics, while Marx and Schumpeter would have argued that the existence of non-competitive (in the neoclassical sense) markets is an inevitable, if a secondary, feature of a dynamic economy driven by technological innovation. Thus, a classic example of market failure in the neoclassical framework, namely, the non-competitive market, is regarded as an inevitable feature of a successful dynamic economy from Schumpeter's or Marx's point of view. Or to put it differently, a market which is perfect in the neoclassical sense (e.g. perfect information, no market power) may look like an absolute failure to Schumpeter because perfect information, which is necessary for a perfectly competitive market to exist, will lead to an instantaneous diffusion of new technology and thus to an instantaneous dissipation of monopoly rents, which means that there will be no incentive for entrepreneurs to innovate and generate new knowledge and new wealth.

The point that I have tried to illustrate with the above examples is that, when we talk about market failures, we need to make it clear what we expect from the ideal market, against which only can the failures of the existing markets be defined. Otherwise, the concept of market failure becomes empty, as in the same market where one person sees a perfection another person can see a miserable failure, and vice versa. Only when we make our own theory of the market clear, can we make our notion of market failure clear.

Now, how much does market failure matter, however we define it? The short answer is that it would matter greatly for neoclassical economists, while it may not matter so much for other types of economists, especially institutionalist economists. Neoclassical economics is, at its core, an economics about the market or, more precisely, about the barter exchange economy, with, to borrow Coase's analogy, "lone individuals exchanging nuts and berries on the edge of the forest" (Coase 1992: 718). In this world, even the firm exists only as a production function, and not as an 'institution of production'. Other institutions that make up the modern capitalist economy (e.g. formal producer associations, informal enterprise networks, trade unions) figure basically as 'rigidities' that prevent the proper functioning of markets (see Chang 1995 for a critique of this).

Therefore, for neoclassical economists, for whom the market is essentially the economy, if the market fails, the economy fails. Of course, many neoclassical economists with neoliberal leanings would argue that market failures do not occur often and that, given the possibility of government failure, it is usually better to live with failing markets than to attempt state intervention. However, as far as they acknowledge the existence of market failure, the only alternative they will seriously contemplate (and ultimately reject) is state intervention, because no intermediate institutions or organisations have a place in their scheme. In contrast, for institutionalist economists, who regard the market as only one of the many institutions that make up the capitalist economic system, market failures may not matter as much, because they know that there are many institutions other than markets and state intervention through which we can organise, and have organised, our economic activities. In other words, when most economic interactions in the modern capitalist economy are actually conducted within organisations and not between them through the market (Simon 1991), the fact that some (or even many) markets are 'failing' according to one (that is, the neoclassical) of many possible criteria may not really make much difference for the performance of the economy as a whole.

For example, in many modern industries where there are high incidences of monopoly and oligopoly, markets are failing all the time according to the neoclassical criterion, but these industries are often very successful in more commonsensical terms because they generate high productivity growth and consequently high standards of living. Such an outcome is due to the success of modern business organisations, which enabled the coordination of a most complex division of labour – so, where neoclassical economists see a 'market failure', institutionalist economists may see an 'organisational success' (Lazonick 1991). And if this is indeed the case, state intervention in these markets, especially interventions of the neoclassical anti-trust variety, may not be very necessary, and indeed under certain circumstances may be harmful.

The point that I am trying to make here is not that market failures do not exist or that they do not matter at all – on the contrary, the real world is full of market failures and they do matter. The real point is that the market is only one of the many institutions that make up what many people call the 'market economy', or what I think is better called capitalism. The capitalist system is made up of a range of institutions, including the markets as institutions of exchange, the firms as institutions of production, and the state as the creator and regulator of the institutions governing their relationships (while itself being a political institution), as well as other informal institutions such as social convention. Thus, focusing on the market (and market failure), as neoclassical economics does, really gives us a wrong perspective in the sense that we lose sight of a large chunk of the economic system and concentrate on one, albeit important, part only. This suggests that we badly need an explicitly 'institutionalist' perspective that incorporates non- market, non-state institutions as integral elements, and not simply as add-ons.

In the neoliberal discourse, the market is seen as a 'natural' economic phenomenon that grows spontaneously out of the universal human nature to exploit gains from trading. While, when pressed, most neoliberal economists would admit that the market itself is an economic institution, their analysis of the market itself involves only a minimal, and often implicit, institutional specification. Usually, some simplified notion of private property rights is all that exists in the neoliberal analysis of the market, although some of them may also consider those institutions that are needed for effective exercise and modification of property rights (e.g. the court system, contract law).

In contrast, institutional political economy highlights the institutional complexity of the market. It argues that, in order to understand the workings of the market, we need to understand a wide range of institutions that affect and are affected by it. These institutions are not, of course, simply formal institutions such as law and state regulation. They also include private-sector self-regulatory institutions (e.g. professional associations, producer associations) and informal institutions such as social conventions, although many of these institutions are supported by formal institutions (e.g. decisions by professional associations or social conventions may, when it comes to the crunch, be enforceable through the legal system). Many of these institutions that need to be incorporated into the analysis of the market are often 'invisible' because the rights–obligations structure that underlies them is taken so much for granted that they are seen as inalienable components of naturally ordered free markets. But, no institution, however 'natural' it may look, can be regarded as such, and although in many cases we may choose to accept many institutions as given, in the final analysis we should be willing and able to subject all institutions that support markets to analytical and political scrutiny.

To begin with, all markets are based on institutions that regulate who can participate. For example, laws may stipulate that certain types of individuals (e.g. slaves, foreigners, women) cannot own property. Banking laws or pension laws may limit the range of assets that banks or pension funds can own and therefore limit the range of asset markets that they can enter. Who can participate in which labour market will be affected not only by formal regulation of the state and by private sector agents (e.g. laws regulating professional qualifications, rules of unions and professional associations) but also by social conventions regarding caste, gender and ethnicity. Company laws and industrial licensing rules will decide who can participate in the product market, while stock market listing rules and brokerage regulations determine who can participate in the stock market.

Second, there are institutions which determine the legitimate objects of market exchange (and, by implication, ownership). In most countries, there are laws outlawing transactions in things such as addictive drugs, 'indecent' publications, human organs or firearms (although different societies have different views on what count as, say, addictive drugs or indecent publications). Laws on slavery, child labour and immigration will stipulate, respectively, that human beings, the labour service of children and the labour service of illegal immigrants may not be legitimate objects of exchange.

Third, even when the legitimate participants in and the legitimate objects of exchange have been stipulated, we need institutions that define what exactly each agent's rights and obligations are in which areas. So, for example, zoning laws, environmental regulations (e.g. regarding pollution or noise), and fire regulations define how property rights in land can be exercised (e.g. what kinds of building can be built where). For another example, the laws regarding health, safety and grievance resolution in workplaces define rights and obligations of workers and employers.

Finally, there are numerous institutions that regulate the process of exchange itself. For example, there are rules regarding fraud, breach of contract, default, bankruptcy and other disruptions in the exchange process, which are backed up by the police, the court system and other legal institutions. Consumer laws and liability laws, to take another example, will stipulate when and how buyers of unsatisfactory or faulty products may annul the act of purchase and/or claim compensation from the sellers. Social conventions (e.g. those regarding fairness and probity) or codes of conduct issued by trade associations (e.g. bankers' association) may also influence the way economic agents behave in economic transactions.

To sum up, understanding the market requires consideration of a much wider range of institutions than what is normally discussed by the neoliberals. In addition to property rights and the legal infrastructure that help their exercise and modification, which the neoliberals focus on, we also need to consider all the other formal and informal institutions that define who can hold which kinds of property and participate in which kinds of exchange, what the legitimate objects of exchange are, what acceptable conducts in the exchange process are, and in what terms different types of agent may participate in which markets, and so on. In other words, neoliberal markets are institutionally very under-specified, and we need a fuller institutional specification of markets, if we are to understand them properly.

Emphasising the institutional nature of the market in the above-discussed way also requires that we have to bring politics explicitly into the analysis of the market and to stop pretending that markets need to be, and can be, 'de-politicised'. Markets are in the end political constructs in the sense that they are defined by a range of formal and informal institutions that embody certain rights and obligations, whose legitimacy (and therefore whose contestability) is ultimately determined in the realm of politics. Consequently, institutional political economy adopts a 'political economy' approach not only in the analysis of the state but also in the analysis of the market. It emphasises the fundamentally political nature of the market and applies the political economy logic to the analysis of the market, and not just to the analysis of the state.

Ha-Joon Chang is Reader in the Political Economy of Development at the University of Cambridge. This chapter is abridged from Breaking the Mould: An Institutionalist Political Economy Alternative to the Neoliberal Theory of the Market and the State, *Cambridge Journal of Economics*, vo. 26, no. 5, 2002, pp. 539-59. © 2002 Oxford University Press. Reproduced with permission of the author and Oxford University Press.

Economic Evolution and Cumulative Causation
George Argyrous

The notion of cumulative causation as a methodological principle for guiding economic analysis was first developed by Thorstein Veblen, one of the founders of the institutionalist movement. Essentially, cumulative causation explains the emergence of mass production and how it spreads throughout the system by forces of its own making. Veblen regarded cumulative causation a vehicle for transforming economics into an evolutionary science, as opposed to the static and mechanistic character it had taken under neoclassical economics. Since Veblen's time the concept of cumulative causation has itself evolved, and now offers a distinct methodology to that used by neoclassical economics.

Neoclassical economics is based on three assumptions. These assumptions are that tastes and preferences of consumers are fixed and unlimited; that the resources available to meet these wants are limited; and that the technology available to transform resources into goods that can satisfy some of these unlimited wants is given. The economic problem is thereby a static one: how to satisfy these unlimited wants with the limited resources available. To solve this problem another assumption is added regarding the strategy economic agents follow in making choices between these unlimited wants. This is the assumption of rational maximization. The details of these assumptions can be found in any standard micro textbook; the important point for the following discussion is the teleological nature of neoclassical methodology. Causality runs in one direction from the assumptions to the variables to be explained (prices, wages, profit, employment, etc.). Once we know the initial conditions the final resting point – equilibrium – is predetermined.

Cumulative causation is based on a different methodology. Rather than unidirectional causality from independent to dependent variables, each variable interacts with the others in a mutually dependent way. Thus tastes and preferences, technology, and available resources change during the course of economic growth. Moreover, the principle of rational maximization as an assumption about behavior is substantially qualified, so that the behavioral rules which agents follow (traditions, social norms, blind habit, rules of thumb, etc.) emerge out of the process of adaptation and evolution to a changing environment, and which in turn affect the environment. Rational maximization may emerge as one of these decision rules – it certainly is relevant in an analysis of the imperatives on business to cut costs – but its relevance is contingent on the context.

The division of labor and the specialization of industry

Even though the model of cumulative causation is one in which 'everything depends on everything else', the foundations of the technological system are given central importance in most discussions. All the key figures who have explicitly developed the notion of cumulative causation begin with the effect that the application of fixed capital and the division of labor has on capitalist growth. The shift from craft production to mass production fundamentally altered the way economic growth occurs. The nature of this shift in production technology is discussed in the work of Allyn Young (1928) and Nicholas Kaldor (1966), who drew on the inspiration of Adam Smith. In the *Wealth of Nations* Smith argued that the division of labor is limited by the extent of the market. By this he meant that the application of heavy machinery and the breakdown of the production process into its component parts is limited by the ability to sell the larger output that such technology generates. With a larger market to cater to, economies of scale can be realized through the division of labor, and thereby bring about an increase in productivity and the social surplus. If this surplus is consumed productively it will bring about further expansion of the market, and thereby encourage the further application of heavy machinery and division of labor. The circular character of these induced changes means that in fact the division of labor is limited by the division of labor!

Adam Smith illustrated this process by analyzing the internal restructuring of the famous pin factory. Young and Kaldor took this one step further and argued that the specialization of tasks and the decomposition of the production process into sequential stages causes a vertical splintering of industry: each layer produces an intermediate product which becomes an input to the next stage in the production process. Each 'layer' of firms produces one component of the final commodity, which ultimately comes together in the final assembly stage. Pasinetti (1981) refers to such a network as a "vertically integrated industry", which is a far cry from the craft shop which would turn raw outputs into final product, and along the way make any machinery and equipment under the one roof.

In short, therefore, a number of vertically integrated firms insert themselves between raw materials and the final product – a process which we may call vertical specialization, and which raises productivity through learning-by-doing and dynamic returns to scale. The application of mass production technology progressively brings down unit prices as productivity grows, which causes the market to expand and open up the field for further extension of mass production within that industry.

This process of vertical specialization, if pushed far enough, leads to the establishment of a layer of firms which focuses specifically on the production of capital goods. Of particular importance is the emergence of a machine tool industry which produces equipment such as lathes, grinders, and milling machines. These pieces of equipment, as Marx pointed out, take over the functions that were once performed by skilled artisans, and which are only viable when substantial economies of scale have been reached. Since individual machines can be used to produce thousands of units of final product, the market for the latter has to expand considerably before a market for specialized equipment emerges. They are, in short, the technology upon which mass production is based and are the means by which thousands of units of identical, standardized products are produced. These machines are used to produce final or intermediate products, or indeed to produce more machines.

Rosenberg (1976) has discussed the way in which the formation of a capital goods sector, and a machine tool industry specifically, gives the evolution of capitalism an added mechanism of cumulative change. This is a learning-by-using process, whereby the users of capital goods identify problems and limitations with existing designs of equipment and relate this information back to the equipment producers. This poses a technological puzzle which equipment producers solve by modifying and adapting successive existing designs. This process feeds on itself as each solution tends to create a new problem – the advent of high speed metal alloys increased the speed of many machine tools, but this required major structural changes in the design of the machines to deal with the vibrations caused by the higher speeds. The result is a technological disequilibrium where new, unforeseen problems emerge out of solutions to old ones.

This incremental development, according to Rosenberg, follows a "compulsive sequence" of problems-solutions-new problems, and is given a specific direction by "inducement mechanisms" and "focusing devices" which set this compulsive sequence in train. These factors ensure that the development path is *historically* conditioned. For example, Rosenberg, citing Marx, points out how disputes between capitalists and workers in Manchester in 1825 directly led to the invention of the self-acting mule to allow for greater control of the labor process. Another common source of direction is provided by wars which cause a major disruption to critical supplies. The implication is that historical accidents will not be 'washed-away' by supposedly permanent and systematic forces that direct the economy toward a long run equilibrium: "the mere cessation of interference will not leave the outcome the same as if no interference had taken place" (Veblen 1919: 116). In modern terminology, cumulative causation is *path-dependent*, since the specific sequence of industries that emerge and the specific nature of the technologies they adopt will usually be affected by historically contingent circumstances that have long-lasting effects. The history of the QWERTY keyboard (discussed in an earlier chapter) illustrates this point.

Cumulative causation across industries

The model of cumulative causation has thus far looked at the way in which the mass production of a particular commodity establishes a process of expansion for the layers of firms that are vertically integrated in its production. As this process takes hold in one industry, though, it then sparks the division of labor in industries producing entirely distinct commodities. The mass production of cars, for example, affects, and is affected by, the same process occurring in the production of shoes and washing machines, so that the production of various commodities becomes interconnected. There are three related transfers which release cumulative forces of expansion across industries: transfers of technological knowledge; transfers of organizational knowledge; and transfers of wage income paid in one industry as demand for the product of other industries.

Transfers of technology

Mass production is built on a set of core, and fairly generic, industrial processes, such as grinding, milling, and planing. All manufactured commodities will involve the application of some, if not all, of these activities. The use of a common set of basic industrial processes means that a solution to a technical problem in one industry can be subsequently used in the production of completely different commodities to solve similar production problems. However, the requirements from industry to industry will not be the exactly same, so that some adaptation of technology must take place. Technology, in other words, has a public and a private dimension (Nelson 1993). In so far as machines are designed for a specific production line the technology is appropriated privately by the user of the machine. However, in so far as it is the application of general engineering and design principles it has a public dimension, and which gives it a potentially wider sphere of application.

Rosenberg illustrates this with the example of the stocking lathe for the shaping of gunstocks which was then applied in the production of hat blocks, handles, wheel-spokes, sculptured busts, oars, and shoe lasts. Moreover, as we noted above, an improvement in any one aspect of technology often disrupts other parts of the system so that new problems arise: "single improvements tend to *create* their own future problems, which compel further modification and revision" (Rosenberg 1976: 29). So there is a leapfrogging process whereby problems are generated and solved, and the solutions are diffused into sectors of the economy other than where they originated, creating, in turn, new production problems to solve.

The other key institution involved in the transfer of technology from one industry to another is the modern research and development division of the large corporation. The pre-eminence of production technology under conditions of mass production, the demands on energy production and use, the importance on fundamental scientific advance render R&D of critical significance. Through the desire of the corporation to take advantage of a new development, scientific breakthroughs quickly gain a wide application. The distinction between knowledge as a private and specific application of generic and public knowledge again feeds the cumulative process. There is a private incentive to apply and extend innovations in order to extract windfall profits and recoup the enormous costs involved in R&D, and this incentive is heightened by the fact that the public nature of the underlying technology could allow competitors to appropriate the returns instead (Nelson 1993: 15-17).

Transfers of organizational knowledge

The transfer of mass production technology involves more than just technical know-how. It calls forth an entire system of business organization: the rise of large industrial corporations. The vertical fragmentation of production brought about by the division of labor and economies of scale requires an immense amount of planning and coordination. Unlike the small craft shop where a commodity was made from scratch under the one roof, mass production splinters productive activity across thousands of separate units. Yet each of these units must coordinate with the others, otherwise the final commodity will not materialize: the smallest discrepancy between screw sizes and screw holes in a panel, for example, and the car will literally not come together. The maintenance of strict standards, the coordination of production runs and of delivery schedules, the regulation of stocks and supplies, and the monitoring of quality control become very large managerial problems which require skills of their own that come to reside, as Galbraith (1971) points out, in the large bureaucratic technostructure of the modern corporation.

Chandler (1990; 1992) has traced the historical evolution of the modern industrial corporation and the way it has facilitated the spread of mass production across industries. He argues that when an industry begins to realize economies of scale, firms who are the 'first-movers' into that industry are able to dominate it for years to come, using their accumulated managerial expertise to keep late-comers out. During a critical period in the late 1800s when mass production technology was emerging on a wide scale in the US, these first-mover firms were able to invest in the three key areas of production, distribution, and management, and thereby 'take hold' of the market. Once established within an industry these large corporations then began to realize economies of *scope*. These are the gains that can be made by using the organizational expertise developed in one market to enter into other markets and thereby continue growth and dominance. The managerial skills that form the technostructure have a generic quality which allows them to be applied across a wide variety of activities. Thus individual corporations provided the institutional framework within which mass production spread cumulatively across sectors. They have an incentive to do this because diversification spreads risk so that problems arising in one market do not undermine the whole company.

The transfer of demand

These two transfer processes, that of production technology and of organizational structure, are not sufficient by themselves to explain the cumulative spread of mass production across industries. These systems only become viable if there is a mass market to cater to, so some explanation of the way in which mass markets grow and in turn feed these other transfers is needed. Craft production is geared toward custom-ordering in which products are 'tailor-made' to the needs of individual orders placed in advance of production. Mass production is based on the manufacture of thousands of units of standardized, identical products, which are produced in anticipation of a large homogenous market. The question is how does one type of market eliminate the other?

It is at this point that the economic sphere of life and broader social processes are most closely tied. The conception of growth as a holistic process in which mutually reinforcing feedbacks between the economic sphere and cultural and political institutions bring about cumulative causation has been most emphatically argued by Gunnar Myrdal (1974: 735-6). According to Myrdal, the problem is not dissected into an economic component and a social component, but rather treated as an indivisible whole.

Central to the explanation of the rise of mass markets is the change that occurs to the character of the household. Households have always had to balance the amount of labor available to them to devote to domestic production, and the amount to be sold in return for paid income. In the pre-industrial era, most families satisfied the bulk of their consumption needs within the home, using any income generated outside domestic production to buy raw materials such as cloth and seed and applying domestic labor to transform them into consumable items. However, this basis for household organization gives way to households in which most labor power is sold for wages, and these wages are used to purchase commercially produced final and intermediate goods. With the formation of an industrial working class, less labor is devoted to domestic production and households become increasingly reliant on produced commodities to satisfy their consumption needs. The household is transformed from being a production unit to a consumption unit and a supplier of wage labor.

How does this actually happen? As labor is drawn in from the countryside when an industry expands, these workers will spend their wage income purchasing goods that they no longer have time to produce in the home, thereby creating markets for other industries. As markets for these other industries expand, the division of labor in these industries takes off to realize economies of scale, and labor drawn into these industries will further expand the market for other wage goods.

This change in the structure and function of the household *vis-a-vis* the market works itself out slowly. Households do not instantly change from being large extended families living in small towns to urban, nuclear families, nor are all production activities transferred to the market *al.* the same time. The stable consumption pattern exhibited by the Engel Curve suggests that some goods are transferred to the market relatively early as income expands, with others entering the bundle of wage goods as demand expands further. The demand for each commodity follows an S-shaped path of growth: the market expands rapidly in initial phases but eventually reaches saturation. The market is then geared to replacement purchases. But as long as incomes are growing, the decline in one set of markets will be offset by an increase in others. Slowly more commodities produced under industrial processes enter into the consumption patterns of households, replacing goods produced within the household itself. This approach to consumption provides a sociological basis for the explanation of consumer demand that takes into account learning processes and emulation between groups of consumers as their incomes increase (rather than following the neoclassical notion of rational choice at a *given* income level) (Pasinetti 1981: 69). An example of such a sociological theory of consumption was provided by James Duesenberry (1967) and his 'relative income hypothesis' which itself built on the work of Veblen.

Picturing the development of the economy in this way as a holistic process of qualitative change affects the method of economic analysis. Myrdal, for example, originally thought that the patterns of causal relations that generate cumulative causation could be "given in the form of an interconnected series of quantitative equations" and this would provide a "truly scientific solution" (1944: 1069) to the problem. However, he later substantially qualified the argument for a quantitative approach (1968: 1866-70), and finally rejected such a position altogether, arguing that the feedback mechanisms were essentially qualitative in character, and therefore not reducible to a set of equations. The "coefficients of interrelation among the various conditions in circular causation are ordinarily not known with quantitative precision" (1978: 774). Instead, detailed historical analysis of the particularity and peculiarities of individual industries and countries is needed. Certain aspects of this process might be amenable to quantitative measurement and formal modelling (especially drawing on evolutionary game theory, time series analysis, and systems theory), but the whole story can never be told this way. Armchair theorizing won't go very far: the methods of anthropologists, sociologists and economic historians (e.g. fieldwork and historical case studies) become relevant to economists as well.

The arrangement of industries around a core sector of capital goods producers presented here may be misleading in one important respect. It may imply that any given industry is as important as any other. However, this is not the case. The three factors we noted which connect change in one industry with change in another, also allow us to construct a hierarchy of industries according to their capacity to spur the cumulative process. The most important for twentieth century development is clearly the automobile. The technical complexity and the ensuing technical puzzles involved in mass producing cars generated many of the major improvements in equipment and machinery, which then fed into other sectors; the firms which dominated the auto industry such as GM and Ford were able to use their organizational strength to move into other sectors such as aeroplane manufacture; and no other single product has so affected the patterns of social organization. The facility that the automobile has given to the process of urbanization and the unification of previously disparate markets has caused the demand for innumerable other products to expand.

Limits to cumulative causation

This discussion of cumulative causation may give the impression that once set in motion, the growth process spirals upward with a vigorous energy of its own making. However, such an impression is misleading because there are factors which retard the process and which in fact can turn a virtuous cycle of growth into a vicious cycle of decline. The first limitation arises from the mutual dependence of variables on each other, which is the very basis of cumulative causation. An example of this arose in the development of the aircraft industry (Holley 1964: 27):

> Low-priced airplanes waited upon the introduction of production techniques in the industry, but high-volume production could be justified only by a mass market, which waited upon low-priced airplanes. Until some escape from this circle could be found, true mass production in the aircraft industry would remain out of reach.

Where everything, in a sense, depends on everything else, there may be system-wide inertia and overall stagnation that may be difficult to overcome on a sectoral basis. Thus some system-wide form of regulation is required, a function usually undertaken by the state. The state can operate as a circuit breaker if such a problem arises. By coordinating the integration of the various components, and by initiating growth in key sectors which trigger expansion elsewhere the state can set a virtuous cycle in motion.

Even if some exogenous nudge has been given to the system so that it begins to cumulate under forces of its own making, such cumulation cannot occur at too rapid a pace. The second force of inertia is due to the *sequential* nature of the causal relations, such that each variable in the sequence can only change within the limits set by the previous changes in the other variables. For example, new technology will raise productivity and lower the real price of the commodity produced. However, it may take time for consumers to incorporate this new commodity into their consumption patterns. It is like trying to walk with shoe laces tied together: the left foot can only step so far in front of the right, and the position of the right foot is itself determined by previous movements of the left. Over time great distances can be travelled, but obviously each foot cannot go too fast without causing the whole body to topple over. Cumulative causation is even more complicated because there are many feet tied together in all sorts of directions.

A particularly important step in this causal sequence, which can limit overall expansion, is the capacity of the machine tool sector. Its pivotal role within the input-output matrix is discussed above, and as Lowe argues this "strategic position" (1976: 30) imposes a constraint on the entire economy:

> One need only to consider an increase in the aggregate demand for coal ... Then we see at once that the critical bottleneck 'in the hierarchy of production' arises in the machine tool stage and that only after capacity has been increased there, can the output of ore, steel, extractive machinery and, finally, coal be increased (1976: 34, n.6).

The bottleneck is compounded though by the fact that capacity in the machine tool industry is directly limited by its own capacity. This is because machine tools are key elements in their own production. The expansion of capacity in other industries necessitates a further expansion in the production of tools and equipment, but this then requires an expansion of tools and equipment!

The third force of inertia relates to the fact that cumulative causation is inherently a process of social and institutional change and such changes do not occur quickly. Institutions and social practices operate on the basis of customs, traditions, and habits which are deeply ingrained and only slowly abandoned and replaced by others. For example, the transfer of productive activity from the household to the family in any given country takes over a century to complete. Households have to learn knew patterns of behavior and new forms of social interaction, largely through emulation; corporations have to adjust their routines and structures (Nelson and Winter 1982). In other words, the involvement of social institutions weakens the coefficients of interrelations, giving the system a level of stability that prevents cumulative growth or decline from accelerating too rapidly: "But certainly the main resistance to change in the social system stems from attitudes and institutions. They are part of an inherited culture and are not easily or rapidly moved in either direction" (Myrdal 1968: 873).

The fourth force of inertia relates to the discrepancy that can arise between individual actions and their collective social outcome. People act with certain objectives in mind following various rules of behavior, but in a social network these objectives may not be realized, so that the goal or the means to attain them need to be adjusted. An unintended outcome at the social level will cause the original basis for decision-making to change. This process of adjustment to environmental changes brought about by past actions is the very driving force of cumulative causation. It is why learning features so prominently in the model: there are no absolute rules to guide behavior at all times, and given the contingent, historical and limited nature of information available, consumers and producers adapt through learning.

In other instances, however, this discrepancy can also lead to stagnation. Of particular importance is the fact that each firm has an incentive to innovate by cost-cutting, especially by replacing workers with machines. For each firm, it essential that they try to raise productivity and to lower costs, but the aggregate effect of this on effective demand is to undermine markets which are the precondition for such innovation. Thus mass production has an in-built tendency to stagnation that can overwhelm the forces that are also present and that facilitate growth and expansion.

A fifth limitation on the cumulative growth process is the finite nature of domestic markets. The satiation of domestic markets for consumer goods may cause the cumulative process to lose steam. Therefore, it is imperative that foreign markets be tapped if growth is to continue, once production for domestic markets has reached a saturation level (Kaldor 1966). This may be a fairly natural progression if the economies of scale realized in meeting home markets are sufficient to allow easy penetration of overseas markets. However, this will not always be the case, so that domestic markets are saturated before sufficient progress has occurred to make goods internationally competitive.

Moreover, other countries will be building up production for home markets as a basis for exporting, so that not all countries can pursue this strategy at once: there are necessarily winners and losers. The determination of winners and losers is not based on any inherent comparative advantage, but rather on the ability of any given economy to facilitate the forces which generate improvements in production. Advantages are created as a result of historical development rather than endowed by nature. And small advantages that one nation has over another at an early phase of development may accumulate over time so that it becomes a very wide discrepancy later, with one country on a virtuous cycle of expansion and the other on a vicious cycle of decline. A similar approach can be taken to explain differences between regions within a country in terms of differential growth rates. Growth rates do not converge across countries or regions, but rather become more pronounced.

A final limitation on the endogenous process of expansion has been discussed in detail by Setterfield (1997; 2001). Setterfield argues that the very process that drives the cumulative process of growth creates, as we discussed above, a high-degree of interrelatedness among the parts of the economics system. But this interrelatedness can 'lock-in' the system to a technology that becomes outdated and uncompetitive with other systems not yet locked-in in this way. The mature system cannot 'lump tracks' easily and adopt fundamentally new technologies, precisely because it is a system and needs to adapt as a *system* rather than as individual parts. This is similar to the phenomenon Veblen described as the 'penalty of being first'. This clearly raises the necessity for such system transformations to be coordinated, probably by the state, so that once advanced economies do not find themselves becoming industrial backwaters.

Conclusion

The model of cumulative causation presented here provides a much greater scope for the government to alter the trajectory of industrial development in a positive way than in the neoclassical approach. A country is not restricted by its natural endowment of resources and comparative advantage – it has greater discretion to follow alternative development paths. Comparative advantage (as discussed by West in his chapter below) is a static concept relating to the relative status of countries at any given point in time. This state of affairs, though, is the outcome of an historical process that can take alternative paths. However, to paraphrase Marx, while nations do make their own history, they are not free to do this at will. The possibilities that are open for policy are limited at any point in time by the historically given conditions in which a nation finds itself. The conception of the economy as a set of mutually dependent institutions means that any aspect of it can only be altered within the limits set by other aspects. It is fundamentally a story of *incremental change*.

George Argyrous is Senior Lecturer, University of New South Wales. Economic Evolution and Cumulative Causation © 2011 George Argyrous.

Institutional Economics: Old and New
Geoffrey M. Hodgson

Institutional economics is now a major sub-discipline, with important applications to studies of business, developing economies, transitional economies, property rights and much else. Prominent names in modern institutional economics include the Nobel Laureates Ronald Coase, Douglass North, Elinor Ostrom and Oliver Williamson. Contemporary 'new institutional economics' was preceded in America in the interwar period by another tradition of 'institutional economics', inspired by Thorstein Veblen, Wesley C. Mitchell, John R. Commons and others. For a time this was pervasive in leading American universities and research institutes (Rutherford 2001, Hodgson 2004). Even after the Second World War, the 'old' institutionalism retained some influence. Simon Kuznets and Gunnar Myrdal declared an affinity with this tradition of institutionalism and won Nobel Prizes in 1971 and 1974 respectively.

This essay discusses some key characteristics of both these 'old' and 'new' institutional economic traditions and suggests the most promising approach for the present century.

A central theme of the 'old' institutional economics

What is the essence of the 'old' or original institutional economics? A common theme pervades institutionalism, from the writings of Veblen in the 1890s to those of John Kenneth Galbraith in more recent decades – a notion that the individual is not given, but can be reconstituted by institutions. For instance, Veblen (1909: 629) wrote:

> The wants and desires, the end and aim, the ways and the means, the amplitude and drift of the individual's conduct are functions of an institutional variable that is of a highly complex and wholly unstable character.

Similarly, Clarence Ayres (1944: 84) explained:

> 'wants' are not primary. They are not inborn physical mechanisms ... They are social habits. For every individual their point of origin is in the mores of his community; and even these traditions have a natural history and are subject to modification in the general process of social change.

The idea that individual tastes are not given but are shaped by institutional circumstances and by particular influences, such as advertising, is also a major theme in the writings of Galbraith. For instance, Galbraith (1969: 152) insisted that individual "wants can be synthesized by advertising, catalysed by salesmanship, and shaped by the discreet manipulations of the persuaders." The theme persists throughout his writings and no author has brought these ideas to the attention of the modern reader more clearly and resolutely than Galbraith. His analysis puts particular emphasis on the effects of advertising on individual wants. Institutionalists more generally recognize the potential influence of institutions on individual habits, conceptions and preferences.

Such ideas permeate the 'old' institutionalism as a whole, distinguishing it from both mainstream economics and most of the 'new institutional economics'. It does not assume a given individual, with given purposes or preference functions. Instead the old institutionalism holds to the idea of interactive and partially malleable agents, mutually entwined in a web of partially durable and self-reinforcing institutions. Although it is not the only difference, no other criterion demarcates as clearly the old institutional economics from new institutional and mainstream economics (Hodgson 1988, 1998, 2004).

The assumption of malleable preferences is often subject to the criticism that it leads to some kind of structural or cultural determinism, or to methodological collectivism. The individual, it is said, is made a puppet of social or cultural circumstances. When Ayres (1961: 175) wrote that "there is no such thing as an individual" he was giving succour to such ideas (Rutherford 1994: 40–1, Hodgson 2004: 347-8). The danger is to see social order as *exclusively* a 'top down' process in which individuals are formed and cajoled by institutions, with a neglect of individual autonomy, variation and agency, and no clear explanation of how this occurs.

However, in the writings of Veblen and Commons there is both upward and downward causation; individuals create and change institutions, just as institutions mould and constrain individuals (Hodgson 2004). This is especially clear in the writings of Veblen (1909: 629-36). The 'old' institutionalism is not necessarily confined to the 'top down' cultural and institutional determinism or methodological collectivism with which it is sometimes associated.

A merit of the institutionalist idea that institutions shape individual behaviour is that it admits an enhanced concept of power into economic analysis. Power is exercised not only by forceful coercion. For Steven Lukes (1974) the overemphasis on the coercive aspect of power ignores the way that it is often exercised more subtly – and often without overt conflict. He points out that supreme power is exercised by orchestrating the thoughts and desires of others. These considerations are almost entirely absent from mainstream economics.

Preference malleability is also important in regard to learning, which typically takes place through and within social structures. Neoclassical economics has difficulty accommodating a full notion of learning because the very idea of 'rational learning' is problematic. It also assumes that our preference function – presumably acquired in the womb – is already fully primed to evaluate options about which we are not yet aware and may not have emerged. However, instead of the mere input of 'facts' to given individuals, learning in practice is a developmental and reconstitutive process. Learning involves adaptation to changing circumstances, and such adaptations mean the reconstitution of the individuals involved. Furthermore, institutions and cultures play a vital role in establishing the concepts and norms of the learning process (Hodgson 1988, 2003, 2004).

In sum, the single most important characteristic of the original institutionalism is the idea that the individual is socially and institutionally constituted. 'Old' institutional economists from Veblen to Galbraith embrace the notion that the individual is moulded by cultural or institutional circumstances. Accordingly, conceptions of social power and learning are placed at the centre of economic analysis. This means that institutionalism is more able to address questions of structural change and long-term economic development, including the problems of less-developed economies and the transformation processes in the former Soviet Bloc countries. On the other hand, the analysis becomes much more complicated and less open to formal modelling. In normative terms, the individual is no longer taken as the best judge of his or her welfare. An alternative type of welfare analysis is required, including those addressing the difficult question of the discernment and evaluation of human needs (Doyal and Gough 1991).

The 'new' institutionalist project and beyond

The 'new institutional economics' has a different focus – to explain the existence of political, legal, or social, institutions by reference to a model of given, individual behaviour, tracing out its consequences in terms of human interactions. The explanatory movement is from individuals to institutions, taking individuals as primary and given.

A focus on individuals as ultimate elements in the explanation is clearly evident, for example, in North's (1981) theory of the development of capitalism, Coase's (1937) and Williamson's (1975; 1985) transaction cost analysis of the firm, and Schotter's (1981) game-theoretic analysis of institutions. Coase and Williamson are pioneers of the transaction cost theory of the firm, but while their analyses yield important results, their comparisons of different institutional structures do not consider the possibility that individual preferences or capabilities way be moulded or facilitated by different institutional circumstances (Hodgson and Knudsen 2007). Similarly, Schotter's pioneering analysis is valuable in showing how institutions facilitate interaction, but does not consider how individuals may be reconstituted through these interactions. In all these cases, the proposal is to start with given individuals and their interactions, and from that starting point to move on to explain institutions.

In particular, Williamson's transaction cost theory of the firm takes its original state of nature as a somehow de-institutionalised market. He writes that 'in the beginning there were markets' (Williamson 1975: 20; 1985: 143). But the market itself is an institution that took time to create. It involves social norms and customs, instituted exchange relations, and – sometimes consciously organized – information networks that also have to be explained (Hodgson 1988, 1998, 2008; McMillan 2002; Mirowski 2007). Markets are not an institution-free beginning.

There are several reasons why the starting point of a given individual is generally misconceived. Choosing requires a conceptual framework to make sense of the world. The reception of information by individuals requires cognitive norms and frames to process and make sense of that information. Further, our interaction with others requires the use of language. Language itself is an institution (Searle 1995; Hodgson 2006). We cannot understand the world without concepts and we cannot communicate without some form of language. As the 'old' institutionalists argue, the transmission of information from institution to individual is impossible without a coextensive process of *enculturation*, in which the individual learns the meaning and value of the sense-data that is communicated. The transmission of information between agents always and necessarily involves such a process of enculturation.

Institutions both constrain and influence individuals. Accordingly, if there are institutional influences on individuals and their goals, then these are worthy of explanation. In turn, the explanation of those may be in terms of other purposeful individuals. But where should the analysis stop? The purposes of an individual could be partly explained by relevant institutions, culture and so on. These, in their turn, would be partly explained in terms of other individuals. But these individual purposes and actions could then be partly explained by cultural and institutional factors, and so on, indefinitely. We are involved in an apparently infinite regress, similar to the puzzle 'which came first, the chicken or the egg?'

All theories must first build from elements which are taken as given. However, the particular problem of infinite regress identified here undermines any 'new institutionalist' claim that the explanation of the emergence of institutions can start from some kind of institution-free ensemble of (rational) individuals in which there is supposedly no rule or institution to be explained. At the very minimum, new institutionalist stories of the development of institutions depend upon interpersonal communication of information. And the communication of information itself requires shared conventions, rules, routines and norms. These, in turn, have to be explained. Consequently, the new institutionalist project to explain the emergence of institutions on the basis of given individuals runs into difficulties, particularly with regard to the conceptualization of the initial state from which institutions are supposed to emerge.

This does not mean that new institutionalist research is without value, but it suggests that the starting point of explanations cannot be institution-free: the main project has to be reformulated as just a part of a wider theoretical analysis of institutions. The reformulated project would stress the evolution of institutions, in part from other institutions, rather than from a hypothetical, institution-free 'state of nature'. What is required is a theory of process, development and learning.

More recently some 'new' institutionalists have taken some of these points on board. Douglass

North has insisted on the general importance of understanding the context and processes of cognition. In his Nobel lecture, he cautioned on the limits of the rational-choice framework, emphasising that 'History demonstrates that ideas, ideologies, myths, dogmas and prejudices matter; and an understanding of the way they evolve is necessary for further progress in developing a framework to understand societal change. ... Belief structures get transformed into societal and economic structures by institutions' (North 1994: 362-3). This recognition of social influences on individual cognition places North's more recent writing very close to the old institutionalist tradition (Syll 1992; Groenewegen et al. 1995; Rutherford 1995).

Other modern institutionalists have abandoned the idea of starting from given individuals alone. For example, Knight (1992) criticizes much of the new institutionalist literature for neglecting the importance of distributional and power considerations in the emergence and development of institutions. Ostrom (1990, 2000, 2005) emphasises the role of culture and norms in establishing and moulding both perceptions and interactions, and Aoki (2001) identifies the problem of infinite explanatory regress in much of the former literature and develops a novel approach. He not only takes individuals as given, but also a historically bestowed set of institutions, and then, using game theory, explores the evolution of further institutions.

Taken together, these recent developments suggest that there is some convergence between elements of the 'new' institutional economics and ideas that can trace their origin to the original institutionalism. The boundaries between the 'old' and the 'new' institutionalism have become less distinct (Dequech 2002).

Institutionalism in the future

A reformulated institutionalist project would stress the evolution of institutions, in part from other institutions, rather than from a hypothetical, institution-free 'state of nature'. Once we take a step in the direction of a more open-ended evolutionary approach, another question is raised. If in principle every component in the system can evolve, then so too can individual preferences. Of course, most economists recognise that preferences are malleable in the real world. But they have often taken the assumption of fixed preferences as a reasonable, simplifying assumption. In contrast, the possibility is raised here that some malleability of preferences may be necessary to explain fully the evolution and stability of institutions. Institutions involve rules, constraints, practices and ideas that can – through psychological and social mechanisms that need to be revealed – sometimes mould individual purposes and preferences in some way. This preference malleability could improve the possibility and stability of an emergent institution and overcome difficulties in some cases where institutions fail to emerge.

Such intuitions can be found in the writings of the 'old' institutionalism. But what is lacking in much of this literature is a clear exposition of the causal processes involved. It is one thing to claim that institutions affect individuals in a process of downward causation. It is another to explain in detail the causes and effects. One of the most satisfactory early explanations of the processes is in the writings of Veblen (1899: 190), who wrote "The situation of today shapes the institutions of tomorrow through a selective, coercive process, by acting upon men's habitual view of things".

From this viewpoint, inspired by pragmatist philosophy and habit-instinct psychology, the key element in this process is *habit*. Habits themselves are formed through repetition of action or thought. They are influenced by prior activity and have durable, self-sustaining qualities. However, contrary to some popular formulations, habit does not mean behavior. It is a *propensity* to behave in particular ways in a particular class of situations (Camic 1986; Murphy 1994; Ouellette and Wood 1998; Wood et al. 2002). Crucially, we may have habits that lie unused for a long time. A habit may exist even if it is not manifest in behaviour. Habits are submerged repertoires of potential behavior; and these habits can be triggered by an appropriate stimulus or context.

In Veblenian institutional economics, cognition and habit have a prior and central place in the story. For Veblen (1909: 628) "institutions are an outgrowth of habit". Knowledge and learning are stressed. But the crucial difference is the insistence that the perception of information is not possible without prior habits of thought to endow it with meaning. Without such habits, agents cannot perceive or make use of the data received by their senses. Habits thus have a crucial cognitive role. As Veblen (1914: 53) put it, "All facts of observation are necessarily seen in the light of the observer's habits of thought". Furthermore, acquired habits and conceptual frameworks are seen to reflect culturally-based social norms and rules.

The Veblenian concept of habit points to a crucial psychological mechanism by which institutions may affect individuals. Insofar as individuals are constrained or motivated to follow particular institutional norms or rules, then they tend to strengthen habits that are consistent with this behaviour. They may then rationalise these outcomes in terms of preference or choice (Hodgson 2003, 2010; Hodgson and Knudsen 2004). Conscious preferences are the outcome of habits, rather than the other way round.

Our habits help to make up our preferences and dispositions. When new habits are acquired or existing habits change, then our preferences alter. John Dewey (1922: 40) thus wrote of "the cumulative effect of insensible modifications worked by a particular habit in the body of preferences". Crucially, institutional changes and constraints can cause changes in habits of thought and behaviour. Institutions constrain our behavior and develop our habits in specific ways. What does happen is that the framing, shifting and constraining capacities of social institutions give rise to new perceptions and dispositions within individuals. Once habits become established they become a potential basis for new intentions or beliefs. As a result, shared habits are the constitutive material of institutions, providing them with enhanced durability, power and normative authority.

A pressing issue for future research is the extent to which these mechanisms of habituation play a role in different cases of institutional evolution. What is being proposed here is; first, the possibility of a viable causal mechanism by which institutions can lead to changes in individual purposes and preferences; second, the possibility that such mechanisms may lead to some degree of conformity; and third, the possibility that such conformism may help to strengthen and sustain the institution in question.

Arguably the Veblenian stream within the original institutional economics offers the most viable theoretical core for institutionalism in the twenty-first century (Hodgson 2004). This does not mean that other streams of institutionalist thinking are irrelevant. For example, the contribution of Commons to the interface of economics and law is still relevant today (Commons 1924, 1925, Vanberg 1989, Hodgson 2009). More work also needs to be done to relate institutionalism to macroeconomics, similar to the contribution of the 'old' institutionalist Mitchell in the interwar period (Hodgson 2004). A number of institutionalists have taken up post-Keynesian ideas but so far only limited progress has been made in developing robust theoretical links between the theoretical analysis of institutions and macroeconomic theory. Finally, all institutional approaches ('old' and 'new') need to develop an alternative grounding for economic policy to rival the patently limited neoclassical welfare approach, where the individual is assumed to be always the best judge of his or her interests. This too is an urgent item on the research agenda.

Conclusion

There is a growing overlap in areas of research and the possibility of fruitful dialogue between old and new institutionalism. This is evidenced by the foundation of the *Journal of Institutional Economics* in 2005 that publishes articles from scholars in both institutionalist traditions, as well as work on institutions by other social scientists. What emerges as 'institutional economics' in the next few decades may turn out to be very different from what was prominent in the 1980s and 1990s, and it may trace its genealogy from the old as well as the more conceptually restricted new institutionalism.

Geoff Hodgson is Research Professor in Business Studies at the University of Hertfordshire. Institutional Economics: Old and New © 2011 Geoffrey M. Hodgson.

THE ECONOMICS OF KEYNES

The course of economic theory and economic policy have been fundamentally altered as a result of Keynes's work, but exactly how, why, and in which direction remain open questions. Some argue that Keynes represented a radical break with orthodoxy while others argue that, despite his rhetoric, Keynes's work was a minor variation on neoclassical economics. Marxists such as Paul Sweezy have been influenced by the *General Theory of Employment, Interest and Money* (1936), but so too was Paul Samuelson, the principal architect of the 'neoclassical synthesis' between the macroeconomics of Keynes and neoclassical microeconomics. Some see the importance of Keynes's work mainly in the realm of theory, while others argue that it was predominantly a revolution in policy that Keynes inspired. All schools of thought, except the extreme free market wing of neoclassical economics, claim Keynes as their own, so that the complex interplay of a theory, its interpretation and its application in policy-making is more difficult to unravel here than probably anywhere else in economics.

The source of this confusion partly resides in the *General Theory* itself. It is not an easy book, and it is not completely consistent in all its arguments. Thus, simply working out 'what Keynes meant' is a never-ending source of controversy. Another source of difficulty is that Keynes wrote in a particular historical context with a very specific end in mind – the alleviation of the Great Depression and the mass unemployment that was its principal socio-economic problem. Can it be applied or adapted to other problems at other times? Is it worth the effort?

That effort was made during the long boom that followed World War II, so that by 1970 it became common to proclaim that 'we're all Keynesians now'. But the onset of 'stagflation' during the subsequent decade made many policy-makers disillusioned about Keynesian policies. The dominant response was a turn to neoliberalism and a more 'hands-off' policy stance. In effect, it was a return to pre-Keynesian economics. The onset of the global financial crisis (GFC) in 2007, and the subsequent economic recession in most capitalist countries, shattered the complacency, creating a major revival of Keynesian economic policy. Again it seemed 'we're all Keynesians now'. As a response to the GFC, Keynesian policies were appropriate and effective in staving off an even deeper recession, but the long-term prospects for Keynesian economic policy remain debateable, as the chapter by Martijn Konings in the opening section of this book argues in more details.

The articles that follow seek to take stock of the Keynesian legacy. The first article is from Keynes himself, taken from the chapter in the *General Theory* where he considers the importance of expectations in shaping the behavior of investors and the problems of having the economy reliant on such an uncertain basis. The next, written by George Argyrous for this book, attempts to present the 'bare bones' of Keynes's *General Theory*. Robert Skidelsky then discusses the underlying political philosophy, and the influence of Keynes and his *General Theory*. Finally, in an article written in 2008 during the depths of the GFC, Nobel prizewinning economist Joseph Stiglitz suggests that the Keynesian approach to economic analysis is alive, well and more important than ever.

Readers interested in exploring the economics of Keynes in more detail can find a wealth of resources on Keynes at the New School's History of Economic Thought website, <homepage.newschool.edu/het//profiles/keynes.htm>. A definitive biography of Keynes is that by Robert Skidelsky, *John Maynard Keynes*, 3 volumes, Viking Penguin, New York.

Investment, Expectations and Speculation

John Maynard Keynes

It would be foolish, in forming our expectations, to attach great weight to matters which are very uncertain. It is reasonable, therefore, to be guided to a considerable degree by the facts about which we feel somewhat confident, even though they may be less decisively relevant to the issue than other facts about which our knowledge is vague and scanty. For this reason the facts of the existing situation enter, in a sense disproportionately, into the formation of our long-term expectations; our usual practice being to take the existing situation and to project it into the future, modified only to the extent that we have more or less definite reasons for expecting a change.

The state of long-term expectation, upon which our decisions are based, does not solely depend, therefore, on the most probable forecast we can make. It also depends on the *confidence* with which we make this forecast – on how highly we rate the likelihood of our best forecast turning out quite wrong. If we expect large changes but are very uncertain as to what precise form these changes will take, then our confidence will be weak.

The state of confidence, as they term it, is a matter to which practical men always pay the closest and most anxious attention. But economists have not analyzed it carefully and have been content, as a rule, to discuss it in general terms. In particular it has not been made clear that its relevance to economic problems comes in through its important influence on the schedule of the marginal efficiency of capital. There are not two separate factors affecting the rate of investment, namely, the schedule of the marginal efficiency of capital and the state of confidence. The state of confidence is relevant because it is one of the major factors determining the former, which is the same thing as the investment demand-schedule.

The outstanding fact is the extreme precariousness of the basis of knowledge on which our estimates of prospective yield have to be made. Our knowledge of the factors which will govern the yield of an investment some years hence is usually very slight and often negligible. If we speak frankly, we have to admit that our basis of knowledge for estimating the yield ten years hence of a railway, a copper mine, a textile factory, the goodwill of a patent medicine, an Atlantic liner, a building in the City of London amounts to little and sometimes to nothing; or even five years hence. In fact, those who seriously attempt to make any such estimate are often so much in the minority that their behavior does not govern the market.

In former times, when enterprises were mainly owned by those who undertook them or by their friends and associates, investment depended on a sufficient supply of individuals of sanguine temperament and constructive impulses who embarked on business as a way of life, not really relying on a precise calculation of prospective profit. The affair was partly a lottery, though with the ultimate result largely governed by whether the abilities and character of the managers were above or below the average. Some would fail and some would succeed … Business men play a mixed game of skill and chance, the average results of which to the players are not known by those who take a hand. If human nature felt no temptation to take a chance, no satisfaction (profit apart) in constructing a factory, a railway, a mine or a farm, there might not be much investment merely as a result of cold calculation.

Decisions to invest in private business of the old-fashioned type were, however, decisions largely irrevocable, not only for the community as a whole, but also for the individual. With the separation between ownership and management which prevails to-day and with the development of organised investment markets, a new factor of great importance has entered in, which sometimes facilitates investment but sometimes adds greatly to the instability of the system. In the absence of security markets, there is no object in frequently attempting to revalue an investment to which we are committed. But the Stock Exchange revalues many investments every day and the revaluations give a frequent opportunity to the individual (though not to the community as a whole) to revise his commitments. It is as though a farmer, having tapped his barometer after breakfast, could decide to remove his capital from the farming business between 10 and 11 in the morning and reconsider whether he should return to it later in the week. But the daily revaluations of the Stock Exchange, though they are primarily made to facilitate transfers of old investments between one individual and another, inevitably exert a decisive influence on the rate of current investment. For there is no sense in building up a new enterprise at a cost greater than that at which a similar existing enterprise can be purchased; whilst there is an inducement to spend on a new project what may seem an extravagant sum, if it can be floated off on the Stock Exchange at an immediate profit. Thus certain classes of investment are governed by the average expectation of those who deal on the Stock Exchange as revealed in the price of shares, rather than by the genuine expectations of the professional entrepreneur. How then are these highly significant daily, even hourly, revaluations of existing investments carried out in practice?

In practice we have tacitly agreed, as a rule, to fall back on what is, in truth, a *convention*. The essence of this convention – though it does not, of course, work out quite so simply – lies in assuming that the existing state of affairs will continue indefinitely, except in so far as we have specific reasons to expect a change ... We are assuming, in effect, that the existing market valuation, however arrived at, is uniquely *correct* in relation to our existing knowledge of the facts which will influence the yield of the investment, and that it will only change in proportion to changes in this knowledge; though, philosophically speaking it cannot be uniquely correct, since our existing knowledge does not provide a sufficient basis for a calculated mathematical expectation. In point of fact, all sorts of considerations enter into the market valuation which are in no way relevant to the prospective yield.

Nevertheless the above conventional method of calculation will be compatible with a considerable measure of continuity and stability in our affairs, *so long as we can rely on the maintenance of the convention.* For if there exist organised investment markets and if we can rely on the maintenance of the convention, an investor can legitimately encourage himself with the idea that the only risk he runs is that of a genuine change in the news *over the near future*, as to the likelihood of which he can attempt to form his own judgment, and which is unlikely to be very large. For, assuming that the convention holds good, it is only these changes which can affect the value of his investment, and he need not lose his sleep merely because he has not any notion what his investment will be worth ten years hence. Thus investment becomes reasonably 'safe' for the individual investor over short periods, and hence over a succession of short periods however many, if he can fairly rely on there being no breakdown in the convention and on his therefore having an opportunity to revise his judgment and change his investment, before there has been time for much to happen. Investments which are 'fixed' for the community are thus made 'liquid' for the individual.

It has been, I am sure, on the basis of some such procedure as this that our leading investment markets have been developed. But it is not surprising that a convention, in an absolute view of things so arbitrary, should have its weak points. It is its precariousness which creates no small part of our contemporary problem of securing sufficient investment ...

Th[e] battle of wits to anticipate the basis of conventional valuation a few months hence, rather than the prospective yield of an investment over a long term of years, does not even require gulls amongst the public to feed the maws of the professional; – it can be played by professionals amongst themselves. Nor is it necessary that anyone should keep his simple faith in the conventional basis of valuation having any genuine long-term validity. For it is, so to speak, a game of Snap, of Old Maid, of Musical Chairs – a pastime in which he is victor who says "snap" neither too soon nor too late, who passes the Old Maid to his neighbour before the game is over, who secures a chair for himself when the music stops. These games can be played with zest and enjoyment, though all the players know that it is the Old Maid which is circulating, or that when the music stops some of the players will find themselves unseated.

Or, to change the metaphor slightly, professional investment may be likened to those newspaper competitions in which the competitors have to pick out the six prettiest faces from a hundred photographs, the prize being awarded to the competitor whose choice most nearly corresponds to the average preferences of the competitors as a whole; so that each competitor has to pick, not those faces which he himself finds prettiest, but those which he thinks likeliest to catch the fancy of the other competitors, all of whom are looking at the problem from the same point of view. It is not a case of choosing those which, to the best of one's judgment, are really the prettiest, nor even those which average opinion genuinely thinks the prettiest. We have reached the third degree where we devote our intelligences to anticipating what average opinion expects the average opinion to be. And there are some, I believe, who practise the fourth, fifth and higher degrees.

If the reader interjects that there must surely be large profits to be gained from the other players in the long run by a skilled individual who, unperturbed by the prevailing pastime, continues to purchase investments on the best genuine long-term expectations he can frame, he must be answered, first of all, that there are, indeed, such serious-minded individuals and that it makes a vast difference to an investment market whether or not they predominate in their influence over the game-players. But we must also add that there are several factors which jeopardise the predominance of such individuals in modern investment markets. Investment based on genuine long-term expectation is so difficult to-day as to be scarcely practicable. He who attempts it must surely lead much more labourious days and run greater risks than he who tries to guess better than the crowd how the crowd will behave; and, given equal intelligence, he may make more disastrous mistakes. There is no clear evidence from experience that the investment policy which is socially advantageous coincides with that which is most profitable. It needs more intelligence to defeat the forces of time and our ignorance of the future than to beat the gun. Moreover, life is not long enough; – human nature desires quick results, there is a peculiar zest in making money quickly, and remoter gains are discounted by the average man at a very high rate. The game of professional investment is intolerably boring and over-exacting to anyone who is entirely exempt from the gambling instinct; whilst he who has it must pay to this propensity the appropriate toll. Furthermore, an investor who proposes to ignore near-term market fluctuations needs greater resources for safety and must not operate on so large a scale, if at all, with borrowed money – a further reason for the higher return from the pastime to a given stock of intelligence and resources.

Finally it is the long-term investor, he who most promotes the public interest, who will in practice come in for most criticism, wherever investment funds are managed by committees or boards or banks. For it is in the essence of his behavior that he should be eccentric, unconventional and rash in the eyes of average opinion. If he is successful, that will only confirm the general belief in his rashness; and if in the short run he is unsuccessful, which is very likely, he will not receive much mercy. Worldly wisdom teaches that it is better for reputation to fail conventionally than to succeed unconventionally ...

These considerations should not lie beyond the purview of the economist. But they must be relegated to their right perspective. If I may be allowed to appropriate the term *speculation* for the activity of forecasting the psychology of the market, and the term *enterprise* for the activity of forecasting the prospective yield of assets over their whole life, it is by no means always the case that speculation predominates over enterprise. As the organisation of investment markets improves, the risk of the predominance of speculation does, however, increase ... Speculators may do no harm as bubbles on a steady stream of enterprise. But the position is serious when enterprise becomes the bubble on a whirlpool of speculation. When the capital development of a country becomes a by-product of the activities of a casino, the job is likely to be ill-done. The measure of success attained by Wall Street, regarded as an institution of which the proper social purpose is to direct new investment into the most profitable channels in terms of future yield, cannot be claimed as one of the outstanding triumphs of *laissez faire* capitalism – which is not surprising, if I am right in thinking that the best brains of Wall Street have been in fact directed towards a different object.

These tendencies are a scarcely avoidable outcome of our having successfully organised 'liquid' investment markets. It is usually agreed that casinos should, in the public interest, be inaccessible and expensive. And perhaps the same is true of Stock Exchanges … The spectacle of modern investment markets has sometimes moved me towards the conclusion that to make the purchase of an investment permanent and indissoluble, like marriage, except by reason of death or other grave cause, might be a useful remedy for our contemporary evils. For this would force the investor to direct his mind to the long-term prospects and to those only. But a little consideration of this expedient brings us up against a dilemma, and shows us how the liquidity of investment markets often facilitates, though it sometimes impedes, the course of new investment. For the fact that each individual investor flatters himself that his commitment is 'liquid' (though this cannot be true for all investors collectively) calms his nerves and makes him much more willing to run a risk. If individual purchases of investments were rendered illiquid, this might seriously impede new investment, so long as *alternative ways* in which to hold his savings are available to the individual. This is the dilemma. So long as it is open to the individual to employ his wealth in hoarding or lending *money*, the alternative of purchasing actual capital assets cannot be rendered sufficiently attractive (especially to the man who does not manage the capital assets and knows very little about them), except by organising markets wherein these assets can be easily realised for money.

The only radical cure for the crises of confidence that afflict the economic life of the modern world would be to allow the individual no choice between consuming his income and ordering the production of the specific capital-asset which, even though it be on precarious evidence, impresses him as the most promising investment available to him. It might be that, at times when he was more than usually assailed by doubts concerning the future, he would turn in his perplexity towards more consumption and less new investment. But that would avoid the disastrous, cumulative and far-reaching repercussions of its being open to him, when thus assailed by doubts, to spend his income neither on the one nor on the other.

Those who have emphasised the social dangers of the hoarding of money have, of course, had something similar to the above in mind. But they have overlooked the possibility that the phenomenon can occur without any change, or at least any commensurate change, in the hoarding of money.

Even apart from the instability due to speculation, there is the instability due to the characteristic of human nature that a large proportion of our positive activities depend on spontaneous optimism rather than on a mathematical expectation, whether moral or hedonistic or economic. Most, probably, of our decisions to do something positive, the full consequences of which will be drawn out over many days to come, can only be taken as a result of animal spirits; of a spontaneous urge to action rather than inaction, and not as the outcome of a weighted average of quantitative benefits multiplied by quantitative probabilities. Enterprise only pretends to itself to be mainly actuated by the statements in its own prospectus, however candid and sincere. Only a little more than an expedition to the South Pole, is it based on an exact calculation of benefits to come. Thus if the animal spirits are dimmed and the spontaneous optimism falters, leaving us to depend on nothing but a mathematical expectation, enterprise will fade and die; though fears of loss may have a basis no more reasonable than hopes of profit had before.

It is safe to say that enterprise which depends on hopes stretching into the future benefits the community as a whole. But individual initiative will only be adequate when reasonable calculation is supplemented and supported by animal spirits, so that the thought of ultimate loss which often overtakes pioneers, as experience undoubtedly tells us and them, is put aside as a healthy man puts aside the expectation of death.

This means, unfortunately, not only that slumps and depressions are exaggerated in degree, but that economic prosperity is excessively dependent on a political and social atmosphere which is congenial to the average business man. If the fear of a Labour Government or a New Deal depresses enterprise, this need not be the result either of a reasonable calculation or of a plot with political intent; – it is the mere consequence of upsetting the delicate balance of spontaneous optimism. In estimating the prospects of investment, we must have regard, therefore, to the nerves and hysteria and even the digestions and reactions to the weather of those upon whose spontaneous activity it largely depends.

We should not conclude from this that everything depends on waves of irrational psychology. On the contrary, the state of long-term expectation is often steady, and, even when it is not, the other factors exert their compensating effects. We are merely reminding ourselves that human decisions affecting the future, whether personal or political or economic, cannot depend on strict mathematical expectation, since the basis for making such calculations does not exist; and that it is our innate urge to activity which makes the wheels go round, our rational selves choosing between the alternatives as best we are able, calculating where we can, but often falling back for our motive on whim or sentiment or chance.

There are, moreover, certain important factors which somewhat mitigate in practice the effects of our ignorance of the future. Owing to the operation of compound interest combined with the likelihood of obsolescence with the passage of time, there are many individual investments of which the prospective yield is legitimately dominated by the returns of the comparatively near future. In the case of the most important class of very long-term investments, namely buildings, the risk can be frequently transferred from the investor to the occupier, or at least shared between them, by means of long-term contracts, the risk being outweighed in the mind of the occupier by the advantages of continuity and security of tenure. In the case of another important class of long-term investments, namely public utilities, a substantial proportion of the prospective yield is practically guaranteed by monopoly privileges coupled with the right to charge such rates as will provide a certain stipulated margin. Finally there is a growing class of investments entered upon by, or at the risk of, public authorities, which are frankly influenced in making the investment by a general presumption of there being prospective social advantages from the investment, whatever its commercial yield may prove to be within a wide range, and without seeking to be satisfied that the mathematical expectation of the yield is at least equal to the current rate of interest, – though the rate which the public authority has to pay may still play a decisive part in determining the scale of investment operations which it can afford.

Thus after giving full weight to the importance of the influence of short-period changes in the state of long-term expectation as distinct from changes in the rate of interest, we are still entitled to return to the latter as exercising, at any rate, in normal circumstances, a great, though not a decisive, influence on the rate of investment. Only experience, however, can show how far management of the rate of interest is capable of continuously stimulating the appropriate volume of investment.

For my own part I am now somewhat sceptical of the success of a merely monetary policy directed towards influencing the rate of interest. I expect to see the State, which is in a position to calculate the marginal efficiency of capital-goods on long views and on the basis of the general social advantage, taking an ever greater responsibility for directly organising investment; since it seems likely that the fluctuations in the market estimation of the marginal efficiency of different types of capital, calculated on the principles I have described above, will be too great to be offset by any practicable changes in the rate of interest.

John Maynard Keynes was a Fellow of Kings College Cambridge and advisor to the British government. This chapter is adapted from *The General Theory of Employment, Interest and Money*, Macmillan, London, 1936, ch. 12.

The Economics of *The General Theory*
George Argyrous

The major economic theories which preceded Keynes, whether the classical-Marxian or the neoclassical, saw economic growth as being limited on the supply-side: that is, by the availability of resources with which to expand. Ricardo, for example, thought that the economy's growth was limited by the supply of fertile land. Neoclassical economists focused on the availability of savings. Even Marx, who came closest to perceiving that demand could be an endemic problem for capitalism, ultimately saw growth as limited by the amount of surplus value allocated to the employment of productive labor. Behind all these otherwise divergent theories was the common assumption that, if supply constraints could be eased then more goods would be produced, and that if more goods were produced then more goods would also be sold. Production cannot be limited by a lack of markets – there is no problem of effective demand.

The problem of effective demand

When we look closely at the nature of production it is not immediately obvious why there should not be a problem of effective demand. When a market economy produces, it actually produces two quantities. One is a collection of goods and services – cars, haircuts, shoes, etc – which together are called *real output*. Some elements of real output can be used for consumption, while others can be used in the production of more goods and services in the future – investment. The other quantity that emerges out of production is *income* to the individuals that comprise society. Income represents a claim over real output, an entitlement to what has been produced. A person's income is a right to claim a certain amount of the real output as their own.

Since income is generated in the course of producing real output, it is a truism to say that total income must equal the value of total output. The question is whether individuals will exercise their respective claims on output – whether they will buy all the shoes, cars, hats, etc. that are sitting on shop shelves. If some goods and services are left over after incomes have been spent, then the level of production is too big and needs to be contracted (and workers need to be laid off). If everything that is produced cannot be sold then cutbacks are required.

It is important to note that this is not a problem of overproduction in *some* markets. There will always be some markets in which producers have been over-optimistic, so that they make too many shoes, for example. But this is part of the normal ebb and flow of the market system, and for each individual market in which supply exceeds demand there will be others in which demand exceeds supply. The problem of effective demand relates to the demand for real output *as whole*: whether *in total* there are more goods produced in relation to the income available to purchase them.

The activity that connects income to output is *expenditure*: people enter the market with their respective claims over output (demand) and producers enter the market with their goods and services (supply) and exchange takes place. There would not be a problem if all income is directly consumed, i.e. if people spent their income during the same period in which it is earned. But they don't spend all their income. At least part of people's income is saved. Saving is simply the act of not consuming, of not exercising a claim over current output. Saving can be used to buy interest-bearing financial assets such as equities and bonds, or held as cash; but regardless of how this portion of income is held, it is by definition not used to purchase final commodities. Saving therefore does not represent a demand on today's output. It is a leakage out of the expenditure stream and unless the loss in demand can find its way back into spending in some other way, some output will remain unsold at current prices.

Compensating for this leakage is the fact that consumers are not the only people making a claim over current output. Capitalists also make a claim over current output, not to satisfy their own consumption needs but to use these resources to produce more commodities in the future. This is the act of investment. It is clear that if the demand for investment goods by capitalists just compensates for the reduction in demand for consumer goods due to saving by households, then the problem of effective demand will not materialize. All goods produced will be absorbed in one way or another: either by consumers purchasing goods to satisfy their immediate needs, or by capitalists purchasing capital goods that can be used in producing more commodities in the future.

This idea – that everything produced will also be sold – is often called Say's Law of Markets, summarized in the statement that 'supply creates its own demand.' This pithy statement, however, can be interpreted in many ways, and not all versions of Say's Law are the same. The version of Say's Law to which Keynes directed his attack was that in the dominant neoclassical theory (which Keynes confusingly called 'classical economics').

Neoclassical economics and the theory of full employment

According to neoclassical economics it is the operation of the capital market that ensures savings are channelled back into investment. Saving is an act of sacrifice; a decision not to exercise a claim over output. The only reason people will be prepared to make such a sacrifice is if they are rewarded, and the reward for saving is interest. People will save up to the point at which the return on saving (interest) is equal to the psychological cost of giving up one more unit of present consumption. The higher the rate of interest, the greater the sacrifice households will be prepared to make. Therefore, higher rates of interest will induce households to supply more saving.

Capitalists will demand savings to finance investment up to the point at which the marginal return on this investment – the extra unit of output which will be generated by one more unit of capital – is equal to the marginal cost. This cost is the interest that has to be paid on borrowing. So the demand for saving to finance investment will go down if the interest rate goes up. Provided interest rates are sufficiently flexible, the competition for funds will ensure that the market establishes a rate of interest whereby all that people want to save is borrowed and invested by capitalists. Households would not forego present consumption unless they received a return for it, and capitalists would not borrow these savings to undertake investment unless they thought it profitable, and the interest rate ensures that the two sets of decisions just balance each other.

In this model, it is really households driving the system. They decide how much labor to supply in the market and how much saving to offer, and the greater the sacrifice they are prepared to make, the more resources that firms will have to produce with. Firms, on the other hand, operate in a ghost-like manner. Given the state of technology which provides a set of blueprints from which they choose the optimum combination of labor and capital, firms simply follow the market signals and allocate resources in the most efficient way. The real decision-making, as we have just noted, is made within the household.

The most important conclusion we reach from this version of Say's Law is that the system, in a competitive state, will always move towards full employment. For example, imagine that at the current real wage there are more workers looking for jobs compared to the number of jobs available. These unemployed workers will compete for jobs and push wages down. Employers will now find it more profitable to increase the level of employment because labor has become relatively cheaper. This increase in employment will mean that there is more total income in the economy then previously, and also that more goods are being produced. Some of this increase in income will be saved and therefore will not directly add to the demand for the new goods. However, these extra savings will lower the rate of interest, inducing firms to increase their investment up to the point where this investment soaks up all the available savings. The operation of the real wage as the price for labor, and the interest rate as the price of capital, will ensure that in a perfectly competitive world both markets will clear: there cannot be a permanent oversupply of capital and labor (unemployment).

All those who are prepared to work at the existing real wage will find a job. There is no macroeconomic role for the government to play. If the government tries to expand the economy by increasing its own expenditure, all it will do is compete away scarce resources from the private sector. The government will have to compete away savings and so push up the rate of interest, thereby reducing private investment. So all that will happen is that public activity substitutes for private activity. In fact, because the government is not regulated by market forces, it is likely to use the scarce resources it has bid away from the private sector less efficiently, and therefore cause total output to decline. This simple logic underlies much of the current arguments for reducing the budget deficit and achieving a budget surplus.

This theory of full employment, based on the idea of perfectly competitive markets equating supply and demand, also contains its opposite – a theory of unemployment. Anything which interrupts the market and stops it from establishing equilibrium prices will also prevent the market from clearing. Trade unions which block the operation of the labor market, or producers' monopolies which block the operation of product markets, will prevent the price from settling at its equilibrium level, and so result in an under-utilization of resources (although the emphasis is usually on problems in the labor market due to unions). So the role of the government is simply to get rid of these micro problems that may occur in individual markets. This is what is meant by microeconomic reform – free up markets so that they can operate as efficiently as possible. The macroeconomic objective of full employment will then follow as a natural outcome of microeconomic processes.

The quantity theory of money

Looking back at this story one might point out that when individuals save they do not have to purchase an interest-bearing financial asset such as a bond or equity which go to finance investment. One can refrain from consumption by simply holding money (cash). However, neoclassical economists would see savings left idle in the form of cash as irrational. Surely a rational person would consume their income, and thereby gain immediate satisfaction, or else lend their income to a capitalist and receive an interest payment that will increase their ability to consume (utility) in the future. Why give up present gratification for no reward when a reward is available? Money is barren – only a miser can get satisfaction from the holding of cash as such.

There are two exceptions to this idea that it is not rational to store income in the form of cash. The first is the *transactions* demand for money. We all need some cash in our pockets to make it between pay periods and to fund day-to-day transactions. We might also want to hold cash for *precautionary* reasons: either to take advantage of unforeseen opportunities, or to guard against unforeseen problems. However, these two reasons for hanging on to cash rather than storing savings in interest-bearing assets are minor and do not lead to any substantial economy wide loss of demand. So although it is possible for full employment to be upset by the existence of money, this is not a possibility that will actually materialize since there is no rational reason for income to be held as cash in any significant way. The role of money is simply to facilitate exchange – to grease the wheels of markets and make it easier for transactions to take place. But the quantity of money itself does not affect what is to be produced or how much, it only helps circulate it.

The conclusion reached by neoclassical economics that the economy naturally tends to full employment equilibrium leads to the Quantity Theory of Money. The QTM argues that changes in the money supply will lead to changes in the price level rather than in real output. To see what the QTM is all about, think of the possible effects that could follow from the government pumping more money – more purchasing power – into the economy. One of two things could happen. Either the extra purchasing power in the hands of consumers will induce capitalists to produce more goods and services, or the volume of goods and services might remain the same, but the prices of all goods increase (inflation).

Which is the most likely situation to follow from an increase in the money supply? The Quantity Theory says the second case – inflation – will eventuate. Why? Because the system is already at or near its peak capacity level. With resources all fully employed through the operation of the free market, the government cannot squeeze any more real output out of the economy by simply increasing purchasing power. The economy cannot respond to the increase in money that the government has injected into the economy by producing more goods, since there is no idle labor or capital available to produce it with.

The only way that real output can be increased is if people were willing to save more of their income at the current rate of interest or work harder at the current wage rate. This will supply more real resources with which to produce more goods, but unless such changes occur in the supply of resources, an increase in purchasing power will only lead to inflation.

The formal way of presenting this is in terms of the Equation of Exchange:

$$PQ = MV$$

The important point is that the value of Q – real output – is already fixed at the full employment level through the operation of competition in the capital and labor markets. The value of V is also fixed. This is the velocity of circulation; the rate at which money 'moves' around the economy. This tends to be determined by institutional factors such as the frequency with which people are paid and the existence of payments systems such as checking facilities and automatic teller machines.

It is clear that if Q and V are already fixed at a certain level, then increasing the money supply (M) will only lead to an increase in the price level (P) – more money chasing the same amount of goods. It is also clear that the QTM depends on the neoclassical version of Say's Law: if the economy did not naturally tend to full employment because effective demand was insufficient to keep it there, then Q is not a fixed value and may respond to a change in money supply rather than the price level. But if Say's Law holds then it is useless to try and squeeze more out of an economy that is already running at full pace; in current terms, the economy will simply 'overheat'. The only way we can get more output is if people are prepared to make sacrifices – to offer more labor at the existing wage, and to save more at the existing interest rate. There is no way of doing it on the cheap by printing more money – we have to make sacrifices.

Enter Keynes and the critique of the quantity theory

John Maynard Keynes attacked the conclusion of the Quantity Theory – that changes in the money supply only affected the level of prices – by destroying the premise upon which it was based. This is the premise that an unregulated market economy naturally tends to full employment. Keynes based this critique of Say's Law and the Quantity Theory on the argument that a modern industrial economy operates on different principles from those implicit in the neoclassical theory. He argued that in a system where production decisions had to be made on the basis of what was expected to happen a long way into the future, and which had very well-developed financial institutions for carrying out these decisions, then the relationship between savings and investment completely changed. The conclusion he reached as a result of his analysis was striking – a perfectly competitive economy had no natural tendency to reach full employment. It could settle at a point at which 5 percent or 6 percent or 10 percent or 20 percent of the labor force was prepared to work but could not find employment, and it could stay there.

The point of departure from the neoclassical theory for Keynes was his explanation of the rate of interest. In a modern economy the rate of interest was no longer determined by the supply of savings. Keynes believed that people did not vary the proportion of income to be saved (rather than consumed) whenever the rate of interest changed. The division of income into consumption and saving was determined by the income level. People with higher incomes tended to save a higher proportion of it, whereas poorer people tended to save very little and spend most of their income.

It is only after income has been divided into a portion for consumption and a portion for saving that the rate of interest entered the story. The rate of interest affects the decision as to how much of this saving is to be held as cash and how much as interest-bearing assets. The rate of interest is not the price, in other words, for getting people to give up present consumption. Instead, the rate of interest is the price foregone for holding savings as cash rather than as interest-bearing assets.

Contrary to the QTM outlined above, Keynes argued that rational individuals could desire to hold money rather then interest-bearing assets. In particular, there was a class of people – financial speculators – who sometimes would prefer to hold cash as a means of making a capital gain from future interest rate fluctuations. In addition to households' transactions and precautionary demands for money now was added the *speculative* demand for money, and this new source of money demand (liquidity preference) changed the entire character of the economy by allowing expected movements in the interest rate to affect the current rate of interest.

How does this work? Imagine that there are only two types of assets in which people can hold their savings: cash and bonds. A bond is a financial asset sold by the government. There are various types of bonds that governments sell, and one type guarantees a certain annual payment, called a 'coupon', to anyone who holds the bond. So, someone who buys this type of bond for $100 with a coupon of $5 a year will be paid $5 by the government for each year that they hold the bond rather than sell it. The government, in other words, is paying an interest rate of 5 percent to get hold of private savings. The annual payment of $5 (the coupon) is guaranteed by the government, but the resale price of the bond is not. In the following year, if the government sold a new issue of bonds which offered an interest rate of 10 percent, what would happen to the value of the initial bond? If someone holding the $100/$5 bond tried to resell it, they obviously would not get the face value of $100. No one would want to pay $100 for a $5 annual payment when under the new issue they need only spend $50 to get the same annual return. The maximum anyone would be prepared to pay would be $50, because the implicit rate of interest on the bond (5/50) would be equal to the rate that they could get elsewhere. So, after being originally bought for $100, the bond can now only be sold for $50: a capital loss of fifty dollars. This is a bit like buying a car. If I pay $10,000 for new car, but a week later a new model is expected to come out at that price, the resale price of my car is immediately affected. What I paid and what I would get if I resold it are not the same, and the difference can either represent a capital gain or a capital loss. Similarly, even though I may pay $100 for a bond, the following year I may only be able to sell it for $50.

In fact, it would have been better to hold on to cash for a year until after the interest rates had gone up and then purchased the new issue of bonds. This is a remarkable result – we have a situation in which it is rational to hang on to cash (liquidity) instead of purchasing an interest-bearing asset. The demand for money is not stable, but varies inversely with the *expected* money rate of interest. If the rate of interest is expected to go up then speculators don't want to be caught holding bonds, so they seek liquidity by holding cash and waiting. Conversely, if they expect interest rates to fall they try to buy up bonds and reduce their holdings of cash.

An interesting conclusion follows. The combined result of all these decisions based on what interest rates are *expected* to be is that these expectations become self-fulfilling. In other words, if people expect the rate of interest to rise, their actions will actually cause the rate of interest to rise. How? The thing to note is that there is only a limited amount of money in circulation – it is put out by the central bank. On one side we have households who need money for transactions and precautionary purposes. On the other side we have speculators who want money for speculative purposes – to make a capital gain. Assume that suddenly these speculators expect interest rates to go up; they will want to sell their bonds and hold cash. Where are they going to get this cash? They can only get it by offering a higher rate of interest to induce households to give up some of their money. If households are already happy holding the amount of cash that they hold, they can only be induced to give up some of it if they receive a higher rate of interest on the asset that they can hold instead of money. So the interest rate will actually be bid up because of expectations that it will go up!

This may seem a bizarre result, but that was Keynes's point. Keynes wanted to show in his liquidity preference theory that modern financial markets operate in a very bizarre way that causes interest rates to 'hang by their own bootstraps'. Interest rates no longer depend on the amount of savings in the economy, but in the form in which people want to hold their savings, either as cash or as assets. So interest rates could be high or low at any given level of savings, depending on the unstable expectations of financial speculators.

The theory of investment

The instability in the demand for money causes the neoclassical theory of Say's Law to unravel. *The problem is not that effective demand falls because more income is lying idle as cash*: the amount of cash circulating is fixed by the central bank. But the increased *desire* to hold this fixed amount of cash has caused the rate of interest to go up, and the reduction in effective demand comes about because the higher rate of interest chokes off investment.

To see why, we need to outline the next piece in Keynes's puzzle, which is the theory of investment. Keynes argued that the amount of investment undertaken is affected, as in neoclassical economics, by the rate of interest. But we have seen that the rate of interest is not tied to the existing level of savings, but to the vagaries of financial speculation. Thus investment takes on an independent existence in Keynes's theory: it is free to vary independently of the existing volume of savings. Having severed the link between what households want to save and what capitalists want to borrow and invest, investment takes on life of its own. Suddenly the impulses that drive our system get reversed and instead of households running the show, it is firms and their (fragile) investment plans that dominate.

To Keynes the neoclassical story oversimplified the basis upon which investment decisions were taken. In a modern industrial economy, which already has in existence a large stock of capital, the long time horizons involved in deciding whether a particular investment will be profitable renders such a decision to be fundamentally uncertain: investment decisions cannot be reduced to simple calculations of probability. Keynes tried to get a handle on this uncertainty in his idea of the marginal efficiency of capital. According to Keynes, capitalists form expectations about the likely profitability of each investment project they can undertake. If Plan A is carried out, a certain entrepreneur may expect to get a return of 15 percent. If she carried out Plan B she might expect to get a return of 12 percent. Plan C may be expected to yield 10 percent, and so on.

In other words, possible investment projects – a new factory, or refitting an old one, or expanding an existing shop – are ranked according to their expected profitability, generating a 'menu' of options. This ordering of investment projects according to their expected profitability Keynes called the Marginal Efficiency of Capital, and the individual schedules for each capitalist can be summed together to produce the MEC schedule for the economy as a whole.

It is fairly obvious that not all investment projects will be undertaken. If the cost of borrowing – the rate of interest – is 11 percent then only those projects with an expected return greater than this will be undertaken. No one will carry out a project if the cost of financing it exceeds the expected returns. Thus expectations enter the picture at two points. They enter in the determination of the rate of interest through the speculative demand for money. They also enter in the MEC through entrepreneurs' expectations of future profitability. And the important factor is that these expectations are often volatile and self-reinforcing so that a wave of pessimism can sweep the markets and cause investment to be choked off. Investment is tied to the vagaries of expectations which are fundamentally uncertain.

The theory of effective demand and the income multiplier

Having established the relative autonomy and instability of investment, we now come to the centrepiece of Keynes's theory of effective demand. This is how investment determines the volume of savings through the income multiplier. The theory of effective demand and the multiplier explain how the system adjusts to whatever amount of investment firms choose to undertake. In effect it reverses the causal relation between savings and investment. Both the neoclassical and Keynes's theory argue that savings equal investment – they have to be equal as a matter of definition. But the two theories differ in terms of what each sees as cause and effect. The multiplier is a story which shows that the volume of savings adjust to the level of investment firms have decided to undertake *through changes in the volume of income.*

The rationale for the multiplier is that one person's expenditure is another person's income, so that an increase in expenditure will increase incomes as well. And since savings are a stable proportion of income, an increase in expenditure will also increase the total amount of savings. Assume that investment increases by $100. I go to a factory and place an order for capital goods of this amount. This initial increase in investment does not have to be financed out of existing savings. The availability of credit facilities extended by banks to business means that investment can increase beyond the amount of funds currently in the banking system. As we shall see, eventually savings will expand to underwrite this increase in investment, but initially the expansion is not limited by available savings.

To meet the increase in demand for investment goods new workers are hired and their income goes up by $100. Assume that they save 20 percent of this ($20) and consume the rest. This $80 of spending is income for somebody else. They then save 20 percent ($16) and spend the remaining $64. This $64 of spending is then more income to somebody else, who also saves a portion of it and consumes the rest, and so on until the amount being passed on as consumption is negligible. The *total* income in the economy will have increased by the sum of all these individual increases. We can write this relationship formally in the following way:

$$Y = \frac{1}{s}(I)$$

In other words, the level of income (Y) will be some multiple of the level of investment (I), and this multiplier is determined by people's propensity to save (s), so that if people tried to save more, income would go down. This is a striking conclusion. The media are constantly informing us that we are not saving enough, that we should be more frugal, and that if we could supply more savings we could restore economic growth. *But the economy as a whole cannot save more than it is prepared to invest*. So the effect of everyone trying to save more will be to reduce total income. Individual action and social outcome diverge. This is the paradox of thrift. The economy as a whole operates on a different principle to the way in which the individuals which comprise it do. And what seems right to the individual is wrong for everybody taken together.

The important conclusion that follows from Keynes's theory of effective demand is that the economy has no natural tendency towards full employment. The economy can settle at any point and stay there: any rate of unemployment can be an equilibrium. Relative prices can go up and down, but that won't help. Even if we could get rid of trade unions and other monopolies, ultimately it is capitalists' expectations about the growth of markets which determines the level of investment and therefore employment.

It may help at this point to look back and summarize the key elements of Keynes's theory of effective demand. This theory of macroeconomic behavior is essentially made up of three pieces: liquidity preference theory, the theory of investment, and the income multiplier. Like a jigsaw puzzle, it is made up of separate pieces, each locking into the next one. The theory of liquidity preference determines the rate of interest, which then becomes an element in the determination of the rate of investment. The rate of investment then determines the level of income and employment. Thus it is a story of sequential and cumulative causation, in which there are no self-correcting properties: a problem at any one point in the chain is passed on down the line with disastrous consequences. Waves of speculation in the financial markets, cycles of pessimism among capitalists, or savings rates that are too high by households, each can set up forces which ultimately cause unemployment to arise.

The major policy implication is that if the economy won't reach full employment on its own account (and it is most unlikely that it will do so), then the government can step in and increase demand. Given the sequential nature of causality in Keynes's model, the state can intervene at each or all of the steps in the chain to increase effective demand. In broad terms, the government can pursue and or all of the following strategies:

1. *Increase the supply of money*. Using monetary policy in this way will mean that speculators won't have to push up the interest rate in order to get hold of cash being held by households. Unlike the Quantity Theory, changes in the amount of money can have permanent effects on the actual quantity of real output, and need not cause inflation.
2. *Manage interest rates*. By lowering interest rates through its bond sales, the government can lower the cost of borrowing throughout the financial markets.
3. *Increase public investment*. If the private sector is unwilling to undertake long term investments due to pessimistic expectations, the government can make up for the deficiency by making its own investments: building roads, ports, schools, etc. This will finance itself as the increase in income that results from the multiplier will generate higher tax revenue to the government.
4. *Redistribute income in order to increase society's propensity to consume*. Keynes thought that advanced countries would have low propensities to consume, which would mean that the multiplier would not be as powerful a force for growth. However, the government can compensate for this through its own expenditure program. In particular, by redistributing income to the poor, who have a higher propensity to consume, and away from the wealthy, the government can alter the value of the multiplier. For any given amount of investment there will thereby be a greater expansion in income.

George Argyrous is Senior Lecturer, University of New South Wales. The Economics of *The General Theory* © 2011 George Argyrous.

Keynes's Political Legacy
Robert Skidelsky

Keynes was a lifelong liberal. By the interwar years the tasks of liberal statesmanship had emerged with painful clarity: to stave off revolution from Left and Right and to make the economic system (or 'capitalism') work more efficiently and humanely. The two tasks were connected, the second being a means to the first, for by the 1930s both communism and fascism were staking their claim to power on liberal capitalism's inability to provide full employment. This premise Keynes set out to refute.

"The authoritarian state systems of today," he wrote in 1936 in *The General Theory*,

> seem to solve the problem of unemployment at the expense of efficiency and freedom. It is certain that the world will not much longer tolerate the unemployment which … is associated – and, in my opinion, inevitably associated – with present day capitalistic individualism. But it may be possible by a right analysis of the problem to cure the disease whilst preserving efficiency and freedom (*Collected Writings*, VII: 381).

Taking a broad historical view, the Keynesian revolution in economics was a key part of what emerged as the dominant western intellectual response to the rise of the totalitarians and, more generally, to the 'rise of the masses'.

This intellectual movement may be called the second liberal revival. Unlike the 'new' liberalism of the turn of the century, it made no serious attempt to reshape the philosophical foundations of liberalism. 'New' liberals were concerned chiefly with the justifications of existing property relations, from the point of view of efficiency and equity, and as affecting the moral growth of the individual. By contrast, the second wave of liberal thinkers took the existing property relationships as given: what they did was to superimpose a managerial philosophy on the theory and practice of 'classic' liberalism. This reflects, on the one hand, a much greater institutional timidity, in face of the violent rearrangement of property relations which had taken place in Russia, and, on the other, a faith that existing institutions could be made to work, provided that government intervened in certain key areas and that the social sciences could provide an ideologically neutral logic of intervention – a faith which may have been born of desperation. A philosophy of *ad hoc* intervention based on disinterested thought was thus twentieth century liberalism's answer to the faith of early-nineteenth-century liberals that institutional reform could secure the conditions of minimalist government – a belief, or course, which Marx also shared. It reflects the extent to which utilitarianism had lost its radical cutting edge.

In Keynes's updated version of liberalism the intellectual has a key part to play in stabilizing society – as social scientist and as manager. Keynes believed that the economic problem of his day was an intellectual and not a structural or institutional problem: the slump was the result of a "frightful muddle" whose cure lay, first, in the realm of thought, and secondly, in that of management.

Keynes has often been criticized for exaggerating the importance of ideas, relative to power, especially class power. According to the Marxist, John Strachey, his *Essays on Persuasion* were so "uniformly unpersuasive" because he ignored the fact that unemployment was a necessary feature of capitalism. Keynes compounded his political naiveté, from this point of view, by writing in the *General Theory*: "But soon or late, it is ideas, not vested interests, which are dangerous for good or evil" (*Collected Writings*, VII: 381).

It is a facile misinterpretation of Keynes's position to say that he believed that ideas triumph by a kind of natural magic. Successful ideas succeed because they have more political utility than the alternatives on offer; smaller interests yield to larger interests, or survive only if they can plausibly attach themselves to coalitions of interests. Here public opinion, as filtered through the electoral process, is ultimately decisive in a democracy. Politicians, being in the business of want satisfaction, have to attend to public opinion sooner or later, if they are to win or retain power; and public opinion will not stand indefinitely for policies which they perceive as bringing about impoverishment. Having said this, it is also true that Keynes was the last person to deny the power of persuasive utterance. He was himself a master of it, and it was through journalism that the educated public, at any rate, became familiar with his general approach to curing the slump.

With intellectuals (and in this case economists) the process of acceptance of new ideas is admittedly more complicated. Economists too have political purposes, and are open to non-rational 'persuasion'. But genuine intellectual conversion also has to take place. Theories must possess formal properties of logical consistency which commend them to specialists. However, it would be wrong to say that Keynes attached excessive importance to this factor. What he tended to require of fellow economists was the power of 'seeing the world' as he saw it; minds must meet intuitively before logical discussion could become fruitful. But such 'meeting of minds' was never for him simply or largely a matter of psychological affinity. His faith was that all rational land competent) persons confronted with the same evidence will attach the same values to various possible conclusions to be drawn from it.

For Keynes, therefore, the success or failure, as well as the truth or falsity, of ideas was always connected to the facts. Those ideas win which have a perceived tendency to maximize contentment; for intellectuals the probable rightness of a theory is a matter of logical intuition applied to the evidence. These are straightforward deductions from his political utilitarianism and from his theory of probability. It is significant that Marxists, who started in the 1930s by saying that Keynes's ideas could not possibly be implemented under capitalism, ended up by explaining that they 'fitted the needs' of capitalism. Keynes could not, I think, have asked for more.

Keynes has also been criticized for his belief in the possibility of disinterested economic argument. Seymour Harris accused him of failing to "reconcile his dislike and distrust of politicians with his determination to thrust upon government serious additional responsibilities". Alternatively, he has been attacked for believing that economic management could be "insulated" from political pressures.

In considering such criticisms it is important to be clear about what Keynes wanted his 'managers' to do. Keynes's (not Keynesian) policies for securing a high, continuous, non-inflationary level of output and employment can be divided into two main parts: "a somewhat comprehensive socialisation of investment", and monetary fine-tuning. Fiscal fine-tuning was not part of his design; budget deficits were to be resorted to only to pull an economy out of a slump. The postwar reliance on managing the economy through budgetary policy, with monetary policy either ignored or reduced to a subsidiary role, was not part of Keynes's original intention. The short answer to Seymour Harris, therefore, is that Keynes did not wish to thrust large extra responsibilities on politicians as such. He can still be held to be politically naive in supposing that they could be prevented from using the potential instruments for manipulating demand to their own political advantage.

In trying to understand how Keynes visualized the political economy of the future a key problem of interpretation is posed by the phrase "a somewhat comprehensive socialization of investment". It is clear enough that Keynes means that the state will become responsible for a major part of total investment. Thus he writes in the *General Theory* "I expect to see the State, which is in a position to calculate the marginal efficiency of capital-goods on long views and on the basis of the general social advantage, taking an ever greater responsibility for directly organizing investments". The problem here is to determine what Keynes means by "the State". It is highly improbable that Keynes wants to identify the state with the government of the day since he can hardly have supposed that politicians elected to govern on the basis of renewable popular consent would be best placed to take 'long views'. At the very least, we must suppose Keynes to mean the permanent officials; but by the state he seems to mean something wider still.

Keynes means by the state that sector of the polity not working for private self-interest, but for the public good. This cuts across the division between the public and private sectors; the state includes bodies which are legally private, but which in the course of their evolution have come to acquire a sense of public purpose. Insofar as politicians were motivated by public purposes, they were part of the state; insofar as they pursued their own interests through politics, they were part of the non-state. Governments were presumably a mixture of both.

In the capitalist era property escaped from vassalage to become fully 'privatized', with its public functions taken over by the Crown-in-Parliament. In effect, Keynes suggested that this tendency was now reversing itself. The state was no longer rigidly separated from private property and private enterprise, rather the two were forging or reforging a corporate relationship. "Time and the Joint Stock Company and Civil Service have silently brought the salaried class into power" Keynes wrote in 1934.

It was through the forging of a new relationship between the civil service and the joint stock companies that Keynes expected the "socialization of investment" to come about.

On the other side, Keynes saw the public service motive growing at the industrial level through the emergence of the "semi-autonomous" corporation: in 1927 he estimated that two-thirds of the capital of large-scale undertakings could not be classed as private any more. The central thread of his argument has to do with the tendency of large-scale industry to 'socialise' itself. By this he meant the divorce of management from ownership, and the transformation of the money-making into the 'public service' motive. He wrote of "the trend of the Joint Stock Institutions, when they have reached a certain age and size, to approximate to the status of the public corporations rather than that of individualistic private enterprise". Keynes welcomed these developments as ridding capitalism of its 'casino' features, while avoiding the dead hand of bureaucratic governmental controls. Interestingly, while left-wing commentators saw in this concentration of private capital a powerful argument for public ownership, Keynes believed it made it unnecessary since the 'managers' were no longer short-term profit maximisers. If large-scale industry was already 'socialised', public ownership was superfluous.

The final assumption which underlay Keynes's vision of the political economy of the future was that all these different parts of the state would be controlled by much the same kind of people. The 'semi-autonomous' corporations would be run neither by Cabinet ministers nor by town councils, but by boards chosen for business ability, adequately remunerated and free from bureaucratic interference. "I do not see," he wrote, "why we should not build up in this country a great public service running the business side of public concerns recruited from the whole population with the same ability and the same great tradition as our administrative Civil Service." Keynes undoubtedly saw the 'socialisation' of large parts of the economy, in the form of legally private, but public-spirited, corporations run by university high-fliers and generating their own investment funds as providing the essential guarantee of a stable high level of investment, since it was this development which would mitigate the large-scale *fluctuations* of investment associated with the psychology of the stock market. Monetary fine-tuning and residual fiscal policy would be in the hands of different members of the same elite at the Bank of England and the Treasury. Thus he saw science, expertise, and public spirit gradually ousting politics and self-interest as governors of a system that remained largely unchanged in its legal, institutional forms. Keynes's intellectual and managerial elitism left little room for "participatory democracy".

The Keynesian revolution in economic policy was a particular manifestation of the general trend towards collectivism which distinguished the first half of the twentieth century from the first half of the nineteenth century. Its success derives from the fact that it offered a logic of collective action within the framework of liberal democracy. It did not raise in acute form issues which liberal democracy cannot easily handle – distributional questions, questions of property rights and questions about the relationship between liberty and legal coercion. The Keynesian logic of intervention offered the benefits of collectivism without any of its costs.

Collectivism is the belief that individual and/or social well-being cannot be achieved by individuals pursuing their own interests within the law, but must be willed and brought about by the action of collective bodies, embodying the 'common will' of their members. The dominant forces behind the collectivist surge in our century are generally taken to be: the quest for economic security by individuals, firms, trade unions and states; the quest for social and/or national efficiency; efforts to control the abuse of private power; and the quest for justice between classes. Twentieth-century collectivism has ranged all the way from centrally planned and owned and politically controlled economies to milder forms of planning and selective public provision of goods and services which have been advocated not only as good in themselves, but as inoculations against the more virulent forms of the disease.

Keynes was certainly a collectivist in the latter sense, but of a very precise kind. "I come next", he wrote in 1924,

> to a criterion of the *Agenda* which is particularly relevant to what is urgent and desirable to do in the near future. We must aim at separating those services which are *technically social* from those which are *technically individual*. The most important *Agenda* of the State relate not to those activities which private individuals are already fulfilling but to those functions which fall outside the sphere of the individual, to those decisions which are made by *no one* if the State does not make them. The important thing for government is not to do things which individuals are doing already, and to do them a little better or a little worse; but to do those things which at present are not done at all (*Collected Writings* IX: 291-2).

Examples of the agenda to government were: (1) control of the business cycle by the central bank; (2) control of the amount of savings and their flow as between domestic and foreign uses; and (3) population policy, including attention to 'quality' as well as to mere numbers.

The main charge against *laissez faire* capitalism was not that private self-interest allocated resources inefficiently or unjustly as between different uses – Keynes specifically denies that it does – but that it failed to ensure full use of the potential resources. This suggested a quite different logic of intervention from that of the reigning socialist and national socialist models, directed as they were to 'planning' for efficiency or national power, or the achievement of distributional justice.

Pre-Keynesian economics had no theory capable of explaining persisting mass unemployment. The fact was that such unemployment was attributed to contractual, institutional or legislative obstacles to the formation of market-clearing prices for labor. The only advice economists had to offer governments was to remove these obstacles, so that the institutional setting would once more be 'appropriate' for the achievement of full employment. Governments shrank by dismantling many of the social and trade union legislation they passed in the previous fifty years.

Keynes's earliest analysis of the unemployment problem – in terms of fluctuations in the quantity of money – had the great political merit of by-passing this set of problems. Given the institutional setting, and particularly the wages policies of employers and unions, the quantity of employment depended (within limits) on the quantity of money supplied by the central bank.

Behind Keynes's concentration on the monetary factor as a cause of unemployment lay a great deal of institutional timidity; he often expressed the view that an old, inflexible economy like England's could not take the classical medicine without the risk of grave social disorder.

Although in Keynes's mature theory the quantity of employment was made to depend (again within limits) on the level of demand (particularly investment demand) rather than on the quantity of money, prevention and cure remained, at least for shallow fluctuations of market demand, the task of monetary policy. Collectivism is confined to two points: provision by the central bank of an appropriate quantity of money, and by the 'state' of an appropriate level of investment. Nothing else is to change. In the mature Keynes, the picture of a sluggishly self-healing economy has given way to one in which an economy which experiences a decline in investment demand subsides, if left to itself, into a state of permanent illness. Yet Keynes remained confident that a change in ideas superimposed on a natural evolution towards corporatism could cure the disease without any need for institutional change.

It remains to consider what is left of Keynes's political legacy today. Is it depleted beyond replenishment? Or does it still have the power to invigorate our thinking? Keynes raises in a variety of ways the central political question of our time, and perhaps all times: what we think a 'central authority' can or should do to bring about a more desirable state of affairs. Three issues deserve particular attention.

The first concerns the relationship between goodness and utility and more generally between ethics and politics. The classical tradition, which runs deep, is that politics is a means to, and part of, the 'good society'. Political utilitarianism broke finally with this by seeing government as a mere contrivance to satisfy certain wants. But much political practice, and the political vocation itself, rests on the older assumption. People may go into politics because they are ambitious, or because they feel that government should be as competent as possible; but they normally feel the need to justify their choice by saying that they aim to 'do good'. Keynes's political thought is for the cool hour, when politicians ask themselves what they really think they are doing, rather than for the platform where they trumpet their faiths.

The second issue concerns the relationship between elites and masses. Keynes's thinking challenges the ideal of a participatory democracy – whether in the form of consumer sovereignty which the Right offers or in the form of popular decision-making advocated by the Left. Keynes clearly saw a conflict between direct government and good government; and while he would not have denied the educative value of popular democracy, he would not have taken too many risks for what would be at best a long-run benefit. It may be we are in a position to go further than Keynes by taking into account different levels of decision-making; direct democracy may be appropriate in some places and not in others. A related question is this: if Keynes was wrong in thinking that certain kinds of high-level decision-making could be insulated from vested interest or vote-catching, how does this affect our judgment about the proper sphere of public action?

Thirdly, there is the relationship between management and reform. Keynes's approach, and that of his generation of liberals, was heavily infected by institutional timidity. This gave a 'demand-side' bias to his economics, which became even more pronounced in the postwar Keynesian regime. Have we now reached the end of this road? Keynes saw institutional reform as fraught with danger for social stability. Moreover, he saw institutions evolving in a manner helpful to his macroeconomic purposes. But to what extent is institutional reform, today and in the near future, a necessary condition of fuller employment? To put it concretely: are the wage-determining and political institutions such that any Keynesian policy is bound to generate, at an early date, unacceptable levels of inflation? It may be that reform has become a less risky option than reliance on unaided management, though management will still be needed. Keynesian liberalism, in other words, may need some of the cutting edge of an earlier, less embattled, liberalism, if good government is to be preserved.

Robert Skidelsky is Emeritus Professor of Political Economy, University of Warwick. This chapter is abridged from Keynes Political Legacy in O.F. Hamouda and J.N. Smithin (eds) *Keynes and Public Policy After Fifty Years*, NYU Press, 1988, ch. 1. © 1988 NYU Press. Reprinted with permission of the author.

The Triumphant Return of JM Keynes
Joseph E. Stiglitz

We are all Keynesians now. Even the right in the United States has joined the Keynesian camp with unbridled enthusiasm and on a scale that at one time would have been truly unimaginable. For those of us who claimed some connection to the Keynesian tradition, this is a moment of triumph, after having been left in the wilderness, almost shunned, for more than three decades. At one level, what is happening now is a triumph of reason and evidence over ideology and interests.

Economic theory had long explained why unfettered markets were not self-correcting, why regulation was needed, why there was an important role for government to play in the economy. But many, especially people working in the financial markets, pushed a type of "market fundamentalism." The misguided policies that resulted – pushed by, among others, some members of US President Barack Obama's economic team – had earlier inflicted enormous costs on developing countries. The moment of enlightenment came only when those policies also began inflicting costs on the US and other advanced industrial countries.

Keynes argued not only that markets are not self-correcting, but that in a severe downturn, monetary policy was likely to be ineffective. Fiscal policy was required. But not all fiscal policies are equivalent. In America today, with an overhang of household debt and high uncertainty, tax cuts are likely to be ineffective (as they were in Japan in the 1990's). Much, if not most, of the February 1998 US tax cut went into savings.

With the huge debt left behind by the Bush administration, the US should be especially motivated to get the largest possible stimulation from each dollar spent. The legacy of underinvestment in technology and infrastructure, especially of the green kind, and the growing divide between the rich and the poor, requires congruence between short-run spending and a long-term vision.

That necessitates restructuring both tax and expenditure programs. Lowering taxes on the poor and raising unemployment benefits while simultaneously increasing taxes on the rich can stimulate the economy, reduce the deficit, and reduce inequality. Cutting expenditures on the Iraq war and increasing expenditures on education can simultaneously increase output in the short and long run and reduce the deficit.

Keynes was worried about a liquidity trap – the inability of monetary authorities to induce an increase in the supply of credit in order to raise the level of economic activity. US Federal Reserve Chairman Ben Bernanke has tried hard to avoid having the blame fall on the Fed for deepening this downturn in the way that it is blamed for the Great Depression, famously associated with a contraction of the money supply and the collapse of banks.

And yet one should read history and theory carefully: preserving financial institutions is not an end in itself, but a means to an end. It is the flow of credit that is important, and the reason that the failure of banks during the Great Depression was important is that they were involved in determining creditworthiness; they were the repositories of information necessary for the maintenance of the flow of credit.

But America's financial system has changed dramatically since the 1930's. Many of America's big banks moved out of the "lending" business and into the "moving business." They focused on buying assets, repackaging them, and selling them, while establishing a record of incompetence in assessing risk and screening for creditworthiness. Hundreds of billions have been spent to preserve these dysfunctional institutions. Nothing has been done even to address their perverse incentive structures, which encourage short-sighted behavior and excessive risk taking. With private rewards so markedly different from social returns, it is no surprise that the pursuit of self-interest (greed) led to such socially destructive consequences. Not even the interests of their own shareholders have been served well.

Meanwhile, too little is being done to help banks that actually do what banks are supposed to do – lend money and assess creditworthiness. The Federal government has assumed trillions of dollars of liabilities and risks. In rescuing the financial system, no less than in fiscal policy, we need to worry about the "bang for the buck." Otherwise, the deficit – which has doubled in eight years – will soar even more.

In September 2008, there was talk that the government would get back its money, with interest. As the bailout has ballooned, it is increasingly clear that this was merely another example of financial markets mis-appraising risk – just as they have done consistently in recent years. The terms of the Bernanke-Paulson bailouts were disadvantageous to taxpayers, and yet remarkably, despite their size, have done little to rekindle lending.

The neoliberal push for deregulation served some interests well. Financial markets did well through capital market liberalization. Enabling America to sell its risky financial products and engage in speculation all over the world may have served its firms well, even if they imposed large costs on others.

Today, the risk is that the new Keynesian doctrines will be used and abused to serve some of the same interests. Have those who pushed deregulation ten years ago learned their lesson? Or will they simply push for cosmetic reforms – the minimum required to justify the mega-trillion dollar bailouts? Has there been a change of heart, or only a change in strategy? After all, in today's context, the pursuit of Keynesian policies looks even more profitable than the pursuit of market fundamentalism!

Ten years ago, at the time of the Asian financial crisis, there was much discussion of the need to reform the global financial architecture. Little was done. It is imperative that we not just respond adequately to the current crisis, but that we undertake the long-run reforms that will be necessary if we are to create a more stable, more prosperous, and equitable global economy.

Joseph E. Stiglitz is Professor of Economics at Columbia University, and recipient of the Nobel Prize in Economics. This chapter is adapted from The Triumphant Return of John Maynard Keynes, *Project Syndicate*, 5 December, 2008. © 2008 Project Syndicate.

POST-KEYNESIAN ECONOMICS

Since Keynes wrote the *General Theory*, his ideas have been adapted in various ways. The standard interpretation of his work in the economics textbooks has taken the form of a mechanized and simplified model of the macro-economy. This is the product of the attempts to fuse Keynesian insights with a neoclassical analysis of markets – the so-called 'neoclassical synthesis' – which was for so long the basis of economic teaching. This is the tendency that Joan Robinson called 'bastard Keynesianism'. It has not gone unchallenged, and those challenges have helped to stimulate further contributions to contemporary political economy. It is in this context that we can talk of post-Keynesian economics, not just as economics since Keynes's time but as a critical current of economic thought, challenging neoclassicism but from a somewhat different stance than Marxist and institutionalist economics.

In part, the concern has been to re-emphasize the original insights of Keynes into the workings of capitalism, with particular stress on the study of economic dynamics and the analysis of decision-making under conditions of uncertainty. The economy is treated as moving through non-reversible historical time, whereby decisions at one point of time foreclose alternative lines of development. This emphasis on the path-dependent nature of economic development, rather than on self-correcting equilibrium, makes post-Keynesianism more compatible with the other currents of political economy than with the treatment of macroeconomics within the neoclassical synthesis.

However, the boundaries and features of post-Keynesian economics as a distinct school of thought are not sharply defined. Substantial internal disagreements (which sympathetic scholars may view as a sign of vitality) run through the post-Keynesian literature. Michal Kalecki's work provides one major inspiration. Writing at the same time as Keynes, Kalecki is credited with being an independent discoverer of the principle of effective demand. His followers and other post-Keynesians, drawing on the work of such writers as Joan Robinson and Nicholas Kaldor, emphasise cyclical growth and the short period. Other post-Keynesians who see the work of Piero Sraffa (and before him, Ricardo) as being of similar importance to Keynes (the so-called neo-Ricardians) tend to focus on problems of value and distribution and the long period.

The articles that follow in this section of the book illustrate post-Keynesian concerns. First is a classic contribution by Kalecki, pointing to the political economic difficulties of achieving full employment in a capitalist economy, despite governments having the technical policy means to achieve that goal. The reasoning has elements in common with Marxian analysis, especially in regard to the view of class character of the capitalist state. The next article by Hyman Minsky emphasizes the sources of financial instability in modern capitalism that are more pronounced today than when Keynes wrote. Indeed, there has been a major surge of interest in Minski's work in the last decade, triggered in large measure by the global financial crisis. Finally, Peter Kriesler's article considers what is distinctive in general about the post-Keynesians' view of the economy, how it should be perceived, and how it can be analysed.

Readers interested in the major issues and approaches of post-Keynesian economics should consult its leading journals, such as the *Journal of Post Keynesian Economics* <www.mesharpe.com/mall/results1.asp?ACR=PKE> and the *Cambridge Journal of Economics* <cje.oxfordjournals.org>.

Political Aspects of Full Employment
Michal Kalecki

A solid majority of economists is now [1943] of the opinion that, even for a capitalist system, full employment may be secured by a government spending program, provided there is in existence an adequate plan to employ all existing labor power, and provided adequate supplies of necessary foreign materials may be obtained in exchange for exports.

If the government undertakes public investment (e.g. builds schools, hospitals, and highways) or subsidises mass consumption (by family allowances, reduction of indirect taxation, or subsidies to keep down the price of necessities), and if, moreover, this expenditure is financed by borrowing and not by taxation (which would affect adversely private investment and consumption), the effective demand for goods and services may be increased up to a point where full employment is achieved. Such government expenditure increases employment, be it noted, not only directly but indirectly as well, since the higher incomes caused by it result in a secondary increase in demand for consumer and investment goods.

It may be objected that the government expenditure financed by borrowing will cause inflation. To this it may be replied that the effective demand created by the government acts like any other increase in demand. If labor, plants, and foreign raw materials are in ample supply, the increase in demand is met by an increase in production. But if the point of full employment of resources is reached and effective demand continues to increase, prices will rise so as to equilibrate the demand for and the supply of goods and services. It follows that if the government intervention aims at achieving full employment but stops short of increasing effective demand over the full employment mark, there is no need to be afraid of inflation.

The above is a very crude and incomplete statement of the economic doctrine of full employment. But it is, I think, sufficient to acquaint the reader with the essence of the doctrine and so enable him to follow the subsequent discussion of the *political* problems involved in the achievement of full employment.

It should be first stated that, although most economists are now agreed that full employment may be achieved by government spending, this was by no means the case even in the recent past. Among the opposers of this doctrine there were (and still are) prominent so-called 'economic experts' closely connected with banking and industry. This suggests that there is a political background in the opposition to the full employment doctrine, even though the arguments advanced are economic. That is not to say that people who advance them do not believe in their economics, poor though this is. But obstinate ignorance is usually a manifestation of underlying political motives.

There are, however, even more direct indications that a first-class political issue is at stake here. In the Great Depression in the 1930s, big business consistently opposed experiments for increasing employment by government spending in all countries, except Nazi Germany. The attitude is not easy to explain. Clearly, higher output and employment benefit not only workers but entrepreneurs as well, because the latter's profits rise. And the policy of full employment outlined above does not encroach upon profits because it does not involve any additional taxation. The entrepreneurs in the slump are longing for a boom; why do they not gladly accept the synthetic boom which the government is able to offer them? It is this difficult and fascinating question with which we intend to deal in this article.

The reasons for the opposition of the 'industrial leaders' to full employment achieved by government spending may be subdivided into three categories: (i) dislike of government interference in the problem of employment as such; (ii) dislike of the direction of government spending (public investment and subsidizing consumption); (iii) dislike of the social and political changes resulting from the *maintenance* of full employment. We shall examine each of these three categories of objections to the government expansion policy in detail.

We shall deal first with the reluctance of the 'captains of industry' to accept government intervention in the matter of employment. Every widening of state activity is looked upon by business with suspicion, but the creation of employment by government spending has a special aspect which makes the opposition particularly intense. Under a *laissez faire* system the level of employment depends to a great extent on the so-called state of confidence. If this deteriorates, private investment declines, which results in a fall of output and employment (both directly and through the secondary effect of the fall in incomes upon consumption and investment). This gives the capitalists a powerful indirect control over government policy: everything which may shake the state of confidence must be carefully avoided because it would cause an economic crisis. But once the government learns the trick of increasing employment by its own purchases, this powerful controlling device loses its effectiveness.

Hence budget deficits necessary to carry out government intervention must be regarded as perilous. The social function of the doctrine of 'sound finance' is to make the level of employment dependent on the state of confidence. The dislike of business leaders for a government spending policy grows even more acute when they come to consider the objects on which the money would be spent: public investment and subsidizing mass consumption.

The economic principles of government intervention require that public investment should be confined to objects which do not compete with the equipment of private business (e.g. hospitals, schools, highways). Otherwise the profitability of private investment might be impaired, and the positive effect of public investment upon employment offset, by the negative effect of the decline in private investment. This conception suits the businessmen very well. But the scope for public investment of this type is rather narrow, and there is a danger that the government, in pursuing this policy, may eventually be tempted to nationalize transport or public utilities so as to gain a new sphere for investment.

One might therefore expect business leaders and their experts to be more in favor of subsidizing mass consumption (by means of family allowances, subsidies to keep down the prices of necessities, etc.) than of public investment; for by subsidizing consumption the government would not be embarking on any sort of enterprise. In practice, however, this is not the case. Indeed, subsidizing mass consumption is much more violently opposed by these experts than public investment. For here a moral principle of the highest importance is at stake. The fundamentals of capitalist ethics require that 'you shall earn your bread in sweat' – unless you happen to have private means.

We have considered the political reasons for the opposition to the policy of creating employment by government spending. But even if this opposition were overcome – as it may well be under the pressure of the masses – the maintenance of full employment would cause social and political changes which would give a new impetus to the opposition of the business leaders. Indeed, under a regime of permanent full employment, the 'sack' would cease to play its role as a 'disciplinary measure'. The social position of the boss would be undermined, and the self-assurance and class-consciousness of the working class would grow. Strikes for wage increases and improvements in conditions of work would create political tension. It is true that profits would be higher under a regime of full employment than they are on the average under *laissez faire*, and even the rise in wage rates resulting from the stronger bargaining power of the workers is less likely to reduce profits than to increase prices, and thus adversely affects only the rentier interests. But 'discipline in the factories' and 'political stability' are more appreciated than profits by business leaders. Their class instinct tells them that lasting full employment is unsound from their point of view, and that unemployment is an integral part of the 'normal' capitalist system.

What will be the practical outcome of the opposition to a policy of full employment by government spending in a capitalist democracy? We shall try to answer this question on the basis of the analysis of the reasons for this opposition given [already]. We argued that we may expect the opposition of the leaders of industry on three planes: (i) opposition on principle to government spending based on a budget deficit; (ii) opposition to this spending directed either towards public investment – which may foreshadow the intrusion of the state into the new spheres of economic activity – or towards subsidising mass consumption; (iii) opposition to *maintaining* full employment and not merely preventing deep and prolonged slumps.

In current discussions of these problems there emerges time and again the conception of counteracting the slump by stimulating *private* investment. This may be done by lowering the rate of interest, by the reduction of income tax, or by subsidising private investment directly in this or another form. That such a scheme should be attractive to business is not surprising. The entrepreneur remains the medium through which the intervention is conducted. If he does not feel confidence in the political situation, he will not be bribed into the investment. And the intervention does not involve the government either 'playing with' (public) investment or 'wasting money' on subsidising consumption.

It may be shown, however, that the stimulation of private investment does not provide an adequate method for preventing mass unemployment. There are two alternatives to be considered here. (i) The rate of interest or income tax (or both) is reduced sharply in the slump and increased in the boom. In this case, both the period and the amplitude of the business cycle will be reduced, but employment not only in the slump but even in the boom may be far from full, i.e. the average unemployment may be considerable, although its fluctuations will be less marked. (ii) The rate of interest or income tax is reduced in a slump but not increased in the subsequent boom. In this case the boom will last longer, but it must end in a new slump; one reduction in the rate of interest or income tax does not, of course, eliminate the forces which cause cyclical fluctuations in a capitalist economy. In the new slump it will be necessary to reduce the rate of interest or income tax again and so on. Thus in the not too remote future, the rate of interest would have to be negative and income tax would have to be replaced by an income subsidy. The same would arise if it were attempted to *maintain* full employment by stimulating private investment: the rate of interest and income tax would have to be reduced continuously.

In addition to this fundamental weakness of combating unemployment by stimulating private investment, there is a practical difficulty. The reaction of the entrepreneurs to the measures described is uncertain. If the downswing is sharp, they may take a very pessimistic view of the future and the reduction of the rate of interest or income tax may then for a long time have little or no effect upon investment, and thus upon the level of output and employment.

Even those who advocate stimulating private investment to counteract the slump frequently do not rely on it exclusively, but envisage that it should be associated with public investment. It looks at present as if business leaders and their experts (at least some of them) would tend to accept [as a last resort] public investment financed by borrowing as a means of alleviating slumps. They seem, however, still to be consistently opposed to creating employment by subsidising consumption and to *maintaining* full employment.

This state of affairs is perhaps symptomatic of the future economic regime of capitalist democracies. In the slump, either under the pressure of the masses, or even without it, public investment financed by borrowing will be undertaken to prevent large-scale unemployment. But if attempts are made to apply this method in order to maintain the high level of employment reached in the subsequent boom, strong opposition by business leaders is likely to be encountered … Lasting full employment is not at all to their liking. The workers would 'get out of hand' and the 'captains of industry' would be anxious to 'teach them a lesson'. Moreover, the price increase in the upswing is to the disadvantage of small and big rentiers, and makes them 'boom-tired'.

In this situation a powerful alliance is likely to be formed between big business and rentier interests, and they would probably find more than one economist to declare that the situation was manifestly unsound. The pressure of all these forces, and in particular of big business – as a rule influential in government departments – would most probably induce the government to return to the orthodox policy of cutting down the budget deficit. A slump would follow in which government spending policy would again come into its own.

The regime of the political business cycle would be an artificial restoration of the position as it existed in nineteenth-century capitalism. Full employment would be reached only at the top of the boom, but slumps would be relatively mild and short-lived.

Should a progressive be satisfied with a regime of the political business cycle? I think he should oppose it on two grounds: (i) that it does not assure lasting full employment; (ii) that government intervention is tied to public investment and does not embrace subsidising consumption. What the masses now ask for is not the mitigation of slumps but their total abolition. Nor should the resulting fuller utilisation of resources be applied to unwanted public investment merely in order to provide work. The government spending program should be devoted to public investment only to the extent to which such investment is actually needed. The rest of government spending necessary to maintain full employment should be used to subsidise consumption (through family allowances, old-age pensions, reduction in indirect taxation, and subsidising necessities). Opponents of such government will then have nothing to show for their money. The reply is that the counterpart of this spending will be the higher standard of living of the masses. Is not this the purpose of all economic activity?

'Full employment capitalism' will, of course, have to develop new social and political institutions which will reflect the increased power of the working class. If capitalism can adjust itself to full employment, a fundamental reform will have been incorporated in it. If not, it will show itself an outmoded system which must be scrapped.

Michael Kalecki worked at the United Nations Secretariat, the Polish Planning Commission, and the Central School of Planning and Statistics. He also taught at the Polish Academy of Sciences. This article is abridged from Political Aspects of Full Employment, *Political Quarterly*, vol. 14 no. 3, 1943, pp. 322-31.

The Financial Instability Hypothesis
Hyman P. Minsky

The financial instability hypothesis has both empirical and theoretical aspects. The readily observed empirical aspect is that from time to time capitalist economies exhibit inflations and debt deflations which seem to have the potential to spin out of control. In such processes the economic system's reactions to any movement of the economy amplify that movement – inflation feeds upon inflation and debt – deflation upon debt-deflation. Government interventions aimed to contain the deterioration seem to have been inept in a number of historical crises. These historical episodes provide evidence supporting the view that the economy does not always conform to the classic precepts of Smith and Walras – that economies can best be understood by assuming that at all times they are equilibrium-seeking and equilibrium-sustaining systems.

As economic theory, the financial instability hypothesis is an interpretation of the substance of Keynes's *General Theory* that also places the latter historically. As *The General Theory* was written in the early 1930s, the great financial and real contraction of the US and other capitalist economies of that time was part of the evidence *The General Theory* aimed to explain. The financial instability hypothesis also draws upon the credit view of money and finance of Joseph Schumpeter.

The theoretical argument of the financial instability hypothesis starts from the characterization of the economy as capitalist, with expensive capital assets and a complex, sophisticated financial system. The economic problem is identified (following Keynes) as the 'capital development of the economy' rather than the neoclassical 'allocation of given resources among alternative employments'. The focus is on an accumulating capitalist economy that moves through real calendar time.

The capital development of a capitalist economy is accompanied by exchanges of present money for future money. Present money pays for resources that go into the production of investment output, whereas future money is the 'profits' that will accrue to the capital asset-owning firms as capital assets are used in production. As a result of the process by which investment is financed, control over items in the capital stock by producing units is financed by liabilities; these are commitments to pay money at dates specified or as conditions arise. For each economic unit the liabilities on its balance sheet determine a time series of prior payment commitments even as the assets generate a time series of conjectured cash receipts.

This structure was well stated by Keynes (1936: 151):

> There is a multitude of real assets in the world which constitutes our capital wealth – buildings, stocks of commodities, goods in the course of manufacture and of transport, and so forth. The nominal owners of these assets, however, have not infrequently borrowed *money* [Keynes's emphasis] in order to become possessed of them. To a corresponding extent the actual owners of wealth have claims, not on real assets, but on money. A considerable part of this financing takes place through the banking system, which interposes its guarantee between its depositors who lend it money, and its borrowing customers to whom it loans money wherewith to finance the purchase of real assets. The interposition of this veil of money between the real asset and the wealth owner is an especially marked characteristic of the modern world.

This Keynesian *veil of money* is different from that of the quantity theory of money. According to the quantity theory veil of money, the exchanges in trading in commodity markets are of goods for money and money for goods. The Keynesian veil implies that money is connected with financing through time. A part of the financing of the economy can be structured as dated payment commitments in which banks are the central players. The money flows are first from depositors to banks and from banks to firms and then, at some later date, from firms to banks and then from banks to their depositors. In the first instance, the exchanges are for the financing of investment; in the second, they fulfill the prior commitments that are stated in the financial contract.

In a Keynesian veil of money world, the flow of money to firms is a response to expectations of future profits, and the flow of money from firms is financed by profits that are realized. In the Keynesian set-up, the key economic exchanges take place as a result of negotiations between generic bankers and generic businessmen. The documents 'on the table' in such negotiations detail the cost and profit expectations of businessmen who interpret them as enthusiasts: the bankers as skeptics.

It follows that in a capitalist economy the past, the present and the future are linked, not only by capital assets and labor force characteristics, but also by financial relations. The key financial relations link the creation and ownership of capital assets to the structure of financial relations and changes in this structure. Institutional complexity may result in several layers of intermediation between the ultimate owners of the community's wealth and the units that control and operate that wealth.

Expectations of business profits determine both the flow of financing contracts to business and the price in the market of existing financing contracts. Profit realizations determine whether the commitments in financial contracts are fulfilled, whether financial assets perform as the *pro formas* of the negotiations indicated they should.

In the modern world the analysis of financial relations and their implications for system behavior cannot be restricted to the liability structures of businesses and the cash flow they entail. The current performance of the economy either validates or does not validate the liability structures of households (in terms of their ability to borrow on credit cards for expensive consumer goods such as automobiles, house purchases and to carry financial assets), governments (with their large floating and funded debts) and international units (as a result of the internationalization of finance). The system may behave differently than in earlier eras due to, first, an increasing complexity of the financial structure and, second, a greater involvement of governments as refinancing agents for financial institutions as well as for ordinary business firms … In particular the much greater participation of national governments in assuring that finance does not degenerate as in the 1929-33 period means that the down-side vulnerability of aggregate profit flows has been much diminished. However, the same interventions may well induce a greater degree of up-side (i.e. inflationary) bias to the economy.

In spite of the greater complexity of financial relations than was true in the past, the key determinant of system behavior remains the level of profits. The financial instability hypothesis incorporates the Kalecki (1969) view of profits in which the structure of aggregate demand determines profits. In the simple model, in each period aggregate profits equal aggregate investment. In more complex though still highly abstract structures, aggregate profits equal aggregate investment plus the government deficit. As expectations of profits depend upon investment in the future and as realized profits are determined by investment, whether or not liabilities are validated depends upon investment. Investment takes place in the present because businessmen and their bankers expect investment to take place in the future.

The financial instability hypothesis therefore is a theory of the impact of debt on system behavior and the way debt is validated. In contrast to the orthodox quantity theory of money, the financial instability hypothesis takes banking seriously as a profit-seeking activity. Banks seek profits by financing activity; like all entrepreneurs in a capitalist economy, bankers are aware that innovation assures profits. Thus using the term generically for all intermediaries in finance (whether they be brokers or dealers), bankers are merchants of debt who strive to innovate in the assets they acquire and the liabilities they market. This innovative characteristic of banking and finance invalidates the fundamental presupposition of the orthodox quantity theory of money to the effect that there is an unchanging 'money' item whose velocity of circulation is sufficiently close to being constant so that changes in this money's supply have a linear proportional relation to a well-defined price level.

Three income-debt relations for economic units – labeled as hedge, speculative and Ponzi finance – can be identified. Hedge-financing units are those which can fulfill all of their contractual payment obligations by their cash flows: the greater the weight of equity financing in the liability structure, the greater the likelihood that the unit is a hedge-financing unit. Speculative finance units are those that can meet their payment commitments on 'income account' on their liabilities even though they cannot repay the principal out of income cash flows. Such units need to 'roll over' their liabilities; i.e. issue new debt to meet commitments on maturing debts. Governments with floating debts, corporations with floating issues of commercial paper and banks are typical hedge units.

For Ponzi units the cash flows from operations are not sufficient to fulfill either the repayment of principal or the interest due on outstanding debts. Such units can sell assets or borrow in order to pay interest; dividends on common stock lower the equity of a unit even as they increase liabilities and the prior commitment of future incomes. Each unit that Ponzi finances lowers the margin of safety that it offers the holders of its debts.

It can be shown that if hedge financing dominates, then the economy is an equilibrium-seeking and deviation-containing system, whereas the greater the weight of speculative and Ponzi finance, the more likely that the economy is a deviation-amplifying system. The first theorem of the financial instability hypothesis is that the economy has financing regimes under which it is stable and financing regimes under which it is unstable. The second theorem is that, over periods of prolonged prosperity, the economy moves from financial relations that make for a stable system to those that make for an unstable system.

In particular, over a protracted period of good times, capitalist economies tend to move from a financial structure dominated by hedge-finance units to one dominated by units engaged in speculative and Ponzi finance. Furthermore, if an economy with a sizeable body of speculative financial units is in an inflationary state and the authorities attempt to exorcise inflation by monetary constraint, then speculative units will become Ponzi units and the net worth of what were previously Ponzi units will quickly evaporate. When this happens, units with cash flow shortfalls will be forced to try to make position by selling out position. This is likely to lead to a collapse of asset values. The financial instability hypothesis is a model of a capitalist economy which does not rely upon exogenous shocks to generate business cycles of varying severity: the hypothesis contends that business cycles of history are compounded out of the internal dynamics of capitalist economies as well as out of the system of interventions and regulations designed to keep the economy operating within reasonable bounds.

Hyman Minsky was Professor Emeritus of Economics in Arts and Sciences, Washington University, St Louis. This chapter is adapted from The Financial Instability Hypothesis, in P. Arestis and Sawyer, M. (eds). *The Elgar Companion to Radical Political Economy*, Edward Elgar, Aldershot, 1994, pp. 153-8. © 1994 Philip Arestis and Malcolm Sawyer. Reprinted with permission of the editors.

Post-Keynesian Economics
Peter Kriesler

Post-Keynesian economics refers to a body of economic analysis inspired by the works of John Maynard Keynes and Michal Kalecki. By its very nature, post-Keynesian theory is not a homogeneous analysis. Unlike modern neoclassical theory, post-Keynesians do not try to present a mathematically elegant general abstract model with little relation to reality. Post-Keynesians are interested in trying to understand the dynamics of actual economies. They follow Kalecki's view that "the Institutional framework of a social system is a basic element of its economic dynamics" (Kalecki 1970: 111) and Joan Robinson's view that we always need to know 'the rules of the game' of the society we are analysing. Since most economies have different institutions, post-Keynesians do not subscribe to a general theory with modifications to allow for institutions and social phenomena, but instead incorporate these into the essence of their models.

Being anchored in the real world, Post Keynesian theory attempts to understand specific aspects of capitalism, so it is concerned with analysing how economic processes function through historical time. This has a number of important implications. First, post-Keynesians deny the validity or usefulness of general theory which can apply to all societies at all times. Rather, because the economy is extremely complex and always evolving, there are many different ways of looking at it, which themselves will be in a state of change. No single way will always be correct, and the best method of interpreting the economy will depend on the purpose of the analysis. Post-Keynesians see the economy as developing though a historical process, with the unchangeable past influencing the present, while the future is uncertain and expectations have a significant and unavoidable impact on economic events. The world is messy and the future unknowable, and decision-makers operate in a world without certainty.

Historical time and uncertainty

Post-Keynesians have a clear definition of historical time and its role in economic theory. Decisions taken today are influenced both by the past, as well as by our expectations of the future. These decisions will, in turn, influence current events and so will lead to different behaviours of individuals and institutions. Historical time refers to the fact that time moves in one direction. The past is unchangeable, though its influence is felt in the present and, therefore, in the future. All aspects of the economy are in a state of flux, changing and evolving as a result of decisions taken currently as well as those taken in the past. Today's events and decisions are profoundly influenced by what has gone on before, by history, so that the sequence of events leading up to the present is extremely important. Future outcomes cannot be predestined, as they also crucially depend on current events and the history of events leading to those outcomes. This fundamental role of historical time is an underlying feature of post-Keynesian economics, and represents a major contrast with neoclassical theory. Post-Keynesians believe that the movement of the economy is determined by the path it has taken and that its destination (if it has one) is also determined by that path.

According to Paul Davidson, the neoclassical analysis of uncertainty is based on "the axiom of ergodicity". He explains this essential feature of neoclassical theory as follows: "In an ergodic system future events are always reliably predictable by using a probabilistic analysis of past and current outcomes" (Davidson 1994: 89). The theory assumes that either we know the future, or we know with certainty the probability distribution of all future events. Post-Keynesian economists, by contrast, deny this axiom. For them the future is unknowable, the world non-ergodic.

It is important to note that uncertainty is something which permeates all economic decisions. Why do we do things today? It is because we have expectations or beliefs about their future consequences. We take actions today in order to reap something from them – usually some 'reward' – in the future. However, according to post-Keynesians, we can never know the future because it is inherently uncertain. Therefore, the ways in which we deal with uncertainty will always have a profound impact on our current actions. It is important in this context to consider how uncertainty differs from risk. To quote Keynes (1937: 223):

By 'uncertain' knowledge ... I do not mean merely to distinguish what is known for certain from what is only probable. The game of roulette is not subject, in this sense, to uncertainty. Or, again, the expectation of life is only slightly uncertain. Even the weather is only moderately uncertain ... The sense in which I am using the term is that in which the prospect of a European war is uncertain, or the price of copper and the rate of interest twenty years hence, the obsolescence of a new invention, or the position of private wealth holders in the social system in [2035]. About these matters there is no scientific basis on which to form any calculable probability whatsoever. We simply do not know.

Because the future is unknowable, the question arises as to what is the basis on which people can act. Keynes's solution, which has been taken up by post-Keynesian economists, is that, faced with an unknowable future, people rely on conventions and institutions as a way of dealing with radical uncertainty. The fact that most people follow these conventions minimizes individual losses. However, conventions can break down outside normal times, and expectations can fluctuate wildly.

As a result of these considerations, most post-Keynesians do not use equilibrium concepts in their analysis of capitalist economies, as they are concerned with cumulative change and dynamic paths. Inherent in their analysis is the concept of cumulative causation, which is destructive of the concept of equilibrium since it implies that any movement away from an initial position will be amplified and generates further movements away from that position. As the institutional economist Gunnar Myrdal said: "Cumulative causation is the idea of reinforcing processes by which the patterns of uneven development between regions, between countries and between economic and social phenomena may be perpetuated and even accentuated" (Myrdal 1957). To quote another pioneering theorist, "change becomes progressive and propagates itself in a cumulative way" (Young 1928).

Institutions

Keynes believed that fundamental uncertainty is a crucial element in any economic processes. In most circumstances, even if probabilities can be estimated, they are meaningless for long period decision-making. Market forces cannot deal with the inherent unpredictability of the long run and we cannot rely on them to do so. When faced with radical uncertainty, people form rules to follow, and institutions arise. In other words, institutions serve the function of allowing people to make decisions in a world which has too much information to process, and where uncertainty permeates most aspects of economic behaviour and inhibits optimising behaviour. In a complex world of ignorance and uncertainty, these procedures and rules of thumb are quite "rational". There are many examples of such rules of thumb in the real world, including mark-up pricing, investment and bureaucratic rules. The principles of mark-up pricing are discussed below, but they are general rules of thumb which guide decision-makers in deciding on price so that they do not have to worry about the uncertain and changing economic environment in which they are operating. They also are derived on the basis of readily available information, and do not lead to frequent and costly changes in price.

These examples show that economic, social and political institutions play a fundamental role in shaping the basic determinate of economic activity.

Macroeconomics

Post-Keynesian economists also believe that macroeconomic phenomena – such as aggregate demand, the level of employment and the inflation rate – behave differently from microeconomic ones. The economy as a whole operates differently from the behaviour of individuals, of firms and of industries. Most importantly, it behaves differently from the simple sum of those individual behaviours. The attempt to derive macroeconomic behaviour from the behaviour at the microeconomic level by aggregating it is known as the fallacy of composition. As Keynes said, "mistakes have been made through extending to the system, as a whole, conclusions which have been correctly arrived at in respect of a part of it taken in isolation (Keynes 1936: xxxii).

Post-Keynesian macroeconomics follows the analysis of Keynes and Kalecki in seeing the main determinant of the level of employment and output as being the level of aggregate demand. This represents an important departure from mainstream economics where the main determinant of the level of employment is the real wage rate which, if sufficiently flexible, is presumed to ensure full employment, The levels of growth and output within mainstream theory are determined by supply side considerations such as the growth in labour force and in productivity. Demand side factors have no long run role. In contrast, aggregate demand plays a key role for post-Keynesian economists.

The central message of Keynes and Kalecki is that there is no automatic mechanism in capitalist economies that will ensure full employment. The economy achieving full employment would be a fluke. Unemployment during a recession is not caused by rigidities in wage rates or in the rate of interest, but by a failure of the level of aggregate demand to generate adequate employment opportunities. In order to terminate a recession and to achieve full employment, the economy needs an injection of demand from an exogenous source, such as government expenditure. Within post-Keynesian analysis there is detailed analysis of all the determinants of aggregate demand, particularly investment. This focus is appropriate because it is the extreme volatility of investment spending which makes it the leading cause of economic cycles. This volatility, in turn, is tied to uncertainty about future returns. Investment represents expenditures today in order to make profits in the future. It is, therefore, tied to expectations of future returns, which themselves are extremely volatile as they cannot be based on actual knowledge.

Post-Keynesians also see a fundamental role for money and credit in the economy. This is another contrast with neoclassical theory, where one of the key features is the assumed long-run neutrality of money. In the post-Keynesian view, money is seen as playing a key role in connecting the irreversible past and the uncertain future. The money supply is not a stock of financial assets, but a flow of debt issued primarily to transfer purchasing power from the future to the present. The assets included in money supply change over time through financial innovations. 'Money' is simply the most liquid of these assets, with most financial assets having well developed second-hand markets where they can be converted into cash. Money markets act quite differently under different circumstances: in particular they act differently under boom conditions than under recession conditions.

It is common to observe that goods markets in modern capitalist economies are imperfectly competitive. Post-Keynesians regard financial markets as imperfectly competitive, too, so that there is no such thing as "efficient markets", as neoclassical economists assume. Rather, interest rates are determined as a mark-up over the cost of funds. The mark-up will vary with the market in which the loans are made, and thus there will be an array of interest rates reflecting the differences in the markets. Access to financial markets depends on the liquidity which firms and businesses bring to that market.

According to post-Keynesians:

- Money is credit created which reflects the state of demand for money in the economy.
- Banks are not restrained in terms of their reserves. The money supply is determined by the demand from the private sector at an interest rate fixed by the central bank.
- Central banks set rates either officially or through open market operations. In doing so, they must consider constraints such as foreign rates and exchange rates, and have institutional constraints on their ability to set interest rates – for example, those implied by inflation targeting.
- Financial markets (for equities and derivatives in particular) are not inherently stable, as traditional theory would suggest. Instability in the financial markets will spread to other markets, and is itself a cause of economic cycles. The important conclusion for post-Keynesian economists is that money and financial assets can affect the real economy in both the short and long run, and can be a source of cycles and recessions in their own right.

Microeconomics

In considering the actions of firms and individuals, post-Keynesians believe that micro behaviour is dependent on the institutional framework of the economy. In particular, modern capitalist economies are typified by a manufacturing or service sector which is far from competitive. As Kalecki (1971: 98) pointed out:

> 'Perfect competition' ... is a most unrealistic assumption not only for the present phase of capitalism but even for the so called competitive capitalist economy of past centuries: surely this competition was always in general very imperfect. Perfect competition when its actual status of a handy model is forgotten becomes a dangerous myth.

The modern capitalist economy is, typically, oligopolistic, with a relatively small number of influential firms controlling each industry. Firms in the manufacturing sector of the economy face constant costs per unit of output up to the level of full capacity. This means that supply is typically elastic, with excess capacity being the norm. As a result, price in the oligopolistic manufacturing sector is not determined by supply and demand, but as a mark-up on constant costs. Post-Keynesians identify two different sources for the determination of mark-ups. On the one hand, the mark-up is determined by competitive factors and market structures. On the other hand, prices help generate internal funds which firms can use to finance investment. This is important because, due to the imperfections of financial markets, firms' access to credit depends directly upon the internal funds they can generate. Which explanation of the determination of the mark-up dominates a particular industry or firm will depend on the economic environment and history of that particular entity.

The important conclusion is that prices do not usually respond directly to changes in demand. Rather, prices are determined on the basis of costs, while demand plays the role of determining how much is actually sold. So, importantly, prices for post Keynesian economists do not serve the role of allocating scarce resources. Therein lies another striking contrast with neoclassical economic theory.

Economic policy

Post-Keynesians see an important role for the state to influence the level of output and employment, both indirectly and directly. Indirect influence comes through the effect of the state on the components of aggregate demand: for example, government taxes will influence the level of consumption, investment and the balance of trade. Directly, government expenditures add to aggregate demand. Post-Keynesians prefer the direct stimulation of demand through fiscal policy, particularly by increased government expenditure on infrastructure which increases productivity, or through increased incentives for private sector investment. Monetary policy – control over interest rates – is seen as a relatively blunt instrument, whose efficacy varies depending on the state of the economy. Post-Keynesians also wish to design policies which affect the level, rate of change and distribution of money incomes: the distribution of income affects the propensity to consume and therefore the level of effective demand, output and employment.

However, Post-Keynesians are also aware of the political constraints on achieving full employment. They understand that unemployment serves important socio-economic functions in modern capitalist economies. This point was emphasised by Kalecki, who argued that unemployment was essential for the survival of capitalism as it was the means by which the capitalist class asserted its control over the working class. Without unemployment, the system would exascerbate the underlying social and political tensions, resulting in problems of discipline and instability. As Kalecki said, "Indeed, under a regime of permanent full employment, the 'sack' would cease to play its role as a disciplinary measure. The social position of the boss would be undermined, and the self-assurance and class-consciousness of the working class would grow" (Kalecki 1943: 351).

Post-Keynesian economists do not advocate a unique set of policies that should always be applied to solve any particular economic problem. Rather, they adopt what Geoff Harcourt (2004) calls a "horses for courses" approach, whereby the most appropriate policies depend on the specifics of the national economy, and the domestic and international environment in which it is operating.

Peter Kriesler is Associate Professor of Economics at the University of NSW. Post-Keynesian Economics © 2010 Peter Kriesler.

III
ALTERNATIVE ECONOMIC PERSPECTIVES

GREEN ECONOMICS

We turn now to four influences on modern political economy of a more interdisciplinary nature. The first three reflect contemporary social movements – regarding the environment, the status of women in society, and development in the Third World. The fourth builds on attempts to link economic analysis with social psychology in developing more sophisticated understandings of actual economic behavior. These areas of concern feed into the reformulation of political economy as part of social science.

The growing awareness of environmental constraints on economic growth has caused a particularly fundamental challenge to conventional economics. Warnings about the bio-physical limits set by natural resource endowments have intensified in recent years. So too have concerns about pollution, both locally and globally, including concerns about global warming and climate change. However, there remain major differences of opinion about what changes to the economic system are needed to create ecological sustainability. Is it necessary to put a severe brake on economic growth? If so, how? If not, what other changes to our economic institutions and methods of allocating resources are warranted?

These are enormous challenges, not least for the discipline of economics. Can economics be reformulated to deal with environmental issues or, more boldly, to embrace a holistic ecological vision of the economy-nature' relationship? Opinions vary. On the one hand, neoclassical economists contend that their theories can be extended to analyse how environmental decay results from 'market imperfections'. According to this view, these imperfections can be corrected simply by extending the market to deal with 'environmental goods' such as clean air and clean water. These resources would be efficiently allocated through market processes if property rights were extended to allow individual ownership of them. Thus, the market is the solution, not the problem. A more radical view is that addressing the problem of environmental decay requires a fundamental assault on existing structures of economic power, the pervasive ideologies of individualism and consumerism, the socioeconomic inequalities which inhibit collective action, and the process of capital accumulation that depletes 'natural capital'. This political economic perspective is fundamentally at odds, conceptually and politically, with mainstream economic thinking.

The following readings reflect some of these controversies. The article by Michael Jacobs demonstrates the inadequacy of conventional economic accounting. It shows that GNP is inherently biased as a measure of economic activity and fundamentally inadequate as a measure of national well-being. Sharon Beder presents a sceptical view of current market-based policy proposals for dealing with the threat of climate change, seeing the need for a more fundamental change in social values and economic practices. James O'Connor indicates how Marxist analysis can be extended to understand the roots of environmental decay and the rise of social movements challenging anti-ecological practices. Finally, Joy Paton explores the notion of sustainable development, pointing to the dangers arising when this notion subordinates ecological to economic concerns and thereby loses its radical edge.

For more on green economics see the journal *Capitalism, Nature, Socialism* <www.cnsjournal.org>, and Sharon Beder's book *Environmental Principles and Policies: An Interdisciplinary Approach*, UNSW Press, Sydney, 2006. The *Journal of Australian Political Economy* released a special issue on climate change in Summer 2010/11, issue 66.

Measuring Success
Michael Jacobs

For the past 150 years, since the end of the first Industrial Revolution, western society has had little doubt about its economic goals. The purpose of the economy is to create wealth. Economic progress can therefore be measured by the size of the national income, along with the base of capital or wealth from which it is generated. Economies are successful when wealth and income rise, allowing higher consumption and therefore higher standards of living. Economic growth, it is assumed, makes people better off.

These claims have been taken by most people as practically self-evident. It is true that there have been disagreements about the nature and distribution of the national income. Those on the left have emphasised that wealth and consumption need not be private, pointing out that public services (from street cleaning to museums) make as valuable a contribution to the living standards as private expenditure. They have argued too that the distribution of income is as important as its creation. But neither caveat challenges the basic view of economic progress as the expansion of monetary wealth. Indeed, many socialists have stressed that it is only by generating wealth that public services can be provided and poverty relieved. Governments of all shades in practically all countries have been committed to the achievement of economic growth.

Yet it is precisely this accepted view of economic success which a concern for the environment throws into question. If the creation of wealth causes environmental damage, should it automatically be counted as progress? Is an economy with a high growth rate of national income and a high growth rate of degradation necessarily performing better than one with lower rates of both? If not, is economic growth society's most appropriate goal?

These questions are essentially about economic objectives. But they can very quickly turn into debates about indicators; that is, about the statistical measures of economic behaviour. If economic progress is defined as the growth of national income, society can only tell whether or not it is progressing if national income can be measured. So the indicators that do this, Gross National or Domestic Product (GNP or GDP), assume considerable significance. GNP, GDP, and their annual growth rates serve to measure the economy's performance. These indicators are both the principal means of judging one country's economic progress over time, and of comparing the economic success of different countries. Arguments over objectives are consequently often expressed as arguments over indicators. The substance of the Green case is that society should not seek higher income levels if this involves environmental damage. But given that national income is measured by GNP, this is equivalent to saying that GNP is the wrong indicator of economic performance. A successful economy, environmentalists argue, should be defined as one which does not experience environmental degradation. But GNP, as a purely monetary statistic, doesn't record degradation. So GNP cannot be maintained as society's chief indicator of economic success.

The Greens' argument against GNP is that its growth rests on two separate but connected observations about the effect of environmental degradation. Degradation directly reduces the current well-being or welfare of the population, through pollution and loss of aesthetic amenity. It also reduces the capacity of the economy to produce future welfare, through the depletion of resources, loss of absorptive capacities and impairment of life support services. Both of these effects might reasonably be said to reflect badly on the performance of the economy. Yet because they don't have monetary measures, neither is recorded in national income.

Indeed, environmental degradation has a rather perverse relationship to GDP. In cases of pollution, for example, national income clearly overstates the actual level of welfare. If GNP is to be used as a measure of how well off people are, it would seem sensible to subtract something to reflect the loss of amenity, damage to health and other ill effects which the pollution causes. Yet the effect of pollution, if anything, is the reverse. If people are less healthy and need more medical care, or if buildings have to be cleaned more often, economic activity increases, which adds to national income. Indeed, the more pollution there is, the higher will be these 'defensive expenditures' (that is, expenditures on things which defend people against the effects of the pollution). If society makes a concerted attempt to control and repair pollution damage, for example by investment in pollution control equipment and clean-up programs, the contribution to GNP will be even greater.

It is not true to say, as some Greens have done, that 'pollution increases GNP'. The extra anti-pollution or defensive expenditure could have been spent on something else, leaving the final level of national income unchanged. But those alternative goods and services might have made a net contribution to welfare, whereas spending on pollution control and repair simply uses up resources to keep welfare exactly where it was to start with. GNP becomes less reliable as a measure of welfare.

The failure of national income to measure the depletion of natural resources is perhaps even more serious. The environment is an essential foundation of economic activity: it may be considered a part of the 'capital' from which the economy derives its income. Yet it is not recorded as such in the national income accounts.

It is one of the first principles of accounting that economic success must be measured by the stock of capital as well as the flow of income. There is little virtue in high income if it is achieved simply by running down reserves or productive capacity. This way lies long-term ruin: when the capital runs out, there will be no income at all. The national income accounts acknowledge this in respect of human-made capital (factories, machines, etc.), by subtracting from GNP an allowance for 'depreciation'. This is the sum which, if reinvested in productive capacity, would maintain the capital stock intact. The result is known as 'Net National Product' (NNP; or its counterpart Net Domestic Product). NNP is actually rarely used, partly because it is very difficult to estimate the appropriate figure for depreciation, and partly because depreciation is assumed to be roughly constant from year to year, so that its effect on the growth of GNP can safely be ignored. But in theory at least NNP is intended to be a measure of 'sustainable income': the amount available for consumption after the sum required to maintain capital has been set aside.

But in fact, environmentalists point out, NNP isn't such a measure, since no allocation is made for the depreciation of 'natural capital' despite the fact that this capital is also being run down, in some cases very rapidly. On the contrary, so far from environmental degradation leading to a subtraction from GNP, it tends to increase it. When a forest is felled for timber, for example, GNP includes all the income earned, but NNP records no loss in future productive capacity. Similarly, when high levels of agricultural production cause soil erosion, GNP rises, but NNP remains unchanged, despite the depletion of the natural capital base.

This mismeasurement of sustainable income can have a particularly damaging effect for countries in the South for whom a large proportion of output comes from natural resources. Rapid depletion of these resources causes high GNP growth, which is taken to mean economic success. But if no allowance is made for the reduction in income which must inevitably follow when the resources are exhausted, such 'success' can only be illusory and short-lived.

Environmentalists' criticisms of the conventional national income measures are therefore not simply academic debating points. Of themselves, indicators such as GNP and NNP are only tools. But choice of the wrong tool measuring the economy's performance by the wrong indicators may lead to wrong policies being adopted, and wrong judgments being made about how successful such policies are. Countries may decide to exhaust their natural resources in the belief that this will lead to a long-term increase in consumption. Reductions in welfare caused by pollution, urban congestion and loss of amenity may simply go unrecognised, and therefore untackled, because policy-makers have assumed that living standards are measured simply by national income. It is this influence on the making and evaluation of economic policy which has made GNP an object of such opprobrium in the Green movement.

Of course, one response to these arguments is to return to the primary issue of objectives. If governments do not believe that environmental degradation matters, because welfare and sustainable income are not the goals of economic policy, the Green case will cut no ice. But let us assume (not unreasonably) that both current and future welfare are considered important objectives. What effect does the environmental critique then have on the choice of economic indicators? For many Greens, the answer is self-evident. The way in which national income is calculated should be changed so that it includes the effects of environmental degradation. Specifically, three kinds of adjustment have been proposed.

First, 'defensive expenditures' (such as pollution control equipment and medical expenditure on pollution-related illnesses) should be subtracted from GNP in its current form. Such expenditures are not net additions to welfare: as 'regrettable necessities' they should be regarded as the costs of consuming other goods and services rather than benefits in their own right. Second, any residual damage to the environment that reduces welfare and has not been made good by defensive expenditure should be valued and also removed from the current GNP. If only defensive expenditures are subtracted, GNP would clearly be higher the more pollution was left untreated. To prevent this, any pollution which remains should also cause a reduction in GNP. Third, NNP should include an allowance for the depletion of natural capital as well as the depreciation of human-made capital. The point of NNP is to measure the potential for future income. It does not do this if no recognition is made that exhaustion of and damage to the economy's natural resource base is effectively a form of capital consumption. Unless new investment is undertaken, environmental damage reduces the possibility of earning future income. (Note that if both the second and third adjustments are made, there is a risk of double counting, since some aspects of the environment that provide welfare, such as forests, are also aspects of 'natural capital'.)

If national income were adjusted in these ways, the environmentalists argue, it would act as a more accurate indicator of the overall performance of the economy and therefore as a better guide to the conduct of policy. Environmental costs would be properly accounted for, both in the measurement of current welfare (through the first two subtractions) and in that of future sustainability (through the third). Growth of an 'Environmentally adjusted Net National Product' would then be a genuinely acceptable economic objective. This seems a reasonable argument, but it is important to note the implicit assumption here. This is that GNP is the best starting point to measure economic performance, even if various subtractions have to be made from it. After all, one response to the inadequacy of GNP might have been to abandon it altogether for evaluative purposes and start again with a different indicator or set of indicators. It is easy to see why the environmentalists have not done this. In the first place, GNP is a measure of income, and it will generally be agreed that income should be an important component of any performance measure. Moreover, incorporating environmental measurement into national income avoids the problem of comparing unlike indicators. If environmental changes are recorded in non-monetary terms, politicians and the electorate must somehow judge whether, for example, a rise in GNP and a fall in environmental performance constitutes a net loss or gain: being expressed in different units there is no easy means of comparison. If both objectives are counted in one indicator, on the other hand, the problem disappears and judgment is (apparently) made easier.

Perhaps most importantly, however, the point of adjusting GNP is to challenge it. GNP is an influential indicator. It is widely used to measure economic success: its rate of growth is announced monthly and features prominently in news broadcasts and economic analysis.

Politicians and economists are accustomed to measuring performance by it. In these circumstances, the environmentalists reason, merely proposing a new, separate indicator will not have the desired effect of dethroning GNP. It has to be replaced directly, by saying not merely that it is inadequate, but that it is inadequate by such-and-such an amount, which they have calculated and can then subtract from it. GNP has to be shown to be wrong, not merely insufficient.

Michael Jacobs is a consultant and Visiting Senior Fellow at the Grantham Research Institute on Climate Change and the Environment at the London School of Economics. This chapter is adapted from Measuring Success, *The Green Economy*, Pluto Press, London, 1991, pp. 222-8. © 1991 Michael Jacobs. Reprinted with permission of the author.

Market Mechanisms, Ecological Sustainability and Equity
Sharon Beder

Economists are commonly asked for advice on environmental policy. In Australia, for example, it was economist Ross Garnaut who was asked by the government to prepare the major report on climate change policy. Not surprisingly, economists tend to advocate market mechanisms to achieve environmental protection. But can market mechanisms achieve ecological sustainability and maintain social equity? In most cases, market mechanisms aim to maximise economic efficiency rather than environmental effectiveness or equity.

The use of emissions trading to reduce greenhouse gases in the atmosphere is a typical policy advocated by mainstream economists. Tradeable pollution rights were originally developed in the US to cut costs to industry and enable economic growth to continue in highly polluted areas. Emissions trading allows firms to trade the right to emit specific quantities of pollutants. It aims to achieve a given level of environmental protection at less cost to industry rather than maximising environmental gains. Indeed, past experience has shown that the environmental gains from emissions trading are far from guaranteed.

Ecological sustainability

Emissions trading is based on the idea some firms can reduce their emissions more cheaply than others. Therefore, it is more cost effective to allow the market to decide where emission reductions will be made than for governments to require uniform reductions across an industry. Firms that find it expensive to reduce emissions are able to buy up emission permits instead. Those that can reduce emissions cheaply can sell on their unwanted permits.

This might be acceptable if only limited pollution reductions are required – that is, if reductions can be limited to what can be done cheaply. However, it makes little sense if substantial reductions are required. If more expensive reductions have to be made, then there is little point in setting up markets that enable some firms to avoid making those expensive reductions so as to minimise overall costs.

This became evident when the German government considered implementing an acid rain emissions programme. The aim of the German programme was a 90 percent reduction in SO_2 between 1983 and 1998. In comparison, the aim of the US emissions trading program was only a

50 percent reduction by 2010. This meant that, in the US, there was much more scope for power stations to find cheaper ways to reduce their emissions, whereas in Germany every power station had little choice but to retrofit their plants with flue gas desulphurisation and selective catalytic reduction for nitrogen oxides. This meant that there was no scope for emissions trading in Germany (Schärer 1999: 144-5).

The US Acid Rain Cap and Trade scheme is consistently cited as a success because it achieved emissions reductions at minimal cost, but how do those reductions compare with what can be achieved with traditional regulation? The UK Environmental Agency (2003: 8) noted that sulphur emissions in the US exceeded those from the EU Member States by 150 percent.

Even proponents of trading admit that there will inevitably be a conflict and an implicit trade-off between the goals of reducing costs and improving environmental quality (Hahn and Hester 1989: 147, Atkinson and Tietenberg 1991: 20-26). This conflict can be seen in the setting of a cap for tradeable emissions programmes. The cap is the total amount of emissions for which permits are issued. There are various reasons for choosing a particular cap. They include (Moore 2004: 2):

- environmental and health protection;
- technical feasibility – available technology;
- economics – balancing costs; and
- politics – influence of vested interests and political acceptability.

In practice, caps tend to be based on economics and politics rather than on what is technically feasible to protect the environment and human health. This is evident in Garnaut's recommendations for emissions trading. His report recommended two levels of reductions for Australia – a 20 percent reduction if a post-Kyoto international agreement is achieved, but, if not, only a 5 percent reduction in Australian greenhouse gases from 2000 levels by 2010. In other words, the cap should reflect political and economic reality, not what is best for the environment (Garnaut 2008: 3).

The Garnaut Review claimed that, even if an international agreement is reached, the aim would only be to stabilise at 550 ppm (compared to current emissions of 455 ppm) of greenhouse gases. This is likely to result in 44-87 percent mortality of coral, 8-39 percent species at risk of extinction, and 12-77 percent likelihood of irreversible melting of the Greenland ice sheet (Garnaut 2008: 33). Even the more ambitious target of ten percent reduction by 2020 is conditional on an international agreement that will not prevent disastrous environmental consequences.

What is good for the environment is not necessarily good for encouraging trade in a market. If the cap is set too low and too few permits are issued, there will be little trading because firms will not have spare permits. Yet such a low cap may be necessary to protect the environment.

When the EU emissions trading system was introduced in 2005, analysts believed that many governments had been too generous in allocating permits to local firms because they feared their local industries would be at a competitive disadvantage if they had to buy extra permits. A study by Ilex Energy Consulting for WWF, examining six EU countries, found that none of them had set caps that went beyond 'business as usual' and that they would meet their agreed Kyoto obligations (ILEX Energy Consulting 2005). Because allowances were not in great demand, the market opened at 8 euros per tonne and settled around 23 euros a few months later, far less than necessary to provide an incentive to reduce emissions (Pearce 1997: 6). Yet Garnaut recommended permits be sold in Australia in 2010 for only $20 per tonne, rising each year by only 4 percent (Garnaut 2008: 2).

Emissions trading has the potential to enable phoney reductions. The most obvious example is the trading of emissions permits with Russia and other eastern European countries that are in economic decline. This has meant that some countries in Eastern Europe are already emitting 30-45 percent less carbon dioxide than in 1990 because of lowered production, yet they can sell to other nations their rights to emissions they were not going to make in return for hard currency, with no net benefit to the planet (Pearce 1997: 22, Corporate Europe Observatory 2000: 13). The reductions that would have occurred *without* emissions trading are now available to affluent countries to avoid their own emissions reductions. They are referred to as 'hot air' or 'phantom' emissions reductions.

In NSW, the Greenhouse Abatement Scheme issued certificates to those who reduced greenhouse gas emissions that could then be sold to electricity retailers who had to meet mandatory emissions reductions. However, a study by researchers at the University of NSW found that 95 percent of the certificates issued in the 18 months leading up to June 2004 were for projects established before the introduction of the scheme, and that more than 70 percent were awarded for emissions reductions that would have occurred anyway (Frew 2005: 1).

Even Australia's oldest and most polluting electricity generators, based in Victoria, were awarded certificates worth millions of dollars. A government spokesman defended the scheme, which is predicted to cost rate payers some $2 billion over 9 years, saying: 'It is not possible to distinguish between production or investment decisions made as a result of the scheme and those that would have been made anyway' (Frew 2005: 11).

It is often argued by economists that markets are more efficient than centralised government decision-making because they automatically gather information, and ensure that supply and demand are balanced and resources allocated efficiently. However, this sort of argument cannot be applied to artificial markets such as those created for pollution rights, since the need for monitoring and enforcement remains and is arguably even greater. For emissions trading to work properly, the regulator needs to know what emissions a company is making so as to check that it has sufficient permits. Too often, inspection and verification does not happen.

In the Australian scheme, according to the government's green paper, firms would estimate their own emissions and very large emitters would have to have their reported emissions audited by a third party (Department of Climate Change 2008: 42). Elsewhere, this is often done by transnational corporations such as PricewaterhouseCoopers that are also consultants and accountants to the companies whose emissions they are auditing. Critics say "This can only lead to a severe conflict of interests, resulting in fraud and ultimately little guarantee of actual emissions reductions" (Bachram *et al.* 2003: 37).

There is even more scope for cooking the books when it comes to carbon sinks, such as tree plantations, because of the lack of accepted methods for calculating how much carbon is temporarily taken up by growing trees. Such trees may release their carbon early as a result of fires, disease or illegal logging, so plantations need to be monitored throughout their life cycles to ensure the carbon credits earned by planting them are deserved; however, governments are only concerned with meeting targets in a comparatively short compliance period (Kill 2001: 10). Emissions trading also tends to protect very polluting or dirty industries by allowing them to buy emission permits rather than meet environmental standards. In this way, trading can reduce the pressure on companies to change production processes and to introduce other measures to reduce their emissions.

An emissions trading scheme will see the price of electricity and manufactured goods rise, but that is no guarantee that market participants will invest in alternatives, especially if polluters can pass on the extra cost to consumers, buy up environmentally dubious offsets, or be compensated for extra costs that might damage their international competitiveness.

Take the example of electricity generation. Currently, electricity generators offer quantities of electricity into the National Electricity Market for a particular price for each time period the next day. If they have to pay for emission permits, their offer price will presumably be higher. The system operator chooses the cheapest electricity for supplying the predicted demand for the next day. It only chooses electricity generated by renewable energy if it is cheaper or if there is not enough other electricity available. For any significant switch to renewable energy, carbon credits have to be expensive enough to make coal and gas-based electricity more expensive than renewable energy. This is not going to happen given the proposed compensation for coal power generators having to buy permits and the proposed low set price for permits.

The oil and fossil fuel dependent companies who want to continue expanding their businesses are the very ones that are promoting emissions trading in the knowledge that it will enable them to continue to do this. A price of $20 per ton of emissions is likely to increase the price of petrol by only 1 or 2 cents per litre, which is tiny compared with daily market fluctuations in oil prices, and anyway, will be counteracted by a reduction in the government fuel levy.

Social equity

Market mechanisms impact social equity in various ways:

- through the impact of the higher prices that are supposed to provide the incentive to change to more environmental behaviour;
- because market mechanisms shift decision-making power about how the environment is protected from the realm of politics to the market, enabling those with most market power to have most say; and
- because they prioritise economic considerations and their ineffectiveness is uncertain, which has consequences that are often felt more by disadvantaged people.

The inequitable impacts of higher prices caused by emissions trading has been recognised by the Australian government. It proposes to compensate poorer households for the expected increased costs. However, this will inevitably undermine the incentive provided by the scheme for change, and highlights the inability of market mechanisms to effectively meet equity, environmental and economic concerns at once. Even with compensation, those on low incomes are less able to afford to buy new, more energy-efficient appliances such as fridges and cars and those on higher incomes will feel the higher prices less and may not have the incentive to become more energy efficient. Both tenants and landlords are less likely to spend money on energy saving measures such as roof insulation or solar water heating, since the tenants cannot be sure of long-term returns in a house they do not own and landlords will not benefit from the energy savings themselves.

Also, higher prices will only work as an incentive to change behaviour if there are alternatives available. Otherwise, they just serve to penalise some sectors of the community and are inequitable. For example, higher fuel prices have most impact on people who have to travel long distances to get to work and do not have access to public transport. Since it is often the poor who are forced to live in the outer suburbs, because that is where the cheapest housing can be found, such a measure would impose its greatest burden on those least able to pay. People in rural areas and on the outskirts of cities will be also worse off because of the longer distances they have to travel. And rural industries will also be badly hit because of the longer distances and the heavy fuel requirements of agricultural machinery.

Emissions trading puts the decisions about how emissions should be reduced into the hands of the market. For example, the Australian scheme allows the use of offsets that are causing problems around the world. Those offering plantations as offsets look for the cheapest land to grow their trees, which is often in poor countries and often is land that is not owned by individuals but rather occupied by indigenous people without formal property rights. Such plantations can suck up ground water needed by local people for their own crops, and the pesticides and fertilisers used on the plantations can pollute rivers, water sources and fish that may be a major source of food and livelihood for local people (Bachram 2004: 8). Corporations and foreign countries in the name of carbon offsets are also usurping existing forests. Critics point out that "projects in countries such as Uganda and Ecuador have already led to thousands of local communities dependant on forest areas being forced off their land as private Northern corporations backed by their governments, engage in a worldwide land-grab at wholesale prices" (Bachram *et al.* 2003: 16).

Within Australia, emission permits are likely to be bought up by the wealthiest companies and by market speculators rather than by those producing products that the community values most highly and those that provide the best employment opportunities.

However, the greatest impact on social equity is likely to be the impact of global warming that will result from the ineffectiveness of emissions trading. The Dutch research institute RIVM calculates that, by allowing emissions trading, the actual reductions in greenhouse gases will be far less than one percent (Bachram 2004: 2). This failure to make significant reductions will have grave consequences for millions of people around the world. A study published in the prestigious science magazine *Nature* reports that climate change is causing a dramatic increase in deaths because it is causing increased malaria, malnutrition and diarrhoea in the poorest nations (Sample 2005: 12). The World Health Organisation (WHO) reported that, in 2000, "more than 150,000 premature deaths were attributed to various climate change impacts" as well as 5 million illnesses. It estimates that this annual toll will double by 2030 (cited in Vidal 2005, Sample 2005).

We know that low-lying island states are particularly at risk. UN scientists have also warned that the severe droughts experienced in 2005 could become a semi-permanent phenomenon as a result of climate change, and that one in six countries are short of food as a result of these (Vidal and Radford 2005). The UN has also predicted that as early as 2010 there could be 50 million environmental refugees, that is, people who have been displaced from their homes by problems such as drought, deforestation and soil degradation (Scheer 2005).

In light of these concerns, it is necessary to ask whether governments should put so much faith in the market to solve environmental problems. Why is it assumed that increasing the cost of fossil fuel emissions will reduce their use rather than just increase everyone's cost of living, something that has most impact on the poor and those on set incomes? Petrol prices have doubled in the past few years, causing much pain to individual and company budgets. Yet petrol usage has not declined significantly. There has been no mass shift to public transport, no major decline in car sales, no flood of affordable hybrid and electric cars onto the market. Why? Because the market has not been able to provide the alternatives required. Large-scale investment in public transport systems and cycleways, land-use planning and car emission standards require government investment and intervention in the market.

We are fooling ourselves if we think there is a cheap solution to global warming. On the one hand we can pay through taxes for cooperative planned investment and suffer the higher prices that strong government regulation may result in. This way we will be paying directly for the changes we want. On the other hand we can pay higher prices in the hope that the market will come up with the right sort of investments and changes. In this case we are likely to be paying escalating prices as the price of carbon becomes a market commodity subject to financial speculation, but with minimal and uncertain environmental benefits.

Sharon Beder is Visiting Professor in the School of Social Science, Media and Communication at the University of Wollongong. Market Mechanisms, Ecological Sustainability and Equity © 2011 Sharon Beder.

Environmental Crisis: An Eco-Marxist Perspective

James O'Connor

Radical green (and green radical) movements today are born from what is arguably the basic contradiction of world capitalism at the start of the twenty-first century. On the one hand, environmental and social problems during the past two or three decades have multiplied beyond any reasonable calculation. On the other hand, during the same period of time, older forms of political, economic, and social regulation of capital and capitalism have been in part or in whole dismantled by neoliberal governments eager to share in the spoils of the new global economy (and to avoid disinvestment, capital flight, and other blows to local economies). Just at the historical moment when the state (and society) need to regulate capital more firmly and intelligently – most particularly with respect to the viability of ecological systems and community collective social skills and norms that are the basis of social solidarity – the state's steering capacities (and society's regulatory capabilities) are becoming increasingly threatened and ineffective.

A political vacuum has thus been created into which all kinds of populist (left, right, centre, ethnic, etc.) and localist politics have rushed in. All imaginable types of local organization and action have arisen to deal with all kinds of socioecological and ecosocial issues the origins of which are regional, national, and international – and systemic – in character. However, in this vacuum, as well, have appeared new radical green and green radical politics.

An extension of Marxist analysis can help in understanding the roots of the contemporary crisis and the political responses. A starting point is the recognition of contradictory features embedded in the capitalist system. One contradiction arises because of the recurrent imbalance between productive capacity and the demand for the products of capitalist businesses. Another arises because capitalist business displace their costs onto other businesses, workers, society and nature. An understanding of these two contradictions, and the economic and environmental crises they generate, is fundamental to understanding modern capitalism.

Two fundamental capitalist contradictions

The first contradiction of capitalism, emphasized throughout Marxist political economy, concerns the exploitation of labor. It arises from capital's social and political power over labor, and is at the root of capitalism's inherent tendencies toward realization crises. For example, if capital exercises much power over labor, the rate of exploitation will be high, and the risk of a realization crisis will be greater. In other words, because wages are depressed, there tends to be inadequate demand for the products of capitalist businesses, so capitalists have difficulty in realizing surplus value (derived from the exploitation of labor) as profits. Hence the need for a vast credit structure, aggressive marketing, constant product innovation; and intensified competition for market shares. This first contradiction of capitalism is internal to capitalism as an economic and social system.

The second contraction of capitalism concerns the broader conditions of production, including the relationship of the capitalist economy to nature. It requires a more complex symbolization: the volume and value content of the goods and services consumed, and of fixed capital; the 'costs of the natural elements entering into constant and variable capital'; ground rent as a deduction from surplus value; and 'negative externalities' (e.g. congestion costs in cities).

In this second contradiction, no single term has the theoretical centrality that the rate of exploitation has in the first contradiction. This is one reason for the corresponding plurality of social movements today. Contestation over the rate of exploitation pitches labor against capital and gives rise to a focus on unions and industrial relations. Contestations arising from the second contradiction precipitate more diverse social movement struggles, including environmental struggles. Yet the terms above are also sociological/political categories, as well as economic categories. For example, the amount of absolute ground rent reflects the relative power of landed capital and industrial capital. The costs of congestion reflect struggles over community and regional transport systems. The cost of raw materials reflects not only ground rent and monopoly power but also capital's power over labor in the raw material sector. One final example: the cost of land and water reflect the power of the ecology movement in relation to the systemic and social power of capital (not to speak of the relationship between the power of environmentalism *vis-a-vis* traditional labor unions). The general point of listing these examples is to suggest that there is even less justification for a purely economistic-type theory of the second contradiction of capitalism then there is for the traditional Marxist theory of the first contradiction.

The first contradiction of capitalism strikes at capital from the demand side; it expresses an over-production of capital. It states that when individual capitals lower costs with the aim of defending or restoring profits, the unintended effect is to reduce total market demand for commodities, and to lower profits. The second contradiction strikes from the cost side; it expresses an under-production of capital. It states that when individual capitals lower costs, i.e. externalize costs on to nature (or on to labor or the urban context) with the aim of defending or restoring profits, the unintended effect is to raise costs on other capitals (at the limit, capital as a whole), and to lower profits.

In the first contradiction, there is no problem producing surplus value, hence for that reason there is a problem of realizing surplus value. In the second contradiction, there is no problem realizing surplus value; hence for that reason there is a problem of producing surplus value. Putting aside the possible actual and conjunctural causes of the second contradiction today, it is clear that, whereas a deficit of markets leads to state Keynesianism, productivity/wage bargains and consumerism, a deficit of surplus value and real profits leads to a devalorization of Keynesianism, a break up of the wage/productivity bargain, and a retrenchment of consumerism.

Causes of the second contradiction

The basic cause of the second contradiction is capitalism's self-destructive appropriation and use of labor power, space, and external nature or environment. The present-day crisis of health, education, and the family; the urban crisis; and the ecological crisis exemplify this self-destructiveness. The form which global capitalist development has taken since the second world war would have been impossible without deforestation, air and water pollution, pollution of the atmosphere, global warming, and the other ecological disasters; without the construction of 'mega-cities', with no regard for congestion, rational land use and transport systems, and the social costs of inappropriate housing and rising rents; and finally, without the reckless disregard for community and family health, physical and emotional, education, and other 'components' of the socialized reproduction of labor power (not to speak of the welfare of future generations).

If global capital had bothered to reproduce or restore the conditions of production as these presented themselves at the end of the reconstruction period after the World War 2, GNP growth rates probably would have been only a fraction of recorded rates.

The causes of the second contradiction are both economic and social. They are 'economic' in the sense that shortages of disciplined wage labor, urban space, and 'environmental resources' push up costs (via 'normal' market forces). They are 'social' in the sense that labor struggles, women's struggles, urban movements, and environmental struggles (all to one degree or another organized to prevent the full capitalization of the conditions of production, or to fight capitalist restructuring of these conditions) have also pushed up costs, and reduced the flexibility of capital in general and the variability of labor power in particular.

In sum, both 'natural' and self-created shortages of wage labor, land, air, space, and so on, and also social struggles organized to protect labor power, urban space, and nature, push up costs of constant capital (both quantity and value content) and variable capital (both the consumption basket and its value content). They also decrease the flexibility of capital by limiting the ways that capital can use labor, space, and land and other resources, as well as slowing down the turnover time of capital.

Consequences of the second contradiction

The first and most obvious consequence of the second contradiction is that capital runs up against 'limits' which are often self-created: limits of space, educated labor power, good soils, clean water, and so on. The bourgeois version of this thesis is the 'limits to growth' argument by the Club of Rome, and a host of imitators. The Marxist version is that capital never faces absolute limits. Rather, shortages of materials, space, and so on, and deficits of flexibility, express themselves in the form of economic crisis. Crises are mainly localized because of the site specificity of production conditions, which is one reason for the uneven, fragmented nature of prosperity and crises ('post-modern' crises).

On a general level, with the eruption of many local crises (or economic and social turning points), one result may be a recession or depression, which relieves shortages, restores discipline, and creates new flexibilities. Another result may be capital relocation. In brief, 'external' barriers to capital show up in the form of economic crisis (as, of course, do internal barriers, or the first contradiction of capitalism). Thus, for example, the shortages of cheap oil in the 1970s did not result in absolute energy scarcities but rather in a redistribution of values from industrial to landed capital (e.g. oil producing states), which, in turn, lowered realized profits in industry. This caused liquidity problems for industry, a slowdown of investment and productivity, inflationary pressures, and, finally, a drive for 'energy efficiency' or conservation, as well as development of alternative energy technologies.

When capital impairs or destroys its own conditions of production (a possibility that Marx never theorized), it threatens itself with economic crisis of a 'cost push' type. The result is that capital will attempt to restructure the conditions of production in order to reduce costs. This typically involves more state planning, i.e. more social forms of producing the conditions of production. Examples are numerous. In Californian agriculture, for example, we have some established agricultural institutions coming out for 'sustainable agriculture', thereby gaining legitimacy for the development of bio-technological approaches to pest control. This is backed by sectors of agribusiness caught by the increasingly costly 'pesticide treadmill'. In Los Angeles, industry and infrastructure are being restructured by new state agencies regulating air quality to attempt to deal with horrible air pollution and congestion problems (a restructuring which, not so incidentally, involves getting rid of small capital in polluting industries such as furniture, paints, and varnishes; that is, consolidating capital as a way to restructure the use of the region's air). It is important to stress that this restructuring is organized by already politicized state planning bodies. Meanwhile urban renewal and mass transit restructure space with the aim of reducing congestion costs. One could cite many more examples today, including attempts to restructure increasingly unviable education and health care systems.

However, capital and the state rarely have a free hand in their attempt to restructure production conditions. These conditions are also means of life, means of survival and consumption, and, in the case of labor power, life itself. Hence we find today much resistance to capitalist restructuring (a struggle over the course of restructuring which expresses itself particularly dramatically in times of 'natural disaster'). Here again we must speak of the crisis emerging from the second contradiction of capitalism as social and political struggle. This is a period in which nothing can be taken for granted, in which the mobilization of resources and good political strategy and leadership will decide, one way or another, whether the conditions of production are defined as desired by capital, or by labor, communities, and urban populations.

Because the state regulates access to, or production of, the conditions of production, all struggles over restructuring production conditions are political struggles. Environmental, urban, feminist, and other movements must face state agencies, prevailing legitimations of state power, state experts, and so on. State agency goals, divisions of labor, lines of authority, and the nature of their 'expertise,' are inevitably thrown into question. Officialdom, norms of impersonality, and the reification of bureaucracy may also be radically questioned. This confrontation raises the stakes of the struggle, and transforms environmental, social, and economic battles into political struggles (pertaining to the way that the state bureaucracy operates). Strategic unity between movements thus needs to be oriented around the theme of 'democratizing the state'. The demand for 'radical democracy', common in 'post-Marxist' circles, can thus be explained, at least in part, in terms of an eco-Marxist theory of capital and its production conditions.

New social movements

Post-structuralist theorists focus on new social movements and radical democracy, 'celebrating difference' and denouncing 'totalistic' approaches to social theory and political practice. They regard the traditional labor movement as irrelevant or dead. But no theory of the rise of new social movements (beyond a shaky 'politics of identity' approach), or of the decline of traditional labor movements, is offered. By contrast, an eco-Marxist theory roots itself in the concept of social labor (now broadened to include the labor of producing the conditions of production) and changes in the international division of labor.

The new international division of labor and the hegemony of transnational capital has weakened labor and workplace struggles world-wide (especially following the tremendous mobilization of the political power of capital in the 1980s). In the mid-1970s, capital had begun to respond to the slow growth of world market demand by raising the rate of exploitation of labor and by allowing the conditions of production to further deteriorate (with the obvious aim of reducing costs of production). The crisis strategy adopted globally by capital and by most nation-states was to exploit labor more, and also to 'exploit' other production conditions, communities and nature, more intensively. If we regard the rate of depletion and pollution of nature as dependent on the rate of accumulation and rate of profit, increases in the rate of labor exploitation will usually increase the profit and accumulation rates, and hence the rates of depletion and pollution. The more capital exploits labor, the more it exploits nature, and *vice versa*. The new competition from East Asia made the situation worse in the US and other regions that were losing the competitive struggle. The weakness or irrelevancy of the labor movement was thus doubly determined: first, by the new international division of labor; second, by the shift in focus by capital and social movements from production to the broader array of production conditions.

The rise of new social movements, organized around the conditions of production, has moved the class struggle from the workplace to communities; from strikes to consumer boycotts; from capital to the state bureaucracy as the primary target of action. Struggles for democracy in the workplace have increasingly come to be aimed at protecting labor power from the ravages of capital, eg. occupational health and safety movements. Struggles for democracy in the community have aimed to protect or restructure general, communal conditions of production and the environment; and struggles for political democracy have aimed to democratize the bureaucracies, to mobilize unregistered voters, to attack campaign financing that favors incumbents, and so on.

In sum, according to an eco-Marxist theory, capital has been self-destructing by raising the costs of health and education and welfare; urban transport and home and commercial rents; and the cost of extracting the 'elements of constant and variable capital' from nature. This is the second contradiction of capital in a nutshell. The policy of individual capitals to lower costs results in higher costs for capital as a whole (all in the context of a growing, inflated, and fragile credit structure). In this account, capital can been seen as totally confused as to the new form of regulation which will provide a coherent framework for a new round of capitalist accumulation. Individual capitals continue to lower costs in every way imaginable; by so doing, they inadvertently raise costs of capital as a whole, not to speak of threatening their own markets, as the first contradiction leads us to believe. In sum, capital today is faced with both rising costs and weak market demand, i.e. with both the first and second contradiction. Is it any wonder that capital today is obsessed both with process innovation and cost-cutting and with product innovation and market expansion, i.e. that we live in a kind of hyper-capitalist world?

Spokespeople for capital as a whole, and far-seeing state managers, are today attempting to end the short-sighted policies of individual capitals and to rebuild and restore the long-neglected, half-destroyed conditions of production. But the trajectory of this long view is being increasingly challenged by the new social movements, which are also addressing health care, education, urban conditions, and environment (with a stress on use value, not exchange value; and with another stress on democratic forms of decision-making, not bureaucratic expertise and the naked power of the state). But these new social movements, commonly founded in their concern for the conditions of production, face increasing surveillance and state 'security management', and, in many places, sheer repression (e.g. oppression against black urban movements and against 'Earth First!' in the USA). The stakes in the struggle thus increase still higher, with the possible result of a gathering general crisis, of economy and society, of ideological hegemony and legitimacy. The outcomes of these crises are today totally unknown; they are turning points, time for decisions, time when what individuals and groups do can make big historical differences.

This is the context of the newly forming configurations of 'red-green-feminist' politics world-wide. All the old issues once addressed by classical socialism (inequality, social injustice, and so on) have reappeared; more new issues addressed by new social movements are also on the political agenda. What better time for labor and the left, labor and the environmental and feminist movements, and community and urban movements and environmental movements to combine into a new eco-socialism, an eco-feminism, and eco-urbanism – in short, into a new movement that can change the history of the world? For the better, this time.

James O'Connor is Emeritus Professor, University of California Santa Cruz. The Second Contradiction of Capitalism: An Eco-Marxist View © 2002 James O'Connor.

Sustainable Development
Joy Paton

Twenty years ago it seemed that 'sustainability' was an idea whose time had come. The United Nations World Commission on Environment and Development released its watershed report – *Our Common Future* (WCED 1987) – and its promotion of 'sustainable development' was subsequently embraced internationally as a key policy principle. Yet after two decades, and despite some positive achievements, global environmental degradation has accelerated and a new wave of environmental concern has emerged around the specifics of climate change (Kovel 2002: 4; UNEP 2007). The UK's *Stern Review* (2006) was a timely *aide memoire* to the ongoing and unresolved question of 'sustainability' while the *Garnaut Review* (2008) sought to tackle this problem directly in the Australian context. Both reviews advocate the use of market-based economic policy instruments for dealing with the prospect of climate change.

Despite the international 'consensus' on sustainable development, the meaning of sustainability remains contested. On the one hand, it has been taken up by corporate leaders and politicians in claiming the green credentials of their economic growth agendas. This 'economic sustainability' position is itself increasingly perceived as contributing to the climate change "tipping point" (Hansen 2006: 949). On the other hand, sustainability can be understood to embody radical normative dimensions that point to the need for an equitable society served by an economy operating within ecological limits. From this latter 'ecological sustainability' perspective, the critical questions are about the way in which society organises production, consumption and reproduction in relation to the natural environment which sustains it. Although a mainstream concept today, sustainability first emerged within this radical tradition as a critical and transformative discourse.

The challenge of ecological sustainability

Throughout the 1970s and early 1980s, the idea of "building a sustainable society" that was both socially equitable and ecologically sustainable was thought by its proponents to be both possible and necessary (Brown 1981). The period provided fertile ground for 'alternative social visions' not just because of the perceived *ecological* crisis, but also because of the broader "policy vacuum" left by the *accumulation* crisis that characterised the collapse of the post-war boom (Bryan 2002: 153). However, neoliberal ideas also penetrated that vacuum and began to hold sway over policy makers looking for solutions to economic stagnation. The need for 'ecological restructuring' thus fell victim to the perceived immediacy of economic concerns, notwithstanding the inseparable links between economy and ecology to which the emergent sustainability literature was drawing attention at that time.

One of the first publications to explicitly use the word "sustainable" in this context was the *1972 Yearbook* of the International Union for the Conservation of Nature (IUCN). It asserted that the natural environment should be conserved and managed "so as to achieve the highest sustainable quality of human life" (in Kidd 1992: 13). Meanwhile, the editors of *The Ecologist* published *Blueprint for Survival* (Goldsmith *et al.* 1972), wherein sustainability appeared unambiguously for the first time as a major theme (Kidd 1992: 13). Echoing some of the concerns expressed in the *Limits to Growth* report (Meadows *et al.* 1972), *Blueprint* argued that the "principal defect of the industrial way of life with its ethos of expansion is that it is not sustainable...*indefinite* growth of whatever type can not be sustained by *finite* resources" (Goldsmith *et al.* 1972: 3). From these concerns with the 'unsustainability' of *growth* economies, 'sustainability' emerged as a critical discourse synonymous with the idea of a *steady-state* economy (Kidd 1992: 15). It was understood as marking the transition from high growth to low or even no-growth societies.

Steady-state theorists argued that unlimited growth was a biophysical impossibility and that sustainability would require a "low throughput" economy (Georgescu-Roegen 1971). In this, they pointed to more than a tension between ecology and economics; they argued there was "an axiomatic incompatibility" between maximising economic growth and the goal of environmental sustainability (Carruthers 2001: 94). However, sustainability was more than a purely economic or, for that matter, ecological concept. While the steady-state perspective emphasised policies related to the reduction of fossil fuel-based energy consumption, it also encompassed broader socio-political goals and ethical values. For example, Daly (1973) argued for 'qualitative development' rather than 'quantitative growth'; while Meadows (1977: 36) suggested sustainability would require such an economy to be consistent with "equity, personal liberty, cultural progress, and the satisfaction of basic physical and psychological needs".

The concerns with sustainability were also recognised as important for developing economies. As early as 1962, a United Nations (UN) resolution recognised the threat that declining natural resources would have on the prospects for economic development in the Third World. Subsequently, the need for conservation and restoration of natural resources laid the basis for linking development, conservation and sustainable resource use (O'Riordon 1981: 35). However, amidst the 'limits' debate, which implied western affluence could not be duplicated, the apparent failures of the 'development paradigm' drove the search for alternative models. At the grassroots level, these focused on paths that would be sustainable and socially just (Dryzek 2005: 148). They emphasised small-scale production, appropriate technology, sensitivity to cultural norms and local knowledge, and redistribution of wealth and resources (Carruthers 2001: 97). These themes became central elements in the idea of 'eco-development' – the forerunner to sustainable development – especially in its radical interpretation where it was understood as "development … within the constraints of local ecosystems" (Dasmann 1984: 20).

In 1972, First and Third World 'stakeholders' were brought together in the landmark UN Conference on the Human Environment held in Stockholm. The conference enabled co-operation at the international level on environmental issues that crossed national borders, creating a basis for the development of international environmental law in the process (Pallemaerts 1996: 626). The conference also focused on the global implications of many environmental problems for biophysical and economic linkages, with such concerns being based on an understanding that economic activity would need to be constrained (White 1980: 189). The economy and the environment were conceived as opposing sides in a zero-sum game that implied trade-offs between economic efficiency and ecological integrity (Sanwal 2004: 17). This 'incommensurability' gave rise to a raft of legislative events for environmental protection that were similar in nature and timing across much of the developed world (Weale 1992: 10).

However, the regulatory response proved to be fragile on two fronts. Unsurprisingly, in the context of accumulation crises and growing influence of neoliberalism, the emergent trend in developed economies was toward *enabling*, rather than *constraining*, the forces of capital. The oppositional way in which economy-environment interactions had been conceptualised at Stockholm also proved problematic for developing countries. Their leaders were suspicious of environmental motives in the North, especially the emphasis on pollution abatement, as a potential restriction on their development aspirations (Weiss *et al*. 1994: 177; Tolba 1998: 1). At the same time, grassroots 'eco-development' initiatives remained marginal to official policies because the apparent prioritisation of ecology over development was perceived by elites as a similar threat (Bernstein 2001: 57). Developing country leaders therefore rejected both low and no-growth scenarios, seeking instead a more equitable engagement with the global economy (Carruthers 2001: 97).

Subsequently, international environmental concern was broadened from the problems of urban industrialisation in developed economies to include those generated by rural poverty in developing countries. The inclusion of poverty as a cause of environmental degradation helped to generate acceptance of the idea that the environment was a problem for the development process (Kidd 1992: 17). Development could then be a pathway for solving both poverty and its attendant environmental problems. Attempts to institutionalise environmental governance after Stockholm therefore focused on integrating the opposing normative frameworks of 'environment' and 'development' (Bernstein 2002: 3-4; Pallemaerts 1996: 626). In stimulating changes to the content and rationale of development programs, the Stockholm conference set in place the foundation for a fundamentally different understanding of 'sustainability' to that which had emerged in the 'no-growth' school (Kidd 1992: 17-18).

'Sustainable development'

In this context, a pre-requisite for 'moving forward' on 'environmental concerns' was their reconstitution as 'economic concerns'. As a result, policy entrepreneurs working within the

OECD and key UN organisations, tried to situate environmental norms within the growing consensus on a liberal economic order by re-conceptualising the environment as an *economic* rather than *ecological* problem. The OECD (1985) actively promoted a model of 'sustainable development' based on strengthening the reciprocity between policies for environmental protection and those for economic growth, advocating a key role for markets in that process. This facilitated international co-operation on environmental issues and helped to move environmental concern into the mainstream of international governance (Bernstein 2002: 8; 2001: 179).

However, the most significant institution to popularise and propel political engagement with the concept of sustainable development was the World Commission on Environment and Development (WCED). Established as an independent body by the UN in 1983, the Commission's report, *Our Common Future* (WCED 1987: 23), argued that the acceleration of global environmental problems required pro-active management and that international co-operation on sustainable development was the appropriate response. In the WCED approach, long standing 'North-South' tensions in the environment-development question seemed to be reconciled (Meadowcroft 2000: 371) and governments across the OECD consequently launched national sustainable development strategy and planning processes.

In Australia, working groups were established in 1990 which resulted in specific recommendations for promoting social, economic and industrial change. This process was notable at the outset for its use of the idea of *ecologically* sustainable development which emphasised the importance of preserving bio-diversity and considering intergenerational issues. However, rather than sustaining ecological systems *per se*, the policy focus of the working groups centred on the areas which required preservation and protection so that *economically* sustainable development could be secured (Rosewarne 1993: 54). By the mid 1990s the national government bureaucracy viewed "ecologically sustainable development" as an obsolete language (Christoff 1995: 72) and in keeping with international trends, the truncated 'sustainable development', with its substantive core of *economic* sustainability, became common parlance.

The world-wide support for this interpretation of sustainable development reached its apogee in 1992 at the United Nations Conference on Environment and Development (UNCED) held in Rio de Janeiro. Creating a "global partnership" for sustainable development, national government delegations at the 'Rio Earth Summit' signed on to *Agenda 21* (UNCED 1992) which committed signatories to developing and implementing national "plans of action" (Lafferty 1996: 194; Jacobs 1995: 1471). However, UNCED's understanding of sustainable development reconstructed the idea that a healthy environment is central to securing continued economic growth in such a way that growth is central to securing a healthy environment. Where sustainable development once implied 'ecological sustainability', it was now commonly promoted as 'economic sustainability'; that is, sustaining the "growth in material consumption" (Lele 1991: 608-609).

While the rhetoric of sustainable development in the WCED tried to make economic growth consistent with goals such as environmental improvement, population stabilisation, international equity, and peace (Dryzek 2005: 148-149), *Agenda 21* (UNCED 1992) made economic growth the means for achieving them, explicitly rejecting the discourse of scarcity and limits (Carruthers 2001: 99). Although the production and consumption habits of developed countries were acknowledged as a major source of environmental problems, UNCED documents recommended more economic growth (in both developed and developing countries) as the solution to such problems (Dryzek 2005: 149). Twenty years after sustainability first emerged as a radical challenge to unlimited economic growth in *Blueprint for Survival* (Goldsmith *et al.*1972), the concept of sustainable development was now being used by global institutions for explicitly promoting such growth (Carruthers 2001: 99).

Despite the enthusiasm surrounding the new discourse of sustainable development, the post-UNCED reality fell somewhat short of 'Rio rhetoric'. Rather than fulfilling the promise of development for those on the periphery of world capitalism, the pursuit of 'market forces' in the name of growth has perpetuated environmental destruction and the gap between rich and poor. As Foster (2003: 4) argues, such forces served to "deepen the economic stagnation of most third world countries" and justified "watering down…meaningful global environmental change". Despite the growing number of international environmental treaties and other initiatives, the period of 'transnational capital' has correlated with a marked deterioration in global environmental quality. Damage to coral reefs, species extinction, and deforestation all persisted, while global emissions of greenhouse gas carbon dioxide continued to climb (Worldwatch Institute 2002: 5). These shortcomings were brought into sharp focus with the 2002 World Summit on Sustainable Development (WSSD) in Johannesburg (Flavin 2002).

The WSSD was convened in order to define the instruments for tackling global poverty and reaching ecosystem security, as well as setting timeframes and targets for *Agenda 21* which had contained no binding agreements for implementation and accountability (von Frantzius 2004: 467; Wapner 2003: 2; La Vina *et al*. 2003: 55). The summit was the largest UN conference that had been held but critics were sceptical of what could be achieved. A number of high profile environmentalists – including Paul Hawken, Hazel Henderson and Anita Roddick – pointed out in *The Jo'burg Memo* that governments at UNCED had already committed to curbing environmental decline and social impoverishment, yet poverty and ecological decline persists "notwithstanding the increase of wealth in specific places" (Sachs 2002: 11). Growth scepticism continues in the wake of the 2009 Copenhagen Summit where international agreement on carbon-pollution reduction targets to address climate change – perhaps the most pressing 'sustainability' issue – failed to materialise.

Co-opted and contested: Reclaiming sustainable development?

Subsuming sustainable development into the imperatives of growth and accumulation has led critics to conclude that the project is tainted and should be abandoned (Richardson 1997: 58). A rather different view, put by Dobson (1996) and Barry (1996), regards 'ecological sustainability' as still being an important concept, albeit currently at the margins of policy relevance. However, according to Meadowcroft (2000: 373), sustainable development should be conceived as a political meta-objective with a suggestive normative core. While acknowledging its ambiguity and potential for various interpretations, that 'core' is often understood as a set of values, norms and goals consistent with social democracy. Thus, Lafferty (1996: 205; 189) argues it is "logically and ethically unsound" for neoliberalism to gain legitimacy from the language of sustainable development and that *Our Common Future* (WCED 1987) embodies an ideological and mobilising function for social and environmental justice that remains unrealised.

Certainly, the social democratic elements of *Our Common Future* (WCED 1987) were important in sustainable development's acceptance by a broad range of interests across the ideological spectrum (Dryzek 2005: 160; Meadowcroft 2000: 370). However, during the time sustainable development has established itself as the leading transnational environmental discourse, neoliberalism has been a more effective global movement in terms of shaping policies, practices, and institutions (Dryzek 2005: 160). As a result, the confidence expressed in *Our Common Future* about the power of human reason to comprehend problems and to "consciously remould social institutions and practices" (Meadowcroft 2000: 382) has been vindicated; but that 'remoulding' has been away from social democratic structures towards those of neoliberalism. Evidently, the sustainable development concept has not just 'gained acceptance'; it has been 'appropriated' by a *particular* ideological perspective with the result that, according to Dryzek (2005: 160-161), "sustainable development's prospects are poor".

However, it is not just that neoliberalism has 'perverted' the institutionalisation of sustainable development. The trans-nationalisation of capitalism and the embrace of sustainable development have been *symbiotic* processes. Thus, while neoliberal imperatives – trade liberalisation, capital mobility and economic growth – were unable to confront limits in nature, in sustainable development the conflict between economic growth and limits in nature is (conceptually) eliminated, thereby legitimising and facilitating neoliberalism (Carruthers 2001: 101). Conversely, at a time when economic stagnation gave impetus to a focus on growth, the language of the market provided a common idiom through which sustainable development could be articulated, firstly via the 'Washington Consensus' and then in the more radical neoliberal form. The establishment of market-based economic norms across developed and developing economies thereby facilitated global co-operation on the environment (Bernstein 2001: 72).

Highlighting sustainable development's social democratic elements is therefore problematic. There is no 'authentic' sustainable development (*Cf.* Carruthers 2001: 102). Its "appealing ambiguity" (Eckersley 1992: 37) has made the concept vulnerable to the prevailing ideological hegemony. As Dryzek (2005: 159) acknowledges, "market liberalism" is a "powerful discourse in the international system … furthered by the same corporations now so active in the … politics of sustainable development". In such a climate, national and international governance has increasingly turned to the market mechanism as a substitute policy delivery system, requiring that sustainable development be made consistent with business profitability and economic growth.

The opportunity for profits embedded in the Garnaut (2008) proposal for trading of carbon emission permits – effectively private property rights in pollution – is symptomatic of this process. Yet, the promise of compatibility between liberal markets and environmental protection has not been substantiated in practice. During the last two decades it has proved difficult to formulate specific responses to global environmental problems. While the theoretical explication and advocacy of market instruments is clear and simple, the 'real-world' introduction of charges and marketable permit schemes rarely occurs in textbook form because of the design and implementation problems they pose (Dryzek 1997: 111). Such policy instruments have proven difficult to put into practice and, once in place, are less successful than anticipated.

There are good reasons for these problems. The "highly restrictive assumptions" that underpin neoclassical economic theory render it problematic for policy development because it "gives no clear guidelines … in most practical circumstances in an imperfect world" (Stilwell 2000: 42). There is no clear evidence that market incentives are superior to regulatory mechanisms. Their choice is often the result of ideological, rather than empirical or effectiveness-based criteria (Majone 1989: 145). Even Jeffrey Sachs (2008), the well known advocate of market 'shock-therapy' for transition economies, has stated that trading schemes, such as that proposed by Garnaut (2008), are more costly and administratively complex than traditional regulatory or taxation mechanisms.

Conclusion

Contemporary environmental priorities have largely been shaped by the imperatives of capital accumulation. Although poverty eradication remains central to the current rhetoric of sustainable development, there is little to connect that goal to the eco-development movements of the 1970s where sustainability was a critical discourse aimed at the established orthodoxies. Compared to its radical roots, a quite different interpretation of 'sustainability' has emerged; one where economic rather than ecological concerns dominate the environment-development discourse. In the process of this political 'compromise', sustainable development has been divorced from its critical content and 'reconfigured' to make it congruent with neoliberal policies (Carruthers 2001: 93).

'Environmental neoliberalism' has gone further in denying that there is any necessary incompatibility between the values of economic growth and environmental protection (Leff 2002; Bernstein 2002: 14). Moreover, its emphasis on economic criteria has furthered the opportunities for profit generation without achieving the promised social and environmental benefits. The shift to a neoliberal interpretation of sustainable development may have facilitated greater global prominence for environmental issues, but its terms of engagement have been costly. 'Government through the market' has failed both 'sustainability' and 'development'. The global environment continues to deteriorate and inequality between North and South continues to widen (UNEP 2002: 1; UNEP 2007: 72). Resisting the current neoliberal trends in environmental policy and governance requires challenging the co-option of sustainability as an 'economic category' and rejecting the dominant imperatives of accumulation and commercialisation.

Joy Paton is Lecturer in Political Economy, School of Social and Political Sciences, University of Sydney. This chapter is adapted from What's Left of Sustainable Development, *Journal of Australian Political Economy*, no. 62, 2008, pp. 94-115. © 2011 Joy Paton.

FEMINIST ECONOMICS

The impact of feminism in mainstream economics has been relatively minor – the citadel remains largely impregnable – but it has been influential in shaping contemporary political economy. Indeed, the challenges posed by feminism are not significantly less for political economy than for the mainstream. These challenges include the need to account for the differential position of men and women in respect to waged labor and non-waged labor, to reappraise the role of the household in the production process, and to broaden the analysis of economic activity to include the role of the household in the process of reproducing the economic and social order.

How do gender relations shape capitalism and *vice versa*? It is difficult to pose this issue within the contours of orthodox economics that does not admit consideration of non-market sources of economic power as an integral part of the analysis. For Marxism, there is a different problem in that its traditional focus on class relations tends to take priority over gender inequalities in terms of the access to the sources of economic power and to income and wealth. Further problems arise in analysing the division of labor according to gender. The notion of non-competing groups in the labor market has a long history, but work in feminist political economy has involved significant advances in the analysis of workforce segmentation as well as the documentation of associated gender inequalities. Of equal importance are the lively debates about the role of non-waged domestic labor, including the relevance of the classical-Marxian distinction between productive and unproductive labor.

The treatment of the household as the basic unit of analysis in neoclassical theory is a major source of problems from this perspective, because many significant inequalities in respect of distribution are thereby concealed. Worse, the neglect of the contributions of non-waged labor in the definition of the economy's overall level of production imparts a significant bias to the analysis of production. The recognition of the role of the family in respect of social reproduction has likewise generated critiques of the economistic focus on production, distribution and exchange.

The following readings introduce some of these concerns. A classic article by Marilyn Waring stresses the need to rethink how we evaluate economic production, drawing attention to gender biases in existing practices of economic accounting. Julie Nelson presents reflections on how economics might be reformulated to take account of feminist insights about 'provisioning' rather than 'choice' – which mainstream economists treat as the focus of economic analysis. Rhonda Sharp's contribution discusses how governments' budgets can be made more sensitive to gender-based concerns. Gillian Hewitson surveys the diverse feminist contributions, emphasising methodological and conceptual issues as well as practical aspects of womens' economic contributions. In all these various respects, feminist analysis raises issues of importance in the reformulation of contemporary political economy.

Further reading on feminist economics could include the journal *Feminist Economics*; Barker, D.K. and S.F. Feiner, *Liberating Economics: Feminist Perspectives on Families, Work, and Globalization*, University of Michigan Press, Ann Arbor, 2004; M.A. Ferber, and J.A. Nelson, (eds), *Feminist Economics Today: Beyond Economic Man*, University of Chicago Press, Chicago, 2003; and N. Folbre, *Greed, Lust and Gender: A History of Economic Ideas*, Oxford University Press, Oxford, 2010.

A Woman's Reckoning
Marilyn Waring

Consider Tendai, a young girl in the Lowveld, in Zimbabwe. Her day starts at 4 a.m. when, to fetch water, she carries a 30 litre tin to a borehole about 11 kilometres from her home. She walks barefoot and is home by 9 a.m. She eats a little and proceeds to fetch firewood until midday. She cleans the utensils from the family's morning meal and sits preparing a lunch of *sadza* for the family. After lunch and the cleaning of the dishes, she wanders in the hot sun until early evening, fetching wild vegetables for supper before making the evening trip for water. Her day ends at 9 p.m., after she has prepared supper and put her younger brothers and sisters to sleep. Tendai is considered unproductive, unoccupied, and economically inactive. According to the international economic system, Tendai does not work and is not part of the labor force.

Ben is a highly trained member of the US military. His regular duty is to descend to an underground facility where he waits with a colleague, for hours at a time, for an order to fire a nuclear missile. So skilled and effective is Ben that if his colleague were to attempt to subvert an order to fire, Ben would, if all else failed, be expected to kill him to ensure a successful missile launch. Ben is in paid work; he is economically active. His work has value and contributes, as part of the nuclear machine, to the nation's growth, wealth, and productivity. That's what the international economic system says.

Ben works. Tendai does not. Those are the rules. I believe that women all over the world are economically productive. You, too, may believe that these women work full days. But according to the theory, science, profession, practice, and institutionalisation of economics, we are wrong.

Blind man's bluff: How economic theory constructs reality

My thinking would have me conclude that Tendai works, that she is productive, and that her economic activity is of value. My technique of thinking leads me to conclude that Ben works, that he is destructive, and that his economic activity is a major cost and threat to the planet. But that is not how the established economic theory views his activities.

Theory is used, first of all, in order to decide what facts are relevant to an analysis. As the lives of Tendai and Ben illustrate, only some everyday experiences are stated, recognised and recorded by economic theory. Overwhelmingly, those experiences that are economically visible can be summarised as what men do.

Most propositions in economics are explained and illustrated by using words and mathematics. These are seen to be alternative languages that are translatable into each other. Mathematical formulas assist the illusion that economics is a value-free science: propaganda is less easily discerned from figures than it is from words. The process of theorising takes place when economists reason about simplified models of an actual economy or some part of an economy. From this model, 'factual predictions' are made. Clearly, if you do not perceive parts of the community as economically active, they will not be in your model, and your 'correct conclusions' based on the model will not include them.

The belief that value results only when (predominantly) men interact with the marketplace, means that few attempts are made to disguise this myopic approach. Feminist theorist Sheila Rowbotham reminds us:

> Language conveys a certain power. It is one of the instruments of domination ... The language of theory censored language only expresses a reality experienced by the oppressors. It speaks only for their world, for their point of view.

Xenophon coined the word *oikonomikos* to describe the management or rule of a house or household. In general usage, the word 'economy' still retains some links with its Greek origins. *Roget's Thesaurus* lists as synonyms management, order, careful administration, frugality, austerity, prudence, thrift, providence, care and retrenchment. These synonyms are unlikely candidates for what is called the 'science' of economics. The meaning of words, our words, change inside a 'discipline'.

Disciples of economics are likely to see it as a science that treats things from the standpoint of price. Words that we think we all understand (such as value, work, labor, production, reproduction and economic activity) have been hijacked into the service of this science. As a result, such words come to have two very different definitions: an economic definition and a non-economic one.

Value

Value is the most important word to understand in its economic and non-economic contexts. The word is derived from the Latin *valere*, meaning 'to be strong or worthy'. The *Oxford English Dictionary* now lists its principal meaning in purely economic terms: "that amount of some commodity, medium or exchange, etc, which is considered to be an equivalent for something else; a fair or adequate equivalent or return". But I know what I think is 'strong or worthy' in my life. I know about the value of friendship, fresh air, daily exercise. I frequently weigh the value of my time: how will I spend it, in which activity?

From the fourteenth to the seventeenth centuries, sources of value were seen, in literature and in politics, to be scarcity, utility, and desirability. Language is power but literary concepts of value find few friends in economics. Like much of our language, this strong, worthy word has been taken from us and led along a very narrow path.

Adam Smith, writing in the eighteenth century, was perhaps the first to use the concept of value in relation to the market. He distinguished 'market' from 'moral' value and identified the market as the place where values are expressed. That this distinction was in itself not objective but a specific moral and political viewpoint does not attract much debate. Writing at the time of the emergence of a new manufacturing class, Smith wanted to know what was responsible for the growth of national wealth. He established the logical foundation for his work by identifying what he thought was essential human nature. He developed an image of humans as materialistic, egotistic, selfish and primarily motivated by pursuits of their own self-interest. Smith did not acknowledge women's (or men's) altruism and benevolence. In ignoring women he characteristically presumed their idiosyncrasies to be those of his 'brethren'.

Economists from Adam Smith onward have maintained that their moral judgment that the market was the source of value was a judgment devoid of self-interest. The concept of value used in articles in modern economic journals is far from metaphysical. The value of much is measured or guessed at. For example, an article entitled 'The Value of Safety' shows economic value at its 'objective' and absurd best:

> If decisions are to be taken in a systematic and consistent manner and scarce resources are to be allocated efficiently and to the greatest advantage, it would seem necessary to have a method of associating explicit values with anticipated improvements in safety and costs with deteriorations in order that these effects can be weighed in relation to other desirable and undesirable consequences of the decision.

Thus, the value of safety is not a moral value of averting injury, saving life, ensuring healthy working conditions. Such considerations play no part. The value of safety is its costs and benefits relative to lost or gained production, possible legal suits, different groups of workers, and the allocation of scarce resources.

I turn back to the mountains. If minerals were found there, the hills would still be worthless until a mining operation commenced. And then as cliffs were gouged, as roads were cut, and smoke rose, the hills would be of value their value would be the price the minerals would fetch on the world market. No price would be put on the violation of the earth, or the loss of beauty, or the depletion of mineral resources. That is what value means, according to economic theory.

Work, labor, and economic activity

Every time I see a mother with an infant, I know I am seeing a woman at work. I know that work is not leisure and it is not sleep and it may well be enjoyable. I know that money payment is not necessary for work to be done. But, again, I seem to be at odds with economics as a discipline, because when work becomes a concept in institutionalised economics, payment enters the picture. Work and labor and economic activity are used interchangeably (though different schools of economics will argue that this is not the case). So my grandmother did not work, and those mothers I see with their infants are not working. No housewives, according to this economic definition, are workers.

The criterion for 'productive' work, proposed over fifty years ago by home economist Margaret Reid, was that any activity culminating in a service or product, which one can buy or hire someone else to do, is an 'economic activity' even if pay is not involved. Yet in major texts used in economics courses, it is not unusual to find sentences such as "Most of us prefer no work to work with no pay". Who is 'us', I wonder. Adam Smith defined work as an activity requiring the worker to give up "his [sic] tranquillity, his freedom and his happiness". Charlotte Perkins Gilman, a leading intellectual of the women's movement in the USA in the early twentieth century, called this a particularly masculine view:

> Following that pitiful conception of labor as a curse, comes the very old and andro-centric (i.e. male-centred) habit of despising it as belonging to women and then to slaves ... for long ages men performed no productive industry at all, being merely hunters and fighters. Our current teachings in the infant science of political economy are naively masculine. They assume as unquestionable that 'the economic man' will never do anything unless he has to; will only do it to escape pain or attain pleasure; and will, inevitably, take all he can get and do all he can to outwit, overcome, and if necessary destroy his antagonist.

But the view of the world that Gilman despised has been institutionalised, so that work, according to Katherine Newland, "is still the primary means by which people establish a claim to a share of production. To be without work is to place that claim in jeopardy". Housewives clearly do not 'work'. Mothers taking care of children are not working. No money changes hands.

Those who are in the grey area of informal work between the recognised labor market and the housewife may not claim to be workers either, in this economic sense. Invisible, informal work includes bartering, the trading of goods in informal settings (for example, in flea markets), and 'off the books' or 'under the table' employment. Workers who do not report work or pay income taxes on earnings and workers who are paid in cash at below minimum wages fall into this category. In addition, volunteer work can be considered informal work. (And note that volunteer work is generally done by women, while financial contributions to voluntary organizations which take place in the market, are tax-deductible, and have special rules within the economic system are generally made by men.)

'Home-based work activities' including housekeeping, home repair and maintenance, do-it-yourself building, and child-care are informal work. So are 'deviant work activities' which include anything from organised crime to petty fraud. The social exchange of services, which is the giving and receiving of services within social networks of relatives, friends, neighbours, and acquaintances, is also regarded as economically unimportant and remains unacknowledged.

The labor force, then, is defined in economics as all members of the working age population who are either employed formally or are seeking or awaiting formal employment. The labor force consists of the employed and unemployed but not the underemployed, the marginally employed, the would-be employed, and certainly not those who work in the informal sector, or who work as housewives.

Production and reproduction

The skewed definitions of work and labor that are used by economists result in an equally skewed concept of production. As we have seen, economists usually use labor to mean only those activities that produce surplus value (that is, profit in the marketplace). Consequently, labor (work) that does not produce profits is not considered production.

So, for example, the labor of childbirth may be work for a paid surrogate mother or for the paid midwife, nurse, doctor, and anaesthetist. Despite the *Oxford English Dictionary's* description of labor as "the pains and effort of childbirth; travail", the woman in labor the reproducer, sustainer, and nurturer of human life does not 'produce' anything. Similarly, all the other reproductive work that women do is widely viewed as unproductive. Growing and processing food, nurturing, educating, and running a household – all part of the complex process of reproduction – are unacknowledged as part of the production system. A woman who supplies such labor is not seen by economists as performing work of value. Yet the satisfaction of basic needs to sustain human society is fundamental to any economic system. By this failure to acknowledge the primacy of reproduction, the male face of economics is fatally flawed.

But what value is a unit of production which cannot guarantee its own continuous and regular reproduction? As a means of reproduction, woman is irreplaceable wealth. Reproducing the system depends on her. Gold, cloth, ivory, and cattle may be desirable, but they are only able to produce and reproduce wealth in the hands of progeny. Control derives ultimately not from the possession of wealth, but the control of reproduction. In terms of value, reproduction of the human species is either the whore, debased, of no worth, or the virgin on the pedestal, valued beyond wealth.

In support of this view, Gerda Lerner, professor of history at the University of Wisconsin, argues that women's reproductive power was the first private property amassed by men, and that domination over women provided the model for men's enslavement of other men.

The basic definitions and concepts in the male analyses of production and reproduction also reflect an unquestioned acceptance of biological determinism. Women's household and child-care work are seen as an extension of their physiology. All the labor that goes into the production of life, including the labor of giving birth to a child, is seen as an activity of nature, rather than an interaction of a woman with nature. 'Nature' apparently produces plants, animals, and homo sapiens unconsciously, and women play no active or conscious part in the process.

Pivotal to this analysis is the fixation on paid labor alone as productive. Even Frederick Engels's brief insight on reproduction is now forgotten. Engels was the long-time friend of Karl Marx and Marx's collaborator on *The Origin of the Family, Private Property and the State*. In it, Engels wrote:

> According to the materialistic concept ... the determining factor of history is, in the final instance, the production and reproduction of the immediate essentials of life. This, again, is of a two-fold character. On the one side, the production of the means of existence of articles of food and clothing, dwellings and of the tools necessary for that production; on the other side, the production of human beings themselves, the propagation of the species.

Yet today the liberal-conservative spectrum of economists speaks of reproduction (in some of its forms) as privatised and domestic (and thus only of its microeconomic significance). The

Marxist economists speak of it (in some of its forms) as having only 'use value'. Reproduction in all its forms is not fully addressed within any discipline: it is generally seen as part of nature and, thus, not within the scope of analysis or change.

Marilyn Waring is Professor of Public Policy at the Institute of Public Policy at AUT University in Auckland, New Zealand. This chapter is adapted from *Counting for Nothing*, George Allen & Unwin, Wellington, 1988, ch. 1, pp. 12-29. © 1988 Marilyn Waring. Reprinted with permission of the author.

Gender and the Definition of Economics
Julie Nelson

So what is economics? Does economics include any study having to do with the creation and distribution of the "necessaries and conveniences of life", as Adam Smith said in 1776? Or is it about goods and services only to the extent that they enter into a process of exchange? Or is the core of economics to be found in mathematical models of individual choice, which sometimes leads to hypothetical exchange? There is no doubt that, while room exists around the fringes for other sorts of studies, the last definition of economics is the one that is currently dominant in the most highly regarded research and in the core of graduate study. This narrowing of the definition of economics reflects particular gender-related biases and that, while significant advances have been made through the mathematical study of exchange, feminist insights can help to reorient the discipline towards a broader and richer economics.

Gender and the Cartesian ideal

Feminists have used techniques of literary criticism, historical interpretation, and psychoanalysis "to 'read science as a text' in order to reveal the social meanings the hidden symbolic and structural agendas of purportedly value-neutral claims and practices" (Harding 1986: 23). There is now a considerable literature that uses such tools to investigate the historical links between social ideals of science and of gender in western society. This literature describes the radical and gendered change in world view that occurred during the sixteenth and seventeenth centuries. In this period, the predominant cultural conception of the relationship between humans and nature changed from one in which humans were seen as embedded in a female, living cosmos to one in which men were seen as potentially detached, objective observers and controllers of nature. In this new conception, nature came to be seen as passive and, eventually, as mechanical. Science became identified with masculinity, detachment, and domination, and femininity with nature, subjectivity, and submission.

Of greater interest for the discussion of the high-status definition of economics is the literature on the gendered nature of Cartesian thought. Descartes regarded sensory input from the *res extensa* as deceptive; therefore, he believed that the only true knowledge is that which can be expressed mentally in the form of theorems and proofs. The Cartesian model of objectivity, based on dispassion and detachment, has been interpreted by Susan Bordo and others as related to anxiety created by the loss of the medieval feeling of connection to nature. Karl Stern's book on philosophy beginning with Descartes is entitled *The Flight from Woman*. James Hillman writes in *The Myth of Analysis*, "The specific consciousness we call scientific, Western and modern is the long sharpened tool of the masculine mind that has discarded parts of its own substance, calling it 'Eve', 'female' and 'inferior'" (quoted in Bordo 1986: 441). The counterpoint to rational detached 'man' is "woman [who] provides his connection with nature; she is the mediating force between man and nature, a reminder of his childhood, a reminder of the body, and a reminder of sexuality, passion, and human connectedness. She is the repository of emotional life and of all the non-rational elements of human experience" (Fee 1983: 12). In the Cartesian view, the abstract, general, detached, emotionless, 'masculine' approach taken to represent scientific thinking is radically removed from, and clearly viewed as superior to, the concrete, particular, embodied, passionate, 'feminine' reality of material life.

The high-status definition of economics

Economics increasingly has come to be defined not by its subject matter but by a particular way of viewing the world. The phrase 'the economic approach to …' is commonly used to mean viewing a problem in terms of choices, especially the individual welfare of profit maximising choices of autonomous rational agents. Lionel Robbins's much-quoted 1935 definition of economics as "the science which studies human behaviour as a relationship between ends and scarce means which have alternative uses" helped to consolidate this view. 'Economic theory' is frequently made synonymous with 'choice theory' or 'decision theory'.

Such a definition is not unrelated to the gendered Cartesian ideal. Defining the subject of economics as individual choice makes the detached *cogito*, not the material world or real persons in the material world, the centre of study. Nature, childhood, bodily needs, and human connectedness, cut off from 'masculine' concern in the Cartesian split, remain safely out of the limelight. The emphasis on the 'scarcity of means' suggests that nature is static, stingy, and hostile, a view of nature perhaps still based on a conception of man as dominating feminine nature, which, while dominated and passive, is still able to frighten.

While one presumably could attempt to pursue this choice-centred approach in a purely verbal manner, one of the advantages of such an approach is that some aspects are easily expressed in mathematical form. The assumptions of this model and the form the analysis takes have been closely linked ever since economics adopted concepts from eighteenth-century physics (Mirowski 1991). When economics is assumed to be centred around mathematical models of individual choice, assumptions about human behaviour take on the status of axioms (Becker 1976) while nature becomes a mathematical 'commodity space' (Debreu 1991). Study of actual markets tends to give way to study of ideal abstract markets or hypothetical games. In fact, the less research has to do with actual economies, the higher its status: purely abstract models are commonly referred to as being 'highbrow', 'capital T', or 'pure' economic theory while models that bring in some institutional detail are only 'middlebrow', 'small t' economic theory, or 'merely applied'. Attempts to explain phenomena that do not include a mathematical model of individual choice are not seen as economic theory at all. Thus the Cartesian voice echoes down through the centuries.

While some feminist economists have been able to stretch the dominant model to address some of their concerns, others believe that the model is too narrow that forcing the analysis of such issues as discrimination, comparable worth, inequality within the household, and non-sexist policy reforms into this framework leaves many of the most crucial questions unanswered.

Thinking about an alternative to masculine economics

When all we know is masculine economics, it is hard to imagine an alternative. The common ways of thinking about gender suggest that the only alternative to macho economics must be emasculated, impotent economics. Given current conceptions of science and masculinity, there is a tendency to think that the only alternative to a definition of economics emphasising rigour, scientificity, and rationality would be one that gives in to, say, sloppiness, subjectivity, and emotionalism. Or that if economics backs down from an emphasis on theory of individual choice, it would degenerate into a dogmatic theory of sociological determinism or a practice of prosaic, theoryless potato counting. The masculine is good; the feminine (trespassing into science from its proper realm) can only be bad or so we are accustomed to thinking.

Envisioning an alternative that is not simply weak and mushy requires a new view of gender, value, and knowledge. Ideas from feminist theory, recent work in the philosophy and sociology of science, and research on cognition and language all play a role in constructing this view. Starting with the concepts of gender and value, we can think of sexism as an unjustified association of masculinity with superiority and of femininity with inferiority at the cognitive as well as social level. But instead of substituting for this the idea that 'feminine is good, too', or turning the tables to 'feminine is good and masculine is bad', we can think of breaking apart the association of gender with value. If gender and value are thought of as orthogonal dimensions, then it becomes possible to think about good and bad aspects of the characteristics cognitively associated with masculinity in our culture, and also the good and bad characteristics of what we think of as feminine. *At the cognitive level, then, sexism can also be seen as the selective blocking from view of the strengths of femininity and the dangers of unmitigated masculinity.* A better economics would neither be purged of all of its distinctively masculine characteristics nor simply have feminine-associated characteristics tacked on indiscriminately; in a better economics we would choose carefully from both 'masculine' and 'feminine' approaches those that result in the best science.

Take as a simple example the idea that a 'hard' economics is preferable to a 'soft' economics. This judgment relies on an association of hardness with positively valued masculine-associated strength, and softness with negatively valued, feminine-associated weakness. However, hardness may also mean rigidity, and softness may also imply flexibility. A pursuit of masculine hardness that spurns association with femininity and hence with flexibility can be thought of as leading to rigidity, just as surely as a pursuit of feminine softness without corresponding strength make us think of weakness. Would not a more balanced and resilient economics be one that is flexible as well as hard?

Alternative methods

The impression, fostered by the Cartesian view, that only theorems that can be proved (*a la* geometry) constitute knowledge tends to block from view alternative kinds of knowledge. The devaluation of language, community, the body, and emotion implied by an emphasis on axiomatic, detached truth has been contested in recent works in feminist theory, the philosophy of science, and studies of cognition and language as well as in economics. These works claim that rationality includes reasoning by analogy, by metaphor, by pattern recognition, by imagination, and by, as Einstein once put it, "intuition, resting on sympathetic understanding of experience".

The crucial advantage of this form of reasoning, is that it can deal with overlapping, interconnected concepts because it is experientially or contextually based. Georgescu-Roegen distinguishes what he calls "arithmomorphic" concepts, that is, concepts that are "discretely distinct" and suitable for manipulation by the laws of logic, from "dialectical" concepts, which overlap with their opposites "over a contourless penumbra of varying breadth" (1971: 14). Far from being trivial, the latter, he argues, constitute "most of our thoughts". Lakoff and Johnson argue that the elevation of set-theoretic categorisation as the basis for objectivist knowledge overlooks important aspects of the way people actually comprehend the world: human categorisation is much more flexible, purpose specific, and open-ended, and tends to be based on family resemblances or prototypes (1980: 122-5). Lakoff and Johnson argue that human understanding is based on metaphors, which in turn are based on bodily experience, and that understanding is inseparable from imagination and emotion. This idea of understanding as connected to experience is reiterated in Keller's (1985: 117) definition of objectivity:

the pursuit of a maximally authentic, and hence maximally reliable, understanding of the world around oneself. Such a pursuit is dynamic to the extent that it actively draws on the commonality between mind and nature as a resource of understanding ... In this, dynamic objectivity is not unlike empathy.

Such reasoning beyond logic makes use of experience and connection rather than suppressing or denying them.

The point here is not that one way of thinking is peculiar to females and the other to males. Indeed this would be a rather odd conclusion, given the number of males who investigate 'imaginative rationality' and the number of females who have worked within disciplines emphasising formal logic. Rather, gender linkages enter at the level of cultural association: females are stereotypically linked with the intuitive approach, where 'intuitive' is taken to mean an effortless, irrational sort of knowledge of mysterious origin. The above analysis suggests that a revaluation of such different-than-logical (not illogical) forms of knowledge, devalued by descendants of Descartes as intuitive and inferior, is in order.

As McCloskey pointed out in *The Rhetoric of Economics* (1985), much economic argument already takes this form, although it does so unselfconsciously. Even in the most high-tech, abstract economics lectures or seminars, the presenter is usually asked to give the 'intuition' behind the model or result, that is, an explanation using analogies or examples that make the value of the exercise clear. Nevertheless, the formal model is generally considered to be the substance of the talk and the rest merely supplementary material.

The broader conception of reasoning outlined above suggests, on the contrary, that the real reasoning comes in the words: the conceptual framework, the applications, the metaphors, and the determination of priorities, within which the role of logic and abstraction is 'to facilitate the argument, clarify the results, and so guard against possible faults of reasoning that is all'. This by no means implies the abandonment or neglect of mathematical, analytical argument as long as it furthers the investigation.

If the neglected strength of feminine-associated knowledge is in 'imaginative rationality', what is the unseen danger of unmitigated masculinity? Georgescu-Roegen calls the enthralment with discrete, arithmomorphic concepts manageable by logic "arithmomania"; he writes that it "ends by giving us mental cramps" (1971: 52, 80). Sound economic reasoning, including (or even especially) about very applied issues and including (or even especially) argument in largely verbal form, should be no reason for apology in economics seminars. The pitfall of empty logic, just as much as of illogic, should be cause for embarrassment.

Alternative in subject

For Robbins, Jevons, and their followers, the question of choice between alternative ends, given the means at hand, is at the heart of economics. While economic theory and choice theory have become synonymous in recent decades, there are still substantial echoes of an order definition of economics: the study of the basis of human material welfare. According to the older alternative, in the words of Alfred Marshall, "Economics is a study of mankind [*sic*] in the ordinary business of life; it examines that part of individual and social action which is most closely connected with the attainment and with the use of the material requisites of well-being" (1920: 1). Rather than defining economics as a particular way of looking at human behaviour, this definition delineates economics in terms of material goods. Of course, as Robbins correctly argued in promoting his definition based on scarcity, the material welfare definition also has its problems. Adam Smith's and Karl Marx's distinction between productive labor, which results in the production of a material object, and unproductive labor, which does not, led to interminable and useless debate. Taken literally, the materialist definition implies that non-tangibles, even such service as health care, lie outside the scope of economics.

Feminist theory suggests that the definition focusing on choice, which looks at human decisions as radically separated from physical and social constraints, and the definition stressing material well-being which ignores non-physical sources of human satisfaction, are not the only alternatives. Such a dichotomy merely reinforces the separation of humans from the world. What is needed instead is a definition of economics that considers humans *in relation* to the world.

Focusing economics on the *provisioning* of human life, that is, on the commodities and processes necessary to human survival, provides such a definition. In contrast to Robbins's view of economics as synonymous with choice, consider the following claim by Georgescu-Roegen: "Apt though we are to lose sight of the fact, the primary objective of economic activity is the self-preservation of the human species. Self-preservation in turn requires the satisfaction of some basic needs which are nevertheless subject to evolution" (1966: 93). Such a definition is not limited to physical concepts. Georgescu-Roegen points out that "purposive activity and enjoyment of life", parts of his definition of self-preservation, are not material variables. In addition, when human survival including survival through childhood is made the core of economic inquiry, non-material services, such as childcare and supervision, as well as attendance to health concerns and the transmission of skills, become just as central as food and shelter.

The concept of needs or necessaries is, of course, itself dialectical and fluid. This is not necessarily a disadvantage: recognition of this fact guards against a slide into a too rigid formalism. It requires a honing of exactly those rational skills that much of the current practice of economics has allowed to atrophy. The line between needs and wants is not distinct, and yet one certainly can say that a Guatemalan orphan needs her daily bowl of soup more than the overfed North American needs a second piece of cake. A refusal to recognise such a distinction on the basis of its logical ambiguity leads to an abdication of human ethical responsibility.

Such a definition of economics need not rule out studies of choice or of exchange, but it does displace them from the core of economics. It does not rule out study of the provision of conveniences or luxuries as well as more basic needs, but it does not give them equal priority. Voluntary exchange is part of the process of provisioning, but so are gift-giving and coercion. Organised, impersonal markets are one locus of economic activity, but so are households, governments, and other more personal or informal human organizations. Issues of the organisation of production, of power and poverty, of unemployment and economic duress, of health care and education become the *raison d'etre* of the economics profession, not the further elaboration of a particular axiomatic theory of human behaviour. The Greek root of both the words 'economics' and 'ecology' is *oikos*, meaning 'house'. Economics could be about how we live in our house, the Earth.

Conclusion

Feminist theory suggests that the Cartesian divisions between rationality and embodiment, and between man and nature, reflect a peculiarly masculinist and separative view of the world. The Cartesian view underlies the prestige given to mathematical models of individual rational choice in the current definition of economics. A richer economics, while not excluding formal models or the study of choice, would be centred around the study of provisioning and make full use of the tools of 'imaginative rationality'. Such an economics would be neither masculine nor feminine but would be a human science in the pursuit of human ends.

Lest this be misunderstood, I am not claiming or advocating that men do one kind of economics and women do another. Nor do I believe that the problem can be solved by asking economists who want a richer approach simply to remove themselves to sociology (as has been suggested more than once). While economists and sociologists certainly could learn more from each other, sociology as it stand has its own problems (as feminist sociologists have been quick to point out); moreover, it deals with social phenomena broader than the provision of the necessaries of life. The material side of the provisioning definition of economics has roots reaching back to several of our own, including Adam Smith and Alfred Marshall, and has survived as an undercurrent, if not as the high-prestige current, in economic thought. Rather than keeping high-status economics as it is and pushing all dissidents out, I suggest that the term economics be reclaimed. Let us start by speaking of the mathematical theory of individual choice as 'the mathematical theory of individual choice' instead of as 'economic theory', of the choice-theoretic approach as 'the choice-theoretic approach' instead of as '*the* economic approach'.

Does it seem too prosaic or worldly to define economics as centrally concerned with the study of how humans, in interaction with each other and the environment, provide for their own survival and health? If it does, perhaps such a judgment reveals more about how we feel about our own bodily (and gendered) existence than it reveals about the correct level of prestige to be attributed to different definitions of economics.

Julie Nelson is Associate Professor of Economics at the University of Massachusetts, Boston and a Senior Research Fellow at the Global Development and Environment Institute, Tufts University. This chapter is adapted from The Study of Choice or the Study of Provisioning? Gender and the Definition of Economics, in M.A. Ferber and J.A. Nelson (eds), *Beyond Economic Man*, University of Chicago Press, Chicago, 1993, pp. 23-36. © 1993 Chicago University Press. Reprinted with permission of Chicago University Press.

Government Budgets: Integrating a Gender Perspective
Rhonda Sharp

When Treasurers (or Ministers of Finance) announce the annual government budget they generally identify ways in which its revenue raising and expenditure activities will impact on the lives of people directly through specific measures and indirectly via its impact on 'the economy'. They outline direct budgetary impacts through the provision of services (health care and education), infrastructure (water and energy), income transfers (family payments, unemployment benefits) and through the provision of public sector jobs. Further significant direct impacts are identified through the determination of types and amounts of taxation and user charges. The Treasurer's budget statement generally also generally identifies the anticipated impacts of the budget on the private sector (e.g. through government contracts to the private sector to supply goods and services) and the macroeconomic impacts on the level of aggregate demand in the economy. These are indirect channels by which budgets impact on people because they in turn affect employment, price levels and economic growth (Elson and Sharp 2010). What Treasurers rarely spell out, however, is that these budgetary impacts are likely to be profoundly different for different groups of people.

Gender responsive budgeting (also termed gender sensitive budgets, gender budgets and women's budgets) has emerged as a strategy for shining a brighter light on government budgets for their gender impacts. That is, the budget is examined for what it has done and not done towards the promotion of economic and social equality between men and women and between different groups of men and women. These assessments form the basis for developing strategies for changing funding, policies, programs and the budgetary decision-making processes so that gender equality and women's empowerment is promoted. Since the world's first 'women's budget' exercise in 1983 under the Hawke Labor government more than 90 countries have introduced gender responsive budget initiatives either by governments or civil society groups.

A gender responsive budget is not a separate budget for women (or men). Rather it is the application of a gender lens to the whole of the government budget and the policies and programs funded with a view to engage in change. In doing so, issues that are overlooked or obscured in conventional budgetary analysis are brought into focus. This includes the role of unpaid work in economic and social outcomes between groups, the distribution of resources between and within families and the level of participation of men and women in budget decision-making processes (Elson and Sharp 2010).

By paying attention to the gender differentiated nature of budgetary impacts and developing actions for change, gender responsive budgeting aims to make governments accountable for their gender equality commitments. Gender responsive budgeting is now seen as a tool for promoting gender equality by monitoring human rights and other international conventions, promoting development and human capabilities, and fostering effective economic governance through ensuring efficiency and equity (Elson 2006; Hewitt and Mukhopadhyay 2002). In some cases gender responsive budgeting has focussed on poverty as well as gender equality. An example is the Tanzania Gender Networking programme, which influenced its government to adopt gender analysis into its budget planning process and to improve the availability of poverty related sex disaggregated data (Elson and Sharp 2010). In Mexico gender responsive budgeting research has directed attention to the plight of poor women in accessing government services (Cooper and Sharp 2007).

While there are variations between countries in the form these exercises have taken, they share similar assumptions about the importance of the government budget for gender. Gender responsive budget exercises recognize that government budgets command substantial resources and that the state is an influential force in shaping gender outcomes. Also, government budgets impact on individuals and groups directly by design and indirectly as part of general policy. By asking questions about the direct and indirect impacts and the equity and efficiency outcomes of government budgets on men and women and different groups of men and women, gender responsive budgets force re-evaluation of a long held assumption that government budgets and economic policies generally are 'gender neutral' in their impact (Sharp and Broomhill 1988; 1990). This perception has been maintained with the traditional presentation of budgets in terms of financial aggregates without specific mention of either women or men. For example, the large amount of taxation concessions Australian federal governments have provided to superannuation contributions and investments have been shown to disproportionately favour high income men, with women much less likely as a group to benefit having about half the superannuation savings as men (Sharp and Austen 2007). Yet these budget allocations are portrayed as ultimately benefitting all in the community. Such presentations belie the fact that women and men tend to occupy different and unequal economic and social positions and roles; they undertake different activities, face different constraints and accordingly make different choices. Consequently, there is considerable scope for women and men to be affected by, and respond differently to, budgetary policy (Elson 1997; Budlender and Sharp 1998; Himmelweit 2002). Gender sensitive budgets provide a mechanism for systematically uncovering these issues, and, in doing so, challenge the 'gender blindness' of traditional economic policy. They also highlight that government policymaking that recognises gender differences and impacts is more likely to achieve not only equity but also efficiency goals (Sharp and Broomhill 2009). Moreover, in the process of 'following the money' and requiring that gender is explicitly discussed and reported upon, the policy evaporation and resistance around gender issues that characterises both industrialised and developing countries is also more visible for challenge (Budlender 2007).

Gender sensitive budget analyses have emerged out of feminist practical politics seeking to change government policies. However, increasingly their theoretical underpinnings and capacities to achieve change are being analysed, providing a new terrain for feminist economic thought.

Two key areas to which theoretical connections have been made are feminist theories of the state and feminist critiques and reconstructions of macroeconomics.

The question of the role of the state in relation to women's economic position has been raised and debated extensively by feminists. Gender sensitive budgets offer opportunities to inform and be informed by this theoretical debate. In Australia, where gender responsive budgets originated, this has been enabled by the fact that feminist politics has for three decades had a significant space within the state itself. Early analysis of women's budgets, as they were called in Australia, argued that the longer-term significance of gender responsive budgets needs to be assessed in the context of the overall role of the state in relation to women's economic position (Sharp and Broomhill 1990). Several feminist analyses of gender responsive budgets acknowledged that these exercises offer a potentially positive role for the state to play in raising women's economic position. In particular, these analyses argue that national machinery introduced for integrating gender into government policy is ultimately limited unless attention is paid to the budgetary dimension (Sawer 1990; Budlender 1996). National machinery for women that provides policy oversight, monitoring and advocacy needs to be scrutinised for its implications for the budget.

Other analyses, however, caution against assuming that the state will respond positively even when the processes or 'machinery of government' for promoting gender equality have been established. Historically, the role of the state in influencing women's economic position in society has been complex, and in some respects, contradictory (Sharp and Broomhill 2002, 1990). While it is clear that the various agencies of the capitalist state, and the government in particular, have played an important role in sustaining the structures within which women are subordinated in society, the state has also acted as an agent for progressive changes to improve women's economic position. Gender responsive budgets themselves reflect this contradiction. On the one hand, their existence illustrates that pressure from feminists in the political process has been successful in forcing governments at least to acknowledge women's specific economic interests. On the other hand, the potentially progressive role of gender responsive budgets envisaged by their architects remains only partially fulfilled as a result of other conservative pressures placed on the state. Paramount among these are the gender blind set of economic policy making assumptions and a strong ideological bias against state intervention to achieve equity goals for specific groups. An important step in making gender responsive budgets more effective requires considerable political pressure to be exerted upon the state by women's groups and their supporters. Ideally this approach would incorporate a feminist politics which pressures the state from within as well as from outside (Sharp and Broomhill 2002).

The second area where feminists have forged theoretical connections has been between gender sensitive budget exercises and the emerging feminist economic critique of macroeconomics. Central to this view is the idea that a gender neutral approach to national budgets can undermine macroeconomic policies by ignoring women's economic contributions in the form of unpaid work in the household, voluntary community work, subsistence and informal sector employment. These economic contributions are deemed significant in how the economy operates. They are based on a gender division of labour that gives rise to gender differences which are structural to the economy. In this way feminist economists have created a space to argue that gender matters for policy efficiency as well as for equity. Studies of developing countries have shown, for example, that reducing gender inequality in education enrolments, the labour market or time burdens leads to rises in productivity, national income, and economic growth (Elson 2002a).

The feminist critique of conventional macroeconomics further argues that effective budgets (as well as other macroeconomic policy instruments) require a conceptual framework that incorporates the gendered care economy into the total flow of national income and output. In so doing, interactions between paid and the unpaid activities critical to macroeconomic policy will be brought into view (Beneria 1995; Cagatay, Elson and Grown 1995; Elson 1997 and 2002b;

Bakker 1997; Himmelweit 2002). A starting point for this analysis has been to introduce the unpaid household and community care sector into the circular flow model of the economy. The unpaid care sector, aided by inputs provided by the public sector, is argued to underpin macroeconomic growth because it plays a crucial role in producing the labour force and developing and maintaining the social context in which economic activities take place (including the creation of social assets such as sense of community, responsibility and trust). Thus, in contrast to conventional macroeconomics, which ignores how the labour force comes into existence, labour is theorized as an input into production which is itself produced. Furthermore, long run decisions about social reproduction influence on the quality and quantity of labour available to the productive or paid economy (Walters 1995). Thus, budgetary policies, through their impact on household decisions, the labour market and the availability of government services, potentially have significant feedback effects on quantity and quality of care activities.

One way in which the interdependency of the paid and the unpaid sectors of the economy has been drawn out has been to stress the complementarity of private production and public investments in health, education, infrastructure and market access, a matter emphasized by 'new growth theory' (Bakker 1997; Palmer 1995). Using this framework feminists have pointed to the positive link between equity and growth while noting that women's economic contribution is characterized by absent and biased markets arising out of inequitable gender relations which need to be taken into account for efficient policy. Segmented labour markets which result in women systematically receiving lower wages than men because of a lower sociocultural value being assigned to women's work is an example of a biased market while significant absent markets characterize much of the reproduction of the labour force which is work primarily done by women without any cost being accounted for by the market based economy. The latter amounts to a socially determined tax being placed on women's labour (Palmer 1995). Conventional macroeconomic theory which advocates policies of cutbacks in public sector investments in areas such as health and education ignores the capacity of these expenditures to reduce gender inequities and promote economic growth by creating or stimulating missing or segmented markets. That is, conventional macroeconomic theory and policy by ignoring the ways in which gender relations contribute to distortions in resource allocations caused by absent and biased markets can advocate budgetary reductions which are likely to aggravate these distortions by 'crowding out' women's contribution to economic growth (Palmer 1995; Elson and Catatay 2000). A key conclusion of the feminist critique of macroeconomics is therefore that gender inequalities are not only unfair but costly.

A number of other theoretical implications will undoubtedly continue to emerge from the experience of gender sensitive budgets. There remains a need for ongoing feminist research that critiques traditional budgets and their resource allocations for their equity, efficiency and effectiveness. Tools of public finance analysis such as public expenditure and taxation incidence need to be evaluated for their capacities to incorporate gender. The research agenda could be fruitfully extended to examine how the value of caring labour might be budgeted for in policy and the capacities of institutions such as treasury, finance and public enterprises to engender their approach to programs and policies. At a broader level there is a need for further research on the gendered impact of globalization and restructuring and the consequences of the state adopting neoliberal policies for women's economic position and gender relations. The implementation of gender responsive budgets in a diverse range of countries has also brought to the forefront additional questions for feminist research agenda. Of particular interest to feminist economists, and feminists more generally, is how a feminist analyses of budgets might take into account women's and men's experiences in terms of gender, race, and class.

Rhonda Sharp is Adjunct Professor, Hawke Research Institute, University of South Australia. Government Budgets: Integrating a Gender Perspective © 2011 Rhonda Sharp.

Principal Currents in Feminist Economics

Gillian Hewitson

During the nineteenth and early twentieth centuries, in Western countries such as the Australia, the United States and Britain, the legal framework within which economic activity took place largely dictated women's economic situation. Some examples include the legal requirement, embedded within the common law of marriage, for wives to provide housework, childrearing and sexual services to their husbands in return for at least a minimal subsistence. Husbands were legally entitled to the wage earnings of working wives. Wives were, in effect, legal chattels. Women's labor-supply decisions were restricted by 'protective legislation' with respect to total hours worked, which hours, and in which occupations. Sex discrimination was legal, and women's wages were determined not by their productivity but by socially-accepted norms such as the widespread belief that women worked for 'pin money' rather than for economic necessity, which allowed employers to pay them badly. Indeed, working class women were frequently unable to support themselves, making marriage an attractive economic proposition. Furthermore, women had limited opportunities, if any, to attend university, and they could not own property in their own names. Despite the restrictions of marriage, then, most women married because their access to economic independence was so limited. Women were assumed to be actual or future wives, and the legal and economic environment ensured that this would be so. Even in the mid-twentieth century, women in certain occupations were terminated if they got married; if a wife had a bank account in her own name, her husband had access to it; and a married woman could not borrow money without her husband's consent.

However, by the 1970s, most, if not all, of the legal restrictions on women's economic activity mentioned above had been eliminated in modern Western countries. Most countries have ratified the Convention on the Elimination of Discrimination Against Women, and now there are laws in place that make it illegal to discriminate against women in employment, hours, earnings and lending. Wives now own their own earnings. Women have become prime ministers and presidential candidates, and they have entered the board rooms of many large companies. And, in Western countries, women make up nearly half the labor force. This environment, in which women appear to have the same ability as men to determine their own economic fates, sometimes makes young people question the relevance of feminist economics in today's world. As this chapter shows, however, the economic system remains a gendered system, and most women's economic outcomes are related to the fact that they are women.

Feminist economics is the area of research and practice within which the gendered economic system is analyzed. Feminist economics is quite recent; the International Association for Feminist Economics was formed in 1992, and its journal, *Feminist Economics*, began in 1995. Feminist economists argue that gender is central to understanding the allocation of economic opportunities, rewards and punishments, and therefore gender is a key determinant of individual economic outcomes. They use a variety of feminist perspectives to understand and change the social and economic institutions and policies that reinforce the economic subordination of women. In common with other schools of heterodox economics, such as ecological economics, (old) institutionalism and social economics, feminist economics is critical of the discipline's mainstream neoclassical economics. Feminist economists, however, make the specific claim that orthodox economics naturalizes women's economic subordination, and have also been critical of some other heterodox schools of thought, such as traditional Marxism, for the same reason.

A brief overview of some of the facts of economic inequality is in order (the following statistics are from the United Nations Development Fund for Women and the USA Census). In the United States, in 2007, full-time female workers earned 80 cents for every dollar earned by full-time male workers. In 2007, 12.5 percent of the US population, and 9.8 percent of all families, lived in poverty. Single parent households are more likely to be poor than two-parent households, and women head 85 percent of single parent households. Of those, 28.3 percent lived in poverty. Of the 15 percent of single parent households headed by males, only 13.6 percent live in poverty. Gender differentials in the global context are even more significant. Of the 1.3 billion people living in extreme poverty around the world, 70 percent are women. Globally, the average gender wage gap is 17 percent, but the range is from 3 percent to 51 percent. Two thirds of the world's working hours are performed by women, including the production of half of the world's food supply, but women receive only one tenth of the world's income and own 1 percent of the world's property (UNIFEM *n.d*; U.S. Census *n.d*).

However, globally and nationally, the differences between women can swamp the differences between men and women. For example, women in Botswana have a life expectancy of 33 years, but women in Hong Kong can expect to live until 86. When women work for pay in Georgia, they earn only 49 cents for every dollar earned by a Georgian man, while Maltese women earn 97 cents for every dollar earned by a Maltese man. In comparison to the earnings of full-time white male workers in the US, full-time white female workers earned 79 cents in the dollar, full-time black female workers earned 68 cents, and full-time Hispanic female workers earned just 60 cents. Thus, many feminist economists are as concerned with the differences between women as they are with differences between men and women.

Feminist economists view these facts as problematic, and symptomatic of an oppressive economic system that distributes economic rewards on the basis of gender, race and ethnicity. They argue that mainstream economics plays an important role in the maintenance of this oppressive gender system through its various absences or silences around women and femininity, as well as race, class, and other signifiers of difference. Their primary aim is to improve the lives of women. But their research agendas can be very different, depending upon the feminist perspective they take and their theoretical or empirical orientation. This plurality of approaches within feminist economics can, for convenience, be aggregated into two broad foci: research which uses gender as a theoretical variable, and research which uses gender as an empirical variable. Those using gender as a theoretical variable are interested in the ways in which economic concepts and categories become gendered, and in developing new theoretical perspectives on economic processes. Those feminist economists who undertake research in which gender is an empirical variable tend to be more practically-minded, being interested in statistical analyses in which gender is a descriptive category, and in developing new statistical models to generate insights into the economic behavior of men and women.

Methodology

Along with other heterodox schools of thought, feminist economists have been highly critical of mainstream claims to scientific objectivity. They reject the idea that neoclassical economics is value-free, and argue that it is underpinned by a conservative set of values based on a belief in individualism, the efficiency of free markets, and a merit-based system of economic rewards. Feminist economists are unique, however, in focusing on gender: they argue further that the value-system underpinning neoclassical economics reflects the needs and preferences of masculinity, as they have been constructed within the history of science.

Modern scientific methods emerged during the Enlightenment, when philosophers constructed a series of dualisms in their quest to understand how knowledge is produced. Rene Descartes, for example, with the dictum that "I think, therefore I am," constructed a mind/body split in which the thinker could be conceptually separated from any particular embodiment: this is the "view from nowhere" which defines the objective stance of the scientific inquirer. To see this, consider the meaning of an alternative, such as 'I feel, therefore I am' – the thinker in this case is necessarily embodied, and embodiment is necessarily sexually-specific and racially-specific, which means that the 'view' or perspective of the 'feeling thinker' is from somewhere, and hence not objective. Francis Bacon wrote about the necessity of conquering and penetrating nature, thereby constructing a subject, the researcher, in opposition to the object of research, and in this can be seen the object/subject, mind/matter and culture/nature distinctions. These distinctions were also gendered: the detached, objective observer with the 'view from nowhere', the penetrator of passive matter and producer of scientific knowledge, was associated with masculinity. Subjectivity, passivity, nature, the body, emotions and materiality were associated, on the other hand, with femininity (see Nelson 1993). These connections persist into the present day – one only need construct a list of contemporary stereotypical masculine and feminine characteristics.

The scientific method reflects a specifically *Western* as well as androcentric perspective. It was the European man, not just any man, who had the capacities of autonomy, independence and objectivity that were necessary for scientific knowledge production. The scientific approach was becoming dominant over the seventeenth to nineteenth centuries, just when the West (or Europe) was discovering, conquering and claiming as European territory the lands occupied by dark-skinned native peoples. The appropriation of non-Western land, labor and resources was justified by science, which was used to establish the superiority of the colonizers and hence the unchallengeable supremacy of their perspective on the world.

The rational economic agent

An important focus of feminist economists who use gender as a category of analysis has been the model of the individual at the centre of all neoclassical theorizing. Several assumptions construct this model. The economic agent is assumed to embody a timeless human nature consisting of a number of critical characteristics: individuals maximize their utility; they are instrumentally rational, always choosing the least-cost means to meet their objectives; they are self-interested, and uninterested in the well-being of others; and they are independent, or entirely separate from others. Socially-significant categories such as race or ethnicity, class, gender, nationality or sexuality are irrelevant to this definition of the economic agent. The characteristics attributed to the economic agent are critical because, without them, the neoclassical edifice of the modeling of individual choices within a constrained environment becomes hopelessly entangled. For example, in neoclassical consumer theory, rational, self-interested and independent consumers maximize their individual well-being by spending their incomes such that the marginal utility of the last dollar spent on each good or service is equal. Now imagine the impact of a different theory of the economic agent: what if consumers care about others, live within complex social arrangements and relationships, and use ethics, rather than self-interest, to determine their shopping cart contents. This interrelatedness of individuals means that the solution to the consumer's utility-maximizing problem is a function of many other people's utility, potentially billions (e.g. when shopping fair trade). No neat mathematical solutions are available: the predictions of individual behavior, and the whole policy framework of free markets that is built on those predictions, collapses.

Feminist economists have developed numerous critical analyses of the assumptions supporting the neoclassical theory of human nature (see England 1993). As mentioned, neoclassical economics claims that this human nature is universal, and pre-exists any social arrangements. This is the basis of the mainstream use of the literary figure of Robinson Crusoe as the representative economic agent. Crusoe was a British slave-trader who was shipwrecked on a deserted island, on which he lived alone for more than two decades, and who then rescued a native, whom he called Friday, from cannibals. To neoclassical economists, the facts of Crusoe's race, sex and class, his socialization in seventeenth century London, the importance of the slave trade to the story, his unusual living conditions, including the absence of women, children, and a family, his assertion of ownership of the island, and virtual enslavement of Friday to his will, are irrelevant to the capacity of the figure of Robinson Crusoe, a white Western colonizing man, to function as an exemplar of the economic agent. It need hardly be said that economic agents begin life as helpless babies, and often end life as helpless elders. Economic agents, then, can, in reality, only exist within particular social and familial relations, relations which entail a fundamental dependence on others, and which are completely absent from the paradigmatic neoclassical story of the individual. Neoclassical economics excludes all these aspects of Crusoe's story, leaving only the fantasy of the autonomous agent, independent of all others, seeking only his own self-interest within competitive market conditions, naturalizing and legitimizing the failure of the mainstream to consider gender, race, history, culture, power relations, and connections to others as absolutely essential to an understanding of the sexual, national and global distribution of economic well-being (see Grapard and Hewitson 2011).

Unpaid work

Unpaid work, including childcare, shopping, subsistence crop production, food preparation, cleaning, laundry, and collecting water and firewood, is essential for the functioning of the market economy, by creating workers and consumers on a daily basis. Unpaid work absorbs as many hours of work as paid work, and the majority is performed by women. Several groups of feminist economists research in this area. Those who use gender as a theoretical category have included Marxist feminist economists who, in the 1970s, pointed out that the home was a site of production as well as consumption. How to integrate the idea that domestic labor is economic production with the existing concepts of Marxist analysis was the subject of the so-called Domestic Labor Debate. Others sought to understand how unpaid work had come to be excluded from mainstream definitions of economic activity, and the implications of this exclusion. Unpaid work as productive economic activity is also vital to the research agendas of empirical feminist economists working in areas such as national accounting, development and labor markets (see the introduction and reprinted essays in Volume 2 of Barker and Kuiper 2009).

Work undertaken within the home lost its definition as work during the nineteenth century, and came to be regarded as something that women did naturally and out of love for their families. We see this transformation of unpaid work and the unpaid worker in the evolution of census categories during the nineteenth century. The censuses documented and categorized the population and its activities; in Britain, every ten years from 1800. The categories used for this documentation were products of generally-held views on gender, and men's and women's proper places, as well as the writings of economists. Early in the century, economists understood labor as the most important source of the wealth of nations; hence, the work that was undertaken by the population was of key significance. In the early decades of the census, those who worked in the home on domestic tasks were deemed to be economically occupied. Later in the century, however, economists excluded all non-market activities from their definition of economic activity, and by the end of the century the census categories also reflected this new theoretical boundary of economic behavior. Thus by the end of the century, women's work in British, Australian and North American homes had no place within the census; rather, those undertaking domestic labor were categorized as economic dependents, or economically unoccupied (see Deacon 1985; Folbre 1991).

This particular history is responsible for many of the seemingly natural categories that are used to define and understand today's economies. For example, the labor force categories of employed, unemployed, and not in the labor force, as well as the national accounting system and GDP, are based on nineteenth century census categories. Until 1993, the System of National Accounts (SNA), which generates estimates of the annual value of the productive activity in an economy (GDP), excluded unpaid work (see Waring 1990). The production boundary, or the division between productive and unproductive activities, enclosed the market and excluded non-market activities. In 1993 the SNA was revised, and the production boundary was extended to all goods for household consumption, whether or not those goods had been acquired through markets (UNIFEM n.d.). Where possible, the value of unpaid work is published in a 'satellite account'. This means that macroeconomics, which is the study of GDP (its definition, how it changes, how its changes affect inflation and unemployment, and how the government can manage it), continues to exclude about half the economic activity actually being undertaken. This is a significant limitation on policy-making.

Research into the value of unpaid work has taken two approaches. The first applies market wages to the hours of work in the home, treating the value of household work as equal to the market value of the labor used in household work. The second approach estimates the value of the output produced in the home, and thereby generates a value for unpaid work which is directly comparable to GDP. When the economic activity of households is measured in this way, the value of the household sector is at least equal to the value of the market sector (see Goldschmidt-Clermont 1992; Ironmonger 1996; Beneria 2003).

The mainstream economic theory of the sexual division of labor is called New Home Economics (NHE) (Becker 1991). NHE models the household as a single unit, within which the wage earner is, in effect, a benevolent dictator who maximizes the household's well-being. His distribution decisions ensure that each family member concurs with his wishes. Because spouses exploit their comparative advantages, the benevolent dictator is usually a husband, since men typically earn more than women, and because women, but not men, are able to take advantage of economies of scale in childbearing and rearing (they can be pregnant while also caring for children).

Feminist economists have been very critical of NHE. They have pointed out that the model relies on circular reasoning. To explain women's specialization in the home, look at women's lower wages: to explain women's lower wages, look at women's specialization in the home. This circular reasoning naturalizes women's role in the home and their lower labor market earnings by leaving out the possibility of labor market discrimination against women and the role of gender ideologies and gendered institutions in shaping and forming value assessments of women's work and skills. NHE's vision of the family is also silent on power relations. But empirical evidence suggests that power relations exist and, in particular, that the person earning the most money wages has the most bargaining power. For example, the more equal are the wages of a husband and wife, the more equal is the division of unpaid labor. Women who specialize in domestic labor lose bargaining power as their labor market skills decline, which problematises the notion that the sexual division of labor is efficient (see Ferber 2003). It also points to the heteronormativity of NHE, or its assumption that natural family relations are heterosexual and reproductive. Anyone who does not fit into such a family is inefficient because they do not take advantage of the complementarity of men and women in reproduction and production, including homosexual people, 'career women,' 'house-husbands', people who do not want to or cannot have children, and people who prefer to remain single. This naturalization of the conjugal family contributes tremendously to economists' and policy-makers' inability to imagine economic activity being organized, and work, income and wealth being distributed differently (see Badgett 1995; Hewitson 2003; Danby 2007).

Paid work

Feminist economists argue that the gendered institutional structures which frame and reproduce the current organization of unpaid work also support women's economic subordination in the realm of paid work. Women's paid work often replicates their unpaid work, reflecting a gender ideology which maps femininity onto service work and work involving the support of men. Thus women dominate in occupations such as maids and housekeeping cleaners, childcare worker, elementary and primary school teaching, secretaries and administrative assistants, nursing and receptionists. These jobs are both derivative of unpaid labor and often badly remunerated. Thus the gender wage gap can also be traced to the sexual division of labor in paid work. NHE justifies this pattern of economic rewards, but does not explain why, when women make up nearly half the labor force, they continue to be responsible for the majority of domestic labor and childcare.

Interest in the interrelatedness of women's domestic role and their occupational distribution within the labor market has led to the development of a new category of analysis called caring labor. Caring labor refers to both paid and unpaid caring work, such as childcare for pay, and unpaid emotional support within the family. Feminist economists have found that caring occupations dominated by women tend to attract a 'caring penalty,' which can be linked to the lack of value attributed to unpaid work, and the lack of esteem with which this work is generally viewed (Folbre 1995; the introduction and reprinted essays in Barker and Kuiper 2009 Volume 2).

Mainstream economists agree that there is a sexual division of labor in paid work, and that there is a gender wage gap. However, they believe that these phenomena result from rational, utility-maximizing, individual choices. Early labor market studies within applied neoclassical economics did not consider women at all. It was only in the 1960s, during an unprecedented movement of white wives into the formal labor market, that a female labor supply function was delineated, and because it referred to wives it necessarily included the opportunity cost of women's time at work – not leisure, but home-produced goods and services. Later, race and sex discrimination moved onto the mainstream agenda, though it was, and continues to be, argued that discrimination is an individual phenomenon ("I don't like black people or women"), analytically having nothing to do with larger social institutions such as the organization of unpaid work, gender ideologies, or the history of colonisation, slavery and associated racism. In the mainstream economic model developed by Becker, racists and sexists are punished by the market with lower profit than their competitors, and hence go out of business.

There is an extensive empirical literature examining gender issues in the labor market from a feminist perspective (see Blau, Ferber, and Winkler 2010; Bergmann 2005). The key results contrast sharply with the mainstream economic analysis. Feminist economists have found that sex discrimination plays a role in the gender wage gap. Women often earn less than men who are doing the same job, and are promoted more slowly than equally or lesser-qualified men. Women also hit a glass ceiling, so that in many occupations men largely take the senior positions, while women's careers have stopped progressing once they have reached some mid-way point up the ladder. Feminist economists also emphasise the importance of 'indirect discrimination,' or the discriminatory impact of the gender system that shapes women's choices. When women choose to enter traditionally-male occupations, they encounter the revolving door: women enter, find the working environment hostile to women, and they leave. Either women or men dominate most occupations, and this occupational segregation also accounts for some of the gender wage gap. But, as already discussed, the evidence for women's low productivity is lacking, and in any case women can earn less even with exactly the same human capital investments as their male counterparts. Experiments have shown that application letters from male (or white) applicants are evaluated more positively, and lead to more invitations to an interview, than application letters which are the same in every relevant respect, but are presented as being from female (or black) applicants.

Because of women's work in the home, feminist economists are very interested in the ways in which these responsibilities fit with the institutional requirements of the labor market, for full-time attendance at a workplace, a forty-hour week, 6pm meetings, and so on. Since the categories of work and the worker are gendered masculine, as the complement of the feminine gendered unpaid work and the housewife (discussed above), the worker is someone without domestic responsibilities. (This is a theoretical point about the concept of the worker, rather than being a point about actual men and women). From this perspective, such mechanisms as 'family-friendly' policies, unpaid maternity and paternity leave are ways in which mothers are added to or fitted into the labor market, leaving mothers, rather than work, as the problem. Fathers, because the notion of worker is already intrinsically dependent on the idea of male breadwinner, have been hesitant to make use of these mechanisms for fear that their commitment to work will be questioned. Indeed, holding other factors constant, men with children earn more than those without, while the opposite is true of mothers, revealing the assumptions regarding the work commitment of breadwinners vs mothers. In other words, anyone not fitting the identity of worker in the same way as unencumbered men is problematic. This points once again to the extent to which gendered institutions naturalize and reproduce an organization of work that is detrimental to women (see Williams 2000; Barker 2005).

Gillian Hewitson is Lecturer in Political Economy, School of Social and Political Sciences, University of Sydney. This chapter is adapted from Feminist Economics in R.C. Free (ed), *21st Century Economics: A Reference Handbook*, Sage, Thousand Oaks, CA, 2010. © 2010 Gillian Hewitson.

DEVELOPMENT FOR WHOM?

Capitalist development has always been uneven – temporally, spatially and socially. A striking manifestation of this unevenness is the vast difference in living standards between the affluent nations and the poorer nations. Within the affluent nations are disadvantaged and marginalised groups who do not share equally in the general prosperity. But it is on a world scale that the starkest inequalities of development are evident. The implicit premise in orthodox economic interpretations has been that, in the fullness of time, the benefits of economic growth would spread more evenly, and that the laggards would (eventually) catch up. Economically marginalized groups would join the economic mainstream, and the fruits of material progress would 'trickle down' to all.

This soothing story has its sophisticated and folksy variants. Within neoclassical economics are theorems positing 'factor price equalization' through trade, and a tendency towards 'inter-regional equity' through the mobility of capital and labor. So, if international trade and factor movements are permitted, the economy will produce a tendency to convergence in terms of living standards. This 'equilibrium' analysis has a correspondingly conservative political message. The market works out for the best, spreading the fruits of economic progress, provided that 'market imperfections' are eradicated. However, these conservative propositions sit awkwardly alongside observations about the persistence of glaring economic inequalities between and within nations. Some formerly underdeveloped countries have experienced spectacular aggregate economic growth and industrialization, but in recent times others remain desperately poor. And, within both the poorer and richer countries, the disadvantages and marginalization experienced by particular groups, commonly distinguished according to gender and/or ethnicity, remain profound. Clearly, economic growth and human development do not necessarily go together.

The readings in this section explore some of these concerns from the perspective of the 'have-nots'. The classic article by the late Gunnar Myrdal, the Swedish institutional economist and winner of the Nobel Prize for Economic Science, suggests the need for a fundamental redefinition of development. New concepts of development must also be complemented by new policies which are more in tune with the needs of the dispossessed. The following extract from the writings of Paul Sweezy emphasizes the importance of class analysis in understanding underdevelopment. Sweezy draws on Marxist economic theory to explain the relationship between the independent development in core regions and the dependent development in the periphery. Susan Engel then shows the different phases through which official policies towards the promotion of development have gone – import substitution, export promotion, extending microfinance, and so on. The gulf between the rhetoric of the developmental agencies and the actual experience of continuing underdevelopment is evident. In the final article in this section, Ahmad Movassaghi turns the attention to Asian nations that have experienced significant growth or development in recent times, seeking to identify the role and characteristics of the state in the processes of developmental transition.

For further reading on development and underdevelopment, see Philip McMichael, *Development and Social Change: a Global Perspective*, Sage, Los Angeles, 2008; Jeffrey Sachs, *The End of Poverty*, New York, Penguin, 2005; and specialist development journals such as the *Journal of Development Studies*, *World Development*, and *Economic Development and Cultural Change*.

What is Development?

Gunnar Myrdal

By development I mean the movement upward of the entire social system, and I believe this is the only logically tenable definition. This social system encloses, besides the so-called economic factors, all non-economic factors, including all sorts of consumption by various groups of people; consumption provided collectively; educational and health facilities and levels; the distribution of power in society; and more generally economic, social, and political stratification; broadly speaking, institutions and attitudes – to which we must add, as an exogenous set of factors, induced policy measures applied in order to change one or several of these endogenous factors.

Many of those large masses of figures quoted in the economic literature on underdeveloped countries are not worth the paper they are printed upon. They have been gathered with the help of concepts that are not adequate to local reality, such as unemployment and underemployment, and more generally have been derived from an analysis that is illogically restricted mainly to the 'economic factors' …

The common usage by economists, journalists, and politicians of gross national product or one of its derivatives as representative of development falls under the theoretical stricture expressed above. But apart from this, much more than is commonly conceded, the production concept is utterly weak statistically for developed countries, and for underdeveloped countries it is even more flimsy. Anyone who has taken the trouble to look into how the figures for GNP have been produced in underdeveloped countries should find them very difficult to use as they now commonly are used.

But keeping here to the theoretical problem, it may be useful to remember how classical economists from the very beginning have made a distinction between production (including exchange in the market) and distribution. More and more regularly after John Stuart Mill's clarification of that distinction it has been used for focusing attention on production, while leaving distribution out of the analysis, usually with only a general reservation. This is the historical origin of the GNP, which is still with us.

The common idea is that it is possible, first, to ascertain what is produced and, second, to determine how the product is distributed. This way of thinking is logically unsatisfactory. Production and distribution must be thought of as determined in the same macro system; they are causally interdependent.

When, nevertheless, an interdependence has been recognized, the common pattern has been – also from classical time to the present – to assume that redistributional reforms carry a cost by hampering the growth of production … Well-planned redistributional reforms, however, can be productive by raising the quality of the labor force and/or by saving individuals and society from future costs. This holds true for even those rich countries which already have raised substantially the level of living of their least affluent strata. But it is even more true for underdeveloped countries, where large masses of people suffer from very serious privation which must hold down their productivity.

There are many examples of how the economic analysis of the development problem of underdeveloped countries has erred under the influence of this exclusive focus on production. One such is the frequent use of growth models which leave out consumption levels. Such models may not lead to very incorrect conclusions about development conditions in countries with relatively high incomes, even in the lower income brackets, an effective social security system, and public services on a high level rendered free to all who need them – although they certainly would not be appropriate for analyzing conditions in US slums. Another example is the lightheartedness economists often demonstrate in asking for increased savings, even by the poorest in underdeveloped countries, as a condition for rapid development.

A further serious flaw in the treatment of the problem of equality by many economists, both in earlier times and today, has been to limit whatever interest they have shown to an analysis in terms of incomes and wealth. Both of these are calculated as aggregates of monetary units (as in the GNP). The analysis may be enlarged to encompass consumption and savings, but all of these aspects usually are restricted to what is accounted for in private budgets. This is unsatisfactory for several reasons. Public consumption also should be analyzed with respect to what actually accrues to people in different strata in the form of goods and services after subtracting charges and taxes. Given the trend toward the socialization of consumption, particularly in the advanced welfare states in the wealthier European countries …, an analysis of only the distribution of private incomes goes viciously wrong …

Even more so than in developed countries, and for somewhat different reasons, the imperfections in traditional economics – the inherited tendency of isolating the equality issue from the issue of productivity, and of thinking in terms simply of money incomes and wealth – have led to a superficial approach to the development problem in underdeveloped countries and, indeed, to an abstention from tackling the real problems by intensive study.

This is so, first, because the two concepts, higher productivity and greater equality, are even more closely tied together than in developed countries. Second, in both respects, successful reforms must entail radical changes of all the non-economic factors, which usually have been excluded from the economic analysis. These factors play a much more forceful and inhibiting role for development in underdeveloped countries that have been stagnant over long periods. In fact, the redistribution of money incomes, particularly in very poor countries, cannot amount to much and may not have favorable effects. First, the rich mostly are few in number. Second, higher taxation of the rich is very difficult to effect since tax avoidance and tax evasion usually are colossal.

Quite aside from this, what the poor masses need is not a little money, the distribution of which ordinarily only would spur inflation, which regularly works to their disadvantage. They do need fundamental changes in the conditions under which they are living and working. The important thing is that these changes regularly must imply both increased productivity and greater equality. The two purposes are inextricably joined. Several significant areas require attention.

In agriculture there is need for a changed relation between man and land. The possibility and incentives must be created to enable man to work more, and more effectively, in order to raise yields and to employ all available resources, beginning with his own labor, for improving the land. In addition, land and tenancy reforms – which can take different forms to suit different conditions – need to be supplemented by auxiliary reforms to provide credits, agricultural extension services, and so forth. But without more fundamental reforms of land ownership, these strivings for 'community development' have proven ineffective. Until now they mostly have been a way of escaping land reform, which is why they have failed.

Similarly, truly effective educational reform, also important for creating both greater equality and a higher productive capability, must aim at much more than merely putting children and youth in schools. The whole educational system must be changed as well as the manner of teaching and the content of what is taught, and its impact on inegalitarian social and economic stratification must be felt. Adult education must be given primary importance. In many underdeveloped countries, adherence to the inherited educational system – often not improved by advice and impulses from the developed countries – merely permits the channels to widen under the pressures which mostly come from the relatively privileged classes. These systems are mainly anti-developmental, partly, but not only, because they support the prejudices against manual work.

The population explosion tends to increase inequality in an underdeveloped country, while simultaneously hampering growth and development. I have concluded that a successful policy to spread birth control among the masses assumes a whole package of reforms which can give people the feeling that they are living in a dynamic society that increasingly opens up to them opportunities to improve their lot.

Underdeveloped countries are usually 'soft states' with grave deficiencies in legislation and the implementation of laws. In such a society laxity and licentiousness spread to all social and economic strata. But it is those who have economic, social, and political power who can exploit fully the lack of social discipline in their environment. The fight against the soft state and, in particular, against corruption, which seems to be on the increase almost everywhere, is, therefore, strongly in the interest of greater equality. That these types of deficiencies in the social order hamper economic progress is undeniable.

Conventional economists, accustomed to think in terms of 'economic factors' and redistribution of aggregate money incomes, until recently have not shown much interest in these types of social reforms and the way productivity and equalization of opportunities are tied together indissolubly. They thus have pleased the elite stratum that holds power in almost all underdeveloped countries, rather independent of their constitutions, and which generally is not so interested in the radical reform of a society in which it has a privileged position …

Gunnar Myrdal was Professor of International Economics at the Stockholm University, and recipient of the Nobel Prize in Economic Science. This chapter abridged from What is Development, *Journal of Economic Issues*, vol. 8, 1974, pp. 729-36. © 1974 reprinted from the *Journal of Economic Issues* by special permission of the copyright holder, the Association for Evolutionary Economics.

Centre and Periphery
Paul Sweezy

Capitalism has from the beginning had two poles – which can be variously described by such terms as independent and dependent, dominant and subordinate, developed and underdeveloped, centre and periphery. The driving force has always been the accumulation process in the centre, with the peripheral societies being moulded by a combination of coercion and market forces to conform to the requirements and serve the needs of the centre.

What is the difference between independent development at the centre and dependent development in the periphery? There are obviously many aspects to the question, but here I shall touch on only two of the most essential.

The first relates to the relationship between agriculture and industry. The heart of the matter was put in its briefest possible form by Samir Amin, a leading figure among Third World Marxists of the post-World War 2 period: "Unlike the countries of the center, where the 'agricultural revolution' preceded the 'industrial revolution', the countries of the periphery have imported the latter without having started the former stage" (1977: 16). Capitalism could never have put down roots in the centre without a sustained increase in the productivity of agriculture and hence also in the agricultural surplus. This was the basis for the release of workers from the countryside; the flourishing of rural-urban trade; the emergence directly and through intermediate forms, like the putting-out system, of manufactures based on wage labor and embodying an increasingly elaborate division of labor; and only finally the introduction of machinery (the 'industrial revolution') as the last step in ushering in full-fledged capitalism. This is the only sequence that could have led to the development of independent self-sustaining capitalist societies. It is an illusion, perhaps widespread but reflecting ignorance of economic history, that industrialization somehow lies at the heart of the process of economic development. On the contrary, it is the final act and the crowning achievement of economic development; and there is no direct route to its successful realization, though of course countries like Germany and Japan, which were relatively late in embarking on the development process, could learn (as well as borrow) from their predecessors and in this way avoid mistakes and shorten the time required. But those countries that, to use Samir Amin's phrase, 'imported' the industrial revolution without laying the necessary agricultural foundation have succeeded only in creating new forms of dependence.

The second aspect of the difference between independent development in the centre and dependent development in the periphery to which I want to call attention is simply this: the rate of exploitation is and always has been vastly higher in the periphery than in the centre. In the centre, the rate of exploitation is for all practical purposes the same as the rate of surplus value. This is not so of the periphery, where only a small part of the workforce is employed as wage laborers in capitalist industry, with a much larger proportion being exploited directly and indirectly by landlords, traders, and usurers, primarily in the countryside but also in the cities and towns. Here all or most of the surplus extorted from the workers not employed in capitalist industry is commercialized and becomes indistinguishably mingled with capitalistically produced surplus value. In these circumstances we can speak of a social rate of exploitation but should not confuse the concept with a rate of surplus value in the usual sense. The high rate of exploitation in the periphery enables local ruling classes and allied elites to live on a level comparable to that of the bourgeoisies of the centre, while at the same time making possible a massive flow of monetized surplus product (in the form of profits, interest, rents, royalties, etc.) from periphery to centre.

The other side of the coin is a miserable, often bare subsistence or below, standard of living for workers, peasants, and the marginalized poor of countryside and urban slums. Well-meaning critics often deplore what they consider to be a drain of surplus out of the periphery that might have been invested in productive facilities catering to the impoverished masses, but this is to put the cart before the horse. The root of the problem is the high rate of exploitation, which both perpetuates poverty and at the same time prevents the growth of a mass market for consumer goods that would attract and justify investment in a local version of Marx's Department II (industries producing consumer goods). And, of course, the high rate of exploitation is built into the very structure of the system and protected by a formidable array of domestic and international institutional arrangements.

The counterpart of the very high (and frequently rising) rate of exploitation in the periphery is a lower (and over time relatively stable) rate of surplus value in the centre. There are two basic and interrelated reasons for this. On the one hand, the working class of the centre is more highly developed and is in a better position to organize and struggle for its own interests. On the other hand, the bourgeoisies of the centre learned through historical experience that a situation that allows the standard of living of the proletariat to rise over time (a stable rate of surplus value combined with rising productivity) is not only functional but even indispensable for the operation of the system as a whole. Without it, the growth of Department II (producing consumption goods) is stunted, the demand for the products of Department I (producing means of production) is held down, and vitally important conditions for the operation of the capital accumulation process are absent. What this means is that a high and rising rate of surplus value, however desirable it may appear from the point of view of the individual capitalist, would be a disaster from the point of view of the capitalist societies of the centre as a whole.

Corresponding to the contrast between the levels of exploitation in centre and periphery is an equally striking contrast between the political systems in the two parts of world capitalism. In the centre, by various routes and over a long period of time, bourgeois democracy became the norm and proved to be the political arrangement most conducive to the maintenance of a stable rate of surplus value and class relations reasonably compatible with the functioning of the accumulation process.

In the periphery, on the other hand, efforts to copy the bourgeois democratic institutions of the centre (very widespread, for example, in Latin America after the Spanish colonies achieved their formal independence and sought to model their constitutions on that of the United States) either produced empty facades or were discarded by dominant classes whose way of life depended on the maintenance of extremely high rates of exploitation and who saw in any concessions to the underlying population a dangerous threat to their continued rule. From the beginning, therefore, and now as much as at any time in the past, the norm in the periphery has been military-police states of one kind or another. They are, in fact, as closely related to high rates of exploitation as two sides of the same coin.

The implications of this analysis for the countries and peoples of the periphery are far-reaching. The extremely high rates of exploitation of which they are the victims are not, as conventional bourgeois wisdom would have it, a heritage of their pre-capitalist past to be overcome by the kind of policies prescribed in economics textbooks and touted by governments and international agencies like the World Bank: foreign aid and investment, transfer of technology, and so on, and so on. All such activities are carried out within the framework of the existing structure and normally have both the intention and the effect of strengthening rather than changing it.

Take, for example, the investment by multinational corporations in the periphery, which has occurred on a large scale in the period since World War 2 and has spurred the growth of modern industry beyond anything known in previous times. The multinationals, based in the advanced countries of the centre, go to countries like Brazil – to supply and profit from markets that already exist and can be expected to grow with the general expansion of global capitalism. Some of these are domestic Brazilian markets fuelled by the spending of perhaps 20 percent of the population in the highest income brackets. Others are international markets for agricultural products, raw materials, and certain kinds of manufactures, the costs of which can be kept low through the employment of cheap labor. But there is one market, potentially by far the largest, that does not exist and that the multinationals have no ambition to create, the market that would be generated by a rising real standard of living for the Brazilian masses.

The reason for what at first sight might seem a paradox is simple: for capitalists, both Brazilian and foreign, the masses are looked upon as costs, not as consumers: the lower their real incomes, the higher the profits from selling to the local upper class and the international market. The dynamic at work here has produced a most startling result: in the fifteen years after the military coup of 1964, a period frequently referred to as that of the Brazilian 'economic miracle', when the Gross National Product rose at annual rates as high as 10 percent, the level of real wages declined by a third or more. No wonder the president of Brazil, on a visit to Washington several years ago, was quoted in the press as saying, "In my country the economy is doing fine, but the people aren't".

Paul Sweezy, one of the leading Marxist economists of the twentieth century, was founder and Editor of *Monthly Review*. This chapter is adapted from *Four Lectures on Marxism*, Monthly Review Press, New York, 1981. © 1981 Paul M. Sweezy. Reprinted with permission of the author.

From Theory to Practice in Development
Susan Engel

As decolonisation movements gathered strength following World War II, independence and development were seen to go hand-in-hand. Thanks partly to US President Truman's 1949 Inaugural Address that linked the fight against communism with development assistance, aid and expertise from countries in the West became a driving force in development programs. Moreover, development economics and development practices have operated in tandem. Structuralist and dependency theory ideas, as outlined in the excerpt by Paul Sweezy earlier in this book, were influential in the postwar period on the practices of developing countries. Donors, though, were more influenced in this period by the Keynesian/neoclassical synthesis emphasising infrastructure and area development programs.

In the 1980s, neoclassical economics in its neoliberal form made a resurgence. In the developing country context, this became policies known as the Washington Consensus because they were hammered out in Washington between the US Treasury, the International Monetary Fund (IMF) and the World Bank. The Washington Consensus, however, did not provide a way forward for most developing countries. The 1980s was labelled the 'lost decade' for Africa. The poor outcomes, along with practical and theoretical critiques from a range of perspectives, led donor country development agencies to change their goals. They now claimed that participatory development, pro-poor policies and promotion of good governance underpinned their support efforts. However, critics observe continuity – that the Washington Consensus commitment to conservative monetary and fiscal policy still frames most donors' overall programs. While they may aim to get the incomes of the poor above $1 per day, that is the extent of their vision – there is no broader goal of equality nor social justice.

In the 1950s and 1960s, the development path of many newly independent states was inspired by structuralist ideas. They tended to centre around three main options for achieving industrialisation and growth: autarky; accessing foreign capital to build the industrial sector; and using the state to accumulate necessary resources for development. Most developing countries opted for a blend of foreign capital and state-led development. This was a key basis of the strategy of import substitution industrialisation (ISI) (Rapley 2002: 21). ISI was seen as a way of generating rapid and self-sustaining growth that would promote economic diversification away from reliance on primary commodities while, at the same time, attracting foreign capital. It promoted increased production of locally manufactured goods for domestic consumption to nurture and strengthen the domestic market.

ISI is a development strategy that uses tariffs and quotas to make the local market more benign for local producers. In other words, it protects domestic producers of manufactured goods so that they can compete against foreign producers, particularly those in already industrialised countries that have better access to technologies, existing economies of scale and skilled workforces. A range of additional policies have been used to support ISI, including overvaluing the domestic currency to make importing capital goods cheap, directing foreign investment to key economic sectors, and providing concessional access to available foreign currency or credit for domestic firms diversifying their production.

Western aid donors usually did not discourage ISI strategies and supported state planning for development, but their focus tended to be on funding infrastructure and, later, on rural development schemes. Infrastructure priorities were roads, railways, ports, dams, electricity generation and the like – often on a grand scale and often with little consideration of social or ecological consequences. By the mid-1960s, water supply and sanitation schemes were supported in both rural and urban areas. Rural development schemes gained prominence, with funding focusing on irrigation, technical support for farmers and access to credit to improve the application of technology to farming. Improvements in the health and education sectors have always received publicity in the development arena but, in fact, they are generally not the focus of donor aid. There have been cases of successful donor-supported programs – South Korea and Taiwan being prominent examples – but, by the late 1960s, it was clear that much done in the name of development did little to help the lives of the poor.

By the end of the 1970s, various scholars and practitioners came to the conclusion that ISI and other state-led development strategies were not working. Certainly, there were problems with the operation of ISI, but attributing the difficulties faced by most developing countries simply to ISI was misleading. Developing countries faced a range of challenges, ranging from low levels of infrastructure and education through to highly concentrated land holdings and economies still largely structured around raw material production for their former colonial powers. The more hostile global environment from the early 1970s was another problem. This period saw the first postwar recession in the West and a subsequent turn towards trade protectionism. The first OPEC oil price shock in 1973 increased balance of payments difficulties in oil-importing developing countries; and the recycling of so-called petrodollars as loans to developing countries fuelled the already growing debt crisis. The second oil price shock in 1979 hit the poorer countries hard and commodity prices fell dramatically. The US economic policies, inspired by monetarist economics to focus on combating inflation as the primary goal, saw large increases in international interest rates from 1979. This increased the flow of money from the developing world to the developed world and facilitated the outbreak of a major debt crisis in 1982. Regardless of the causes, the overall faith in the developmentalist paradigm of state planning began to fade; and neoclassical and neoliberal political economic influences increased.

There were exceptions to the poor development and growth outcomes in the developing world. The 'Asian Tigers' achieved ongoing high levels of growth. These nations – South Korea, Taiwan, Singapore and Hong Kong – generally started out utilising ISI strategies but often selectively and with conditions on industrialists benefiting from the policy. From the early 1970s, they started to switch towards a policy of encouraging manufacturers to export their products – a strategy that became known as Export Oriented Industrialisation (EOI). It is worth noting, however, that they still selectively pursued some ISI elements, for example protecting new 'infant industries.' Further, the EOI strategy involved detailed industrial policies, often pursing the growth of industries outside the country's 'natural' comparative advantage. This is important because many of the neoliberal critics of state-led development strategy tended to ignore this component of the Tigers' development.

Although the neoliberal diagnosis of developing countries' problems dates back to the 1940s, the framework did not become mainstream amongst development economists until the 1970s. Its analysis of the problems in developing countries comprised three interrelated ideas (Toye 1993: 70):

i   that the public sector was over-extended;
ii   that there had been too much emphasis on physical capital formation, often at the expense of human capital formation; and
iii that the Third World had developed too many market-distorting economic controls.

This analysis dominated orthodox development economics for two decades. Further, neoliberal analysis became widely accepted amongst policy-makers because its rise coincided with the economic crises of the 1970s for which it purportedly had an explanation and a solution. Well-funded 'think-tanks', World Bank researchers and many in the press set out to disseminate neoliberal views. However, it was the election of the Reagan Administration in the US that broadly legitimised neoliberal economics and facilitated its global implementation through its own aid programs and through its influence on international institutions like the World Bank and IMF. Not all developing countries needed persuasion to adopt neoliberal development strategies; domestic elites in a number of countries held neoliberal beliefs and promoted EOI strategies too.

The Washington Consensus quickly achieved widespread acceptance, and, by the early 1980s, a common set of policy prescriptions for developing countries was being vigorously pursued. The Washington Consensus essentially involved two phases of 'reform'. The first phase was policies to achieve short-term macroeconomic stabilization that were carried out quickly via 'big bang' reforms. The focus here was cutting the budgets of developing nations, devaluing national currencies, and ending price controls and subsidies. The second phase involved a whole range of long-term, structural and prescriptive microeconomic policy 'reforms' that were aimed at making markets and private property central institutions in developing countries whilst minimizing the role of the state. Achieving the first phase of reforms was generally seen the IMF's responsibility, while the second phase was the realm of the IMF, World Bank and bilateral donors jointly. In the wake of the 1982 debt crisis, making the provision of loans and aid conditional upon governments implementing neoliberal policies was the main way to achieve adherence to neoliberalism.

Neoliberal policy prescriptions for development have been no more successful than state-led ones. Indeed, in following these prescriptions many countries in sub-Saharan Africa ended the 1980s and 1990s worse off. As with state-led development programs, the failures resulted in a questioning of both policy prescriptions and theoretical frameworks. However, we have not yet witnessed a fundamental overturning of this particular development paradigm. Instead the current consensus – the post-Washington Consensus – maintains the Washington Consensus commitment to conservative monetary and fiscal policy. This, above all, frames and constrains development programs. The continuity is despite, or perhaps because of, the growing influence of New Institutional Economics (NIE) in development economics. NIE expands the analysis of what constitutes market failures to include information failures and transaction costs. This leads to a view of markets with extensive imperfections, as opposed to the neoliberal view of perfectly working markets, but remains firmly within the neoclassical tradition.

Joseph Stiglitz is one of the most prominent economists in the NIE tradition working on development issues today. One of his key contributions concerns the extent of information asymmetry in markets. Markets are regarded as subject to extensive imperfections, with the implication that government action can be efficient in many more circumstances than allowed for by neoliberal policies and neoclassical economic analysis. If this is true for developed countries, it is more the case in developing ones, where Stiglitz turned his attention after becoming Chief Economist of the World Bank in 1997. This was precipitous timing, just months before the onset of the Asian Financial Crisis. Stiglitz became a well-known critic of the IMF, its one-size-fits-all approach to development and the neoliberal push for 'big bang' capital market liberalization (Stiglitz 2002: 16, 65-67). He argues that there is little evidence that capital market liberalisation promotes economic growth and that, without attention to the order and timing of reforms, it can cause more harm than good (Broad 2004: 138).

In terms of development programs, the most striking change of the post-Washington Consensus period has been large-scale donor support for programs of 'good governance.' This is a generally ill-defined term that often sees donors funding (mostly Western) consultants to help recipient governments seek to improve budgeting, financial systems and auditing. While these are important areas for reform, donors' technocratic approaches have all too often involved transposing Western models, systems and laws to developing countries. The outcome is a lot of money spent for systems that have little relevance to the historical, cultural, organisational and political economic context of the recipient country.

Recent aid efforts have seen some increased support for social support systems, although not as much as donors' public pronouncements would usually have us believe. Health and education remain small components of the World Bank and many other donors' programs. So-called participatory community development schemes and microfinance have been the big winners in aid funding. The rest of this chapter explores the operation of these programs in order to give critical insights into the nature of the post-Washington Consensus support for poverty reduction.

Participatory community development schemes are an evolution of the rural area development schemes of the 1970s. The participatory focus was borrowed from non-governmental organisations that had emphasised participation as a counter to top-down donor development models that ignored community knowledge and power structures. These had often left communities worse off and exacerbated inequalities. However, in the hands of the major bilateral and multilateral donors, participation became a narrow, instrumental concept and tool. For example, in World Bank funded rural electrification programs in Vietnam, the community participation part of the project was actually just a formal household agreement to pay for electricity connection! In other projects, participatory development has been more invasive. Community participation is the language that donors (and some governments) use to justify structure and organising 'civil society' to manage their own development projects. Communities are organised in parallel to existing local governance structures to manage the construction of local infrastructure and social support services. They are trained in 'proper' community consultation methods and in (neoliberal) managerial techniques, and kept busy ensuring there is no 'misallocation' of resources, rather than being involved in socially and politically transformative reflection or action.

Microcredit can also be part of a neoliberal strategy, making individuals responsible for their own development, though it did not fully start out this way. It was developed simultaneously by Ela Bhatt in India in 1974 and Mohammad Yunus in Bangladesh in 1976 in response to economic and institutional conditions that limited the productive potential of skilled artisans. These pioneers were particularly concerned with the lack of access to saving and loans mechanisms, forcing the poor to use informal channels for their personal finance such as money lenders who charged exorbitant interest rates. Microcredit has the appeal of offering poor small loans at more manageable interest rates.

The most common model of microfinance provision in practice involves the formation of small groups (5-6 people), who initially make regular savings deposits into the scheme for a period of three to six months. This forms the group collateral, the savings and the group's commitment. After establishing group collateral, one or two members of the group can then take out loans, the purpose of which must be creating or expanding a microenterprise. If loans are successfully repaid over a period, other group members become eligible for loans. This system has produced very high repayment rates for most schemes. In the past decade, microcredit has expanded to include a broader range of financial services (savings, insurance) for poor people, so it is now generally called microfinance.

Microfinance has had a potentially transformative agenda, yet it has not always lived up to the claims made for it. It has become increasingly commercialised and, through that process, less supportive of pro-poor change. Operating a small loans program is costly, so microfinance programs charge high interest rates – the global average is 37 percent per annum, but in Mexico it is 70 percent and there are reports of institutions even charging 125 percent (MacFarquhar 2010). These high interest rates have attracted increasing numbers of private institutions, with the result that non-government organisations are now only responsible for servicing about 35 percent of clients. Private providers do not support most of the rights-based microfinance agenda.

Most microfinance loans are targeted at women and claim to empower them as well as help them out of poverty. These claims are problematic, as running businesses often adds to women's already high workload and their changed role in the family can strain marriages. Husbands sometimes use or control loans, yet expect their wives to make the repayments. Group collateral has been shown to lead to pressure tactics being applied to ensure members make repayments. Most schemes require immediate weekly repayments, meaning micro-business investments need to make immediate and high returns. Loans are often used for immediate consumption, and often new loans are taken to repay existing ones. Microfinance does not always reach the poorest of the poor, nor challenge women's traditional roles.

Microfinance programs are therefore not the panacea to global poverty that has sometimes been claimed. They do not eliminate the need for basic social and infrastructure services, end vulnerability to economic shocks, nor create economic opportunities for the poor. The odds are still stacked against the self-employed in the global marketplace. Microfinance is best regarded, from a political economic perspective, as a policy response to crises that follows from structural adjustment programs. It is "… a neo-liberal safety net *for* neoliberal political restructuring" (Weber 2004: 360).

Examining donors' social support programs under the post-Washington Consensus reveals minimal support for improved health care and education. There is more support for a range of self-help development schemes, but these do not address the broader political economic structures that constrain the life chances of the poor in developing countries. The goal of ending the most extreme forms of poverty is the extent of most donors' ambitions. This limited ambition is the product of both mainstream development economics and the main donor countries' political economic agendas.

Susan Engel is Lecturer, School of History and Politics, University of Wollongong. From Theory to Practice in Development. © 2011 Susan Engel.

Developmental Transition in Asia
Ahmad Movassaghi

Development is not just economic growth in its pure economic and technical sense of increasing GNP or per capita income. It is the result of socio-economic, political and institutional arrangements which allocate resources effectively, produce wealth permanently, and distribute it evenly among people. According to Todaro (1990: 23), economic and social developments are often impossible without corresponding changes in the social, political and economic "institutions" of a nation; and development economics must be concerned with "the formulation of appropriate public policies designed to affect major economic, institutional, and social transformations of entire societies in the shortest possible time". In addition to improvements in incomes and output, development typically involves "radical changes in institutional, social, and administrative structures as well as in popular attitudes and, in many cases, even customs and beliefs" (Todaro 1990: 62). Gilpin (2001: 332) remarks that economic development is not a technical economic problem involving factor accumulation and getting the "fundamentals right"; it is "a social process that cannot be completed unless the state creates economic institutions, fosters social behavior, and pursues policies favorable to economic development".

In the mainstream development thinking, the major dichotomy is between socialism and capitalism, or the state and market. But, there is a third model or strategy, with a long history, which is called mercantilism or economic nationalism, based on *temporary* intervention of the state in economy by providing public goods and institutional arrangements and protecting infant industries and private sector in order to make them competitive globally. The state leads structural changes and industrialization incrementally in the process of transition, and prepares the necessary conditions for the well functioning of the market. Government intervention in the early stages of development may be, though, through import substitution industrialization (ISI), providing temporary protectionism for newly established industries. A shift to a liberal state, with export orientation, free trade and a market economy can then occur. This so-called state capitalism is different from the liberal model for its emphasis on the role of the state in the process of transition, and also different from the socialist model because it gives key roles to the state *temporarily* and within the context of a capitalist economy. Historically, "the transition from non-market to market organization has been managed be the state" (Barnett 1989: 130). In this process, institutional arrangements are important in order to reduce or prevent "the risk of arbitrary or capricious government action" and to make possible "a stable policy environment in which governments can make policy commitments that are credible into the future" (MacIntyre 2003).

Thus, development, as a shift that is both incremental and systemic, is not possible without a *developmental state*. In the historical European context, the role and functions of the state in economy were much more than what the neoclassical theories of development assume. The state was important in mobilizing resources, creating infrastructures, eradicating pre-capitalist economic and social institutions, and removing unproductive social groups from key positions. It established the rule of law, political conditions for security and stability, and an encouraging climate for individual initiatives. It fostered competition, private capital formation and accumulation, and investment and property rights. It also created a secular national culture, developed policies conducive to economic growth, and established a rational bureaucratic administration. These were, and are, all key functions of the state for development. The transition or take-off from a pre-modern society (or feudalism) to a modern society (or capitalism) requires different ideas, institutions and policies. Politics and political arrangements or institutions, and especially the state, are the main factors determining the economic policies and performances for both public and private sectors and the relationship between them, even in the era of globalization. The *developmental transition* is led by a *developmental state*.

The developmental state

The idea of developmental state is historically and theoretically rooted in mercantilist theories and practices, in Alexander Hamilton's ideas in the United States, and in the ideas of the German economist Friedrich List who promulgated the 'National Order of Political Economy'. Chalmers Johnson's (1982) seminal work on "MITI and the Japanese Miracle" was a major, more recent contribution on this issue, which explicitly posed the role of "developmental state" in Japan. Chalmers Johnson differentiated the "plan-rational" capitalist developmental state, conjoining private ownership with state guidance. At the core of the developmental state and the reason for its success were close ties among government, local banks, and industry which "facilitated channeling bank capital into promising industries and thus promoted rapid industrialization" (Gilpin 2001: 319). According to Linda Weiss (2003: 247), transformative goals, a pilot agency and institutionalized government-business cooperation are the three essential ingredients of a developmental state.

Chalmers Johnson (Johnson 1999: 60) later noted that "developmental state" means that both industrial policy and the market use each other "in a mutually beneficial relationship to achieve developmental goals and enterprise viability". Chang (2003: ch. 1), from an institutionalist perspective, argues that effective structural change requires coordinated changes in many components of the economy, and formulating a choice set in which the state, as the central agent and an entrepreneur, can play an important role. Structural change involves 'creative destruction' of existing productive routines and institutions (Chang 2003: 63). Development becomes a profoundly political process involving new ways in which all manner of resources – both internal and external – are mobilized, directed and deployed to promote growth and welfare. This requires a central "coordinating intelligence" or "coordinating capacity", i.e. the state, or rather that kind of state with the structure and capacity to do so (Leftwich 2000: 7). The developmental states are those states "whose politics have concentrated sufficient power, autonomy, capacity and legitimacy at the centre to shape, pursue and encourage the achievement of explicit developmental objectives" (Leftwich 2000: 155). According to Leftwich (2000: 160), several major characteristics or components of the developmental state model are: a determined developmental elite; relative autonomy of the developmental state; a powerful, competent and insulated economic bureaucracy; a weak and subordinated civil society; the capacity for effective management of private economic interests; and an uneasy mix of repression, poor human rights (especially in the non-democratic developmental states), legitimacy and performance.

East Asia

The initial conditions, as well as the external context, of East Asian countries were important elements through which the role and functions of the states became positive and effective for economic development. These countries had a long period of social dislocation with the consequence of important and radical changes in social structure and elimination of influential special interest groups (Grabowski 1994: 415). The Japanese use of market mechanisms for developmental purposes has been successfully emulated in the 'four tigers' of East Asia – South Korea, Taiwan, Singapore, and Hong Kong – and recently in China. It is often called the 'flying geese' pattern of Asian growth (Ozawa 2009: 25).

The existence of strong external threats, especially for South Korea and Taiwan, and a large flow of Western aid during the Cold War years, set a significant context for this approach to development. Other crucial elements were the implementation of land reforms that eliminated the landlord class, improvements in agricultural productivity and incomes, growing demands for manufactured goods, and strong links between agriculture and industry. The early ISI strategy, involving the protection of infant industries, then led to a policy shift towards export-oriented industrialization (EOI) together with growing competition, efficiency and productivity (resulting from the adaptation of new technologies). Limiting free-riding and rent-seeking, and the imposition of discipline on firms, were further features of hard, autonomous and developmental states. They had great disciplinary and transformative capacities and ethos, with strong links to the powerful rural middle classes (Chowdhury and Islam 1995: 7).

The average annual GDP growth rates of the 'four tigers' during 1965-80 was between 8 to 10 percent, while during 1980-92 they ranged between 6.7 percent and 9.4 percent (Camilleri 2000: 84). The extent of inequality in the income distribution declined and the quality of life in all 'four tigers' became close to those of developed countries (Chowdhury and Islam 1995: 26). However, the four countries differ significantly from one another in both the structures and the strategies of their respective states, with different tools used, and also in links between the state and the capitalist class (Pempel 1999: 149; So and Wing-Kai Chiu 2004: 58-81). Korea went much further in developing advanced and heavy industry than Taiwan, relying primarily on capital goods imports, technology licensing and other technology-transfer agreements to acquire technology, using reverse engineering, adaptation and own-product development to build upon these arm's-length technology imports and developing its own capabilities. It had the highest level of R&D expenditures in the developing world, rising to more than three percent of GDP – higher than Japan during 1999-2007 (Lall 1996: 19; Palat 2004: 135).

All of the tiger countries were highly creative in the generation and channeling of capital, but capital mobilization had different institutional roots and forms. In Japan, most banks are private and often linked to industrial groups, but the keystone of the system, the Bank of Japan, is controlled by the government's Ministry of Finance, while the public postal savings system is a key component of the entire system; foreign capital inflows have been limited (Pempel 1999: 149-50). The export-orientation is centralized in Korea, decentralized in Taiwan, and oligopolistic and highly competitive in Japan (Pempel 1999: 151). However, as Pempel (1999: 179) has concluded, these Asian countries have created "a capitalism with few national political guarantees for organized labor, little impetus toward the social welfare state, high degrees of mercantilism, limited penetration by foreign investment" and are exceptionally dependent on access to the US market (and, for Korea and Taiwan, on the Japanese market as well). But, despite increased dependence on the world market, both Korea and Taiwan managed to remain relatively autonomous from international capital (Lee 1993: 16).

One pillar of Korean technological strategy is particularly notable. This was the deliberate creation of large private conglomerates, the *chaebols*, by giving a range of subsidies and privileges, including the restriction of MNC entry, in return for furthering the strategy of setting up capital- and technology-intensive activities geared to export markets (Lall 1996: 19). This particular Export-Oriented Industrialization strategy changed the demographic composition, the political balance of class power, and the overall economic structure of the nation. However, after the assassination of President Park in 1979, the *chaebols* started influencing government policy in ways that he had sought to avoid, "growing and profiting in unparalleled fashion with a new, more friendly administration in power" (Davis 2004: 139, 154), and this was a major cause of trouble for South Korea in the 1997 Asian financial crisis.

Hong Kong's historical experience was quite different from South Korea's, having been a private-enterprise, free-market economy, even though the government did intervene from time to time and, most notably, has maintained a fixed exchange rate vis-a-vis the US dollar since 1984. The government of Taiwan has been more activist or interventionist but, by and large, it has been content to let the market work where it can. In both Hong Kong and Taiwan, the predominant mode of ownership of enterprises is private, in fact family owned, and almost all of the successful large enterprises in both of them are family controlled; in 1997 Hong Kong became a 'special administrative region' of the People's Republic of China.

The experience of economic development in the People's Republic of China has been exceptional. Its political status has been that of a communist nation and, despite its economic reforms since 1979, is probably the least marketized of the East Asian countries. China's non-state sector, comprised less than 10 percent of Chinese GDP in 1979. However, the introduction of 'open-door policy' by Deng Xiaoping in 1978 transformed China from a centrally planned economy with low incomes to a global 'socialist market' economy with high levels of economic growth. ∤

The transition of Chinese agriculture from a collective system to an essentially private individual household system (with land leases) resulted in large gains in efficiency of the order of between 30 and 40 percent from 1979 to 1985, holding inputs constant, which laid the foundations of its subsequent success in the other (mostly non-state) sectors, including the township and village enterprises (TVEs) (Lau 1997: 49-9). Local government and locally managed firms were given strong incentives to promote growth through external linkages which led to the growth of rural industry and, by 1991, TVEs accounted for more than 26.6 percent of China's industrial production which increased to 44 percent in 1996, and about 25 percent of total exports and joint ventures (Zhu 2003: 146-47). However, the state still controls 56 percent of the country's industrial assets and is responsible for 70 percent of GDP (Chowdhury and Islam 2007: 11).

China's average annual growth rate during 2005-2008 was 11.2 percent, and by 2008 China had become the world's second largest exporter, behind Germany but surpassing the United States (United Nations 2010: 99, 157). An important contributing factor to China's economic development was the large inflow of foreign direct investment (FDI), encouraged particularly by the establishment of Special Economic Zones (SEZs). It amounted to $133 billion during 1979-95, making China the second largest recipient of FDI flows worldwide. The exports of foreign-owned enterprises as a proportion of total exports grew from 0.3 percent in 1984 to 42.3 percent in 1995 and 44.1 percent in 1998 ($80.96 billion) (Camilleri 2000: 107-8; Lee 1993 ch. 7). In 2002, the amount of FDI in China was $52.7 billion, compared to $2.3 billion in India, and its total merchandise exports in 2003 was $438.4 billion, compared with India's $49.3 billion (Das 2005: 44). It is argued that the state in China is becoming like the developmental states of East Asia, especially increasingly similar to Taiwan in the early stage of its development. However, the high level of corruption, the low level of the state's flexibility, and the central-local relations in China differentiates it from those states (Zhu 2003: ch. 7).

The relationship between the nations is also an important factor in understanding development in the region. The interdependent commercial and economic ties between China, Hong Kong and Taiwan rested on a well-integrated division of labor, in which Hong Kong provided China with capital as well as financial and marketing expertise; Taiwan, using Hong Kong as an intermediary, supplied China with capital and technology (Camilleri 2000: 109; Lee 1993: ch. 10). The largest amount of investment by Southeast Asian states in China belongs to Singapore, and even joint governmental companies between Singapore and China have been created (Suryadinata 1997: 7-8). Thus, China's regional interaction and also its ties with the core industrial economies, especially United States and Japan, are increasing (Shirk and Twomey 1996).

In the age of globalization, as Weiss (2003: 246) remarks, in Taiwan, the state's capacity to coordinate structural change has been enhanced by economic liberalization, and in Korea, even before the Asian crisis, important dismantling of the developmental state had occurred and "a newly created state agency has been hastening chaebol restructuring and preparing firms to withstand the entry of foreigners". In all four "neo-developmental states" of Korea, Japan, Taiwan and Singapore, increasing openness is compatible with the strengthening of national governance, and industrial policy is constantly shifting in character and focus in the process of *adaptive* change (Weiss 2003: 267-8).

Comparisons

Generalising from country-specific experiences is always fraught with dangers. Generalising from the East Asian states to other countries of South-East Asia is particularly problematic. The East and Southeast Asian countries differ profoundly with respect to size, population, natural endowments, history, regime type, social and cultural structures and religion as well as economic policy. These societies have many important differences: the huge populations of China and Indonesia in contrast to Singapore; the valuable and exportable raw materials of Indonesia (oil) that Korea and Thailand do not have. Some nations are 'plural' in their socio-cultural or ethnic structures, like Malaysia and Indonesia, but others, like Taiwan and Thailand, are more homogeneous culturally. Most have not sustained democratic or quasi-democratic politics, and economic policy and practice have varied widely among them (Leftwich 2000: 154; Reilly 2006). Even the processes of nation-building and state-making have been extremely different among these countries (Boyd and Ngo 2006).

State-society relationship, nationalism, social capital and social cohesion are major determinants of strong states that differentiate East and Southeast Asian societies. In contrast to East Asia, the influx of Chinese and Indian people in the Southeast Asian nations led to the creation of a series of ethnic divisions of labor, dominating the modernizing sectors of processing, manufacturing, mining and estate production, which reinforced unevenness in access to resources and economic and political power, resulting in serious problems for almost all the regions' governments in the post-colonial period (Dixon and Drakakis-Smith 1997: 6). The Chinese business communities have significant roles in the region's economies. They hold majority ownership of 50 percent of listed companies in the Philippines, 61 percent in Malaysia, 73 percent in Indonesia, and 81 percent in both Thailand and Singapore (Camilleri 2000: 109).

According to Perkins (1994: 655-6), there are at least three quite distinct developmental state models in this broad region: the manufactured export-led state interventionist models of Japan, Korea, and Taiwan; the free port service, commerce-dominated model of Singapore and Hong Kong; and the models of Indonesia, Malaysia and Thailand, rich in natural resources (at least at the beginning) but not in human resources. All three countries of East Asia (South Korea, Japan, and Taiwan) had a long period of social dislocation, with the consequence of important and radical changes in social structure that transformed the country completely and eliminated influential special interest groups (Grabowski 1994: 415). Jomo (2003: 178) makes a distinction between two groups, arguing that Thailand, Malaysia and Indonesia followed the 'export-led' – but not 'open economy' of Hong Kong and Singapore – model more than Japan, Korea and Taiwan, which promoted exports very actively, while also "protecting domestic markets, at least temporarily, to develop domestic industrial and technological capabilities in order to compete internationally".

According to Davis (2004), the East Asian states have had great disciplinary capacity and ethos with strong link with powerful rural middle classes. In Singapore, Korea, Malaysia and Hong Kong, a new middle class is well established, but in China and Indonesia it is still weak and the majority of people are poor (Beng-Huat 2000: 23-24). In both Vietnam and China, at the beginning of the 1990s, three in five people lived below the poverty line, although by 2005 that number was down to one in five (United Nations 2010: XXI).

As Weiss (1998) points out, state involvement does not necessarily mean its transformative capacity, and it is the strength or weakness of domestic institutions that determine the consequences of external economic pressures on national economies and public policies. In other words, institutional arrangements and the state's close interaction with key economic actors are important for developmental transition. The different roles and functions of the state among East and Southeast Asian countries' economies also have large implications and great impacts on their political developments. The East Asian countries of Japan, Taiwan, and South Korea, and to some extent Singapore and Malaysia from Southeast Asia, have consolidated democracies or rule of law and have become "democratic developmental states" (Robinson and White 1998). Other countries of the region, like Indonesia, Thailand, the Philippines, Vietnam, Myanmar and Cambodia, have social conflict, political instability, corruption and oppression, despite growing middle class and civil society (Guan 2004; Jones 1997: ch. 3). However, as Reilly (2006: 195) points out, if these states can "transform their institutional architecture and make the transition from fragmented, personalized, and unstable political systems to cohesive, programmatic, and stable ones", their prospects for both democracy and development, and also their ability to manage internal conflicts, will be significantly enhanced. Regional and global interdependences and interactions, together with the emergence of the new generation of elites, may determine the future of Asia as a prosperous and developed region.

Ahmad Movassaghi is Associate Professor in the Department of Political Science at the University of Tehran. Developmental Transition in Asia © 2011 Ahmad Movassaghi.

BEHAVIOURAL ECONOMICS

Behavioral economics is a relatively new current in economic analysis. It focuses attention on the assumptions about human behavior that lie behind the economic theories introduced in earlier sections of this book. Drawing especially from the discipline of psychology, it has particularly focused on how human beings make choice-based decisions, and whether they behave in the way assumed by neoclassical economics. The study of behavioral economics now has an established position in economic discussion, and Nobel Prizes in economics have been awarded to some of its leading propents, such as Herbert Simon and Daniel Kahneman.

Behavioral economics has made novel contributions on at least two fronts. At a theoretical level it has provided new insights into the processes by which people make choices, especially the effects of notions of trust, reciprocity and fairness. At a methodological level it has contributed to the growth of experimental economics as a means of testing key economic assumptions, and it has linked up with game theory as a means of modelling the interaction of people.

The relationship between behavioral economics and the rest of economic discourse, however, is not clear-cut. It can be viewed as a school of thought in itself, providing a framework for understanding a market economy. It can also be viewed as providing the microeconomic foundations for heterodox schools of thought, in so far as it makes explicit some of the behavioral assumptions that have been implicit in these schools. For example, Keynes's discussion of financial speculation that appears earlier in this text alludes to some of the major findings that behavioral economists have subsequently explored in greater detail. In other respects behavioral economics may be regarded as a critique of neoclassical economics, proving that the assumption of *homo economicus* or rational economic man – greedy, insatiable and selfish – cannot be justified. Human beings are more than that. Yet another perspective argues that behavioral economics still fits within the neoclassical paradigm, providing it with more realistic assumptions about human motivation but leaving the rest of the theoretical edifice in place.

The articles in this section introduce the key concerns of developments in behavioral economics. Herbert Simon, in his Nobel Prize award speech, abridged here, argues that there is an alternative theory of human decision-making to that provided by the notion of rational economic man. He argues that people do not maximize, but rather *satisfice*; they search until they find a choice that meets some minimum set of requirements, even though they may be aware that better options are still 'out there'. He argues that people make 'rational' choices, but rationality is evaluated on different terms to those presumed by orthodox neoclassical theory. Ross Gittins provides an overview of the key features of behavioral economics and its major implications for theory and policy. Shaun Hargreaves-Heap looks at the way in which experimental methods have helped us uncover the crucial role that trust in other people plays in economic activity. Peter Earl concludes this section by drawing out the policy implications of behavioral economics, providing a challenge to the neoliberal orthodoxy guiding much of contemporary economic policy.

For further reading, see the *Handbook of Contemporary Behavioral Economics: Foundations and Developments*, M.E. Sharpe, Armonk, New York, 2006; the internet source Behavioral Economics: Unifying Psychology and Economics <behavioraleconomics.blogspot.com>; and the *Journal of Economic Behavior and Organization* and *The Journal of Economic Psychology*.

Rational Decision Making in Business Organizations

Herbert A. Simon

The classical theory of omniscient rationality is strikingly simple and beautiful. Moreover, it allows us to predict (correctly or not) human behavior without stirring out of our armchairs to observe what such behavior is like. All the predictive power comes from characterizing the shape of the environment in which the behavior takes place. The environment, combined with the assumptions of perfect rationality, fully determines the behavior. Behavioral theories of rational choice theories of bounded rationality do not have this kind of simplicity. But, by way of compensation, their assumptions about human capabilities are far weaker than those of the classical theory. Thus, they make modest and realistic demands on the knowledge and computational abilities of the human agents, but they also fail to predict that those agents will equate costs and returns at the margin.

It may well be that classical theory can be patched up sufficiently to handle a wide range of situations where uncertainty and outguessing phenomena do not play a central role – that is, to handle the behavior of economies that are relatively stable and not too distant from a competitive equilibrium. However, a strong positive case for replacing the classical theory by a model of bounded rationality begins to emerge when we examine situations involving decision-making under uncertainty and imperfect competition. These situations the classical theory was never designed to handle, and has never handled satisfactorily.

The principal forerunner of a behavioral theory of the firm is the tradition usually called Institutionalism. It is not clear that all of the writings, European and American, usually lumped under this rubric have much in common, or that their authors would agree with each other's views. At best, they share a conviction that economic theory must be reformulated to take account of the social and legal structures amidst which market transactions are carried out.

In 1934-35, in the course of a field study of the administration of public recreational facilities in Milwaukee, which were managed jointly by the school board and the city public works department, I encountered a puzzling phenomenon. Although the heads of the two agencies appeared to agree as to the objectives of the recreation program, and did not appear to be competing for empire, there was continual disagreement and tension between them with respect to the allocation of funds between physical maintenance, on the one hand, and play supervision on the other. Why did they not, as my economics books suggested, simply balance off the marginal return of the one activity against that of the other?

Further exploration made it apparent that they didn't equate expenditures at the margin because, intellectually, they couldn't. There was no measurable production function from which quantitative inferences about marginal productivities could be drawn; and such qualitative notions of a production function as the two managers possessed were mutually incompatible. To the public works administrator, a playground was a physical facility, serving as a green oasis in the crowded gray city. To the recreation administrator, a playground was a social facility, where children could play together with adult help and guidance.

How can human beings make rational decisions in circumstances like these? How are they to apply the marginal calculus? Or, if it does not apply, what do they substitute for it?

The phenomenon observed in Milwaukee is ubiquitous in human decision-making. In organization theory it is usually referred to as subgoal identification. When the goals of an organization cannot be connected operationally with actions (when the production function can't be formulated in concrete terms), then decisions will be judged against subordinate goals that can be so connected. There is no unique determination of these subordinate goals. Their formulation will depend on the knowledge, experience, and organizational environment of the decision maker. In the face of this ambiguity, the formulation can also be influenced in subtle, and not so subtle, ways by his self-interest and power drives.

On examination, the phenomenon of subgoal identification proved to be the visible tip of a very large iceberg. The shape of the iceberg is best appreciated by contrasting it with classical models of rational choice. The classical model calls for knowledge of all the alternatives that are open to choice. It calls for complete knowledge of, or ability to compute, the consequences that will follow on each of the alternatives. It calls for certainty in the decision maker's present and future evaluation of these consequences. It calls for the ability to compare consequences, no matter how diverse and heterogeneous, in terms of some consistent measure of utility. The task, then, was to replace the classical model with one that would describe how decisions could be (and probably actually were) made when the alternatives of search had to be sought out, the consequences of choosing particular alternatives were only very imperfectly known both because of limited computational power and because of uncertainty in the external world, and the decision maker did not possess a general and consistent utility function for comparing heterogeneous alternatives.

Several procedures of rather general applicability and wide use have been discovered that transform intractable decision problems into tractable ones. One procedure already mentioned is to look for satisfactory choices instead of optimal ones. Another is to replace abstract, global goals with tangible subgoals, whose achievement can be observed and measured. A third is to divide up the decision-making task among many specialists, coordinating their work by means of a structure of communications and authority relations. All of these, and others, fit the general rubric of "bounded rationality," and it is now clear that the elaborate organizations that human beings have constructed in the modern world to carry out the work of production and government can only be understood as machinery for coping with the limits of man's abilities to comprehend and compute in the face of complexity and uncertainty.

In Administrative Behavior, bounded rationality is largely characterized as a residual category: rationality is bounded when it falls short of omniscience. And the failures of omniscience are largely failures of knowing all the alternatives, uncertainty about relevant exogenous events, and inability to calculate consequences. There was needed a more positive and formal characterization of the mechanisms of choice under conditions of bounded rationality.

Two concepts are central to the characterization: search and satisficing. If the alternatives for choice are not given initially to the decision maker, then he must search for them. Hence, a theory of bounded rationality must incorporate a theory of search. This idea was later developed independently by George Stigler in a very influential paper that took as its example of a decision situation the purchase of a second-hand automobile. Stigler poured the search theory back into the old bottle of classical utility maximization, the cost of search being equated with its marginal return. In my 1956 paper, I had demonstrated the same formal equivalence, using as my example a dynamic programming formulation of the process of selling a house.

But utility maximization, as I showed, was not essential to the search scheme – fortunately, for it would have required the decision maker to be able to estimate the marginal costs and returns of search in a decision situation that was already too complex for the exercise of global rationality. As an alternative, one could postulate that the decision maker had formed some aspiration as to how good an alternative he should find. As soon as he discovered an alternative for choice meeting his level of aspiration, he would terminate the search and choose that alternative. I called this mode of selection satisficing. It had its roots in the empirically based psychological theories, due to Lewin and others, of aspiration levels. As psychological inquiry had shown, aspiration levels are not static, but tend to rise and fall in consonance with changing experiences. In a benign environment that provides many good alternatives, aspirations rise; in a harsher environment, they fall.

In long run equilibrium it might even be the case that choice with dynamically adapting aspiration levels would be equivalent to optimal choice, taking the costs of search into account. But the important thing about the search and satisficing theory is that it showed how choice could actually be made with reasonable amounts of calculation, and using very incomplete information, without the need of performing the impossible – of carrying out this optimizing procedure.

Thus, by the middle 1950s, a theory of bounded rationality had been proposed as an alternative to classical omniscient rationality, a significant number of empirical studies had been carried out that showed actual business decision-making to conform reasonably well with the assumptions of bounded rationality but not with the assumptions of perfect rationality, and key components of the theory – the nature of the authority and employment relations, organizational equilibrium, and the mechanisms of search and satisficing – had been elucidated formally.

Although they have played a muted role in the total economic research activity during the past two decades, theories of bounded rationality and the behavioral theory of the business firm have undergone steady development during that period.

First, there has been work in the psychological laboratory and the field to test whether people in relatively simple choice situations behave as statistical decision theory (maximization of expected utilities) say they do. Second, there has been extensive psychological research, to discover the actual microprocesses of human decision-making and problem solving. Third, there have been numerous empirical observations – most of them in the form of "case studies" – of the actual processes of decision-making in organizational and business contexts. Fourth, there have been reformulations and extensions of the theory of the firm replacing classical maximization with behavioral decision postulates.

The general features of bounded rationality – selective search, satisficing, and so on – have been taken as the starting points for a number of attempts to build theories of the business firm incorporating behavioral assumptions.

Characterized in this way, there seems to be little commonality among all of these theories and models, except that they depart in one way or another from the classical assumption of perfect rationality in firm decision-making. A closer look, however, and a more abstract description of their assumptions, shows that they share several basic characteristics. Most of them depart from the assumption of profit maximization in the short run, and replace it with an assumption of goals defined in terms of targets – that is, they are to greater or lesser degree satisficing theories. If they do retain maximizing assumptions, they contain some kind of mechanism that prevents the maximum from being attained, at least in the short run. In the Cyert-March theory, and that of Leibenstein, this mechanism can be viewed as producing "organizational slack," the magnitude of which may itself be a function of motivational and environmental variables.

The presence of something like organizational slack in a model of the business firm introduces complexity in the firm's behavior in the short run. Since the firm may operate very far from any optimum, the slack serves as a buffer between the environment and the firm's decisions. Responses to environmental events can no longer be predicted simply by analyzing the 'requirements of the situation', but depend on the specific decision processes that the firm employs. However well this characteristic of a business firm model corresponds to reality, it reduces the attractiveness of the model for many economists, who are reluctant to give up the process-independent predictions of classical theory, and who do not feel at home with the kind of empirical investigation that is required for disclosing actual real world decision processes.

But there is another side to the matter. If, in the face of identical environmental conditions, different decision mechanisms can produce different firm behaviors, this sensitivity of outcomes to process can have important consequences for analysis at the level of markets and the economy. Political economy, whether descriptive or normative, cannot remain indifferent to this source of variability in response. At the very least it demands that – before we draw policy conclusions from our theories, and particularly before we act on those policy conclusions – we carry out sensitivity analyses to test how far our conclusions would be changed if we made different assumptions about the decision mechanisms at the micro level.

If our conclusions are robust – if they are not changed materially by substituting one or another variant of the behavioral model for the classical model – we will gain confidence in our predictions and recommendations; if the conclusions are sensitive to such substitutions, we will use them warily until we can determine which micro theory is the correct one.

As reference to the literature cited earlier in this section will verify, our predictions of the operations of markets and of the economy are sensitive to our assumptions about mechanisms at the level of decision processes. Moreover, the assumptions of the behavioral theories are almost certainly closer to reality than those of the classical theory. These two facts, in combination, constitute a direct refutation of the argument that the unrealism of the assumptions of the classical theory is harmless. We cannot use the *in vacua* version of the law of falling bodies to predict the sinking of a heavy body in molasses. The predictions of the classical and neoclassical theories and the policy recommendations derived from them must be treated with the greatest caution.

What then is the present status of the classical theory of the firm? There can no longer be any doubt that the micro assumptions of the theory – the assumptions of perfect rationality – are contrary to fact. It is not a question of approximation; they do not even remotely describe the processes that human beings use for making decisions in complex situations.

Moreover, there is an alternative. If anything, there is an embarrassing richness of alternatives. Today, we have a large mass of descriptive data, from both laboratory and field, which show how human problem solving and decision-making actually take place in a wide variety of situations. A number of theories have been constructed to account for these data, and while these theories certainly do not yet constitute a single coherent whole, there is much in common among them. In one way or another, they incorporate the notions of bounded rationality: the need to search for decision alternatives, the replacement of optimization by targets and satisficing goals, and mechanisms of learning and adaptation. If our interest lies in descriptive decision theory (or even normative decision theory), it is now entirely clear that the classical and neoclassical theories have been replaced by a superior alternative that provides us with a much closer approximation to what is actually going on.

But what if our interest lies primarily in normative political economy rather than in the more remote regions of the economic sciences? Is there then any reason why we should give up the familiar theories? Have the newer concepts of decision-making and the firm shown their superiority 'for purposes of economic analysis'?

If the classical and neoclassical theories were, as is sometimes argued, simply powerful tools for deriving aggregative consequences that held alike for both perfect and bounded rationality, we would have every reason to retain them for this purpose. But we have seen, on the contrary, that neoclassical theory does not always lead to the same conclusions at the level of aggregate phenomena and policy as are implied by the postulate of bounded rationality, in any of its variants. Hence, we cannot defend an uncritical use of these contrary-to-fact assumptions by the argument that their veridicality is unimportant. In many cases, in fact, this veridicality may be crucial to reaching correct conclusions about the central questions of political economy. Only a comparison of predictions can tell us whether a case before us is one of these.

The social sciences have been accustomed to look for models in the most spectacular successes of the natural sciences. There is no harm in that, provided that it is not done in a spirit of slavish imitation. In economics, it has been common enough to admire Newtonian mechanics (or, as we have seen, the law of falling bodies), and to search for the economic equivalent of the laws of motion. But this is not the only model for a science, and it seems, indeed, not to be the right one for our purposes.

Human behavior, even rational human behavior, is not to be accounted for by a handful of invariants. It is certainly not to be accounted for by assuming perfect adaptation to the environment. Its basic mechanisms may be relatively simple, and I believe they are, but that simplicity operates in interaction with extremely complex boundary conditions imposed by the environment and by the very facts of human long-term memory and of the capacity of human beings, individually and collectively, to learn.

If we wish to be guided by a natural science metaphor, I suggest one drawn from biology rather than physics.

Herbert Simon was an American political scientist, sociologist and psychologist, Professor at Carnegie Mellon University, and recipient of the Nobel Prize in Economics. This chapter is abridged from Rational Decision-Making in Business Organizations, Nobel Memorial Lecture, 8 December, 1978. © 1978 The Nobel Foundation.

An Economics Fit for Humans
Ross Gittins

Two aspects of psychological research present significant challenges to conventional economics: the study of how people make decisions and the study of happiness or 'subjective well-being'. What I want to do here is draw out the respects in which these advances challenge various aspects of economic theory and the policy prescriptions conventionally flowing from the theory. The first challenge – concerning decision-making – is being taken quite seriously by the economics profession. The thriving school of economic thought it has given rise to is known as 'behavioural economics', and the psychologist who did most to inspire it, Daniel Kahneman, was awarded the Nobel Prize in economics in 2002. The second challenge to conventional economics – from the burgeoning happiness research – is taking longer to win converts among economists. But I'm enough of an optimist to hope that we're witnessing the early stages of another revolution in economics, one to match or even exceed the influence of the Keynesian revolution of the 1940s and 1950s. (John Maynard Keynes, by the way, is now being hailed as one of the earliest behavioural economists – though his contemporary followers largely ignored that aspect of his contribution.)

Psychology's first challenge to microeconomic theory strikes at one of its central elements: the assumption of *Homo Economicus*. Economic man is assumed to be rational and self-interested. He or she always carefully evaluates all the options before making any decision, and always with the object of maximising his or her personal 'utility' or satisfaction. But cognitive psychologists have demonstrated that humans simply lack the neural processing power to make the carefully calculated decisions economists assume. People aren't rational, they're intuitive. And altruism is often an important consideration in their decision-making. People can't choose correctly between three options where no option is obviously best. Rather than carefully thinking through the pros and cons of every decision, people tend to rely on mental shortcuts ('heuristics') which often serve them well enough, but also lead them into systematic biases. People are often slow to learn from their mistakes. They are frequently capable of reacting differently to choices that are essentially the same, just because the choices have been 'framed' (packaged) differently.

This means that, rather than being coldly rational, people's decisions are often influenced by emotional considerations.

All this means that *Homo Sapiens* differs from *Homo Economicus* in many important respects. He doesn't conform to economists' assumption of 'fungibility' (one dollar is indistinguishable from another). He's often not bothered by opportunity cost and thus has a strong bias in favour of the status quo. He doesn't ignore 'sunk costs' as he's supposed to and often can't order his preferences consistently. He's not averse to risks so much as averse to losses and he focuses more on changes in his wealth than on its absolute level.

Unlike *Homo Economicus*, *Homo Sapiens* cares deeply about fairness. Experiments show people will walk away from deals they consider treat them unfairly, even though those deals would leave them better off. People are prepared to pay a price to punish others they consider to have been behaving badly towards the group. Often people are concerned about 'procedural fairness' – how things are done, not just how they end up.

What are the policy implications of all this? Well, I think it has powerful implications for the aspect of the neoclassical model that economic rationalists (particularly right-wing rationalists) find so attractive: its elevation and celebration of individualism. The individual should be free to choose, and governments should be most circumspect in how they constrain individuals' freedom, including by taxing them to pay for the public provision of services and to redistribute income. This elevation of the individual and, by implication, denigration of a more communitarian approach, turns out to rest heavily on the assumption that individuals are rational. If individuals are rational decision-makers then it follows, as the rationalists keep asserting, that governments can never know what's good for you better than you know yourself. Governments should therefore tax individuals as little as possible, and maximise the private provision of such things as education and health care. If individuals are not particularly rational in their decisionmaking, however, then there may well be a case for government paternalism in certain circumstances. Add to this the findings that people's decisions are often influenced by altruism, their concerns about fairness, their willingness to punish people who act contrary to the interests of the group, and that their behaviour is often influenced by the behaviour of those around them, and you get a further argument in support of communitarian interventions and income redistribution.

A second strand of policy implications also flows from abandoning the assumption that people are rational. It calls into question the economists' adherence to 'consumer sovereignty' – their belief that consumers should and do determine what producers produce. When consumers' decisions can be influenced by the way propositions are framed, and when decisions are frequently influenced by emotions, producers can use advertising and other marketing to manipulate consumer demand. This contravenes a basic tenet of market economics that, in Keynes's phrase, consumption is 'the sole end and object of all economic activity'. If producers can use advertising to increase as well as manipulate consumption, this puts the cart before the horse; it reverses the direction of causation in the economic system, turning means into ends.

Economists don't like talking about advertising. To make it fit their model they have to assume that it's purely informational, whereas we all know that smart advertisers sell the sizzle not the steak. They prey on our inadequacies and irrationalities, subtly selling us propositions which become absurd as soon as someone puts them into words: that buying certain products will at last put us among the beautiful people or give us a healthy, happy family. But if advertising is antithetical to consumer sovereignty, why are economists usually so disapproving of proposals to limit or ban advertising?

Now let's turn to psychology's second challenge to economic theory, arising from the rapidly growing body of research into happiness. There's not a big difference between subjective well-being and the economists' goal of maximising utility or satisfaction. So this is an area of research that ought to be of considerable relevance to economists. One common reservation they have, however, is that it's all so subjective – asking people to rate their satisfaction with life on a scale of one to 10. But psychologists have demonstrated that people's own assessment of their happiness has a high correlation with other people's assessments of them and with physical measurements of brain EEGs (electroencephalogram readings).

The most surprising finding of the happiness research is that the link between life satisfaction and income and wealth is quite weak. It exists, but it's small. Once a nation's income per person exceeds about $US15,000 a year, the acquisition of further income is subject to rapidly diminishing returns. And, as was first pointed out 30 years ago by the US economist Richard Easterlin, in the period since World War II the correlation between GDP and happiness has broken down. In America, for instance, real GDP per person has trebled while subjective well-being has been unchanged. Similar results are found for other developed countries where life satisfaction has been regularly measured.

This is a devastating conclusion for economists – and particularly economic rationalists – whose whole practical motivation has been based on the assumption that helping the community raise its productivity and increase its production and consumption of goods and services will leave it unequivocally better off. There's no doubt that, materially, we are better off than we were even 10 years ago: our homes are bigger and better, our cars are better, our food and clothing are fancier and we have any number of wonderful new gadgets to save us labour or entertain us. But though we are better off, we don't feel better off. Why not? Why is it that the acquisition of income does so little to increase our satisfaction?

Psychologists (and a few economists) have proposed two main explanations. First, it's a characteristic of humans that we adapt surprisingly quickly to our changed circumstances. We get a promotion, move into a better house or buy a new car and, for a while, we really feel better off. But all too soon we adapt to our new circumstances and absorb them into the status quo. People who win the lottery are no happier than normal a year later but, by the same token, most accident victims who suffer paraplegia end up being no unhappier than normal. The thing that's surprising about all this is our failure to learn from all the times the buzz from an acquisition has worn off so quickly. We keep striving to acquire another new toy in the hope it will be the one that finally delivers nirvana. This amnesia – which, in terms of the economists' model, constitutes a major information failure – is why psychologists describe us as being trapped on a 'hedonic treadmill'.

The second part of the explanation for the diminishing marginal utility of money is rivalry. The economic model assumes that what satisfies us is absolute increases in our income or wealth. This is because we're all individualists, who not only don't care about the well-being of others, but also don't ever compare ourselves with others. In truth, we are highly social animals, obsessed by what those around us think of us and what we think of them. And remember that great quote from Gore Vidal: 'when I see a friend succeed … a little part of me dies'. Evolution has made us a species highly conscious of our social status. We care deeply about how we rank in the pecking order, and are always striving to advance our status – or avoid slipping back – by the promotions we get, the size of our incomes, the location and opulence of our homes, the newness and foreignness of our cars, the private schools we send our kids to and the private hospitals we use when sick. In our mania for getting ahead of the Joneses, what we care about is not absolute increases in our income, but relative increases.

The trouble with this rivalry, however, is that it is a zero-sum game. To the extent that I succeed in making myself happy by moving up in the pecking order, those people I move ahead of suffer a loss of status that makes them unhappy. In economists' jargon, my efforts to advance myself generate offsetting 'negative externalities' for those I pass. And what's more, the whole leapfrogging game tends to leave us perpetually anxious about slipping back in the race for status.

What are the policy implications arising from the happiness research? There are many and I will only scratch the surface. The economist Richard Layard of the London School of Economics says that, beside adequate income, the research shows six main factors affect happiness: mental health, satisfying and secure work, a secure and loving private life, a secure community, freedom, and moral values.

So my first policy implication is that reducing unemployment should be given a much higher priority by the economic policy- makers. Research shows that being unemployed makes people particularly unhappy, a lot more unhappy than can be explained by the loss of income they suffer by not having a job. What people miss is the sense of self-identity and self-worth that comes from a job, and also, no doubt, the social contact. Economists may protest that they're already giving high priority to reducing unemployment but, in truth, their pursuit of this goal is conditional. Their concern with the 'efficient' allocation of resources means they frown on any solutions (job sharing, job-creation schemes, public sector employment, for instance) that involve modest inefficiencies. The truth is that the overwhelming goal of economists is to hasten the growth in the economy's production of goods and services, and the jobs generated in this process are just a fortunate by-product.

My second policy implication is that governments and employers could do a lot to raise subjective well-being if they put more emphasis on the enrichment of jobs – increasing job satisfaction by giving workers more personal control, opportunity to use their skills, variety in tasks, respect and status, and contact with others. Taken literally, the economists' model assumes that all work is unpleasant – a 'disutility' – and is undertaken purely to gain the money to buy the things that bring utility. Like the rest of us, economists know that, in reality, work carries much intrinsic satisfaction. But they don't follow this realisation through to their policy prescriptions. They're perpetually advocating 'labour market reform' aimed at ensuring labour is used more efficiently, treating labour as though it were just another inanimate economic resource, and ignoring the feelings of the human beings attached to the labour. The various ways labour can be used more efficiently make life unpleasant and even unhealthy for the workers involved: ever-changing casual hours, rolling shift work, split shifts and companies continually moving their staff between cities. When we pursue efficiency at the expense of people, economists have got things round the wrong way, trashing ends so as to advance means.

A third implication is that economic policy-makers should recognise the benefit of stability. People like stability – it makes them feel secure and happy. What's more, it breeds a highly valuable commodity: trust. People don't like continuous change. Macroeconomic management is aimed at stabilising the rate of growth in demand, and that's good. But micro-economists perpetually advocate change ('reform') aimed at increasing efficiency, raising productivity and quickening the production of goods and services – the very objective we now know doesn't make people any happier. Often, micro reform involves 'displacing' workers from the reformed industries where their labour wasn't being used efficiently. This is a process that causes no heart searching among economists because their model: (a) assumes alternative employment will be readily forthcoming, (b) ignores the intrinsic satisfaction of work, and (c) assumes unemployed workers will have a whale of a time enjoying all their new-found leisure.

A fourth policy implication is that the thing economists celebrate as 'competition' and are always trying to encourage because it acts as a spur to efficiency and growth, is actually 'rivalry' that creates losers as well as winners and thus generates roughly as much unhappiness as happiness. Rivalry is hardwired into our brains, but a case can be made that social comparison is not something we should be encouraging. Seen in this light, we should think twice about the unceasing calls for us to do this or do that to preserve or improve the economy's 'international competitiveness'. But why? It's just rivalry on a global scale. It is saying, we must make sure foreigners don't get richer at a faster rate than we do, or even overtake us on the league table.

Fifth, instead of merely unquestioningly promoting consumption, economists should be doing something they rarely do: studying it. They need to see whether there are some forms of consumption that yield more satisfaction than others. It may be that, in our striving for social status, we're devoting too much of our time and income to the purchase of 'positional goods' (conspicuous consumption) and too little to activities empirical research now tells us would yield greater satisfaction. The US economist Robert Frank says the 'gains that endure' are more likely to include social life, time with our kids, less travel time to work, more job security and better health care. Layard says we should be spending a lot more on fighting glaring evils – and sources of profound unhappiness – such as depression.

Sixth, the evidence that income is subject to diminishing marginal utility strengthens the case for redistributing income from rich to poor, since such transfers should increase total happiness. As yet there is mixed evidence on the question of whether people who live in countries with a narrower gap between rich and poor are happier.

Finally, we should look sceptically at the incessant calls for lower tax rates to encourage people to work harder. By its very nature, the economists' model assumes away all non-monetary motives for work. We do it only for the money. But the reminder of the intrinsic satisfaction we derive from work also reminds us that higher income-earners in particular have powerful non-monetary motives for working long and hard: job satisfaction and the pursuit of power and status. Reducing tax rates would merely allow us to run faster on the hedonic treadmill, whereas I think we should slow down. The drive for reduced government spending and lower taxes would leave people with more disposable income they could use to purchase education and health care privately, in the hope that these positional goods would enhance their social standing. Layard warns we should worry lest leisure, public goods and inconspicuous consumption (consumption that's not compared with the consumption of others) are under-produced because people focus so much on conspicuous consumption.

My conclusion is not that economics should be abolished but that it, rather than the economy, is what's in desperate need of radical reform. Neoclassical economics is a product of the state of man's knowledge during the eighteenth and nineteenth centuries, and has advanced surprisingly little since then. It needs to assimilate the considerable knowledge we've acquired since then, particularly our vastly superior understanding of human decision- making and motivations. The community will always need the advice of people who specialise in studying the economic aspects of our lives, but those specialists need to rebuild their models using more realistic assumptions about human behaviour. This would give us an economics fit for humans.

Ross Gittins is Economics Editor, *The Sydney Morning Herald*. This chapter is adapted from The Ronald Henderson Oration, August 5, 2004. © 2004 Ross Gittins. Reprinted with permission of the author.

Trust: Experiments and Behaviour
Shaun Hargreaves-Heap

Behavioural economics is the field within economics that has focussed on what is known about how people *actually* behave. This knowledge is largely based on what laboratory and field experiments reveal about behaviour, and I illustrate the approach here with a discussion of trusting behaviour.

Trust is a key ingredient in many exchanges. An employer and employee, for instance, may prefer a high wage accompanied by high effort on the job to a low wage with low effort. However, the employer will not agree to the high wage unless he or she can trust that the worker, once hired at the high wage, will expend a high effort. Since taking it easy is usually preferred to working up a sweat, such trust may not be warranted and the pair will likely settle, in its absence, for the inferior low wage and low effort combination. More generally, trust is potentially important in this way whenever a supplier of a good has some discretion over the quality of what they supply. Of course, the problem of trust (or rather its absence) can be overcome, if quality can be monitored, by writing a contract that makes the high price depend on the delivery of high quality. Alternatively when the exchange is potentially repeated, the threat of not repeating the purchase may ensure the supplier produces a high quality product. But quality cannot always be measured and, even when it can, such contracts can be expensive to draw up and enforce; and exchanges are not always repeated. It would be much better if people could just trust each other. Indeed, such a simple ability to trust (or its absence) arguably helps explain why markets grew historically faster in some places and why some populations are relatively more successful economically than others (Seabright 2004; Fukuyama 1995).

Experiments provide one source of insight into when and if people are able to trust each other in this sense. I sketch the experimental approach next, before reviewing some of the key results and concluding with a discussion of the broader implications for economics of these results.

The trust game and the experimental method

The behavioural approach distills the essence of trusting behaviour into a relatively simple decision problem known as the trust game. In this game, there are two people (or 'players') who interact anonymously. One person has an endowment, say $100, and he or she must decide whether to give any of this to the other person. Whatever is given (call it $x) is multiplied by three (so the other person receives $3x), then the other person must decide how much, if any, to return to the first person (call this amount $y). Since the interaction occurs under conditions of anonymity, a selfish second person will not want to return any of the $3x that they receive. Knowing this, a selfish first person will not want to give any in the first place (since whatever they give simply diminishes their initial $100). Thus there is a clear prediction that selfish players will give nothing. However, if the first person can trust the second to act in some non-selfish way and return a reasonable proportion of what they receive, then they could both be much better off because whatever is given is multiplied by three. For instance, if the first person gave the full $100 to the second, the second would receive $300 and if he or she returned anything more than $100, both would be better off than the case where there is no trust and none is given. For this reason, the extent to which the first person gives some of his or her endowment ($x/100$) is treated as an index of the trust the first person has in the second, and the proportion returned ($y/3x$) is an index of the second's trustworthiness.

The game is played anonymously between randomly drawn people from a population to avoid other considerations, such as a prior social relation or the prospect of the interaction being repeated, entering into each person's decision. Siblings, after all, might have special reasons for trusting (or not trusting!) each other that do not apply more generally to most exchanges and one wants to avoid picking up these effects. The insights into the determinants of people's behaviour with this approach come from carefully controlled variations in the details of the decision problem. The essence of careful control for this purpose is to introduce changes singly so that any alteration in behaviour can be associated unambiguously with the changed feature of the decision problem. This is the hallmark of the experimental approach and it offers a major advantage over other types of empirical investigation in economics that use real world data on behaviour. Observations on behaviour from outside the laboratory are typically generated under conditions where many of the potential causes of behaviour are changing at the same time, making it difficult, even when the econometrics are sophisticated, to disentangle their respective contributions. Nevertheless, this distillation of the problem to be studied and its careful manipulation does entail an obvious possible drawback. Such a forensic examination of trusting behaviour, by removing so much of the flesh and blood found in real decisions, raises a question about the relevance of the results in the laboratory for interpreting behaviour outside. This is called the problem of 'external validity'.

Some experimental results

The first arresting experimental result is that people typically do not behave as selfish people would: they exhibit trust and trustworthiness by giving 40-60 percent in the first place, while the second person returns approximately 33 percent. This leaves the first person no worse off usually and often slightly better off than if they had given nothing, while the second person is much better off. It is also commonly found that the variation in individual return rates is related to the variation in giving rates: people who give a lot tend to have a larger proportion returned than those who give less (i.e. there is reciprocation).

One type of controlled variation in the experiment is designed to examine the character of the non-selfish motivations that people reveal in their behaviour. In the standard rational choice model of individual behaviour in economics, where people have preferences over outcomes and are assumed to be rational because they select actions that best satisfy those preferences, these non-selfish motivates are captured by the idea that people have 'other regarding' or 'social' preferences as well as purely self-regarding ones. This simply means they care about others' welfare as well as their own and act accordingly. In these terms, one obvious explanation of people's behaviour in the trust game is that they have a particular 'social' preference for equality (i.e. they are averse to inequality) because, on average, with a gift of say 50 percent and a return rate of 33 percent, both players leave the lab with $100 when one started with nothing and the other had $100. However, when the second player receives an equally sized endowment (for turning up over which they make no decisions) only slightly less is given by the first player and not a lot more is returned. So, even if inequality aversion is at play, it is not the only kind of 'social' preference. Indeed, when the productivity attached to any gift is varied (i.e. how much the $x is multiplied by), the amount given seems to vary. Thus people's 'social' preferences also seem to embody a concern for efficiency; and this is consistent with results regarding the character of people's social preferences from experiments with other decision problems.

There is also evidence that trust behaviours vary across countries. While people typically give around 50 percent of their endowment, there are some populations that give notably less and some more. For example, subjects in the US and the UK often give at the high end of 60 percent, in China and Japan the giving rate can be even higher, closer to 70 percent, while Kenya and Uganda have produced the relatively low rates of 30 percent or below. This provokes an obviously interesting question as to what might account for these cross-country differences. A version of this question has recently been investigated, not in relation to inclinations towards trust, but for a related 'social' preference for fairness revealed in two different game: the so called Ultimatum and Dictator games. In the former, the first player must decide on the division of a resource and the second decides whether to accept this division. If they accept, then each gets whatever has been proposed and accepted. If the second person rejects the proposal, both get zero. The Dictator version corresponds to the first part of the Ultimatum game: the first person simply decides on the division of the resource and this is implemented. In both games, the first player's decision can be interpreted as reflecting their commitment to fairness, although in the Ultimatum game it is complicated by a fear of rejection that might come from the second person holding a different view of what is fair. When these games are played in different countries in what are otherwise identical experimental conditions, the amount offered varies across countries and it appears that this can be partially accounted for by by the cross country differences in the importance of the market as a regulator of economic activity and the extent of religious belief (see

Henrich *et al.* 2010).

This suggestion that the intensity of a 'social' preference might depend in part on the background social context of the interaction is reinforced by the results of experiments where the controlled variation of conditions focuses specifically on these possible influences. The membership or otherwise of a group is one such aspect of social context that has been studied. In treatments where players are identified by the membership of a group (even when the identification is quite minimal in the sense that it is through a blue or red identifier on their screen), their behaviour depends on whether they are interacting with a fellow member of the group or with someone from a different group. People trust non-members less than fellow members; and this in-group favoratism seems to be explained by negative discrimination against outsiders rather than specially high levels of trust among insiders. Inequality between players also seems to have complicated effects on behaviour. For instance, trustworthiness falls, but not trust. However, if the interaction is given a market context (i.e. it explicitly takes place over the sale of a good where the first person sets the price and the second decides on the quality through a decision over how much effort to expend) both trust and trustworthiness fall. There are also some status related effects: the poor (or low status) are trusted less than the rich (high status). But this largely disappears in the market version of the game. The verdict on the effect of the institutional context of the market is, therefore, rather more nuanced in the trust game experiments than in the Heinrich *et al.* (2010) cross country study of fairness: markets do seem to encourage fairness in the sense of people being treated equally, but the adverse effect on trust when there is inequality is worse in markets than in non-market settings.

There is also evidence for this sensitivity of 'social' preferences to institutional context in experiments that examine how the introduction of additional mechanisms of control affect trusting behaviours. In the market exchange version of the trust game, a control mechanism is introduced, for instance, in the form of an ability to make the price/wage depend on quality/effort, to see whether it improves the the quality/effort of the supplier/employee. It does not. This somewhat paradoxical result is sometimes explained by appealing to a common finding in experimental psychology that an explicit financial reward supplies an extrinsic reason for making an effort that can undermine the intrinsic reason for doing a good job that comes from professional pride which otherwise governs behaviour. Support for this idea comes explicitly from experiments in which a control mechanism is introduced that effectively sets a minimum effort level. People who are inclined to shirk work more when this control is introduced, but who would naturally work above whatever is the controlled minimum level, become de-motivated by the control and work less intensely than they would without the control device. The two effects seemingly roughly cancel out in the aggregate.

Implications of behavioural economics

Textbooks in economics often assume that people are selfish, but this is only a convenient simplification. The great virtue of the rational choice model is that it can accommodate many kinds of action because it is usefully quiet about the character of people's preferences. People can be selfish, altruistic, spiteful, or whatever. All that is required is that people's actions are coherent in the sense that one can talk about having such a thing as preferences in the first place (e.g. if people say they prefer A to B now, they will prefer A to B when faced with the same question one hour later). From this perspective, the behavioural discovery that people trust each other poses no obvious explanatory difficulty for the rational choice model. It can be explained by an apparent 'fact' about people's preferences: they are sometimes 'social' or 'other' regarding.

The real challenge posed by behavioural economics in this regard comes from the way that the strength of these 'social' preferences seems to depend on the social context of the interaction (e.g. whether it occurs in the market, among groups, between people who are unequal, in the context of control mechanisms, etc). This need not matter for explanation and prediction in economics so long as this dependence is understood, but it will matter for prescriptive or normative economics. This is because the standard by which different outcomes are judged (and advice is given) in mainstream economics is the extent to which people's preferences are satisfied, but this only makes sense if people's preferences can be taken as exogenous. The difficulty, then, is that behavioural economics suggests that preferences may be endogenous rather than exogenous and so fail to provide this standard. This is most acute when the advice relates to the choice of institutions governing these contextual factors. The usual basis for advice is how well the different possible institutional arrangements satisfy people's preferences. But this makes no sense when people do not have fixed antecedent preferences. When the preferences themselves depend on the choice of institution, this choice is in part a decision over what preferences to have and not just how best to satisfy them. There is nothing in conventional welfare economics that helps answer this new question about what preferences to have.

This point is liable to be more general because of what we know from other experiments. The standard tool of applied welfare economics is cost-benefit analysis. This framework places a monetary values on all the advantages (benefits) and disadvantages (costs) associated with some project and recommends only implementing those that have a net benefit, starting with those that have the highest net benefit. This is because, in principle, those who lose (the value of the costs) can be more than compensated by those who benefit (the value of the benefits) when there is a net benefit, leaving the surplus monetary value associated with the project as an index of how people can be potentially made better off through it. This only makes sense, though, so long as people's willingness to pay for something is an index of their preferences, so that if a person values apples at $1 each and bananas at fifty cents, then the person is made better off by substituting an apple for a banana in their lunchbox.

When this assumption is tested in a fairly simple experimental setting of what is called the 'P/$' experiment, it does not fare well. These experiments involve a choice between a P-bet and a $-bet, where the P-bet offers a relatively high chance of a modest prize and the $-bet offers a relatively large prize but with a small probability. Subjects make a straight choice between the two options and they are also asked to place a monetary value on each option. The worrying result is that a significant number of subjects switch from preferring the P-bet to placing a higher valuation on the $-bet, whereas there are relatively very few subjects who do the reverse. The fact that the reversals largely occur in one direction is important because it suggests that the revealed inconsistency in behaviour *cannot* be simply accounted for by some general tendency for the hand to tremble (i.e. make random mistakes). Instead, it seems some people's behaviour is systematic rather than random, but this systematic component just cannot be captured by the idea, which is necessary if cost-benefit analysis is to be used to guide policy, that people's behaviour reveals their preferences. Some people either do not have well behaved preferences or, if they do, they are not always guided by them.

It is not surprising that this experimental result has attracted a lot of attention. It has been very carefully examined for its 'internal validity': that is, for whether it is a correct and general inference about people's behaviour in the laboratory. In addition, this result, like the earlier ones regarding the endogeneity of 'social' preferences, will only *really* trouble mainstream normative or prescriptive economics if the laboratory results are granted 'external validity'. This is perhaps the more difficult area. One type of check for this comes from looking at whether the experimental results are consistent with what we know about people's behaviour from other sources. Unfortunately, these sources are not always as clear as the experimental insights, for the reasons noted earlier. Nevertheless, what we know from survey evidence on people's trust broadly supports many of the experimental findings sketched here.

Shaun Hargreaves-Heap is Professor of Economics, University of East Anglia. Trust: Experiments and Behaviour. © 2011 Shaun Hargreaves-Heap.

Behavioural Economics and Economic Policy

Peter E. Earl

From the standpoint of mainstream economics, the role of policy is to address market failure and distributional concerns. People are viewed as constrained merely by the time and wealth at their disposal and as if they act optimally given the information to which they have access. Given this, policies have to focus on making information easier to obtain and on changing incentives, property rights and/or the distribution of wealth. In reality, people face an additional constraint, namely, their limited cognitive capacity. Behavioural economics takes account of what is known about how this affects decision-making processes. It leads to a different view of what can be achieved by economic policy and what needs to be kept in mind by those trying to devise effective policies. From the behavioural perspective, there is scope for policy to be designed to work by affecting whether people think they need to take a decision, how they evaluate the options they discover, and how they choose between alternatives. These issues are explored in sequence in this chapter.

Policies that work by causing problems that promote search and discovery

Problems in gathering and processing information commonly preclude the computation of optimal strategies and leave decision-makers unsure about what they can achieve. Herbert Simon's Nobel Prize-winning work, therefore, portrays economizing behaviour as a 'satisficing' activity rather than as constrained optimization: people focus on trying to reach targets that they have based on past experience and their inferences about what it is currently reasonable to expect. If they do better (worse) than expected, they wait to see if this is a one-off outcome rather than jumping to the conclusion that they should raise (lower) their aspirations. Aspirations thus follow attainments with a lag.

Decision-makers are typically busy trying to implement plans, aware that problems may arise and impede their progress, so they tend to avoid using up their cognitive capacity by looking for ways of doing better in areas where they believe they are on track to meeting their targets. Policy-makers may therefore be able to induce higher attainments by producing situations in which those working in firms are more likely to search for ways of improving productivity and consumers are more likely to discover products that give them a better 'bang for their bucks'.

Policies aimed at opening up markets to greater competition – for example, by reducing tariffs and other barriers to imports – may make it harder for firms to meet their targets with their established routines. New competitors provide stimuli to find cheaper ways of producing a given product and/or more demanding external reference points for the non-price standards at which they should be aiming. Under such pressures, firms may discover ways of achieving levels of performance that they had not previously thought possible.

Policies aimed at changing the extent of competition within organizations may produce similar results. Many privatization policies and structural reforms in public service and tertiary education in recent years have been designed to raise employees' expectations about what they will have to deliver in order to keep their jobs or achieve promotion. However, while such policies may increase worker productivity in the short term, they are not guaranteed to produce welfare gains. The top-heavy management structures needed to run such systems may chew up much of the revenue gains, while line workers may find it harder to meet other aspirations, such as those regarding their work-life balance and their stress levels (see the analysis of economic reforms in New Zealand offered by Hazledine (1998) and the work of Carr (1994) on the impact of managerialism in Australia's education sector). Furthermore, encouraging growth in the number of competitors in a market can be a mixed blessing for customers: while privatization and exposure to competition may force phone companies that previously were sleepy state monopoly to set higher standards, consumers may find themselves bewildered by the range of unfamiliar suppliers competing for their business.

From a behavioural perspective, decision-makers economise on the costs of deciding among a set of options by taking the default option. This tendency to settle on a default option often produces missed opportunities in the economic system. Those who take the default option may end up with poor value for money, so policy may have a role in shaping the kind of options they face. Consider financial services, for example. Waterson (2003) suggests that the fact that insurance is a much more hotly contested area than banking may be due partly to insurance products having an annual renewal notice (which may provoke search if it seems to involve a big increase) whereas deposit and credit card accounts are open ended. (Even with insurance, the default option – accept the renewal quotation – favours the existing provider, especially if the customer has already arranged automatic payments by direct debit.) Customers have to be proactive if they want to ensure they are not sent, and billed for, a new credit card when their existing one expires. An implication of this for financial regulators is that consumers might be more choosey if they had to act periodically to determine which firm they wanted to provide their deposit or credit accounts. One might even go so far as to require them to provide evidence (for example, via an authorization code picked up via a visit to a website run by the regulator) of having checked alternatives before they could authorize that current arrangements be renewed.

Policies aimed at steering people away from traditional default options also have great potential to reduce damage to the environment: for many consumers, getting into their cars is the default option even though, if they bothered to check things out, they could discover viable alternatives that reduced their greenhouse footprints. Changing the incidence of congestion by introducing bus-lanes and raising the costs of finding parking spaces by reducing their number (rather than simply raising meter charges) are obvious ways of getting motorists to rethink their behaviour. Similarly, if manufacturers are required to meet pollution reduction schedules, rather than being allowed the possibility of simply paying carbon taxes and then passing the costs on to their customers, they may be more likely to search for ways of reducing pollution. In the process they may discover solutions that result in their businesses becoming both greener and more profitable.

Sometimes, however, it may make sense to design policies that involve *creating* a default for consumers that will be in their own interests, given their tendency to adopt the default position. Superannuation is an obvious case, given that (a) workers tend not to switch their superannuation accumulations out of the fund into which they are deposited by default, and (b) well-managed not-for-profit industry superannuation funds will tend to give higher returns than for-profit funds that are open to all, due to smaller fees and not needing to pay dividend to shareholders. Policy-makers might thus serve consumers well by requiring that employers must use the former kind of superannuation fund as the default option.

Evaluation of options: Twisted and twistable

Economics normally avoids the question of how decision-makers work out the possible costs and benefits of the alternative courses of action that they consider. In reality, once an option has been discovered, its costs and benefits are not self-evident, even in probabilistic terms. Rather, assessments of the implications of selecting one option rather than another are mental constructs. They are therefore open to being twisted by cognitive processes that may involve self-deception through wishful thinking or denial where it is cognitively difficult to face up to the presence of tradeoffs and dilemmas. This is particularly likely where at stake is the chooser's ability to maintain ideas that they use as key foundations for constructing their view of themselves and the world in general. Awareness of such processes leads to recognition of both the need for policy interventions and barriers to making economic policies work.

Consider for example a person who is in an electrical appliance store and is tempted by the idea of using their credit card to buy an enormous plasma television currently offered at a 'special' price. This could be a bad thing if the person would have trouble paying the credit card bill. Moreover, the energy consumption of such a television is far higher than that of a smaller, less ostentatious LED television. However, instead of seeing these downsides, the consumer may end up reasoning that (a) it is a good idea to buy it right now because of the special price (despite the fact that the prices of these product, like those of computers, tend to fall over time), (b) the credit card debt will be paid off rapidly (wishful thinking), and (c) although the mandatory energy efficiency label gives it a poor rating, this will be a product that reduces the consumer's energy use since it will reduce the number of occasions when they drive into town to watch movies at cinemas (a conclusion reached without any serious attempt at calculation).

Wishful thinking about credit card servicing capacity is relatively easy to prevent via a central database of credit cards and a prohibition on financial institutions issuing credit cards whose credit limits will allow the cardholder to exceed a particular ratio of total credit to income. Product labelling is less likely to have as much clout. For example, what should consumers in the UK make of Carbon Trust labelling that enables them to see that making a packet of Walker's salt and vinegar potato crisps involves 120g of CO_2 emissions? As Pollard (2010) points out, this is slightly worse than driving one kilometre in a BMW316d. Depending on whether they are feeling peckish or want to travel in a modern symbol of affluence, they can 'spin' the information either way.

Personality differences determine the kind of spin that individual decision-makers give to a piece of information. This complicates life for policymakers. However, there is scope for designing policies around what is known about *general* tendencies for 'heuristics and biases' to affect what people make of the situations in which they find themselves. For example, it is widely observed that people tend to treat high probabilities as certainties, and ignore *very* low probabilities, whilst taking *fairly* low probabilities much more seriously than economists would normally expect. It is also common for people to make erroneous assessments of risk due to the way information is presented. In consequence, they often place bets that make little sense in terms of statistics and expected utility theory. For example, people are much more likely to purchase extended product warranties (which make little sense over a lifetime in which one buys many appliances, only a few of which will fail prematurely) than insurance against becoming physically unable to work, while some fail to inoculate their children against diseases such as whooping cough because of fears about relatively rare side-effects.

By designing policies in the light of knowledge of these information processing biases, it may be possible to manipulate choices, whether to protect people against their own shortcomings or to get them to behave in a way that suits the interests of the policy-makers. Hanson and Kysar (1999a, 1999b) offer a comprehensive guide to the how firms do this to consumers, but similar principles can be applied by public agencies seeking to meet social goals (Thaler and Sunstein 2008). For example, a behavioural health economist would point out that how information is framed can make all the difference: '90 percent fat-free' sounds much more appealing than '10 percent fat'.

In addition to policies aimed at protecting consumers from their cognitive shortcomings by managing the information environment that they face, it may also be necessary to set rules about what firms are allowed to offer. For example, in attempting to achieve or maintain particular levels of social status, consumers will be prone to delude themselves about the financial commitments they can safely make. If firms in the financial services sector are willing to allow them to risk mortgage stress and bankruptcy by letting them step up their debt/income ratios, they can try to buy more expensive properties and other status symbols for themselves and their offspring. As Frank (2007) argues, this kind of behaviour is akin to an arms race and consumers typically will fail to end up feeling any better off despite the debts they have incurred. Worse still, they may typically not end up in bigger homes unless they are prepared to incur bigger commuting costs from the city fringes. The trouble is that the products they are trying to afford are 'positional goods': there is a limited supply of homes with waterfront views or convenient location, so attempts to chase the limited supply mainly serve to push up prices. The 'soccer moms' who drive larger and larger 4WDs in attempting to out-do each other and protect their children from other people's vehicles likewise mostly cancel out each other's efforts. If they all travelled in smaller, lighter vehicles, they would all be safer and pollution would be reduced.

If policy-makers wish to restrain real estate prices and reduce the incidence of personal bankruptcy and financial stress, the simple way to do this is to impose rules for the repayment periods of loans and the maximum ratios of monthly repayments to income. To limit the availability of huge 4WDs for family motoring, policy-makers might use strategically designed rules regarding weight and height of private passenger vehicles, or their ability to avoid rolling over when swerving at a required speed to avoid an obstruction representing a moose or kangaroo.

Policies to reduce confusion and address the consequences of intolerant decision rules

Cognitive constraints often drive decision-makers to choose without first searching to discover a comprehensive list of alternatives and carefully sizing them up. Familiar brands or recommendations from trusted authorities provide quick solutions to problems. Where decision-makers do engage in extended problem-solving, they will be prone to run out of cognitive capacity. People can consciously process only about ten bits of information per second (Marschak 1968), and can only keep in mind about seven things at a time (Miller 1956). They may thus fail to notice changing incentives or be unable to remember information they have come across. They may also get confused and make mistakes in the process of trying to make sense of whatever information they have at hand. Given these constraints, they may be prey to groups of firms that operate as a 'confusopoly' by trying to overload them with information in ways that may conceal the relative value for money offered by rival products. If regulators try to intervene by demanding more comprehensive product disclosure statements, they may make matters even worse.

Consider how mobile phone service providers offer an enormous choice of products, each of which is specified via a contract offer that contains extensive 'fine print'. To work out which one is best, after making some assumptions about future conditions, consumers need to be able to decipher the wording with the skill of a contract lawyer and then to perform complex calculations across hundreds of rival plans. In such situations, consumers clearly will have to adopt a simplifying strategy, and they run the risk of being led in particular directions by firms whose marketers are applying knowledge of cognitive biases (Ayal 2009). It will be hard to know whether a firm that offers a 'simple, no-nonsense' deal is actually offering something that will be cheaper or trying to prey upon those who find it altogether too confusing to try to work out which supplier is actually offering the kind of service they want at the lowest price.

Similar issues arise with financial services. O'Shea (2010) tested how well consumers from a wide variety of backgrounds understood credit contracts. Most of them failed dismally and said that what they wanted was not more information but summaries that simply told them what the total cost of a given loan would be if repaid via a particular sum per month.

Markets that operate as confusopolies do not inherently require regulatory intervention. In some case, consumers may be able outsource cognitive effort and expertise to websites that provide comparison services. However, these may be expensive to programme accurately and difficult to offer in a way that is profitable, so in some cases they may be unreliable or absent. For providers of such services and for public policy designers alike, there is also the problem that the confusopolists may keep changing their products to retaliate against attempts to make them easier to compare. For example, if regulators try to make life simpler for supermarket customers by requiring unit pricing signals to be given, food processing companies may attempt to increase the differentiation of their products in non-price terms via taste, quality of ingredients, convenience of packaging, and so on. It should also be noted that public policy itself may be a cause of confusion, an obvious example being taxation systems that in some countries are so complex that it is unwise to complete a tax return without employing the services of a professional tax advisor.

Policy-makers need to know how consumers will try to cope with information overload as well as with perceived gaps in information. The use of decision rules is central to these processes. The discussion above provides an example of such a rule, namely, 'if choice is too complicated, try to outsource it to a specialist website'. Where consumers try to solve decision problems themselves, they seem to change which kind of decision rule they use depending on the amount of information they have to process (Payne, Bettman and Johnson 1993). It is difficult to compute trade-offs across a wide variety of alternatives that differ significantly across many characteristics. In such situations, people are more likely to choose using non-compensatory decisions rules that involve eliminating any option that does not 'tick all the boxes' on a checklist. Another workable strategy is to eliminate options progressively by applying a set of tests in order of priority until only one remains. A compensatory, trade-off-based approach to choice may prove workable if applied to a shortlist of options that meet an entire set of checklist criteria, but in some cases a simpler way of selecting from the shortlist may be used, such as 'choose the cheapest'.

Even if a trade-off is made at the end of a decision process, the use of intolerant decision rules to derive a shortlist remains significant. Options that are dismissed at an early stage due to failing to pass a particular test are not given further consideration, regardless of their strengths in other areas. In other words, it is as though a kind of discrimination is going on. Policymakers in recent decades have often focused on designing frameworks to prevent people from suffering discrimination in labour markets and in access to public services on the basis of age, gender, disability or sexual orientation, but the significance of non-compensatory decision rules runs far wider. This is particularly the case if there are also barriers to making substitutions on the production side due to certain activities requiring specific skills.

For example, consider a situation in which domestic car producers are failing to produce vehicles that meet the checklists that potential customers have evolved (for example, because domestically produced vehicles are falling behind global standards in safety, fuel efficiency, luxury or build quality). If so, imports may rise and exports may be lost. Conventional wisdom suggests that the firms should concentrate on offering products whose features reflect their comparative advantage, and that the emerging trade imbalance may be thwarted if the domestic currency is allowed to depreciate. The behavioural perspective, by contrast, implies that a change in relative prices of exports and imports will have limited impact so long as the imported vehicles still come within the budget ranges of potential buyers. For the domestic cars to sell better, they need to be improved in areas where they are being deemed inadequate rather than being improved in areas where they are already seen as satisfactory. To achieve the necessary improvements, the manufacturers may need to develop new capabilities, which in turn may require immigration policies that are more flexible, enabling them to bring in workers with key skills. In the long run, it may be necessary to change attitudes and academic programmes so that it is easier to attract top students into fields such as engineering that they would otherwise 'rule out' in favour of, say, commerce subjects. In other words, where non-compensatory decision rules are producing 'no go areas' in an economic system, the policy problem is how to inculcate substitutability in related parts of the system such that the resources that are prerequisites for solving the key problem become available.

Conclusion

The behavioural economist's view of the cognitively constrained real-world decision-maker has both bad and good new for the policy-maker. The bad news is that policies may fail dismally due to incentives not being noticed or acted upon in the way that mainstream economics might predict. The good news is that there is potentially a much bigger role for policy interventions to help people cope better with the problem of choice, or to 'nudge' them (see for example Thaler and Sunstein 2008) into taking decisions that will increase the productivity and well-being of the nation.

Peter E. Earl is Associate Professor of Economics, University of Queensland. Behavioural Economics and Economic Policy © 2011 Peter E. Earl.

IV
FROM ECONOMIC ANALYSIS TO ECONOMIC POLICY

THE STATE AND THE ECONOMY

We now turn more explicitly to questions of economic policy. The preceding sections of this book – concerned with identifying economic problems and considering the frameworks within which they can be analysed – lead inexorably to this concern with 'what is to be done'. A commitment to economic development and social progress requires appropriate responses. It requires consideration of what changes to the economy would contribute positively to social well-being – what would make the society more prosperous, equitable and sustainable. It also raises the question of which institutions are to be the agents of change.

We commonly look to governments for this purpose. Indeed, some say it is their *raison d'etre*. In seeking political office, politicians commonly promise, if elected, to implement policies that will contribute to economic and social improvements. The governments they form seek credit when there is 'a good set of figures' for the national economy (while usually blaming adverse outcomes on variables beyond their control). However, in addition to government, other elements within the state apparatus have a major influence on economic outcomes. In Australia, such elements include the Reserve Bank, FairWork Australia (which has specific responsibilities for overseeing industrial relations), and key sections of the public service such as the Treasury. Moreover, it is not necessarily true that governments and these other public institutions can actually solve economic problems in practice. Their attempts to do so are often severely constrained. Sometimes, it seems, they may not even try. So a critical analysis of the state in the economy is needed.

Unfortunately, coherent analysis of the state has been a casualty of the disciplinary separation of mainstream economics from politics. All too often, mainstream economists make facile assumptions about the state, commonly regarding it as outside the economy but engaging in 'government intervention' to steer the economic system, for better or for worse. Some problems with this terminology, and the underlying notion of the state, have been considered in the earlier chapter by Evan Jones. From a political economic perspective, it is more sensible to regard the state as integral to the economy – establishing and enforcing the property rights on which the whole system depends, creating markets and developing the 'rules of the game' as well as directly producing goods and services, distributing incomes and ensuring social order.

This section begins with a reading by Frank Stilwell that emphasises the array of possible assumptions that can be made about the role of the state in economic life. This is a brief introduction to issues which are at the core of political economy, integrating the study of politics and economics. Then comes the late J.K. Galbraith's magisterial reflections on what role the state can play in creating 'the good society'. The third item is by Michael Johnson, looking at state capacity and the problems arising from attempts at public sector reform, showing that corporatization of public sector enterprises has had markedly different outcomes from what the proponents of that restructuring claimed. These chapters are a prelude to the chapters in the final section in this book that look at particular policy issues.

For further reading on the character of the state and its interpretation, significant books include Robert R. Alford and Roger Friedland, *Powers of Theory: Capitalism, the State, and Democracy*, Cambridge University Press, Cambridge, 1985; Arthur McEwan, *Neoliberalism or Democracy: Economic Strategy, Markets and Alternatives for the Twenty-first Century*, Zed Books, London, 1999; and Robert Manne and David McKnight (eds), *Goodbye to All That? On the Failure of Neoliberalism and the Urgency of Change*, Black Inc, Melbourne, 2010.

The State: Competing Perspectives
Frank Stilwell

The simplest definition of the state is as an interconnected set of institutions – comprising the government, public service, judiciary, armed forces and police, political parties and parliamentary assemblies. These are the institutions of national and sub-national administration. A systematic analysis of this state apparatus is a key focus of political economy. But how does the state work? Whose interests does it serve? Broadly speaking, there are three currents of analysis, according to whether the state is regarded as democratic, capitalist or bureaucratic.

The *democratic* character of the state is its most evident feature where the selection of government from among the contesting political parties occurs through an electoral process. However, other elements of the state – such as the judiciary, the police or the central bank – are not normally subject to such democratic procedures. And in some countries it has been common for the government to be taken over by military or other despotic autocrats who dispense with democracy altogether. Successive military dictatorships in the Pacific island state of Fiji in recent years provide an example. We cannot blithely assume that the state is innately democratic. However, democratic processes commonly give some impetus to use the power of the state for public purposes and provide some checks on the abuse of that power.

What about the state's *capitalist* character? Formally, the state stands aside from capitalism, in that ownership of capital does not directly confer official state power. Being a businessman and an elected member of government are quite different roles. However, the state is *capitalist* to the extent that its activities are shaped and/or constrained by the prevailing economic system. Ensuring the conditions for capital accumulation and the legitimacy of capitalism is a recurrent concern for the state, if only because failure to do so can be expected to cause economic and political crisis.

Bureaucratic characteristics are also commonly in evidence. Managing the array of public policies – economic, social and environmental – is a task usually requiring a considerable state apparatus. Legions of public servants carry the burden. In the process some may develop interests and practices not in harmony with either the formal requirements of the democratically elected governments or the needs of capital. On this reasoning, the state is unlikely to function purely as the embodiment of the democratic ideal or as the 'ideal collective capitalist'. Internal state structures and interests shape how public policies are developed and implemented in practice.

This trilogy of democratic, capitalistic and bureaucratic features of the state needs emphasis because so much disagreement about the state – as a vehicle for social progress, an instrument of class domination or a parasitic institution – is traceable back to a different emphasis on these three aspects. The disagreements are reflected in the different questions that people often pose about the functions of the state. Does it serve the national interest, albeit in difficult economic circumstances partly beyond its own making? Or, in responding to various sectional interests, does it recurrently violate the national interest? Is the state more like an arena of struggle in which competing class and sectional interests confront each other? Then again, does it act in a managerial role, serving its own interests instead of the national interest or particular class interests? If we are to avoid a purely descriptive account of economic and social policies, it is useful to set our discussion in the context of these competing political economic views.

A democratic state

The first possibility is a liberal pluralist view which sees the state implementing public policies in response to the interests expressed by the people. A focus on electoral processes and pressure-group politics commonly leads to this interpretation of the state in the democratic process. We can usefully distinguish two principal variants, one seeing public policy as serving the national interest and the other seeing it as violating the national interest. In the former case, the state may be limited to correcting minor sources of 'market failure', or it may undertake more large-scale government intervention to correct the various inefficiencies and injustices associated with a market system. Galbraith's notion of the state as a source of "countervailing power" to monopoly capital is a strong version of this view of the state. The Keynesian economists' conception of the state as an instrument for macroeconomic management sits reasonably comfortably here too. The state's activities are regarded as generally benign, tempering the worst excesses of the free market economy with some elements of macroeconomic stability, redistributive justice, and social regulation.

A negative variant suggests that the state's activities, although responsive to political demands, tend to be harmful. This view dovetails with neoliberal ideology. It is exemplified by the 'private interest theory of the state' that sees the state accommodating to sectional interests in ways that violate the national interest. Tariff policy is often cited as a classic case – protectionism being interpreted as the consequence of the government 'caving in' to demands from firms and unions in various industries, resulting in a macroeconomic outcome that impedes economic restructuring and efficiency. Similarly, regional policy is interpreted as a pragmatic accommodation to parochial demands for special consideration, leading to outcomes that are economically inefficient. Critics of the 'country independents' who held the balance of power in the Australian parliament after the 2010 general election accused them of putting their own regional interests ahead of national interests in this way. This is not to say that democracy in practice *is* necessarily inefficient or wasteful; only that its critics are sceptical that its outcomes have overall coherence in terms of a national interest. Some go further in denying the possibility of identifying a 'national interest'.

A capitalist state

Class-based analyses present a quite different picture of the state as serving dominant class interests. It is a view that is most evident in the traditional Marxist interpretation of the capitalist state as "the executive for managing the common affairs of the whole bourgeoisie". From this perspective, the state can be expected systematically to serve the requirements of capitalists (although it may be noted that Marx's own empirical studies did not treat the state simply as an obedient tool of a monolithic ruling class). The interests of the class *as a whole* are of paramount importance here. This is because individual capitalists often do not perceive their common interests (or, if they do, they cannot coordinate their activities towards that end without 'external' assistance). Hence the need for a state with 'relative autonomy' from the capitalist class. This makes it a more effective instrument for maintaining the social order required for a capitalist economy. Since, according to this view, the interests of capital and labor are fundamentally opposed, the state can be expected to implement policies that work against the long-term interests of the working class, although interim concessions may be made to secure legitimacy and social reproduction.

Expressed in this way, an underlying determinism is evident – the actions of the state follow more or less directly from the needs of the capitalist class. Analysis of the state therefore begins with an analysis of the requirements of capital – for accumulation and legitimation. Economic and social policies are interpreted as helping to open up new opportunities for capital accumulation and/or as providing legitimacy for continuing class-domination. This is a powerful means of integrating economic and political analysis. However, a tendency to tautology may exist because, by definition, all government policies are encompassed. Either policy directly facilitates capital accumulation or, if it involves progressive redistribution of income to workers and welfare recipients, it must be serving the needs of capital for legitimation of the *status quo*. The possibility that policies might go against to general interests of capital is precluded. The reasoning also tends to deny that any great significance attaches to which different political parties form government. The 'logic of capital' rules.

A variation on this class-based approach to understanding the state that is less prone to these determinist tendencies emphasises how the state relates to the broadened political conflict between capital and labor. This is the view of the state as *an arena of class struggle*. On this reading, the state is not simply an instrument of class domination nor even an instrument of class mediation. It neither automatically serves the interests of one class nor some idealized notion of a national interest. Rather, it is continually contested terrain. This view differs from the more traditional Marxist view of the state because of its greater emphasis on the extension of class and intra-class struggle from the economic to the political sphere. It accords major significance to struggles between and within political parties. It allows for the possibility of significant working class gains, even an evolutionary transition to some sort of socialism. On the other hand, the view of the state as an arena of class struggle differs from the liberal pluralist view because it recognises the existence of fundamental antagonisms between classes that shape the state's role. It also emphasises that political possibilities are rooted in, and limited by, the economic system.

One important aspect of this 'revisionist' view of the state as an arena of class struggle is the consideration of conflict between fractions of capital. For example, high rents from urban land usually benefit the owners of urban property at the expense of industrial capital; so there arises the recurrent possibility of a political alignment between the working class and industrialists, particularly the small business sector, in support of policies for shifting the burden of taxation towards land owners. Intra-class conflicts, according to the more orthodox Marxist view, strengthen the need for the state to act on behalf of the capitalist class as a whole. However, according to this revisionist view, they also open up the possibility for the working class, or sections thereof, to exploit such conflicts in their own interests, thereby gaining more control over the state apparatus. Taking this chain of reasoning to the limit, there arises the possibility of the state being used for the transformation of capitalism into quite different type of economy and society based on socialist principles. This, in essence, is the Fabian socialist perspective that was influential in the early stages of the development of labour parties (which have more recently jettisoned any such socialist ambitions). Even shorn of explicitly socialist goals, the revisionist view regards the state as having the capacity to use its policy instruments as part of a comprehensive program of radical reforms.

A managerial state

What about the internal structures and interests within the state? A third view of the state focuses on the organizations and the interests of the key players within the state apparatus. Again, there are two variations on the general theme, the first emphasizing a 'gatekeeper' role for state and the second seeing the state as a self-serving institution.

The 'gatekeeper' view stresses how the state personnel guard access to public resources from the diverse claimants within the community. To carry out this function requires the government and state employees to act as gatekeepers, in which capacity they have the potential to develop their own ways of working and allocative criteria. It is a view that has resonance in respect of industry and regional policies, for example. State employees carry out the gatekeeper role by saying "yes" to some industries and regions and "no" to others in the allocation of funding. The industry and regional plans that they formulate favor development in some industries and localities and deny it in others. It is a process which is both technical (involving the application of planning techniques), and value-laden (reflecting distinctive values shaped within the state apparatus itself). The state officials are not merely tools of capitalist class interests, not disinterested functionaries, nor just mediators of diverse private interests. Their own identity and interests shape how the state operates.

Pushing this line of reasoning to its limits leads to the view of the state as a self-serving institution, as the 'property' of officials that they control and use for their personal advancement. There were elements of this view in early Marxist writings on the state. It is more fully developed in currents of anarchist thought where the oppressive consequences of the state are regarded as even more problematic than the exploitative consequences of capitalism. Interestingly, this view of the state also has an echo in the writings of right-wing economists such as Milton Friedman and George Stigler (see section 2 of this book) who contend that the expansion of the state has been the product of misguided reformism, frustrating the achievement of goals of economic efficiency and individual freedom. Anarchist and neoliberals make strange bedfellows, it seems. The common element is a libertarian philosophy that is deeply sceptical about the state, if not downright hostile to it. The difference is that, whereas the anarchist perspective generally has a libertarian socialist character, the Friedmanite perspective evaluates the state from a standpoint favoring free-market capitalism.

Conclusion

The various political economic perspectives on the state lead to markedly different forms of analysis and political conclusions. Indeed, this is one of the most controversial areas of debate in political economy. The principal views are summarized in the following table:

The state: Competing perspectives

Analytical focus	Dominant view	Alternative view
Liberal-pluralism	State serving the national interest	State responding incoherently to private interests
Class analysis	State serving capitalist class	State as arena of class struggle
Managerialism	State officials as gatekeepers	State as self-serving institution

This taxonomy and the preceding discussion in this chapter, although quite complex, are not exhaustive. It could be extended, for example, by looking at insights into the sources of state power coming from *post-structuralist* theories. Herbert-Cheshire and Lawrence (2002) argue that Foucault's analysis can be adapted to understand the state, not in terms of its formal structures, but in relation to "a complex network of local power relations ... made up of shifting alliances between individuals and groups, which fracture and re-form according to different issues and interests". The state authorities can, in effect, 'govern at a distance' because citizens 'freely' choose to align their conduct with the *status quo*. Antonio Gramsci, the radical Italian thinker, had previously stressed the importance of 'hegemony' as a process whereby people come to accept the fundamentally exploitative or oppressive system, thereby making the explicit exercise of the coercive power of the state only intermittently necessary. These may be regarded as essentially class-based views, but recognises that the economic dimension of class intersects in complex ways with social position, including gender and ethnicity, and that class consciousness is more the exception than the rule in our dealings with the economy and state.

All political economists recognise that the state is central to the functioning of modern capitalism. However, as we have seen in this chapter, its interpretation remains contentious. The competing perspectives on the state provide a basis for interpreting the experience of particular economic and social policies. Herein lies much of the 'political' in political economy.

Frank Stilwell is Professor of Political Economy, School of Social and Political Sciences, University of Sydney. The State: Competing Perspectives © 1995 Frank Stilwell.

The State and 'The Good Society'
John Kenneth Galbraith

Since the collapse of communism in Eastern Europe and the former Soviet Union, it has been taken for granted in the USA, as also in Canada, Western Europe, Japan and in the emergent industrial countries of the Pacific, that there is economic and social success. This is being much celebrated.

Sadly, in much of the world, and notably in Africa and Asia, deep poverty persists. And we must ask if the situation in the fortunate world is wholly the success that is commonly averred. Should our satisfaction be somewhat tempered? What very specifically should be the economic standards of achievement of the good or even the tolerable economic society? These are questions which, running against the current wave of self-congratulation, I seek to ask. And what can and should be done for improvement – for a good society?

We must begin with the very great change in social and economic structure in the economically advanced lands in modern times. Once all economic and social thought turned on a bilateral economic and social structure. There were capital and labor, the capitalist and the worker. There were also, to be sure, farmers. And intellectuals and others. But capital versus labor, that was the basic dialectic. Marx had an authority here that would have surprised even him.

This is no longer the case in the advance industrial countries. The great political dichotomy – the capitalist and the working masses – has retreated into the shadows. It survives not as reality but as mental commitment. In place of the capitalist there is now the modern great corporate bureaucracy. Not capitalists but managers. The labor movement and the trade union survive but no longer as a strongly combative force on behalf of the denied and deprived. Decimated by the decline or migration of mass-production industry, the union, as often as not, finds itself in tacit alliance with the management for their joint survival. Reference to the class struggle has, indeed, a markedly antique sound.

Politically dominant now are the corporate bureaucracy, the diverse smaller entrepreneurs, the public bureaucracy and the lawyers, physicians, educators, members of the many professions, the cultural elite, as it has been called, and the large pensioned and rentier community. These all lay claim to political influence and power. We have now a new class structure that embraces, on the one hand, the comfortably situated and on the other the large number of lesser income and the impoverished. The latter do the work that makes life pleasant, even tolerable, for what I have elsewhere called "the culture of contentment". The modern equivalent of the one-time industrial proletariat is now an underclass in the service of the numerous and comfortably situated. This underclass does much of the heavy repetitive industrial work that still survives, and its members render the multitude of services that the comfortable community requires. They clean our streets, harvest our fruits and vegetables, collect our garbage. Here in the USA there is a modern reserve army of the unemployed and the poorly employed available for the unpleasant tasks of modern life. It extends on to the poverty-stricken masses in the great cities.

The modern underclass is not active in the political process. Some are excluded for lack of citizenship. Some do not vote because they do not see a sufficient difference between the two political parties. Both of the latter appeal to the more fortunate community, for that is where voice, money and political activism are to be found. We speak much of democracy. But democracy can be an imperfect thing. So it is when the most needful and most vulnerable of people do not participate in the political process and do not have voice and influence. Nor is this situation consistent with a tranquil and civilised life. Those who have no other outlet for political expression may well take to the streets in protest or they escape civilised reality into drugs and crime. That this should be their recourse should surprise no-one.

In the good society there cannot, must not, be a deprived and excluded underclass. Those who heretofore have comprised it must be fully a part of the larger social community. There must be full democratic participation by all, and from this alone can come the sense of community which accepts and even values ethnic and other diversity. Also, as a very practical matter, there will be a much better, much more civilised attitude towards minorities, recent migrants, the unfortunate in general, if it is known that they are politically active. In the USA we have seen a marked improvement in attitudes towards our black minority as its voting power has become evident. But a full participation of the now-excluded will not be brought about by plea or prayer. It requires some very practical, very concrete steps on the part of the modern state.

There is, first, the absolute, inescapable requirement that everyone in the good, even decent society have a basic source of income. And if this is not available from the market system, as now it is called – the word capitalism is no longer politically quite correct – it must come from the state. Nothing, let us never forget, sets a stronger limit on the liberty of a citizen than a total absence of money. In the USA and in lesser measure in the other fortunate lands there is repetitive comment on the moral damage that comes from giving public support to the poor – to those living on welfare. There could be no more convenient doctrine for those who see themselves as paying for such support. With others I wish to see a society in which everyone has an opportunity for useful, remunerative employment. However, where and when that opportunity is absent, an alternative form of income – public support – is an absolute essential. There must similarly be support for those who, from infirmity or family situation, cannot work. There can be no claim to civilised existence when such a safety net is not available. And there should be no condemnation of those who live thereon. Their suffering is already sufficient.

Next, there must be help for those who are seeking escape from the underclass. Social tranquillity is best served by the hope of upward movement, if not for this generation, then for the next. There is no novelty as to what is required here; it is good, effective education, sometimes made more reputable by calling it human investment. The situation in the USA on this matter is far from satisfactory. We have excellent universities, good suburban and private schools for the comfortable class. But many in the underclass in our cities are condemned to an education that perpetuates their dismal economic position, their poverty. And on need only look at the larger world to see the power of this point. There is, over the globe, no well-educated, literate population that is poor; there is no illiterate population that is other than poor.

In the good society there must also be emphasis on the other essential services of the state. This is not a matter to be decided by formula – capitalism or socialism, public ownership or privatization. It is a matter for considered, practical judgment in the particular case.

The market system provides excellently, abundantly, a large range of producer and consumer goods and services. There is no case for change here. Once there was fear of the power endowed by capital and capitalism in the production of such goods. This was central in the classical case for socialism. Now no longer; here in the USA we often worry far more about corporate power. The basic market system and its managerial efforts and achievements the good society accepts.

But there are some things the market system does not do either well or sometimes even badly. These must be the responsibility of the state. Some of the tasks for government action are evident. In no country does the market system provide good low-cost housing. This must everywhere be a public responsibility. Few things are more visibly at odds with the good society than badly housed or homeless people. Health care for the needful is also a public responsibility. No-one can be consigned to continuing poor health, illness or death because of insufficient income.

Essential also are the more conventional services of the state. It must always be in mind that many of these services – public works, parks and recreational facilities, police, libraries, and many others – are more important for, more needed by, the poor than by the affluent. Those who mount the modern attack on the services of government are frequently those who can afford to provide similar services for themselves. Or they accept that we should have clean houses and filthy streets; elegant, expensive if sometimes violent television and poor schools.

In the good society there must also be attention to a range of activities that are beyond the time horizons of the market economy. This is true in the sciences, not excluding medical research. And notably in the arts. The market system, by its nature, invests for relatively short-run return. Much scientific discovery and the development of a strong artistic tradition do not offer early or certain pecuniary return. To support them there remains, pre-eminently, the state.

The most progressive economies of these past years, notably Japan and Germany, have gone beyond military matters, have recognised and strongly supported this function. And some of our most important American achievements of recent generations – the great improvement in agricultural productivity, modern air transport, advanced electronics – have depended heavily on public investment. Success here is a mark of the good and progressive society. So also – a matter we are beginning, if sometimes reluctantly, to recognise – is investment and regulation in the interest of the environment, the protection and improvement of life in its planetary dimension.

There remain two final requirements of the good society. It must have an effectively working economy. And it must be at peace with itself and the world at large. I am inclined to believe that the tendency of the market system to boom and bust is basic, a part of its deeper character and motivation. The good society must deal in a very practical way with the problem of recession and depression, however, caused, and thus alleviate the consequent social dislocation and despair.

A central step is to ensure a more equitable distribution of income than the market system provides of itself. This may have some effect in curbing speculative excess. More important, it will assure a steadier flow of purchasing power in time of recession. The rich have the choice between spending and not spending (or not investing) their income. Those of more moderate income do not. I do not foresee or advocate rigid equality in economic reward. I do urge that a reasonably equitable distribution of income is not only socially good but also economically functional. It is a mark of a good society, and it contributes to economic stability.

The tendency of the modern market economy to periods of despondency and depression must be more specifically addressed. This requires positive government intervention. Prediction and prayer, the instruments of policy in past years, will not serve. Nor is there any economic magic in monetary policy. Its role is much exaggerated, partly because it is politically and administratively convenient to do so. In times of recession governments must move aggressively to employ people, mitigate economic distress. The wealth so created, the distress so relieved, are glowing alternatives to unemployment. When recovery is assured there must then be the discipline that brings restraint and allows the reduction of government expenditure – the deficit.

This is not a wholly popular political design; there are many in the culture of contentment whose income is secure and who do not find recession and poor economic performance particularly uncomfortable. They greatly prefer them to the corrective measures, including government support to the economy. To this position the good economic society can make no concession. The discomfort and social disarray from unemployment and associated deprivation must always be in mind, as also the measures for mitigation. The good society does not allow some of its people to feel useless, superfluous and deprived.

My specification for the good society is not complete. I want, especially in the USA, to see demilitarization. To a distressing degree, the military establishment has become a power in its own right. It decides as to its weapons and force levels, then has the political power, in the Executive and the Congress, that provides the requisite funds in support. If you can decide what you want and then command what pays for it, your authority is complete. Again the imperfect democracy.

From our arms expenditure, as well as from a more equitable tax system, could come the funds for the rescue of the poor, for ensuring a peaceful upward movement of our distressed population. In the good society I wish also to see an effective curb on the arms trade. Nothing is more appalling in our time than the flow of lethal weapons from rich countries to the poor – to countries that obtain arms for the slaughter of their own people and their neighbours but do not have the food to keep their children alive.

This affirms the further obligation of the good society. That is to recognise that its good fortune is not universal – to see that a large part of the human community survives, if does survive, in deep poverty. People are people wherever they live, and the pain from hunger, illness and general deprivation is the same for human beings wherever they suffer it.

There is further issue here. In our time the economically fortunate countries live peacefully together. Modern industry, communications, travel, the arts and entertainment, all lead to a closer association between countries. For this reason the modern advanced economy is inherently transnational. Once capitalism was thought to be the source of international competition and conflict, and the capitalist was thought the parent or progenitor of war. Now no longer. It is poor of the world who destroy each other. That is the tendency of people who have little for which to live.

Religion, alas, also plays a part. If life in this world is deprived and painful, it can be believed that in the next life things will be better. This is a risk that the economically more favoured are less inclined to run. They are more disposed to value life here; they worry that after death they may be left trying to pass through that needle along with the camels. Be this as it may, the lesson is clear: the hope and reality of economic improvement is one of the pacifying influences of our time.

Accordingly, we in the fortunate countries must have strongly and effectively in mind those who live in the reverse of our well-being. And out of the resources and experience that so favour us we must extend help. Conscience cannot allow us to ignore the poor either at home or abroad – to be less poor than concerned, less than generous. And it is thus, over time, that we will help to assure for others and for ourselves a better, more peaceful world.

Let us not rest in satisfaction over what we have accomplished. Let us not rest in comfort in the politics of the comfortable. Let us see how great is the task that remains and let us on that now begin.

John Kenneth Galbraith was Paul M. Warburg Emeritus Professor of Economics, Harvard University. The Good Society © 1995 John Kenneth Galbraith.

Transforming the Public Sector
Michael Johnson

The public sector played a key role in the formulation and implementation of macroeconomic and microeconomic policy in Australia after 1945. From the late 1970s, its effectiveness in this role was progressively undermined until the global financial crisis that began in 2007 reversed this trend. The crisis led to new and widespread government intervention to prop up the private sector, directly and indirectly, and stimulate the economy in countries like the United States, Britain and Australia. Intervention partly took the form of an active fiscal policy that is now forcing a re-evaluation of the importance of public spending in macroeconomic policy and infrastructure provision (Nevile 2009). It has also reinforced the awareness of the value of creating an effective public sector to implement public policy.

Between World War II and the end of the 1970s, the emphasis was on the developmental role of the state and the application of Keynesian economic ideas to stabilize and grow the economy. Three aspects of this view of the public sector in that earlier period were distinctive. Firstly, public expenditure was seen as a key contributor to macroeconomic economic growth, stimulating investment and aggregate demand to secure increases in output, rising incomes, and reasonably full employment (Kriesler 2009). Secondly, government budgets were managed to play an important role in the stabilization of an otherwise uneven economic growth path, in combination with administered interest rate adjustments and exchange rate policies. Thirdly, governments sought efficiency and equity through a combination of microeconomic industry policies to enhance productivity growth, and incomes policies to control cost increases and redistribute income. Finally, governments played the central role in building the infrastructure and services required to build the stock of human capital and physical infrastructure to support and sustain economic development and an improvement in living standards over the longer term.

All this changed quickly in the 1980s. The activity of the public sector was transformed as a result of the systematic application of neo-classical economic principles, including the theory of public choice. The public sector's role in economic development was progressively neutralized as a result of restructuring the institutions of government and the processes employed to achieve government objectives. The influence of neoliberalism, the political expression of the view that the role of the government in the economy should be minimal and the role of the public sector limited (Woodward 2005: 33), became pervasive until deficits in the supply of public services that emerged in the 1990s and the global financial crisis (GFC) that began in 2007 highlighted the errors in this strategy.

At the core of the neoliberal approach remains the fundamental belief of key policy makers, heavily influenced by the business sector, that the organizing principles for the public sector should be based primarily on the market efficiency propositions of neoclassical economics and on the private business models of organisation. The dominant emphasis in reform derived from this approach has been on applying the principles of 'public choice' at the political level, and the principles of 'competitive commodity markets' and the 'business enterprise' at the administrative level. The 'reforms' derived from the analytical elements of neoclassical microeconomics (supply, demand, choice, competition and market clearing) have been progressively transferred into the internal operations of government (Johnson and Guthrie 1993). The changes led to the re-structuring of public organizations, and changes to the 'mix' of goods, services and regulatory functions that governments provide. The 'reforms' also reinforced the 'openness' of the domestic economy to the global economy and contributed to the need for a period of Keynesian economic stimulus and new forms of government intervention, in the Australian financial sector in particular, when the GFC unfolded in 2007.

At the macroeconomic level, the focus of the public sector reforms that gathered pace after the election of a Labor Government in 1983 was on limiting the impact of government on the economy through tighter controls on government expenditure, the adoption of debt reduction targets, commitments to balanced or surplus budgets, and the generation of 'efficiency dividends' from government agencies. Similar goals were sought on the income side of government budgets through changes to the tax system, designed to reduce the tax paid by corporations and high-income earners, and a switch in the tax burden to consumers through a widening of the consumption tax base when the Commonwealth Government introduced a value-added goods and services tax (GST) in 2000. These reforms, contrary to agreements made at the time, led to new difficulties in delivering public services like public education and health by the Australian states, because their tax base was reduced to make way for the reforms. At the microeconomic level, this process has also seen continuing restructuring of the administrative and service delivery organizations within the public sector, and integrating substantial parts of them into the private sector.

These changes impact at a number of different levels. The first of these was the separation, through legislation to reinforce their independence, of some agencies dealing with national economic management, such as the Reserve Bank of Australia, and the establishment of independent boards for some regulatory agencies, like the National Competition Council (NCC). This process has separated these agencies from the direct control of central government departments and their ministers who are responsible to parliaments. At the Commonwealth Government level, the NCC and its implementation agency, the Australian Consumer and Competition Commission (ACCC), regulate competition in the private sector and increasingly in the wider public sector, at arms length from governments (see Michael 2006; Woodward 2005). In undertaking these functions they reinforce the pressures to apply market principles to the public sector by enforcing 'competitive neutrality' for all activities that potentially overlap between the public and private sectors. These regulatory bodies have also reinforced tendencies towards increasing corporatisation and privatisation of public sector activities, since the detailed regulation is based on private sector principles of markets, accounting and pricing which are being extended to increasing numbers of public sector activities.

The second aspect of restructuring taking place within the agencies of government is the break up of 'vertical' connections between the management and service delivery functions of government, and the 'horizontal' separation into programs of distinctive management activities and services within government departments. These public sector reform initiatives began in the mid-1980s, setting out to better identify objectives, improve services, contain costs and rationalize the organizations delivering them. These goals were linked to the adoption of new management technologies to form a new management paradigm (Johnson 2001) called New Public Management (NPM). This paradigm was marketed as 'new', but was in fact an approach and style derived from older principles based on a neo-classical competitive market model. The steps adopted were to improve product focus, to open public sector activities to competition, and to contract them out to the private sector where possible. An example was the opening up of the Commonwealth (un)employment programs to private sector competition, with the result that they are now largely provided by the private sector, including the profit seeking arms of 'not-for-profit' organizations like the Salvation Army (see Considine 2001). The reform elements making up NPM continue to be implemented, but NPM as a management 'style' has been discredited (see Dibben, *et al.* 2004) and has been replaced by new styles like 'egovernment' and 'networked' governance that have their own critics (see Dunleavy *et al.* 2006).

The result of these changes has been the progressive 'hollowing out' of the public sector. Instead of public sector expenditures being spent on producing and delivering public services directly to the community, many have become 'pass through' transfer payments to pay for private enterprises contracted to provide services to citizen-consumers. How much of government expenditure is of this form is not precisely known because governments do not systematically report on it, other than some reporting on the use of consultants in the annual reports of government agencies. What is not in doubt, however, is that increasing amounts of public sector services and their management are being undertaken by private sector product and service suppliers. Whether there is a positive impact in terms of reduced costs and increased efficiency of service delivery is less certain. Major costs have been incurred and losses have been made by the Commonwealth Government in attempting to outsource, for example, government IT programs (see Quiggin 1996). The Commonwealth's home insulation program (discontinued in 2010), introduced as a fiscal stimulus program to counter the recessionary effects of the GFC by supporting the private sector, is another example of both the success and failure of this type of activity (see Commonwealth Auditor General 2010). The program generated employment and economic growth at a critical time, but at the cost of some of the private sector insulation installers' lives because of the poor quality of both public sector management and occupational health and safety standards in some of the private sector businesses that were contracted to do the installations. There were also complex questions about ministerial culpability for these failures in relation to the program (see Mulgan 2006).

As a consequence of contracting-out and internal efficiency programs, Commonwealth public sector employment levels have fallen (with a loss of expertise and memory as exhibited in the case of the recent insulation program), but levels of expenditure since the turn of the century have not. The changes in the public-private mix have also affected the government's budget flexibility by 'locking in' expenditure for the private provision programs over longer periods and the 'locking out' the public provision of competing services in others.

The third dimension of structural change taking place is the progressive dis-establishment of those parts of government departments providing services similar to private sector ones and the privatization of government business enterprises. This ongoing activity was initially designed to improve economic efficiency, support the development of the private sector, increase the community's capital 'stake' in it, and retire public debt. The case for so doing was reinforced by the 'twin deficits' theory – with its now discredited claim that public sector budget deficits cause the nation to have a higher external trade deficit. The steps in this program that adopted a private business model in public organisations included, initially, establishing all the elements of private market institutions inside the public entities delivering marketed goods and services. These included: changing the capital structure of organizations, establishing corporations with boards of directors, shedding social services, or just selling the activities to a private sector organization.

The privatization process has been carried out in a wide variety of forms such as: sales of public enterprises, contracting out and in, and shedding activities (Walker and Walker 2000, 2010; Johnson 2008). Privatisation increased the exposure of the Australian economy to the cost of the transactions and the forces of international competition; and this is one factor that helps explain why public sector expenditure in the medium term did not fall *in aggregate terms* at any level of government in the near decade and a half to 2008. Then the effects of the GFC began to be felt in some areas, e.g. local governments forced to curtail their expenditures because they had placed their capital in insecure investments. Public expenditure levels generally stayed up, though, despite the proponents of the reforms claiming that the benefits of the lower costs of services would eventually accrue to offset the loss of revenue from these services to governments. There is also the unknown quantum of costs to all Australia's governments and taxpayers resulting from the growth in public sector 'tax expenditures' – those forms of tax relief (together with a wide array of other project incentives) given to induce new private sector investments into areas like infrastructure.

Program delivery has also been affected by the introduction of microeconomic reform and NPM. There have been significant changes to the composition of the public sector 'mix' of the services delivered and the ways in which they are delivered. The focus on internal reforms has been on establishing a distinct product and program focus for each service delivered. This has created difficulties, in addition to those that normally arise in a federal system where different tiers and agencies of government are involved, of coordinating and delivering an appropriate range and consistency of services across the country. The 'bundling' of services by a mix of private and public providers in a way that meets the needs of those requiring multiple services, like the aged or those reliant on children's services, is more difficult. The process of introducing market institutions has transferred many generic services to private sector providers through privatization and contracting, but some have been retained and others have been transferred back to the public sector because their costs could not be recovered or because profits could not be earned by the private sector. A case in point has been the Port Macquarie Hospital in New South Wales. In general, the mix of public and private providers of public services has made managing those services even more complex and challenging. The situation has been made more complex as the Commonwealth Government, seeking to address a shortage of essential services like housing, health and education, has taken control of these areas and injected more resources into them than state governments can provide.

Accountability and transparency are further problems. The introduction of market institutions into the public sector has created a major obstacle to maintaining the necessary accountability and transparency expected in a democratic country. The traditional institutions of governance, such as the political institutions, legal frameworks, administrative rules and auditors, continue to cover the bulk of the public sector. However, the work of these institutions is made more difficult as the 'veil' of commercial secrecy is pulled over an ever-increasing share of public sector activity (see Johnson 2007). At the same time, the creation of independent policy agencies and the process of privatization and contracting-out markedly shift the responsibility for the setting of economic policy at the macro and micro levels. The effects are to neutralize the economic role and effectiveness of the public sector, and to entrench the influence of key business interest groups in policy-making.

Does all this indicate significantly new directions for the public sector in Australia? As in other developed OECD countries, the public sector has been changing its *modus operandi*, if not its size, since the 1980s. The results are still becoming apparent. Governments at local, regional, and the central level have been fundamentally reorganized in terms of their goals, structures and functions. While public expenditures in Australia and elsewhere have continued to grow, this growth has been partly necessary to offset the social costs of the changes taking place within the public sector. Underlying the changes is the adoption of a different paradigm for guiding the objective-setting and management of the public sector, transforming the way that policy makers see the role of government and how its role is carried out. The influence of the neoclassical economic paradigm, which is at the core of the public sector reforms of the last decade, has been linked to the claim that the role of the public sector in developed countries should be 'steering' not 'rowing' the economy (Osborne and Gaebler 1992). This metaphor has proved misplaced because steering and rowing are in fact usually integrated activities – the better rowers steer while rowing. The steering capacity is being lost by the public sector, despite claims to the contrary by Michael Keating, the former head of the Commonwealth Department of Prime Minister and Cabinet (Keating 2004).

The short-term benefits of the public sector reform program have been some efficiencies generated in service delivery for regulated services and a reduction in public debt. However, the reductions in public debt and the adoption by Commonwealth and state governments of balanced budget rules, recently resurrected after being suspended in 2008 for the GFC, has created a problem in at least two key areas of Australian macroeconomic policy. Firstly, the reduction in debt has taken place at the expense of the level of the public investment, thereby also reducing the 'crowding in' of private investment that would lift the overall growth rates of output and employment and the community's amenities and welfare (Aschauer 1989a). There is no economically logical reason why governments with significant assets cannot do what households and private businesses do – borrow to grow – while recognizing that the amount and its servicing costs must be managed appropriately.

Secondly, the reduction in public debt has posed questions about the capacity of the relevant regulatory institutions, like the Reserve Bank, to ensure the stability of interest rates in the long term. This problem was temporarily solved by the issue of public debt to fund the fiscal stimulus during the GFC, but trying to repay the debt in a short period reduces the governmental capacity to regulate output and prices in future. Responding to this situation when it emerged before the onset of the GFC, the Commonwealth Treasury established a national private equities fund, the Future Fund, in 2006. This was capitalized with the proceeds of privatizations, with the goal of delivering a return that would act as a marker for setting interest rates. It was envisaged that this would replace the government bond rate – the interest rate used for raising funds to finance the national debt – that had declined in significance as public debt fell. The Future Fund has provided valuable capital for use in public investment. However, a much better long-term solution would be a judicious increase in public borrowing to directly fund investment in social and economic infrastructure so as to generate an increase in employment, output and living standards in Australia (Johnson 1995, 2001; Sardoni and Palazzi 2000; Nevile 2009). That strategy is not as viable in the medium term in other countries, like Britain and the United States, where governments have taken over failing financial institutions and provided capital to the private sector (Lucarelli 2008) to increase the level of sovereign debt, much of which must now be paid by taxpayers. In Australia, a rapid short-term increase in Commonwealth public debt was very effectively engineered to fund counter-cyclical spending to offset the impact of the GFC, reduce increases in unemployment, and counter the trend towards negative growth.

In summary, the application of neoclassical market ideas to the institutions of the state has ostensibly been directed at achieving microeconomic efficiencies in the agencies of government. In practice it has involved the transfer of public sector activity to the private sector and, to a lesser extent, to the 'not-for-profit' sector. This has led to the creation of what some are now calling the 'service' state (Wanna, Butcher and Freyens 2010: 16). The political economic cost, despite the national economic growth achieved since the mid-1990's, has been a loss of public sector 'steering' capacity at the micro and macro level that was only partially recovered through the responses to the global financial crisis. The costs of the past organizational reforms, and the resurrection of balanced budget rules and debt reduction targets as the GFC has moved into a new phase, still leaves a critical and unnecessary shortage of services like health and public transport services. These problems can only be reversed in the long term by the adoption of a more comprehensive role for the public sector in the economy based on the way the economy really works.

Michael Johnson is Associate Professor, School of Social Sciences and International Studies, University of New South Wales. Transforming the Public Sector © 2011 Michael Johnson.

CURRENT POLICY ISSUES

We turn now to specific aspects of economic policy. In practice, this means focusing on the policies of particular governments at particular times, trying to discern the principles embodied in those policies, evaluating them and identifying alternatives. There are both analytical and prescriptive elements here. The analytical aspect involves identifying the economic ideologies, interests and political practices that shape policy. The prescriptive element involves critique and the advocacy of alternatives which better serve the same objective or which serve more worthy objectives. Therein lies much scope for personal judgment.

In discussing contemporary policy challenges, there is also an essential element of strategic thinking, of anticipating trends, and of considering political and economic opportunities. This raises the big issues of social change. Can reform achieve a more productive, sustainable or equitable economy? Our earlier exploration of competing currents in political economy necessarily leaves this question open to alternative interpretations.

This section includes articles that illustrate the judgments involved in the analysis of policy issues in contemporary Australia. The first article, by John Quiggin, looks at desirable reforms to the financial system in the wake of the global financial crisis. John Phillimore then puts a case for policies to develop a 'high road' to economic development, drawing on ideas derived from Joseph Schumpeter, an economist who does not fit neatly into the main schools of thought we have previously identified. Lynne Chester considers the looming energy crisis, its policy underpinnings and possible responses. Alan Morris looks at the housing crisis and housing policies. George Argyrous considers what government budgetary policy can achieve and reveals the fallacies that underpin the current fetishism with budget surpluses. Michael Johnson looks at the reasons for more focus on infrastructure policies. Jon Altman then discusses policies for policy alleviation in remote Indigenous communities, emphasising the need for recognition of the mix of economic activities pursued there. Finally, turning to the conditions of labour, John Buchanan and his colleagues explore the changing nature of employment and some principles that could underpin policies to improve the character of working life.

These articles do not cover all the important areas of political economic policy. Others have been considered earlier in the book, especially when dealing with alternative economic perspectives – green, feminist, developmental and behavioral. The articles in this section are invitations to on-going debates about public policy. They generally assume a key role for the state in redirecting capitalist economic development at the national level. In the terminology introduced by Evan Jones earlier in the book, they are all explorations of 'strategic intervention.' In various ways they also reflect the influence of the competing currents of economic thought set out in this volume. They are a sharp reminder that the differences between competing schools of economic thought, as surveyed in the preceding pages, are not mere academic exercises. How we analyse economic phenomena has implications for public policy and for possibilities of social progress.

For more on Australian public policies, see the website of the Centre for Policy Development <www.cpd.org.au>. For an introduction to a critical perspective on the 'economic rationalist' approach to policy, see Lindy Edwards, *How to Argue With an Economist*, Cambridge University Press, Melbourne, 2007. Articles on Australian policy issues regularly appear in the *Journal of Australian Political Economy*, *Labour and Industry*, *Economic and Labour Relations Review*, and in the *Journal of Economic and Social Policy*.

Financial Regulation After The Crisis
John Quiggin

One of the most striking developments of the late twentieth century was the explosion in the volume, speed and complexity of international financial transactions, and the resulting breakdown of effective regulatory control over the global financial system. Equally striking has been how quickly this process has more recently gone into reverse.

Transactions in the global foreign exchange market, once confined to financing trade flows, peaked at around $4 trillion per day in mid-2008. At that pace, two days of foreign exchange trading would be sufficient to finance an entire year's trade flows. The growth of private credit reached an annualised rate of $10 trillion at the same time.

The market collapsed in the crisis of late 2008. According to the International Monetary Fund's *Global Financial Stability Report Market Update* (January 2009), private sector credit growth fell by 90 percent, and 'Emerging bond markets virtually shut down for a period of time in the fourth quarter'.

Although rescue measures by governments have restored credit flows, the system remains weak and unstable. The challenge facing governments and regulators will be to construct a new financial system and a regulatory architecture strong enough to prevent a recurrence of the bubble and meltdown that has largely destroyed the existing unregulated system.

The essential features of a system of financial regulation to support market stability and prevent another meltdown are:

- linking and integrating national financial systems to produce a sustainable international financial architecture;
- decoupling exchange rates from the vicissitudes of financial markets – through the introduction of the Tobin tax;
- guaranteeing and regulating the banks;
- regulating innovation; and
- introducing an effective ratings system.

A new financial architecture

The idea of a 'global financial architecture' is both misleading and unattainable. The keystone for any financial architecture is the institution that acts as lender of last resort for others. This function is, and is likely to remain, one undertaken by national governments and their central banks. It follows that there can be no global financial architecture. Rather, national systems of financial regulation must be linked and integrated to produce a sustainable international financial architecture. To achieve this, there must be no 'offshore' financial system, outside the agreements that govern the international financial architecture, but nevertheless allowed to transact with institutions inside the system. This issue has already arisen in relation to international tax avoidance and evasion, and will arise in an even more acute form in relation to the Tobin tax, discussed below.

Fortunately, the OECD has already developed a strategy to address tax avoidance that will serve as a model for financial regulation. The Financial Stability Board, established as part of the response to the global financial crisis, has already indicated that the tax haven model will be applied to 'regulatory havens' offering lax financial regulation. As with taxation, the process will undoubtedly be slow, but the mechanisms are in place to ensure that evasion of financial regulation through the use of offshore transactions can be prevented.

The Tobin tax

The long-advocated and long-resisted idea of a small tax on financial transactions, commonly called a Tobin tax, is the most promising option for ensuring that exchange rate movements reflect the economic fundamentals of trade and long-term capital flows, rather than the vicissitudes of financial markets. In its simplest version, though not necessarily the most practical, the tax would be applied to all exchanges of one currency into another, and would be collected by an international authority.

A tax at a rate of 0.1 percent would be insignificant in relation to the transaction costs associated with international trade or long-term investments. On the other hand, daily transactions of $3 trillion would yield revenue of $30 billion per day, or nearly $1 trillion per year. Since this amount exceeds the total profits of the financial sector (profits that are likely to be much smaller in future), an effective Tobin tax would imply a drastic reduction in the volume of short-term financial flows. It follows that the revenue from a Tobin tax, while significant, would not be sufficient to replace the main existing sources of taxation, such as income tax.

The large literature on Tobin taxes has identified two significant problems with the simple proposal for a tax on international financial transactions.

First, it is possible to replicate spot transactions on foreign exchange markets with combinations of forward, futures and swap transactions. To make a Tobin tax effective, it would have to be applied to all financial transactions, including domestic transactions. During the bubble era, when the few remaining taxes on domestic financial transactions were being scrapped to facilitate the growth of the financial sector, this was seen as a fatal objection. It has become apparent, however, that the destabilising effects of explosive growth in the volume of financial transactions are much the same, whether the transactions are domestic or international.

The fact that a Tobin tax on international financial transactions would be integrated with taxes on domestic transactions suggests that, in all probability, revenue would be collected and retained by national governments. However, the suggestion that at least some of the revenue should be used to fund global projects, such as the international development goals of UNCTAD, remains worthy of consideration.

The second problem is that the tax would require global co-operation, since otherwise financial market activity would migrate to jurisdictions that did not apply the tax. Although this will remain a problem in the post-crisis world, it is likely to be less severe than indicated by earlier discussions because of the smaller number of separate jurisdictions that would need to agree, following the emergence of the euro. It seems inevitable that most remaining European currencies, with the possible exception of the British pound, will disappear in the wake of the crisis, and that a Europe-wide regulatory system will emerge.

To address the problem of 'offshore' financial centres, such as Caribbean island states, a Tobin tax on transactions among complying jurisdictions may have to be supplemented by a punitive tax, at a rate of, say 10 percent, on transactions with non-compliant jurisdictions. This would effectively ensure that non-compliant jurisdictions were excluded from global financial markets, though the penalty would be modest as regards trade and long-term investment flows.

Regulating the banks: Guarantees, regulation or narrow banking

The core of financial regulation is the existence of a (partial or total) guarantee that bank depositors who exercise ordinary prudence will not lose their money. Until October 2008, the guarantee system in Australia was carefully ambiguous. Governments and the Reserve Bank implicitly assured both the general public and wholesale lenders that our major banks were completely safe, while simultaneously denying that their liabilities were guaranteed. As was both predictable and predicted, the contradictions in this stance were exposed the first time the system faced a serious crisis. The result was the unlimited guarantee Australia currently has.

We must now consider whether to maintain, modify or withdraw the guarantee. Whatever we do, the crucial issue that has not been faced so far is that publicly-guaranteed institutions require closer regulation than is consistent with policies of financial deregulation.

So, there are three policy options available.

1. The first is the maintenance of the existing guarantee, and a comprehensive re-regulation of the system. This would not mean a return to the system that prevailed before the 1970s (no such return is ever possible), but it would require direct control over the allowable range of products, the setting of interest rates, fees and charges, and the allocation of lending between sectors of the economy.
2. Current government rhetoric suggests the desire to return to something like the old system, with deposit guarantees being withdrawn once the crisis is over. But clearly, we cannot go back to the old ambiguity. If the guarantee is withdrawn, this will be a clear statement to depositors that they must make their own judgements about the safety of their money. It was in this context that the idea of a publicly-owned and publicly guaranteed savings bank was suggested.
3. The third option, in some ways a compromise, is that of narrow banking, in which publicly guaranteed banks stick to a tightly regulated range of well-understood activities. This allows for a completely separate set of financial institutions, of which stock markets are the exemplar, where government guarantees are ruled out in advance. These would offer higher returns but no possibility of transferring risk to the public. This is my preferred option.

Narrow banking

Post-crisis financial regulation should begin with a clearly defined set of institutions (such as banks and insurance companies) offering a set of well-tested financial instruments with explicit public guarantees for clients, and a public guarantee of solvency, with nationalisation as a last-resort option. Financial innovations must be treated with caution, and allowed only on the basis of a clear understanding of their effects on systemic risk.

In this context, it is crucial to maintain sharp boundaries between publicly guaranteed institutions and unprotected financial institutions, such as hedge funds, finance companies, stockbroking firms and mutual funds. Institutions in the latter category must not be allowed to present a threat of systemic failure that might precipitate a public sector rescue, whether direct (as in the global financial crisis) or indirect (as in the 1998 bailout of Long Term Capital Management). A number of measures are required to ensure this:

- Ownership links between protected and unprotected financial institutions must be absolutely prohibited, to avoid the risk that failure of an unregulated subsidiary will necessitate a rescue of the parent, or that an unregulated parent could seek to expose a bank subsidiary to excessive risk. Long before the latest crisis, these dangers were illustrated by Australian experience with bank-owned finance companies, most notably the rescue, by the Reserve Bank, of the Bank of Adelaide in the 1970s.
- Banks should not market unregulated financial products such as share investments and hedge funds.
- The provision of bank credit to unregulated financial enterprises should be limited to levels that ensure that even large-scale failure in this sector cannot threaten the solvency of the regulated system.

In the resulting system of 'narrow banking', the financial sector would become, in effect, an infrastructure service, like electricity or telecommunications. While either public or private enterprises might undertake the provision of financial services, governments would accept a clear responsibility for the stability of the financial infrastructure.

Financial innovation

The prevailing rule has been to allow, and indeed encourage, financial innovations unless they can be shown to represent a threat to financial stability. With an unlimited public guarantee for the liabilities of large financial institutions, this rule is a guaranteed, and proven, recipe for disaster, offering huge rewards to any innovation that increases both risks (ultimately borne by the public) and returns (captured by the innovators). There must be a reversal of the burden of proof in relation to financial innovation.

The process of financial innovation, involving either the creation of new financial instruments or the design of new financial strategies for firms (often termed 'financial engineering') was, a central feature of the era of market liberalism. The growth of finance has been almost unstoppable. Seemingly major financial crises like the stock market crash of 1987 or the NASDAQ crash of 2000 stimulated the development of yet more innovative responses. Even the exposure of spectacular fraud at the Enron Corporation, which had been nominated by Fortune magazine as 'America's most innovative' for six years in succession, did little to dent faith in the desirability of innovation.

It is now clear that unrestricted financial innovation played a major role in the advent of the financial crisis by facilitating the growth of unsound lending and by undermining systems of regulation. There is an inherent inconsistency between unrestricted financial innovation and a regulatory system aimed at preventing the failure of financial systems or at insuring market participants against such failures. Guarantees create 'moral hazard' by allowing financial institutions to capture the benefits of risky investments, while shifting some or all of the losses to government-backed insurance pools.

Moral hazard can only be offset by the design of regulatory mechanisms that discourage excessive risk-taking. But, as the literature on mechanism design has shown, the effectiveness of such mechanisms depends on the existence of stable relationships between the observable variables that are the subject of regulation and the risk allocation that generates them. Financial innovation changes the relationship. In the presence of moral hazard, therefore, there is an incentive to introduce innovations that increase the underlying level of risk while leaving regulatory measures of risk unchanged. It follows that the only sustainable approach to financial innovation is one in which proposed innovations are introduced only after the implementation of necessary changes to regulatory requirements and risk measures. If reliable risk measures cannot be computed, the associated innovations should not be permitted.

A public ratings system: Capital adequacy, transparency and risk assessment

Another important regulatory adjustment will be the end of the system by which prudential regulation has been, in effect, outsourced to ratings agencies such as Standard & Poor's and Moody's. Agency ratings have been enshrined in regulation, for example through official investment guidelines that require regulated entities to invest in assets with a high rating (AAA in some cases, investment grade in others) or provide those responsible for making bad investment decisions with a 'safe harbour' against claims of negligence if the assets in question carried a high rating. For these purposes at least, an international, publicly-backed non-profit system of assessing and rating investments is required.

Conclusion

The temptation to put off until calmer times questions about our financial vulnerability has proved irresistible so far. Looking at the current global scene, however, it seems unlikely that economic calm will return any time soon. A careful examination of the vulnerabilities in our financial system is an urgent task for Australia and the world.

John Quiggin is Professor and Australian Research Council Federation Fellow, University of Queensland.

Industry and Innovation:
Neo-Schumpeterian Economics
John Phillimore

In the 1990s, there was much discussion about the prospects of a 'third way' situated between traditional social democracy and a rejuvenated neoliberalism. Spearheaded by the Blair Labour Government in Britain, the 'third way' aimed to refashion the welfare state and its delivery of health, education and social services.

The 'third way' was, however, notably silent on macroeconomic, industry and labour market policy. In these spheres, neoliberal orthodoxy was virtually unchallenged. Fiscal restraint, financial and product market deregulation, lower corporate taxation, less progressive income tax scales, privatisation, reduced union power and increased labour flexibility were the basic underlying governing principles throughout the industrial world. Only with the onset of the global financial crisis (GFC) in 2008-9 was there a return to more interventionist governments.

However, the basic structure and philosophy of policymaking have not fundamentally changed. There appears to be little appetite among governments for active (as opposed to rescue-based) re-nationalisation, large public sector deficits are already leading to severe cutbacks to public expenditure and welfare programs in many countries, and the extent of re-regulation in the financial sector has been strictly limited. Globalisation has made 'go-it-alone' Keynesianism extremely difficult. In many respects, the neoliberal regime remains untouched.

The absence of a sustained challenge to neoclassical economic orthodoxy is a major problem for progressive politics in general. An important part of the Left's optimism and strength in the post-war boom was its possession of a seemingly coherent economic view of the world, which offered guidance on how to act in a variety of circumstances (e.g. keep up aggregate demand in the face of impending recessions through increased public expenditure, support unions and higher wages). Keynesian policies helped form the basis of a coherent and sustainable political coalition: trade unions, the public sector, welfare recipients. Neoclassical economic theory played a similar role from the early 1980s – it provided policy-makers with ready-made answers (not solutions) to problems in almost every policy area (i.e. promote markets, introduce competition, reduce public expenditure), while also having clear benefits for certain interest groups. With the Keynesian revival appearing to be stillborn – or at best narrow in application – in the aftermath of the GFC, progressive politics is yet to find a coherent alternative economic guidance mechanism.

However, all is not lost. Just as a viable political coalition was once built around Keynesian economic policy, it may be possible for such a coalition to be formed around an economic approach associated with the legacy of Joseph Schumpeter. The main focus of neo-Schumpeterian economics (NSE), though, is not on aggregate demand (as with the old Left), or on competition and free markets (as with the new Right), but rather "the innovation-driven development of economic systems" (Hanusch and Pyka 2007: 4).

? Political economy of coalition?

Schumpeter and the economics of 'creative destruction'

Schumpeter's main concern as an economist was the process of capitalist growth and development (Schumpeter 1934). Neo-classical economics, as a theory of equilibrium, did not really have a theory of economic growth, or of innovation and technical change. Schumpeter, by contrast, saw these as the central elements of the capitalist system and the main challenge for economic theory to explain. There is not space here for a detailed analysis or description of Schumpeter's economic theory (see Freeman 1994). However, several key ideas deriving from his work have helped form the basic principles underlying neo-Schumpeterian economics.

Perhaps the most significant was Schumpeter's recognition of the crucial role which innovation (often, but not always, the product of scientific and technological advance) played in economic growth and the development of capitalism. Innovation – in products, processes, work organisation, finance and markets – enabled entrepreneurs to secure monopoly profits, at least temporarily. The search for such profits was the main cause of the process of 'creative destruction' that Schumpeter saw as endemic to capitalism. Creative destruction – the replacement of products and processes (and the firms associated with them) by other, invariably superior products and techniques – propelled capitalist growth, primarily through the imitation and diffusion of innovations and through the efforts of entrepreneurs to improve on them in order to secure a share of the newly created or altered market. Competition was crucial to the process, but it was competition between entrepreneurs aiming at securing monopoly profits (or a share of them), not competition in the neoclassical sense of price-based competition in perfectly competitive markets. Indeed, Schumpeter argued in his later work that innovation was increasingly centred on oligopolistic markets which enabled large firms to earn sufficient profits to invest in R&D and market development and thereby 'routinise' innovation, at least to some extent (Schumpeter 1942: 132-34).

Schumpeter also held that the interaction between innovation and competition gave rise to fluctuations in economic growth that recurred over time, thus providing a link to theories of 'long waves' of capitalist developed by Kondratiev and others (Freeman and Louca 2001). This link between the micro dynamics of innovation in firms and their macro implications is an important strand that has been taken up by Schumpeter's followers (e.g. Perez 2010).

See "business cycle"

Neo-Schumpeterian economics: Basic tenets

So what are the key principles of neo-Schumpeterian economics? The first thing to note is that NSE builds on but does not blindly follow Schumpeter's insights. For example, there is a long-standing debate within NSE about Schumpeter's view that large firms and oligopolistic markets are more conducive to innovation than small firms and competitive markets. Schumpeter also focused mainly on radical innovation, and had less to say about incremental innovation and the important role that the diffusion of innovation plays in generating economic growth. In addition, Schumpeter tended to treat technology and social institutions as exogenous to the economy, focusing more on their impact on the wider economy. By contrast, NSE places the generation and diffusion of innovation and technology at its heart – and sees institutions as crucial to these processes. Finally, many authors writing in the NSE tradition write from a social democratic perspective, in contrast to Schumpeter's own more conservative political outlook.

Rather than give a comprehensive account of NSE or the innovation literature here (see Dodgson and Gann 2010; Fagerberg et al. 2005; Freeman and Soete 1998; Hanusch and Pyka 2007), the main features can be summarised as follows:

- First, innovation is best understood as a *system* in which innovative firms operate 'in the context of the institutions, government policies, competitors, suppliers, customers, value systems, and social and cultural practices which determine their opportunities' (DIST 1995: 1). These systemic features constitute the 'selection environment' in which firms find themselves and evolve (Marceau *et al.* 1997: ES.5).

- These systems of innovation have both geographic and industry features, and so both sectoral and regional innovation systems can be detected, analysed and potentially influenced through policy (Carlsson 2007).

- As the OECD notes, 'understanding the linkages among the actors involved in innovation is the key to improving technological performance' (OECD 1997: 9). In fact, the linkages and flows within the system are as important as the actors themselves.

- Innovation often occurs in clusters rather than in 'lone' firms, and involves much more than producers. For example, the role of large and demanding users is crucial in many clusters – retailers for the clothing industry, hospitals for the scientific equipment industry, etc. (Porter 1990; Marceau 1996).

- National systems of innovation are extremely significant, despite globalisation, since it is national institutions, values and culture which govern the behaviour of many of the actors and the quality and extent of linkages between them (DIST 1995; Edquist 1997; Marceau *et al.* 1997; Lundvall 1992; Nelson 1993; OECD 1997).

- The institutional basis of the innovation system means that its functioning 'is limited by past practices and existing industrial structures' (Marceau *et al.* 1997: ES.5). In other words, innovation is to a large extent path-dependent, both at the firm and the national level. Consequently, 'countries specialise technologically and seem not to converge as much as has often been thought' (Marceau *et al.* 1997: ES.5).

- Knowledge is a crucial factor of production. Accessing and using knowledge in commercially successful ways requires the development of 'complementary assets' such as management skills, marketing and distribution channels, manufacturing facilities, good labour relations, etc. in order to fully exploit the knowledge gained (Marceau *et al.* 1997: ES.6);

- Firms and countries tend to respond to changing patterns of world demand either through technology/innovation development or through wage and exchange rate adjustments (Marceau *et al.* 1997: ES.6).

- In contrast to neoclassical economics' emphasis on the micro world of representative households and firms, NSE focuses on structural and qualitative changes at the meso (i.e. industry dynamics) level, which are themselves propelled by innovation, learning and entrepreneurship at the firm level and subsequently determine to a great extent growth and competitiveness at a macro level (Harnusch and Pyka 2007).

- Finally, innovations vary by type and significance. Innovation occurs in processes and in products. It can also be incremental or radical (Freeman and Soete 1998). Some innovations – and in particular some technologies – are of such a radical nature that they spawn whole new branches of industry (and destroy others), and impact significantly on the economy, employment and society at large. This in turn affects the direction, speed and shape of economic growth and trade (Perez 2010).

Policy implications

The policy implications of NSE are not as clear-cut as in neoclassical economics, partly because the institutional and historical approach which NSE adopts necessarily means that policy preferences will be determined to a large extent by the specific circumstances and histories of the companies, industries and countries concerned. There is no one policy that can fit all circumstances. Nevertheless we can list some broad principles of NSE relating to innovation policy:

- A technology/innovation-driven response to changing world demand is correlated with higher wages and employment growth, while a response based on exchange rate and wage flexibility is associated with lower wages and reduced employment growth. The former path represents 'the high road', the latter 'the low road', to economic development. But getting onto the high road is not an easy task, especially given the significance of path-dependence in innovation and institutions. Therefore, 'unless strategic policies are implemented to shift the direction of development', existing specialisation patterns are likely to continue (Marceau *et al.* 1997: ES.5).

- Policy needs to be sensitive to the idiosyncratic needs of firms and sectors (Dodgson and Bessant 1996). This is especially important in less populous countries, such as Australia, where some sectors are dominated by a very small number of companies (Marceau *et al.* 1997: ES.9).

- The importance of learning, knowledge flows, industry clusters, etc. means that 'the key function of a national system of innovation is to promote learning by its constituent economic actors' (Marceau *et al.* 1997: ES.5). This requires innovation to focus on clusters and sectors rather than individual companies, and to promote linkages between actors, including an important role for intermediaries and consultants in promoting innovation (Dodgson and Bessant 1996).

- The focus on learning means it is vital to maintain diversity and general competencies within the system (e.g. in education, research and industry structure), and there is an accompanying need to avoid over-emphasising the benefits of 'efficiency' at the expense of flexibility (Streeck 1991).

- Improving firms' innovative capabilities is a crucial policy aim. This may involve addressing resource deficiencies within companies, often through active intervention and support mechanisms rather than relying on companies to take the initiative themselves (Dodgson and Bessant 1996).

- Knowledge is tacit and not easy to transfer. Therefore firm-specific knowledge is not easily imitated and not always in need of strict legal protection for firms to make a return on their knowledge investment. As a result, NSE tends to favour a narrower scope for intellectual property laws such as patents, in order to increase the potential for learning and experimentation throughout the economic system (Metcalfe 2007).

- Some technologies have particularly significant growth-inducing potential and require special emphasis in order to assist their roll-out and diffusion in such a way that firms and society can maximise benefit from them. These include 'general purpose technologies' (such as ICT and biotechnology) and new energy, transport and telecommunications infrastructures (Helpmann 1998).

NSE has many affinities with Keynesianism on macroeconomic issues, and recognises the importance of expansive macro settings in achieving growth and reducing unemployment. But NSE argues that Keynesians have neglected the supply side of the economy (Streeck 1991) and that the quality of the innovation system determines to a large extent the response of the supply side (i.e. firms) to particular investment and fiscal stimuli. For NSE, not all forms of investment and consumption are equal; some provide greater learning opportunities and spillover benefits than others.

By contrast, NSE agrees with neoclassical economics on some issues, for example, the need generally to promote competition and free trade (e.g. Porter 1990). But it differs on many issues too, or provides an alternative rationale for policy, even if the end result is sometimes the same. So while both approaches accept that there is a case for government to support R&D, NSE does so not simply because of the existence of a static notion of 'market failure' (the neoclassical rationale), but also because of the importance of R&D to learning capabilities more generally (Nelson 2009). In essence, the heuristic or 'rule of thumb' that governs NSE in policy terms is that of learning and innovation, rather than the neoclassical emphasis on correcting market failure and promoting market-defined static efficiency.

An example of how NSE differentiates itself from both Keynesian and neo-classical economic policies could be seen in industry policy debates in Australia in the late 1990s (Phillimore 1998). At that time, the mainstream view was prepared to concede the need for a basic set of generic support programs for R&D, export promotion, etc. in opposition to those (mainly from industry) who wished to add investment attraction through tax concessions, grants, subsidies, etc. as a way of showing that Australia was 'open for business'.

From an NSE perspective, there was little to choose between the two groups: both relied on 'sound' macroeconomic policy, competitive microeconomic settings and lower input costs as the most important keys to economic growth and industry development. Neither suggested that government needs to think about the way in which Australian industry is structured, either in terms of the balance between sectors or within sectors, or where growth is going to come from. By contrast, an NSE-influenced report published at this time (Marceau *et al.* 1997) argued that industry policy needed to go beyond microeconomic reform, cost reductions and attracting footloose capital, without harking back to 'old style' support for tariffs or subsidies. Agnosticism about industry structure is not acceptable; governments must actively strive to shift the economy towards greater knowledge and innovation intensity. Policy proposals included measures aimed at encouraging business and industry networks, promoting R&D, building global marketing and distribution channels for local industry, and investing heavily in public infrastructure, etc.

As it turned out, Australian economic performance was dominated by extensive growth based on natural resource exports, and debates about industry policy largely disappeared. However, under the Federal Labor Government elected in 2007, an innovation policy explicitly structured around greater understanding and development of Australia's national innovation system was initiated (Commonwealth of Australia 2009a). Furthermore, key technology investments such as the National Broadband Network and the Green Car Initiative were introduced which could be seen to be consistent with NSE thinking, while policy proposals for R&D tax credits and patent law reform also had NSE origins (Cutler 2008; DIISR, 2010).

A neo-Schumpeterian policy approach

NSE provides opportunities for progressive politics in several areas, many of which are not directly related to innovation policy *per se*. However, NSE views innovation as a *systemic* process, and therefore involves many institutions and actors which may have an indirect impact on the innovative capacity of the economic system and society as a whole. In these circumstances, an NSE-inspired policy regime will focus on promoting innovation and learning as an additional or replacement rationale in many policy areas, just as neoclassical economics has promoted competition and market-based rationality. The crucial difference is that an innovation-based labour market or environment policy has much greater progressive possibilities, in policy and political terms, than does a neoclassical policy heuristic.

Labour

An innovation-driven economic policy has several potential advantages for workers and trade unions, one of the traditional support bases of social democracy. In contrast to the familiar nostrums of neoclassical economists about 'labour market reform', NSE is concerned that "policies aiming at a greater degree of labour market flexibility may be successful in the short run, but harmful to innovation and economic performance in the longer run" (Kleinknecht 1998:

388). Drawing on the experience of the Netherlands, Kleinknecht (1998: 393) argues that wage moderation creates a threefold problem from a neo-Schumpeterian perspective:

- it lowers the rate of labour productivity growth due to an ageing of the capital stock (since labour is now relatively cheaper, capital replacement is delayed) which in turn slows income growth and reduces the economy's technological capacity;
- it slows the process of 'creative destruction' by allowing less efficient firms to compete through means of lower wages rather than innovation; and
- it reduces the size of effective demand which discourages product innovation, particularly for smaller firms.

'Flexible' industrial relations have a similar effect: they 'give an extra competitive option to non-innovating firms' and as a result 'innovating firms have less chance to out-compete them' (Kleinknecht 1998: 394). Unions can break the cycle by making higher wage claims or by resisting non-innovative 'labour flexibilities' and translating productivity gains into shorter working hours and increased jobs (Kleinknecht and Naastepad 2007).

Environment

A similar concern with non-innovative competition can be found in relation to environmental regulation. Several authors (e.g. Banks and Heaton 1995; Porter and van den Linde 1995; Kleinknecht 1998) have argued that tougher environmental standards can create innovative advantages for companies and countries alike. For companies, tough standards prevent firms from undercutting each other via a 'race to the bottom' in environmental performance; more innovative solutions are then required for environmental problems, and there is a greater incentive for companies to invest in risky R&D to achieve them.

Education, training and research

Education and training, and research and development (R&D) are acknowledged areas of market failure in neoclassical economics and, as such, government intervention to promote these activities is generally supported. Nevertheless, there are differences even here between neoclassical orthodoxy and NSE which suggest that the latter provides a surer avenue of support to interests concerned with public education, training and research – again, groups traditionally associated with the Left.

On schools, neo-Schumpeterians are convinced of the importance of a sound general and technical education for all students, since they believe that information flows and innovation are promoted by having competent people at all levels of the production process. In that sense, they oppose a strongly differentiated education system that caters primarily to an elite rather than providing a good basic educational grounding for all students. Similarly, the vocational education and training system should ensure that as many workers as possible receive appropriate training.

NSE is not agnostic about the educational choices of students and is loathe to leave them solely or mainly to market forces. Certain fields of research and education – in particular engineering and some scientific disciplines – have an extremely important role within the national system of innovation in enabling countries to generate and absorb technological advances (Marceau et al. 1997) and therefore the future supply of people educated in these subjects cannot be left solely to the changing preferences of students as expressed, for example, through a voucher system. Planning and active support for these study options is required from government to ensure that society has a basic competence in key areas of science and technology.

Basic research is an extremely important part of the innovation system, not just for generating new ideas but also for providing new graduates and skills which transfer into and are available for use by companies and other research performers (Pavitt 1991; Gersbach 2009). NSE argues that it is important for a country to maintain a basic level of competency in a range of research disciplines and skills, and for diversity to flourish. The NSE approach also acknowledges the importance of public sector research agencies (such as CSIRO) to the innovation system, and is reluctant to break them up or cut them too severely, especially if the private sector is not taking up the challenge (Ewer 1995). However, NSE is aware of the importance of developing networks between the different players in the research system and encourages collaborative R&D among companies and among industry, universities and public sector research agencies.

Cities and regions

For NSE, proximity matters. Information flows and networking activity are more likely to occur within national (and regional) borders than outside them. Regional clusters of innovative firms in particular industries have been identified in a number of studies; the innovative nature of the sectors stems at least partly from the dense communication and other networks which have formed, often between ostensible competitors (Castells and Hall 1994; Cooke and Schall 2007; Piore and Sabel 1984). NSE advocates the identification and development of regional industry clusters and policies to assist in the process. Again, there is political potential in such an approach, as declining regions and industries can be offered assistance to chart a new future based on existing capabilities being exploited in new directions, rather than being at the mercy of one or two major employers in cost-based industries such as clothing or steel.

The public sector

Government has several very important roles to play in NSE. Not all of them require the expenditure of large amounts of funds, but the state is definitely not a 'nightwatchman', as in the neoclassical ideal. Some of the more important tasks that the public sector must carry out under a NSE framework include:

- establishing strong regulatory standards for labour relations, products, environmental performance, etc., in order to promote 'virtuous' rather than 'vicious' competition;
- maintaining strong public sector research agencies with a clear understanding of the industries to which they are linked;
- using public expenditure to boost innovation. At the macro level, Freeman and Soete (1994) have argued that solving unemployment requires a combination of Keynes (boosting aggregate demand through increased investment) and Schumpeter (targeting such investment in key new technologies such as ICT, biotechnology and renewable energy). At the micro level, an NSE approach would involve using public procurement policy to promote and encourage innovation and develop industry capabilities;
- providing access to information and technology for companies and encouraging networking and sharing among companies;
- investing heavily in education, training and research; and
- easing the transition from declining industries to growing industries through appropriate retraining programs.

Neo-Schumpeterian economics and the 'third way'

Neo-Schumpeterian economics is not a panacea. However, it does have the virtue of establishing an underlying policy framework centred around support for innovation which also provides arguments for related policy positions in areas which many progressives hold dear – support for unions, collective bargaining, tougher environmental protection, a larger role for education and the public sector, regional programs, etc. In doing so, it contains the seeds of a viable political constituency that can attract support from the traditional Left as well as reaching out to other groups such as environmentalists, innovative companies and people involved in the knowledge economy. Moreover, it argues for these positions from an economic perspective which has strong evidence that such policies are more likely to promote innovation and growth than those based on a neoclassical approach. By also complementing Keynesian macroeconomic policies and neoclassical views on competition and trade policy, NSE can truly be said to be a 'third way' in economic policy with promising political possibilities.

John Phillimore is the Executive Director of The John Curtin Institute of Public Policy, Curtin University. Industry and Innovation: Neo-Schumpeterian Economics © 2011 John Phillimore.

An Inevitable or Avertable Energy Crisis?

Lynne Chester

Australia faces an energy crisis due to an overwhelming reliance on the market to deliver its energy needs. It is becoming increasingly evident that the market will not provide adequate generation capacity to meet the growing demand for electricity whilst delivering increasingly unaffordable electricity for more and more Australian households, creating a new form of deprivation called energy poverty. Political indecision on substantive, albeit market-based, policy responses to climate change further threatens Australia's long term energy security, as does a wide range of contradictory and poorly designed public policies. Avoiding an energy crisis can be averted with timely political decisions to adjust a handful of core policies and establish a holistic policy framework to deliver adequate, reliable, affordable and sustainable energy to all, not a few, Australians.

Australia produces around three times more primary energy than it consumes domestically. It is the world's largest coal exporter, one of the largest exporters of uranium and liquefied natural gas but a net importer of liquid fuels. Coal (41 percent) and oil (36 percent) dominate primary energy consumption. Total energy consumption has more than doubled in the last thirty years and is currently growing by around 2-3 percent each year. Australia's three largest energy users are electricity generation, transport and manufacturing. Since the early 1990s total electricity consumption has increased by more than 50 percent and is forecast to grow by more than 60 percent from 2006 to 2030. More than 90 percent of Australian electricity is generated by fossil fuels (76 percent coal, 2 percent oil and 15 percent gas) and contributes nearly 40 percent to Australia's greenhouse gas emissions. Coal is currently the most cost-effective fuel for base-load capacity but one of the highest contributors to greenhouse gas. Australia's *per capita* emissions are the highest in the OECD and among the highest in the world. Every Australian household and business is dependent on electricity (ABARE 2008; DRET 2008; Energy Futures Forum 2006; Garnaut 2008).

These are the dynamics and characteristics of Australia's energy 'mix' and use. Yet these distinctive features also pose significant threats to Australia's energy security. The requirements for energy security dimensions are fourfold – availability, adequacy of capacity, affordability and sustainability delineate energy (Chester 2010). Each of these dimensions is being threatened by an overwhelming reliance on the market to deliver Australia's energy needs, political indecision on climate change, and contradictory and poorly designed policies. The extent to which an energy crisis will materialise will depend very much on the Australian electricity sector given its pivotal role in meeting energy needs and its unequalled contribution to greenhouse gas emissions.

Australia's electricity sector and its generation capacity

The 1990s delivered a decade of structural change, with astonishing rapidity, to electricity sectors around the world. Australia's electricity restructuring has been hailed by the International Energy Agency (IEA) as a role model against which other countries should benchmark their own progress. The functions of generation and retail are exposed to competition and the natural monopoly functions of transmission and distribution are regulated to support competition. Electricity companies have generally become single function operations although, like elsewhere internationally, there is increasing re-integration of generation and retail activities. Former government monopolies have been broken up and some have been sold. The overwhelming majority of electricity generated and consumed in Australia is traded through the mandatory wholesale National Electricity Market (NEM) which commenced in late 1998. Retail competition has been also progressively introduced and most Australian households can choose their electricity supplier, although the majority has not exercised this option.

Thirty-four government electricity companies existed in 1990. By September 2010, the National Electricity Market (NEM) had 150 registered participants compared to 77 when the market commenced in late 1998 (AEMO 2010c). Across the NEM, private ownership currently accounts for around 30 percent of generation and transmission capacities respectively, 52 percent of services to distribution customers and more than 60 percent of services to retail customers (Chester 2007). Offshore transnationals dominate private ownership, just like other electricity sectors around the world, and ownership changes are an ongoing feature. Regulation has been increasingly transferred from State governments to Federal authorities and, like the UK and European Union, electricity and gas regulation has been merged within exceedingly complex regulatory regimes. A core feature of this sector's restructuring has been to place far greater reliance on the market to determine pricing and investment outcomes.

A key contributor to the looming energy crisis is inadequate investment in electricity generation base-load capacity. As of 2009, installed generation capacity across Australia was nearly 51,000 MegaWatts (MW) of which about 90 percent is within the NEM, about 60 percent is fuelled by coal and a third is more than 26 years old (ESAA 2009, 2010; Owen 2007). Non-grid generation provides a further 5,170MW of capacity. The three eastern states of NSW, Queensland and Victoria collectively account for 85 percent of the NEM's generation capacity. Since the mandatory wholesale market began in 1998, installed NEM capacity has increased by 21 percent. The two States of Queensland and South Australia, and gas-fuelled peaking plants, have overwhelming dominated this increase (Chester 2008a; ESAA 2010). Additional base-load capacity has essentially been minor augmentation to existing plants (ESAA 2003; IEA 2003).

Only a small proportion of proposed generation reaches construction stage. A little more than 8 percent of the total proposed during the five years to 2005 led to an actual increase in capacity (Chester 2007). In 2009, some 41,450MW of intended new generation capacity was reported, of which 84 percent is 'proposed', 9 percent in the stage of 'advanced planning' and seven percent 'under construction' (ESAA 2010). Gas accounts for a little over 41 percent of this intended additional capacity and wind, although significant in terms of the number of projects, for some 27 percent. Of the more than 100 proposed generation projects listed by the AEMO (2010d), only four have a firm construction date.

According to neoclassical economic theory, it would be expected that higher electricity prices would lead to increased generation capacity. The level of wholesale prices – particularly, its volatility or 'spikes' (particularly high prices for short durations) – is claimed to signal the need for investment in additional generation capacity (COAG *Energy Market Review* 2002; NEMMCO 2005). Price volatility within the NEM has been widely acknowledged (ABARE 2002; Department of Prime Minister and Cabinet 2004; Productivity Commission 2005b). The critical aspect of this volatility is not its occurrence but the extent of the price spike and its duration.

Fluctuations in demand have not been the principal driver of NEM price volatility, nor can this volatility be attributed to shortages of supply due to transmission congestion or capacity being offline for scheduled maintenance (Chester 2007, 2008a; COAG Energy Market Review 2002). It has, however, been observed that the NEM's permitted re-bidding practices do not result, in the majority of cases, in re-bids that reflect the marginal cost of bringing extra capacity into production – assumed by the market's design – but a higher price to yield a more advantageous financial outcome for the generation company concerned (Bardak Ventures 2005). These wholesale price spikes have been at levels well below maximum demand. Thus generators are able to make substantial financial gains by exercising their market power, without breaching the NEM's bidding rules, and these same generation companies have made substantial annual dividend and tax equivalent payments to their government owners (Chester 2007).

The increase in wholesale prices is not stimulating investment in base-load capacity, but the demand for electricity is forecast to continue to grow strongly (AEMCO 2010a). As noted earlier, total electricity consumption has increased by more than 50 percent, since the early 1990s, and is forecast to grow by more than 60 percent from 2006 to 2030. This expected growth requires additional base-load generation capacity as well as additional peaking capacity when extreme temperatures occur.

The Australian Energy Market Operator (AEMO 2010b) 'expects' sufficient supply capacity to be available to meet forecast peak demand during the next two years, although the picture becomes a little more grim a short time later. Additional capacity is forecast to be needed for Queensland in 2013-14, and Victoria and South Australia in 2015-16 (AEMO 2010a). The Australian Energy Regulator (AER) claimed that the "NEM has generated sufficient investment capacity to keep pace with rising demand ... and to provide a 'safety margin' of capacity to maintain the reliability of the power system" (AER 2007: 73). The foregoing discussion has signalled a number of reasons which may well prevent this situation from continuing.

The AER (2007) posited that mixed ownership within the sector has led to an 'uneasiness' about investment which privatisation of electricity assets still in public ownership would overcome. A report to the NSW Government contended that public ownership inhibited private sector generation investment which will occur "when wholesale prices and market-related conditions point to a decision based upon commercial criteria" (Owen 2007: vii). If this is the case, no new private sector investment will occur until all generation assets are privatised. Yet only marginal augmentation to base-load capacity has occurred since the 1990s privatisation of Victorian and South Australian generation assets.

In summary, Australian electricity demand is growing rapidly, especially peak demand when extreme temperatures occur. Generation capacity has increased, although predominantly in Queensland peaking plants. Timely investment in new base-load generation capacity to meet forecast demand and reliability standards is not being stimulated by long-term NEM prices because they barely cover the long run marginal, and hedging costs, of existing generators without them exerting market power (Chester 2007, 2008a). But all Australian governments are relying on market-determined price signals to determine new investment.

Political indecision on climate change

Political indecision on climate change is a second critical contributor to Australia's looming energy crisis. Climate change and greenhouse gas emissions have become major community concerns with an intensified political debate since 2007. The IEA has cited Australia as facing a unique challenge because emission intensity is very high at 1.5 percent of global greenhouse gas and 43 percent above the IEA average (IEA 2005). Divergent Federal and State government greenhouse gas abatement schemes have been criticised as unsustainable policy and a serious impediment to generation investment (ESAA 2004; Port Jackson Partners Limited 2005;

Productivity Commission 2005a). Electricity generation produces around 40 percent of Australia's greenhouse gas emissions, coal being primarily responsible. ✓

The Federal Coalition Government led by John Howard (1996-2007) announced its intention to establish an emissions trading system but no targets were defined. Following its election in late 2007, the Federal Labor Government led by Kevin Rudd injected considerable energy into developing Australia's response to climate change. The Kyoto Protocol was ratified not long after office was assumed, a Minister for Climate Change was appointed and the 2008-09 Federal Budget included $2.3 billion for new programs to address climate change. A 516-page Green Paper for a *Carbon pollution reduction scheme* (CPRS) was released by the government in July 2008, followed in September by the 634-page final report of *The Garnaut Climate Change Review*, and then by a 292-page report of the potential impacts of an ETS (Commonwealth Treasury 2008) accompanied by its own 'low pollution' website. An expanded Renewable Energy Target of 20 percent by 2020 was implemented. Complementary programs have also been introduced, although some, such as the green loans program and home insulation program, were abandoned at considerable cost in 2010 following serious unintended consequences due to extremely poor implementation.

The CPRS, as it progressed through a number of incarnations, proposed weak mitigation targets and increasingly generous assistance to the biggest emitters, the coal generators, by giving them free permits to continue their emissions over 10 years. The Senate's refusal to pass the CPRS legislation led to the Federal Government abandoning, in the words of Prime Minister Rudd, the "greatest moral challenge of our time". His successor, Prime Minister Gillard, subsequently committed to considering a CPRS once community support is evident and there is greater clarity on the climate change actions of the major world economies although her own bureaucracy has advised "too much time has already been wasted – for which the Australian community will necessarily pay a high price" (Commonwealth Treasury 2010: 11).

Critical to considering new investment in electricity generation will be the potential for adverse environmental impacts and the additional costs that may be incurred to meet government emission trading or other forms of abatement schemes. Policy uncertainty is created once a government has announced an intention but the precise details and time of implementation are unclear. The longer the period of policy uncertainty, as is occurring with Australia's approach to tackling greenhouse gas emissions, as well as the time needed to develop new commercially viable technologies, makes generation investment planning tenuous at best. The longer the period without unequivocal commitments for investment in new generation capacity, capacity constraints will continue to tighten.

Higher electricity prices for households

A key outcome of the electricity sector's restructuring, over the past 15 years, has been that all households have paid significantly higher electricity prices although, for the vast majority, these prices are set by regulation. Further increases are imminent. Policies addressing climate change will also increase electricity prices, given Australia's high reliance on fossil fuels for electricity generation (Commonwealth Treasury 2008).

Following the progressive introduction of retail contestability, should a household elect to change suppliers, the final end-use price is set by the new provider. Should a household make no change in supplier, State government regulators determine its electricity prices. The vast majority of Australian households pay 'regulated' or 'capped' electricity prices.

The electricity prices paid by all Australian households have substantially increased in all Australian States and Territories. In the last three years, electricity prices have risen by more than 35 percent (Ferguson 2010). From 2010, prices for NSW households are expected to rise between 20 percent and 42 percent by 2012-13 (IPART 2010). Queensland can expect to pay a further 21-

26 percent during 2010-11 following a 12 percent rise in the previous year (QCA 2009). In Western Australian, household electricity prices rose by at least 25 percent in 2009, and the WA State Government is projecting further increases of more than 40 percent in the following three years (Office of Energy 2010).

In 2006, the Council of Australian Governments agreed to phase out the regulation of household electricity prices subject to evidence of effective competition. Victoria led the way from 1 January 2009. This means that end-use electricity prices, paid by households, will be set by electricity suppliers. Overseas experience following the removal of similar regulation has shown households paying electricity prices of up to 60 percent higher (Showalter 2007). Victorian households, supplied by AGL, since May 2010 have faced a 35 percent electricity price hike for energy used on weekdays instead of late at night or weekends (Johnston 2010)

There is strong evidence emerging from Australia and overseas of increasing proportions of disposable income needed to pay ever-increasing electricity bills, of low-income households suffering considerable hardship to pay energy bills, of increasing arrears on utility bills, and growing evidence of self-disconnection to manage energy costs (CALC 2010; Gibbons and Singler 2008; PSIRU 2008).

UK households paying pay more than 10 percent of disposable income to meet energy costs are considered to be in 'fuel poverty'. Higher energy prices, low incomes and poor energy efficiency are causing increasing numbers to be experiencing fuel poverty (EPEE 2009; OFGEM 2008). Strong correlations have been found between fuel poverty and excess winter mortality, expenditure trade-offs between food and energy, self-disconnection when a pre-payment energy meter has been installed, a range of 'energy coping strategies' across household type, adverse impacts on physical and psychological health, and strong linkages between fuel poverty, social exclusion and marginalisation.

It has also been found that particular low-income households are more vulnerable to fuel poverty: these households include the aged, the permanently sick and disabled, those in rural isolated communities, those with low literacy levels and those without access to the internet. Social tariffs, cold weather and winter fuel payments, prepayment meters, and low income home energy assistance are examples of policy responses introduced in the UK, US and Europe in response to fuel poverty. However, these measures have not prevented the escalation in households experiencing fuel poverty and do not overcome the root causes.

The rising numbers in fuel poverty is strongly prevalent in those countries which have similarly restructured their electricity sectors to Australia. The steps taken and policy tools used to restructure their respective electricity sectors are virtually identical, although Australia is regarded as the exemplar being one of the most liberalised energy sectors in the world. One point of policy difference with the UK and EU, however, has been the retention, to date, of regulated electricity prices for Australian households.

Australian households do not experience the same climatic conditions as Northern hemisphere households, particularly below freezing winter temperatures, and thus would not be expected to experience as much fuel poverty as in the UK, for example. However, Australian households have experienced substantial increases in energy costs which are projected to continue, and it has been found that low income single-person households spend about 15 percent of income on energy compared to 5 percent for high income households and around 9 percent on average for all Australian households (Hatfield-Dodds and Denniss 2008). There is also evidence strongly signalling a growing problem of low-income households experiencing forms of stress and deprivation due to the impact of escalating energy bills (Babbington and King 2008; PIAC 2009). Australian households are experiencing energy poverty due to higher electricity prices. The prevalence, and consequences, of Australian energy poverty will become more widespread as further substantive rises in electricity prices occur.

Contradictory and poorly designed public policies

Australia has no national energy security strategy. The Rudd Federal Labor Government announced an intention to prepare a White Paper on energy. However, after a series of issues papers and consultations, this was jettisoned in March 2010 after the Opposition did not support passage of the CPRS legislation (Ferguson 2010). This hiatus will continue until there is a clear commitment by the Federal Government to tackling climate change which, as noted above, could take some time. In the meantime, a range of existing policies – in conjunction with market reliance for generation investment and the determination of electricity prices – are impacting on the adequacy, availability, affordability and sustainability of Australia's energy security.

Australia's short and long term energy security is under threat because of this conjunction of policies, all of which have been specifically implemented to address objectives other than energy security, albeit often within the energy sector. This contention is supported by an assessment of a range of policies against each of the four dimensions of energy security (Chester 2008b). The policies considered include: nuclear energy prohibition; subsidies to energy and transport; promotion of energy renewables; new technology development (e.g. clean coal and biofuels); energy efficiency; smart meters; solar rebates and feed-in-tariffs; the mandatory renewable energy target; the offshore petroleum exploration program; the governance and operation of electricity and gas markets; reliability standards; regulation of monopoly network infrastructure; water resource management; end-use price regulation; as well as assistance to those on low incomes.

The following table (adapted from Chester 2008b) presents an updated synthesis of the assessment. The energy dimensions against which public policies are assessed are defined as follows:

- *Adequacy of capacity:* the net outcome of demand for energy and the capacity available to provide energy in response to that demand.

- *Availability:* this refers to continuity and reliability of the energy supply. The capacity to provide energy may exist but it needs to be available when demanded.

- *Affordability:* Energy affordability is not equivalent to energy being 'competitively priced'. Residential energy affordability shows considerable variation by household type and income level ranging from 5-15 percent of income.

- *Sustainability:* This is generally used to mean that non-renewable sources should only be used within the rate of substitution by alternatives and renewable resources should be used no faster than they are able to be renewed. For the purposes of this broad assessment, the meaning has been taken less literally and has been used in the sense of moving to a higher reliance on renewable energy sources.

This broad assessment indicates multiple policies, across a wide range, are exerting detrimental impacts, individually and in conjunction, on Australia's energy security.

There is a very high preponderance of policies 'detracting' rather than 'supporting' adequacy of capacity, indicating the most serious immediate and longer-term threat to Australia's energy security lies in the capacity available to provide energy in response to demand. The most significant of these 'detractive' policies rely on the market – market reliance for new capacity investment in the production, transmission, storage and distribution of all energy sources; new technology development such as clean coal and biofuels; and, offshore petroleum exploration. Secondly, there is evidence of policy 'push-pull' i.e. some policies are 'pushing' in a supportive direction for an energy security dimension but other policies are diluting, or counteracting, this impact by 'pulling' in a contrary direction. There is also evidence that a policy can impact on more than one energy securityy dimension but the direction of that impact may not always be the

Policies impacting on Australian energy security

Common name of public policy or primary policy area	Energy security dimensions			
	Adequacy of capacity	Availability	Affordability	Sustainability
Market reliance for new capacity investment	x	x		
ERET and State Government GG schemes	x	x		
Abandoned Carbon Pollution Reduction Scheme	x		x	+
Regulation of transmission and distribution networks	x	x		
Tax: current review, condensate tax, frontier exploration tax, FBT	x			
Nuclear energy prohibition	x			
Subsidies for fossil fuel use	x			x
State government energy concessions/end-user electricity pricing	x		+	
Programs to develop renewable energy sources	+	x	x	+
New technology development (e.g. clean coal, biofuels)	x		x	x
Energy efficiency	+			+
Smart meters	?			?
Solar rebates and feed-in-tariffs	?			+
Offshore petroleum exploration acreage release program	+			x
Gas retail price cap for small use customers			+	
Energy market operation (e.g. AEMO, IMO, Gas Bulletin Board)		+		
Reliability standards		+		
Water resource management/desalination plants		x	x	x
Trade Practices Act		x		

+ Supportive of energy security dimension
x Detractive of energy security dimension
? Indeterminate

same. For example, policies to develop renewable energy sources (such as solar and biofuels) may be supportive of adequate capacity but detract from affordability and sustainability; policies to develop new technology may be supportive of adequate capacity but not for sustainability; and, water resource management policies may impact negatively on availability and sustainability.

Can an energy crisis be averted?

An energy crisis can be averted but whether this eventuates lies squarely with the actions of the Australian Federal Government. The recent political indecision about tackling climate change, and subsequent jettisoning of an energy White Paper, coupled with the seemingly fragile relations of a minority government, does not bode well. Timely understanding and clear acknowledgment of the issues impacting on Australia's energy security is needed. In particular, there needs to be a strong recognition of the contradictory forces being exerted by a labyrinth of public policies. Moreover, equivocation on policy responses to climate change will heighten the probability of an energy crisis.

Australia's short and long-term energy security, through all its dimensions, is complex and, as such, is akin to a 'wicked' policy problem. Increasingly complex problems have been termed 'wicked' because of being seemingly intractable or highly resistant to resolution. Traditionally many problems for policy makers could be resolved by the systematic application of technical expertise. But this is not the case with a wicked problem which is difficult to define, has many interdependencies, can be explained in many ways, evolves as steps are being taken to address it, does not belong to a class of similar problems able to be solved in similar ways, has no clear solution but many possible options although none of which can be judged as right or wrong and can lead to unforeseen consequences. These problems require new ways of thinking and pose substantive challenges to governance.

A key Federal Government agency, the Australian Public Service Commission, has developed expertise in the recognition of 'wicked' problems (APS 2007). Much depends in this case on the political will to tackle the overwhelming reliance on heavily regulated markets which lie at the heart of the looming energy crisis. Ongoing reliance on markets needs to be questioned, given the obvious weaknesses occurring in the capacity to deliver electricity to all Australians. Moreover, market reliance is increasingly pushing more and more Australian households into energy poverty, a legacy of which no government should be proud. This could be reversed by the adoption of a holistic approach to energy security and abolition of the current policy antagonisms.

Lynne Chester is Lecturer in Political Economy, School of Social and Political Sciences, University of Sydney. Policy to Avert a Looming Energy Crisis? © 2011 Lynne Chester.

Housing Crisis and Housing Policy
Alan Morris

In an advanced economy like Australia we would expect that something as fundamental as adequate, affordable and secure housing would be available to all. It is a foundation for a decent life. Research has shown that individuals who find themselves in a tenuous and inadequate housing situation are more likely to have poor physical and mental health (Best 1999; Burrows and Nettleton 1998). However, in practice, the housing market and housing policy are not able to provide affordable housing for an increasing proportion of the population, leading to what many scholars and policy-makers consider to be a housing crisis. This chapter considers the crisis and policy responses to it.

Dimensions of the housing crisis

Homelessness is the most dramatic manifestation of the housing crisis. On any given night in Australia about 105,000 people are homeless. There are various gradations of homelessness. The 2006 Census found that 16,375 people were enduring 'primary homelessness', defined as having no access to conventional accommodation and having to 'sleep rough' in parks, stations, vehicles, etc. Another 66,714 people were suffering from what has been labelled 'secondary homelessness'. This grouping had no access to permanent accommodation and were 'couch-surfing', staying in garages or temporarily sharing with friends or relatives. A further 21,596 people were living in boarding houses, where privacy is minimal, the kitchen and bathroom facilities have to be shared and often the accommodation is in poor condition. This situation has been termed "tertiary homelessness" (Chamberlain and MacKenzie 2008).

A second, less dramatic but more widespread, dimension of the housing crisis is 'housing stress' and associated housing affordability problems. When low-income households, defined here as those with incomes in the bottom 40 percent, have to use 30 percent or more of their income for housing (rent or mortgage), they are officially classified as experiencing housing stress (National Housing Strategy 1992). Housing stress and housing affordability problems go hand-in-hand: "Housing affordability problems arise when a household's income is insufficient to meet the various non-housing costs of living after paying for a dwelling of reasonable basic standard, appropriate to the size and structure of the household" (Berry 2006: ii). Households suffering from housing affordability problems often have to cut back on what are usually considered necessities, while luxuries would be off-limits.

In 2005-6 it was estimated that close to 23 percent of all Australian households spent more than 30 percent of their disposable income on housing, compared to 19 percent in 1995-6 (Tanton, Nepal and Harding 2007). Low-income households were far more likely to be in housing stress; about 28 percent of all low-income households were suffering from housing stress in 2002-3, up from 24 percent a decade earlier (Yates and Milligan 2007). At this time about 400,000 low-income households were suffering from severe housing stress – using more than 50 percent of their income for housing (Yates and Gabriel 2006). An important finding is that housing stress and housing affordability problems are often long-lasting: "There is a 60 percent chance that a household in stress in one year will be in housing stress in at least one of the next 2 years. Almost 70 percent of households surveyed saw their housing cost problems as ongoing" (Yates and Milligan 2007: 5).

In 2009 it was estimated that there was shortfall of about 251,000 rental houses for low-income families (FaHCSIA 2009). Older (65 plus) private renters who were living by themselves and whose sole income was the age or veteran's pension were particularly vulnerable; 80 percent were using more than 30 percent of their income for accommodation and 53 percent more than half (ABS 2008).

A third dimension of the housing problem is the chronic insecurity of tenure that a large proportion of Australian households have to endure. Renters in the private rental market (just under a quarter of Australian households) have minimal security of tenure once the written agreement (the lease) comes to an end. In Australia, private renters usually have a six-month or, at most, a twelve-month lease. When the lease ends the landlord is entitled to increase the rent by whatever margin s/he feels is reasonable. A tenant can appeal to the Consumer, Trader and Tenancy Tribunal if they feel that the increase is not justified. In order for their appeal to succeed, the tenant has to prove that the rent increase is excessive: appeals are rarely successful, as tenants are seldom able to show this (personal communication from the Tenants Union of NSW). If the landlord wants the tenant to vacate, the only requirement is that s/he must give the tenant two months' written notice once the fixed-term lease has ended.

For many households the insecurity of tenure and the possibility that they may be forced to vacate due to a rent increase, or the apartment being renovated or sold, creates enormous anxiety and psychological distress (Morris 2007). For many private renters the slightest rent increase may force them to vacate. For people in low-income households who have to move finding affordable and adequate accommodation can be an extremely challenging task, especially if they are frail, have a disability or are a sole person household.

The fourth manifestation of the crisis in housing is that the increasing cost of housing has resulted in a downward pressure on the proportion of the population that are homeowners. Between 1976 and 2001, the proportion of homeowners among persons aged 25 to 29 dropped by 11 percent; for the 30 to 34 year-old age group it dropped by 10 percent and for the 35-39 year-old age group it dropped by six percent (Yates 2008). These declining home-ownership rates among younger age-groups can be expected to flow through eventually into lower overall home owndership rates (Yates and Bradbury 2010: 207) The affordability crisis is already reflected in the drop in the proportion of households that own their home outright. The 2006 Census found that fewer homes were owned outright in 2006 than had been owned outright in 1996 (ABS

2007a). In percentage terms, 41 percent of homes were owned outright in 1996 and 33 percent in 2006.

The decline in homeownership is significant as it means that an increasing proportion of households are permanently dependent on the volatile private rental market. Private rental is often sustainable when household members are working, but once they are no longer in the labour force this housing tenure may become extremely precarious. An increasing proportion of households will also be retiring with a mortgage. A mortgage can usually be serviced when a household has employed members, but unemployment or retirement invariably results in a substantial fall in income, often making it difficult or impossible to service the mortgage.

Why is there a housing crisis?

Three primary reasons help to explain why Australia is experiencing a housing crisis – the high cost of homeownership; the limited and declining public housing sector; and the inadequacy of Commonwealth Rent Assistance (CRA) in metropolitan areas.

The *high cost of homeownership* is a fundamental reason why many homeowners are suffering from housing stress. In their annual review of housing markets in 272 cities in six countries, Cox and Pavletich (2010), rated 22 of the 23 Australian cities surveyed as 'severely unaffordable'; Sydney was found to be the second most expensive city after Vancouver. Increases in the price of housing have consistently outpaced increases in household real income in Australian cities: "Between 1960 and 2006 real house prices increased at an average of 2.7 per annum, ahead of a 1.9 percent per annum growth in per household real incomes" (Yates and Milligan 2007: 9). The gap between household income and housing costs increased markedly at the turn of the millennium; between 2001 and 2006, gross income grew by 31.2 percent, whereas housing costs grew by 62 percent (Ngu *et al.* 2008). The household income required to buy a median priced first home more than doubled between 1984 and 2006 (Yates and Milligan 2007). In the year ending March 2010, house prices nationally increased by 20 percent (Zappone, 2010a).

The global financial crisis appears to have added to the housing crisis. The increase in casual and part-time employment and unemployment has meant that thousands more homeowners are struggling to service their loans. The Mortgage and Finance Association of Australia /Bankwest Home Finance Index, indicated that, in November 2009, 15.9 percent of respondents "were struggling to make home repayments", up from 11.7 percent in May, 2009. In Western Australia, where a substantial increase in house prices resulted from the mining boom, 25 percent of respondents were struggling (Zappone, 2010b). In a recent survey in South Australia of 1250 clients from the Salvation Army Emergency Relief, "10% of people presenting for emergency relief had recently bought their own home. Those presenting for relief who owned their homes were paying, on average, 48.8% of their budget on housing, while for renters the equivalent figure was 53.5%" (Access Economics 2008: 24).

There is a range of interrelated reasons for the high cost of Australian housing. In the metropolitan areas the cost of land is high and demand for housing has been outstripping supply due to strong immigration and reduction in household size. The property and developer lobby argues that a major contributor is state and local governments not releasing enough land and imposing high charges for services. For new homes, local councils can charge as much as $60,000 a lot. Others argue that high prices are due mainly to the tax system. Negative gearing allows investors to buy property and limit their tax burden by claiming expenses, which encourages speculation in the housing market. The absence of a capital gains tax on owner-occupied property is also viewed as encouraging excessive renovation and investment in housing. The easy availability of credit historically has pushed up property prices (Gittins 2010).

The *decline of public housing* is a second contributory factor in the housing crisis. Although public housing has never exceeded about six percent of Australia's housing stock, it has played an important role in providing accommodation for low-income households who have not been able to access homeownership or the private rental market. Public housing for low-income households is potentially enormously beneficial, as rents are s*et al.* a maximum of 25 percent of income and security of tenure is virtually guaranteed (Morris 2009). However, during the period of office of the last Liberal-National Coalition government (1996-2007) there was a substantial cut in funding for public housing. Funding for public housing in real terms, using 2000-01 dollars, dropped from $1643.5 million in 1995-96 to $1229.6 million in 2002-03 (ACOSS 2002). Not surprisingly this funding cut was accompanied by a substantial decline in the public housing stock; the number of mainstream public housing dwellings declined from a high of about 388,601 in 1995 to approximately 333,000 in 2005 (AIHW 2008; McIntosh 1997).

This decrease meant that public housing became exceedingly difficult to access. No longer is a low income adequate for being placed on the priority waiting list. An individual now has to have complex needs in addition to a low income. In New South Wales older, healthy people whose only source of income is the age pension will only be placed on the priority list if they are "aged 80 years and over, or [c]onfirmed to be an Aboriginal person or Torres Strait Islander and aged 55 years and over" (NSW Government 2006).

The inadequacy of Commonwealth Rent Assistance (CRA) is a third element underlying the housing crisis. The shortage of public housing has meant that a large proportion of low-income households are forced to depend on the relatively expensive private rental market. CRA was viewed by government as a policy that would allow low-income households access to the private rental market without falling victim to housing stress. Accordingly, expenditure on CRA increased from approximately one quarter of spending on public housing in 1984-85 to approximately one and a half times the expenditure on public housing by 1994-95 (McIntosh and Phillips 2001). In March 2006, 941,319 'income units' ("an income unit is defined as a single person with or without dependant children, or a couple with or without dependant children") were receiving CRA (ABS 2007a). In 2008 it was estimated that 37 percent of private renters were paying more than 30 percent of income on rent, but that if CRA was not in place close to two thirds would be in housing stress (Commonwealth of Australia 2009b).

Although CRA does alleviate hardship, the maximum amount individuals or couples are eligible to receive is often not enough in tight rental markets like Sydney. In June 2010 the average median rent for a one-bedroom apartment in Sydney was $380 a week, in the inner areas it was $420, in the middle areas it was $360 and in the outer areas it was $250 (NSW Housing, 2010). Thus, even in the outer suburban areas, a single older person paying the median rent and drawing the full age pension and the maximum CRA would have to use about 60 percent of their income for rent; a person dependent on Newstart would be using about 90 percent of their income.

Government housing policy initiatives

When the federal Labor government took office in November 2007, housing policy and the expansion of affordable housing took centre-stage. The global financial crisis in the second half of 2008 led to an even greater emphasis on housing as concern spread that the housing market and the construction industry could collapse. A range of measures has been put in place to stimulate the construction industry and to expand the proportion of citizens who could access affordable accommodation. Milligan and Pinnegar (2010) estimate that between 2007 and 2012 the housing budget will be about $18 billion.

One policy was to replace the Commonwealth State Housing Agreement (CSHA) with the National Affordable Housing Agreement (NAHA) in January 2009. Under this new arrangement the federal government committed $6.1 billion to the States over five years. The NAHA intergovernmental agreement committed to a number of measures "including social housing;

assistance to people in the private rental market; support and accommodation for people who are homeless or at risk of homelessness; and home purchase assistance ..." (COAG 2008). The Labor government also allocated about $6 billion for the building of public housing and it is envisaged that this will allow for the building of approximately 19,300 dwellings.

The commitment to halve the number of homeless people by 2020 was also an important initiative, but the achievement of that goal would mean that in a decade over 50,000 people will still be homeless on any given night.

Turning to new construction of new homes, other government policy initiatives have included the Housing Affordability Fund. This is directed towards increasing the supply of private housing by partially funding the building of infrastructure in newly released areas and giving local government the capacity to lower development charges.

Finally, the National Rental Affordability Scheme involves the federal government providing developers with subsidies to encourage the building of 'affordable' rental properties, which are rented out at 20 percent below market value.

It is evident that the depth of the housing crisis means that resolving it will take time and a good deal of innovative policy and government expenditure. The government initiatives that have been put in place since 2007 have made a contribution, but the crisis persists. More policy initiatives are needed.

One initiative that could help dissipate housing stress would be to change the CRA formula to take account of locational differences in the strength of the rental market. For private renters in regional areas it is probable that CRA is an effective mechanism for alleviating housing stress, but for low-income households in the metropolitan areas the maximum CRA allowed is usually not enough to overcome housing stress. A reformulation of the CRA policy that takes account of the variations in the rental markets could have a significant and immediate impact. The potential drawback is that an increase in CRA could lead to landlords increasing rents. Some form of rent control could counter this – perhaps pegging rent increases to annual changes in the Consumer Price Index (CPI) plus 2 percent.

Another policy option would be for government to increase the supply by building more public housing. This has been done before. Between 1985 and 1995, during the era of the Hawke-Keating governments, about 120,000 public houses were built. However, some of these homes were of poor quality and concentrated in distant areas, creating concentrated islands of disadvantage. What is now required is massive government intervention to increase the number of good quality, well-located public housing units. This is a daunting task but it has been done in many European countries.

Government does not have to be solely responsible for the supply of social housing. Research has indicated that there is substantial potential to rapidly expand the role of not-for-profit organisations in the supply of housing. Milligan *et al.* (2010) have identified about 40 not-for-profit organisations in Australia that have had experience in the production of affordable housing. In countries where the not-for-profit housing sector has been successful, its growth 'has been underpinned by long-term public funding commitments and incentives' (Milligan *et al*, 2010: 4). Government needs to play a major role in the supply of land and infrastructure, capacity building and skill development, and the creation of strong and consistent regulatory systems that ensure quality and affordability.

Examples of governments, in collaboration with the non-profit sector, supplying large quantities of good quality, affordable housing abound. Milligan *et al.* (2010) discuss the remarkable success of the Vienna-Limited Profit model which provides 48 percent of Vienna's rental housing. This sector accounts for 22 percent of all Austria's housing and is controlled by a range of social landlords – municipalities, private companies, cooperatives, unions, etc. The sector is strongly protected and backed up by government that ensures access to capital and strong regulation. Social housing accounted for 35 percent of housing in the Netherlands in 2004; 25 percent of housing in Austria; 21 percent in Denmark; 20 percent in Sweden and 17 percent in France (Scanlon and Whitehead 2007). In these contexts low-income families will almost always have the possibility of accessing affordable accommodation.

Conclusion

The lack of a right to housing underpins the housing problem in Australia. Despite the right to affordable and adequate housing being a part of International Conventions, most notably the *International Covenant on Economic, Social and Cultural Rights (ICESCR)*, Australia citizens do not have a right to housing and the government does not have a legal obligation to ensure that the population has access to affordable and adequate housing. There is the general notion that housing is a good that it is the responsibility of the individual to procure. This allows governments to insist that the market should be the primary provider of housing.

However, as argued above, the interrelated problems of homelessness, housing cost, insecurity of tenure and falling levels of home ownership require active policy responses from government. The housing policy initiatives launched by the Rudd government in 2008 clearly represented a step forward, but much more needs to be done before we can say that Australia is a country where all citizens have the ability to access adequate, secure and affordable housing.

Allan Morris is Senior Lecturer, School of Social Sciences and International Studies, University of New South Wales. Housing Policy in Australia © 2011 Alan Morris.

International Trade Policy
Jonathan West

The concept of comparative advantage is perhaps the single most powerful idea in economics. It is taught to every undergraduate and printed in every introductory textbook. It has all the hallmarks of a great theory: simple, non-obvious, logically irrefutable, with sweeping implications. And adherence to it promises a better world.

Never expressed better than by David Ricardo, its originator, the theory states that even if England is more efficient than Portugal at producing both textiles and wine, but Portugal is relatively better at producing wine than textiles, both countries would prosper if England produced all the textiles needed by the two countries and Portugal all the wine. The idea is to allow free markets to allocate resources to the sector(s) in which a nation has a relative productivity advantage and then trade freely to enjoy the benefits. In turn, free trade nudges the economy to concentrate on its comparative advantage.

Nowhere has this proposition had more impact than in Australia. Indeed, many would have it define the destiny of the nation. Comparative advantage stands today at the core of the free-trade ideology that dominates public discourse about the future. Applied to Australia, the theory proposes that this country stop trying to produce goods or services in which we lack a relative advantage – say, manufacturing and tradable services – and focus on exporting those in which we do, namely resources. And that's exactly what the Australian economy has been doing in recent years: narrowing, largely with the support of official policy.

Yet, in spite of its logical power and its promise of a painless path to superior economic performance, the idea of comparative advantage has always struggled for supremacy in Australia.

Over the course of this country's economic development, comparative advantage has repeatedly been dethroned by another proposition: that, rather than narrow its focus to resources, Australia should broaden its economy, using its natural resource advantages as a platform from which to build other sectors.

Deliberate broadening appears to fly in the face of the prescriptions of comparative advantage and its companion, free trade. It implies protectionism and deliberate, government-directed industry policy. Today, these notions are almost universally rejected by economists and are even out of favour among political leaders of all stripes. Nevertheless, the impetus to broaden seems not to die, and every few years it re-emerges to shape the nation's view of its future. Indeed, the history of Australian economic policy can be seen as a century-long battle between these two propositions.

Why cannot such a great idea as comparative advantage – logical, simple and with the power to make everyone better off – achieve lasting dominance, particularly in Australia, which seems so obviously to be blessed by a compelling comparative advantage? How does such a seemingly discredited idea as protectionism keep reappearing? Put simply, why should the Portuguese (or Australians) exert extra effort to turn out five metres of woven cloth when, for the same amount of work, they could take advantage of their blissful climate and rich soil to produce six barrels of wine, trade three with England for perhaps ten metres of cloth and keep three barrels for their own enjoyment?

The answer is that, as a guide to the economic future and policy-making to shape the future, comparative advantage turns out to be fatally flawed. While as a snapshot fixed in time and limited to the economic sphere, it is beyond reproach, looked at over time it ignores three vital dimensions of economic development: differential industry growth, technological improvement and the divergent social consequences of concentration in different types of economic activity. In fact, the theory of comparative advantage ignores economic development entirely – including the vital issue of the origins of comparative advantage itself. And therein lies its downfall, both as a concept and as a guide to good policy-making.

Let's consider each of these three problems for comparative advantage. First, industries tend to grow at very different rates as societies become richer. Demand for meat grows faster than for rice, for automobiles faster than for bicycles, for televisions faster than for radios. This has an important implication for nations specialising in their comparative advantage. In Ricardo's illustration, for example, history shows that as Europe emerged from the centuries-long grip of poverty, demand for England's textiles grew much faster – by up to five times – than did demand for Portugal's wine. Clothing is much more 'income elastic' than wine; as people break out of poverty they buy many more sets of clothes than they do casks of wine. The result was that by specialising in their respective comparative advantages, Portugal's economy stagnated, growing only as fast as population, but Britain's roared. It matters a great deal in which products your economy specialises and has comparative advantage. The East Asian nations that have improved so dramatically in recent decades have done so by specialising in fast-growing manufacturing sectors, not slow-growing traditional parts of the economy.

Second, as with growth rates, industries have very different technological potentials over time. England's textile producers spectacularly increased their output during the industrial revolution by introducing a string of new machines, driving productivity to hitherto unimagined heights; Portugal's wine makers, by contrast, were forced to continue growing grapes and pressing juice from them, with only marginal increases in output over time. This effect is even more marked today, with huge disparities among industries in average technology-driven productivity growth rates, particularly in the fields closest to the twin revolutions of computers and biotechnology.

Third, and perhaps most importantly, different industries have divergent social consequences. Which industries a society specialises in can exert important influence over the type of society that emerges: its relative equality, its social cohesion, its propensity to democracy, and even its sustenance or otherwise of such intangibles as personal self-respect and the arts. Some industries generate novel skills, and with them equality and self-reliance. The English textile industry created new classes of skilled workers, managers, fashion designers, equipment engineers and dye chemists, all of who were well rewarded for their skill and experience. The industry further supported a network of educational, technical and scientific institutions – which in turn spawned further technological advance. The textile industry also demanded increasingly sophisticated and complex machinery, which led to the birth of other industries, in a virtuous cycle. The Portuguese wine industry, with its time-honoured – and massively unequal – mix of peasants, winemakers and landowners, needed, and generated, little external support.

Indeed, it can be argued that the textile industry was important not only for creating the wealth that made England the richest country in the world in its day, but also for laying the foundations for the broadening of democracy to the majority of the population, and the flowering of science and the arts that was so apparent in eighteenth and nineteenth-century Britain. Portugal's wine industry offered no such potential. In general, a society dominated by industries in which artisans and small enterprises are the natural form of economic organisation (textiles) can be expected to develop a very different character to one in which a single wealthy and powerful landowner employs the other members of society (Portuguese winemaking), or in which most people work for – or receive income without work from – the government.

Had the eighteenth-century Portuguese been able to divine the future, they would have been much better off ignoring Ricardo's advice and imposing a prohibitive tariff on English textile imports, giving their own textile industry a chance to survive and potentially even expand.

The proponents of comparative advantage and free trade would respond that Portugal's citizens would have seen their living standards lowered by any such decision, and that in any case England might retaliate with a tariff on wine. They would be right. Residents of Portugal would have had to put up with lower-quality and probably more expensive clothes, and would likely have sold less wine. But in Ricardo's example, there was no other way for Portugal to escape what became its fate over the next two centuries.

Without deliberately setting their sights on industries against their comparative advantage, Portugal could not develop. And indeed, no country has broken the grip of underdevelopment without ignoring the theory, at least as it is traditionally understood. The United States in the nineteenth century, Japan in the twentieth, Europe after World War II, East Asia in the 1980s and 1990s, and China today: all nations that have developed have done so contrary to the precepts of comparative advantage. Far from being a guide to good policy for aspiring nations, the theory has been a poverty trap.

In the principal industries that have driven economic development over the past two centuries – manufacturing and services – comparative advantage is not endowed by God but created by human effort, ingenuity and organisation: comparative advantage can be brought into existence by deliberate investment and sustained commitment. This recognition makes all the difference. Because the theory is mute on the origins of comparative advantage and how it changes over time, it offers no guidance to how it can be constructed. Instead of insisting that nations stick to what they start with, we should ask how comparative advantage is created and what can be done to change a nation's destiny.

Actually, most economists, or at least those even slightly acquainted with history and the real economy, know this. They know that no nation has developed by applying the theory of comparative advantage, and they are aware that in the most important industries that advantage is deliberately created.

But they are reluctant to admit they know it. The real reason most economists espouse comparative advantage and free trade has nothing to do with economic theory. It stems from political judgement. Economists fear that conceding the possibility that comparative advantage might be created by the tools of government policy – tariffs, quotas, import prohibitions, low-interest loans, tax exemptions, subsidies, targeted education, government-funded research and development, military spin-offs, to name but a few – will open the floodgates to government-mandated protection for monopolies that have no hope of ever standing on their own feet. They worry that government will be captured by special interests, and industry policy will become merely a cloak for the kind of inefficient and expensive government-connected industries that are so common in the Third World. Economists commonly fear that democracies are especially prone to such capture, and that, rather than building the industries of the future, the slogans of 'nation-building' will merely shelter dinosaurs.

The fear is valid. It may well be true that modern western democracies are no longer capable of sustaining commitment to future-oriented industrial development strategies, and that they will inevitably lapse back into pork-barrelling and special-interest protection. As western nations fragment into squabbling tribes, rancorously fighting over ever more hardened ideologies, perhaps we have lost the cohesion required to deliberate and to act. Certainly, the contemporary world offers plenty of evidence for such concern.

But if we accept this pessimistic view, it is important to be aware of the consequences. With the exception of a lucky few who do enjoy an insurmountable God-given comparative advantage, such a failure will likely doom western democracies to long-term economic decline. Successive waves of technological development rapidly supersede today's comparative advantage. If nations allow markets to narrow their bets to today's advantage and industries built in prior eras, they risk their industries being replaced as rapidly as the products they once made.

In this sense, all industries today are infant industries, the one exception allowed by the free-trade theorists. Technological change and targeted support from rivals can render a once healthy, grown-up industry a helpless infant within a few years. And along with these industries goes the service infrastructure that is intimately connected to them: banking, insurance, financial services, advertising and consulting. If assistance is denied to these industries, due to a fear of protectionism and in the face of competition from nations deliberately building new comparative advantage with every tool at their disposal, the overtaken industries will wither.

The overwhelming majority of Australia's manufacturing industry has already suffered this fate; much of North America's has gone down the same path. Failure to commit decisively to an alternative comparative advantage will lead inevitably to further narrowing towards our natural endowment in resources.

The consequences will be not only economic but social and, for many, personal. Loss of the non-resource industries will transform our culture in as yet unimagined ways. But before we admit defeat, it is worth considering very seriously whether any other future is possible. Might we not be able to build a new comparative advantage? And what would be required?

One set of answers might come from our own past. The character of contemporary Australia, especially of its economy but also many of its social values, was forged more than a hundred years ago. In the decade following Federation, Australia's political parties negotiated an economic consensus that aimed to create the future desired by the population of the time.

This consensus survived largely intact until the late 1970s, and still underlies public assumptions about and expectations of government. The strategy was to draw upon the nation's natural comparative advantage in farming and resources to finance a shift to manufacturing. Key planks in the platform were tariff barriers to protect and promote manufacturing, racial and workforce insulation (the White Australia policy and the protection of wage workers from foreign competition went hand in hand), needs-based wages and judicially determined industrial relations, equalisation of revenues among the states, and a growing welfare role for the federal government.

These commitments were funded directly, through taxes on the resource and farming exporters, and indirectly, through tariffs and restrictive immigration. This 'Federation settlement' took eight difficult years to agree upon, during which time Australia had three elections, nine minority governments and two failed efforts to fuse the non-Labor parties. Stability came only in 1909, with the merger of the non-Labor parties as a credible alternative to the Labor Party.

It was a deliberate, and successful, effort to build a particular type of economy that would shape a particular type of society – essentially, the one Australians live in today. The structure of the Australian economy was purposefully transformed, as investment and employment shifted from farming and mining into manufacturing. Farming and mining employment declined from 30 percent of the workforce in 1901 to 12 percent in 1968, while manufacturing employment rose over the same period from 12 percent to 27 percent. Services (termed 'Other' in the statistics) remained largely stable, shifting only from 58 percent to 61 percent. To reiterate, this transformation was not a 'natural' shift or a simple response to 'market forces', but a consciously targeted and implemented political and social vision.

To succeed in the transformation, Australia's leadership had to understand comparative advantage in a novel way: not as an imperative to narrow the economy to a few advantaged sectors, which would export while the rest of the things the nation wanted to consume were imported; rather, as a source of finance to build the kind of economy that would support the liberal-democratic, diversified, middle-class nation in which Australians aspired to live.

What was not undertaken, though, was the construction of a new comparative advantage. Australia's economic vision throughout most of the twentieth century was to continue exporting resources, while diversifying its economy into sectors that remained largely domestically focused and sheltered behind tariff walls. Unlike in other nations, tariffs were not employed as a means to construct infant industries that would ultimately prove to be export-capable. As the domestic economy diversified, Australia's export portfolio remained relatively unchanged.

Consequently, as the burden of protection increased in the 1970s, with a long-term decline in resource and farm-based global commodity prices (relative to the price of imports), Australia's manufacturing and service industries were generally incapable of competing globally. They had not built a comparative advantage – unsurprisingly, since they were never intended to.

With the progressive removal of tariffs in the 1970s and 1980s, the trade-exposed portions of manufacturing and services shrank. Manufacturing declined as a share of gross domestic product, from a high of 28 percent in 1956 to 11 percent in 2007; and of employment, from a high in 1954 of 28 percent to today's 10 percent.

In recent years, the narrowing of Australia's economy, especially its export portfolio, has accelerated. Today the nation's exports are more dominated by resources than almost ever before. Minerals alone accounted for 59 percent of merchandise exports in 2006 and 63 percent in 2007, with iron ore and concentrates rising from $5.3 billion to $12.5 billion, and exports of coal from $10.9 billion to $24.4 billion. This concentration in resources is in marked contrast to any other developed country, even other resource-rich nations such as Canada that have broadened their economies and exports.

The implications of this narrowing focus, and the domination of public discussion of the nation's economic future by notions of nature-based comparative advantage and free trade, are likely to be profound. At the purely economic level, although primary production remains a small proportion of the overall economy (less than an eighth), the prosperity of the growing service sectors and of the remaining manufacturing sector – to say nothing of the finances of the

Australian Government, which underwrites a substantial proportion of household income – depends greatly on the resource sector. Should that falter, for example due to a downturn in East Asia, Australia would rapidly encounter difficulty in servicing its mounting foreign debt. (Although there are frequent assertions to the contrary, Australia is one of the most foreign-indebted nations in the world, but the debt is private rather than government.)

Of perhaps even greater concern are the long-term effects on the character of Australian society of an ever greater economic narrowing and resource focus. Resource-rich societies tend to come in two variants: either the resources are privately controlled, usually by a shrinking number of larger companies, or the government gains control, 'redistributing' the wealth more or less widely. In the long run, even if successful – and there are many examples of failed resource-exporting nations – neither offers an attractive future. While privately controlled resource-rich nations can have high average incomes, the average almost always disguises a bifurcated population: a few rich who own or are employed by the resource-extraction industries, alongside many poor who don't, and little in between. The all-important middle class is absent, and with it the economic and social bulwark of democracy and opportunity.

Government is usually captured by the resource owners. And resource industries have traditionally proven to be weak multipliers of income and opportunity across society. In particular, they provide few opportunities for education- and skill-based advancement, and almost none for entrepreneurial achievement (outside of a very few exploration and service companies, usually critically dependent on connections with government and the large companies).

It is not an attractive picture. Fortunately, however, this is the least likely scenario. Most Australians would strenuously resist such an outcome, and the long-term strength of democratic institutions in Australia would almost certainly prevent the nation evolving into a kind of Saudi Arabia Down Under.

Much more probable, given Australia's history and social expectations, is that government will incrementally expand its control over the resource industries, seizing an ever expanding share of the proceeds. Indeed, around the world, from Russia and Brazil, through Norway and the Middle East, this is the model towards which resource-rich nations are gravitating. It is the one that fits best with the long-term Australian commitment to government as a guarantor of living standards, welfare and economic risk-bearing. In early 2010 it was reflected in new tax proposals under consideration by the federal government and at least two states.

But with fewer of the well-paid, skill-intensive jobs in manufacturing and non-resource-oriented areas, what would such a government-dominated society look like? As government is able to provide for its citizens more and more directly, its share of national economic activity would inexorably expand, and with it the dependence of the citizenry on government for economic well-being. The result would be a society in which the ability to undertake a task effectively is less important than getting along well with government, a society in which politics dominates self-reliance. It's ultimately a society in which the citizens are infantilised, as they remain lifelong mendicants of government. This can occur directly, with a growing proportion of the population dependent on government payments (in my home state of Tasmania, 34 percent of households now have as their sole or primary source of income a Commonwealth Government payment), or indirectly, with a rising proportion of the population employed by government or government-owned entities.

Could Australia use its comparative advantage to avoid – rather than fall into – this fate? It did in the past, through tariffs and domestically focused manufacturing. But that will not work in the future. With vastly improved freight to reduce import costs, and dramatically cheaper manufacturing in China and elsewhere, the cost gap of any attempt to resurrect the Federation settlement and manufacture most items in Australia would be prohibitive. That path is, in practical terms, blocked. Any simple-minded reintroduction of tariff protection will not achieve the aim of building comparative advantage in desirable Australian industries. It will breed non-capable industries, possessed of comparative disadvantage, sheltered behind ever more expensive walls.

Two other alternatives are possible. Both focus on building new human-derived comparative advantage on the back of natural advantage, and both test themselves in global competition. One looks to value-adding in resources, by employing the income flows from minerals and energy to support massive new infrastructure and capital equipment investment. The other seeks to build on traditional strengths in industries in which the product is low-technology, such as food, by adding science and know-how to provide safer, more environmentally sustainable solutions.

But neither will be achieved by market forces alone, or by following comparative advantage as conceived by the economists. Economics is the study of markets: interactions and transactions among individuals and organisations. Why some individuals, organisations, regions or nations come to be better than others at performing the tasks that matter in market transactions is seen by most economists as being outside the scope of economic theory, a matter for historians, business analysts or organisation theorists. Yet, at its heart, comparative advantage is about just such economic capability: the ability to meet human wants better than rivals can.

Unfortunately, media coverage of economic issues rarely focuses on capability. It tends to dwell instead on eye-catching stories of managerial blunders or power struggles, mergers, acquisitions, business cycles, currency exchange and interest rates, taxes, fluctuations in energy prices. But none of these is fundamental. They can at best be thought of as contributing to shallow capability: short-term pricing and cost issues. Shifts in exchange rates, tax levels and interest rates might buffet companies' business and financial performance, inflating or deflating earnings for a year or two, but they are surface phenomena. Underlying the dramas that surround these topics are the permanent or enduring factors that determine sustainable prosperity.

Because the media focuses on the shallow factors, so too often do political leaders, ignoring the deep capabilities that develop more gradually and last longer. These include accumulations of strategic resources and proprietary knowledge, which demand for their realisation organisational routines and employee commitment, and in turn enable superior problem-solving. Deep capabilities are thus those aspects of the economy that are difficult for others to emulate and that support ongoing gains in competitiveness. To develop new capabilities – comparative advantage – we need to move from a static to a dynamic perspective. In the contemporary economy, deep capabilities are created more by human effort, skill, and organisational and institutional effectiveness than gifted from God. In reality, countries mostly make their own 'luck'.

Three characteristics of economic capability are of particular interest when considering the construction of comparative advantage. First, in their traded sectors, economies tend to specialise according to their comparative advantage. That is, they concentrate in the fields in which they have acquired or built deep capability. Products and services from these sectors in a particular geography can generally out-compete those from others. While all developed economies include large and relatively similar proportions of largely non-trade-exposed sectors – health, education, community services, security, home-building, retail, personal services – in their traded sectors economies can be remarkably concentrated. And the traded sector is especially important for two reasons: first, non-traded sectors generally grow only roughly in line with population and per capita income, whereas traded sectors can generate far greater expansion as they tap distant and overseas markets. In a modern economy, especially a small one, many of the goods and services citizens want can be obtained only from afar; generating the income to pay for these imports depends on what the community can sell to the world. The economic fate of relatively small communities, such as Australia, can thus rest on a surprisingly narrow base of capability in very few fields. Ensuring the long-term strength of these sectors ought to be a high priority for any community and its government.

Capability is commonly geographically concentrated. Successful industries show a marked tendency to cluster in quite small regions. Such clusters include famous names like Silicon Valley in technology and the City of London and Manhattan in finance, but also such less-known locations as Aalsmeer, twenty kilometres south-west of Amsterdam, the global cut-flower trading capital (with 60 percent of the global trade), and Surat, in the Indian state of Gujarat, which cuts 92 percent of the world's diamonds. Capability concentrates regionally because much of the basis for capability within firms exists and is maintained outside firms, in educational and research institutions, finance, local industry and community bodies, support and allied service industries, and community memory. The combination of these elements can be thought of as the local capability platform, and the health of these platforms is of vital interest to the future of these communities.

Capability also assumes different forms, and is created by different processes, in different sectors. If capability can be thought of as the ability to perform tasks that matter in competition, what matters in competition varies industry by industry.

These three observations lead to an important implication: the construction of comparative advantage implies geographic and sectoral decentralisation. To promote capability and comparative advantage effectively, government policy ought to focus on sectors in which the economy specialises, and be geographically specific. There can be no effective one-size-fits-all 'best' economic policy.

How, then, might we navigate between the twin – but opposite – evils of, on the one hand, undesirably narrowing and potentially atrophying comparative advantage; and, on the other, coddling long-term state mendicants? We must expose candidates for strengthened comparative advantage to competition, while improving their ability to survive in that competition.

Consider coal and iron ore, Australia's most important exports. While a necessary precondition for the nation's prominent position in international trade in these sectors is a surplus of raw materials over domestic needs, that alone does not create global comparative advantage. In commodity competition, it is not sufficient simply to have been endowed with a surplus of the material in the ground. The tasks that matter in such commodities are the ability to deliver the right product (that is, with precisely the right specifications), to the right customer, in the right place, in the right quantity, at the right time – and all at the right price.

Achieving that requires far more than a mere surplus endowment. Otherwise, Africa would dominate almost every commodity sector. To be successful in the coal and iron ore sectors, Australia has had to develop a wide capability that ultimately comprises its comparative advantage, and much of its has been supported or provided by government and other non-firm institutions. To begin with, these industries require effective systems for financing and performing mineral exploration and discovery. Australia has built these.

It possesses the world's foremost risk-capital market for financing early stage mineral-discovery, with highly sophisticated market rules and governance for ensuring that potential investors can properly compare claims and evaluate risk in exploration ventures. The Australian Stock Exchange has invested in this capability over many years, and Australia leads the world in the field, with the result that the nation possesses the world's broadest and deepest markets for financing mineral exploration. The ASX includes hundreds of firms active in these fields – firms that must be able to tap a body of geological expertise and methodologies for engaging knowledge to create efficient search systems. Again, the country has invested in these, and leads the world in this field.

The rules for controlling ownership and access to raw materials must be designed and enforced without corruption. Australian government bodies are ahead in this area. Beyond discovery, highly complex and scale-intensive development projects must be financed. Australia's banks, financial institutions and resource companies lead the world in large-scale project finance and management. Logistics systems of great complexity must be designed, constructed, maintained and operated. Australia has built these. (To understand the scale of these systems, it is necessary only to note that more than half of all world trade, by weight, is in a single product: iron ore.)

Comparative advantage stems from the combination of all these organisational, institutional and individual capabilities, which must be deliberately nurtured and sustained, including often through downturn periods when markets don't yet want to pay for them, and whose interaction must be co-ordinated.

Australia has built similar, if not yet so obvious, comparative advantage in other fields. Consider wheat, humanity's most important food source. Wheat is grown on 500 million acres worldwide, taking more space than any other crop. Australia produces a surplus over domestic needs, and while it is not a major grower of wheat, it is able to be a major trader. Its farmers produce high yields. But comparative advantage in this case comes also from superior genetics – Australia is pre-eminent in wheat genetics and genomics, an unsung national treasure – along with superior logistics and trading.

These examples illustrate not only that comparative advantage in the modern world must reach far beyond natural endowment, even in areas that would appear most dependent on nature, but also that comparative advantage is continuously dynamic, changing all the time. Possession of comparative advantage must be deliberately led, to ensure that it stays abreast of the future.

This is not a matter of government planning and control, but of strategic investment to create the capabilities, incentives and rules through which private industry can succeed in competition. A vital part of government economic policy must be to consider which forms of comparative advantage the nation wants to build and sustain, and to help construct them; for that will shape the future.

Jonathan West is Professor and founding Director of the Australian Innovation Research Centre, University of Tasmania. This chapter is adapted from More than a Gift from the Gods, *Griffith REVIEW*, edition 28, 2010. © 2010 Griffith and Jonathan West. Reprinted with permission of the author.

Government Budgets: A Surplus of Funds, a Deficit of Logic

George Argyrous

Each year the Commonwealth and each state government deliver their respective budgets. The budget reports the amount of revenue the government has received in the previous financial year, along with details of the amount it has paid out (outlays). If revenue exceeds spending the budget is in surplus; if the government spends more than it receives the budget is in deficit.

The budget, however, is more than just an accounting of how government spending and revenue stacked up in the previous year. It is a policy document that charts the government's plans for the future and what this is expected to produce in terms of a surplus or deficit in the coming years. It details where the government will direct its expenditure and how it finance it. It is the government's blueprint for its *fiscal policy*.

The actual outcome may differ from the budgeted outcome. In determining the revenue and outlays for the coming financial year, a number of assumptions about the economy need to be made. Judgments about the unemployment rate, for example, will affect how much the government decides to set aside for payment of unemployment benefits. Similarly, assumptions about overall economic growth, locally and internationally, will affect how much revenue the government expects to receive. This problem of forecasting key economic variables so that the government can construct its list of spending and revenue-raising activities for the year ahead is complicated by the fact that, at any point in time, public sector operations can be between 30-40 percent of the total economic activity in the nation. Thus the government's own actions have an impact on the assumptions upon which these actions are based.

The budget is affected by the ups and downs of the economy. Recessions push the budget into deficit as tax revenues shrink, and welfare and unemployment benefits increase. Economic upswings conversely push the budget into surplus. Such movements in the budget outcome are termed *automatic stabilizers*, as they provide a spending boost during recessions when the economy needs it, and withdraw spending in boom times when the economy no longer requires it.

Since the neoliberal ascendancy from the mid 1970s, official policy has been to keep the budget balanced over the course of the business cycle. This *stated* objective, however, differs from the *practice*. In practice, governments have been singularly focussed on achieving budget surpluses. Each year government fiscal policy has been focussed on ensuring that spending does not exceed the amount of revenue it receives. A self-reinforcing spiral has set in where the preceding year's surplus becomes the benchmark for the following year's target outcome; unless a bigger surplus is achieved than the previous one, the government is seen to be failing as a 'responsible economic manager'. The process of achieving annual surpluses is called *fiscal consolidation*. This involves cuts to government spending, rather than taxes being increased, to generate the excess of revenue over outlays. Indeed, spending cuts have been pursued at the same time as reductions in income tax, especially for high-income earners.

'Crowding-out' and the obsession with surplus budget outcomes

Why have governments become obsessed with achieving continuous budget surpluses? There are several interlocking forces at work. The first is the underlying economic argument, grounded in a particular, and simplistic, version of neoclassical theory, which emphasizes the 'crowding out' of private sector activity by the public sector. According to this theory, any government spending comes at the expense of the private sector: the resources that the government purchases cannot be used by the private sector. Similarly, the income the government draws away from households and business when it taxes them or imposes charges on their activities can no longer be used by those households and businesses to make purchases in private markets. And, as the private sector is seen as inherently more productive and efficient than the public sector, because it is subject to the forces of competition, this transfer of resources from the private sphere to the public sector comes at the expense of economic growth. This 'crowding-out' hypothesis is the basis for attempts to reduce the overall size of government activity by setting targets for the total size of government relative to GDP, which are meant to decline over time. In 2009-10, Commonwealth government revenue was around 23 percent of GDP and expenditure around 26 percent of GDP (Commonwealth of Australia 2010b: 1). This is around one-quarter of the economic pie, according to the 'crowding-out' hypothesis, which the private sector would be using, if the government were not 'interfering' in the economy.

The notion of 'crowding-out' is also applied in a more specific sense. Neoliberals regard a government budget deficit, regardless of the total size of the budget, as particularly harmful to the economy. The harm is done through a deficit's impact on interest rates. The government can only spend more than it receives by going into debt. This debt is 'financed' by diverting domestic savings away from households, and it does this by offering a higher rate of return on government securities. These higher interest rates reduce private investment in proportion to the size of the deficit, and this reduction in private investment constitutes the 'crowding-out' caused by excessive government spending. As we noted above, in 2009-10 government expenses as a percentage of GDP exceeded that for revenue by over three percent (or around $50 billion), and this represents an increase in public debt, which denies the private sector of finance it would use to expand its own economic activity.

The domestic imbalance caused by government deficits is further extended to explain the imbalance in trade; if the private sector is squeezed out of the domestic capital market by excessive government spending, businesses must turn to foreign sources if they want to maintain the same level of activity. The higher interest rates that the public debt is said to have caused push up the exchange rate between Australian dollars and other currencies, so that the competitiveness of Australian firms in foreign markets is undermined, bringing about a decline in exports and an increase in imports. Thus the government's budget deficit is said to produce a 'twin deficit' in the form of imports exceeding exports.

The policy implication arising from this analysis of financial 'crowding-out' is that the government should plan for budget surpluses. These extra funds allow the government to buy back government securities that it had previously issued, reducing its future debt obligations. This puts savings back in the hands of private households, so that they can be borrowed by businesses that are prepared to invest more as a result of the fall in interest rates. In all of this, the banking system operates as a neutral intermediary; making sure that all the income that households are willing to save, and which are not diverted to the public sector, flows through into private investment.

This financial 'crowding-out' argument is the 'intellectual' foundation for the pursuit of ever-larger budget surpluses. It has been widely influential both in theory and in practice. Having taken hold in policy-making, the surplus budget objective has taken on a life of its own, and holds sway over decision-making independently of the underlying economic argument. A number of interlocking forces operate to entrench this budget objective.

- *Budget surpluses as a Treasurer's performance measure.* Government Treasurers are often assessed by other politicians and economic commentators under the sway of neoliberal ideas in terms of how big a surplus they are able to generate. The bigger the surplus the more 'responsible' they are deemed to be at economic management, irrespective of the underlying economic arguments for achieving a surplus or the particular state of the economy.
- *Private ratings agencies.* Part of the obsession of Treasurers with surpluses is that they help to ensure the government receives a Triple-A credit rating from agencies such as Moodys and Standard and Poor's. Such a rating allows governments to borrow at the lowest possible interest rates on world markets. However, it is worth noting that governments always receive preferential interest rates in financial markets because they represent such low risk, even if their rating moved from AAA to a slightly lower rating of AA+. The extra borrowing cost that is incurred when a government is downgraded on these rating scales is actually insignificant (Walker and Walker 2008). And it is ironic that the way in which governments achieve the AAA rating is by not borrowing, which makes redundant the need to have this rating in the first place.

- *Private economic modelling.* The impact of the government's budget is assessed by private modelling agencies such as Access Economics. These agencies build the 'crowding-out' hypothesis into their models, biasing their assessments against government spending.
- *Media commentators.* Journalist, with notable exceptions such as Ross Gittins and Kenneth Davidson, take as given that any increase in public debt will push up interest rates. They reinforce the negative 'spin' that is placed on budget deficits.

Why 'crowding-out' does not happen

The 'crowding-out' hypothesis, which gives theoretical justification to the pursuit of budget surpluses, does not stand up to critical scrutiny. One line of criticism is empirical; although politicians and most media commentators accept as a 'fact' increases in public debt directly cause increases in interest rates, there is little statistical evidence that this relationship holds in practice. The Commonwealth Treasury has reviewed past studies and concluded that the evidence linking public debt to interest rates is ambiguous at best (Yan and Brittle 2010). Its own statistical analysis found no relationship in the short-run and a small but negligible association in the long-run.

This empirical observation should not come as a surprise. The Commonwealth deficit in Australia in 2009-10 totals $50 billion is trivially small relative to the size of financial markets. It is not surprising that a relatively small increase in the demand for finance, which may result from a government deficit, has no measurable impact on a market in which trillions of dollars are traded.

At a more fundamental level, however, there are strong theoretical arguments for rejecting the 'crowding-out' hypothesis. 'crowding-out' of private investment by public debt *assumes that the economy is operating at or near full employment.* If resources, especially labor and households savings, are already fully employed by the private sector, the government can only run a deficit by drawing away some of these resources away for its own use. The notion that a capitalist market economy normally operates at full employment, however, has been heavily criticised on a number of fronts. Within the neoclassical paradigm itself, more sophisticated macroeconomic models than the simplistic version used to justify the 'crowding-out' hypothesis have been developed whereby unemployment is a normal condition. These 'advanced' neoclassical models point to particular imperfections, especially with the effect of imperfect information, that 'clog-up' the workings of markets and prevent them moving toward full employment equilibrium. The problem is that policy-makers and media commentators seldom learn more than the simple neoclassical model where markets work perfectly and the economy always tend to full employment.

We have seen in earlier readings in this text that there are more radical theories of capitalism that see large-scale unemployment as a natural feature of a market economy, rather than a result of 'market imperfections'. Unemployment arises, not because markets fail to work, but rather *because* they work. Keynes showed that private investment can be insufficient to generate enough jobs for all those willing to work because of uncertainty about the future and speculative activity in the financial markets. Marx argued that technological change creates a 'reserve industrial army of unemployed' precisely because competition drives capitalists to find more efficient, usually labor-saving, methods of production. Whichever theoretical justification one provides to argue that the economy does not operate at full employment, the implication for government spending is clear. A budget deficit may not come at the expense of private activity, but rather help stimulate it. By making use of resources that would otherwise be idle, the government does not crowd-out the private sector. Indeed, the increase in the level of economic activity that this spending generates, through the operation of the income multiplier, will generate the additional revenue in the future, through taxes and other payments, that may counter-balance a short-run deficit.

Crowding-out or crowding-in?

Another criticism of the 'crowding-out' hypothesis comes from the work of Aschauer (1989a, 1989b). The simple neoclassical model views all government spending as inherently unproductive; it is all lumped together into one numerical aggregate. Aschauer, on the other hand, argues that government spending needs to be differentiated into its current and capital components. He argues that the decline in public capital accumulation, especially in core infrastructure areas of roads, highways, water systems, sewers, and airports, explains a large part of the productivity slowdown that has taken place in the United States since the 1970s. Along with this decline in productivity has come a decline in private profitability and, subsequently, private investment. The implication is that spending that is directed toward the development of key infrastructure, by raising private productivity and profitability, may 'crowd-in' private investment, contrary to the conventional wisdom. Rather than the public and private sectors being in conflict with each other, they are complementary.

The problem is that, to achieve a budget surplus, governments tend to slash infrastructure spending, which is ironically the type of spending that should be sustained in order to keep the economy expanding. To achieve a budget surplus in the short-run, the conditions for long-term growth are undermined, with the result that bigger deficits are incurred in the future. In other words, a little wise spending now may more than pay for itself in the future by raising the productivity of the economy.

What to do?

It will take a considerable effort to change perceptions about the impact that government deficits, surpluses, and debt have on the overall economy. The simplistic neoclassical model is so ingrained in the discourse over 'appropriate' levels of government spending that a different vision will not replace it easily. But there is hope. At the very least, economic reality cannot be permanently ignored. The Federal Labor government under Kevin Rudd realized this when confronted with the economic consequences of the Global Financial Crisis. Before being elected Rudd argued that he was a 'fiscal conservative'; he would go further than previous governments and try to keep the budget in continuous surplus rather than balance it over the course of the business cycle. Almost as soon as he we was elected Prime Minister the impossibility of meeting this objective was obvious, as the world entered the biggest economic downturn since the Great Depression of the 1930s.

Around the world, government budgets moved into deficit as unemployment worsened and tax revenues declined. The Labor Government abandoned as futile the pursuit of surpluses, and instead took a proactive approach. Its fiscal stimulus package injected spending into a faltering economy, keeping Australia from suffering the recessions experienced by the rest of the world and keeping the unemployment rate well below that in comparable countries. The budget went into deficit but, by spending in advance of the economic downturn, it prevented the worst effects of this downturn. The economic growth that followed is pushing the budget back toward surplus earlier than had originally been predicted.

The obvious success of this spending program, however, has not completely removed from people's minds the simplistic notion that 'public debt is bad'. With the fear of recession subsiding, both the newly re-elected Labor Government and the Opposition are clamouring for a quick return to surplus and warning of the 'upward pressure' on interest rates that public debt is supposedly creating. This perception is misleading and needs to be changed. In particular, we need to change the view that the budget outcome is itself an *objective* of policy, and instead see it as an *instrument* of policy. There is nothing inherently good or bad about a budget deficit or surplus; it depends on the type of spending and revenue raising that produces the outcome and where on the business cycle the economy happens to be.

Once we see the budget outcome as an instrument to be used in pursuing macroeconomic objectives, we can also begin to change the prevailing view as to what these objectives should be. In particular, we need to reassert the significance of persistent unemployment as the key problem that requires attention. In the perverse world of neoliberal policy-making, inflation is seen as the major threat to the economy. The belief that the economy is at full employment means economic managers in central agencies, such as Treasury, Finance, and the Reserve Bank, always see inflation as likely to accelerate, and that any increase in government spending will fuel the inflation fire. To accommodate this view, perceptions of what constitutes 'full employment' change so that they are compatible with whatever the measured unemployment rate happens to be. Thus an economy with a *measured* unemployment rate of five percent (which implies a real unemployment rate around twice this value) is seen as operating near capacity and suffering from labor shortages. This strange definition of the 'full employment rate of unemployment' needs to be challenged at every opportunity. Unemployment remains the primary macroeconomic problem, and should be restored as the principal focus of policy-making. This can then inform the decision about the appropriate size of budget deficit or surplus. A target rate of measured unemployment, much like the current inflation targeting of the Reserve Bank, should be specified, and there is no reason why this canno be set at a rate of two percent, which the far less productive and less flexible economy of the post-war period successfully achieved.

The other policy objective that should be pursued through the budget process is a predetermined amount of public infrastructure spending as a proportion of GDP. Government capital outlays have been the big casualty of the obsession with surpluses, falling from seven percent of total government spending in 1984 to around one percent in recent times. It has been too easy to cut back infrastructure spending to achieve a budget surplus, but there has been a long-term cost to economic productivity. By making capital spending a specific objective of budget policy it may be shielded from being slashed in the short run. If the target rate of infrastructure spending can only be achieved by putting the budget into deficit, then so be it.

The other reform to pursue, which follows on from the previous point, is to change the way in which the budget accounts are kept and presented. Currently there is an almost singular focus on the 'headline deficit or surplus'. This ignores the longer term trends in the flow of spending and revenue. At the very least it is important to distinguish between the *cyclical* components of government budget outcomes, which are affected by the ups and downs of the business cycle, and the *structural* components, which give a sense of the budget outcome over the course of the whole business cycle. The amount that the government spends on capital, including items of infrastructure, should also be made more explicit so that it is clear whether any deficit is a result of necessary expenditure on basic economic resources. Just as businesses and households understand that occasionally they need to go into debt to finance large but crucial expenditures – such as buying a house or replacing worn out machinery – government expenditure that pushes the budget into deficit can be more readily justified if it is seen to contribute to fundamental nation building. Similarly, this explicit accounting for government capital spending can help to expose governments that pursue surpluses by slashing infrastructure spending. Just as deficits are regarded as 'something that has to be paid for', we can also see that surpluses come at a cost. This cost is the loss of all the projects that are necessary to keeping the economy healthy and growing but which are cut to meet short term political expediency.

Conclusion

Governments in recent years have been obsessed with bringing down budget surpluses. But the basic premise that justifies this obsession does not hold. Full employment is rarely, or never, achieved. The economy is not at full employment, so that budget deficits, and the increase in public debt they imply, do not push up interest rates or cause 'crowding-out' of private economic activity. In fact, depending on the type of spending that is cut to achieve a surplus, the economy may not grow as rapidly, putting pressure on government spending and tax revenues in the future. A better approach is to treat the budget outcome – surplus or deficit – as a tool for achieving other objectives, rather than an end in itself. These objectives are more jobs, better infrastructure, and the reorientation of the economy to a more environmentally and socially sustainable footing.

George Argyrous is Senior Lecturer, School of Social Sciences and International Studies, University of New South Wales. Government Budgets: a Surplus of Funds, a Deficit of Logic © 2011 George Argyrous.

Meeting Australia's Infrastructure Needs
Michael Johnson

The global economic shock that unfolded in 2007 received immediate attention from economic policy makers, even if the interventions have not led to the fundamental economic reforms required to prevent the crisis from recurring. Other pressing economic problems, such as the lack of sufficient and appropriate economic and social infrastructure to provide goods and services, have also received attention, especially as they become obvious. Trains that are full or run late, or public hospitals that cannot find beds for patients, force governments to attend to the underlying issue of inadequate infrastructure. However, there are many other cases of infrastructure shortage, where the costs of insufficient infrastructure of appropriate quality are spread over many sectors and reflected in less than optimal levels of productivity, employment, output and living standards. The infrastructure crisis that confronts Australia at the start of the twenty-first century is greater than generally recognised. The current policy and investment responses will have to be expanded significantly if Australia's infrastructure needs are to be met.

The nature and causes of the infrastructure crisis are complex. Firstly, there is an infrastructural 'deficit' caused by successive governments over three decades neglecting to adequately maintain existing infrastructure. This problem has been made worse by a failure to plan and invest in new infrastructure to meet the economic and social needs of a growing population. The investments have not taken advantage of the opportunities presented by new technologies and rising living standards. There are also new problems that constrain Australia from solving its development problems in old ways, like the over-exploitation of finite resources such as water in some major water catchments. Global warming will make some of the old infrastructure redundant and require major and sustained new investment, for example in new energy technologies. There is also less opportunity for capital widening than there was in the past. For example, the potential to extend human settlement inland is limited by the need today for rapid capital deepening in places like the cities where populations already live. Finally, public investment in infrastructure has been inadequate because the current policy approach still depends on the private sector (to which much of the publicly-owned infrastructure was sold from the 1980s onwards). Investing in infrastructure has not been a high priority at a time when the supply of private capital is limited and the private sector is being selective in what it will or will not invest.

In the past governments invested in sufficient infrastructure to meet the needs of population growth and rising living standards. They also recognised that such investment often had a long gestation period before any services were delivered. Starting in the late1980s, this capacity began to decline, unnoticed except by isolated public inquiries like the Langmore Inquiry of 1987 and a few agencies like the Commonwealth Government Economic Planning and Advisory Council (EPAC). EPAC was an agency, created in 1983, that focussed its attention on measures to develop private infrastructure – before it was absorbed by the Productivity Commission in 1998 (Johnson 1995). Private infrastructure provision, however, did not meet Australia's needs, as its advocates had hoped, and a shortage in the supply of infrastructure began to have an impact on every person, community group and business in Australia. These impacts emerged in the form of increasing traffic congestion, over-crowded trains, longer hospital waiting lists, rising dwelling costs and decaying school buildings, indicating a crisis in the supply and stock of Australia's infrastructure (Johnson 2001; Business Council of Australia 2005; Engineers Australia 2005; Chester and Johnson 2006). The question being asked was: why, if the benefits of sufficient infrastructure were so obvious, was so little was being done to address it? Part of the answer is related to the inherent nature and complexity of infrastructure investment, but also in part related to the decline in the capacity and willingness of the government to address the problem.

What is infrastructure and what economic role does it play?

Infrastructure is defined in a number of different ways. In its most general sense, infrastructure can be thought of as the physical and human resources that build economic and social capacity or deliver essential public services. Economic infrastructure ranges from roads to power stations and fibre optic cables. Social infrastructure ranges from school buildings to hospitals that serve and support sustainable economic and social activity over time. As Strategic Economics notes, these infrastructure components "are generally costly, provide intergenerational benefits and provide goods and/or services" (Strategic Economics 2005: 7). Chester and Johnson note the economic "definition and measure of infrastructure underpinning most discussion by government and business groups has been that it is the stock of physical 'economic' assets (e.g. telecommunications, ports, roads, railways, electricity, gas and water), assets that are 'networked' and required to sustain economic activity and promote growth" (2006: 69). This list should be expanded to include such amenities as employment services, and fire and police stations, because these provide services essential for maintaining the stock of human capital, for people to realise their capabilities, and for maintaining social order.

The economic benefits generated by infrastructure investment can include reducing costs at the microeconomic level and, at the macroeconomic level, the generation of further productive investment, employment, output and development (Nevile 2009). New infrastructure investment, whether in public goods such as railways or cabled telecommunications capacity, creates access to new resources, markets, social or business opportunities. Investment in private infrastructure, like shopping precincts that attract new retailers, service providers and customers, also generates further investment and economic growth. Investment in public infrastructure, in the form of physical assets like roads and schools, creates long term 'networks' that are re-usable and contribute to increases in labour and capital productivity (through boosting the scale and speed of economic activity, increasing the amount of human capital available, and raising productivity in the case of social infrastructure). In a dynamic process, public investment deepens the capital stock by 'crowding-in' further private investment (see Aschauer 1989a; Otto and Voss 1994, 1995) to the longer-term benefit of the economy (Johnson 2002).

A key role in infrastructure provision for government?

The primary role in infrastructure provision, historically in Australia, has been taken by governments. For example, they have built roads and ports, even though the investment process was sometimes initiated by private capital (e.g. in the case of railways and electricity services) or not-for-profit institutions (e.g. schools and hospitals). There were some basic economic reasons for governments taking this leadership role. First, many infrastructure services have the characteristic of being natural monopolies (e.g. in the case of water services, electricity and telecommunications industries) where entry into the industry was both costly, difficult and the industries themselves required close regulation to prevent the misuse of market power. Secondly, there were often strong infrastructure links to environmental assets, such as in the case of dams and irrigation infrastructure for water resources (that generate what some economists call externalities). These assets are often costly to develop and often require ownership and regulation separate from the users of the resources to ensure they are managed properly. Thirdly, there are some infrastructure services that have the characteristics of public goods, which are not easily divisible and are difficult to charge for their use (e.g. air navigation and roads), although modern technologies are addressing some of these problems. Given these strong microeconomic economic justifications for public investment in and management of infrastructure, why were governments not investing in infrastructure after the 1970s?

Up until the late 1970s, governments in Australia were prepared to find the resources through income generation and borrowing to invest in the provision of infrastructure. Governments could (and still can) borrow capital at lower rates of interest than the private sector; and the public sector was equipped with the resources and skills to build and manage the infrastructure. Despite this capability, the central role of government in the economy and in infrastructure provision was questioned in the late 1970s by a range of critics, some of whom were to earn fees, commissions and other benefits from their advocacy, as was the case with Macquarie Bank (see Jeffries and Stilwell 2006). The private sector claimed the private sector could mobilise the required capital and deliver the goods and services more efficiently and cheaply than the public sector could. Politically, they won the argument, which led to the start of a massive and ongoing program of infrastructure privatisation (Walker and Walker 2000) and the start of a slow withdrawal by governments from the public provision of infrastructure.

The Commonwealth and the state governments' withdrawal from infrastructure spending was accelerated by a slow-down in global and Australian economic growth. Public debt levels rose and there was resistance to increased taxation and public spending. The previous use of Keynesian stabilisation policy, using fiscal (government spending) measures to boost investment (much of it in infrastructure), was challenged by advocates of the neoliberal model in which economic policy is designed and guided by the ideals of perfectly competitive markets (the believers in this approach sometimes being called economic 'economic rationalists'). Neoliberal ideas gave primacy to developing the economic role of the private sector through deregulation of the economy and reducing public expenditure and public debt. On the basis of these ideas, all governments in Australia were committed to generating budget surpluses until 2007-8, when the Rudd Government recognised the need for a big deficit to fund its stabilisation policy in the face of the global financial crisis (see the chapter above by Argyrous).

Seeking a solution to the problem of infrastructure provision since the 1980s through the privatisation of public infrastructure also involved encouraging private investment to reverse falling levels of public investment. That encouragement included introducing tax incentives for private investors in infrastructure by 1994 (Chester and Johnson 2006: 70). The sale of public monopolies like public transport also introduced the necessity for extensive and ongoing regulation of the public/private services markets to control access and producer prices. The result was the creation of a wide range of public regulators, including the Independent Pricing and Regulatory Tribunal in New South Wales (regulating areas like public transport) and the Australian Consumer and Competition Commission (regulating areas such as communications). There was also a shift to a dependence on what were called Public/Private Partnerships (PPPs) to supply new infrastructure.

The impact of privatisation and PPPs on the supply of infrastructure

Widespread privatisation began with the corporatisation of government business enterprises (GBEs) and then their sale, reaching a peak in the 1990s when in excess of $95 billion in receipts were generated by Australian governments from asset sales (Walker and Walker 2000: 17). Privatisations that occurred early in this period took the form of sales of assets to the general public, usually at below the market values of those assets (to attract purchasers), and at a high cost in commissions, consultants and marketing. The hoped-for efficiency gains in the delivery of services from the major studies of the results of privatisation, however, were often unclear (Johnson 2008: 62-63). At the Commonwealth Government level, the privatisations comprised a wide range of activities, including Medibank Private, large parts of Telstra, and the Commonwealth car fleet. Australia Post was slated for sale before 2005 and this asset continues in 2010 to be a future target for privatization (Aulich and Wettenhall 2005). At the State government level, there were sales of electricity, water, and railway infrastructure (Walker and Walker 2000) and these asset sales also continue. In 2010 the privatization of the majority of the capital in QR National – the publicly owned bulk freight component of Queensland Railways – is in process, as are the sale of some electricity generating assets in New South Wales (Johnson 2008). In the Queensland case the privatization of QR National and other assets is being pursued despite the fact that the Queensland government has no significant debt and budgetary problems (Walker and Walker 2010). As well as asset sales, there was also a major increase in the contracting out of the provision of infrastructure services by governments, though the exact scale and impact on infrastructure provision of this activity is still unknown.

The proceeds of privatisation have been used by governments to retire some old debt and to pay for the social costs of the removal of public services in rural and other areas, where those activities are deemed to be uneconomic by the private operators of the infrastructure. New resources have also been needed, as some advocates for privatisation like Michael Keating have recognised, for regulating the privatised activity (Keating 2004: 75). The retained or transferred services in the public sector have included those having so-called community service obligations, like transport and other concessions for the aged and the provision of telecommunications services to rural areas. Where such services have then been cancelled this has tended to exacerbate the trend towards growing inequality in incomes and wealth and regional disparities in access to infrastructure.

There is also the unknown quantum of costs from the privatisation of infrastructure to all Australia's governments and taxpayers from the growth in public sector 'tax expenditures' – those forms of tax relief (together with a wide array of other project incentives) given to induce new private sector investments into areas like infrastructure. This issue is also of concern in the case of the Commonwealth Government's planned $43 billion National Broadband Network, which began in July 2009, and with the first services available in 2010. This is because, while the project marks a renewed awareness in the Commonwealth Government of the justifications for public ownership in a field such as high-speed national open access broadband infrastructure, it remains a network that is dependent for its extension on a whole range of commercial deals with private telecommunications operators like Telstra. The full cost to taxpayers arising from these deals will likely remain unknown.

Public-private partnerships (PPPs) are particularly problematic from the viewpoint of privatising benefits while socialising costs and risks. The resumption of higher levels of economic growth from the mid-1990s to 2007 increased private sector infrastructure investment in new infrastructure, supported by a range of tax and other incentives, and the most favoured method was the development of PPPs. They are joint ventures between private sector investors and governments to build infrastructure. PPPs have features that may include one or more of "a long term service contract between a public sector entity and a private sector partner; the provision of capital assets and associated services by a private sector operator; the payment by government for the provision of a service, not acquisition of an asset, often through upfront 'fees' to the operator and/or a subsequent stream of payments; project design, construction, financing and operation services provided by a private sector operator; other features such as off-balance sheet treatment of the project so that it is not included in government borrowings or debt levels" (Chester and Johnson 2006: 78). Examples include water treatment works, tollways, railways and other infrastructure, some of which, like the Sydney Cross City Tunnel, have failed, losing money for private investors.

Many of the PPPs agreed between governments and companies have included a wide range of concessions (incentives) to the infrastructure developers for which the Treasury officials and the politicians approving them, especially in the state governments, have been unaccountable. They have included a range of payments to operators that are contrary to the public interest; guarantees of revenue flows to operators and agreements not to compete on nearby roads and public transport in a wide range of cases, such as the Sydney M7 Tollway (Chester and Johnson 2006: 77). A wide range of PPPs, like the Sydney Airport Rail Link, Cross City Tunnel, hospitals at Latrobe in Victoria, Modbury in South Australia and Port Macquarie in New South Wales, have failed in various ways. The eventual cost to taxpayers of projects is often unknown (Chester and Johnson 2006: 80). A basic problem in many PPP projects is that they have been designed to make short-term returns for the proponents rather than meet the long-term infrastructure needs of the community. The total value of PPPs in 2004 was about $20 billion (National PPP Forum 2004) but the failures of PPPs since then, and the onset of the global financial crisis in 2007 put an end to most new PPP projects, at least for the time being.

The effective end of new private sector spending on infrastructure in 2007 was partly offset by a rapid increase in government borrowing and counter-cyclical expenditure (including investment in infrastructure) in 2008. The new pattern of expenditure that will continue until 2012-13 has offset at least part of the fall in private infrastructure investment. As a result, some of the problems identified by Chester and Johnson's survey of studies of infrastructure shortage in 2006 have been partially addressed. They included some new investment to reduce road congestion in cities; while low urban dam water levels have been redressed temporarily by higher rainfall in 2010. There has also been a significant increase in investment in public housing to reduce waiting list numbers; and initiatives by the Commonwealth to improve health infrastructure. However, the scale of investment is still insufficient to address the crisis in public transport in cities like Sydney, while some areas like higher education have also been neglected.

Future reform in the management of infrastructure

Among the macroeconomic consequences of continuing privatization and contracting out of public sector infrastructure has been a reduced capacity to respond to macroeconomic 'steering' objectives, and ensure appropriate levels of investment to sustain high levels of development across Australia. The evidence of Aschauer (1989) and others demonstrated that public investment 'crowds in' additional private investment and contributes significantly to increased productivity and economic development. Reducing public investment produces the opposite effect and also reduces the capacity of governments to stabilize the trade cycle through adjustments to the expenditure side of the budget. Tax expenditures continue to be offered as incentives for the private sector to invest, but the fiscal base of government itself has been weakened. In addition, the steering capacity has been reduced, as the extension of private property and contract rights (called 'locked boxes' by some analysts) to infrastructure have also reduced the capacity of citizens to influence the policies and programs of governments and enforce accountability for the infrastructure decisions made.

The budgetary spending on infrastructure by the Rudd/Gillard Governments as part of their response to the global financial crisis, helped to address the deficits in social infrastructure in schools and funded some economic infrastructure in areas like urban rail. However, it has not fixed the fundamental problems arising from the shortcomings of the use of PPPs. Some of the deficiencies of Australian infrastructure policies and programs have been addressed by the Commonwealth Government through its creating a new body in 2008 called Infrastructure Australia. Infrastructure Australia also has had carriage of introducing the Council of Australia Governments' endorsed National Public Private Partnership Policy and Guidelines, issued in November 2008, guidelines to which "all Australian, State and Territory Government agencies will now apply" (Industry Australia 2010a). The guidelines also aim to help improve the quality and outcomes of PPPs and may contribute to improving the transparency of PPP contracts that is currently lacking in the management of infrastructure (see Johnson 2007; Wanna, Butcher and Freyens 2010).

Industry Australia's role is also to "provide advice to Australian governments about infrastructure gaps and bottlenecks that hinder economic growth and prosperity. It will also identify investment priorities and policy and regulatory reforms that will be necessary to enable timely and coordinated delivery of national infrastructure investment", with a Building Australia Fund to resource some of the required investments (Infrastructure Australia 2010b). Its report on Australia's infrastructure building priorities includes proposals for the $43bn National Broadband Network, energy infrastructure, the national rail freight network, urban infrastructure and indigenous communities infrastructure (Infrastructure Australia 2010c).

These initiatives take important steps towards addressing areas of previous neglect in Australia's stock of infrastructure. However, a more substantial amount of capital investment is required to address the infrastructure deficit created over the last three decades and to deal with the infrastructure shortage that will be intensified in the medium and long term if climate change accelerates as predicted. These challenges will need to be addressed through substantially increased revenue raising, public borrowing or more directive policies in relation to national savings that ensure that a greater proportion is invested in infrastructure (see Ramsay and Lloyd 2010). The initiatives will also require increased support by the Commonwealth for the state governments that are responsible for the delivery and upkeep of the bulk of Australia's economic and social infrastructure.

Michael Johnson is Associate Professor, School of Social Sciences and International Studies, University of New South Wales. Meeting Australia's Infrastructure Needs © 2011 Michael Johnson.

Alleviating Poverty in Remote Indigenous Australia: The Hybrid Economy
Jon Altman

While Australia is one of the world's richest countries in both absolute and *per capita* terms, many of its Indigenous peoples live in poverty. This article seeks to elucidate some avenues for addressing poverty in remote Indigenous Australia via appropriate pro-poor growth strategies. An economic development perspective is appropriate. First, there are many similarities in the development problems facing Indigenous poor in Australia living within a rich developed nation and poor people in developing Third World nations. Second, Australia's development discourse and aid practice offshore generally focuses on failed states, problems of governance and policy failure, while conveniently ignoring economic development problems at home.

The dominant Indigenous policy approach in Australia somewhat myopically promulgates a view that Indigenous economic development can only be achieved via 'mainstreaming'. This term that refers to orthodox engagement with the market either through sale of labour or through operation of commercial business. The alternative approach that is championed here is a 'livelihoods' approach. It is argued that such an approach would be more successful than mainstreaming in both economic and cultural terms in addressing Indigenous poverty. This approach, referred to as 'the hybrid economy model', emphasises that the customary or non-market sector has a crucially important role to play in addressing Indigenous poverty in Australia.

Poverty in remote Indigenous Australia

The focus here is on people who at first glance appear land rich but cash poor. Because Indigenous Australians live within a rich state as an encapsulated minority, their *per capita* cash incomes are relatively high by Third World standards, owing to the operations of the welfare state safety net. So the focus has to be re-cast to emphasise activity poverty (and associated social ills) rather than cash poverty and relative rather than absolute poverty.

We also need to recognise the marked variations evident in official statistics disaggregated by the Accessibility/Remoteness Index of Australia (ARIA). According to the 2006 Census, only about 26 percent of Australia's Indigenous population resided in remote and very remote Australia, with the majority living in metropolitan and inner and outer regional areas. These approximately 120,000 Indigenous people in remote and very remote areas comprise less than one percent of Australia's population. The majority of them live on what is increasingly referred to as the Indigenous estate, an area that covers over 20 percent of the Australian continent or about 1.7 million square kilometres, mainly made up of environmentally intact desert and tropical savannah. They live in about 1200 small geographically dispersed communities that are almost invariably distant from markets and commercial opportunities and service centres (see Altman 2006: 18-19 for maps of these communities).

Using standard poverty measures, it can be demonstrated that more than 40 percent of this Indigenous population lives below the Australian poverty line (Hunter 2006). And this population demonstrates many characteristics that are distinctly Third World. According to estimates based on the 2006 Census, 35 percent of Indigenous people in remote and very remote Australia are aged less than 15 years (reflecting high fertility) and only eight percent of the population are aged 55 years or over (reflecting in part historically low life expectancies). Additional data from the 2008 National Aboriginal and Torres Strait Islander Social Survey (NATSISS) identify low levels of formal education and employment. For example, only 34 percent of people have wages and salaries as their main source of income and another 18 percent work for the dole. In addition, household income levels are low and people are poorly housed, often living in extremely over-crowded conditions.

The policy debate

The current policy discourse in Australia, dominant since the abolition of the Aboriginal and Torres Strait Islander Commission in 2004, seeks to address Indigenous poverty via a re-enactment of the modernisation paradigm, the development theory behind the failed assimilation era of the 1950s and 1960s in Indigenous affairs.

In the last five years there has simultaneously been a growing chorus highlighting policy failure, with much reference to the experience of continuing Indigenous economic and social disadvantage during the last 30 years. This is despite available official statistics for the period 1971-2006 that actually suggest that many social indicators have improved, at least at the national level. For example, life expectancies, labour force participation rates and median weekly incomes have improved in both absolute and relative (ratio of Indigenous to non-Indigenous) terms (Altman et al. 2008).

The discourse of failure, even in the face of this evidence, has seen a dramatic policy shift away from self-determination and self-management as the central terms of policy to a re-embrace of the assimilation approach. The new terms used in policy include mainstreaming, shared responsibility, mutual obligation and 'normalisation'. These principles have perhaps been most clearly embodied in the Australian Government's 'Northern Territory Emergency Response' intervention that, in its reincarnation of assimilationist principles, can be seen as a form of 'new paternalism' (see Altman and Hinkson 2007). By focusing on 'Closing the Gap' between Indigenous and other Australians in statistical terms, the Australian Government has also de-emphasised the aspirations of some Indigenous people to pursue livelihood options beyond the mainstream (Altman 2009).

The state's revisiting of such an approach is hardly puzzling, given the dominance of economic liberalism in public policy generally. The views of some influential Indigenous spokespeople, like Noel Pearson (see Phillpot 2006), also provide the requisite moral authority for such revisitation. Policy makers argue that the pro-growth approach that has been successful at the national level should now be transferred cross-regionally and cross-culturally. Some suggest that the free market can succeed in remote and very remote Australia. Others suggest that, in the absence of mainstream commercial opportunities at remote Indigenous communities, it is imperative to move the people to the opportunities. The latter approach is naive at best, because it ignores people's agency and their active links to the ancestral lands that they now own. Also, given Indigenous people's low educational and health status and their economic marginality, labour migration could be disastrous for migrants, as well as for the communities to which they move.

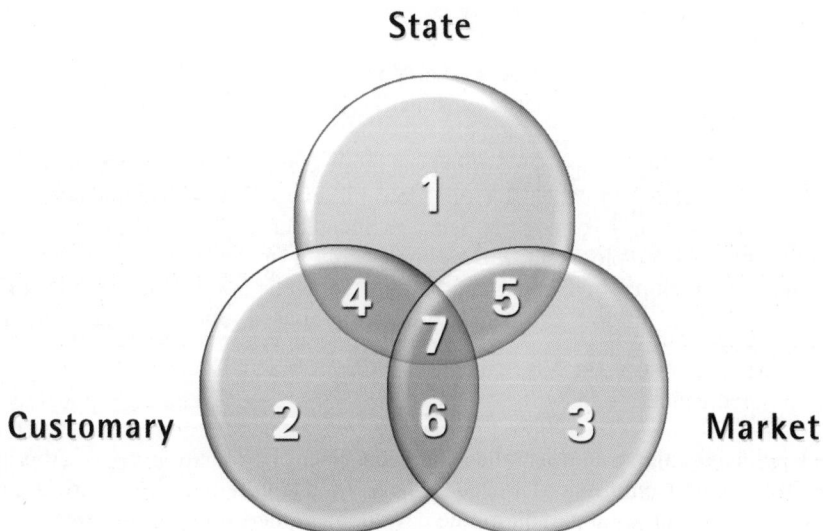

Figure 1: The hybrid economy

The alternative hybrid economy model

The currently dominant policy orthodoxy misunderstands and mis-specifies the nature of the economic problem in remote Indigenous Australia. This is due, in part, to an overstatement of the powers of the market and an understatement of some of the poverty traps that Indigenous people face. In reality, there is limited market opportunity for both Indigenous and non-Indigenous people in much of remote and very remote Australia. This is partly why so much land here was unalienated and available for successful Indigenous land rights and native title claim since the late 1970s. A mix of access to welfare and limited mainstream opportunity means that poverty traps are very significant and income replacement ratios (the amount one needs to earn to offset welfare entitlements) are extraordinarily high.

Current policy approaches also conveniently ignore the colonial processes and Indigenous cultural prerogatives that have created underdevelopment. Despite a general perception of high public expenditure on Indigenous people, in reality under-expenditure has historically been the norm. On any needs-based equitable criteria there has been under-expenditure on Indigenous people in the areas of housing and infrastructure, health and education, and employment services. This has left a legacy of neglect that is evident in poor housing, limited social and physical infrastructure at remote communities, and poor access to financial services. In making this important point, it is not being suggested that enhanced state expenditure alone will be the solution to Indigenous poverty. However, there are significant contemporary shortfalls that do require urgent attention.

There are also cultural prerogatives at work. Many people who were hunter-gatherers in pre-colonial times (as recently as in the 1950s in parts of Arnhem Land) retain a livelihood approach today. Many groups also demonstrate strong ongoing connections to their traditional lands.

Under such circumstances, an alternate model is urgently needed to understand the nature of the economy. Based on empirical research undertaken since 1979 in central Arnhem Land in the tropical savannah, a very different 'hybrid economy' model has been developed (Altman 2005). This model represents the economy as having three sectors; the public (or state), the non-market (or customary) and the private (or market) rather than the more standard two-sector (private/public) model. The model was developed from case study research among Kuninjku-speaking people that showed that, in 1979-80, the imputed value of the customary sector (hunting, fishing and gathering returns) was the dominant component of the local economy, totalling 64 percent, with welfare (the state sector) accounting for 26 percent and art sales (the market) for ten percent (Altman 1987). Subsequently, in 2002-2003, a new set of data were collected, in collaboration with the same people in the same region, showing that the customary sector remained important, alongside state income support and earnings from the sale of art (Altman 2003).

The hybrid economy model is depicted conceptually in Figure 1. While it is made up of three sectors represented by the circles marked 1, 2 and 3, a crucially important feature of the model is the articulations (or inter-linkages) between these sectors that are depicted by the segments 4, 5, 6 and 7. Another important feature of this model is that the relative scale of the three sectors and four points of articulation can, and probably do, vary from one local context to another. In remote Australia, many Indigenous people regularly move between these seven occupational niches, with the mobility evident in pre-colonial times in the food quest now evident in livelihood adaptations. For example, an individual might participate in customary wildlife harvesting, the production of an artefact for market sale and in engagement with the state through the publicly-funded Community Development Employment Projects (CDEP) scheme, all on the same day. Clearly, in such circumstances people are not just reliant on state welfare, nor just on the customary sector, nor just on income from the sale of art. The emerging post-colonial adaptation that is observed here can be seen, at least partly, as a risk-minimising livelihoods diversity that sees engagement in all sectors of the local economy. It is interesting to note that while CDEP has underpinned this livelihood approach since the late 1970s, current policy seeks to wind back this scheme in the hope participants will move into jobs in the mainstream labour market. A more likely outcome of this attempt at mainstreaming will be increased reliance on welfare in the absence of appropriate alternative employment options.

What differentiates the Indigenous Australian situation from many other Third World situations is the centrality of the state in supporting both customary and market activity. This support occurs directly, for example, by the provision of some income support and indirectly, for example, through the provision of limited state patronage of community-controlled art centres that broker the sale of arts and crafts.

The National Aboriginal and Torres Strait Islander Survey

Historically, the argument made above – that the customary sector remains of significance – could be dismissed as being generalized from an atypical case study focused on a particular region – central Arnhem Land in the tropical savannah – where colonisation only arrived in the last 50 years. However, there is a growing body of official statistics that suggest that the Arnhem Land case might not be so exceptional and that allow some scaling up of findings.

In 1994, the Australian Bureau of Statistics (ABS) conducted the National Aboriginal and Torres Strait Islander Survey that showed that the customary sector (then termed the voluntary sector) was significant (Smith and Roach 1996). More recently, the 2002 and 2008 NATSISS included some questions on the customary sector, at least in remote and very remote regions. Although the survey is broad-brush, and the survey methodology clearly has limitations in measuring the economic significance of customary activity, it does suggest that the customary sector remains robust.

The responses indicate that more than 80 percent of Indigenous people over the age of 15 and living at remote Community Areas (discrete communities) hunted or fished as a group, with those living on homelands most likely to do so. The survey also showed that 16 percent of Indigenous people living in remote or very remote areas were involved in arts or crafts, and of those, 13 percent were paid for their involvement. The customary arts sector appears particularly significant in remote and very remote areas of the Northern Territory, with around one in five adults participating in art or craft activities, and a high proportion (68 percent) being paid for some of those activities.

In these survey results there is certainly some indication that, where land rights and native title is strongest, people are more likely to engage in the customary sector or to combine customary skills with contemporary economic opportunity in the production of art for sale in the market.

Payment for environmental services

At present, climate change and associated national concerns about water quantity and quality and potential loss of biodiversity are all high priorities. In Figure 2, a conceptual outline is provided that shows how the Indigenous estate overlaps with the national conservation reserve system. Maps showing Indigenous land ownership illustrate that many parts of the Indigenous estate abut the conservation estate. Research undertaken in 2006 shows that the Indigenous estate includes some of the most biodiverse lands in Australia. Official natural resource atlas maps produced by the now disestablished Land and Water Australia indicate that many of the most intact and nationally-important wetlands, riparian zones, forests and rivers and waterways are located on the Indigenous estate. Mapping also shows that these lands are at risk of species contraction and face major threats from feral animals, exotic weeds, changed fire regimes, pollution and overgrazing (see Altman, Buchanan and Larsen 2007). The latest available climate science suggests that substantial biodiversity impacts are inevitable.

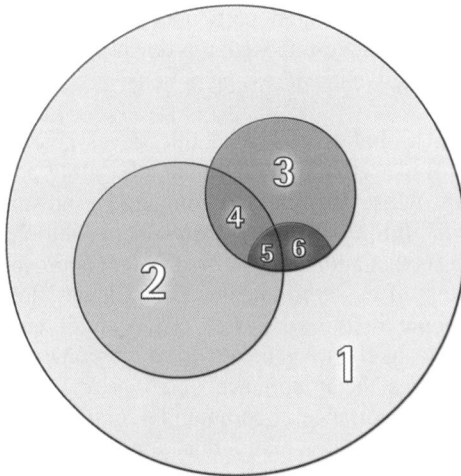

1. **Australia**
   7.7 million sq kms

2. **The Indigenous Estate**
   c.1.7 million sq kms,
   22% of Australia

3. **National Reserve System**
   890,000 sq kilometres,
   11.4% of Australia

4. **Indigenous Protected Areas**
   230,000 sq kilometres,
   23% of NRS, 2.6% of Australia

5. **Joint Management
   (Aboriginal-owned)**
   c. 69,300 sq kilometres,
   0.9% of Australia

6. **Cooperative Management
   Arrangements**

Figure 2: The Indigenous estate

Unfortunately, NATSISS 2002 and 2008 did not ask Indigenous people in remote Australia and living on the Indigenous estate about their participation in natural resource management activities. However, there is a growing body of evidence that in the last decade community-based rangering activity, often undertaken while participating in customary activity, is generating environmental benefit. Such activity is highly variable and includes fire management, weed eradication and feral animal control (see Northern Land Council 2006). A recent project in Western Arnhem Land has seen a multinational corporation, Conoco Phillips, pay Indigenous rangers to abate 100,000 tonnes of carbon emissions per annum via wildfire management. And the Australian Government supports an Indigenous Protected Areas program at 40 sites on the Indigenous estate. It has also established the Working on Country program to pay Aboriginal rangers proper wages for environmental work.

There is a crucially important potential role for Indigenous people in environmental management of the Indigenous lands they own. This is an area where Indigenous ecological knowledge and Western science can be linked and where Indigenous people seek enhanced engagement. While much is already undertaken, only 600 Indigenous people are currently remunerated under the Working on Country program (see May 2010). There are significant opportunities to enhance such Indigenous engagement in natural and cultural resource management as an element of the hybrid economy.

Improving livelihood options

Much of the policy debate in Australia in recent years has focused on the need for enhanced Indigenous engagement with the 'real' economy in remote Australia (Pearson 2000). This article argues that there is statistical evidence that indicates that the real Indigenous economy in remote regions includes the customary sector. Conversely, it is argued that the free market alone will not deliver pro-poor outcomes in remote Indigenous Australia for a wide range of historical, structural, resource endowment and cultural reasons. Nevertheless, there are many livelihood opportunities in remote Australia; and poverty alleviation policies could benefit by recognising the complex nature of the three-sector hybrid economy in such situations and the sectoral articulations between market, state and customary sectors. Policies need to be crafted that recognise this reality and diversity. Simultaneously, communities and individuals need to be empowered to pursue a livelihood approach that suits their particular circumstances. There is much evidence in the development literature that a state-imposed, top down and monolithic form of imposed development is unlikely to prove effective in addressing poverty.

A paternalistic and assimilationist approach to Indigenous economic development in remote Australia will not work and runs the danger of exacerbating rather than alleviating poverty. Such an approach is limited because it fails to recognise the role and comparative advantage of the hybrid economy with a customary sector or the futility of forcing mainstream solutions onto very non-mainstream situations. This article suggests that a fundamentally different approach is needed that empowers communities to grow all sectors of the hybrid economy to alleviate local poverty. The possibility of engaging Indigenous people in the wholesale provision of environmental services on the massive Indigenous estate is likely to generate local, regional and national benefits. A livelihoods approach that recognises the importance of all sectors in the 'hybrid economy' – including the customary – and the importance of community-control of development processes will alleviate poverty more readily than any monolithic approach currently being promulgated.

Jon Altman is a research professor at the Centre for Aboriginal Economic Policy Research, Research School of Social Sciences, the Australian National University, Canberra. This is an updated version of an article published in *Development Bulletin*, no. 72, 2007 © 2011 Jon Altman.

Where Next for Working Life Policy?
John Buchanan, Ian Watson, Chris Briggs, and Iain Campbell

It is commonly argued by mainstream policy advocates that the key challenge for contemporary Australia is to overcome market rigidities. In working life these are defined as awards, unfair dismissal laws and state support for multi-employer unions (e.g. BCA 1989; IMF 2004; OECD 2004; ACCI 2005). On the contrary, we argue that the major problems in Australian working life are intellectual rigidities associated with neoliberal economic ideas and backlash social policy. A particularly powerful discourse holds that 'deregulation' is needed to allow a spontaneous order to flourish in both economic and social life. The reality is quite different. The issue is not more or less regulation – it is the form regulation takes. Neoliberal economic policies attempt to impose the fantasy that all economic relations are merely commodity exchanges mediated by markets. Backlash social policies mobilise disenchantment generated by the dislocation associated with neoliberal policies that do little to ameliorate and often intensify the periodic upheaval associated with market economies. Such social policies purport to provide order based on 'proper' notions of households (especially concerning gender relations) and the nation (especially concerning race relations). The ascendancy of this neoliberal/neo-conservative policy mix has been associated with contradictory legacies for Australian working life – some gains (e.g. increased choices for some concerning part-time work) but increasing problems for nearly all in the labour market (ACIRRT 1999; Buchanan *et al.* 2001; Watson *et al.* 2003).

There has been fragmentation in working life policy and practice. Diverse forms of employment have emerged to replace the once dominant 'male breadwinner' model of work. Wages and hours of work have become more unequal – driven partly by a wages 'breakout' amongst the top deciles and partly by growth in involuntary part-time and extended hours workers. Working life transitions involving education/training, family formation and retirement are often difficult and people's capacities to navigate them are unequally distributed. This is because, for high income earners, market services (e.g. child care) can be bought to ease the pressures of balancing work with life beyond it. For many people, however, navigating transitions can only be achieved by working as a casual and/or significantly compromising the subjective quality of life as discretionary time is squeezed out of households. Hence, while fragmentation of the older model has provided the potential for increased diversity, it has resulted in a deepening and reconfiguration of inequality. The cost and risks of working life have been shifted away from employers and the state and increasingly onto households in general, but especially more marginal participants in the labour market (Watson *et al.* 2003). Low-income and middle-income households where women are the secondary earner have been particularly big losers (Apps 2004, 2006).

Five key challenges need to be addressed if research and policies concerning Australian working life are to be improved.

Challenge 1: To the traditional 'standards' approach to promoting fairness

Wage outcomes are becoming more unequal, and hours of work are fragmenting. While this has desirable outcomes for some people, especially part-timers with caring responsibilities, for others it is undesirable. Approximately 40 percent of males working part-time want longer hours, and two-thirds of females working extended hours want shorter hours. Clearly, traditional approaches to addressing these issues are not working, as most of these developments commenced *before* neoliberal and neoconservative ideas gained policy ascendancy. New approaches need to be developed.

The problems of fairness related to work are not just about renewing standards for the traditional issues. New issues must also be addressed. Non-standard work is on the rise and many of the jobs emerging in new industries and occupations are limited in the skills required and the wages and conditions associated with them. Work intensification is becoming an increasingly serious problem for growing numbers of workers. Special attention also needs to be devoted to ensuring workers' skills are more effectively developed on the job. Finally, changing roles at home and at work raise profound challenges. While households have proven to be adaptable in adjusting to the labour market, the labour market has not been as adaptable in adjusting to the needs of households.

Challenge 2: To free market inspired approaches to 'flexibility' are not working

The policy of 'deregulation' in the name of 'flexibility', far from solving problems concerning fairness at work, has merely exacerbated them. Wages policies have created increased wage inequality. Nor have they delivered lasting reductions in the level of unemployment. While unemployment did fall as real wages fell in the later 1980s, this proved to be only a temporary achievement. Even sixteen years of economic growth, from 1992 to 2008, did not reduce the official unemployment rate below 5 percent, and the global financial crisis – although less severe in Australia than in other nations – was a reminder of how elusive economic security is. Unemployment and especially underemployment remain at unacceptably high levels. 'Deregulation' has, however, made an enduring contribution to a reduction in job quality, especially at the lower end of the labour market. The major result of recent changes appears to have been an increase in the number of workers moving between unemployment and low paid casual jobs. Meanwhile, at the top of the labour market, high earners have drawn further away from the mainstream.

In a similar vein, it is now clear that enterprise bargaining during the last two decades has successfully facilitated changing working time standards, but this has not given flexibility to individuals and allowed them to strike their own balance between life and work. Rather, it has created growing numbers of people dissatisfied with their hours of work and the balance between their work and life beyond it.

Challenge 3: Capturing the benefits of coordination with autonomy

There are potential benefits for both fairness and efficiency if coordination in the labour market is improved. Coordination needs to be improved amongst employers to ensure that better management of the risks associated with hiring and managing labour occurs, so that economies of scale can be realised. Improved coordination amongst workers is needed to ensure the risks and benefits associated with work and working life are more fairly distributed. This finding is supported by recent research from scholars working in disciplines as diverse as economics, sociology, education, industrial relations and law. Over the course of the 1990s a growing body of research has highlighted the benefits for both efficiency and fairness in simultaneously capturing the benefits of coordination at sectoral and national levels and adaptability at the workplace and regional levels (Briggs 2002).

Workers are neither as 'standardised' nor as 'unique' as commonly assumed. It is more accurate to recognise that they often share experiences and circumstances which make it possible to increase choices for individuals by better coordinating the provision of services for people in common situations. Consider the issue of work/life balance, for example. This is a growing problem for many people. These problems are not, however, unique to each household – many households face very similar pressures. Amongst households with working parents most problems emerge within four distinct situations (Buchanan and Thornthwaite 2001):

- the 'traditional' model of one full-time worker and one full-time carer;
- the 'career couple' model of two full-time workers;
- the 'one plus' model with one full-timer and on part-time worker;
- the 'sole parent' model.

The pressures involved in managing work and family life for employed parents are not unique and, because of this, they are not efficiently solved on a workplace-by-workplace or household-by-household basis. If people are to have the capacity to choose between these different arrangements, support will need to be available in terms of child care, flexible rostering arrangements and possibly home-help arrangements. These are the kind of arrangements for which there can be considerable economies of scale when needs are co-ordinated through new collective structures. Traditionally, Australia has nurtured a dynamic community-based child care sector to provide quality, affordable child care. These and similar initiatives need to be developed further as social innovations that enhance the choices available to individuals and households.

Defining choice in terms of a range of pathways offers a more useful way of thinking about both standards and flexibility. The issue is not identifying one universal standard and imposing it on all people. Equally, the issue is not allowing unlimited 'choice' through supposedly 'individual' contracts of employment. Rather, the challenge is to work with the reality of a limited range of work-parenting pathways and make access to them as equally accessible to all, so that choices are made on preferred modes of child-rearing and interest in work and not primarily on capacity to pay.

Developing standards for flexibility also requires the development of new approaches to the classic working life issues: hours of work, skill formation and wages. Hours of work provide a particularly good example of how standards for flexibility can achieve better outcomes than either totally 'standardised' or totally 'flexible' arrangements. For extended hours workers this could take the form of having a cap on the number of overtime hours worked over a six-month period. Once all workers in a work area filled their quota, management would be required to recruit additional labour to meet further demands and reduce work-intensification problems. This would facilitate flexibility in the short run and nurture sustainability in the longer term. The issue of skill formation provides another good example of how coordinated flexibility can achieve superior outcomes. The essence of a new approach would involve establishing arrangements which pool the risk of training so that the individuals and employers who take responsibility for nurturing skills do not acquire a cost disadvantage for doing so.

In relation to wage determination, greater attention needs to be given to the potential benefits of coordinating bargaining on a multi-employer basis. Coordination need not necessarily mean rigid prescriptions in pay rates and movements. If properly managed, it can deliver both stability at national and sector levels and adaptability at local and workplace level. In dealing with the problem of excessive executive pay, consideration could be given to devising taxation-based incomes policies. Movements in the living wage could be linked to movements in the total earnings of the top 5 percent of the population – to prevent levels of inequality spiralling out of control (Waltman 2004). Such arrangements do not prevent adaptation at enterprise level, but they send a powerful signal about how wage relativities should be handled.

Challenge 4: Keeping working life in perspective

Powerful economic forces shape the extent and nature of the key problems in working life – like unemployment, wage inequality, fragmentation in working time and sub-standard forms of employment. Improved policies on working life alone will not resolve issues such as these. Policies concerning full employment and industry development are particularly important. To ensure that increased profits and savings are put back into positive and sustainable economic development new institutions need to be established to ensure priority is accorded to creating quality, sustainable jobs. Such institutions could take the form of an enlarged and invigorated public sector – especially in education, health and social services. Wage earner funds, which involve the redistribution of excess profits through networks of regionally elected local economic development councils, offer another possible basis for shaping more desirable forms of economic and social growth (Pontusson 1992; Quiggin and Langmore 1994).

There is also a need to have a more active industry policy. This is necessary if we are to directly shape the industry and occupational composition of employment. In short, any serious improvement in working life will require that policy on work is no longer regarded as a discrete area of policy. Instead, a commitment to promoting sustainable, quality employment must become the defining feature of the overall mix of public policies directed at shaping economic and social development in general (Buchanan and Pocock 2002; Briggs, Cole, Evesson, Larcombe and Saddler 2006).

Challenge 5: Building new linkages in policy and practice

Too often responses to new issues in working life occur on an *ad hoc* basis. It is necessary to identify ways in which issues can be linked to address traditional and emerging concerns simultaneously. Making links among different issues requires establishing links across a range of social groups. For example, problems of work intensification for nurses arise from the steady rise in influence of concerns with controlling costs (as opposed to providing quality care) becoming the defining feature of labour management strategies in public hospitals today (Buchanan and Considine 2002).

Skill shortages in manufacturing are linked to an industry policy environment that encourages the sweating rather the development of labour assets, i.e. a process akin to farmers eating their seed (Buchanan, Evesson and Briggs 2002). And problems in work/family balance for shop assistants have as much to do with wage rates, rosters and levels of public funding for child care as they do with any fancy 'work/family' packages promoted by employers (Buchanan and Thornthwaite 2001). In short, achieving a fairer future for work is intimately linked to establishing a broad coalition committed to achieving a fairer society.

Unequal freedoms or cohesive diversity?

Our major conclusion is that policy objectives need to be clarified and the categories that guide working life analysis and policy need to be updated and refined. Neoliberal notions of free individuals and flexible firms are failing to deliver diversity that offers real choices to growing numbers of workers. Equally, traditional approaches to working life intervention, based as they were on gendered notions of breadwinner households, have failed to grapple with changed labour market realities and workers' (especially women's and young people's) aspirations.

The notion of transitional labour markets (TLMs) provides a powerful framework for thinking about these issues. The transitions involve profound social experiences like learning, caring for the young, aged and infirm, experiencing unemployment and living life beyond work. More thought and resources need to be devoted to new institutional arrangements that actively assist or facilitate the fairer sharing of the costs and risks of making these transitions. Such arrangements need to be designed so as to achieve, simultaneously, the benefits of coordination and increased choice for workers and workplaces. In short, *the key challenge for working life policy today is to ensure that fragmentation diversifies options and does not deepen and reconfigure inequality.* This means particular attention has to be devoted to rethinking notions of equality and diversity. How can both be achieved simultaneously? In particular, how can we ensure that increasing diversity does not simply result in reconfigured inequality or that increased equality does not just result in the annihilation of difference through the imposition of uniformity? For us the key idea needing further development to answer these questions is 'cohesive diversity'.

Promoting cohesive diversity will be difficult. It also means breaking with the fictions underpinning neoliberalism – especially the fantasy that human labour is a tradeable commodity. Most challenging of all, it also means recognising the limitations of what some US researchers have termed 'money liberalism' and traditional notions of tax-transfer payments as the primary tool for achieving equality (Waltman 2000). The redistribution of income can only, at best, reduce inequality in the consumption of market goods and services. Such a strategy has a number of limitations. The market just does not meet social needs (e.g. the provision of quality care for children and the aged) – it only addresses solvent demand. In addressing social need we need social innovation, deepening social capacity.

In all societies only a limited range of choices are possible at any one time. The key issue is identifying what these are and ensuring access to the really key opportunities is available to all – not just the well off. As we noted earlier, this is not simply a matter of redistributing income. It is also a matter of ensuring that the options available are of a decent quality. From our research, the key issue is support structures that help mediate complexities associated with the supply and demand for labour. For individuals the issue is accessible pathways available to navigate the key transitions identified in the TLM framework. For workplaces the key issue is structures that more fairly share the costs and risks.

Encouragingly, organisational forms are emerging that can deliver improved outcomes. The clearest examples in Australia are provided by the better group training schemes (Buchanan and Evesson 2004). These arrangements ensure that no one employer has to bear the risk of training an individual, and means that more training places than would otherwise emerge are offered by employers. Greater attention needs to be devoted to identifying, nurturing and developing arrangements such as these. Unless greater attention is devoted to them, the choices available to growing numbers of people will be limited and the future will be marked by increasingly unequal freedoms, not cohesive diversity.

John Buchanan is the Director of the Workplace Research Centre, University of Sydney. Ian Watson is Visiting Senior Research Fellow, Macquarie University and Social Policy Research Centre, UNSW. Chris Briggs is a Senior Research Fellow at the Workplace Research Centre, University of Sydney. Iain Campbell is a Senior Research Fellow, School of Global Studies, Social Science and Planning, RMIT. This chapter is adapted from J. Buchanan, I. Watson, C. Briggs and I. Campbell, Beyond Voodoo Economics and Backlash Social Policy: Where next for Working Life Research and Policy, *Australian Bulletin of Labour*, vol. 32, no. 2, 2006, pp. 183-201. © 2006 John Buchanan, Ian Watson, Chris Briggs and Iain Campbell.

BIBLIOGRAPHY

For readers who are not totally exhausted by this stage, a comprehensive consideration of concepts and currents in political economy can be found in P.A. O'Hara (ed), *Encyclopaedia of Political Economy*, Routledge, London, 1999.

Access Economics. 2008. *The Impact of the Global Financial Crisis on Social Services in Australia.* Issues paper prepared for Anglicare, Salvation, Catholic Social Services and Uniting Care, Sydney.

ACIRRT. 1999. *Australia at Work: Just Managing*, Prentice Hall, Sydney.

Akerlof, G. and Dickens, W. 1982. The Economic Consequences of Cognitive Dissonance. *American Economic Review*, vol. 72, pp. 307-19.

Alhadeff, D. 1982. *Microeconomics and Human Behavior: Toward a New Synthesis of Economics and Psychology*, University of California Press, Berkeley.

Altman, J.C. 1987. *Hunter-gatherers Today: An Aboriginal Economy in North Australia*, Australian Institute of Aboriginal Studies, Canberra.

Altman, J.C. 2003. People on Country, Healthy Landscapes and Sustainable Indigenous Economic Futures: The Arnhem Land Case. *The Drawing Board: An Australian Review of Public Affairs*, vol 4, no. 2, pp. 65-82.

Altman, J.C. 2005. Development Options on Aboriginal Land: Sustainable Indigenous Hybrid Economies in the Twenty-First Century. In L. Taylor, G.K. Ward, G. Henderson, R. Davis and L.A. Wallis (eds). *The Power of Knowledge, the Resonance of Tradition*, Aboriginal Studies Press, Canberra.

Altman, J.C. 2006. In Search of an Outstations Policy for Indigenous Australia, *CAEPR Working Paper 34*, Centre for Aboriginal Economic Policy Research, Australian National University, Canberra.

Altman, J.C. 2009. Beyond Closing the Gap: Valuing diversity in Indigenous Australia, *CAEPR Working Paper 54*, Centre for Aboriginal Economic Policy Research, Australian National University, Canberra.

Altman, J.C., Biddle, N. and Hunter, B.H. 2008. How Realistic are the Prospects for 'Closing the Gaps' in Socioeconomic Outcomes for Indigenous Australians? *CAEPR Discussion Paper No. 287*, Centre for Aboriginal Economic Policy Research, Australian National University, Canberra.

Altman, J.C., Buchanan, G. and Biddle, N. 2006. The Real 'Real' Economy in Remote Australia. In B.H. Hunter (ed). *Assessing the Evidence on Indigenous Socioeconomic Outcomes: A Focus on the 2002 NATSISS*, ANU E Press, Canberra.

Altman, J.C., Buchanan, G. and Larsen, L. 2007. The Environmental Significance of the Indigenous Estate: Natural Resource Management as Economic Development in Remote Australia, *CAEPR Discussion Paper No. 286*, Centre for Aboriginal Economic Policy Research, Australian National University, Canberra.

Altman, J.C. and Hinkson, M. (eds) 2007. *Coercive reconciliation: Stabilise, normalise, exit Aboriginal Australia*, Arena Publications Association, North Carlton.

Amin, S. 1977. Self-Reliance and the New International Economic Order. *Monthly Review*, July-August, pp. 1-21.

Amin, S. 1980. *Class and Nation*, Monthly Review Press, New York.

Aoki, M. 2001. *Toward a Comparative Institutional Analysis*, MIT Press, Cambridge.

Apps, P. 2004. The High Taxation of Working Families. *Australian Review of Public Affairs*, vol. 5, no 1, pp. 1–24.

Apps, P. 2006. *Family Taxation: An Unfair and Inefficient System*, <heifer.ucc.usyd.edu.au/law/FMPro?-db=lawstaff.fp5 &-format=academicstaff_detail2.htm&-lay=web&StaffID=PatriciaApps&-find>.

Arthur, W.B. 1983. *On Competing Technologies and Historical Small Events: The Dynamics of Choice Under Increasing Returns*, Technological Innovation Program Workshop Paper, Department of Economics, Stanford University, November.

Arthur, W.B., Ermoliev, Y.M., and Kaniovski, Y.M. 1983. On Generalized Urn Schemes of the Polya Kind. *Kibernetika*, no. 1, pp. 49-56 (translated from the Russian in *Cybernetics*, 1983, vol. 19, pp. 61-71.

Arthur, W.B., Ermoliev, Y.M., and Kaniovski, Y.M. 1985. Strong Laws for a Class of Path-Dependent Urn Processes. *Proceedings of the International Conference on Stochastic Optimization*, Kiev, Springer-Verlag, Munich.

Aschauer, D.A. 1989a. Is Public Expenditure Productive? *Journal of Monetary Economics*, vol. 23, pp. 177-200.

Aschauer, D.A. 1989b. Does Public Capital Crowd Out Private Capital? *Journal of Monetary Economics*, vol. 24, pp. 171-88.

Atkinson, S. and Tietenberg, T.H. 1991. Market Failure in Incentive Based Regulation: The Case of Emissions Trading. *Journal of Environmental Economics and Management*, vol. 21, no. 1, pp. 17-31.

Aulich C. and Wettenhall R. (eds) 2005. *Howard's Second and Third Governments; Australian Commonwealth Administration*, UNSW Press, Sydney.

Australian Bureau of Agricultural and Resource Economics ABARE. 2002. Competition in the Australian National Electricity Market. *Current Issues*, vol. 2, no. 1, pp. 1-12.

Australian Bureau of Agricultural and Resource Economics ABARE. 2008. *Energy in Australia 2008*, Department of Resources, Energy and Tourism, Australian Government, February, Canberra.

Australian Bureau of Statistics. 2007a. *Fewer Australian Homes are Paid Off*, Media Fact Sheet, 27 June.

Australian Bureau of Statistics. 2007b. *Household Wealth and Wealth Distribution, Australia, 2005-06*, cat. 6554.0.

Australian Bureau of Statistics. 2007c. *Year Book Australia, 2007, Housing Assistance*, cat. no. 2050.0.

Australian Bureau of Statistics. 2008. *Census 2006*, (unpublished data).

Australian Bureau of Statistics. 2009. *Household Income and Income Distribution, Australia, 2007-08*, cat. 6523.0.

Australian Bureau of Statistics. 2010. *E08_aug96 – Employed Persons by Sex, Occupation, State, Status in Employment, August 1996 Onwards*, data cube.

Australian Chamber of Commerce and Industry. 2005. Structural Labour Market Reform: The Key to Sustaining Lower Unemployment. *ACCI Review*, January, pp. 4-8.

Australian Council of Social Service. 2002. *Public & Community Housing: A Rescue Package Needed*, ACOSS, Sydney.

Australian Energy Market Operator 2010b. *Power System Adequacy: Two Year Outlook*, August, <www.aemo.com.au/electricityops/psa2010.html>, accessed 25 September 2010.

Australian Energy Market Operator. 2010a. *Electricity Statement of Opportunities for the National Electricity Market*, Executive Briefing, August, <www.aemo.com.au/planning/esoo2010.html>, accesed 25 Sepember 2010.

Australian Energy Market Operator. 2010c. *Registered Participants in the NEM*, <www.aemo.com.au/registration/registration.html>, accessed 25 September 2010.

Australian Energy Market Operator. 2010d. *Proposed Generation Projects*, <www.aemo.com.au/data/gendata_prop.shtml>, accessed 25 September 2010.

Australian Energy Regulator. 2007. *State of the Energy Market 2007*, AER, Melbourne.

Australian Institute of Health and Welfare. 2008. *Housing Assistance in Australia*, AIHW, Canberra.

Australian Public Service Commission. 2007. *Tackling Wicked Problems: A Public Policy Perspective*, Australian Government, Canberra: Australian Public Service Commission.

Ayal, A. 2009. Consumers' Freedom of Choice: Lessons From the Cellular Market. *Working Paper*, 16 April, <papers.ssrn.com/sol3/papers.cfm?abstract_id=1386189>.

Ayres, C. 1944. *The Theory of Economic Progress*, University of North Carolina Press, Chapel Hill.

Ayres, C. 1952. *The Industrial Economy*, Houghton-Mifflin, Boston.

Ayres, C. 1961. *Toward a Reasonable Society: The Values of Industrial Civilization*, University of Texas Press, Austin.

Babbington, S. and King, S. 2008. *Helping with Cost of Energy*, Report of Anglicare Sydney's 2006 EAPA Data Collection, Policy Unit Research Paper, Anglicare, Sydney.

Bachram, H. 2004. Climate Fraud and Carbon Colonialism: The New Trade in Greenhouse Gases. *Capitalism Nature Socialism*, vol. 15, no. 4, pp. 1-16.

Bachram, H., Bekker, J., Clayden, L., Hotz, C. and Ma'anit, A. 2003. *The Sky Is Not the Limit: The Emerging Market in Greenhouse Gases*, Amsterdam, Carbon Trade Watch, January.

Backhouse, R.E. and Fontaine, P. 2010. *The History of the Social Sciences Since 1945*, Cambridge University Press, Cambridge.

Badgett, M.V.L. 1995. Gender, Sexuality, and Sexual Orientation: All in the Feminist Family? *Feminist Economics*, vol.1, no. 1, pp. 121-39.

Bakker, I. 1997. *Integrating Paid and Unpaid Work into Economic Growth and Human Development Strategies*. Paper presented at the United Nations Development Program sponsored workshop on Integrating Paid and Unpaid Work into National Policies, Seoul, Republic of Korea, May, pp. 28-30.

Banks, R.D. and Heaton, G.R. 1995. An Innovation-Driven Environmental Policy. *Issues in Science and Technology*, Fall, pp. 43-51.

Bardak Ventures. 2005. *The Effect of Industry Structure on Generation Competition and End-user Prices in the National Electricity Market*, Report prepared for the Energy Users Association of Australia, the Energy Action Group, the Energy Markets Reform Forum, the Electricity Consumers Coalition of South Australia and the Energy Users Coalition of Victoria, Bowman, 2 May.

Barker, D.K. 2005. Beyond Women and Economics: Rereading 'Women's Work.' *Signs*, vol. 30, no. 4, pp. 2189-209.

Barker, D.K. and Kuiper, E. 2009. *Feminist Economics*, New York, Routledge.

Barnett, T. 1989. *Social and Economic Development*, The Guilford Press, New York and London,.

Barry, J. 1996. Sustainability, Political Judgement and Citizenship: Connecting Green Politics and Democracy. In B. Doherty and M. de Geus (eds). *Democracy and Green Political Thought: Sustainability, Rights and Citizenship*, Routledge, London.

Becker, G.S. 1968. Crime and Punishment: An Economic Approach. *Journal of Political Economy*, vol. 76, pp. 169-217.

Becker, G.S. 1976. *The Economic Approach to Human Behavior*, Chicago University Press, Chicago.

Becker, G.S. 1991. *Treatise on the Family*, revised edition, Harvard University Press, Cambridge.

Becker, G.S. 1996. *Accounting for Tastes*, Harvard University Press, Cambridge Mass.

Beder, S. 2000. *Global Spin: The Corporate Assault on Environmentalism*, Scribe, Melbourne.

Beder, S. 2006. *Environmental Principles and Policies*, UNSW Press, Sydney.

Beneria, L. 1995. Towards a Greater Integration of Gender in Economics. *World Development*, vol. 23, no. 11, pp. 1839-50.

Beneria, L. 2003. *Gender, Development and Globalization*, Routledge, New York.

Beng-Huat, C. 2000. *Consumption in Asia*, Routledge, London.

Bengsston, J. 1989. The New Economy: The Need for Innovation and Integration. *Asia Pacific Human Resource Management*, February, pp. 48-55.

Bergmann, B. 2005. *The Economic Emergence of Women*, second edition, Palgrave Macmillan, New York.

Bernstein, S. 2001. *The Compromise of Liberal Environmentalism*, Columbia University Press, New York.

Bernstein, S. 2002. Liberal Environmentalism and Global Environmental Governance. *Global Environmental Politics*, vol. 2, no. 3, pp. 1-16.

Berry, M. 2006. *Housing Affordability and the Economy: A Review of the Labour Market Impacts and Policy Issues*, Australian Housing and Urban Research Institute, Melbourne.

Best, R. 1999. Health Inequalities: the Place of Housing in D. Acheson, D. Gordon, M, Shaw, D. Dorling and G. Davey Smith (eds), *Inequalities in Health: The Evidence*, Bristol: Policy Press.

Blau, F.D., Ferber, M.A., and Winkler, A.E. 2010. *The Economics of Women, Men and Work*, sixth edition, Prentice Hall.

Bordo, S. 1986. The Cartesian Masculinization of Thought. *Signs*, 11, pp. 439-56.

Boreham, P., Dow, G. and Leet M. 1999. *Room to Manoeuvre: Political Aspects of Full Employment*, Melbourne University Press, Melbourne.

Bourdieu, P. 1986. The Forms of Capital. In Richardson (ed). *Handbook of Theory and Research for the Sociology of Education*, Greenwood Press, New York.

Boyd, R. and Ngo, T-W. 2006. *State Making in Asia*, Routledge, London.

Boyer, R. 1990. *The Regulation School: A Critical Introduction*, Columbia University Press, New York.

Bramble, T. and Kuhn, R. 2010. *Labor's Conflict: Big Business, Workers and the Politics of Class*, Cambridge University Press, Melbourne.

Briggs, C. 2002. Overview of the Debate on Coordinated Flexibility. In J. Buchanan, C. Briggs and C. Wright (eds). *A Critique of the Productivity Commission's Review of Automotive Assistance*, acirrt, University of Sydney, <www.acirrt.com/pubs/carindustryreport.pdf>.

Briggs, C., Cole, M., Evesson, J., Gleeson, K., Lacomb, G. and Saddler, H. 2006. *Going with the Grain? Skills and Sustainable Business Development – Key Findings and Policy Directions*, Report Prepared for the NSW Board of Vocational Education and Training, Sydney

Broad, R. 2004. The Washington Consensus Meets the Global Backlash: Shifting Debates and Policies. *Globalizations*, vo. 1, no. 2, pp. 129-54.

Brown, L.R. 1981. *Building a Sustainable Society*, W.W. Norton & Co, New York.

Bryan, D. 2002. Alternative Economic Strategies: An Evaluation. *Journal of Australian Political Economy*, no. 50, p153-162.

Bryan, M. and Potter, B. 2000. Labor Missing out on Net Gains: Alston, *Australian Financial Review*, 4 August, p. 58.

Buchanan, J. 1986. *Liberty, Market, and State: Political Economy in the 1980s*, Wheatsheaf Books, Brighton.

Buchanan, J. and Considine, G. 2002. *'Stop Telling us to Cope!' NSW Nurses Explain why they are Leaving the Profession*, Report Prepared for NSW Nurses Association, Sydney.

Buchanan, J. and Evesson, J. 2004. *Creating Markets or Decent Jobs? Group Training and the Future of Work*, NCVER, Adelaide, <www.ncver.edu.au>.

Buchanan, J., Evesson, J. and Briggs, C. 2002. *Renewing the Capacity for Skill Formation: The Challenge for Victorian Manufacturing*, A Report for the VLESC/MICC: Melbourne, <www.det.vic.gov.au/otte>.

Buchanan, J. and Pocock, B. 2002. Responding to Inequality Today: Eleven Theses Concerning the Redesign of Policies and Agents for Reform. *Journal of Industrial Relations*, vol. 44, no. 1, pp. 108–35.

Buchanan, J., Schofield, K., Briggs, C., Considine, G., Hager, P., Hawke, G., Kitay, J., Meagher, G., Macintyre, J., Mounier, A., and Ryan, S. 2001. *Beyond Flexibility: Skills and Work in the Future*, NSW Board of Vocational Education and Training, Sydney, <www.bvet.nsw.gov.au>.

Buchanan, J. and Thornthwaite, L. 2001. *Paid Work and Parenting: Charting a new Course for Australian Families*, Chifley Research Centre, Canberra (and acirrt working paper).

Budlender, D. (ed). 1996. *The Women's Budget*, Institute for Democracy in South Africa, Cape Town.

Budlender, D. (ed). 1997. *The Second Women's Budget*, Institute for Democracy in South Africa, Cape Town.

Budlender, D. 2007. *Financing for Development: Aid Effectiveness and Gender-Responsive Budgets*. Background paper prepared for the Eighth Commonwealth Women's Affairs Ministers Meeting of the Commonwealth Countries, Kampala, Uganda, Commonwealth Secretariat, London.

Budlender, D. and Sharp, R. with Kerrie, A. 1998. *How to do a Gender-Sensitive Budget*, AusAid, Commonwealth Secretariat, London.

Burrows, R. and Nettleton, S. 1998. Mortgage Debt, Insecure Home Ownership and Health: An Exploratory Analysis. *Sociology of Health & Illness*, vol. 20, no. 5.

Business Council of Australia. 1989. *Enterprise Based Bargaining Units. A Better Way of Working*, BCA, Melbourne.

Business Council of Australia. 2005. *Infrastructure Action Plan for Future Prosperity*, BCA, Melbourne.

Butlin, N.G., Barnard, A., and Pincus, J. 1982. *Government and Capitalism: Public and Private Choice in Twentieth Century Australia*, Allen & Unwin, Sydney.

Cagatay, N., Elson, D. and Grown, C. 1995. Introduction to Gender, Adjustment and Macroeconomics. *World Development*, vol. 23, no. 11, pp. 1827-36.

Callinicos, A. and Harman, C. 1987. *The Changing Working Class: Essays on Class Structure Today*, Bookmarks, London.

Camic, C. 1986. The Matter of Habit. *American Journal of Sociology*, vol. 91, no. 5. pp. 1039-87.

Camilleri, J.A. 2000. *States, Markets and Civil Society in Asia Pacific*, Edward Elgar, Cheltenham.

Carchedi, G. 1975. On The Economic Identification of the New Middle Class. *Economy and Society*, vol. 4, no. 1, pp. 1-86.

Carlsson, B. 2007. Innovation Systems: A Survey of the Literature from a Schumpeterian Perspective. In Hanusch, H. and Pyka, A. (eds). *Elgar Companion to Neo-Schumpeterian Economics*, Elgar, Cheltenham.

Carr, A.M 1994. The 'Emotional Fallout' of the New Efficiency Movement in Public Administration in Australia: A Case Study. *Administration and Society*, vol. 26, pp. 344-58.

Carruthers, D. 2001. From Opposition to Orthodoxy: The Remaking of Sustainable Development. *Journal of Third World Studies*, vol. 18, Issue 2, pp. 93-113.

Castells, P. and Hall, P. 1994. *Technopoles of the World: The Making of 21st Century Industrial Complexes*, Routledge, London.

Chamberlain, C and MacKenzie, D. 2008. *Australian Census Analytic Program: Counting the Homeless 2006*, ABS cat. no. 2050.0, <www.abs.gov.au/AUSSTATS/abs@.nsf/DetailsPage/2050.02006?OpenDocument>.

Chandler, A.D. 1990. *Scale and Scope: The Dynamics of Industrial Capitalism*, Belknap, Harvard University Press, Cambridge.

Chandler, A.D. 1992. Organizational Capabilities and the Economic History of the Industrial Enterprise. *Journal of Economic Perspectives*, vol. 6, no. 3, pp. 79-100.

Chang, H-J. 1995. Exploring 'Flexible Rigidities' in East Asia. In T. Killick (ed). *The Flexible Economy*, Routledge, London.

Chang, H-J. 2003. *Globalization, Economic Development, and the Role of the State*, Zed Books Ltd, London.

Chester, L. 2007. *What are the Outcomes and Who Benefits from the Restructuring of the Australian Electricity Sector?* Unpublished PhD thesis, University of New South Wales, <www.library.unsw.edu.au/~thesis/adt-NUN/public/adt-NUN20071017.113919/>.

Chester, L. 2008a. The Parlous Investment Environment for Australian Electricity Generation and Transmission. *IAEE Energy Forum*, second quarter, pp. 29-35.

Chester, L. 2008b. The (Default) Strategy Determining the Security of Australia's Energy Supply. In Cabalu, H. and Marinova, D. (eds) *Second International Association for Energy Economics (IAEE) Asian Conference: Energy Security and Economic Development under Environmental Constraints in the Asia-Pacific Region*, Refereed papers, November, Curtin University of Technology, Perth, pp. 97-122.

Chester, L. 2010. Conceptualising Energy Security and Making Explicit its Polysemic Nature. *Energy Policy*, vol. 38, no. 2, pp. 887-95.

Chester, L. and Johnson, M. 2006. *A New Approach Needed for Australia's Infrastructure*. In P. Kriesler, M. Johnson and J. Lodewijks (eds). Essays in Heterodox Economics, Refereed Papers of the 5th Australian Society of Heterodox Economists Conference, University of New South Wales, December, pp. 66-86.

Chick, V. and Dow, S.C. 2001. Formalism, Logic and Reality: A Keynesian Analysis. *Cambridge Journal of Economics*, vol. 25, no. 6, pp. 705-21.

Chowdhury, A. and Islam, I. 1995. *The Newly Industrializing Economies of East Asia*, Routledge, London.

Chowdhury, A. and Islam, I. (eds) 2007. *Handbook on the Northeast and Southeast Asian Economies* Edward Elgar, Cheltenham.

Christoff, P. 1995. Whatever Happened to Ecologically Sustainable Development? *Cappuccino Papers*, vol. 1, pp. 69-74.

Coase, R. 1937. The Nature of the Firm. *Economica*, vol. 4, November, pp. 386-405.

Coase, R. 1992. The Institutional Structure of Production. *American Economic Review*, vol. 82, no. 4, pp. 713-19.

Coleman, J. 1988. Social Capital in the Creation of Human Capital. *American Journal of Sociology*, vol. 94, Supplement, pp. S95-S120.

Comim, F. 2000. Forms of Life and 'Horses for Courses': Introductory Remarks, *Economic Issues*, vol. 4, no. 1, pp. 21-37.

Commons, J.R. 1924. *Legal Foundations of Capitalism*, Macmillan, New York.

Commons, J.R. 1925. Marx To-Day: Capitalism and Socialism. *Atlantic Monthly*, November, pp. 682-93.

Commonwealth Auditor General. 2010. *Audit Report: Performance Audit: Home Insulation Program*, Australian National Audit Office, Report No.12, 2010–11, <resources.news.com.au/files/2010/10/15/1225939/149214-home-insulation.pdf>.

Commonwealth of Australia. 2009a. *Powering Ideas: An Innovation Agenda for the 21ˢᵗ Century*, AGPS, Canberra.

Commonwealth of Australia. 2009b. *Factsheet, Housing Delivery of Commonwealth Rent Assistance*, Steering Committee for the Review of Government Service Provision, Canberra.

Commonwealth of Australia. 2010a. *Australia's Future Tax System Review, Report to the Treasurer, Part 2: Detailed Analysis*, volume 1, December 2009.

Commonwealth of Australia. 2010b. *Final Budget Outcome 2009-10*, Canberra.

Commonwealth Treasury. 2008. *Australia's Low Pollution Future: The Economics of Climate Change Mitigation*, Canberra.

Commonwealth Treasury. 2010. *Incoming Government Brief*, August 2010, <www.treasury.gov.au/contentitem.asp?ContentID=1875&NavID=007>, accessed 25 September 2010.

Considine, M. 2001. *Enterprising States: The Public Management of Welfare to Work*, Cambridge University Press, Cambridge.

Consumer Action Law Centre CALC. 2010. *Payday loans: Helping Hand or Quicksand? An Examination of High-cost Short-term Lending in Australia, 2002-2010*, September, Consumer Action Law Centre , Melbourne.

Cooke, P. and Schall, N. 2007. Schumpeter and Varieties of Innovation: Lessons from the Rise of Regional Innovation Systems Research. In Hanusch, H. and Pyka, A. (eds) *Elgar Companion to Neo-Schumpeterian Economics*, Elgar, Cheltenham.

Cooper, J and Sharp, R. 2007. Engendering Accountability in Government Budgets in Mexico. In M. Griffin-Cohen and J. Brodie (eds). *Remapping Gender in the New Global Order*, Routledge, New York, pp. 205-22.

Corporate Europe Observatory. 2000. *Greenhouse Market Mania*, Amsterdam, November.

Council of Australian Governments COAG. 2002. *Towards a truly National and Efficient Market*, Final Report, Energy Market Review, AusInfo, Canberra, 20 December.

Council of Australian Governments COAG. 2008. *National Affordable Housing Agreement Factsheet*, Canberra.

Cox, E. 1995. *A Truly Civil Society*, 1995 Boyer Lectures, ABC Books, Sydney.

Cox, W. and Pavletich, H. 2010. *Sixth Annual Demographia, International Housing Affordability Survey 2010*, Cox Consulting, Belleville, Illinois.

Csikszentmihalyi, M. and Rochberg-Halton, E. 1981. *The Meaning of Things: Domestic Symbols and the Self*, Cambridge University Press, Cambridge.

Cutler, T. 2008. *Venturous Australia – Building Strength in Innovation: Report on the Review of the National Innovation System*, Melbourne.

Daly, H.E. (ed) 1973. *Toward a Steady-State Economy*, W.H. Freeman,

Danby, C. 2007. Political Economy and the Closet: Heteronormativity in Feminist Economics. *Feminist Economics*, vol. 13, no. 2, pp. 29-54.

Das, D.K. 2005. *Asian Economy and Finance*, Springer, Ontario.

Dasmann, R. 1984. An Introduction to World Conservation. In F. Thibodeau and H. Field (eds). *Sustaining Tomorrow: A Strategy for World Conservation and Development*, University Press of New England, London.

David, P.A. 1971. The Landscape and the Machine: Technical Interrelatedness, Land Tenure and the Mechanization of the Corn Harvest in Victorian Britain. In D. McCloskey (ed). *Essays on a Mature Economy: Britain after 1840*, Methuen, London.

David, P.A. 1975. *Technical Choice, Innovation and Economic Growth: Essays on American and British Experience in the Nineteenth Century*, Cambridge University Press, New York.

Davidson, N. 2002. *The Origins of Scottish Nationhood*, Pluto, London.

Davidson, P. 1994. *Post Keynesian Macroeconomic Theory: A Foundation for Successful Economic Policies for the Twenty-first Century*, Edward Elgar, Aldershot

Davis, D.D. 2004. *Discipline and Development*, Cambridge University Press, Cambridge.

Deacon, D. 1985. Political Arithmetic: The Nineteenth Century Australian Census and the Construction of the Dependent Woman. *Signs*, vo. 11, no. 1, pp. 27-47.

Debreu, G. 1991. The Mathematization of Economic Theory. *American Economic Review*, vol. 8l, pp. 1-7.

Department of Climate Change. 2008. *Carbon Pollution Reduction Scheme: Green Paper*, Canberra.

Department of Families, Housing, Community Services and Indigenous Affairs. FaHCSIA. 2009. *Regulation and Growth of the Not-For-Profit Housing Sector*, Discussion Paper, Canberra, <www.facs.gov.au/sa/housing/pubs/homelessness/not-for-profithousingsector/Pages/affordable_housing.aspx>.

Department of Industry, Science and Technology DIST. 1995. *Australian Business Innovation: A Strategic Analysis*, AGPS, Canberra.

Department of Innovation, Industry, Science and Research DIISR. 2010. *Australian Innovation System Report 2010*, DIISR, AGPS, Canberra.

Department of Prime Minister and Cabinet. 2004. *Securing Australia's Energy Future*, Canberra.

Department of Resources, Energy and Tourism DRET. 2008. *Energy Facts, Statistics and Publications*, Australian Government, <www.ret.gov.au/energy/facts/Pages/EnergyFacts.aspx>, accessed 25 October 2008.

Dequech, D. 2002. The Demarcation Between the 'Old' and the 'New' Institutional Economics: Recent Complications. *Journal of Economic Issues*, vol. 36, no. 2, pp. 565-72.

Dewey, J. 1922. *Human Nature and Conduct: An Introduction to Social Psychology*, Holt, New York.

Dibben P, Wood G. and Roper, I (eds) 2004. *Contesting Public Sector Reforms: Critical Perspectives*, Palgrave Macmillan, Basingstoke.

Diesendorf, M. 2007. *Greenhouse Solutions with Sustainable Energy*, UNSW Press, Sydney.

Diesendorf, M. 2009. *Climate Action*, UNSW Press, Sydney.

Dixon, C. and Drakakis-Smith, D. 1997. *Uneven Development in Southeast Asia*, Ashgate, Aldershot and Brookfield.

Dobson, A. 1996. Environment Sustainabilities: An Analysis and a Typology. *Environmental Politics*, vol. 5, no. 3, pp. 401-28.

Dodgson, M. and Bessant, J. 1996. *Effective Innovation Policy*, Routledge, London.

Dodgson, M. and Gann, D. 2009. *Innovation: A Very Short Introduction*, Oxford University Press, Oxford.

Dore, R. 2000. Will Global Capitalism be Anglo-Saxon Capitalism? *New Left Review*, no. 6, pp. 101-19.

Dow, S.C. 1996. *The Methodology of Macroeconomic Thought: A Conceptual Analysis of Schools of Thought in Economics*, Elgar, Cheltenham.

Dow, S.C. 1997. Methodological Pluralism and Pluralism of Method. In A. Salanti and E. Screpanti (eds). *Pluralism in Economics: New Perspectives in History and Methodology*, Elgar, Cheltenham.

Downs, A. 1957. *An Economic Theory of Democracy*, Harper, New York.

Doyal, L. and Gough, I. 1991. *A Theory of Human Need*, Macmillan, London.

Dryzek, J. S. 1997. *The Politics of the Earth: Environmental Discourse*, Oxford University Press, Oxford.

Dryzek, J.S. 2005. *The Politics of the Earth: Environmental Discourses*, second edition, Oxford University Press, Oxford.

Duesenberry, J. 1967. *Income, Saving, and the Theory of Consumer Behavior*, Oxford University Press, New York.

Dunleavy P. Margetts H. Bastow, S and Tinkler, J. 2006. New Public Management is Dead-Long Live Digital-Era Governance, *Journal of Public Administration Research and Theory*, vol. 61, no. 3, pp. 467-94.

Eckersley, R. 1992. Sustainable Development and the Politics of Language. *Canberra Bulletin of Public Administration*, no. 69, pp. 36-41.

Edgeworth, F.Y. 1881. *Mathematical Psychics*, Kegan Paul, London.

Edquist, C. (ed.) 1997. *Systems of Innovation: Technologies, Institutions and Organisations*, Pinter, London.

Edwards, R. 1979. *Contested Terrain: Transformation of the Workplace in the Twentieth Century*, Basic Books, New York.

Ehrlich, I. 1973. Participation in Illegitimate Activities: A Theoretical and Empirical Investigation. *Journal of Political Economy*, vol. 81, pp. 521-65.

Einstein, A. 1961[1916]. *Relativity: The Special and the General Theory*, Random House, New York.

Eliasoph, N. 1998. *Avoiding Politics: How Americans Produce Apathy in Everyday Life*, Cambridge University Press, Cambridge.

Elson, D. 1997. *Gender-neutral, Gender-blind, or Gender-sensitive Budgets? Changing the Conceptual Framework to Include Women's Empowerment and the Economy of Care*. Background paper for the Preparatory Mission to South Africa to Integrate Gender into National Budgetary Policies and Procedures in the Context of Economic Reform, Commonwealth Secretariat, London.

Elson, D. 2002a, Integrating Gender into Government Budgets within a Context of Economic Reform. In D. Budlender, D. Elson, G. Hewitt and T. Mukhopadhyay (eds). *Gender Budgets Make Cents: Understanding Gender Responsive Budgets*, Commonwealth Secretariat, London.

Elson, D. 2002b. Gender Responsive Budget Initiatives; Some Key Dimensions and Practical Examples. In Judd, K. (ed). *Gender Budget Initiatives: Strategies, Concepts and Experiences*, United Nations Investment Fund For Women, United Nations, New York.

Elson, D. 2006. *Budgeting for Women's Rights: Monitoring Government Budgets for Compliance with CEDAW*, UNIFEM: New York.

Elson, D. and Catatay, N. 2000. The Social Context of Macroeconomic Policies. *World Development*, vol. 28, no. 7, pp. 1347-64.

Elson, D. And Sharp, R. 2010. Gender Responsive Budgeting and Women's Poverty. In S. Chant (ed). *The International Handbook of Gender and Poverty*, Edward Elgar, Oxford, pp. 522-27.

Energy Futures Forum. 2006. *The Heat is on: The Future of Energy in Australia*, CSIRO, Canberra.

Energy Supply Association of Australia. 2003, 2004, 2009, 2010. *Electricity Gas Australia 2010*, ESAA, Melbourne.

Engineers Australia 2005. *Australian Infrastructure Report Card*, Engineers Australia, Barton.

England, P. 1993. The Separative Self: Androcentric Bias in Neoclassical Assumptions. In M.A. Ferber and J.A. Nelson (eds). *Beyond Economic Man*, University of Chicago Press, Chicago.

European Fuel Poverty and Energy Efficiency EPEE. 2009. *European Fuel Poverty and Energy Efficiency: EPEE Project*, November.

Ewer, P. (ed). 1995. *For the Common Good: CSIRO and Public Sector Research and Development*, Pluto Press, Sydney.

Fagerberg, J., Mowery, D. and Nelson, R.R. (eds). 2005. *The Oxford Handbook of Innovation*, Oxford University Press, Oxford.

Fee, E. 1983. Women's Nature and Scientific Objectivity. In M. Lowe and R. Hubbard (eds). *Women's Nature: Rationalization of Inequality*, Pergamon, New York.

Ferber, M.A. 2003. A Feminist Critique of the Neoclassical Theory of the Family. In K.S. Moe (ed). *Women, Family and Work*, Blackwell, Oxford.

Ferguson, M. 2010. *Re-focussing the Energy Market Policy Agenda*, Minister for Resources, Energy and Tourism, Speech to Energy Supply Association of Australia, Brisbane, 20 March, <minister.ret.gov.au/TheHonMartinFerguson MP/Pages/RE-FOCUSSINGTHEENERGYMARKETPOLICYAGENDA.aspx.html>, accessed 26 March 2010.

Fine, B. 2010. *Theories of Social Capital: Researchers Behaving Badly*, Pluto Press, London.

Fine, B. and Milonakis, D. 2009. *From Economics Imperialism to Freakonomics: The Shifting Boundaries between Economics and Other Social Sciences*, Routledge, London.

Flavin, C. 2002. Climbing a Steep Summit. *World Watch*, vol. 15, no. 5, pp. 39.

Folbre, N. 1991. The Unproductive Housewife: Her Evolution in Nineteenth Century Economic Thought. *Signs*, vol. 16, no. 3, 463-84.

Folbre, N. 1995. 'Holding hands at midnight': The Paradox of Caring Labor. *Feminist Economics*, vol. 1, no. 1, 73-92.

Foster, J. Bellamy. 2003. A Planetary Defeat: The Failure of Global Environmental Reform. *Monthly Review*, vol. 54, no. 8, pp. 1-9.

Frank, R.H. 2007. Does Context Matter More for Some Goods than Others? In M. Bianchi (ed.). *The Evolution of Consumption: Theory and Practice. Advances in Austrian Economics*, Volume 10, JAI/Elsevier, Oxford.

Frantzius, I. von. 2004. World Summit on Sustainable Development Johannesburg 2002: A Critical Analysis and Assessment of the Outcomes. *Environmental Politics*, vol. 13, no. 2, pp. 467-73.

Freeman, C. 1994. The Economics of Technical Change. *Cambridge Journal of Economics*, vol. 18, pp. 463-514.

Freeman, C. and Louca, F. 2001. *As Time Goes By: From the Industrial Revolutions to the Information Revolution*, Oxford University Press, Oxford.

Freeman, C. and Soete, L. 1994. *Work for All or Mass Unemployment? Computerised Technical Change into the 21st Century*, Pinter, London.

Freeman, C. and Soete, L. 1998. *The Economics of Industrial Innovation*, third edition, Pinter, London.

Frew, W. 2005. Green Millions Squandered. *Sydney Morning Herald*, 14 September.

Frey, B. and Stutzer, A. 2002. *Happiness and Economics*, Princeton University Press, Princeton, New Jersey.

Friedman, M. 1953. The Methodology of Positive Economics. In *Essays on Positive Economics*, University of Chicago Press, Chicago.

Fukuyama, F. 1995. *Trust*. Penguin Books, London.

Fusfeld, D. 2002. *The Age of the Economist*, ninth edition, Pearson Education, Boston.

Gagliardi, F. 2009. Financial Development and the Growth of Cooperative Firms. *Small Business Economics*, vol. 32, no. 4, pp. 439-64.

Galbraith, J.K. 1969. *The Affluent Society*, second edition, Hamilton, London.

Galbraith, J.K. 1971. *The New Industrial State*, Houghton-Mifflin, Boston.

Garnaut, R. 1989. *Australia and the Northeast Asian Ascendancy*, AGPS, Canberra.

Garnaut, R. 2008. *Targets and Trajectories: Supplementary Draft Report*, Canberra, Climate Change Review, September.

Garnaut, R. 2008. *The Garnaut Climate Change Review Final Report*, Cambridge University Press, Melbourne, <www.garnautreview.org.au/index.htm>.

Garnett, R., Olsen, E.K. and Starr, M. (eds). 2010. *Economic Pluralism*, Routledge, London.

Georgescu-Roegen, N. 1966. *Analytical Economics*, Harvard University Press, Cambridge.

Georgescu-Roegen, N. 1971. *The Entropy Law and the Economic Process*, Harvard University Press, Cambridge.

Gersbach, H. 2009. Basic Research and Growth Policy. In D. Foray, (ed). *The New Economics of Technology Policy*, Elgar, Cheltenham.

Gibbons, D. and Singler, R. 2008. *Cold Comfort: A Review of Coping Strategies Employed by Households in Fuel Poverty*, Report for EnergyWatch, Centre for Social and Economic Inclusion, London.

Gilpin, R. 2001. *Global Political Economy*, Princeton University Press, Princeton.

Gittins, R. 2010. At Last a Strategy that will Ease the Housing Shortage. *Sydney Morning Herald*, 9 June.

Goldschmidt-Clermont, L. 1992. Measuring Households' Non-monetary Production. In P. Ekins and M. Max-Neef (eds). *Real-Life Economics*, Routledge, New York.

Goldsmith, E. *et al*. 1972. *Blueprint for Survival (by the editors of The Ecologist)*, Houghton Mifflin, Boston.

Gordon, D., Edwards, R. and Reich, M. 1982. Long Swings and Stages of Capitalism. In D. Kotz, T. McDonough and M. Reich (eds). *Social Structures of Accumulation: The Political Economy of Growth and Crisis*, Cambridge University Press, Cambridge.

Grabowski, G. 1994. The Successful Developmental State: Where Does It Come From? *World Development*, vol. 22, no. 3.

Granovetter, M. 1973. The Strength of Weak Ties. *American Journal of Sociology*, vol. 78, no. 6, pp. 1360-80.

Grapard, U., and Hewitson, G.J. (eds). 2010. *Robinson Crusoe's Economic Man*, Routledge, New York.

Gray, M.C. and Altman, J.C. 2006. The Economic Value of the Harvesting Wild Resources to the Indigenous Community of the Wallis Lake Catchment, NSW. *Family Matters*, vol. 75, pp. 10-19.

Groenewegen, J., Kerstholt, F. and Nagelkerke, A. 1995. On Integrating the New and Old Institutionalisms: Douglass North Building Bridges. *Journal of Economic Issues*, vol. 29, no. 2, pp. 467-75.

Guan, L.H. 2004. *Civil Society in Southeast Asia*, Nias Press, Singapore.

Guardian, 26 April 2001.

Hahn, R. and Hester, G. 1989. Where Did All the Markets Go? An Analysis of EPA's Emissions Trading Program. *Yale Journal of Regulation*, vol. 6, no. 1, pp 109-53.

Hamilton, C. 2003. *Growth Fetish*, Allen & Unwin, Sydney.

Hamilton, C. and Denniss, R. 2005. *Affluenza: When Too Much is Never Enough*, Allen & Unwin, Sydney

Hansen, J, Sato, M, Ruedy, R and Lo, K. 2009. 2008 *Global Surface Temperature in GISS Analysis*, <www.columbia.edu/~jeh1/mailings/2009/20090113_Temperature.pdf>, 13 January.

Hansen, J. 2006. Can We Still Avoid Dangerous Human-made Climate Change? *Social Research*, vol. 73, no. 3, pp. 949-74.

Hansen, J. 2008. Tell Barack Obama the Truth – The Whole Truth. *Letter to the President-Elect*, revised 29 December, <www.columbia.edu/~jeh1>.

Hansen, J., Sato, M., Kharecha, P., Beerling, D., Berner, R., Masson-Delmotte, V., Pagani, M., Raymo, M., Royer, D.L. and Zachos, J.C. 2008. Target atmospheric CO_2: Where should humanity aim? *Open Atmospheric Science Journal*, 2, pp. 217-31.

Hanson, J.D. and Kysar, D.A. 1999a. Taking Behavioralism Seriously: The Problem of Market Manipulation. *New York University Law Review*, vol. 74, pp. 630–749.

Hanson, J.D. and Kysar, D.A. 1999b. Taking Behavioralism Seriously: Some Evidence of Market Manipulation. *Harvard Law Review*, vol. 112, pp. 1420–572.

Hanson, W. 1984. Bandwagons and Orphans: Dynamic Pricing of Competing Technological Systems Subject to Decreasing Costs. *Technological Innovation Program Workshop Paper*, Department of Economics, Stanford University, January.

Hanusch, H. and Pyka, A. 2007. Introduction. In H. Hanusch, and A. Pyka, (eds). *Elgar Companion to Neo-Schumpeterian Economics*, Elgar, Cheltenham.

Harcourt, G.C. 2004. The Economics of Keynes and its Theoretical and Political Importance: Or, what would Marx and Keynes have made of the Happenings of the past 30 years and More? *Post-Autistic Economics Review*, no. 27

Harcourt, G.C. 2006. *The Structure of Post-Keynesian Economics: The Core Contributions of the Pioneers*, Cambridge University Press, Cambridge.

Harding, S. 1986. *The Science Question in Feminism*, Cornell University Press, Ithaca.

Hatfield-Dodds, S. and Denniss, R. 2008. *Energy Affordability Living Standards and Emissions Trading: Assessing the Social Impacts of Achieving deep Cuts in Australian Greenhouse Emissions*, Report to The Climate Institute, June, CSIRO, Canberra.

Hausman, D.M. 1992. The Limits of Economic Science. *Essays on Philosophy and Economic Methodology*, Cambridge University Press, Cambridge.

Hazledine, T. 1998. *Taking New Zealand Seriously: The Economics of Decency*, HarperCollins, Auckland.

Helpmann, E. (ed). 1998. *General Purpose Technologies and Economic Growth*, MIT Press, Cambridge MA.

Henrich, J., Ensminger, J., McElreath, R., Barr, A., Barrett, C., Bolyanatz, A., Cardenas, J.C., Gurven, M., Gwako, E., Henrich, N., Lesorogol, C., Marlowe, F., Tracer, D. and Ziker, J. 2010. Markets, Religion, Community Size, and the Evolution of Fairness and Punishment. *Science*, vol. 327, no. 1480.

Herbert-Cheshire, L. and Lawrence, G. 2002. Political Economy: The Challenge of Governance. *Journal of Australian Political Economy*, no. 50, pp. 135-45.

Hewitson, G.J. 2003. Domestic Labor and Gender Identity: Are all Women Carers? In D.K. Barker and E. Kuiper (eds). *Toward a Feminist Philosophy of Economics*, Routledge, New York.

Hewitt, G. and Mukhopadhyay, T. 2002. Promoting Gender Equality Through Public Expenditure. In D. Budlender, D. Elson, G. Hewitt, and T. Mukhopadhyay (eds) *Gender Budgets Make Cents: Understanding Gender Responsive Budgets*, Commonwealth Secretariat, London, pp. 49-82.

Hicks, J.R. 1953. The Long-run Dollar Problem. *Oxford Economic Papers*, vol. 2, pp. 117-35.

Himmelweit, S. 2002. Making Visible the Hidden Economy: The Case for Gender Impact Analysis of Economic Policy. *Feminist Economics*, vol. 8, no. 1, pp. 49-70.

Hirschman, A. 1982. Rival Views of Market Society. *Journal of Economic Literature*, vol. 48, no. 4, pp. 1463-84.

Hirschman, A. 1997. *The Passions and the Interests: Political Arguments for Capitalism Before its Triumph*, Princeton University Press, Princeton.

Hodgson, G.M. 1988. *Economics and Institutions: A Manifesto for a Modern Institutional Economics*, Polity Press and University of Pennsylvania Press, Cambridge and Philadelphia.

Hodgson, G.M. 1998. The Approach of Institutional Economics. *Journal of Economic Literature*, vol. 36, no. 1, pp. 166-92.

Hodgson, G.M. 2000. From Micro to Macro: The Concept of Emergence and the Role of Institutions. In L. Burlamaqui, A. Célia Castro and H. Chang (eds). *Institutions and the Role of the State*, Edward Elgar, Cheltenham.

Hodgson, G.M. 2001. *How Economics Forgot History: The Problem of Historical Specificity in Social Science*, Routledge, London.

Hodgson, G.M. 2003. The Hidden Persuaders: Institutions and Individuals in Economic Theory. *Cambridge Journal of Economics*, vol. 27, no.2, pp. 159-75.

Hodgson, G.M. 2004. *The Evolution of Institutional Economics: Agency, Structure and Darwinism in American Institutionalism*, Routledge, London.

Hodgson, G.M. 2006. What Are Institutions? *Journal of Economic Issues*, vol. 40, no. 1, pp. 1-25.

Hodgson, G.M. 2008. Markets. *New Palgrave Dictionary of Economics*, second edition, Macmillan, Basingstoke.

Hodgson, G.M. 2009. On the Institutional Foundations of Law: The Insufficiency of Custom and Private Ordering. *Journal of Economic Issues*, vol. 43, no. 1, pp. 143-66.

Hodgson, G.M. 2010. Choice, Habit and Evolution. *Journal of Evolutionary Economics*, vol. 20, no. 1, pp. 1-18.

Hodgson, G.M. and Knudsen, T. 2004. The Complex Evolution of a Simple Traffic Convention: The Functions and Implications of Habit. *Journal of Economic Behavior and Organization*, vol. 54, no. 1, pp. 19-47.

Hodgson, G.M. and Knudsen, T. 2007. Firm-Specific Learning and the Nature of the Firm: Why Transaction Costs May Provide an Incomplete Explanation, *Revue Économique*, vol. 58, no. 2, pp. 331-50.

Hodgson, G.M. and Knudsen, T. 2010. *Darwin's Conjecture: The Search for General Principles of Social and Economic Evolution*, University of Chicago Press, Chicago.

Holley, I.B. 1964. *Buying Aircraft: Materiel Procurement for the Army Air Forces*, The United States Army in World War II: Special Studies, no.7, U.S. Government Printing Office, Washington D.C.

Honeyman, K. and Goodman, J. 1991. Women's Work, Gender Conflict and Labor Markets in Europe, 1500-1900. *Economic History Review*, vol. 44, no. 4, pp. 608-28.

Howard, J. 2001. Election night speech. Sydney, 10 November, <pandora.nla.gov.au/pan/10052/20031121/www.pm.gov.au/news/speeches/2001/speech1326.htm>.

Humphries, J. 1979. Class Struggle and the Persistence of the Working Class Family. *Cambridge Journal of Economics*, vol. 2 no. 3, pp. 241-58.

Hunter, B.H. 2006. Revisiting the Poverty War: Income Status and Financial Stress among Indigenous Australians. In B.H. Hunter (ed). *Assessing the Evidence on Indigenous Socioeconomic Outcomes: A Focus on the 2002 NATSISS*, ANU E Press, Canberra.

ILEX Energy Consulting. 2005. *The Environmental Effectiveness of the EU ETS: Analysis of Caps*, World Wide Fund for Nature, October 2005

Independent Pricing and Regulatory Tribunal IPART. 2010. *Electricity Price Rises Change*, Media release, 28 April.

Infrastructure Australia 2010a. *National Public Private Partnership Policy and Guidelines*, accessed 10 October, <www.infrastructureaustralia.gov.au/public_private_partnership_policy_guidelines.aspx>.

Infrastructure Australia 2010b. *Infrastructure Australia*, accessed on 10 October, <www.infrastructureaustralia.gov.au/>.

Infrastructure Australia 2010c. National Infrastructure Priorities, accessed on the 10 October, <www.infrastructure australia.gov.au/publications.aspx>.

International Energy Agency. 2003. *Power Generation Investment in Electricity Markets*, OECD/IEA, Paris.

International Energy Agency. 2005. *Energy Policies of IEA Countries: Australia 2005 Review*, OECD/IEA, Paris.

International Monetary Fund IMF. 2004. Australia: 2004 Article IV Consultation – Staff Report, Staff Statement, and Public Information Notice on the Executive Board Discussion, *IMF Country Report No 04/353*, November, International Monetary Fund, Washington.

International Union for Conservation of Nature and Natural Resources IUCN. 1972. *Yearbook*, Gland, Switzerland.

IPCC. 2007a. *Climate Change 2007: The Physical Science Basis*, Summary for Policymakers, Intergovernmental Panel on Climate Change.

IPCC. 2007b. *Climate Change 2007: Impacts, Adaptation and Vulnerability*, Intergovnernmental Panel on Climate Change.

Ironmonger, D. 1996. Counting Outputs, Capital Inputs and Caring Labor: Estimating Gross Household Product. *Feminist Economics*, vol. 2, no. 3, pp. 37-64.

Jacobs, M. 1995. Sustainable Development: Assumptions, Contradictions, Progress. In J. Lovenduski and J. Stanyer (eds). *Contemporary Political Studies*, Political Studies Association, Belfast.

Jeffries, C. and Stilwell, F. 2006. Private Finance for Public Infrastructure: The Case of the Macquarie Bank, *Journal of Australian Political Economy*, no. 58, pp. 44-61.

Jessop, B. and Sum, N-L. 2006. *Beyond the Regulation Approach: Putting Capitalist Economies in their Place*, Edward Elgar, Cheltenham.

Johnson, C. 1982. MITI *and the Japanese Miracle*, Stanford University Press, Stanford.

Johnson, C. 1999. The Developmental State: Odyssey of a Concept. In. M. Woo-Cumings (ed). *The Developmental State*, Cornell University Press, Ithaca.

Johnson, H. 1955. Economic Expansion and International Trade. *Manchester School of Social and Economic Studies*, vol. 23, pp. 95-112.

Johnson, M. 1995. Infrastructure and Australia's Economic and Social Development Through the 1990's: Assessing the Problem and the Priorities. In Economic Planning Advisory Council. *Private Infrastructure Task Force, Interim Report: Commissioned Studies*, AGPS, Canberra.

Johnson, M. 2001. The Impact of New Public Management on the Reform of Transportation Infrastructure in Sydney. In L. Jones, J. Guthrie, and P. Steane (eds). *Learning From Public Management Reform: Research in Public Policy Analysis and Management*, Elsevier Science, Amsterdam.

Johnson, M. 2007. Is the Existing Ethical Framework Sufficient to Manage the Current Extension of Contracting and Competition In The Australian Public Sector? *Australian Journal of Applied and Professional Ethics*, vo. 2, no. 9, pp. 96-105.

Johnson, M. 2008. Privatisation, Myopia and the Long Run Provision of Economic Infrastructure, *The Economic and Labour Relations Review*, vol. 19, no.1, November, pp. 57-72.

Johnson, M. and Guthrie, J. 1993. Commercialisation of the Public Sector: Why, How and For What? A Prospective View. In K. Wiltshire (ed). *Australian Governance and Economic Efficiency*, CEDA, Melbourne.

Johnston, M.M. 2010. *New Meters, New Protections: A National Report on Customer Protections and Smart Meters*, St Vincent de Paul Society National Council, Deakin West.

Johnston, R. 1996. The New Drivers of Innovation in the Knowledge Economy. In P. Sheehan *et al.* (eds). *Dialogues on Australia's Future*, Centre for Strategic Economic Studies, Victoria University of Technology, Melbourne.

Jomo K.S. 2003. Growth and Vulnerability before and after the Asian crisis: The Fallacy of the Universal Model. In M. Andersson and C. Gunnarsson (eds). *Development and Structural Change in Asia-Pacific*, Routledge, London.

Jones, D.M. 1997. *Political Development in Pacific Asia*, Blackwell, Cambridge.

Jones, E. 1999. Historical School. In P.A. O'Hara (ed). *Encyclopedia of Political Economy*, Routledge, London, pp. 446-49.

Kaldor, N. 1966. *Causes of the Slow Rate of Economic Growth of the United Kingdom*, Cambridge University Press, Cambridge.

Kalecki, M. 1943. Political Aspects of Full Employment. *The Political Quarterly*, vol.14, no. 4, October, pp. 322-31.

Kalecki, M. 1969, *Theory of Economic Dynamics*, Allen & Unwin, London.

Kalecki, M. 1970. Theories of Growth in Different Social Systems. *Scientia*, no.s 5-6, pp. 311-16. Reprinted in J. Osiatynski, (ed). 1993. *Collected Works of Michal Kalecki, Volume IV: Socialism: Economic Growth and Efficiency of Investment*, Clarendon Press, Oxford.

Kalecki, M. 1971. Class Struggle and Distribution of National Income. *Kyklos*, vol. 24, pp. 1-9. Reprinted in J. Osiatynski, (ed). 1993. *Collected Works of Michal Kalecki: II: Capitalism: Economic Dynamics*, Clarendon Press, Oxford.

Kaletsky, A. 2009. *Goodbye, homo economicus*, Prospect, London.

Karoly, D. 2009. Bushfires and Extreme Heat in South-east Australia. *Real Climate*, 16 February, <www.realclimate.org/index.php/archives/2009/02/bushfires-and-climate>.

Katz, M. and Shapiro, C. 1983. Network Externalities, Competition, and Compatibility. *Woodrow Wilson School Discussion Paper in Economics*, no. 54, Princeton University, September.

Keating M. 2004. *Who Rules? How Government Retains Control of a Privatised Economy*, The Federation Press, Annandale.

Keen, S. 2001. *Debunking Economics*, Pluto Press, Sydney.

Keen, S. 2004. Deregulator: Judgment Day for Microeconomics. *Utilities Policy*, vol. 12, pp. 109-25.

Keen, S. and Standish, R. 2006. Profit Maximization, Industry Structure, and Competition: A Critique of Neoclassical Theory. *Physica A: Statistical Mechanics and its Applications*, vol. 370, no. 1, pp. 81-85.

Keller, E.F. 1985. *Reflections on Gender and Science*, Yale University Press, New Haven.

Kelly, P. 1994. *The End of Certainty: Power, Politics and Business in Australia*, revised edition, Allen & Unwin, St Leonards NSW.

Keynes, J.M. 1921. *A Treatise on Probability*. In *The Collected Writings of John Maynard Keynes*, Volume VIII, Macmillan and Cambridge University Press, London, edited by D. Moggridge.

Keynes, J.M. 1930. A Treatise on Money. In *The Collected Writings of John Maynard Keynes*, Macmillan and Cambridge University Press, London, edited by D. Moggridge, V and VI.

Keynes, J.M. 1933. Robert Malthus 1766-1835: The First of the Cambridge Economists. *Essays in Biography*, Mercury Books, London.

Keynes, J.M. 1936. *The General Theory of Employment, Interest and Money*, Macmillan, London.

Keynes, J.M. 1937. The General Theory of Employment. *The Quarterly Journal of Econommics*, February, pp. 209-23. Reprinted in J.M. Keynes. 1973. *The General Theory and After, Collected Writings*, vol. XIV, Macmillan, London pp. 109-23

Keynes, J.M. 1972. *The Collected Writings of John Maynard Keynes*, Macmillan and Cambridge University Press, London, edited by D. Moggridge.

Kidd, C. V. 1992. The Evolution of Sustainability. *Journal of Agricultural and Environmental Ethics*, vol. 5, no. 1, pp. 1-26.

Kill, J. 2001. *Sinks in the Kyoto Protocol: A Dirty Deal for Forests, Forest Peoples and the Climate*, Brussels, Fern.

King, A. 1998. Income Poverty Since the 1970's. In R. Fincher and J. Nieuwenhuysen (eds). *Australian Poverty: Then and Now*, Melbourne University Press, Melbourne.

Klein, N. 2007. *The Shock Doctrine*, New York, Metropolitan.

Kleinknecht, A. 1998. Is Labour Market Flexibility Harmful to Innovation? *Cambridge Journal of Economics*, vol. 22, pp. 387-96.

Kleinknecht, A. and Naastepad, C.W.M. 2007. Flexible Labour Markets and Labour Productivity Growth: Is There a Trade-off? In H. Hanusch, and A. Pyka, (eds). *Elgar Companion to Neo-Schumpeterian Economics*, Elgar, Cheltenham.

Knight, J. 1992. *Institutions and Social Conflict*, Cambridge University Press, Cambridge.

Koopmans, T. 1957. *Three Essays on the State of Economic Science*, McGraw-Hill, New York.

Kotz, D.M. 2008. Contradictions of Economic Growth in the Neoliberal Era: Accumulation and Crisis in the Contemporary US Economy. *Review of Radical Political Economics*, vol.40, no. 2, Spring, pp. 174-88.

Kovel, J. 2002. *The Enemy of Nature: The End of Capitalism or the End of the World?* Zed Books, London.

Kriesler P. 2009. The Current financial Crisis: Causes and Policy, *The Economic and Labour Relations Review*, vol. 19, no.2, July, pp. 17-25.

Kuhn, R. (ed). 2005. *Class and struggle in Australia* Pearson, Frenchs Forest.

Kuhn, T. 1970. *The Structure of Scientific Revolutions*. Chicago University Press, Chicago.

Kurz, H.D. and Salvadori, N. 2000. On Critics and Protective Belts. In H.D. Kurz and N.Salvadori (eds). *Understanding 'Classical' Economics: Studies in Long-Period Theory*, Routledge, London.

La Vina, A.G.M., G. Hoff, and A. M. DeRose. 2003. The Outcomes of Johannesburg: Assessing the World Summit on Sustainable Development. *SAIS Review*, vol. 23, no. 1, pp. 53-70.

Lafferty, W.M. 1996. The Politics of Sustainable Development: Global Norms for National Implementation. *Environmental Politics*, vol. 5, no. 2, pp. 185-208.

Lakoff, G. and Johnson, M. 1980. *Metaphors We Live By*, Chicago University Press, Chicago.

Lall, S. 1996. *Learning from the Asian Tigers*, Macmillan Press, London.

Lau. L.J. 1997. The Role of Government in Economic Development: Some Observations from the Experience of China, Hong Kong, and Taiwan. In M. Aoki, H-K. Kim and M. Okuno-Fujiwara (eds). *The Role of Government in East Asian Economic Development*, Clarendon Press, Oxford.

Lazear, E. 2000. Economic Imperialism. *Quarterly Journal of Economics*, vol. 115, no.1, pp. 99-146.

Lazonick, W. 1991. *Business Organization and the Myth of the Market Economy*, Cambridge University Press, Cambridge.

Lee, K. 1993. *New East Asian Economic Development*, East Gate, New York.

Leff, E. 2002. Alternatives to Environmental Neoliberalism. *Notable Writings*, Tierramerica, <www.tierramerica.net/2002/0728/igrandesplumas.shtml>.

Leftwich, A. 2000. *States of Development, on the Primacy of Politics in Development*, Polity Press, Cambridge and Oxford.

Lele, S. M. 1991. Sustainable Development: A Critical Review. *World Development*, vol. 19, no. 6, pp. 607-21.

Levi-Faur, D. 1997. Friedrich List and the Political Economy of the Nation-State. *Review of International Political Economy*, vol. 41, Spring, pp. 154-78.

List, F. 1841. *The National System of Political Economy*, Longmans Green, London.

Lowe, A. 1976. *The Path of Economic Growth*, Cambridge University Press, Cambridge.

Lucarelli, B. 2008. The United States Empire of Debt: The Roots of the Current Financial Crisis. *Journal of Australian Political Economy*, no. 62, pp. 16-38.

Lukács, G. 1971. *History and Class Consciousness*, Merlin, London.

Lukes, S. 1974. *Power: A Radical View*, Macmillan, London.

Lundvall, B. (ed). 1992. *National Systems of Innovation: Towards a Theory of Innovation and Interactive Learning*, Pinter, London:

Macfarquhar, N. 2010. Be Careful What you Wish for: 'We Created Microcredit to Fight the Loan Sharks; We didn't Create Microcredit to Encourage New Loan Sharks'. *Pittsburgh Post-Gazette*, 18 April.

MacIntyre, A. 2003. *The Power of Institutions*, Cornell University Press, Ithaca.

Majone, G. 1989. *Evidence, Argument and Persuasion in the Policy Process*, Yale University Press, New Haven.

Mann, M. 1993. *The Sources of Social Power, vol. 2: The Rise of Classes and Nation-States*, 1760-1914, Cambridge University Press, Cambridge.

Marceau, J. 1996. Refashioning Industry Policy: Let's Use What We Know! In P. Sheehan *et al.* (eds). *Dialogues on Australia's Future*, Centre for Strategic Economic Studies, Victoria University of Technology, Melbourne.

Marceau, J., Manley, K., and Sicklen, D. 1997. *The High Road or the Low Road? Alternatives for Australia's Future*, Australian Business Foundation, Sydney.

Marschak, J. 1968. The Economics of Inquiring, Communicating, Deciding. *American Economic Review*, vol. 58 (supplement), pp. 1-18.

Marshall, A. 1920. *Principles of Economics*, eighth edition, Macmillan, London.

Marx, K. 1975 [1847]. *The Poverty of Philosophy*, Progress, Moscow.

Marx, K. 1976 [1867]. *Capital*, vol. 1, Penguin, Harmondsworth.

Marx, K. 1981 [1894]. *Capital*, vol. 3, Penguin, Harmondsworth.

May, K. 2010. Government Support for Indigenous Cultural and Natural Resource Management in Australia: The Role of the Working on Country Program. *Australian Journal of Social Issues*, vol. 45, no. 3, pp. 395-416.

McCloskey, D. 1985. *The Rhetoric of Economics*, University of Wisconsin Press, Madison.

McCloskey, D. 1997. *The Vices of Economics: The Virtues of the Bourgeoisie*, Amsterdam University Press, Amsterdam.

McDonough, T. 2008. Social Structures of Accumulation: The State of the Art. *Review of Radical Political Economics*, vol. 40, no. 2, pp.153-73.

McHugh, F.P. 1993. Christian Social Theory. In W. Outhwaite and T. Bottomore (eds). *The Blackwell Dictionary of Twentieth-century Social Thought.* Blackwell, Oxford.

McIntosh, G. 1997. *Reforming Public Housing, Current Issues, Brief 31, 1996-97.* Parliament of Australia, Parliamentary Library, Canberra.

McIntosh, G. and Phillips, J. 2001). *The Commonwealth-State Housing Agreement.* Parliament of Australia, Parliamentary Library, Canberra.

McMillan, J. 2002. *Reinventing the Bazaar: A Natural History of Markets*, Norton, New York and London.

Meadowcroft, J. 2000. Sustainable Development: A New(ish) Idea for a New Century?. *Political Studies*, vol. 48, no. 2, pp. 370-87.

Meadows, D.H. 1972. *The Limits to Growth: A Report for the Club of Rome's Project on the Predicament of Mankind*, Earth Island, London.

Meadows, D.L. (ed). 1977. *Alternatives to Growth I: A Search for Sustainable Futures*, Ballinger, Cambridge MA.

Metcalfe, S. 2007. Policy for Innovation. In H. Hanusch, and A. Pyka, (eds). *Elgar Companion to Neo-Schumpeterian Economics*, Elgar, Cheltenham.

Michael, E. 2006. *Public Policy: The Competitive Framework*, Oxford University Press, South Melbourne.

Miller, G.A. 1956. The Magic Number Seven Plus or Minus Two: Some Limits on Our Capacity for Processing Information. *Psychological Review*, vol. 63, pp. 81-97.

Milligan, V. and Pinnegar, S. 2010. Policy Review: The Comeback of National Housing Policy in Australia: First Reflections. *International Journal of Housing Policy*, vol. 10, no. 3, pp. 325-44.

Milligan, V., Gurran, N., Lawson, J., Phibbs, P. and Phillips, R. 2010. *Innovation in Affordable Housing in Australia: Bringing Policy and Practice for Not-for-profit Housing Organisations Together: Final Report*, 134, Melbourne: Australian Housing and Urban Research Institute.

Milonakis, D. and Fine, B. 2009. *From Political Economy to Economics: Method, the Social and the Historical in the Evolution of Economic Theory*, London, Routledge.

Mirowski, P. 1991. The When, the How, and the Why of Mathematical Expression in the History of Economic Analysis. *Journal of Economic Perspectives*, vol. 5, no. 1, pp. 145-57.

Mirowski, P. 2007. Markets Come to Bits: Evolution, Computation and Markomata in Economic Science. *Journal of Economic Behavior and Organization*, vol. 63, no. 2, pp. 209-42.

Moore, C.A. 2004. Marketing Failure: The Experience with Air Pollution Trading in the United States. *Health and Clean Air Newsletter*, vol. 3 February.

Morris, A. 2007. On the Edge: the Financial Situation of Older Renters in the Private Rental Market in Sydney. *Australian Journal of Social Issues*, vol. 42, no. 3, pp. 337-50.

Morris, A. 2009. Living on the Margins: Comparing Older Private Renters and Older Public Housing Tenants in Sydney. Australia, *Housing Studies*, vol. 24, no. 5, pp. 697–711.

Mulgan, R. (2006) Government Accountability for Outsourcing Services, *Australian Journal of Public Administration*, vol. 65, no. 2, pp 48-58.

Murphy, J. 1994. The Kinds of Order in Society. In P. Mirowski (ed). *Natural Images in Economic Thought: Markets Read in Tooth and Claw*, Cambridge University Press, Cambridge.

Musgrave, A. 1981. 'Unreal Assumptions' in Economic Theory: The F-twist Untwisted, *Kyklos*, vol. 34, pp. 377-87.

Myers D. G. and Diener, E. 1996. The Pursuit of Happiness. *Scientific American*, no. 274, pp. 54-56.

Myrdal, G. 1944. *An American Dilemma*, Harper & Brothers, New York.

Myrdal, G. 1957. *Economic Theory and Underdeveloped Regions*, Gerald Duckworth & Co, London.

Myrdal, G. 1960. *Beyond the Welfare State: Economic Planning in the Welfare States and its Economic Implications*, Duckworth, London.

Myrdal, G. 1968. *Asian Drama*. Pantheon, New York.

Myrdal, G. 1974. What is Development? *Journal of Economic Issues*, vol. 8, no. 4, pp. 729-36.

Myrdal, G. 1978. Institutional Economics. *Journal of Economic Issues*, vol. 12, no. 4, pp. 771-83.

National Electricity Market Management Company. 2005. *An Introduction to Australia's National Electricity Market*, sixth edition, NEMMCO, Melbourne.

National Housing Strategy. 1992. *National Housing Strategy: Summary of Papers*, AGPS, Canberra.

National PPP Forum. 2004. *National PPP Projects Approach $20bn*, National PPP Forum, Melbourne, Media Release, 5 November.

Nell, E.J. 1998. *The General Theory of Transformational Growth: Keynes after Sraffa*, Cambridge University Press, Cambridge.

Nelson, J.A. 1993. The Study of Choice or the Study of Provisioning? Gender and the Definition of Economics. In M.A. Ferber and J.A. Nelson (eds). 1993. *Beyond Economic Man*, University of Chicago Press, Chicago.

Nelson, R. (ed). 1993. *National Innovation Systems: A Comparative Analysis*, Oxford University Press, Oxford.

Nelson, R. 1993. Technical Changes as Cultural Evolution. In R. Thomson (ed). *Learning and Technological Change*, St Martins Press, New York.

Nelson, R. 2009. Building Effective 'Innovation Systems' Versus Dealing with 'Market Failures' as ways of Thinking about Technology Policy. In D. Foray (ed). *The New Economics of Technology Policy*, Elgar, Cheltenham.

Nelson, R. and Winter, S. 1982. *An Evolutionary Theory of Economic Growth*, Belknap, Harvard University Press, Cambridge.

Nevile J. 2009. The Current Crisis has a Silver Lining. *The Economic and Labour Relations Review*, vol. 19, no.2, pp. 27-38.

New South Wales Government, Department of Housing. 2006. *Housing Assistance for Elderly Clients*, Sydney, <www.housing.nsw.gov.au/Forms+Policies+and+Fact+Sheets/Policies/Housing+Assistance+for+Elderly+Clients+-+ALL0030D.htm>.

New South Wales Government, Department of Housing. 2010. *Rent and Sales Report, no. 92*, Sydney, <www.housing.nsw.gov.au/NR/rdonlyres/1F7062CE-EF2F-483D-82CD-E57336FA7DB5/0 /RandSReport92.pdf>.

Ngu, Q., Harding, A., Tanton, R., Nepal, B. and Yogi, V. 2008. *Advance Australia Fair?* National Centre for Social and Economic Modelling (NATSEM) and AMP, Canberra.

North, D.C. 1981. *Structure and Change in Economic History*, Norton, New York.

North, D.C. 1990. *Institutions, Institutional Change and Economic Performance*, Cambridge University Press, Cambridge.

North, D.C. 1994. Economic Performance Through Time. *American Economic Review*, vol. 84, no. 3, pp. 359-67.

Northern Land Council 2006. *Celebrating Ten Years of Caring for Country: A Northern Land Council Initiative*, NLC, Darwin.

O'Riordon, T. 1981. *Environmentalism*, Pion, London.

O'Shea, P. 2010. *Simplification of Disclosure Regulation for the Consumer Credit Code: Empirical Research and Redesign: Final Report Prepared for Standing Committee of Officials of Consumer Affairs*, Uniquest Pty Ltd, St Lucia, Queensland, <www.consumer.gov.au/html/latest_news.htm>, accessed July 2010.

Obama, B. 2009. *President Obama's Speech on Financial Regulatory Overhaul*, <www.bloomberg.com/apps/news?pid=newsarchive&sid=aHv0yUF5xRp0>.

OECD. 1985. *Environment: Resource for the Future*, OECD, Paris.

OECD. 1996. *The Knowledge-Based Economy*, OECD, Paris.

OECD. 1997. *National Innovation Systems*, OECD, Paris.

OECD. 1998. *Content as a New Growth Industry*, OECD, Paris.

OECD. 2000. *Is There a New Economy?* OECD, Paris.

OECD. 2004. *OECD Economic Surveys: Australia*, OECD, Paris.

Office of Energy. 2010. *Electricity Tariff Increases*, <www.energy.wa.gov.au/2/3263/64/ electricity_tariff_increases.pm>, accesed 2 February 2010.

Office of Gas and Electricity Markets. 2008. *Energy Supply Probe: Initial Findings Report*, 6 October, OFGEM, London.

Okun, A. 1975. *Equality and Efficiency: The Big Tradeoff*, Brookings Institution, Washington.

Ollman, B. 1976. *Alienation: Marx's conception of Man in Capitalist Society*, second edition, Cambridge University Press, Cambridge.

Osborne, D and Gaebler, T. 1992. *Reinventing Government: How the Entrepreneurial Spirit is Transforming the Public Sector, From Schoolhouse to Statehouse, City Hall to the Pentagon*, Addison Wesley, Reading.

Ostrom, E. 1990. *Governing the Commons: The Evolution of Institutions for Collective Action*, Cambridge University Press, Cambridge.

Ostrom, E. 2000. Collective Action and the Evolution of Social Norms. *Journal of Economic Perspectives*, vol. 14, no. 3, pp. 137-58.

Ostrom, E. 2005. *Understanding Institutional Diversity*, Princeton University Press, Princeton.

Otto, G. and Voss, G. 1994. Public Capital and Private Sector Productivity, *The Economic Record*, vol.70, pp. 121-32.

Otto, G. and Voss, G. 1995. Public Capital and Private Sector Productivity: A Review of the Empirical Evidence, *Economic and Labour Relations Review*, vol. 6, no. 1, pp. 52-70.

Ouellette, J.A. and Wood, W. 1998. Habit and Intention in Everyday Life: The Multiple Processes by which Past Behavior Predicts Future Behavior, *Psychological Bulletin*, vol. 124, pp. 54-74.

Owen, A.D. 2007. *Inquiry into the Electricity Supply in NSW*, September, NSW Government, Sydney.

Ozawa, T. 2009. *The Rise of Asia*, Edward Elgar, Cheltenham and Northampton.

Palat, R.A. 2004. *Capitalist Restructuring and the Pacific Rim*, Routledge, London.

Palestrant, V. 1996. Phone Wars, *Sydney Morning Herald*, 11 September.

Pallemaerts, M. 1996. International Environmental Law in the Age of Sustainable Development: A Critical Assessment of the UNCED Process. *Journal of Law and Commerce*, vol. 15, no. 2, pp. 623-76.

Palmer, I. 1995. Public Finance from a Gender Perspective. *World Development*, vol. 32, no. 11, pp. 1981-86.

Pareto, V.1971 [1927]. *Manual of Political Economy*, A.M. Kelley, New York.

Parker, R. 2001. Australia's Social System of Production. In G. Dow and R. Parker (eds). *Business, Work and Community: Into the New Millennium*. Oxford University Press, Melbourne

Parkin, E 1972. *Class, Inequality and Political Order*, Paladin, London.

Pasinetti, L.L. 1981. *Structural Change and Economic Growth*, Cambridge University Press, Cambridge.

Pavitt, K. 1991. What Makes Basic Research Economically Useful? *Research Policy*, vol. 20, pp. 109-19.

Payne, J.W., Bettman, J.R. and Johnson, E.J. 1993. *The Adaptive Decision Maker*, Cambridge University Press, Cambridge.

Pearce, F. 1997. Countdown to Chaos. *New Scientist*, 29 November, p. 22.

Pearson, N. 2000. *Our Right to Take Responsibility*, Noel Pearson and Associates, Cairns.

Pecci, G.V. (Leo XIII). 1891. The Condition of Labour (*Rerum Novarum*). Reprinted in A. Fremantle (ed). 1963. *The Social Teachings of the Church*, Mentor-Omega, New York.

Pempel. T.J. 1999. The Developmental Regime in a Changing World Economy. In Woo-Cumings, M. (ed). *The Developmental State*, Cornell University Press, Ithaca.

Perez, C. 2010. Technological Revolutions and Techno-Economic Paradigms. *Cambridge Journal of Economics*, vol. 34, 185-202.

Perkins, D.H. 1994. There Are At Least Three Models of East Asian Development. *World Development*, vol. 22, no. 4, 1994, pp. 655-56.

Phillimore, J. 1998. Which Way Ahead for Australian Industry Policy? *The Journal of Contemporary Issues in Business and Government*, vol. 41, pp. 73-5.

Phillpot, R. 2006. The 'Gammon Economy' of Cape York: Lessons for Nation Building in Pacific Island Countries. *Development Bulletin*, no. 70, pp. 29-32.

Piore, M. and Sabel, C. 1984. *The Second Industrial Divide: Possibilities for Prosperity*, Basic Books, New York.

Pittock, AB. 2009. *Climate Change: The Science, Impacts and Solutions*, CSIRO Publishing and Earthscan, Collingwood.

Polanyi, K. 1944. *The Great Transformation: The Political and Economic Origins of our Time*, Beacon Press, Boston.

Pollard, T. 2010. The Great CO_2 Debate and a Packet of Crisps. *Car Magazine*, 29 July <www.carmagazine.co.uk/Community/Car-Magazines-Blogs/Tim-Pollard-Blog2/The-great-CO2-debate-and-a-packet-of-crisps/>, accessed August 2010.

Pontusson, J. 1992. *The Limits of Social Democracy: Investment Politics in Sweden*, Cornell University Press, Ithaca.

Port Jackson Partners Limited. 2005. *Reforming and Restoring Australia's Infrastructure*, Report prepared for the Business Council of Australia, March, Sydney.

Porter, M. 1990. *The Competitive Advantage of Nations*, Free Press, New York.

Porter, M. 1998. *Clusters and the New Economics of Competition*, Harvard Business Review, vol. 76, issue 6, pp. 77-91.

Porter, M.E. and van den Linde, C. 1995. Green and Competitive: Ending the Stalemate. *Harvard Business Review*, September, pp. 120-34.

Posner, R. 1977. *The Economic Analysis of Law*, Little, Brown & Co, Boston.

Productivity Commission. 2005a. *Review of National Competition Policy Reforms*, Inquiry Report No. 33, February, Productivity Commission, Canberra.

Productivity Commission. 2005b. *Modelling Impacts of Infrastructure Industry Change over the 1990s: Supplement to Review of National Competition Policy Reforms*, Inquiry Report No. 33, February, Productivity Commission, Canberra.

Public Interest Advocacy Centre. 2009. *Cut-off II: The Experience of Utility Disconnections*, Final report prepared by URBIS, January, PIAC, Sydney.

Public Services International Research Unit. 2008. *Poor Choices: The Limits of Competitive Markets in the Provision of Essential Services to Low-income Consumers*, University of Greenwich, London.

Putnam, R. 1993. *Making Democracy Work: Civic Traditions in Modern Italy*, Princeton University Press, Princeton.

Queensland Competition Authority QCA. 2009. *Notified Electricity Prices: Draft Decision*, 18 December.

Quiggin, J. 1996. Competitive Tendering and Contracting in the Australian Public Service. *Australian Journal of Public Administration*, vol. 55, no. 3, pp. 49-57.

Quiggin, J. and Langmore, J. 1994. *Work for All: Full Employment in the Nineties*, Melbourne University Press, Carlton.

Ramsay, T. and Lloyd, C. 2010. Infrastructure Investment for Full Employment: A Social Democratic Program of Funds Regulation, *Journal of Australian Political Economy*, no. 65, pp. 59-87.

Rapley, J. 2002. *Understanding Development: Theory and Practice in the Third World*, second edition, Lynne Rienner Publishers, Boulder.

Reich, R.B. 1991. *The Work of Nations*, Alfred A. Knopf, New York.

Reidy, C. 2008. *Energy and Transport Subsidies in Australia: 2007 Update*, Final report prepared for Greenpeace Australia Pacific, UTS Institute for Sustainable Futures, Sydney.

Reilly, B. 2006. *Democracy and Diversity: Political Engineering in the Asia-Pacific*, Oxford University Press, Oxford.

Reinert, E. 1995. Competitiveness and its Predecessors. *Structural Change and Economic Dynamics*, vol. 61, pp. 23-42.

Reinert, E. 1999. The Role of the State in Economic Growth. *Journal of Economic Studies*, vol. 26, no.s 4-5, pp. 268-326.

Reinert, E. 2007. *How Rich Countries Got Rich … and Why Poor Countries Stay Poor*, Constable, London.

Reinert, S.A. and Reinert, E.S. 2006. An 'All Too Human' Question: Nietzsche, Die Soziale Frage, and the German Historical School of Economic. In J.G. Backhaus and W. Drechsler (eds). *Friedrich Nietzsche (1844-1900): Economy and Society*, Springer, New York.

Ricardo, D. 1951[1817]. *On the Principles of Political Economy and Taxation*, edited by P. Sraffa, Cambridge University Press, Cambridge.

Richardson, D. 1997. The Politics of Sustainable Development. In S. Baker, M. Kousis, D. Richardson, and S Young (eds). *The Politics of Sustainable Development: Theory, Policy, and Practice within the European Union*, Routledge, London.

Robbins, L. 1952 [1935]. *An Essay on the Nature and Significance of Economic Science*, Macmillan, London.

Robinson, J. 1953. *On Re-reading Marx*, Cambridge University Press, Cambridge.

Robinson, J. 1971a. Michal Kalecki. In *Collected Economic Papers*, vol. 4, Basil Blackwell, Oxford.

Robinson, J. 1971b. The Second Crisis of Economic Theory. In *Collected Economic Papers*, vol. 4, Basil Blackwell, Oxford.

Robinson, M. and White, G. 1998. *The Democratic Developmental State*, Oxford University Press, Oxford.

Rosenberg N. 1976. *Perspectives on Technology*, Cambridge University Press, Cambridge.

Rosewarne, S. 1993. Selling the Environment: a Critique of Market Ecology. In S. Rees, G. Rodley and F. Stilwell (eds). *Beyond the Market: Alternatives to Economic Rationalism*, Pluto Press, Sydney.

Rothstein, B. 2001. Social Capital in the Social Democratic Welfare State. *Politics & Society*, vol. 29, no. 2, pp. 207-41.

Royston, M.G. 1982. Making Pollution Prevention Pay. In D. Huising and V. Bailey (eds). *Making Pollution Prevention*

Pay: Ecology with Economy as Policy, Pergamon, New York.

Rudd, K. 2007. The Victory Speech. *Sydney Morning Herald*, 26 November, <www.smh.com.au/news/national/the-victory-speech/2007/11/25/1195975870615.html>.

Rueschemeyer, D. and van Rossen, R. 1996. The *Verein für Sozialpolitik* and the Fabian Society: A Study in the Sociology of Policy-relevant Knowledge. In D. Rueschemeyer and T. Skocpol (eds). *States, Social Knowledge and the Origins of Modern Social Policies*, Russell Sage Foundation, Princeton.

Rutherford, M.H. 1994. *Institutions in Economics: The Old and the New Institutionalism*, Cambridge University Press, Cambridge.

Rutherford, M.H. 1995. The Old and the New Institutionalism: Can Bridges be Built? *Journal of Economic Issues*, vol. 29, no. 2, pp. 443-51.

Rutherford, M.H. 2001. Institutional Economics: Then and Now. *Journal of Economic Perspectives*, vol. 15, no. 3, pp. 173-94.

Ryan, E. and Conlon, A. 1989. *Gentle Invaders: Australian Women at Work*, second edition, Penguin, Ringwood, Victoria.

Sachs, J. 2008. Confronting Global Challenges. *Keynote Address*, China Update, Australian National University, Canberra.

Sachs, W. (ed). 2002. *The Jo'Burg Memo: Fairness in a Fragile World*, Heinrich Boll Foundation, Berlin, <www.joburgmemo.org>.

Sample, I. 2005. Climate Change Will Fuel Disease among Poor. *Sydney Morning Herald*, 18 November.

Sanwal, M. 2004. Trends in Global Environmental Governance: The Emergence of a Mutual Supportiveness Approach to Achieve Sustainable Development. *Global Environmental Politics*, vol. 4, no. 4, November, pp. 16-22.

Sardoni, C. and Palazzi, P. 2000. Public Investment and Growth. In Bougrine, H. (ed). *The Economics of Public Spending: Debts, Deficits and Economic Performance*, Edward Elgar, Cheltenham.

Sawer, M. 1990. *Sisters in Suits: Women and Public Policy in Australia*, Allen & Unwin, Sydney.

Scanlon, K. and Whitehead, C. (eds). 2007. *Social Housing in Europe*, LSE, London.

Schärer, B. 1999. Tradable Emission Permits in Germany Clean Air Policy: Considerations on the Efficiency of Environmental Policy Instruments. In S. Sorrell and J. Skea (eds). *Pollution for Sale: Emissions Trading and Joint Implementation*, Cheltenham, UK, Edward Elgar.

Scheer. R. 2005. UN Predicts 50 Million Environmental Refugees by 2010. *E Magazine*, 19 October, <www.emagazine.com/view/?2904>.

Schor, J. 1998. *The Overspent American*, Basic Books, New York.

Schotter, A. 1981. *The Economic Theory of Social Institutions*, Cambridge University Press, Cambridge.

Schumpeter, J.A. 1918. The Crisis of the Tax State. Translated in R. Swedberg (ed). 1954. *Economic Sociology*, Edward Elgar, Cheltenham.

Schumpeter, J.A. 1934. *The Theory of Economic Development: An Inquiry into Profits, Capital, Credit, Interest, and the Business Cycle*, Harvard University Press, Cambridge.

Schumpeter, J.A. 1942. *Capitalism, Socialism and Democracy*, Harper and Row, New York.

Seabright, P. 2004. *The Company of Strangers: A Natural History of Economic Life*. Princeton University Press, Princeton.

Searle, J.R. 1995. *The Construction of Social Reality*, Allen Lane, London.

Seccombe, W. 1986. Patriarchy Stabilized: the Construction of the Male Breadwinner Wage Norm in Nineteenth Century Britain. *Social History*, vol. 11, no. 1, pp. 53-76.

Sen, A.K. 1977. Rational Fools: A Critique of the Behavioral Foundations of Economic Theory. *Philosophy and Public Affairs*, vol. 6, pp. 317-44.

Setterfield, M. 1997. 'History versus Equilibrium' and the Theory of Ecnomic Growth. *Cambridge Journal of Economic*, vol. 21, pp. 365-78.

Setterfield, M. 2001. Cumulative Causation, Interrelatedness ad the Theory of Economic Growth: A Reply to Argyrous and Toner. *Cambridge Journal of Economic*, vol. 25, pp. 107-12.

Sharp, R. 1999. Women's Budgets. In J. Peterson and M. Lewis (eds). *The Elgar Companion to Feminist Economics*, Elgar, Cheltenham.

Sharp, R. and Broomhill, R. 1988. *Shortchanged: Women and Economic Policies*, Allen & Unwin, Sydney.

Sharp, R. and Broomhill, R. 1990. Women and Government Budgets. *Australian Journal of Social Issues*, vol. 25, no. 1, pp. 1-14.

Sharp, R. and Broomhill, R. 2002. Budgeting for Equality: The Australian Experience. *Feminist Economics*, vol. 8, no. 1, pp. 25-47.

Sharp, R. and Broomhill, R. 2009. Gender. In J. Spoehr (ed). *State of South Australia: From Crisis to Prosperity?* Wakefield, Adelaide, pp. 152-76.

Sharp, R. Austen, S. 2007. The 2006 Federal Budget: A Gender Analysis of the Superannuation Taxation Concessions. *Australian Journal of Labour Economics*, vol. 10, no. 2, pp. 61-77.

Shirk, S.L. and Twomey, C.P. 1996. *Power and Prosperity, Economics and security Linkages in Asia-Pacific*, Transaction Publishers New Brunswick and London.

Showalter, M. 2007. *Electricity Price Trends in Deregulated vs Regulated States*, November, Power in the Public Interest,

Olympia.

Sills, D. and Merton, R. 1991. *International Encyclopaedia of the Social Sciences*, vol. 19 Social Science Quotations, MacMillan, New York.

Simon, H. 1955. A Behavioral Model of Rational Choice. *Quarterly Journal of Economics*, vol. 69, pp. 99-118.

Simon, H. 1959. Theories of Decision Making in Economics and Behavioral Science. *American Economic Review*, vol. 49, no. 3, pp. 253-83.

Simon, H. 1991. Organisations and Markets. *Journal of Economic Perspectives*, vol. 5, no. 2.

Skocpol, T. 1985. Bringing the State back In: Strategies of Analysis in Current Research. In P. Evans, D. Rueschemeyer and T. Skocpol (eds). *Bringing the State Back In*, Cambridge University Press, Cambridge.

Smith, A. 1937. [1776]. *An Inquiry into the Nature and Causes of the Wealth of Nation*, Random House, New York.

Smith, A. 1976 [1759]. *The Theory of Moral Sentiments*, Liberty Classics, Indianapolis.

So, A. and Wing-Kai Chiu, S. 2004. The Semiperipheralization of the Newly Industrializing Economies. In R.P. Appelbaum (ed). *Introduction to Global Studies*, Kendall/Hunt Publishing Company, Lowa.

Smith, D.E. and Roach, L.M. 1996. Indigenous Voluntary Work: NATSIS Empirical Evidence, Policy Relevance and Future Data Issues. In J.C. Altman and J. Taylor (eds). *The 1994 National Aboriginal and Torres Strait Islander Survey: Findings and Future Prospects*, Centre for Aboriginal Economic Policy Research, Australian National University, Canberra, pp. 65-76.

Stern, N. 2006. *The Stern Review Report on the Economics of Climate Change*, HM Treasury, UK Government, <www.hmtreasury.gov.uk/independent_reviews/stern_review_economics_climate_change/stern_review_report.cfm>.

Stigler, G.J. 1957. Perfect Competition, Historically Contemplated. *The Journal of Political Economy*, vol. 65, no. 1, pp. 1-17.

Stiglitz, J. 2002. *Globalization and its Discontents*, Penguin Books, London.

Stilwell, F. 2000. *Changing Track: A New Political Economic Direction For Australia*, Pluto Press, Sydney.

Stilwell, F. and Jordan, K. 2007. *Who Gets What? Analysing The Distribution of Income and Wealth in Australia*, Cambridge University Press, Melbourne.

Strategic Economics. 2005. *Financing our Future: The Case for Change in the Financing of Australia's Infrastructure Needs*, Report prepared for the Rail, Tram and Bus Union, Australian Education Union, Australian Nursing Federation, Community and Public Sector Union, and Australian Manufacturing Workers Union, Sydney, May.

Streeck, W. 1991. On the Institutional Conditions of Diversified Quality Production. In E. Matzner and W. Streeck (eds). *Beyond Keynesianism: The Socio-Economics of Full Employment*, Edward Elgar, London.

Streeck, W. 1997. Beneficial Constraints: On the Economic Limits of Rational Voluntarism. In J. Hollingsworth and R. Boyer (eds). *Contemporary Capitalism: The Embeddedness of Institutions*, Cambridge University Press, Cambridge.

Streeck, W. and Yamamura, K. (eds). 2001. *The Origins of Nonliberal Capitalism: Germany and Japan in Comparison*, Cornell University Press, Ithaca.

Stroeve, J, Holland, M.M., Meier, W., Scambos, T. and Serreze, M. 2007. Arctic Sea Ice Decline: Faster than Forecast. *Geophysical Research Letters*, 34, L09501.

Suryadinata, L. 1997. *Southeast Asian Chinese and China, The Politico-Economic Dimension*, Times Academic Press, Singapore.

Syll, L.P. 1992. Notes on Neoinstitutional Economics. *Scandinavian Economic History Review*, vol. 40, no. 2, pp. 21-33.

Szreter, S. 1999. A New Political Economy for New Labour: The Importance of Social Capital, *Renewal*, vol. 71, pp. 30-44.

Tanton, R., Nepal, B. and Harding, A. 2008. *Wherever I Lay my Debt that's my Home*, National Centre for Social and Economic Modelling (NATSEM) and AMP, Canberra.

Thaler, R.H. and Sunstein, C.R. 2008. *Nudge: Improving Decisions about Health, Wealth and Happiness*, Yale University Press, New Haven and London.

The Australian. 2000. Advance Australia Where? June 17 and June 24.

Todaro, M.P. 1990. *Economic Development in the Third World*, fourth edition, Longman, New York.

Tolba, M.K. 1998. *Global Environmental Diplomacy: Negotiating Environmental Agreements for the World, 1973-1992*, MIT Press, Cambridge MA.

Toon, O.B, Turco, R.P, Robock, C., Bardeen1, C., Oman, L., and Stenchikov, G.L. 2007. Atmospheric Effects and Societal Consequences of Regional Scale Nuclear Conflicts and Acts of Individual Nuclear Terrorism. *Atmospheric Chemistry & Physics*, 7, pp. 1973-2002.

Toye, J. 1993. *Dilemmas of Development*, Blackwell, Oxford.

Toynbee, A. 1969 [1884]. *Lectures on the Industrial Revolution in England, Popular Addresses, Notes and other Fragments*, Newton Abbott (Devon), David and Charles Reprint.

UK Government Environment Agency. 2003. *Summary of the Responses to the Discussion Document on the Feasibility of a Trading Scheme for Nox and SO2 Emissions from Large Combustion Plant*, May.

UNESCO. 1996. *Our Creative Diversity: Report of the World Commission on Culture and Development*, UNESCO, Paris.

UNIFEM. 2009. United Nations Development Fund for Women, <www.unifem.org/> accessed March 2.

United Nations Conference on Environment and Development UNCED. 1992. *Agenda 21: A Blueprint for Action for Global Sustainable Development into the Twentyfirst Century*, New York.

United Nations Environment Program. 2007. GEO Indicators. *Global Environmental Outlook Year Book*, <www.

unep.org/geo/yearbook/yb2007/>.

United Nations Environment Programme. 2002. *Global Environment Outlook 3: Past, Present and Future Perspectives*, Nairobi.

United Nations. 2000. *Human Development Report*, <hdr.undp.org/reports/global/2000/en/pdf/ hdr_2000_cho.pdf>.

United Nations. 2010. *Statistical Yearbook For Asia And The Pacific 2009*, United Nations Publication.

United States Government. 2009. *United States Census* [Online], <www.census.gov>.

Vanberg, V.J. 1989. Carl Menger's Evolutionary and John R. Commons' Collective Action Approach to Institutions: A Comparison. *Review of Political Economy*, vol. 1, no. 3, pp. 334-60.

Veblen, T.B. 1898. Why is Economics not an Evolutionary Science? *Quarterly Journal of Economics*, vol. 12, pp. 373-97.

Veblen, T.B. 1899a. *The Theory of the Leisure Class*, Viking Penguin, New York.

Veblen, T.B. 1899b. The Preconceptions of Economic Science. *Quarterly Journal of Economics*, vol. 13. Reprinted in *The Place of Science in Modern Civilization and Other Essays*, Capricorn, New York.

Veblen, T.B. 1909. The Limitations of Marginal Utility. *Journal of Political Economy*, vol. 17, no. 9, pp. 620-36.

Veblen, T.B. 1914. *The Instinct of Workmanship, and the State of the Industrial Arts*, Macmillan, New York.

Veblen, T.B. 1915. *Imperial Germany and the Industrial Revolution*, Macmillan, New York.

Veblen, T.B. 1919. *The Place of Science in Modern Civilisation and Other Essays*, Huebsch, New York.

Vidal, J. 2005. Environmental Decline Killing Poor. *The Age*, 7 October.

Vidal, J. and Radford, T. 2005. One in Six Countries Facing Food Shortage. *The Guardian*, 30 June.

Walker B. and Walker B. 2000. *Privatisation: Sell-off or Sell-Out? The Australian Experience*, ABC Books, Sydney.

Walker, B. and Walker, B.C. 2008. *Electricity Privatisation, Budget Black Holes and Credit Ratings*, Briefing Paper, <www. asuqld.asn.au/index.php?option=com_docman&task=doc_ download&gid=697>.

Walters, B. 1995. Engendering Macroeconomics: A Reconsideration of Growth Theory. *World Development*, vol. 23, no. 11, pp. 1839-50.

Waltman, J. 2000. *The Politics of the Minimum Wage*, University of Illinois Press, Urbana, Illinois.

Waltman, J. 2004. *The Case for a Living Wage*, Algora Publishing, New York.

Wanna J. Butcher J. Freyens, B. 2010. *Policy Action: The Challenge of Service Delivery*, UNSW Press, Sydney.

Wapner, P. 2003. World Summit on Sustainable Development: Towards a Post-Jo'burg Environmentalism. *Global Environmental Politics*, vol. 3, no. 1, pp. 1-10.

Waring, M. 1990. *If Women Counted*. Harpercollins, New York.

Waterson, M. 2003. The Role of Consumers in Competition and Competition Policy. *International Journal of Industrial Organization*, vol. 21, pp. 129-50.

Watson, I., Buchanan, J., Campbell, I. and Briggs, C. 2003. *Fragmented Futures: New Challenges in Working Life*, Federation Press, Sydney.

WCED. 1987. *Our Common Future: World Commission on Environment and Development* (The Brundtland Report), Oxford University Press, Oxford.

Weale, A. 1992. *The New Politics of Pollution*, Manchester University Press, Manchester.

Weber, H. 2004. The 'New Economy' and Social Risk: Banking on the Poor? *Review of International Political* Economy, vol. 11, no. 2, pp. 356-86.

Weber, M. 1922. *Economy and Society: An Outline of Interpretive Sociology*, 2 volumes, edited by R. Günther and C. Wittich, 1978. Translated by Ephraim Fischoff *et al.*, University of California Press, Berkeley.

Weiss, L. 1998. *The Myth of the Powerless State*, Cornell University Press, Ithaca.

Weiss, L. 2003. *States in the Global Economy: Bringing Domestic Institutions Back In*, Cambridge University Press, Cambridge.

Weiss, T.G., Forsythe, D.P. and Coate, R.A. 1994. *The United Nations and Changing World Politics*, Westview Press, Boulder.

White, G.F. 1980. Environment. *Science*, vol. 209, no. 4452, pp. 183-90.

Wilensky, H. 2002. *Rich Democracies: Political Economy, Public Policy and Performance*, University of California Press, Berkeley.

Wilkinson R. and Pickett, K. 2009. *The Spirit Level: Why More Equal Societies Almost Always Do Better*, Allen Lane, London.

Wilkinson, R. 1996. *Unhealthy Societies: The Afflictions of Inequality*, Routledge, London.

Wilkinson, R. 2005. *The Impact of Inequality: How to Make Sick Societies Healthier*, W.W. Norton, New York.

Wilkinson, R. and Marmot, M. (eds). 1998. *The Solid Facts*, World Health Organization, London.

Williams, J. 2000. *Unbending Gender*, Oxford University Press, Oxford.

Williams, R.M. 1993. Race, Deconstruction, and the Emergent Agenda of Feminist Economic Theory. In M.A. Ferber and J. A. Nelson (eds). *Beyond Economic Man*, University of Chicago Press, Chicago.

Williamson, O.E. 1975. *Markets and Hierarchies: Analysis and Anti-Trust Implications: A Study in the Economics of Internal Organization*, Free Press, New York.

Williamson, O.E. 1985. *The Economic Institutions of Capitalism: Firms, Markets, Relational Contracting*, Macmillan, London.

Wilson, S. Gibson, R. Meagher, G. Denemark, D. and Western, M. 2005. *Australian Social Attitudes*, UNSW Press, Sydney.

Wood, W., Quinn, J.M. and Kashy, D. 2002. Habits in Everyday Life: Thought, Emotion, and Action. *Journal of Personality and Social Psychology*, vol. 83, pp. 1281-97.

Woodward D. 2005. *Australia Unsettled: The Legacy of Neo-liberalism*, Pearson Education Australia, Sydney.

World Economic Forum, 2009, *The Global Gender Gap Report 2009*, World Economic Forum, Geneva, <www.weforum.org/pdf/gendergap/report2009.pdf >.

World Institute for Development Economic Research. 2006. *The World Distribution of Household Wealth*, United Nations University, Helsinki

Worldwatch Institute. 2002. *State of the World 2002: A Worldwatch Institute Report on Progress Toward a Sustainable Society*, W.W. Norton & Co, New York.

Yan, Y.H. and Brittle, S. 2010. *Reconsidering the Link Between Fiscal Policy and Interest Rates in Australia.* Treasury Working Paper, September.

Yates, J. 2008. Australia's Housing Affordability Crisis. *The Australian Economics Review*, vol. 41, no.2.

Yates, J. and Bradbury, B. 2010. Home ownership as a (Crumbling) Fourth Pillar of Social Insurance in Australia. *Journal of Housing and the Built Environment*, vol.25, pp.193-211.

Yates, J. and Gabriel, M. 2006. *Housing Affordability in Australia*, Research Paper 3 for National Research Venture 3: Housing Affordability for Lower Income Australians, Australian Housing and Urban Research Institute, Melbourne.

Yates, J. and Milligan, V. with Berry, M., Gabriel, M., Phibbs, P. Pinnegar, S. and Randolph, B. 2007. *Housing Affordability: A 21st Century Problem: National Research Venture 3: Housing Affordability for Lower Income Australians*, Australian Housing and Urban Research Institute, Melbourne.

Young, A. 1928. Increasing Returns and Economic Progress. *Economic Journal*, vol. 38, December, pp. 527-42.

Zappone, C. 2010a. House Prices Surge Record 20%. *The Age*, 3 May.

Zappone, C. 2010b. House Price Rises to Weather Rate Hikes: Report. *The Sydney Morning Herald*, 29 January.

Zhu, T. 2003. Building Institutional Capacity for China's New Economic Opening. In L. Weiss (ed). *States in the Global Economy*, Cambridge University Press, Cambridge.

INDEX